Studies and reports in hydrology
Études et rapports d'hydrologie
Estudios e informes de hidrología
Исследования и доклады по гидрологии

21

World catalogue of very large floods

A contribution to the International Hydrological Programme

Répertoire mondial des très fortes crues

Une contribution au Programme hydrologique international

Catálogo mundial de grandes crecidas

Una contribución al Programa Hidrológico Internacional

Всемирный каталог больших паводков

Вклад в Международную гидрологическую программу

The Unesco Press
Les Presses de l'Unesco
Editorial de la Unesco
Издательство ЮНЕСКО

Published in 1976 by the Unesco Press
7, Place de Fontenoy, 75700 Paris
Printed by Offset Aubin, Poitiers

Publié en 1976 par les Presses de l'Unesco
7, place de Fontenoy, 75700 Paris
Offset Aubin, Poitiers

Publicado en 1976 por la Editorial de la Unesco
7, place de Fontenoy, 75700 Paris
Impreso por Offset Aubin, Poitiers

Издано в 1976 г.
Издательство ЮНЕСКО
7, place de Fontenoy, 75700 Париж
Отпечатано в Offset Aubin, Poitiers

ISBN 92-3-001310-2

The designations employed and the presentation of the material do not imply the expression of any opinion whatsoever on the part of Unesco concerning the legal status of any country or territory, or of its authorities, or concerning the frontiers of any country or territory.

Les dénominations employées et la présentation des divers éléments n'impliquent de la part de l'Unesco aucune prise de position à l'égard du statut juridique de l'un quelconque des pays et territoires en cause, de son régime politique ou du tracé de ses frontières.

Las designaciones empleadas y la presentación del material no entrañan ningún juicio de la Unesco con respecto a la situación jurídica de un país o territorio, o a sus autoridades, ni con respecto a la delimitación de las fronteras de cualquier país o territorio.

Подразумевается, что указания и оформление материала не выражают ни в коей мере мнения Юнеско относительно юридического положения той или иной страны или территории, их властей или границ этих стран или территорий.

Preface

This work is the twenty-first volume to appear in the series "Studies and Reports in Hydrology", publication of which was begun by Unesco, along with that of the series "Technical Papers in Hydrology", within the programme of the International Hydrological Decade.

The International Hydrological Decade, which has just come to an end in 1974, was launched in 1965 by the General Conference of Unesco at its thirteenth session. Its purpose was to advance knowledge of scientific hydrology by promoting international co-operation and by training specialists and technicians. At a time when the demand for water is constantly increasing as a result of the rise in population and of developments in industry and agriculture, all countries are endeavouring to make a more accurate assessment of their water resources and to use them more rationally. The IHD has been a valuable means to this end.

In 1974, National Committees for the Decade had been formed in 110 of Unesco's 135 Member States to carry out national activities and contribute to regional and international activities within the programme of the Decade. The implementation of this programme was supervised by a Co-ordinating Council, composed of 30 Member States selected by the General Conference of Unesco, which studied proposals concerning the programme, recommended the adoption of projects of interest to all or a large number of countries, assisted in the development of national and regional projects and co-ordinated international co-operation. The promotion of collaboration in developing hydrological research techniques, diffusing hydrological data and organizing hydrological networks was a major feature of the programme of the IHD, which encompassed all aspects of hydrological studies and research. Hydrological investigations were encouraged at the national, regional and international level, to strengthen and improve the use of natural resources in view of both local and global needs. The programme enabled countries well advanced in hydrological research to exchange information and developing countries to benefit from such exchanges in order to elaborate their own research projects and plan their own hydrological networks, taking advantage of the most recent developments in scientific hydrology.

The purpose of the series "Studies and Reports in Hydrology" is to set forth the data collected and the main results of hydrological studies undertaken within the framework of the Decade, as well as to provide information on the hydrological research techniques used. The proceedings of symposia dealing with this subject are also included. It is hoped that these volumes will furnish material of both practical and theoretical interest to hydrologists and governments and meet the needs of technicians and scientists concerned with problems of water in all countries.

A great deal remains to be done, in particular with regard to the study of the water cycle and the scientific methods used in the world to assess water resources, and also the evaluation of the influence of man's activities on the water cycle in relation to environmental problems as a whole.

For this reason the General Conference of Unesco decided to launch, in 1975, a long-term intergovernmental programme, to be known as the International Hydrological Programme, which will be focused on the scientific and educational aspects of hydrology and in particular on the study of the problems mentioned above.

Unesco will therefore continue to publish "Studies and Reports in Hydrology", which will remain an important means of collecting and disseminating the accumulated experience of hydrologists throughout the world.

Préface

Ce volume est le vingt et unième de la collection « Études et rapports d'hydrologie », dont la publication a été entreprise par l'Unesco, avec celle de la série « Notes techniques d'hydrologie », dans le cadre du programme de la Décennie hydrologique internationale.

La Décennie hydrologique internationale, qui vient de prendre fin en 1974, avait été ouverte en 1965 par la Conférence générale de l'Unesco à sa treizième session. Son but était de faire progresser la connaissance de l'hydrologie scientifique en encourageant la coopération internationale et la formation de spécialistes et de techniciens. La demande d'eau étant en augmentation constante par suite de l'expansion démographique, industrielle et agricole, tous les pays s'efforcent d'évaluer avec plus de précision leurs ressources en eau et de les exploiter plus rationnellement. La DHI s'est avérée un auxiliaire précieux à cette fin.

En 1974, il existait des comités nationaux pour la Décennie dans 110 des 135 États membres de l'Unesco ; ces comités étaient chargés de mener à bien les activités nationales et de participer aux activités régionales et internationales entreprises dans le cadre du programme de la Décennie hydrologique internationale. Ce programme a été exécuté sous la direction d'un Conseil de coordination composé de 30 États membres désignés par la Conférence générale de l'Unesco, qui a étudié les propositions faites pour le programme, a recommandé l'adoption des projets intéressant la totalité ou la grande majorité des pays, a aidé à mettre sur pied des projets nationaux et régionaux et a coordonné la coopération à l'échelon international. Le programme de la DHI, qui portait sur tous les aspects des études et des recherches hydrologiques, visait essentiellement à développer la collaboration aux stades de l'élaboration de techniques de recherche hydrologique, de la diffusion des données hydrologiques et de la mise en place de réseaux d'observations hydrologiques. Il a permis d'encourager les recherches hydrologiques nationales, régionales et internationales visant à accroître et à améliorer l'utilisation des ressources naturelles pour répondre aux besoins locaux et mondiaux. Il a donné aux pays où la recherche hydrologique était déjà bien avancée l'occasion d'échanger des informations, et aux pays en voie de développement la possibilité de tirer parti de ces échanges pour élaborer leurs projets de recherches et planifier leurs réseaux hydrologiques en fonction des derniers progrès de l'hydrologie scientifique.

La collection « Études et rapports d'hydrologie » a pour but de présenter les données recueillies et les principaux résultats obtenus à la suite des études hydrologiques effectuées dans le cadre de la Décennie et de fournir des renseignements sur les techniques de recherche. On y trouve aussi les Actes de colloques. On espère que ces volumes fourniront aux hydrologues et aux gouvernements des matériaux d'un intérêt tant pratique que théorique et qu'ils répondront aux besoins des techniciens et des hommes de science qui s'occupent, dans tous les pays, des problèmes de l'eau.

Il reste beaucoup à faire, notamment en ce qui concerne l'étude du cycle de l'eau et des méthodes scientifiques utilisées dans le monde pour mesurer les ressources en eau, et l'évaluation de l'influence des activités humaines sur le cycle de l'eau, compte tenu de l'ensemble des problèmes liés à l'environnement.

Pour cette raison, la Conférence générale de l'Unesco a décidé de lancer, en 1975, un programme intergouvernemental à long terme, dit Programme hydrologique international, qui sera axé sur les aspects scientifiques et éducatifs de l'hydrologie et, plus particulièrement, sur l'étude des problèmes indiqués plus haut.

L'Unesco continuera donc de publier « Études et rapports d'hydrologie » qui restera un moyen important de rassembler et diffuser l'expérience accumulée par les hydrologues dans le monde entier.

Prefacio

Esta obra es el vigésimo-primer volumen de la serie de "Estudios e informes de hidrología", cuya publicación inició la Unesco, junto con la de la serie "Technical papers in hydrology", con arreglo al programa del Decenio Hidrológico Internacional.

Este Decenio, que terminó en 1974, fue establecido en 1965 por la Conferencia General de la Unesco en su 13.ª reunión, con la finalidad de promover los conocimientos de hidrología científica, fomentando para ello la cooperación internacional y formando especialistas y técnicos. Al estar aumentando constantemente la demanda de agua, debido al crecimiento de la población y a la evolución de la agricultura y de la industria, todos los países se afanan por llegar a una evaluación más exacta de sus recursos hídricos y por utilizarlos de un modo más racional. El DHI ha sido un medio muy valioso para alcanzar este fin.

En 1974 había comités nacionales del Decenio en 110 de los 135 Estados Miembros de la Unesco, con objeto de llevar a cabo actividades nacionales y colaborar en las de carácter regional e internacional con arreglo al programa del Decenio. La realización de este programa fue supervisada por el Consejo de Coordinación, integrado por 30 Estados Miembros designados por la Conferencia General, que estudió las propuestas relativas al programa, recomendó la adopción de proyectos de interés para todos los países o para un gran número de ellos, contribuyó al establecimiento de proyectos nacionales y regionales y se encargó de la cooperación internacional. El fomento de la colaboración en la preparación de técnicas de investigación hidrológica, la difusión de datos hidrológicos y la organización de redes hidrológicas fue una característica capital del programa del DHI, que abarcó todos los aspectos de las investigaciones y estudios hidrológicos. Se estimularon las investigaciones hidrológicas en los planos, nacional, regional e internacional, a fin de consolidar y mejorar la utilización de los recursos naturales en función de las necesidades nacionales y mundiales. Gracias a este programa los países adelantados en el campo de la investigación hidrológica pudieron intercambiar información, y los países en desarrollo se beneficiaron de ese intercambio para preparar sus propios proyectos de investigación y organizar sus propias redes hidrológicas, aprovechando los progresos más recientes de la hidrología.

La finalidad de esta colección de "Estudios e informes de hidrología" consiste en exponer los datos compilados y los resultados principales de los estudios hidrológicos llevados a cabo en el marco del Decenio, así como en proporcionar información sobre las técnicas de investigación hidrológica utilizadas. También se publican en ella las actas de los simposios que tratan de este tema. Cabe esperar que estos volúmenes proporcionarán materiales, de interés a la vez teórico y práctico, a los hidrólogos y a los gobiernos, y permitirán atender las necesidades de los científicos y técnicos que se dedican a los problemas del agua en todos los países.

Queda todavía mucho por hacer, en especial por lo que se refiere al estudio del ciclo del agua y los métodos científicos utilizados en el mundo para calcular los recursos hídricos, así como la evaluación de la influencia de las actividades del hombre sobre el ciclo del agua en relación con los problemas mesológicos en general.

Por esta razón, en 1974, la Conferencia General de la Unesco decidió establecer un programa intergubernamental a largo plazo, que recibirá el nombre de Programa Hidrológico Internacional y que se centrará en los aspectos científicos y educativos de la hidrología, y en particular en el estudio de los problemas antes citados.

Por ello, la Unesco seguirá publicando los "Estudios e informes de hidrología", que continuarán siendo un medio importante para compilar y difundir la experiencia acumulada de los hidrólogos de todo el mundo.

Предисловие

Эта работа является двадцать первом томом серии « Исследования и доклады по гидрологии », публикация которой была начата ЮНЕСКО вместе с серией « Технические доклады по гидрологии » в рамках программы Международного гидрологического десятилетия.

В 1965 г. тринадцатая сессия Генеральной конференции ЮНЕСКО положила начало проведению Международного гидрологического десятилетия, которое завершилось в 1974 году. Его целью было расширить познание научной гидрологии путем развития международного сотрудничества и подготовки специалистов и техников. В то время, как потребности в воде постоянно возрастают в связи с увеличением населения и расширением промышленности и сельского хозяйства, все страны стремятся наиболее точно оценить имеющиеся у них водные ресурсы и более рационально использовать их. МГД было важным средством достижения этой цели.

В 1974 г. в 110 государствах-членах ЮНЕСКО из 135 имелись национальные комитеты по Десятилетию, созданные для проведения национальных мероприятий и участия в региональных и международных мероприятиях программы Десятилетия. Выполнение программы координировалось Координационным советом, состоявшим из 30 государств-членов, избираемых Генеральной конференцией ЮНЕСКО. Этот Совет изучал предложения, касающиеся развития программы, рекомендовал к принятию проекты, представляющие интерес для всех или для большого числа стран, оказывал помощь в развитии национальных и региональных проектов и координировал международное сотрудничество. Важным направлением программы МГД, которая охватыала все аспекты гидрологических научных исследований, являлось содействие сотрудничеству в разработке методов гидрологических исследований, распространению

гидрологических данных и организации гидрологических сетей. Гидрологические исследования поощрялись на национальном, региональном и международном уровнях, с тем чтобы укрепить и улучшить использование естественных ресурсов как в местном, так и в глобальном плане. Эта программа позволила странам, в которых гидрологические исследования получили значительное развитие, обмениваться информацией, а развивающимся странам извлекать пользу из этого обмена информацией для разработки своих собственных исследовательских проектов и учитывать новейшие достижения в области научной гидрологии при планировании своих собственных гидрологических сетей.

Серия « Исследования и доклады по гидрологии » имеет целью регистрацию собранных данных и основных результатов гидрологических исследований, предпринятых в рамках Десятилетия, а также распространение информации об используемых методах гидрологических исследований. В этом выпуске также публикуются отчеты о симпозиумах. Мы надеемся, что эти тома будут содержать как практические, так и теоретические материалы, представляющие интерес для гидрологов и правительств, и удовлетворять требования ученых и специалистов, занимающихся проблемами воды во всех странах.

Много еще предстоит сделать, в частности, в области исследования гидрологического цикла и научных методов, используемых для оценки водных ресурсов во всем мире, а также оценки влияния деятельности человека на гидрологический цикл в связи с проблемами окружающей среды.

По этой причине Генеральная конференция ЮНЕСКО постановила положить в 1975 г. начало долгосрочной межправительственной программе под названием « Международная гидрологическая программа », которая будет сосредоточена на научных и образовательных аспектах гидрологии и, в частности, на изучении проблем, изложенных выше.

Поэтому ЮНЕСКО будет продолжать публикацию « Исследований и докладов по гидрологии », которые будут оставаться важным средством сбора и распространения опыта, приобретенного гидрологами во всем мире.

Contents

Table des matières

1. Since going to press with the body of this work, the Republic of Dahomey has changed its name to the People's Republic of Benin.

1. Au moment de mettre cet ouvrage sous presse, nous apprenons que la République du Dahomay a changé son appellation : elle devient désormais la République populaire du Bénin.

Índice

Содержание

1. En el momento de imprimirse esta obra, la República de Dahomey ha cambiado su nombre en República Popular del Benin.

1. Во время передачи данной работы в типографию стало известно, что Республика Дагомея изменила свое название: отныне она называется Народная Республика Бенин.

Contents   Table des matières

Foreword

One of the main tasks assigned to the Working Group on Floods and their Computation, set up by the Co-ordinating Council of the International Hydrological Decade was "to determine the regional distribution of flood flow from rain and snowmelt". The scope of the Working Group was later extended to cover low flow also. It was realized that world-wide co-operation was essential to carry out this task, and the Working Group at its first session (Leningrad, 1967) decided to prepare a world catalogue of very large floods. At its second session, the Working Group elaborated the draft programme of such a catalogue and submitted it to the IHD National Committees for comment. The comments received were taken into consideration, and the programme for the study and compilation of data for the *World Catalogue of Very Large Floods* was accepted as final at the fourth session of the Working Group (May 1971). The standard forms for the collection of data were then sent to the IHD National Committees.

The Working Group was composed as follows: Mr. B. M. Abbas (Bangladesh); Mr. S. K. Banerjee (India); Mr. S. Cavazza (Italy); Dr. W. Meyer (Poland); Professor H. Kikkawa (Japan); Mr. F. F. Snyder (U.S.A.); Professor A. A. Sokolov (U.S.S.R.); Dr. V. Al. Stanescu (Romania); Dr. H. G. Kreutzer (FAO); Dr. K. Szestay (IAHS/COWAR); Mr. N. A. Bochin and later Mr. Y. N. Bogoyavlensky (Unesco); Dr. M. Podani (WMO). The secretariat was provided by Unesco.

The following also took part in the preparation of the programme for the catalogue: Dr. J. Rodier (IAHS); Mr. G. A. N. Rao (India); Mr. J. A. Murray (India); Mr. M. Roche (WMO); Dr. L. Dorigo (Italy); Dr. A. G. Kovzel (U.S.S.R.).

The chief editors of the *World Catalogue of Very Large Floods,* appointed by the Working Group, were Professor H. Kikkawa (Japan) and Dr. V. Al. Stanescu (Romania).

This work is the outcome of the joint efforts of 35 countries to supply flood information. The Secretariat expresses its gratitude to the National Committees for the IHD of Albania, Bangladesh, Bulgaria, Canada, People's Republic of the Congo, Czechoslovakia, Dahomey, Federal Republic of Germany, Finland, France, Gabon, Ghana, Guyana, Hungary, India, Italy, Ivory Coast, Japan, Jordan, Madagascar, Malaysia, Morocco, Norway, Panama, Poland, Romania, Singapore, Sri Lanka, Sweden, Thailand, Tunisia, U.S.S.R., United Kingdom, United States of America, and Uruguay which have provided data essential for the catalogue. It is hoped that in the future more countries will provide data, thus making it possible to widen the coverage still further. The Secretariat wishes to express its appreciation to Professor Kikkawa and Dr. Stanescu, the chief editors of the catalogue.

All National Committees for the International Hydrological Programme are invited to send comments on the contents of the catalogue and to forward complementary scientific material. The information will be collected by the IHP secretariat with a view to its later publication.

Avant-propos

L'une des principales tâches assignées au groupe de travail sur les crues et leur évaluation, créé par le Conseil de coordination de la Décennie hydrologique internationale, était « de déterminer la répartition géographique des crues dues à la pluie et à la fonte des neiges ». Par la suite, le mandat du groupe a été étendu aux étiages. Il est apparu que la coopération mondiale était indispensable à l'exécution de cette tâche et, à sa première session (Leningrad, 1967), le groupe a décidé d'établir un répertoire mondial des très fortes crues. A sa deuxième session, il élabora un projet de programme pour ce répertoire et le soumit ensuite pour commentaires aux comités nationaux de la DHI. Les observations reçues furent prises en considération et le programme pour l'étude et le rassemblement des données en vue de l'établissement du *Répertoire mondial des très fortes crues* a été définitivement mis au point par le groupe de travail à sa quatrième session (mai 1971). Les formulaires destinés au rassemblement des données ont été adressés ensuite aux comités nationaux pour la DHI.

La composition du groupe de travail était la suivante :

MM. B. M. Abbas (Bangladesh); S. K. Banerjee (Inde); S. Cavazza (Italie); W. Meyer (Pologne); H. Kikkawa (Japon); F. F. Snyder (États-Unis d'Amérique); A. A. Sokolov (URSS); V. Al. Stanescu (Roumanie); H. G. Kreutzer (FAO); K. Szestay (AISH-COWAR); N. A. Bochin, puis Y. N. Bogoyavlensky (Unesco); M. Podani (OMM). Les services de secrétariat étaient assurés par l'Unesco.

Ont également pris part à la préparation du programme relatif au répertoire : MM. J. Rodier (AISH); G. A. N. Rao (Inde); J. A. Murray (Inde); M. Roche (OMM); L. Dorigo (Italie); A. G. Kovzel (URSS).

Les rédacteurs en chef du *Répertoire mondial des très fortes crues,* désignés par le groupe de travail, étaient MM. H. Kikkawa (Japon) et V. Al. Stanescu (Roumanie).

Le présent travail a pu être réalisé grâce aux renseignements sur les crues fournis par les comités pour la DHI des 35 pays suivants : Albanie, République fédérale d'Allemagne, Bangladesh, Bulgarie, Canada, Congo, Côte-d'Ivoire, Dahomey, États-Unis d'Amérique, Finlande, France, Gabon, Ghana, Guyane, Hongrie, Inde, Italie, Japon, Jordanie, Madagascar, Malaisie, Maroc, Norvège, Panama, Pologne, Roumanie, Royaume-Uni, Singapour, Sri Lanka, Suède, Tchécoslovaquie, Thaïlande, Tunisie, URSS et Uruguay. L'Unesco leur exprime sa gratitude et formule l'espoir qu'à l'avenir d'autres pays fourniront également des données sur les crues, ce qui permettra d'élargir encore la portée de l'ouvrage. L'Unesco tient à remercier MM. Kikkawa et Stanescu, rédacteurs en chef du répertoire.

Tous les comités nationaux pour le Programme hydrologique international sont invités à envoyer des observations sur le contenu du répertoire et à communiquer des données scientifiques complémentaires. Les renseignements seront rassemblés par le secrétariat du PHI en vue de leur publication ultérieure.

Prólogo

Uno de los principales cometidos encomendados al grupo de trabajo sobre las crecidas y su evaluación, establecido por el Consejo de Coordinación del Decenio Hidrológico Internacional consistía en determinar la distribución regional de las crecidas provocadas por las lluvias y la fusión de la nieve. Más tarde se amplió esta misión, y quedaron también comprendidos los caudales de estiaje. Se observó que, para llevarla a cabo, resultaba indispensable una cooperación mundial, y, en su primera reunión (Leningrado, 1967), el grupo de trabajo decidió preparar un *Catálogo mundial de grandes crecidas*. En su segunda reunión, el grupo de trabajo estableció el proyecto de programa y el formato de dicho catálogo, y lo presentó a los comités nacionales del DHI para que hicieran los oportunos comentarios. Se tomaron en consideración los que se recibieron, y en la cuarta reunión del grupo de trabajo (mayo de 1971) se aceptó como definitivo el programa de estudio y compilación de datos para el *Catálogo mundial de grandes crecidas*. Tras ello se enviaron a los comités nacionales del DHI los formularios normalizados de compilación de datos.

El grupo de trabajo tenía la siguiente composición: Sr. B. M. Abbas (Bangladesh); Sr. S. K. Banerjee (India); Sr. S. Cavazza (Italia); Dr W. Meyer (Polonia); Prof. H. Kikkawa (Japón); Sr. F. F. Snyder (Estados Unidos de América); Prof. A. A. Sokolov (URSS); Sr. V. Al. Stanescu (Rumania); Dr. H. G. Kreutzer (FAO); Dr. K. Szestay (AICH/CCIH); Sr. N. A. Bochin y más tarde Sr. Y. N. Bogoyavlensky (Unesco); y Dr. M. Podani (OMM).

La secretaría corrió a cargo de la Unesco.

En la preparación del programa del *Catálogo* intervinieron también las siguientes personas: Dr. J. Rodier (AICH); Sr. G. A. N. Rao (India); Sr. J. A. Murray (India); Sr. M. Roche (OMM); Dr. L. Dorigo (Italia) y Dr. A. G. Kovzel (URSS).

Los responsables principales de preparar la edición del *Catálogo mundial de grandes crecidas* fueron el profesor H. Kikkawa (Japón) y el Dr. V. Al. Stanescu (Rumania).

Este trabajo es el resultado de la labor conjunta de 35 países que facilitaron información sobre crecidas. La Secretaría expresa su agradecimiento a los comités nacionales del DHI de Albania, República Federal de Alemania, Bangladesh, Bulgaria, Canadá, República Popular del Congo, Costa de Marfil, Checoslovaquia, Dahomey, Estados Unidos de América, Finlandia, Francia, Gabón, Chana, Guayana, Hungría, India, Italia, Japón, Jordania, Madagascar, Malasia, Marruecos, Noruega, Panamá, Polonia, Reino Unido, Rumania, Singapur, Sri Lanka, Suecia, Tailandia, Túnez, URSS y Uruguay, que aportaron datos esenciales para el *Catálogo*. Cabe esperar que, en el futuro, otros países suministrarán datos, con lo que podrá ampliar aún más su alcance. La Secretaría desea dar las gracias al profesor Kikkawa y al Dr. Stanescu, responsables principales de la edición del *Catálogo*.

Se invita a todos los comités nacionales del Programa Hidrológico Internacional a enviar comentarios sobre el contenido del *Catálogo* y a remitir materiales científicos complementarios. La información será compilada por la secretaría del Programa Hidrológico Internacional con miras a una publicación ulterior.

Вступление

Одной из основных задач, возложенных на Рабочую группу по паводкам и их расчетам, образованной Координационным советом Международного гидрологического десятилетия, было « определение регионального распределения дождевого и снегового паводочного стока ». В последующем полномочия Рабочей группы были расширены и в ее компетенции были также проблемы исследования низкого стока. Было признано, что широкое международное сотрудничество является важным элементом успешного выполнения этой задачи и Рабочая группа на своей первой сессии (Ленинград, 1967 г.) решила подготовить *Всемирный каталог больших паводков*. На своей второй сессии Рабочая группа разработала проект программы и форму такого каталога и представила их национальным комитетам по Международному гидрологическому десятилетию для обсуждения. Полученные замечания были учтены и программа по изучению и сбору данных для Всемирного каталога больших паводков была принята четвертой сессией Рабочей группы (май 1971 г.). Затем стандартные формы для сбора данных были направлены национальным комитетам по Международному гидрологическому десятилетию.

В состав Рабочей группы входили : проф. А. А. Соколов (СССР), г-н Ф. Снайдер (США), проф. Каваза (Италия), проф. Киккава (Япония), д-р В. Мэйер (Польша), г-н С. К. Бенерджи (Индия), д-р Станеску В. (Румыния), г-н Б. Н. Аббас (Бангладеш), д-р Крейцер (ФАО), д-р К. Сестаи (МАНГ/КОВАР), г-н Н. А. Бочин и позднее г-н Ю. Н. Богоявленский (ЮНЕСКО), д-р М. Подани (ВМО). Секретариатское обслуживание обеспечивалось ЮНЕСКО.

В подготовке программы каталога также принимали участие : д-р Ж. Родье (МАГН), д-р Г. А. Н. Рао (Индия), г-н Ж. А. Мюррей (Индия), г-н М. Рош (ВМО), д-р Л. Дориго (Италия), д-р А. Г. Ковзель (СССР).

Главными редакторами *Всемирного каталога больших паводков*, назначенными Рабочей группой, были проф. Киккава (Япония), и д-р В. Ал. Станеску (Румыния).

Эта работа является результатом совместных усилий 35 стран, представивших информацию по паводкам. Секретариат выражает свою благодарность национальным комитетам по Международному гидрологическому десятилетию Албании, Бангладеш, Болгарии, Канады, Народной Республики Конго, Чехословакии, Дагомеи, Федеративной Республики Германии, Финляндии, Франции, Габона, Ганы, Венгрии, Индии, Италии, Берега Слоновой Кости, Японии, Иордании, Мадагаскара, Малейзии, Марокко, Норвегии, Панамы, Польши, Румынии, Сингапура, Шри Ланка, Швеции, Таиланда, Туниса, СССР, Соединенного Королевства, США и Уругвая, которые представили основные данные для каталога. Мы выражаем надежду, что в будущем еще большее число стран предоставит данные, что позволит увеличить репрезентативность стран, участвующих в составлении каталога. Секретариат выражает свою признательность профессору Киккава и доктору Станеску, главным редакторам каталога.

Национальным комитетам по Международной гидрологической программе предлагается прислать свои замечания по содержанию каталога, а также дополнительный научный материал. Эта информация будет собираться Секретариатом Международной гидрологической программы для ее последующей публикации.

Introduction

Water management and flood control practice rely a great deal on data concerning the variability of floods in space and time, their formation and propagation.

Several methods and techniques for dealing with the computation problems involved have been developed, beginning with the regionally-based peak discharge computations and leading to sophisticated mathematical models meant to simulate the complex process of flood formation. Characteristic flood processing techniques based on statistics have been widely employed. When using mathematical models, whether deterministic or stochastic, any future projection of model parameters should, as a general rule, be based on the longest possible series of hydrological data encompassing the various characteristics of floods.

Often, a minimum of basic information such as peak discharge could be useful for flood control procedures. The specific maximum discharges (the ratio between the peak discharge and the corresponding area of the basin) are often closely related to the area of the catchments. Thus, an appraisal of certain flood hydrograph elements may be made on the basis of geographical interpolation. This is frequently done when hydrological data are lacking or insufficient.

Finally, in some circumstances, even a general picture of the streamflow régime for areas having a similar physiography might prove useful, to give an idea at least of the order of magnitude of peak discharge for areas from which data are unavailable.

The main aim of the *World Catalogue of Very Large Floods* is to present an overall picture of the global flood situation. However, while preparing the catalogue, it was felt that the inclusion of additional information would permit the use of more elaborate methods of data processing. Thus, for instance, Table I gives a minimum of physiographical information related to flood-prone basins in terms of surface and mean altitude, and also provides other physiographical information such as slopes, cover, soils, etc. which may be taken into account for more complex geographical interpolation studies.

Table II presents available statistical data on flood peak discharge and volume which may be useful in statistical processing, and supplies information on the statistical parameters that may, in turn, be used for areas from which data are insufficient or unavailable.

Table III and IV give a minimum of flood evaluation information such as peak discharge, volume of hydrograph, and other flood characteristics together with information on flood-forming rainfall, antecedent precipitation, probabilities of peak discharge and volume, etc. All these might aid in the introduction of more complete methods of flood computation.

Sketch maps of the countries show the locations for which data are given.

Introduction

En matière de gestion des ressources en eau et de lutte contre les crues, la pratique dépend pour beaucoup des données concernant la variabilité des crues dans l'espace et dans le temps, leur formation et leur propagation. Pour résoudre les problèmes de mesure, plusieurs méthodes et techniques ont été mises au point, depuis le calcul des débits de pointe sur une base régionale jusqu'à l'élaboration de modèles mathématiques compliqués pour simuler le processus complexe de la formation des crues. Des techniques fondées sur des statistiques ont été largement employées. Avec l'emploi de modèles mathématiques, de caractère déterministe ou stochastique, toute projection future des paramètres des modèles doit, en règle générale, s'appuyer sur la plus longue série possible de données hydrologiques englobant les diverses caractéristiques des crues.

Souvent, un minimum de renseignements fondamentaux sur le débit de pointe, par exemple, pourraient être utiles pour lutter contre les crues. Les débits maximaux spécifiques (c'est-à-dire le rapport entre le débit de pointe et la surface correspondante du bassin) sont souvent étroitement liés à la superficie du bassin. Ainsi, une évaluation de certains éléments de l'hydrogramme des crues peut être faite sur la base d'interpolations géographiques. Cela est fréquemment le cas lorsque les données hydrologiques manquent ou sont insuffisantes.

Enfin, dans certaines circonstances, une description, même générale, du régime de l'écoulement pour des bassins ayant une physiographie similaire pourrait s'avérer utile, en donnant une idée au moins de l'ordre de grandeur du débit de pointe pour des zones sur lesquelles on manque de données.

Le principal but du *Répertoire mondial des très fortes crues* est d'offrir une vision d'ensemble de la situation des crues dans le monde entier. Toutefois, lors de sa préparation, on a pensé que l'insertion de renseignements supplémentaires permettrait d'employer des méthodes plus élaborées de traitement des données. Ainsi, le tableau I donne un minimum d'informations physiographiques sur les bassins exposés aux crues (superficie et altitude moyenne), mais il contient aussi d'autres renseignements physiographiques (pentes, couverture, sols, etc.) qui peuvent être pris en compte pour des études plus complexes fondées sur l'interpolation géographique.

Le tableau II présente les données statistiques disponibles sur les débits et volumes maximaux qui peuvent être utiles pour les traitements statistiques et fournit des renseignements sur les paramètres statistiques qui peuvent à leur tour être employés pour des zones où les données sont insuffisantes ou inexistantes.

Les tableaux III et IV donnent un minimum de renseignements pour l'évaluation des crues (par exemple, débit de pointe, volume de l'hydrogramme et autres caractéristiques des crues), ainsi que des renseignements sur les précipitations qui causent les crues, les précipitations antérieures, les probabilités concernant les débits et volumes maximaux, etc. Toutes ces indications pourraient contribuer à l'introduction de méthodes plus complètes d'évaluation des crues.

Des cartes-croquis des pays montrent les points pour lesquels des données sont fournies.

Introducción

La ordenación de los recursos hídricos y la lucha contra las inundaciones dependen en gran medida de la disponibilidad de datos sobre la variabilidad de las credidas en el tiempo y en el espacio, su formación y su programación.

Existen varios métodos y técnicas para solventar los problemas de cálculo, empezando por los cálculos del caudal máximo, de carácter regional, y terminando por unos complicados modelos matemáticos que se proponen simular el complejo proceso de formación de las crecidas. Se han empleado ampliamente técnicas de tratamiento de crecidas características, basadas en las estadísticas. Al utilizar los modelos matemáticos, ya sean deterministas o estocásticos, en general toda futura proyección de los parámetros del modelo deberán basarse en la serie más larga posible de datos hidrológicos que abarquen las diversas características de las crecidas.

Con frecuencia, puede resultar útil un mínimo de información básica como por ejemplo el caudal máximo, en las actividades de lucha contra las inundaciones. Los caudales máximos específicos (relación entre el caudal máximo y la superficie de la cuenca) están a menudo estrechamente relacionados con la superficie de la cuenca de recepción. Por ello, se podrá hacer una evaluación de ciertos elementos del hidrograma de una crecida a partir de una interpolación geográfica, como se hace frecuentemente cuando los datos hidrológicos son insuficientes o inexistentes.

Por último, en ciertas circunstancias, puede resultar útil hasta una descripción general del régimen del caudal fluvial en aquellas zonas de fisiografía similar, a fin de tener por lo menos una idea del orden de magnitud del caudal máximo, cuando no se disponga de datos sobre esas zonas.

La finalidad principal del *Catálogo mundial de grandes crecidas* consiste en presentar una descripción global de las crecidas mundiales. Ahora bien, al preparar este *Catálogo* se estimó que la inclusión de información adicional permitiría utilizar métodos más complejos de tratamiento de datos. Así por ejemplo, el cuadro I da un mínimo de información fisiográfica relacionada con las cuencas propensas a las crecidas, en términos de superficie y altitud media, así como otros tipos de información fisiográfica, como las referentes a las pendientes, la cubierta, los suelos, etc., que podrán tenerse en cuenta en unos estudios más complejos de interpolación geográfica.

El cuadro II presenta los datos estadísticos disponibles sobre el volumen y el caudal máximos, que pueden resultar útiles a efectos de tratamiento estadístico, y se facilita información sobre los parámetros estadísticos, que podrán emplearse, a su vez, en las zonas en las que los datos sean insuficientes o inexistentes.

En los cuadros III y IV se aporta un mínimo de información sobre la evaluación de las crecidas —caudal máximo, volumen de hidrograma y otras características de las crecidas—, así como información sobre las lluvias que provocan crecidas, la participación anterior, las probabilidades de volumen y caudal máximo, etc. Todo ello podría facilitar la aplicación de métodos más completos de cálculo de las crecidas.

Hay también mapas simplificados de los países, en los que se indican los puntos a los que corresponden los datos.

Введение

Водное хозяйство и защита от паводков в значительной мере основываются на данных об изменчивости паводков во времени и пространстве, об их формировании и распространении.

Разработан ряд методов и приемов расчета паводков, начиная с региональных формул для расчета максимального расхода паводка и до сложных математических моделей для моделирования процесса формирования паводков. Широко используются статистические методы обработки данных по паводкам. При использовании математических моделей, будь то детерминистические или стохастические модели, расчет основных параметров должен основываться, по возможности, как правило, на более длинном ряду гидрологических данных, включающих различные характеристики паводков.

Часто даже минимум основной информации, например, максимальный расход, может быть полезным для разработки методов защиты от паводков. Максимальный модуль стока (соотношение между максимальным расходом и площадью водосбора) часто тесно связан с площадью бассейна. Таким образом, оценка некоторых элементов гидрографа паводка может быть сделана на основе географической интерполяции, что часто делается при отсутствии или недостаточности гидрологических данных.

В конечном счете при некоторых обстоятельствах даже знание общей картины режима речного стока для районов, имеющих сходные физико-географические условия, может оказаться полезной для представления, по крайней мере, о порядке размера максимального расхода для районов, по которым отсутствуют данные.

Основная цель *Всемирного каталога больших паводков* — дать общую картину паводков земного шара. Однако при подготовке каталога сложилось мнение, что включение дополнительной информации позволило использовать более детальные методы обработки собранных данных. Таким образом, например, в Таблице I приводится минимум физико-географических характеристик бассейнов : средняя высота, характер поверхности, уклон, тип почвы и т.д., которые могут быть использованы для более комплексных исследований.

Таблица II содержит статистичеекие данные о максимальных расходах воды и объемах, которые могут быть полезны при обработке данных, и приводится информация о статистических параметрах, которые могут быть использованы для районов, по которым данные недостаточны или отсутствуют.

В таблицах III и IУ приводятся характеристики паводков — максимальный расход, объем гидрографа и другие данные, а также данные об осадках, формирующих паводок, и осадках за предшествующие дни, вероятных максимальных расходах и объемах и т.д. Все это может помочь для использования наиболее совершенных методов расчета паводков.

Схематические карты стран показывают бассейны, по которым приводятся данные.

Explanatory note

1 Selection of flood

The catalogue has been conceived so as to provide the maximum of available information on floods recorded in the world. The choice of the catchments and floods entered in the catalogue was based on physiographical diversity at world-wide level in order to provide wide representation. In this context, the twin criteria of macroclimate and river catchment surface area were adopted with a view to the best selection and analysis of basins having a flood record.

The basins were graded as follows:
Surface area less than 100 km²
Surface area between 100 and 5,000 km²
Surface area between 5,000 and 10,000 km²
Surface area between 10,000 and 50,000 km²
Surface area between 50,000 and 200,000 km²
Surface area between 200,000 and 1,000,000 km²
Surface area over 1,000,000 km².

The main purpose of the catalogue is to supply data on representative floods occurring under different physiographical conditions. Thus, certain countries with great variations in climatic and physiographical conditions have selected more than one basin in the same range of basin area.

For each country, the number of selected floods for which data are supplied was established as follows:

(a) more than 50 years of observation—at least five floods

(b) 20 to 50 years of observation—2 to 5 floods

(c) 10 to 20 years of observation—1 to 2 floods.

In the context of this catalogue, which deals particularly with very large floods, a "large flood" is a flood with an exceedance probability of at least 10 per cent. This probability of 10 per cent refers to the peak discharge and/or to the volume of the flood. Thus, the catalogue may list floods with peak discharges having a probability greater than 10 per cent but with flood volumes having probabilities of less than 10 per cent.

2 Explanation of the content of the tables

2.1 TABLE I — CHARACTERISTICS OF BASIN

	GAUGING STATION								BASIN			
	River					Distance (km) from gauging site					Altitude (m)		
No.	River system	Name	Period of records	Co-ordinates Lat.	Long.	to remotest point of river system L_{rs}	to projection of centre of basin on main course L_{ca}	Mean slope of river I_r (%)	Area A (km²)	Mean H_m	Max. H_{max}	Min. H_{min}
1	2	3	4	5	6	7	8	9	10	11	12	13

						BASIN					
	Width (km)		Mean slope I_b (%)			Weighted lake area P_L (%)	Swamps R_s (%)	Mean annual precipitation P (mm)	Annual runoff Q (mm)	Mean annual temperature T (°C)	Regulating capacity of reservoirs α
No.	Mean B_m	Max. B_{max}		Soils	Cover						
1	14	15	16	17	18	19	20	21	22	23	24

Column 4 *Period of record.* The period mentioned in this column is not necessarily the whole period of record of the station.

Column 5 and 6 *Co-ordinates* give the geographical co-ordinates (latitude and longitude) in degrees, minutes and seconds.

For example:

N

15:12:42 means $15°12'42''$ north latitude.

Column 9 *The mean slope of the river, I_r (%),* is computed by the formula:

$$I_r = \frac{H_1 - H_n}{10\,L}$$

where L is the length of the river (km); H_1 and H_n are the maximum and minimum elevations respectively (m).

Column 11 *The mean altitude of the basin, H_m,* is computed by the formula:

$$H_m = \frac{\sum_{i=1}^{h} a_i h_i}{A}$$

where A is the area of the basin; a_i is the area of the surface between two successive contour lines (km²); h_i is the mean altitude (m) of a_i (the half sum of the heights of the two successive isolines). For large basins, the mean altitude is not a representative characteristic of the basin and therefore is not usually provided.

Column 14 *The mean width of the basin, B_m,* is computed by the formula:

$$B_m = \frac{A}{L}$$

where A is the area of the basin; and L is the distance from the gauging site to the remotest point of the basin.

Column 16 *The mean slope of the basin, I_b (%),* is computed by the formula :

$$I_b = \frac{\left(\dfrac{l_0 + l_n}{2} + \sum_{i=1}^{h} l_i\right)\Delta h}{10\,A}$$

where Δh is the equidistance of the contour lines (m); $l_0, l_i \ldots l_n$ are the lengths (km) of each of the contour lines; A is the area of the basin (km²).

Column 17 *Soils:* the types of soils are indicated by the code numbers, as shown in the following list:

Code	Type of soil
1	Tundra soil
2	Podzolic soil
3	Grey forest soil
4	Brown forest soil
5	Chernozem and prairie blackearth
6	Steppe chestnut-coloured soil
7	Brown steppe soil
8	Red and yellow subtropical soil
9	Subtropical steppe black-red soil
10	Forest cinnamonic soil
11	Subtropical steppe grey-cinnamonic soil
12	Serozem
13	Tropical and subtropical desert soil
14	Laterites
15	Savanne red soil
16	Tropical forest red-cinnamonic soil.

In certain tables the percentage of the total area of the basin for each type of soils is given after the code number in brackets. For example: 2 (45), 3 (55) means Podzolic soils 45 per cent and Grey forest soil 55 per cent. Certain countries considered that the classification mentioned above did not correspond to their natural conditions, and therefore they listed other types of soils. Such supplementary types are not given in codified from, but are described by their local names.

Column 18 *Cover:* given in a codified form, as follows:

F   Forest
C   Cultivated area
U   Uncultivated area (meadows, urban areas, etc.)

Some tables contain, in brackets after the code, the percentage of each type of cover. For example, F (30), C (68), U (2) means Forest 30 per cent, Cultivated 68 per cent, and Uncultivated 2 per cent.

Column 19 *The weighted lake area index of the basin, P_L%,* is expressed as a dimensionless index given by:

$$P_L\% = 100\,\frac{\sum A_{li}\, a_i}{A^2}$$

where A_{li} is the surface area of the lake i (km²)
a_i is the catchment area of the lake i (km²)
A is the area of the basin (km²)

In some cases this index is computed as the ratio between the total area of the lakes and the area of the basin.

Column 20 *The percentage of swamps, R_s (%),* is calculated as the ratio of area covered by swamps to the basin area.

Explanatory note

Column 24 *The regulating capacity of reservoirs* is expressed by the dimensionless coefficient α :

$$\alpha = \frac{W_R}{W_m}$$

where W_R is the volume of the reservoir (10^6 m²)
W_m is the average annual runoff volume.
The remaining columns are self-explanatory.

2.2 TABLE II — ANNUAL MAXIMUM DISCHARGES AND VOLUMES

Date	Maximum discharge (m³/s) resulting from:		Maximum volume (10^6 m²) corresponding to max. discharge resulting from:	
	Rainfall	Snowmelt	Rainfall	Snowmelt
1	2	3	4	5

Column 1 *Date* shows the date of the peak discharge. For example: 12-06-68 means 12 June 1968.

The values of maximum discharges and volumes resulting from mixed feed (snowmelt and rainfall) are also listed in columns 3 and 5, respectively. The figures in brackets after "country" correspond to the number of the gauging station given in Table I, column 1.

For example: "Country: Finland (3)" refers to the gauging station no. 3 selected in Table I.

2.3 TABLE III — CHARACTERISTICS OF SNOWMELT FLOODS

No.	River	Gauging station	Characteristic elements							Type of probability curve	
			Q_{max} (m³/s)	Date	h (mm)	T_T (hours)	t_i (hours)	P_w (%)	P_{Qmax} (%)	for P_w	for P_{Qmax}
1	2	3	4	5	6	7	8	9	10	11	12

No.	Method of curve fitting		Snow cover		Rainfall during snowmelt (mm)	Monthly precipitation before soil freezing (mm)	Mean monthly temperature before snowmelt (°C)
	for W	for Q_{max}	Water equivalent (mm)	Layer thickness (cm)			
1	13	14	15	16	17	18	19

In Table III the following symbols are used :
Column 4 Q_{max} : peak discharge.

Column 5 *Date of the peak discharge*
For example:
12-06-68 means 12 June 1968
12-06-90 means 12 June 1890
12-06-40* means 12 June 1840
12-06-40** means 12 June 1740

Column 6 $h = \dfrac{W}{A}$

depth of runoff, where W is the flood volume

Column 7 T_T
total duration of the flood

Column 8 t_i: time to peak

Columns 9 and 10 P_W, P_Q
exceedance probabilities of volume and peak discharge, respectively.

In columns 17, 18 and 19 the values are given as average values for the whole area of the basin or representative values.
The remaining columns are self-explanatory.

2.4 TABLE IV — CHARACTERISTICS OF RAINFALL FLOODS

No.	River	Gauging station	Q_{max} (m³/s)	Date	h (mm)	T_T (hours)	t_i (hours)	P_W (%)	P_{Qmax} (%)	Type of probability curve for P_W	for P_{Qmax}
										Characteristic elements	
1	2	3	4	5	6	7	8	9	10	11	12

No.	Method of curve fitting for W	for Q_{max}	Rainfall forming flood (mm)	Snowmelt during floods (mm)	Maximum daily rainfall (mm)	Date	Hourly maximum rainfall (mm)	Date	Antecedent precipitation for 10 days (mm)	30 days (mm)
1	13	14	15	16	17	18	19	20	21	22

In Table IV, the symbols are the same as in Table III.

As a general rule, the values of maximum daily rainfall are listed for basins with an area of less than 10,000 km².

The values of hourly maximum rainfall are usually given for small basins.

In columns 15, 16, 17, 19, 21 and 22 the values are given as mean values or representative values valid for the whole basin.

2.5 SKETCH MAPS

In the sketch maps of the basins, the locations of selected gauging stations are identified by the serial numbers of the stations as listed in Table I (column 1).

Notice explicative

1 Choix des crues

Le répertoire a été conçu de façon à fournir le maximum de renseignements disponibles sur les crues enregistrées dans le monde. Le choix des bassins de réception et des crues s'appuie sur leur diversité physiographique au niveau mondial de façon à assurer une large représentation. Dans cette optique, on a adopté le double critère du macroclimat et de la superficie du bassin de réception de façon à choisir et à analyser au mieux les bassins exposés aux crues.

Les bassins ont été classés comme suit :
Superficie inférieure à 100 km²
Superficie comprise entre 100 et 5 000 km²
Superficie comprise entre 5 000 et 10 000 km²
Superficie comprise entre 10 000 et 50 000 km²
Superficie comprise entre 50 000 et 200 000 km²
Superficie comprise entre 200 000 et 1 000 000 de km²
Superficie supérieure à 1 000 000 de km².

Le but principal du répertoire est de fournir des données sur les crues représentatives qui se produisent dans différentes conditions physiographiques. Ainsi, certains pays où les conditions climatiques et physiographiques varient beaucoup ont retenu plus d'un bassin dans la même catégorie de superficie.

Pour chaque pays, le nombre des crues choisies pour lesquelles des données sont fournies s'établit comme suit :
a) Plus de 50 ans d'observation : au moins 5 crues,
b) De 20 à 50 ans d'observation : 2 à 5 crues,
c) De 10 à 20 ans d'observation : 1 à 2 crues.

Dans le contexte de ce répertoire, qui est consacré plus particulièrement aux très fortes crues, on entend par « forte crue » une crue affectée d'un coefficient de probabilité de 10 % au moins. Cette probabilité de 10 % concerne le débit de pointe ou le volume de la crue. Aussi, le répertoire peut-il mentionner des crues avec des débits de pointe ayant une probabilité supérieure à 10 %, mais avec des volumes de crue ayant des probabilités inférieures à 10 %.

2 Contenu des tableaux

2.1 TABLEAU I — CARACTÉRISTIQUES DU BASSIN

| | Station de jaugeage | | | | | | | | Bassin | | | | |
| | | | | | | Distance (en km) entre la station de jaugeage et | | | | | Altitude (en m) | | |
N°	Cours d'eau	Nom	Période d'enregistrement des données	Coordonnées Lat.	Long.	Le point le plus éloigné du réseau hydrographique L_{rs}	La projection du centre du bassin sur le cours principal L_{ca}	Pente moyenne du cours d'eau I_r (%)	Superficie A (km²)	Moy. H_m	Maxi. H_{max}	Mini. H_{min}
1	2	3	4	5	6	7	8	9	10	11	12	13

| | Bassin | | | | | | | | | | |
| | Largeur (en km) | | Pente moyenne I_b (%) | | | Superficie lacustre pondérée P_L (%) | Maré-cages R_s (%) | Préci-pitation annuelle moyenne P (en mm) | Ruisselle-ment annuel Q (en mm) | Température annuelle moyenne T (en °C) | Capacité régulatrice des réservoirs α |
N°	Moy. B_m	Maxi. B_{max}		Sols	Couverture						
1	14	15	16	17	18	19	20	21	22	23	24

Colonne 4 *Période d'enregistrement des données*. Cette période n'est pas nécessairement la période totale d'enregistrement de la station.

Colonnes 5 et 6 *Coordonnées*. Coordonnées géographiques (latitude et longitude) en degrés, minutes et secondes. Par exemple :

N

15:12:42 signifie $15°12'42''$ de latitude nord.

Colonne 9 *Pente moyenne du cours d'eau, I_r (%)*. Elle se calcule au moyen de la formule :

$$I_r = \frac{H_1 - H_n}{10\,L}$$

ou L représente la longueur du cours d'eau (en kilomètres), H_1 et H_n représentent respectivement les hauteurs maximale et minimale (en mètres).

Colonne 11 *Altitude moyenne du bassin, H_m*. Elle se calcule à l'aide de la formule :

$$H_m = \frac{\sum_{i=1}^{n} a_i h_i}{A}$$

dans laquelle A est la superficie du bassin ; a_i représente la superficie (en kilomètres carrés) de la zone située entre deux courbes de niveau successives ; h_i est l'altitude moyenne (en mètres) de la zone a_i (soit la demi-somme des hauteurs des courbes de niveau successives). Pour les grands bassins, l'altitude moyenne n'étant pas une caractéristique représentative n'a pas été fournie en général.

Colonne 14 *Largeur moyenne du bassin, B_m*. Elle se calcule à l'aide de la formule :

$$B_m = \frac{A}{L}$$

où A est la superficie du bassin et L la distance entre la station de jaugeage et le point le plus éloigné du bassin.

Colonne 16 *Pente moyenne du bassin, I_b (%)*. Elle se calcule à l'aide de la formule :

$$I_b = \frac{\left(\dfrac{l_0 + l_n}{2} + \sum_{i=1}^{n} l_i\right)\Delta h}{10\,A}$$

où Δh est l'équidistance des courbes de niveau (en mètres); $l_0, l_i \ldots l_n$ correspondent à la longueur (en kilomètres) de chacune des courbes de niveau; A est la superficie du bassin (en kilomètres carrés).

Colonne 17 *Sols*. Les types de sols sont indiqués par des numéros selon le code suivant :

Code	Type de sol
1	Sol de toundra
2	Sol podzolique
3	Sol gris forestier
4	Sol brun forestier
5	Sol noir de chernozem et de prairie
6	Sol châtain des steppes
7	Sol brun steppique
8	Sol rouge et jaune subtropical
9	Sol brun-rouge des steppes subtropicales
10	Sol forestier cannelle
11	Sol subtropical de steppe gris ou cannelle
12	Sierozem
13	Sol désertique tropical ou subtropical
14	Latérites
15	Sol rouge de savane
16	Sol forestier tropical cannelle rougeâtre.

Dans certains tableaux, le pourcentage de la superficie totale du bassin pour chaque type de sol est indiqué entre parenthèses après le numéro de code. Ainsi 2 (45), 3 (55), signifie : 45 % de sols podzoliques et 55 % de sol gris forestier. Estimant que la classification mentionnée ci-dessus ne correspondait pas à leurs conditions naturelles, certains pays ont indiqué d'autres types de sols. Ces types supplémentaires ne sont pas signalés sous une forme codifiée, mais désignés par leur appellation locale.

Colonne 18 *Couverture*. Elle est indiquée sous une forme codifiée, comme suit :

F Zones boisées

C Zones cultivées

U Zones non cultivées (prairies, zones urbaines, etc.).

Certains tableaux donnent entre parenthèses, après le code, le pourcentage de chaque type de couverture. Ainsi : F (30), C (68), U (2), signifie 30 % de zones boisées, 68 % de zones cultivées et 2 % de zones non cultivées.

Colonne 19 *Superficie lacustre pondérée du bassin, P_L %*. Cette superficie est exprimée sous la forme d'un indice sans dimension, selon la formule :

$$P_L \% = 100\,\frac{\Sigma\, A_{li}\, a_i}{A^2}$$

dans laquelle A_{li} représente la superficie du lac i (en km²) a_i représente la superficie de réception du lac i (en km²) A est la superficie du bassin (en km²).

Dans certains cas, cet indice est le rapport entre la superficie lacustre totale et la superficie du bassin.

Colonne 20 *Pourcentage de marécages, R_s (%)*. Il s'obtient en calculant le rapport entre la superficie couverte en marécages et la superficie totale du bassin.

Notice explicative

Colonne 24 *Capacité régulatrice des réservoirs*. Elle est exprimée par le coefficient sans dimension ci-après (α) :

$$\alpha = \frac{W_{\mathrm{R}}}{W_m}$$

où W_{R} représente le volume des réservoirs (en millions de m³) et W_m le volume moyen annuel du ruissellement.

Les autres colonnes se passent d'explications.

2.2 TABLEAU II — DÉBITS ET VOLUMES ANNUELS MAXIMAUX

Date	Débit maximal (en m³/s)		Volume maximal (en millions de m³) correspondant au débit maximal	
	Résultant de chutes de pluie	Résultant de la fonte des neiges	Résultant de chutes de pluie	Résultant de la fonte des neiges
1	2	3	4	5

Colonne 1 *Date*. Il s'agit de la date du débit de pointe. Ainsi : 12-06-68 signifie 12 juin 1968.

Les valeurs des débits et volumes maximaux provenant à la fois des chutes de pluie et de la fonte des neiges sont indiquées aussi dans les colonnes 3 et 5, respec-tivement. Les chiffres entre parenthèses apparaissant après le mot « pays » correspondent au nom de la station de jaugeage indiquée dans la colonne 1 du tableau I.

Ainsi : « Pays : Finlande (3) » se réfère à la station de jaugeage n° 3 choisie dans le tableau I.

2.3 TABLEAU III — CARACTÉRISTIQUES DES CRUES NIVALES

N°	Cours d'eau	Station de jaugeage	Q_{max} (m³/s)	Date	h (en mm)	T_{T} (en heures)	t_i (en heures)	P_{W} (%)	$P_{Q_{max}}$ (%)	Courbe de probabilité utilisée	
						Éléments caractéristiques				Pour P_{W}	Pour $P_{Q_{max}}$
1	2	3	4	5	6	7	8	9	10	11	12

N°	Méthode d'ajustement de la courbe		Couverture de neige		Chutes de pluie pendant la fonte des neiges (en mm)	Chutes de pluie mensuelles antérieures au gel du sol (en mm)	Température mensuelle moyenne de l'air avant la fonte des neiges (en °C)
	Pour W	Pour Q_{max}	Équivalent en eau (en mm)	Épaisseur de la couche (en cm)			
1	13	14	15	16	17	18	19

Colonne 4 Q_{max} : Débit de pointe maximal.

Colonne 5 *Date du débit de pointe maximal*.
Par exemple :
12-06-68 signifie 12 juin 1968,
12-06-90 signifie 12 juin 1890,
12-06-40* signifie 12 juin 1840,
12-06-40** signifie 12 juin 1740.

Colonne 6 $h = \dfrac{W}{A}$

Lame d'eau écoulée, W étant le volume de la crue.

Colonne 7 T_{T}
Durée totale de la crue.

Colonne 8 t_i : Temps compris entre le début et le maximum de la crue (débit de pointe).

Colonnes 9 et 10 P_{W}, P_{Q}
Probabilité d'un volume et d'un débit supérieurs.

Dans les colonnes 17, 18 et 19, les valeurs indiquées sont les valeurs moyennes pour toute la surface du bassin ou des valeurs représentatives.

Les autres colonnes se passent d'explications.

2.4 TABLEAU IV — CARACTÉRISTIQUES DES CRUES PLUVIALES

			Éléments caractéristiques							Courbe de probabilité utilisée	
Nº	Cours d'eau	Station de jaugeage	Q_{max} (m³/s)	Date	h (en mm)	T_T (en heures)	t_1 (en heures)	P_w (%)	P_{Qmax} (%)	Pour P_w	Pour P_{Qmax}
1	2	3	4	5	6	7	8	9	10	11	12

	Méthode d'ajustement de la courbe		Chutes de pluie provoquant la crue en (mm)	Fonte de neige pendant la crue (en mm)	Intensité journalière maximale des préci- pitations (en mm)		Intensité horaire maximale des préci- pitations (en mm)		Chutes de pluies antérieures (mm) pendant	
Nº	Pour W	Pour Q_{max}				Date		Date	10 jours (en mm)	30 jours (en mm)
1	13	14	15	16	17	18	19	20	21	22

Dans le tableau IV, les symboles sont les mêmes que dans le tableau III.

En règle générale, les valeurs des précipitations journalières maximales sont indiquées pour les bassins d'une superficie inférieure à 10 000 km².

La valeur des précipitations horaires maximales est habituellement indiquée pour les bassins de faible étendue.

Dans les colonnes 15, 16, 17, 19, 21 et 22, les valeurs indiquées sont des valeurs moyennes ou des valeurs représentatives valables pour l'ensemble du bassin.

2.5 CARTES SOMMAIRES

Sur les cartes croquis des bassins, l'emplacement des stations de jaugeage choisies est indiqué par les numéros de série des stations précisés au tableau I (colonne 1).

Nota explicativa

1 *Selección de las crecidas*

Se ha concebido el *Catálogo* de modo tal que proporcione el máximo de información sobre las crecidas observadas en el mundo. La elección de las crecidas y de las cuencas de recepción que figuran en el *Catálogo* se basa en la diversidad fisiográfica en el plano mundial, con objeto de obtener una amplia representación. En este orden de cosas, se adoptaron los dos criterios gemelos del macroclima y de la superficie de la cuenca, con miras a establecer una selección y análisis óptimos de las cuencas en las que se han observado las crecidas.

Se clasificaron las cuencas como sigue:
Superficie de menos de 100 km²
Superficie entre 100 y 5 000 km²
Superficie entre 5 000 y 10 000 km²
Superficie de 10 000 a 50 000 km²
Superficie de 50 000 a 200 000 km²
Superficie de 200 000 a 1 000 000 km²
Superficie de más de 1 000 000 de km².

La finalidad principal del *Catálogo* consiste en proporcionar datos sobre unas crecidas representativas que se producen en condiciones fisiográficas distintas. Por ello, ciertos países que tienen grandes variaciones de clima y de condiciones fisiográficas han escogido más de una cuenca de una misma categoría de superficie.

Con respecto a cada país, se estableció como sigue el número de crecidas seleccionadas para las que se suministran datos:
a) más de 50 años de observación: 5 crecidas por lo menos,
b) de 20 a 50 años de observación: de 2 a 5 crecidas,
c) de 10 a 20 años de observación: de 1 a 2 crecidas.
En este *Catálogo*, que se refiere de modo especial a las grandes crecidas, se definen éstas como las que tienen una probabilidad de excedencia de un 10 por ciento por lo menos. Esta probabilidad del 10 por ciento se refiere al caudal máximo y/o al volumen de la crecida. Por ello pueden figurar en el *Catálogo* crecidas con unos caudales máximos que tengan una probabilidad superior al 10 por ciento pero con unos volúmenes de crecida que tengan una probabilidad inferior al 10 por ciento.

2 *Explicación del contenido de los cuadros*

2.1 CUADRO I — CARACTERÍSTICAS DE LA CUENCA

	Estación de aforo								Cuenca				
						Distancia (km) desde el punto de aforo							
	Río					al punto más remoto del sistema fluvial	a la proyección del centro de la cuenca sobre el curso de agua principal	Pendiente media del río			Altitud (m)		
N.º	Sistema fluvial	Nombre	Periodo de observación	Coordenadas Lat.	Long.	L_{rs}	L_{ca}	I_r (%)	Superficie A (km²)	Media H_m	Máx. H_{max}	Mín. H_{min}
1	2	3	4	5	6	7	8	9	10	11	12	13

						Cuenca						
	Anchura (m)		Pendiente		Superficie ponderada de los lagos		Precipitación anual media	Escorrentía anual	Temperatura anual media	Capacidad de regulación de los embalses
N.º	Media B_m	Máx. B_{max}	Suelos máx. I_b (%)	Cubierta	P_L (%)	Pantanos R_s (%)	P (mm)	Q (mm)	T (°C)	α
1	14	15	16	17	18	19	20	21	22	23	24

Columna 4 *Periodo de observación*. El periodo mencionado en esta columna no es necesariamente el periodo total de observación de la estación.

Columnas 5 y 6 *Coordenadas*. Se dan las coordenadas geográficas (latitud y longitud) en grados, minutos y segundos. Por ejemplo:

N
15:12:42 quiere decir $15°12'42''$ de latitud Norte.

Columna 9 *La pendiente media del río, I_r (%)* se calcula con la fórmula:

$$I_r = \frac{H_1 - H_n}{10\,L}$$

en donde L es la longitud del río (en km) y H_1 y H_n las elevaciones máxima y mínima, respectivamente (en metros).

Columna 11 *La altitud media de la cuenca, H_m*, se calcula con la formula:

$$H_m = \frac{\sum_{i=1}^{n} a_i h_i}{A}$$

en donde A es la superficie de la cuenca, a_i es la superficie comprendida entre dos líneas de nivel sucesivas (en km²), h_i la altitud media (en metros) de a_i (suma media de las alturas de las dos isolíneas sucesivas). En el caso de grandes cuencas, la altitud media no es una característica representativa de la cuenca, y por ello no suele indicarse.

Columna 14 *La anchura media de la cuenca, B_m* se calcula con la fórmula:

$$B_m = \frac{A}{L}$$

en done A es la superficie de la cuenca y L la distancia desde el punto de aforo hasta el más remoto de la cuenca.

Columna 16 *La pendiente media de la cuenca, I_b (%)* se calcula con la fórmula:

$$I_b = \frac{\left(\dfrac{l_0 + l_n}{2} + \sum_{i=1}^{h} l_i\right) \Delta h}{10\,A}$$

en donde Δh es la equidistancia de las líneas de nivel (en metros), $l_0, l_i \dots l_n$ las longitudes (en km) de cada una de las líneas de nivel, y A la superficie de la cuenca (en km²).

Columna 17 *Suelos*. Se indican los tipos de suelo con arreglo a los siguientes números de referencia:

Número de referencia	*Tipo de suelo*
1	Suelo de tundra
2	Suelo podsólico
3	Suelo podsólico de bosque
4	Suelo pardo de bosque
5	Tierras negras de pradera y chernozem
6	Suelo castaño de estepa
7	Suelo pardo de estepa
8	Suelo rojo y amarillo subtropical
9	Suelo rojo-negro de estepa tropical
10	Suelo cinamome de bosque
11	Suelo gris-cinamome de estepa subtropical
12	Sierozem
13	Suelo de desierto tropical y subtropical
14	Lateritas
15	Suelo rojo de sabana
16	Suelo rojo-cinamono de bosque tropical.

En ciertos cuadros se indica entre paréntesis, después del número de referencia, el porcentaje de la superficie total de la cuenca correspondiente a cada tipo de suelo. Por ejemplo 2 (45), 3 (55) quiere decir un 45 % de suelos podsólicos y un 55 % de suelos podsólicos de bosque. Algunos países consideraron que la clasificación antes expuesta no se ajustaba a sus condiciones naturales, y por ello indicaron otros tipos de suelos. Estos tipos suplementarios no figuran en forma cifrada, sino que se describen con arreglo a sus nombres locales.

Columna 18 *Cubierta*. Se indica en forma cifrada como sigue:

F   Bosques
C   Superficies cultivadas
U   Superficies no cultivadas (praderas, zonas urbanas, etc.)

En ciertos cuadros se indica entre paréntesis, después del símbolo, el porcentaje de cada tipo de cubierta, por ejemplo: F (30), C (38), U (2) quiere decir un 30 por ciento de bosques, un 68 por ciento de tierras cultivadas y un 2 por ciento de superficies no cultivadas.

Columna 19 *El índice ponderado de la superficie de lagos de la cuenca, P_1 %*, se expresa como un índice adimensional:

$$P_L \% = 100 \frac{\Sigma A_{li}\, a_i}{A^2}$$

en donde A_{li} es la superficie del lago i (en km²), a_i la superficie de la cuenca del lago i (en km²) y A la superficie de la cuenca general (en km²).

En ciertos casos, este índice se calcula como la relación entre la superficie total de los lagos y de la cuenca general.

Columna 20   *El porcentaje de pantanos, R_s (%)* es la relación entre la zona cubierta por pantanos y la de la cuenca.

Columna 24   *La capacidad de regulación de los embalses.* Se expresa con el coeficiente adimensional α:

$$\alpha = \frac{W_R}{W_m}$$

en donde W_R es el volumen del embalse (en 10^6 m³) y W_m el volumen anual medio de escorrentía.

Las demás columnas no requieren explicación.

2.2 CUADRO II — VOLÚMENES Y CAUDALES MÁXIMOS ANUALES

	Caudal máximo (m³/s) debido a:		Volumen máximo (10^6 m³) correspondiente a un caudal máximo debido a:	
Fecha	Lluvia	Fusión de la nieve	Lluvia	Fusión de la nieve
1	2	3	4	5

Columna 1   *Fecha.* Indica la fecha del caudal máximo.

Por ejemplo: 12-06-68 quiere decir 12 de junio de 1968.

Los valores de los caudales máximos y volúmenes debidos a causas mixtas (fusión de la nieve y lluvias) se indican también en las columnas 3 y 5, respectivamente. Las cifras entre paréntesis después del "país" corresponden al número de la estación de aforo que se indica en la columna 1 del cuadro I.

Por ejemplo: "País: Finlandia (3)" remite a la estación de aforo n⁰. 3 seleccionada en el cuadro I.

2.3 CUADRO III — CARACTERÍSTICAS DE LAS CRECIDAS PROVOCADAS POR LA FUSIÓN DE LA NIEVE

N.º	Río	Estación de aforo	Q_{max} (m³/s)	Fecha	h (mm)	T_T (horas)	t_i (horas)	P_w (%)	P_{Qmax} (%)	Curva de probabilidad utilizada	
						Elementos característicos				para P_w	para $P_{Qma,}$
1	2	3	4	5	6	7	8	9	10	11	12

N.º	Método del ajuste de curvas		Capa de nieve		Lluvias durante la fusión de la nieve (mm)	Precipitación mensual antes de que se congele el suelo (mm)	Temperatura mensual media del aire antes de la fusión de la nieve (°C)
	para W	para Q_{max}	Equivalente en agua (mm)	Espesor del estrato (cm)			
1	13	14	15	16	17	18	19

Columna 4 Q_{max}: caudal máximo.

Columna 5   *Fecha del caudal máximo*
Por ejemplo:
12-06-68   quiere decir 12 de junio de 1968
12-06-90   quiere decir 12 de junio de 1890
12-06-40*   quiere decir 12 de junio de 1840
12-06-40**   quiere decir 12 de junio de 1740.

Columna 6 $h_{mm} = \dfrac{W}{A}$

Altura del escurrimiento, siendo W el volumen de la crecida

Columna 7 T_T
Duración total de la crecida

Columna 8 t_i: Horas hasta el caudal máximo

Nota explicativa

Columnas 9 y 10 P_W, P_Q
Probabilidades de excedencia del volumen y del caudal
máximo, respectivamente.

En las columnas 17, 18 y 19 se indican los valores como
promedios de toda la superficie de la cuenca o valores
representativos. Las demás columnas no requieren
explicación.

2.4 CUADRO IV — CARACTERÍSTICAS DE LAS CRECIDAS PROVOCADAS POR LAS LLUVIAS

N.º	Río	Estación de aforo	Q_{max} (m³/s)	Fecha	h (mm)	T_T (horas)	t_i (horas)	P_W (%)	P_{Qmax} (%)	para P_W	para P_{Qmax}
						Elementos característicos				Tipo de curva de probabilidad	
1	2	3	4	5	6	7	8	9	10	11	12

N.º	Método del ajuste de curvas		Lluvia que provoca la crecida (mm)	Fusión de la nieve durante la crecida (mm)	Precipitación diaria máxima (mm)	Fecha	Precipitación máxima por hora (mm)	Fecha	Precipitación anterior correspondiente a	
	para W	para P_{Qmax}							10 días (mm)	30 días (mm)
1	13	14	15	16	17	18	19	20	21	22

En el cuadro IV se emplean los mismos símbolos que
en el cuadro III.

En general, los valores de la precipitación diaria
máxima se refieren a cuencas que tienen una superficie
inferior a 10 000 km².

Los valores de la precipitación máxima por hora
suelen corresponder a cuencas pequeñas.

En las columnas 15, 16, 17, 19, 21 y 22 los valores
se indican como promedios o valores representativos
aplicables a toda la cuenca.

2.5 MAPAS SIMPLIFICADOS

En los mapas simplificados de las cuencas, se indica
el emplazamiento de las estaciones de aforo seleccionadas por el número de serie de las estaciones que figuran
en el cuadro I (columna 1).

Пояснительная записка

1 *Критерий для отбора паводков*

Каталог был задуман таким образом, чтобы включать в себе максимум имеющейся информации по наблюденным паводкам земного щара. Отбор водосборов и паводков, вошедших в Каталог, был произведен с учетом различных физико-географических условий, с тем чтобы добиться большей репрезентативности. Для этого были приняты два критерия : критерий макроклимата и площади водосбора — с тем чтобы обеспечить отбор и анализ наиболее репрезентативных бассейнов с зарегистрированными паводками.

Бассейны были дифференцированы следующим образом :

Площадь водосбора меньше, чем 100 км²
Площадь водосбора от 100 до 5 000 км²
Площадь водосбора от 5 000 до 10 000 км²
Площадь водосбора от 10 000 до 50 000 км²
Площадь водосбора от 50 000 до 200 000 км²
Площадь водосбора от 200 000 до 1 000 000 км²
Площадь водосбора свыше 1 000 000 км².

Основная цель каталога — привести данные по репрезентативным паводкам, имевшим место в различных физико-географических условиях. Таким образом, некоторые страны, имеющие различные климатические и физико-географические условия, отобрали больше, чем один бассейн в одной и той же зоне.

Для каждой страны число отобранных паводков, по которым приводятся данные, было установлено следующим образом :

a. более 50 лет наблюдений — по крайней мере 5 паводков
b. 20-50 лет наблюдений — 2-3 паводка
c. 10-20 лет наблюдений — 1-2 паводка.

В каталоге помещены, в частности, очень большие паводки, « большой паводок » — это паводок по крайней мере 10 % вероятности. 10 % вероятность основывается на максимальном расходе и/или объеме паводка. Таким образом, в каталоге могут приводится паводки с максимальным расходом более 10 % вероятности, но с объемом менее 10 % вероятности.

2 *Пояснения к таблицам*

2.1 ТАБЛИЦА I — ХАРАКТЕРИСТИКИ БАССЕЙНА

	ГИДРОМЕТРИЧЕСКАЯ СТАНЦИЯ							БАССЕЙН			
					Расстояние в км от гидрометрической станции					Высота (м)		
	Река		Период наблюдений	Координаты		до самого удаленного пункта речной системы L_{rs}	до проекции центра бассейна на основное русло L_{ca}	Средний уклон реки I_r (%)	Площадь A (км²)			
№	Речная система	Название		Широта	Долгота					Средняя H_m	Макс. H_{max}	Мин. H_{min}
1	2	3	4	5	6	7	8	9	10	11	12	13

	ВАССЕЙН									
	Ширина (км)		Средний уклон I_b (%)	Почвы	Характер местности	Взвешенная озерная площадь P_L (%)	Болота R_s (%)	Средние годовые осадки P (мм)	Годовой сток Q (мм)	Среднетемпература T (C°)	Регулирующая способность водохранилищ α
№	Средн. B_m	Макс. B_{max}									
1	14	15	16	17	18	19	20	21	22	23	24

Графа 4 *Период наблюдений*. Период, упомянутый в этой графе — не обязательно для всего периода наблюдений станции.

Графы 5 и 6 *Координаты*. Приводятся географические координаты (широта и долгота) в градусах, минутах и секундах.

Например :

N

15 : 12 : 42 означает 15°12'42″ северной широты.

Графа 9 *Средний уклон реки*, I_r (%) может быть подсчитан по следующей формуле :

$$I_r = \frac{H_1 - H_n}{10\, L}$$

где : L — длина реки (км), H_1 и H_n — соответственно максимальная и минимальная высота (м).

Графа 11 *Средняя высота бассейна*, может быть подсчитана следующим образом :

$$H_m = \frac{\sum\limits_{i=1}^{h} a_i\, h_i}{A}$$

где : A — площадь бассейна; a_i — площадь между двумя последовательными горизонталями (км²); h_i — средняя высота (м) площади a_i (полусумма высот двух соседних горизонталей). Для крупных бассейной средняя высота не является репрезентативной характеристикой бассейна и поэтому она часто не приводится.

Графа 14 *Средняя ширина бассейна*, B_m подсчитывается следующим образом :

$$B_m = \frac{A}{L}$$

где : А площадь бассейна; и L — расстояние от гидрометрической станции до самой удаленной точки бассейна.

Графа 16 *Средний уклон бассейна*, I_b (%), может быть подсчитан по следующей формуле :

$$I_b = \frac{\left(\dfrac{l_0 + l_n}{2} + \sum\limits_{i=1}^{h} l_i\right)\Delta h}{10\, A}$$

где : Δh — определяется по разности высот горизонталей (м); l_0, l_i..., l_n — длина каждой горизонтали (км); A — площадь бассейна (км²).

Графа 17 *Типы почв*. Типы почв приводятся в закодированной форме как показывается ниже :

Индекс	Типы почвы
1	Тундровые почвы
2	Подзолистые почвы
3	Серые лесные почвы
4	Бурые лесные почвы
5	Черноземные и степные черноземные почвы
6	Каштановые почвы (степная зона)
7	Бурые почвы (степная зона)
8	Красные и желтые субтропические почвы
9	Темнокрасные субтропические почвы
10	Лесные коричневые почвы
11	Субтропические степные серо—коричневые почвы
12	Сероземы
13	Тропические и субтропические почвы пустыни
14	Латериты
15	Красные почвы саванн
16	Тропические лесные краснокоричневые почвы

В некоторых таблицах процент от всей площади бассейна для каждого типа почв приводится после индексового номера в скобках. Например : 2 (45) 3 (55) Подзолистые почвы — 45 проц. и серые лесные почвы — 55 проц. Некоторые страны считают, что классификация, о которой идет речь выше, не соответствует их природным условиям и по этой причине они включили в список другие типы почв. Такие дополнительные типы почв не даются в закодированной форме, а обозначаются их местными названиями.

Графа 18 *Характер местности* : дан в закодированной форме следующим образом :

F   Леса

C   Обрабатываемые площади

U   Необрабатываемые земли (луга, города и т.д.) Некоторые таблицы содержат в скобках после индекса площадь каждого типа местности в процентах. Например, F (30), C (68), U (2) означает леса-30 проц., обрабатываемые земли- 68 проц. и необрабатываемые-2 проц.

Графа 19 *Взвешенная озерность бассейна* P_L %, может рассчитываться как безразмерный индекс по формуле :

$$P_L\,\% = 100\,\frac{\Sigma\, A_{li}\, a_i}{A^2}$$

Пояснительная записка

где :

A_i — площадь поверхности i-го озера (км²)
a_i - водосборная площадь i-го озера (км²)
A - площадь бассейна (км²)

В ряде случаев этот коэффициент рассчитывается как соотношение между общей площадью озер и площадью бассейна.

Графа 20 *Процент заболоченности* R_s (%) подсчитывается как отношение между площадью занимаемой болотами и площадью бассейна.

Графа 24 *Регулирующая емкость водохранилищ* может быть выражена в виде следующего безмерного коэффициента (α).

$$\alpha = \frac{W_R}{W_m}$$

где :

W_R — объем водохранилища (10^6 м³)
W_m - приблизительный объем годового стока (10^6 м³)

Остальные графы не требуют пояснений.

2.2 ТАБЛИЦА II — ГОДОВЫЕ МАКСИМАЛЬНЫЕ РАСХОДЫ И ОБЪЕМЫ

Дата	Максимальный расход в м³/сек. в результате		Максимальный объем (10^6м³), соответствующий максимальному расходу в результате	
	Дождя	Снеготаяния	Дождя	Снеготаяния
1	2	3	4	5

Графа 1 *Дата.* Указана дату максимального расхода.
Например : 12-06-68 означает 12 июня 1968 г.
Величнны максимальных расходов и объемов, вызванных смешанным поступлением воды (снеготаяние и дождь), также включены в таблицу, соответственно, в графы 3 и 5. Цифры в скобках после « страна » соответствуют номеру гидрометрической станции, данной в Таблице *I*, графа 1.

Например : « Страна : Финляндия (3)″, соответствует гидрометрической станций, приведенной в таблице 1.

2.3 ТАБЛИЦА III — ХАРАКТЕРИСТИКИ ПАВОДКОВ, ВЫЗВАННЫЕ СНЕГОТАЯНИЕМ

№	Река	Гидрометрическая станция	Q_{max} (м³/с)	Дата	h (мм)	T_1 (часы)	t_i (часы)	P_w (%)	P_{Qmax} (%)	Использованная кривая вероятности	
										для P_w	для P_{Qmax}
1	2	3	4	5	6	7	8	9	10	11	12

№	Метод вычерчивания кривой		Снежный покров		Жидкие осадки во время снеготаяния (мм)	Месячные жидкие осадки до замерзания почвы (мм)	Среднемесячная температура воздуха до снеготаяния (C°)
	для W	для Q_{max}	Водный эквивалент (мм)	Толщина покрова (см)			
1	13	14	15	16	17	18	19

В таблице *III* используются следующие обозначения :

Графа 4 Q_{max} : максимальный расход

Графа 5 *Дата максимального расхода*
Например :
12-06-68 означает 12 июня 1968 г.

12-06-90 означает 12 июня 1890 г.
12-06-40* означает 12 июня 1840 г.
12-06-40** означает 12 июня 1740 г.

Графа 6 $h = \dfrac{W}{A}$

глубина паводка, где W — объем паводка

Графа 7 T_{T}
общая продолжительность паводка

Графа 8 t_i
время максимума

Графа 9 и 10 P_{W}, P_{Q}
соответственно вероятный объем и расход.

В графах 17, 18 и 19 должны быть указаны средние величины для бассейна или же репрезентативные.

Остальные графы не требуют пояснений.

2.4. ТАБЛИЦА IУ — ХАРАКТЕРИСТИКИ ДОЖДЕВЫХ ПАВОДКОВ

№	Река	Гидро-метри-ческая станция	Характеристики							Тип кривой вероятности	
			Q_{max} (м³/с)	Дата	h (мм)	T_{I} (часы)	t_i (часы)	P_{W} (%)	$P_{Q_{max}}$ (%)	для P_{W}	для $P_{Q_{max}}$
1	2	3	4	5	6	7	8	9	10	10	12

№	Метод вычерчивания кривой		Жидкие осадки, образующие паводок (мм)	Снеготаяние во время паводка (мм)	Максимальные жидкие осадки (мм)	Дата	Максимальные часовые осадки (мм)	Дата	Осадки за пре-дыдущие дни (мм)	
	для W	для Q_{max}							10 дней	30 дней
1	13	14	15	16	17	18	19	20	21	22

В Таблице *IV* обозначения те же, что и в Таблице *III*.

Как правило максимальные суточные жидкие осадки приводятся для бассейнов с площадью менее чем 10 000 км².

Максимальные часовые осадки обычно приводятся для малых бассейнов.

В графа 15, 16, 17, 19, 21 и 22 приводятся средние или репрезентативные величины для всего бассеина.

2.5 СХЕМАТИЧНЫЕ КАРТЫ

На схематичных картах бассейнов местонахождение отобранных гидрометрических станций идентифицируется серийными номерами станций, указанными в Таблице *I* (графа 1).

Data on very large floods in the world

Données relatives aux très fortes crues dans le monde

Datos sobre las grandes crecidas del mundo

Данные по большим паводкам мира

Albania / Albanie / Албания

TABLE I – CHARACTERISTICS OF BASIN

				GAUGING STATION					BASIN				
						Distance (km) from gauging site					Altitude (m)		
No.	River River system	Name	Period of records	Co-ordinates Lat.	Long.	to remotest point of river system L_{rs}	to projection of centre of basin on main course L_{ca}	Mean slope of river I_r (%)	Area A (km²)	Mean H_m	Max. H_{max}	Min. H_{min}
1	2	3	4	5	6	7	8	9	10	11	12	13
1	Shkumbini	Papër	20 years	N 41:03	E 19:57	117		2.05	1960	889	2370	62

	BASIN											
	Width (km) Mean B_m	Max. B_{max}	Mean slope I_b(%)	Soils	Cover	Weighted lake area P_L (%)	Swamps R_s (%)	Mean annual precipitation P (mm)	Annual runoff Q (mm)	Mean annual temperature T (°C)	Regulating capacity of reservoirs α
No.											
1	14	15	16	17	18	19	20	21	22	23	24
1	17.3	42						1410	887	15.1	

TABLE IV – CHARACTERISTICS OF RAINFALL FLOODS

			Characteristic element							Type of probability curve	
No.	River	Gauging station	Q_{max} (m³/s)	Date	h (mm)	T_T (hours)	t_i (hours)	P_W (%)	$P_{Q_{max}}$ (%)	for P_W	for $P_{Q_{max}}$
1	2	3	4	5	6	7	8	9	10	11	12
1	Shkumbini	Papër	1430	16–11–62	96	78	24		5	Kritskij-Menkel	
			1640	01–01–71	78	77	38		3		"

	Method of curve fitting		Rainfall forming flood (mm)	Snowmelt during floods (mm)	Maximum daily rainfall (mm)		Hourly maximum rainfall (mm)		Antecedent precipitation for	
No.	for W	for Q_{max}				Date		Date	10 days (mm)	30 days (mm)
1	13	14	15	16	17	18	19	20	21	22
1		Method of moments	144		100	15–11–62			226	328
		"	137		68.3	31–12–62			180	222

SUPPLEMENTAL DATA

No.	River	Gauging station	Q_{max} (m³/s)	Date
1	Shkodër	Buna	2000	16–11–62
2	Dejë	Drini	4920	13–01–63
3	Sallmanaj	Erzeni	975	
4	Dorzë	Vjosa	3320	01–01–71

Bangladesh / Бангладеш

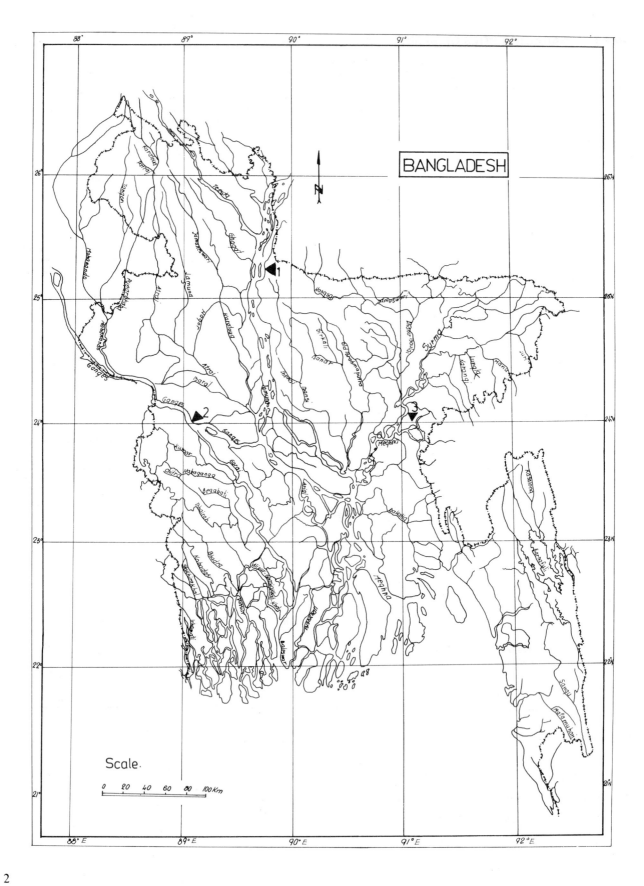

TABLE I — CHARACTERISTICS OF BASIN

No.	River / River system	Name	Period of records	Co-ordinates Lat.	Co-ordinates Long.	Distance (km) from gauging site to remotest point of river system L_{rs}	Distance (km) from gauging site to projection of centre of basin on main course L_{ca}	Mean slope of river I_r (%)	Area A (km^2)	Altitude (m) Mean H_m	Altitude (m) Max. H_{max}	Altitude (m) Min. H_{min}
1	2	3	4	5	6	7	8	9	10	11	12	13
				N	E							
1	Brahmaputra	Bahadurabad	1956–72	25:09.3	89:40.5	105		0.00748	4930	33.3	65.5	16.8
2	Ganges	Hardings Bridge	1934–72	23:04.3	89:02.3	129		0.00482	4770	37.5	76.2	13.7
3	Meghna	Bhairab Bazar	1956–72	24:02.7	90:59.7	386		0.00245	20700		61.0	3.05

No.	Width (km) Mean B_m	Width (km) Max. B_{max}	Mean slope I_b(%)	Soils	Cover	Weighted lake area P_L (%)	Swamps R_s (%)	Mean annual precipitation P (mm)	Annual runoff Q (mm)	Mean annual temperature T (°C)	Regulating capacity of reservoirs α
1	14	15	16	17	18	19	20	21	22	23	24
1	46.9	80	0.0346	Interstream deposits	C	0	0	2030		25	0
2	37.0	85	0.0603	Older alluvial deposits	C	0	0	1780		25.5	0
3	47.4	232		Stream deposits	C	0	18.2	3180		25	0

TABLE II – ANNUAL MAXIMUM DISCHARGES AND VOLUMES

Country: **Bangladesh (1)**
River: **Brahmaputra**
Gauging Station: **Bahadurabad**

| Date | Maximum discharge (m³/s) resulting from: | | Maximum volume (10⁶m³) corresponding to max. discharge resulting from: | |
| | Rainfall | Snowmelt | Rainfall | Snowmelt |
1	2	3	4	5
02–09–65	47700			
26–08–66	69100			
17–07–67	68700			
01–07–68	58600			
22–07–68	56900			

Country: **Bangladesh (3)**
River: **Meghna**
Gauging Station: **Bhairab Bazar**

| Date | Maximum discharge (m³/s) resulting from: | | Maximum volume (10⁶m³) corresponding to max. discharge resulting from: | |
| | Rainfall | Snowmelt | Rainfall | Snowmelt |
1	2	3	4	5
21–08–65	12000			
13–07–66	14800			
26–08–67	9700			
20–07–68	12900			
06–09–69	11300			

Country: **Bangladesh (2)**
River: **Ganges**
Gauging Station: **Hardinge Bridge**

| Date | Maximum discharge (m³/s) resulting from: | | Maximum volume (10⁶m³) corresponding to max. discharge resulting from: | |
| | Rainfall | Snowmelt | Rainfall | Snowmelt |
1	2	3	4	5
01–09–61	73200			
08–08–65	28900			
27–08–66	38500			
18–09–67	50100			
28–08–68	44400			
27–08–69	54700			

TABLE IV — CHARACTERISTICS OF RAINFALL FLOODS

No.	River	Gauging station	Q_{max} (m^3/s)	Date	h (mm)	T_T (hours)	t_i (hours)	P_W (%)	$P_{Q_{max}}$ (%)	Type of probability curve for P_W	for $P_{Q_{max}}$
1	2	3	4	5	6	7	8	9	10	11	12
1	Brahmaputra	Bahadurabad	76600	28—07—70		720	264				
2	Ganges	Hardings Bridge	73200	01—09—61					24		Empirical
			54700	27—08—69		696	432				
3	Meghna	Bhairab-Bazar	14400	03—09—66		696	264				

No.	Method of curve fitting for W	for Q_{max}	Rainfall forming flood (mm)	Snowmelt during floods (mm)	Maximum daily rainfall (mm)	Date	Hourly maximum rainfall (mm)	Date	Antecedent precipitation for 10 days (mm)	30 days (mm)
1	13	14	15	16	17	18	19	20	21	22
1										
2		Maximum Likelihood								
3										

Bulgaria / Bulgarie / Болгария

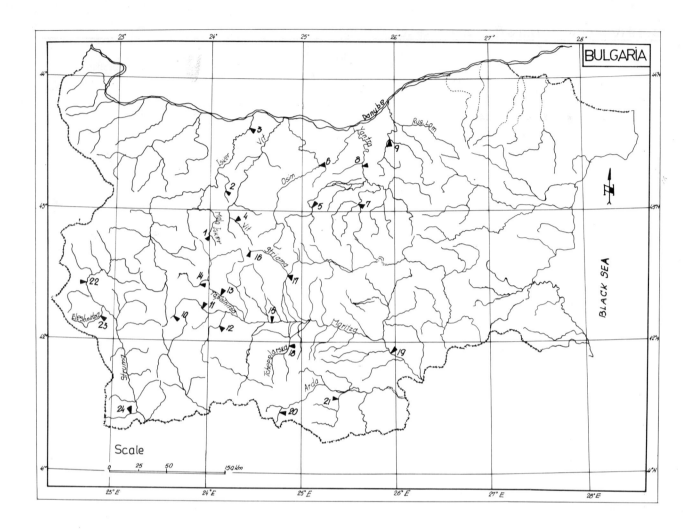

TABLE I – CHARACTERISTICS OF BASIN

	GAUGING STATION								BASIN				
						Distance (km) from gauging site					Altitude (m)		
No.	River River system	Name	Period of records	Co-ordinates Lat.	Long.	to remotest point of river system L_{rs}	to projection of centre of basin on main course L_{ca}	Mean slope of river I_r (%)	Area A (km^2)	Mean H_m	Max. H_{max}	Min. H_{min}
1	2	3	4	5	6	7	8	9	10	11	12	13
1	Malak Iskar	Etropole	1946–70			11.6		6.2	54.3	1160		
2	Zlatna Panega	Petrovene	1939–70			15.6		0.66	180	338		
3	Iskar	Oriahovitza	1935–70			340		0.73	8370	706	2930	33.2
4	Beli Vit	Teteven	1938–70			27.2		2.3	315	1070		376
5	Rositza	Sevlievo	1922–70			61.9		0.71	1090	604	2380	188
6	Osim	Gradiste	1929–70			175		0.13	1770	517		53.7
7	Yantra	Ciolokovitzi	1932–70			69.2		0.65	1290	545		135
8	Yantra	Rodanovo	1936–65			201		0.64	6570	440	2380	36.3
9	Tscherni Lom	Sirokovo	1948–70			88.3		0.18	1380	282		92.5
10	Maritza	Kota 1400	1950–70			11.1		9.3	39.9	2230	2930	
11	Maritza	Belovo	1912–70			66.2		3.4	741	1170	2930	314

	BASIN										
	Width (km)		Mean slope I_b (%)			Weighted lake area P_L (%)	Swamps R_s (%)	Mean annual precipitation P (mm)	Annual runoff Q (mm)	Mean annual temperature T (°C)	Regulating capacity of reservoirs α
No.	Mean B_m	Max. B_{max}		Soils	Cover						
1	14	15	16	17	18	19	20	21	22	23	24
1	4.68	23	34.5	4(81), 3(15), 12(4)				1080	570		
2	11.5	20	13.6	3(100)	F(25), C(75)			675	133		
3	24.6	90	16.3		F(33), C(67)			730	202		
4	11.6	21	38.2	4(54), 3(37), 10(9)	F(90), C(10)			1040	380		
5	17.6	45	20.4	3(78), 4(15), 12(5), 10(2)	F(33), C(67)			876	284	9.20	
6	10.2	45	19.2	3(49), 1(40), 4(17), 2(14)	F(51), C(49)			777	224		
7	18.6	32	22.9	3(85), 4(13), 1(1), 12(1)	F(34), C(66)			880	236	9.56	
8	32.6	142	18.2		F(19), C(81)			762	192	10.0	
9	15.6	25	12.2	1(41), 2(29), 3(25)	F(11), C(89)			602	57		
10	3.59	10.5	41.7	10(55), 4(45)	F(99), C(1)			1100	760		
11	11.2	31.5	28.4	6(42), 4(36), 10(13)	F(75), C(25)			750	365		

TABLE I – CHARACTERISTICS OF BASIN (cont'd)

				GAUGING STATION					BASIN			
	River / River system	Name	Period of records	Co-ordinates Lat.	Long.	Distance (km) from gauging site: to remotest point of river system L_{rs}	to projection of centre of basin on main course L_{ca}	Mean slope of river I_r (%)	Area A (km²)	Altitude (m): Mean H_m	Max. H_{max}	Min. H_{min}
No.												
1	2	3	4	5	6	7	8	9	10	11	12	13
12	Cepinska	M. Nicolov	1913–73			55.1		1.48	881	1210		
13	Topolnitza	Lesichevo	1911–62			125		0.69	1620	837		281
14	Mativir	Sersem Kale	1929–73			52.2		0.69	386	787		
15	Maritza	Plovdiv	1912–73			199		1.67	7930	915	2930	157
16	Striama	Klisura	1952–70			13.5		8.42	49.5	1110		
17	Striama	Bania	1913–73			58.6		1.04	833	833	2380	270
18	Tchepelarska	Batchkovo	1911–73			55.4		1.60	825	1240		147
19	Maritza	Harmanli	1912–73			328		0.87	19700	603	2930	64.0
20	Elhovska	Rudovem	1951–66			18.2		1.63	83.7	1160		
21	Virbitza	Djebel	1950–70			88.2		0.38	1150	584		229
22	Struma	Rajdavitza	1950–70			121		0.33	2170	884	2290	490

								BASIN				
No.	Width (km) Mean B_m	Max. B_{max}	Mean slope I_b(%)	Soils	Cover	Weighted lake area P_L (%)	Swamps R_s (%)	Mean annual precipitation P (mm)	Annual runoff Q (mm)	Mean annual temperature T (°C)	Regulating capacity of reservoirs α
1	14	15	16	17	18	19	20	21	22	23	24
12	16.0	28	27.4	4(91), 6(9)	F(80), C(20)			690	255		
13	12.9	41	25.5	6(49), 4(37), 12(8) 8(3), 5(2), 10(1)	F(57), C(43)			683	180		
14	7.40	18	18.3	6(76), 8(12), 10(6), 12(5), 4(1)	F(58), C(42)			578	104		
15	39.8	123	17.3		F(57), C(43)			695	200		
16	3.66	9		4(96), 10(4)				810	460		
17	14.2	24	22.2	4(65), 12(14), 6(9), 10(6), 5(4), 7(2)	F(68), C(32)			795	280		
18	14.9	36	34.9		F(81), C(19)			794	395		
19	60.0	142	13.1		F(50), C(50)			663	165		
20	4.59	9		4(100)	F(100), C(0)			1010	600		
21	13.0	39	24.2	6(95), 4(3), 12(2)	F(34), C(66)			904	529		
22	18.0	70	19.5		F(32), C(68)			805	148		

TABLE I — CHARACTERISTICS OF BASIN   (cont'd)

No.	River River system	Name	Period of records	Co-ordinates Lat.	Long.	to remotest point of river system L_{rs}	to projection of centre of basin on main course L_{ca}	Mean slope of river I_r (%)	Area A (km^2)	Mean H_m	Max. H_{max}	Min. H_{min}
						GAUGING STATION			BASIN		Altitude (m)	
						Distance (km) from gauging site						
1	2	3	4	5	6	7	8	9	10	11	12	13
23	Elesnitza	Vaksevo	1950—70			44.0		1.74	315	1060		
24	Strumesnitza	Mitino	1937—70			111		0.34	1890	641		

No.	Mean B_m	Max. B_{max}	Mean slope I_b(%)	Soils	Cover	Weighted lake area P_L (%)	Swamps R_s (%)	Mean annual precipitation P (mm)	Annual runoff Q (mm)	Mean annual temperature T ($^\circ$C)	Regulating capacity of reservoirs α
	Width (km)							BASIN			
1	14	15	16	17	18	19	20	21	22	23	24
23	7.15	15	14.0	6(56), 4(35), 10(8), 12(1)	F(55), C(45)			828	284		
24	17.0	37	26.4	5(40), 12(30), 4(17), 6(10), 10(3)	F(45), C(55)			680	177		

TABLE II – ANNUAL MAXIMUM DISCHARGES AND VOLUMES

Country:	Bulgaria (11)
River:	Maritza
Gauging Station:	Belovo

Date	Maximum discharge (m³/s) resulting from: Rainfall	Snowmelt	Maximum volume (10^6m³) corresponding to max. discharge resulting from: Rainfall	Snowmelt
1	2	3	4	5
29–06–11	370			
12	615			
16–05–13	90			
06–07–14	170			
14–05–15	150			
27–04–16	95			
09–12–16	240			
09–10–18	85			
08–05–19	255			
30–05–20	150			
16–08–21	160			
21–06–22	130			
07–07–23	460			
10–06–24	20			
15–05–25	23			
30–06–26	60			
20–01–27	80			
25–04–28	230			
17–04–29	35			
21–06–30	165			
24–02–31	133			
25–04–32	50			
22–05–33	30			
27–07–34	70			
23–06–35	202			
18–03–36	182		21.0	
02–07–37	292		19.9	
24–05–38	50		2.40	
04–07–39	204		12.9	
07–04–40	80		11.7	

Country:	Bulgaria (11) cont'd
River:	Maritza
Gauging Station:	Belovo

Date	Maximum discharge (m³/s) resulting from: Rainfall	Snowmelt	Maximum volume (10^6m³) corresponding to max. discharge resulting from: Rainfall	Snowmelt
1	2	3	4	5
04–01–41	44		7.02	
26–06–42	40		6.19	
16–05–43	125		26.8	
07–03–44	115		14.8	
15–11–44	90		14.8	
12–12–45	88		10.5	
25–06–47	110		16.2	
25–06–48	95		12.2	
22–03–49	135		15.4	
31–10–50	580		19.7	
30–01–51	255		50.2	
21–06–52	91		3.28	
23–05–53	116		10.1	
14–07–54	61		3.99	
15–04–55	80		7.13	
15–02–56	203		41.0	
05–09–57	710		31.7	
15–01–58	168		11.5	
13–08–59	70		9.5	
13–06–60	87		13.9	
29–05–61	51		5.6	
16–03–62	156		15.9	
23–05–63	132		25.9	
30–05–64	49		8.12	
25–05–65	74.6		16.1	
08–12–66	104		12.5	
21–05–67	90		14.3	
06–02–69	58		6.9	
11–06–70	46.8		11.0	

Bulgaria / Bulgarie / Болгария

TABLE II – ANNUAL MAXIMUM DISCHARGES AND VOLUMES   (cont'd)

Country:	Bulgaria (14)
River:	Mativir
Gauging Station:	Sersem Kale

Date	Maximum discharge (m³/s) resulting from:		Maximum volume (10⁶m³) corresponding to max. discharge resulting from:	
	Rainfall	Snowmelt	Rainfall	Snowmelt
1	2	3	4	5
24–09–30	67		3.39	
23–02–31	123		12.50	
20–04–32	145		8.79	
31–07–33	55		2.71	
19–07–34	21		0.67	
23–06–35	47		1.11	
30–05–36	73		6.10	
19–06–37	103		5.70	
13–02–38	86		7.34	
04–07–39	49		1.66	
07–04–40	75		9.05	
05–01–41	46		6.69	
25–04–42	39		3.72	
06–09–43	36		0.80	
04–08–44	102		6.03	
20–09–45	60		1.68	
11–03–46	32		4.51	
25–08–47	109		1.91	
11–04–48	40		2.70	
19–08–49	68		4.15	
03–03–50	42		6.77	
06–04–51	66		6.23	
10–10–52	34		1.02	
24–06–53	45		1.32	
18–06–54	38		1.37	
10–01–55	51		5.81	
15–05–56	57		9.07	
05–09–57	248		17.2	
15–01–58	68		4.21	
28–06–59	22		1.69	

Country:	Bulgaria (14) cont'd
River:	Mativir
Gauging Station:	Sersem Kale

Date	Maximum discharge (m³/s) resulting from:		Maximum volume (10⁶m³) corresponding to max. discharge resulting from:	
	Rainfall	Snowmelt	Rainfall	Snowmelt
1	2	3	4	5
24–02–60	37		3.14	
23–03–61	39		5.26	
16–03–62	43		5.99	
11–03–63	49		12.0	
31–05–64	20.7		3.21	
04–03–65	37.7		3.64	
03–06–66	21.4		1.87	
22–05–67	31.7		4.82	
22–11–68	74.2		4.38	
06–02–69	75.3		6.94	
05–07–70	22.9		0.94	

TABLE II – ANNUAL MAXIMUM DISCHARGES AND VOLUMES   (cont'd)

Country:	Bulgaria (17)
River:	Striama
Gauging Station:	Bania

Date	Maximum discharge (m³/s) resulting from:		Maximum volume (10⁶m³) corresponding to max. discharge resulting from:	
	Rainfall	Snowmelt	Rainfall	Snowmelt
1	2	3	4	5
01–10–14	80			
07–07–15	140			
26–04–16	68			
12–06–17	120			
31–05–18	14			
19–07–19	150			
13–12–19	180			
03–06–21	20			
15–10–22	110			
14–03–23	150			
09–06–24	57			
22–05–25	20			
01–06–26	220			
03–04–27	54			
04–05–28	52			
16–02–29	79			
30–01–30	50			
04–06–31	40			
13–01–32	33			
22–05–33	160			
16–07–34	86			
01–08–35	76			
25–04–36	44		3.43	
01–11–36	68		3.43	
14–02–38	50		5.11	
25–12–38	44		5.11	
08–04–40	105		3.53	
03–07–41	126		11.1	
02–06–42	122		8.31	
15–05–43	85		15.3	

Country:	Bulgaria (17) cont'd
River:	Striama
Gauging Station:	Bania

Date	Maximum discharge (m³/s) resulting from:		Maximum volume (10⁶m³) corresponding to max. discharge resulting from:	
	Rainfall	Snowmelt	Rainfall	Snowmelt
1	2	3	4	5
13–07–44	150		14.6	
31–03–45	69		3.84	
09–12–45	95		3.84	
25–06–47	45		7.08	
08–05–48	40		3.57	
20–08–49	82		8.72	
04–03–50	45		2.31	
25–08–51	320		26.0	
31–03–52	44		6.13	
09–01–53	72		19.1	
30–03–54	86		12.4	
10–01–55	60		6.14	
15–05–56	148		31.6	
27–06–57	247		40.8	
15–01–58	94.2		31.4	
12–06–59	111		10.4	
24–06–60	112		11.9	
11–12–60	79		11.9	
08–03–62	82		10.5	
06–02–63	127		5.91	
24–09–64	77.5		7.83	
15–05–65	103		17.0	
08–12–66	113		21.6	
25–05–67	40.3		10.60	
23–11–68	43.8		11.6	
07–09–69	66		10.3	
18–01–70	39.6		14.1	

TABLE II – ANNUAL MAXIMUM DISCHARGES AND VOLUMES   (cont'd)

Country:	Bulgaria (18)	Country:	Bulgaria (18) cont'd
River:	Tchepelarska	River:	Tchepelarska
Gauging Station:	Batchkovo	Gauging Station:	Batchkovo

Date	Maximum discharge (m³/s) resulting from:		Maximum volume (10⁶m³) corresponding to max. discharge resulting from:		Date	Maximum discharge (m³/s) resulting from:		Maximum volume (10⁶m³) corresponding to max. discharge resulting from:	
	Rainfall	Snowmelt	Rainfall	Snowmelt		Rainfall	Snowmelt	Rainfall	Snowmelt
1	2	3	4	5	1	2	3	4	5
28–10–12	110				09–01–42	50		6.72	
09–11–12	120				16–05–43	155		48.2	
26–06–14	147				13–02–44	65		8.98	
26–02–15	108				25–11–44	62		8.98	
23–09–16	42				07–04–46	36		27.6	
29–01–17	100				17–02–47	67		12.3	
31–10–18	36				13–12–47	96		8.69	
10–06–19	105				20–07–49	94		6.96	
24–06–20	77				30–05–50	162		20.6	
27–04–21	47				05–09–51	170		4.22	
06–05–22	130				30–03–52	92		20.1	
14–03–23	170				07–01–53	187		24.3	
09–06–24	172				28–03–54	68		7.86	
24–03–25	50				09–01–55	290		41.0	
01–04–26	22				13–01–56	205		32.3	
21–01–27	37				29–06–57	410		55.8	
28–03–28	69				13–01–58	200		35.6	
05–04–29	99				12–06–59	95		13.1	
08–02–30	56				12–01–60	374		30.6	
16–02–31	215				16–06–61	147		27.6	
01–01–32	65				06–11–61	530		27.6	
22–05–33	71				05–02–63	258		47.1	
17–07–34	18				28–09–64	97		20.2	
07–04–35	118				14–05–65	149		32.2	
05–02–36	280				01–05–66	300		34.3	
01–11–36	390				01–04–67	62		22.4	
16–12–37	163				18–02–68	138		15.6	
27–06–39	83		4.31		06–02–69	132		22.9	
02–09–40	80		11.7		17–01–70	56		14.3	
09–12–40	105		11.7						

13

TABLE II − ANNUAL MAXIMUM DISCHARGES AND VOLUMES (cont'd)

Country:	Bulgaria (19)
River:	Maritza
Gauging Station:	Harmanli

| Date | Maximum discharge (m³/s) resulting from: | | Maximum volume (10⁶m³) corresponding to max. discharge resulting from: | |
| | Rainfall | Snowmelt | Rainfall | Snowmelt |
1	2	3	4	5
07−07−14	820			
19−02−15	575			
21−05−16	235			
10−03−17	560			
07−10−18	475			
31−01−19	1030			
09−04−20	695			
22−01−21	280			
08−05−22	445			
15−03−23	890			
10−06−24	500			
24−03−25	645			
02−07−26	350			
19−04−27	420			
28−04−28	525			
17−02−29	755			
26−09−30	455			
09−06−31	850			
02−01−32	605			
24−05−33	445			
05−01−34	225			
30−01−35	985			
19−03−36	1120		286	
11−02−37	880		217	
08−12−38	700		274	
31−03−39	440		154	
07−04−40	1300		359	
10−12−40	1250		359	
12−02−42	1080		550	
17−05−43	770		279	

Country:	Bulgaria (19) cont'd
River:	Maritza
Gauging Station:	Harmanli

| Date | Maximum discharge (m³/s) resulting from: | | Maximum volume (10⁶m³) corresponding to max. discharge resulting from: | |
| | Rainfall | Snowmelt | Rainfall | Snowmelt |
1	2	3	4	5
01−05−44	995		567	
12−01−45	610		210	
11−03−46	680		412	
15−02−47	845		317	
10−05−48	925		531	
24−03−49	840		451	
05−03−50	835		282	
02−02−51	890		278	
02−04−52	380		226	
10−01−53	1110		379	
09−03−54	1260		928	
09−01−55	1600		702	
13−02−56	1280		627	
01−07−57	1640		500	
17−01−58	1020		453	
14−06−59	1480		183	
14−07−60	625		187	
17−06−61	1140		195	
17−07−62	1190		16.3	
07−02−63	1800		461	
27−09−64	390		83.0	
12−05−65	1050		192	
02−05−66	615		177	
08−12−66	1460		285	
24−11−68	414		105	
07−02−69	1030		317	
21−03−70	706		297	

TABLE III – CHARACTERISTICS OF SNOWMELT FLOODS

No.	River	Gauging station	Q_{max} (m^3/s)	Date	h (mm)	T_T (hours)	t_i (hours)	P_W (%)	$P_{Q_{max}}$ (%)	Type of probability curve for P_W	for $P_{Q_{max}}$
1	2	3	4	5	6	7	8	9	10	11	12
19	Maritza	Harmanli	1800	07–02–63	23			24	2.3	Log-normal	Log-normal
21	Virbitza	Djebel	2640	03–02–63	168	68	46	7.5	3.0	"	"
22	Struma	Rajdavitza	354	10–01–55	30	110	60		6.7	"	"
24	Strumesnitza	Mitino	318	05–02–63	51	168	66	3.8	4.2	"	"

No.	Method of curve fitting for W	for Q_{max}	Snow cover Water equivalent (mm)	Layer thickness (cm)	Rainfall during snowmelt (mm)	Monthly precipitation before soil freezing (mm)	Mean monthly temperature before snowmelt (°C)
1	13	14	15	16	17	18	19
19	Graphical	Graphical					
21	"	"					
22	"	"					
24	"	"					

Bulgaria / Bulgarie / Болгария

TABLE IV — CHARACTERISTICS OF RAINFALL FLOODS

No.	River	Gauging station	Q_{max} (m³/s)	Date	h (mm)	T_T (hours)	t_i (hours)	P_W (%)	$P_{Q_{max}}$ (%)	Type of probability curve for P_W	for $P_{Q_{max}}$
1	2	3	4	5	6	7	8	9	10	11	12
1	Malak Iskar	Etropole	52	12—06—60	104	96	38	8.6	9.0	Log-normal	Log-normal
2	Zlatna Panega	Petrevene	112	06—04—51	74	86	14	24	10	''	''
3	Iskar	Oriahovitza	940	29—06—57	47	192	56		10	''	''
4	Beli Vit	Teteven	323	24—09—64	104	118	38	4.0	3.0	''	''
5	Rositza	Sevlievo	1160	28—06—57	134	124	42	3.7	6.5	''	''
6	Osim	Gradiste	280	16—07—54	46	108	20	4.6	7.0	''	''
7	Yantra	Ciolokovitzi	1190	04—06—66	75	85	35	3.5	1.8	''	''
8	Yantra	Rodanovo	1340	29—06—57					1.9		''
9	Cerni Lom	Sirokovo	170	25—06—55	15	90	20	4.8	4.0	''	''
10	Maritza	Kota 1400	18.6	29—06—57	125	126	60	2.8	10	''	''
11	Maritza	Velovo	710	05—09—57	43	23.5	10	10	1.3	''	''
12	Cepinska	M. Nicolov	410	29—06—57	66	146	53	0.5	0.6	''	''
13	Topolnitza	Lesichevo	510	05—09—57	14	47	10	9	1.0	''	''
14	Mativir	Sersem Kale	248	05—06—57	84	36	10	1.7	0.9	''	''

No.	Method of curve fitting for W	for Q_{max}	Rainfall forming flood (mm)	Snowmelt during floods (mm)	Maximum daily rainfall (mm)	Date	Hourly maximum rainfall (mm)	Date	Antecedent precipitation for 10 days (mm)	30 days (mm)
1	13	14	15	16	17	18	19	20	21	22
1	Graphical	Graphical								
2	''	''								
3	''	''								
4	''	''								
5	''	''								
6	''	''								
7	''	''								
8		''								
9	''	''								
10	''	''	140							
11	''	''	107							
12	''	''	108							
13	''	''	83							
14	''	''	113							

16

TABLE IV – CHARACTERISTICS OF RAINFALL FLOODS (cont'd)

No.	River	Gauging station	Q_{max} (m³/s)	Date	h (mm)	T_T (hours)	t_i (hours)	P_W (%)	$P_{Q_{max}}$ (%)	Type of probability curve for P_W	for $P_{Q_{max}}$
1	2	3	4	5	6	7	8	9	10	11	12
15	Maritza	Plovdiv	1270	29–06–57	40	202	48	2.2	0.8	Log-normal	Log-normal
16	Striama	Klisura	150	27–06–57	21	107	20	0.4	0.6	"	"
17	Striama	Bania	320	25–08–51	29	69	17	11	1.4	"	"
18	Tchepetarska	Batchkovo	530	06–11–61	34			32	1.7	"	"
20	Elhovska	Rudovem	300	06–11–61	429	84	24	0.12	5.0	"	"
23	Elesnitza	Vaksevo	350	19–06–54	20	24	8	4.2	2.7	"	"

No.	Method of curve fitting for W	for Q_{max}	Rainfall forming flood (mm)	Snowmelt during floods (mm)	Maximum daily rainfall (mm)	Date	Hourly maximum rainfall (mm)	Date	Antecedent precipitation for 10 days (mm)	30 days (mm)
1	13	14	15	16	17	18	19	20	21	22
15	Graphical	Graphical	118							
16	"	"								
17	"	"								
18	"	"								
20	"	"								
23	"	"								

Canada / Canadá / Канада

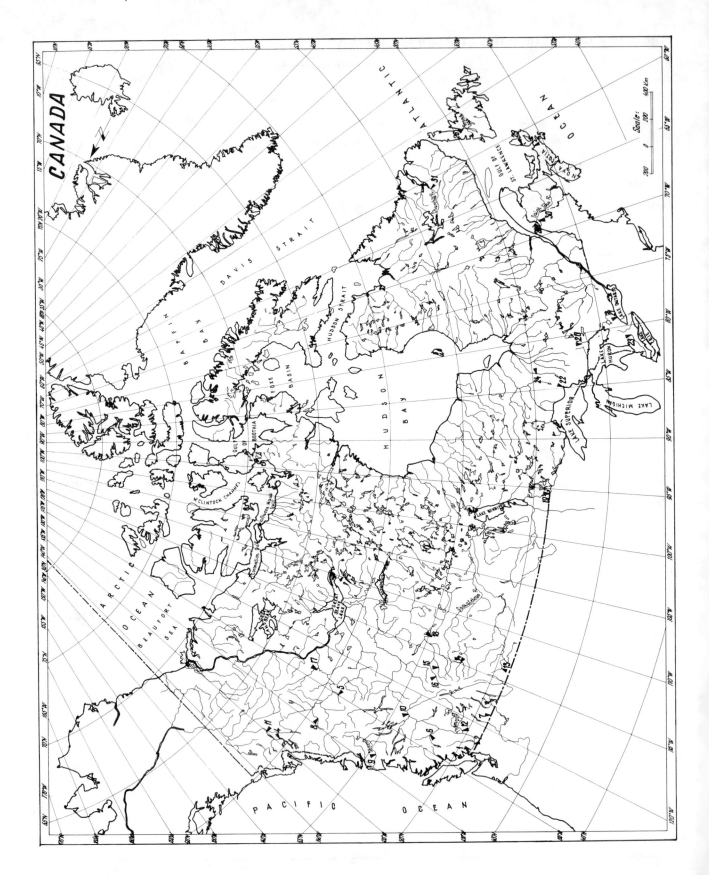

TABLE I — CHARACTERISTICS OF BASIN

		GAUGING STATION							BASIN			
						Distance (km) from gauging site		Mean slope of river I_r (%)	Area A (km^2)	Altitude (m)		
No.	River / River system	Name	Period of records	Co-ordinates		to remotest point of river system L_{rs}	to projection of centre of basin on main course L_{ca}			Mean H_m	Max. H_{max}	Min. H_{min}
				Lat.	Long.							
1	2	3	4	5	6	7	8	9	10	11	12	13
				N	W							
1	Kanaka Fraser	Webster Corners 08MH076	1960–72	49:12:25	122:22:05	12.5	5.9	5.3	47.7	351	914.0	152.0
2	Chilliwack Fraser	Outlet of Chilliwack Lake 08MH016	1923–72	49:05:02	121:27:24	24.5	13.3	4.1	339	1250	1830	610
3	Slocan Columbia	Crescent Valley 08NJ013	1913–72	49:27:38	117:33:52	87.0	44.8	1.4	3280	1540	2290	762
4	M'Clintock Yukon	Whitehorse 09AB008	1955–72	60:36:45	134:27:27	47.2	17.2	2.0	1550	1080	1830	762
5	Toad Mackenzie	Above Nonda Creek 10BE004	1961–72	58:51:20	125:22:50	63.1	34.3	1.8	2570	1600	2440	914
6	Chilko Fraser	Redstone 08MA001	1927–72	52:04:25	123:32:00	125	85.6	1.2	8370	1630	2740	914
7	Kettle Columbia	Ferry 08NN013	1928–72	48:58:53	118:45:55	130	54.2	1.1	5750	981	2130	305
8	Dease Mackenzie	Mcdame 10AC002	1957–72	59:11:20	129:12:44	98.2	49.1	0.8	6990	1260	1830	914

			BASIN								
No.	Width (km)		Mean slope I_b(%)	Soils	Cover	Weighted lake area P_L (%)	Swamps R_s (%)	Mean annual precipitation P (mm)	Annual runoff Q (mm)	Mean annual temperature T (°C)	Regulating capacity of reservoirs α
	Mean B_m	Max. B_{max}									
1	14	15	16	17	18	19	20	21	22	23	24
1	4.2	5.6	7.5	4,2	F, C, U	0.0	0.0	1940	1960	9.8	
2	12.5	18.6	12.5	4	F	4.7	0.0	1570	1770	9.9	
3	37.5	57.6	23.4	2	F	1.8	0.0	529	842	8.0	
4	32.7	35.1	12.1	4	F	0.3	1.8	267	205	4.2	
5	40.3	57.1	28.3	4,3	F	0.1	0.5	465	539	−3.0	
6	56.2	73.6	4.2	3,4	F, U	3.5	0.0	422	351	2.2	
7	44.2	57.0	7.9	5	C, U	0.0	0.0	520	233	4.8	
8	70.5	105	5.4	4	F	0.3	0.0	547	953	−2.9	

TABLE I – CHARACTERISTICS OF BASIN (cont'd)

						GAUGING STATION				BASIN			
	River River system	Name	Period of records	Co-ordinates Lat.	Long.	Distance (km) from gauging site to remotest point of river system L_{rs}	to projection of centre of basin on main course L_{ca}	Mean slope of river I_r (%)	Area A (km²)	Altitude (m) Mean H_m	Max. H_{max}	Min. H_{min}	
No.	2	3	4	5	6	7	8	9	10	11	12	13	
1				N	W								
9	Skeena	Usk 08EF001	1928–72	54:37:50	128:25:40	250	100	0.4	42200	1110	2130	305	
10	Fraser	Shelley 08KB001	1950–72	54:00:40	122:37:00	332	101	0.5	32400	1280	2740	914	
11	Teslin Yukon	Whitehorse 09AF001	1951–72	61:29:21	134:46:35	342	188	0.2	35500	1180	1680	762	
12	Thompson Fraser	Spences Bridge 08LF051	1951–72	50:21:14	121:23:33	287	127	0.7	55900	1250	2740	305	
13	Castle Nelson	Near Beaver Mines 05AA022	1945–72	49:29:20	114:08:40	36.6	19.7	1./	826	1630	2130	1220	
14	Clearwater Nelson	Rocky Mountain House 05DB001	1914–72	52:20:40	114:56:10	113	52.3	1.1	3130	1880	2050	1220	
15	Mcleod Mackenzie	Near Wolf Creek 07AG001	1915–72	53:39:15	116:16:50	101	59.3	1.0	6520	1210	2130	610	
16	Athabasca Mackenzie	Hinton 07AD002	1961–72	53:24:45	117:35:15	134	61.0	0.9	10400	1850	2440	914	

	BASIN										
No.	Width (km) Mean B_m	Max. B_{max}	Mean slope I_b(%)	Soils	Cover	Weighted lake area P_L (%)	Swamps R_s (%)	Mean annual precipitation P (mm)	Annual runoff Q (mm)	Mean annual temperature T (°C)	Regulating capacity of reservoirs α
1	14	15	16	17	18	19	20	21	22	23	24
9	169	297	3.0	3,4	F	0.4	0.0	601	689	5.6	
10	97.1	174	6.7	3,2	F	0.1	0.0	631	814	3.3	
11	104	181	2.3	4	F	2.6	0.0	267	293	4.2	
12	190	267	4.8	5	F, U	2.7	0.0	531	448	6.3	
13	22.4	32.2	15.9	4,3	F	0.0	0.0	539	665	3.7	
14	28.2	44.2	9.3	4,3	F	0.0	3.1	655	258	1.2	
15	66.9	91.5	1.8	3,4	F	0.2	0.0	554	192	1.7	
16	73.9	151	6.3	4,3	F	1.5	0.0	458	554	2.6	

TABLE I — CHARACTERISTICS OF BASIN (cont'd)

						GAUGING STATION			BASIN			
						Distance (km) from gauging site		Mean slope of river I_r (%)	Area A (km²)	Altitude (m)		
	River River system	Name	Period of records	Co-ordinates		to remotest point of river system L_{rs}	to projection of centre of basin on main course L_{ca}			Mean H_m	Max. H_{max}	Min. H_{min}
No.				Lat.	Long.							
1	2	3	4	5	6	7	8	9	10	11	12	13
				N	W							
17	South Nahanni Mackenzie	Above Clausen Creek 10EC001	1959—72	61:15:10	124:02:10	346	159	0.3	33400	1340	2130	914
18	Athabasca Mackenzie	Athabasca 07BE001	1938—72	54:43:20	113:17:10	401	186	0.3	76700	1040	2440	610
19	Sprague Nelson	Sprague 05OD031	1928—72	48:59:30	95:39:43	23.8	11.7	0.1	438	341	366	335
20	Junction St. Lawrence	Sudbury 02CF005	1958—72	46:29:20	80:59:45	12.3	7.7	0.4	89.1	275	305	244
21	Highland St. Lawrence	West Hill 02HC013	1956—72	43:46:45	79:10:26	11.4	8.2	0.6	88.1	163	183	91.4
22	Magpie St. Lawrence	Michipicoten 02BD003	1939—72	47:56:10	84:50:00	90.7	49.6	0.2	1930	382	599	305
23	Nith St. Lawrence	Canning 02GA010	1924—72	43:11:26	80:27:17	65.2	34.0	0.1	1030	349	396	274
24	Missinaibi Moose	Mattice 04LJ001	1920—72	49:37:00	83:15:48	184	11.3	0.11	8940	326	488	213

							BASIN					
	Width (km)		Mean slope I_b (%)			Weighted lake area P_L (%)	Swamps R_s (%)	Mean annual precipitation P (mm)	Annual runoff Q (mm)	Mean annual temperature T (°C)	Regulating capacity of reservoirs α
No.	Mean B_m	Max. B_{max}		Soils	Cover						
1	14	15	16	17	18	19	20	21	22	23	24
17	95.4	168	7.2	4	F	0.0	0.0	449	444	−5.0	
18	185	302	1.7	3	F	0.3	1.8	503	177	1.3	
19	18.9	25.5	0.1	3	F	0.0	18.2	579	128	1.9	
20	6.1	9.2	1.3	2	F	0.0	0.0	779	543	4.2	
21	8.7	12.8	1.1	3	U, C	0.0	0.0	790	259	7.5	
22	21.8	40.5	21.4	2,4	F	3.3	0.6	903	440	1.7	
23	15.1	18.6	0.7	3,4	C, U	0.01	1.0	842	321	6.8	
24	47.2	68.1	0.24	2	F	0.4	9.1	870	370	0.9	

TABLE I — CHARACTERISTICS OF BASIN (cont'd)

				GAUGING STATION					BASIN			
	River River system	Name	Period of records	Co-ordinates		Distance (km) from gauging site		Mean slope of river I_r (%)	Area A (km²)	Altitude (m)		
No.				Lat.	Long.	to remotest point of river system L_{rs}	to projection of centre of basin on main course L_{ca}			Mean H_m	Max. H_{max}	Min. H_{min}
1	2	3	4	5	6	7	8	9	10	11	12	13
				N	W							
25	Clam Harbour	Birchtown 01ER001	1957–72	45:28:06	61:27:36	9.9	5.6	0.5	45.1	145	152	91
26	Upper Humber	Seal Pond 02YL001	1928–72	49:14:26	57:21:45	61.6	39.5	0.5	2120	313	640	91.4
27	Rocky	Colinet 02ZK001	1948–72	47:13:29	53:34:06	33.2	14.0	0.5	285	81.6	244	31
28	St. Francis	Outlet of Glasier Lake 01AD003	1951–72	47:12:25	68:57:25	72.1	31.9	0.4	1350	348	549	183
29	Northeast Margaree	Margaree Valley 01FB001	1916–72	46:22:10	60:58:36	30.3	14.3	0.9	368	344	457	152
30	St. John	Fort Kent 01AD002	1926–72	47:15:25	68:35:35	172	80.1	0.1	14700	420	610	305
31	Churchill	Muskrat Falls 03OE001	1948–72	53:15:30	60:45:00	465	288	0.1	74700	519	762	152

							BASIN					
No.	Width (km)		Mean slope I_b (%)	Soils	Cover	Weighted lake area P_L (%)	Swamps R_s (%)	Mean annual precipitation P (mm)	Annual runoff Q (mm)	Mean annual temperature T (°C)	Regulating capacity of reservoirs α
	Mean B_m	Max. B_{max}									
1	14	15	16	17	18	19	20	21	22	23	24
25	3.6	3.3	1.0	2	F	0.13	0.0	1290	1200	6.2	
26	33.9	51.9	3.4	2	F	2.4	14.0	1010	1230	3.9	
27	9.1	17.6	1.6	2	F	9.9	1.1	1450	1220	5.2	
28	18.6	36.8	3.6	2	F	2.7	0.0	905	566	3.1	
29	11.6	17.9	7.6	2	F	0.0	1.8	1300	1440	5.6	
30	91.6	133	1.0	2	F	0.3	0.0	964	571	3.0	
31	171	315	1.0	2	F	13.1	18.9	884	640	−2.2	

Canada / Canadá / Канада

TABLE II – ANNUAL MAXIMUM DISCHARGES AND VOLUMES

Country: Canada (2)
River: Chilliwack River
Gauging Station: 08MH016

| Date | Maximum discharge (m³/s) resulting from: | | Maximum volume (10⁶m³) corresponding to max. discharge resulting from: | |
| | Rainfall | Snowmelt | Rainfall | Snowmelt |
1	2	3	4	5
12–12–24		61		
21–05–25		64		
09–06–27		72		
23–05–28		66		
24–05–29		54		
12–06–30		48		
09–06–31		46		
28–02–32		85		
16–06–33		86		
06–11–34		81		
27–01–35		92		
03–06–36		68		
23–06–37		67		
27–05–38		61		
20–05–39		61		
21–10–40	54			
03–12–41		68		
27–05–42		47		
04–07–43	68			
19–06–44		36		
22–06–45		54		
27–05–46		73		
11–06–48		109		
25–11–49	88			
19–06–50		94		
03–12–58		56		
06–06–59		64		
04–06–60		63		
07–06–61		86		
26–06–62		50		

Country: Canada (2) cont'd
River: Chilliwack River
Gauging Station: 08MH016

| Date | Maximum discharge (m³/s) resulting from: | | Maximum volume (10⁶m³) corresponding to max. discharge resulting from: | |
| | Rainfall | Snowmelt | Rainfall | Snowmelt |
1	2	3	4	5
07–02–63		54		
11–06–64		74		
12–06–65		54		
18–12–66		61		
22–06–67		95		
03–06–68		87		
25–05–69		75		
22–07–71	72			
20–06–72		116		

TABLE II – ANNUAL MAXIMUM DISCHARGES AND VOLUMES (cont'd)

Country: Canada (3)
River: Slocan
Gauging Station: 08NJ013

Date	Maximum discharge (m³/s) resulting from:		Maximum volume (10⁶m³) corresponding to max. discharge resulting from:	
	Rainfall	Snowmelt	Rainfall	Snowmelt
1	2	3	4	5
16−06−33		634		
13−06−35		411		
02−06−36		473		
23−06−37		323		
30−05−38		430		
16−05−39		354		
25−05−40		408		
17−05−41		262		
25−05−42		374		
17−06−43		357		
12−06−44		233		
11−06−45		416		
28−05−46		484		
09−05−47		362		
07−06−48		708		
14−05−49		413		
21−06−50		518		
24−05−51		402		
20−05−52		377		
13−06−53		501		
01−07−54	490			
23−06−55		617		
02−06−56		651		
19−05−57		436		
25−05−58		510		
22−06−59		479		
17−06−60		405		
07−06−61		719		
26−06−62		413		
31−05−63		402		

Country: Canada (3) (cont'd)
River: Slocan
Gauging Station: 08NJ013

Date	Rainfall	Snowmelt	Rainfall	Snowmelt
1	2	3	4	5
15−06−64		541		
12−06−65		402		
10−06−66		408		
22−06−67		640		
03−06−68		643		
05−06−69		484		
05−06−70		388		
13−05−71		515		
01−06−72		665		

24

TABLE II — ANNUAL MAXIMUM DISCHARGES AND VOLUMES (cont'd)

Country:	Canada (6)
River:	Chilko
Gauging Station:	08MA001

| Date | Maximum discharge (m^3/s) resulting from: | | Maximum volume (10^6m^3) corresponding to max. discharge resulting from: | |
| | Rainfall | Snowmelt | Rainfall | Snowmelt |
1	2	3	4	5
12–07–28		289		
14–08–29		247		
16–08–30		297		
02–08–31		279		
28–08–32		303		
19–08–33		265		
14–06–34		286		
25–07–35		377		
03–06–36		331		
29–07–37		292		
26–06–38		283		
06–08–39		309		
17–07–40		289		
20–07–41		368		
21–08–42		320		
02–08–43		258		
29–07–44		314		
15–05–45		276		
31–07–46		256		
09–06–47		216		
20–06–48		445		
16–07–49		246		
20–06–50		479		
16–06–51		303		
13–08–52		283		
12–07–53		256		
25–08–54		289		
18–07–55		388		
23–07–56		326		
26–06–58		348		

Country:	Canada (6) cont'd
River:	Chilko
Gauging Station:	08MA001

| Date | Maximum discharge (m^3/s) resulting from: | | Maximum volume (10^6m^3) corresponding to max. discharge resulting from: | |
| | Rainfall | Snowmelt | Rainfall | Snowmelt |
1	2	3	4	5
26–07–59		306		
21–07–60		297		
16–07–61		309		
03–08–62		273		
22–07–63		266		
20–06–64		348		
27–08–65		274		
17–07–66		286		
24–06–67		405		
12–06–68		351		
20–06–69		394		
28–06–70		238		
26–06–72		300		

TABLE II – ANNUAL MAXIMUM DISCHARGES AND VOLUMES   (cont'd)

Country:	Canada (7)
River:	Kettle
Gauging Station:	08NN013

| Date | Maximum discharge (m³/s) resulting from: | | Maximum volume (10⁶m³) corresponding to max. discharge resulting from: | |
	Rainfall	Snowmelt	Rainfall	Snowmelt
1	2	3	4	5
15–05–31		225		
22–05–32		292		
17–06–33		396		
25–04–34		326		
23–05–35		314		
03–06–37		281		
17–05–39		294		
26–05–40		281		
02–05–41		264		
27–05–42		515		
27–05–43		225		
02–06–44		234		
31–05–45		365		
29–05–46		385		
08–05–47		257		
29–05–48		600		
14–05–49		408		
15–06–50		340		
13–05–51		425		
21–05–52		419		
14–06–53		334		
20–05–54		442		
13–06–55		408		
21–05–56		484		
20–05–57		462		
23–05–58		351		
24–05–59		351		
13–05–60		317		
08–06–61		425		
28–05–62		253		

Country:	Canada (7) cont'd
River:	Kettle
Gauging Station:	08NN013

| Date | Maximum discharge (m³/s) resulting from: | | Maximum volume (10⁶m³) corresponding to max. discharge resulting from: | |
	Rainfall	Snowmelt	Rainfall	Snowmelt
1	2	3	4	5
24–05–63		297		
07–06–64		385		
30–05–65		303		
10–05–66		215		
04–06–67		413		
03–06–68		348		
11–05–69		408		
26–05–70		255		
14–05–71		473		
01–06–72		470		

TABLE II – ANNUAL MAXIMUM DISCHARGES AND VOLUMES (cont'd)

Country:	Canada (9)
River:	Skeena
Gauging Station:	08EF001

Date	Maximum discharge (m³/s) resulting from:		Maximum volume (10⁶m³) corresponding to max. discharge resulting from:	
	Rainfall	Snowmelt	Rainfall	Snowmelt
1	2	3	4	5
26–06–52		4300		
20–05–53		5100		
10–06–54		6090		
25–06–55		5210		
20–05–57		6800		
29–05–58		5720		
13–06–59		4250		
29–06–60		4670		
08–06–61		6140		
28–06–62		4840		
23–05–63		4250		
11–06–64		7530		
03–06–65		4810		
18–06–66		4900		
07–06–67		5640		
22–05–68		5720		
13–06–69		4640		
05–06–70		5320		
24–06–71		5130		
12–06–72		8100		

Country:	Canada (10)
River:	Fraser
Gauging Station:	08KB001

Date	Maximum discharge (m³/s) resulting from:		Maximum volume (10⁶m³) corresponding to max. discharge resulting from:	
	Rainfall	Snowmelt	Rainfall	Snowmelt
1	2	3	4	5
20–05–52		3090		
20–05–53		2790		
04–07–54		3000		
28–06–55		3680		
07–06–56		3430		
21–05–57		3430		
31–05–58		3230		
05–06–59		3090		
01–07–60		3260		
07–06–61		3230		
28–06–62		3310		
13–06–63		3000		
14–06–64		4080		
04–06–65		3200		
11–06–66		3260		
04–06–67		4130		
29–06–68		3230		
06–06–69		2440		
06–06–70		3960		
16–06–71		3280		
14–06–72		5010		

TABLE II – ANNUAL MAXIMUM DISCHARGES AND VOLUMES (cont'd)

Country:	Canada (12)
River:	Thompson
Gauging Station:	08LF051

Date	Maximum discharge (m³/s) resulting from:		Maximum volume (10⁶m³) corresponding to max. discharge resulting from:	
	Rainfall	Snowmelt	Rainfall	Snowmelt
1	2	3	4	5
28–05–52		2680		
16–06–53		2540		
05–07–54		3110		
29–06–55		3570		
07–06–56		3030		
24–05–57		3600		
04–06–58		3310		
25–06–59		2690		
04–07–60		2970		
10–06–61		3310		
19–06–62		2500		
22–06–63		2340		
19–06–64		3510		
15–06–65		2710		
13–06–66		2470		
24–06–67		3480		
14–06–68		2970		
09–06–69		2760		
08–06–70		2540		
11–06–71		3400		
15–06–72		4130		

Country:	Canada (13)
River:	Castle
Gauging Station:	05AA002

Date	Maximum discharge (m³/s) resulting from:		Maximum volume (10⁶m³) corresponding to max. discharge resulting from:	
	Rainfall	Snowmelt	Rainfall	Snowmelt
1	2	3	4	5
06–06–45		145		9.4
22–05–48		442		26.9
13–05–49		73.9		6.1
16–06–50		128		6.4
14–05–51		145		2.9
27–04–52		92.3		7.9
08–06–53		283		17.6
19–05–54		215		20.4
19–05–55		124		10.6
21–05–56		183		14.4
21–05–57		115		5.0
18–05–58		144		5.3
05–06–59		138		28.4
13–05–60		119		14.1
27–05–61		176		5.9
25–04–62		67.4		6.6
30–06–63		89.2		16.3
08–06–64		510		40.4
17–06–65		294		36.0
22–05–67		227		32.5
23–05–68		157		8.0
26–06–69		159		14.5
13–06–70		210		18.6
28–05–71		125		9.5
01–06–72		213		19.1

TABLE II – ANNUAL MAXIMUM DISCHARGES AND VOLUMES (cont'd)

Country: Canada (14)
River: Clearwater
Gauging Station: 05DB001

| Date | Maximum discharge (m³/s) resulting from: | | Maximum volume (10⁶m³) corresponding to max. discharge resulting from: | |
	Rainfall	Snowmelt	Rainfall	Snowmelt
1	2	3	4	5
17–08–22	75.3		19.6	
01–05–24		153		6.7
17–08–25	328		26.2	
28–07–27		117		4.7
19–06–28		267		27.9
03–06–29		253		17.9
24–06–52		425		39.4
04–06–53		171		10.5
26–08–54	385		59.5	
13–06–55		96.3		11.1
30–04–57		78.4		0.6
02–07–58		104		5.3
28–06–59		146		13.4
03–07–60		63.7		3.4
31–07–61		63.1		6.5
21–05–62		62.0		4.6
17–07–63		147		19.1
07–05–64		189		21.9
19–06–65		524		44.0
04–07–66		180		10.9
01–06–67		152		7.7
21–07–68		74.2		5.0
07–07–69		286		43.3
17–06–70		397		59.0
07–06–71		146		20.8
26–06–72		167		65.1

Country: Canada (18)
River: Athabasca
Gauging Station: 07BE001

| Date | Maximum discharge (m³/s) resulting from: | | Maximum volume (10⁶m³) corresponding to max. discharge resulting from: | |
	Rainfall	Snowmelt	Rainfall	Snowmelt
1	2	3	4	5
08–06–22		940		126
17–06–23		1910		250
01–09–24	1580		145	
19–06–28		2240		156
18–06–44		5040		431
01–08–47	2080		148	
18–06–50		1630		144
26–06–52		2450		411
10–06–54		5660		595
03–06–55		2350		352
08–06–56		1810		192
14–08–57	1170		129	
01–07–58	2400		487	
30–06–59		1760		81
28–06–60		2890		1230
03–07–61	1150		101	
22–05–62		1640		139
29–04–63		1610		191
22–06–64		1630		82
30–06–65		3680		668
31–08–66	1790		222	
21–06–67		1660		184
15–06–68		1290		205
09–08–69	3110		636	
19–06–70		1630		136
11–07–71	4560		548	
28–06–72		3540		472

TABLE II — ANNUAL MAXIMUM DISCHARGES AND VOLUMES (cont'd)

Country:	Canada (19)
River:	Sprague
Gauging Station:	05OD031

Date	Maximum discharge (m³/s) resulting from:		Maximum volume (10⁶m³) corresponding to max. discharge resulting from:	
	Rainfall	Snowmelt	Rainfall	Snowmelt
1	2	3	4	5
30–05–29	4.8		5.0	
13–05–30	29.4		26.0	
09–04–31		4.7		7.0
14–04–32		11.5		23.3
20–04–33		16.4		22.7
07–04–34		0.7		0.3
27–04–35		4.5		6.6
20–04–36		17.3		19.9
17–07–37	44.2		25.9	
11–05–38	21.1		25.4	
04–06–39	0.9		0.6	
30–04–40		2.0		1.0
26–09–41	53.2		43.8	
01–09–42	58.6		29.1	
10–04–43		22.8		20.8
26–06–44	30.6		20.8	
28–03–45		30.0		20.9
23–03–46		8.5		18.1
12–06–47	41.6		22.2	
21–04–48		28.6		32.4
15–04–49		11.8		12.3
12–05–50		41.6		71.2
01–05–51	11.0		15.8	
04–07–52	2.0		3.2	
03–06–53	6.7		6.6	
30–04–54		14.6		24.0
06–06–55	15.8		13.0	
05–07–56	24.4		10.7	
15–06–57	12.0		9.0	
10–07–58	4.7		3.0	

Country:	Canada (19) cont'd
River:	Sprague
Gauging Station:	05OD031

Date	Maximum discharge (m³/s) resulting from:		Maximum volume (10⁶m³) corresponding to max. discharge resulting from:	
	Rainfall	Snowmelt	Rainfall	Snowmelt
1	2	3	4	5
07–05–59	16.8		12.9	
15–04–60		20.0		15.9
24–03–61		3.3		0.9
25–05–62	24.4		21.8	
10–04–63		20.0		12.5
20–06–64	13.2		8.3	
07–05–65	35.4		22.3	
18–04–66		26.4		50.4
22–04–67		31.1		28.9
11–06–68	24.4		17.5	
13–04–69		24.6		26.9
28–04–70		33.4		34.7
19–04–71		9.7		12.1
23–04–72		13.5		21.6

Canada / Canadá / Канада

TABLE II — ANNUAL MAXIMUM DISCHARGES AND VOLUMES   (cont'd)

Country: **Canada (27)**
River: **Rocky**
Gauging Station: **02ZK001**

| Date | Maximum discharge (m³/s) resulting from: | | Maximum volume (10⁶m³) corresponding to max. discharge resulting from: | |
| | Rainfall | Snowmelt | Rainfall | Snowmelt |
1	2	3	4	5
11−03-49		112		
05−10−50	77.6			
26−01−51		120		
06−02−52		120		
27−12−53	161			
09−12−54	148			
13−02−55		103		
10−11−56	140			
06−09−57	119			
31−05−58	110			
11−11−59	118			
06−04−60		73.1		
28−03−61		112		
11−02−62		187		
15−11−63	88.3			
19−12−64	144			
02−03−65		90.3		
15−12−66	111			
06−01−67		87.8		
27−08−68	116			
30−10−69	117			
27−02−70		146		
27−11−72	150			

Country: **Canada (28)**
River: **St. Francis**
Gauging Station: **01AD003**

| Date | Maximum discharge (m³/s) resulting from: | | Maximum volume (10⁶m³) corresponding to max. discharge resulting from: | |
| | Rainfall | Snowmelt | Rainfall | Snowmelt |
1	2	3	4	5
02−05−52		189		150
04−04−53		165		116
25−04−54		230		147
06−05−55		248		331
17−05−56		116		62.5
01−05−57		150		113
26−04−58		306		257
28−04−59		139		87.4
12−05−60		203		279
16−05−61		326		278
09−05−62		96.3		64.1
07−05−63		191		210
03−05−64		134		117
15−05−65		62.9		16.8
26−04−66		142		87.6
06−05−67		144		79.0
18−04−68		227		181
12−05−69		368		288
04−05−70		251		221
13−05−71		206		244
19−05−72		225		216

TABLE II — ANNUAL MAXIMUM DISCHARGES AND VOLUMES (cont'd)

Country:	Canada (29)
River:	Northeast Margaree
Gauging Station:	0!FB001

Date	Maximum discharge (m³/s) resulting from:		Maximum volume (10⁶m³) corresponding to max. discharge resulting from:	
	Rainfall	.Snowmelt	Rainfall	Snowmelt
1	2	3	4	5
13—11—43	303			
09—05—44		146		
19—05—45		202		
14—05—46		260		
02—05—47		264		
30—05—48		527		
26—11—49	303			
23—04—50		164		
26—08—51	221			
24—01—52		176		
09—02—53		242		
27—02—54		129		
21—09—55	193			
07—01—56		210		
04—11—57	197			
28—11—58	231			
13—12—59		190		
26—10—60	177			
29—12—61		270		
02—04—62		493		
03—05—63		175		
25—05—64		196		
18—11—65	184			
05—10—66	146			
24—11—67	558			
26—08—68	569			
20—05—69		365		
27—05—70		240		
21—11—71	311			
17—05—72		279		

Country:	Canada (30)
River:	St. John
Gauging Station:	01AD002

Date	Maximum discharge (m³/s) resulting from:		Maximum volume (10⁶m³) corresponding to max. discharge resulting from:	
	Rainfall	.Snowmelt	Rainfall	Snowmelt
1	2	3	4	5
26—04—34		2710		1940
02—05—35		2140		1200
23—03—36		2320		1310
01—05—37		1720		1550
22—04—38		1990		1440
11—05—39		3260		2430
05—05—40		2460		1930
22—04—41		3090		1700
05—05—42		3260		2590
13—05—43		2520		2010
07—05—44		2080		1270
03—04—45		2210		1050
18—05—46		1960		996
09—05—47		3230		1880
10—05—48		1700		982
04—05—49		1390		581
23—04—50		1890		674
10—04—51		2200		1410
30—40—52		1960		1400
01—04—53		2140		1450
24—04—54		2750		1570
05—05—55		2410		2080
16—05—56		1370		694
24—04—57		1420		612
26—04—58		3340		2220
28—04—59		1490		839
08—05—60		2580		2300
16—05—61		3710		3050
08—05—62		1320		555
03—05—63		2170		1330

TABLE II – ANNUAL MAXIMUM DISCHARGES AND VOLUMES (cont'd)

Country:	Canada (30) cont'd
River:	St. John
Gauging Station:	01AD002

Date	Maximum discharge (m³/s) resulting from:		Maximum volume (10⁶m³) corresponding to max. discharge resulting from:	
	Rainfall	Snowmelt	Rainfall	Snowmelt
1	2	3	4	5
29—04—64		1270		632
14—05—65		702		158
21—05—66		1660		728
05—05—67		1910		830
17—04—68		2570		1490
11—05—69		3650		2280
03—05—70		2690		1770
71		2540		1610
17—05—72		2490		1910

Country:	
River:	
Gauging Station:	

Date	Maximum discharge (m³/s) resulting from:		Maximum volume (10⁶m³) corresponding to max. discharge resulting from:	
	Rainfall	Snowmelt	Rainfall	Snowmelt
1	2	3	4	5

TABLE III — CHARACTERISTICS OF SNOWMELT FLOODS

			Characteristic elements							Type of probability curve	
No.	River	Gauging station	Q_{max} (m³/s)	Date	h (mm)	T_T (hours)	t_i (hours)	P_W (%)	$P_{Q_{max}}$ (%)	for P_W	for $P_{Q_{max}}$
1	2	3	4	5	6	7	8	9	10	11	12
2	Chilliwack	08MH016	73	27–05–46					37		Lognormal
			99	11–06–48					7		"
			86	07–06–61					17		"
			54	12–06–65					80		"
			116	10–06–72					1.6		"
3	Slocan	08NJ013	430	30–05–38					58		"
			722	07–06–61					3.1		"
			541	15–06–64					24		"
			643	03–06–68					8		"
4	M'Clintock	09AB008	69	23–05–68							
			113	01–06–72							
5	Toad	10BE001	535	11 07 63							
			236	31–05–72							
6	Chilko	08MA001	368	20–07–41					14		Lognormal
			479	20–06–50					0.5		"
			309	16–07–61					46		"
			394	20–06–69					7		"
7	Kettle	08NN013	515	27–05–42					5		"
			600	29–05–48					1.1		"
			340	15–06–50					53		"
			425	13–05–51					20		"

	Method of curve fitting		Snow cover		Rainfall during snowmelt (mm)	Monthly precipitation before soil freezing (mm)	Mean monthly temperature before snowmelt (°C)
No.	for W	for Q_{max}	Water equivalent (mm)	Layer thickness (cm)			
1	13	14	15	16	17	18	19
2		Maximum Likelihood					
		"					
		"					
		"					
		"					
3		"					
		"					
		"					
		"					
4			5.1	25.4	10.9	–3.6	
			43.2	39.1	13.5	–4.4	
5							
6		Maximum Likelihood					
		"					
		"					
7		"					
		"					
		"					
		"					

TABLE III — CHARACTERISTICS OF SNOWMELT FLOODS (cont'd)

No.	River	Gauging station	Q_{max} (m³/s)	Date	h (mm)	T_T (hours)	t_i (hours)	P_W (%)	$P_{Q_{max}}$ (%)	Type of probability curve for P_W	for $P_{Q_{max}}$
1	2	3	4	5	6	7	8	9	10	11	12
8	Dease	10AC002	739	03—06—61							
			968	31—05—72							
9	Skeena	08EF001	6800	20—05—57					10		Lognormal
			6140	08—06—61					23		"
			5130	24—06—71					60		"
			8100	12—06—72					1.4		"
10	Fraser	08KB001	3680	28—06—55					27		"
			3430	07—06—56					44		"
			4130	04—06—67					9		"
											"
11	Teslin	09AF001	1860	28—06—62							
			1060	20—06—66							
12	Thompson	08LF051	2680	28—05—52					77		Lognormal
			3110	05—07—54					40		"
			3600	24—05—57					12		"
			4130	15—06—72					1.7		"
13	Castle	05AA022	442	22—05—48	32.6	72	34	11	2.6	Lognormal	"
			283	08—06—53	21.3	96	26	30	14	"	"
			510	08—06—64	48.8	102	32	2.9	1.4	"	"
			210	13—06—70	22.6	216	20	27	30	"	"

No.	Method of curve fitting for W	for Q_{max}	Snow cover Water equivalent (mm)	Layer thickness (cm)	Rainfall during snowmelt (mm)	Monthly precipitation before soil freezing (mm)	Mean monthly temperature before snowmelt (°C)
1	13	14	15	16	17	18	19
8				49.5	36.1	35.3	−5.6
				34.3	49.5	76.7	−10.8
9		Maximum Likelihood					
		"					
		"					
		"					
10		"					
		"					
		"					
		"					
11				33.0	70.0	16.3	−11.2
				19.1	46.0	31.5	−10.2
12		Maximum Likelihood					
		"					
		"					
		"					
13	Maximum Likelihood	"		2.5	188	88.1	−3.2
	"	"		0.0	353	4.1	−2.4
	"	"		2.5	198	70.4	−5.7
	"	"		17.8	179	6.1	−4,1

TABLE III — CHARACTERISTICS OF SNOWMELT FLOODS (cont'd)

			Characteristic elements							Type of probability curve	
No.	River	Gauging station	Q_{max} (m^3/s)	Date	h (mm)	T_T (hours)	t_i (hours)	P_W (%)	$P_{Q_{max}}$ (%)	for P_W	for $P_{Q_{max}}$
1	2	3	4	5	6	7	8	9	10	11	12
14	Clearwater	05DB001	524	19—06—65	14.1	136	34	8	2.9	Lognormal	Lognormal
			180	04—07—66	3.5	130	37	64	44	"	"
			286	07—07—69	13.8	161	79	8	18	"	"
			399	17—06—70	18.8	198	74	3.6	7	"	"
15	Mcleod	07AG001	954	01—06—65	19.3	144	34				
			1180	26—06—72	23.0	138	35				
16	Athabasca	07AD002	864	18—06—67	16.7	438	108				
			1270	13—06—72	13.2	198	114				
18	Athabasca	07BE001	5040	18—06—44	5.6	120	81	22	4	Lognormal	Lognormal
			5660	10—06—54	7.7	158	104	11	2.2	"	"
			2350	03—06—55	4.6	252	40	31	42	"	"
			3540	28—06—72	6.1	222	52	18	15	"	"
19	Sprague	05OD031	22.8	10—04—43	53.3	624	244	38	22	"	"
			28.6	21—04—48	82.8	792	229	16	12	"	"
			41.6	21—05—50	182	1200	672	1.5	3.6	"	"
			13.5	23—04—72	49.3	720	305	36	55	"	"
20	Junction	02CF005	37.9	30—03—63	197	444	186				
			32.6	20—04—72	261	504	210				
21	Highland	02HC013	36.0	10—02—65	46.4	228	92				
			39.9	15—02—72	35.5	144	65				

	Method of curve fitting		Snow cover		Rainfall during snowmelt (mm)	Monthly precipitation before soil freezing (mm)	Mean monthly temperature before snowmelt (°C)
No.	for W	for Q_{max}	Water equivalent (mm)	Layer thickness (cm)			
1	13	14	15	16	17	18	19
14	Maximum Likelihood	Maximum Likelihood		74.9	185	24.1	−9.3
	"	"		57.2	260	32.0	−9.7
	"	"		66.0	205	30.0	−10.6
	"	"		38.1	133	40.4	−7.6
15				61.0	125	1.3	+2.4
				71.1	245	9.9	−14.8
16				45.7	101	33.3	−6.4
				63.5	113	8.6	−12.7
18	Maximum Likelifood	Maximum Likelihood		19.1	247	2.0	−11.7
	"	"		27.9	159	15.2	−7.2
	"	"		14.5	107	17.3	−9.8
	"	"		71.1	163	13.2	−15.6
19	"	"		20.3	1.3	22.1	−15.7
	"	"		44.2	32.3	33.5	−14.7
	"	"		10.2	44.5	39.6	−2.4
	"	"		15.2	53.3	20.6	−17.4
20				53.3	54.6	34.5	−12.0
				40.6	53.6	73.9	−10.3
21							
				7.6	36.8	61.2	−7.8

TABLE III — CHARACTERISTICS OF SNOWMELT FLOODS (cont'd)

No.	River	Gauging station	Q_{max} (m^3/s)	Date	h (mm)	T_T (hours)	t_i (hours)	P_W (%)	$P_{Q_{max}}$ (%)	Type of probability curve for P_W	for $P_{Q_{max}}$
1	2	3	4	5	6	7	8	9	10	11	12
22	Magpie	02BD003	208	11−05−64	272	1920	698				
			136	03−05−72	141	1490	512				
23	Nith	02GA010	354	11−02−65	58.4	274	111				
			295	04−04−67	101	480	228				
24	Missinaibi	04LJ001	1200	17−05−60	333	1440	709				
			728	20−05−67	251	1610	1120				
25	Clam Harbour	01ER001	49.0	05−04−59							
			36.0	02−04−62							
26	Upper Humber	02YL001	566	11−05−60							
			433	06−07−67							
27	Rocky	02ZK001	120	06−02−52					38		Lognormal
			103	13−02−55					61		"
			112	28−03−61					50		"
			187	11−02−62					2.4		"
28	St. Francis	01AD003	248	06−05−55				5.2	21	Lognormal	"
			326	16−05−61				10	6	"	"
			191	07−05−63				25	45	"	"
			368	12−05−69				9	2.9	"	"

No.	Method of curve fitting for W	for Q_{max}	Snow cover Water equivalent (mm)	Layer thickness (cm)	Rainfall during snowmelt (mm)	Monthly precipitation before soil freezing (mm)	Mean monthly temperature before snowmelt (°C)
1	13	14	15	16	17	18	19
22				66.0	96.0	65.0	−6.8
				45.7	16.8	166	−9.8
23				15.2	50.8	141	−6.7
24				76.2	153	125	−9.6
				64.8	143	141	−15.4
25				20.3	115	173	−5.0
				12.7	48.5	162	−4.9
26					104	82.3	−4.2
				91.4	99.6	68.1	−2.7
27		Maximum Likelihood			126	153	−3.9
		"		15.2	57.9	208	−2.0
		"		50.8	87.1	173	−7.0
		"		10.2	161	110	−5.7
28	Maximum Likelihood	"			68.8	86.4	−8.6
	"	"			107	63.2	−10.2
	"	"		122	90.2	118	−12.4
	"	"		104	111	55.6	−5.2

TABLE III — CHARACTERISTICS OF SNOWMELT FLOODS   (cont'd)

No.	River	Gauging station	Q_{max} (m^3/s)	Date	h (mm)	T_T (hours)	t_i (hours)	P_W (%)	$P_{Q_{max}}$ (%)	Type of probability curve for P_W	for $P_{Q_{max}}$
1	2	3	4	5	6	7	8	9	10	11	12
29	Northeast Margaree	01FB001	146	09—05—44					87		Lognormal
			260	14—05—46					39		"
			527	30—05—48					2.2		"
			164	23—04—50					80		"
			493	02—04—62					3.2		"
30	St. John	01AD002	3260	05—05—42				6	25	Lognormal	"
			2080	07—05—44				54	50	"	"
			3710	16—05—61				2.5	19	"	"
			3650	11—05—69				10	19	"	"
31	Churchill	03OE001	6820	27—06—57							
			3400	29—05—61							

No.	Method of curve fitting for W	for Q_{max}	Snow cover Water equivalent (mm)	Layer thickness (cm)	Rainfall during snowmelt (mm)	Monthly precipitation before soil freezing (mm)	Mean monthly temperature before snowmelt (°C)
1	13	14	15	16	17	18	19
29		Maximum Likelihood		25.4	83.8	163	−5.5
		"		12.7	201	209	−1.2
		"		33.0	330	156	−9.2
		"		33.0	176	191	−8.1
		"			73.4	159	−7.0
30	Maximum Likelihood	"		81.3		122	−7.5
	"	"		43.1	76.5	164	−8.8
	"	"		127	140	84.6	−8.9
	"	"		112	140	73.2	−8.9
31	"	"		12.7	190	84.3	−7.6
	"	"		30.5	97.5	63.0	−9.0

TABLE IV — CHARACTERISTICS OF RAINFALL FLOODS

No.	River	Gauging station	Q_{max} (m³/s)	Date	h (mm)	T_T (hours)	t_i (hours)	P_W (%)	$P_{Q_{max}}$ (%)	Type of probability curve for P_W	for $P_{Q_{max}}$
1	2	3	4	5	6	7	8	9	10	11	12
1	Kanaka	08MH076	110	20–01–68							
			78	26–01–71							
15	Mcleod	07AG001	515	17–08–25	16.1	144	48				
			326	08–09–26	8.1	240	72				
16	Athabasca	07AD002	1060	06–08–69	20.6	254	38				
17	South Nahanni	10EC001	8210	17–06–62	4.0	124	21				
			2250	17–08–70							
18	Athabasca	07BE001	1580	01–09–24	1.9	176	82				
			2080	01–08–47	1.9	152	48				
			1170	14–08–57	1.7	240	66				
			3110	09–08–69	8.3	262	46				
19	Sprague	05OD031	44.2	17–07–37	66.3	480	63	14	9	Lognormal	Lognormal
			58.6	01–09–42	74.2	432	91	10	3.6	"	"
			41.6	12–06–47	56.9	432	189	21	10	"	"
			13.2	20–06–64	19.1	312	60	80	70	"	"
			24.4	11–06–68	39.6	408	171	34	33	"	"
20	Junction	02CF005	20.8	14–09–61	36.4	176	33				
			32.0	24–09–70	44.3	138	6				

No.	Method of curve fitting for W	for Q_{max}	Rainfall forming flood (mm)	Snowmelt during floods (mm)	Maximum daily rainfall (mm)	Date	Hourly maximum rainfall (mm)	Date	Antecedent precipitation for 10 days (mm)	30 days (mm)
1	13	14	15	16	17	18	19	20	21	22
1			272	0	126	18–01–68	10	19–01–68	154	358
			182	0	61.5	25–01–71	10	25–01–71	120	282
15			94.0	0	65.5	16–08–25			13.7	48.0
			32.5	0	16.5	06–09–26			34.3	70.4
16			83.1	0	81.5	04–08–69			26.4	78.5
17										
			54.6	0	36.8	16–08–70			53.1	98.0
18			34.0	0	33.8	29–08–24			30.5	104
			41.7	0	39.4	29–07–47			27.2	73.9
			75.2	0	31.5	10–08–57			19.1	77.5
			70.1	0	45.9	04–08–69			29.7	100
19	Maximum Likelihood	Maximum Likelihood	179	0	78.0	16–07–37			30.7	37.1
	"	"	88.6	0	60.5	29–08–42			44.2	159
	"	"	56.9	0	30.0	12–06–47			53.6	85.6
	"	"	60.2	0	26.7	20–06–64			77.5	101
	"	"	61.5	0	43.7	11–06–68			38.9	61.5
20			89.9	0	56.9	13–09–61	10	14–09–61	14.2	30.2
			56.9	0	50.8	24–09–70	37	24–09–70	30.5	128

TABLE IV — CHARACTERISTICS OF RAINFALL FLOODS (cont'd)

No.	River	Gauging station	Q_{max} (m³/s)	Date	h (mm)	T_T (hours)	t_i (hours)	P_W (%)	$P_{Q_{max}}$ (%)	Type of probability curve for P_W	for $P_{Q_{max}}$
1	2	3	4	5	6	7	8	9	10	11	12
21	Highland	02HC013	26.2	10—11—62	19.4	204	9				
			31.2	13—07—64	27.9	219	66				
22	Magpie	02DB003	261	20—07—68	112	520	132				
23	Nith	02GA010	228	09—12—66	42.1	181	58				
24	Missinaibi	04LJ001	600	22—06—63	36.5	210	94				
25	Clam Harbour	01ER001	79.6	31—08—68							
			134	09—11—69							
26	Upper Humber	02YL001	455	31—10—62							
			555	23—09—55							
27	Rocky	02ZK001	77.6	05—10—50				99			
			119	06—09—57				53			
			116	27—08—68				59			
			117	30—10—69				57			
			161	27—12—53				6.3			
29	Northeast Margaree	01FB001	221	26—08—51					62		Lognormal
			193	21—09—55					73		''
			558	24—11—67					4.3		''
			569	26—08—68					3.9		''
			311	21—11—71					33		''

No.	Method of curve fitting for W	for Q_{max}	Rainfall forming flood (mm)	Snowmelt during floods (mm)	Maximum daily rainfall (mm)	Date	Hourly maximum rainfall (mm)	Date	Antecedent precipitation for 10 days (mm)	30 days (mm)
1	13	14	15	16	17	18	19	20	21	22
21			71.6	0	54.9	09—11—62	10	10—11—62	6.1	65.3
			38.1	0	38.1	13—07—64	14	13—07—64	75.9	159
22			61.2	0	32.5	17—07—68			51.8	105
23			66.8	5.1	36.6	06—12—66	5	09—12—66	32.5	97.0
24			50.5	0	34.0	19—06—63			42.2	83.8
25			118	0	83.8	09—11—69	17	09—11—69	87.9	134
			120	0	95.2	30—08—68	33		41.9	64.8
26			46.5	0	23.9	29—10—62	6	29—10—62	30.7	93.5
			85.6	0	64.0	21—09—55			18.5	74.2
27			63.5	0	63.5	04—10—50			13.2	32.3
			78.5	0	34.5	06—09—57			21.1	88.9
			57.2	0	40.1	27—08—68	8	27—08—68	55.6	71.9
			82.3	0	38.6	28—10—69	5	29—10—69	36.8	94.2
			117	0	104	26—12—53			77.2	208
29		Maximum Likelihood	120	0	89.4	24—08—51			52.1	86.4
		''	98.0	0	72.1	22—09—55			8.6	106
		''	66.8	0	51.6	23—11—67	7	23—11—67	66.8	157
		''	63.5	0	56.6	25—08—68	9	25—08—68	41.7	77.5
		''	55.1	0	43.9	20—11—71			62.7	128

Congo / Конго

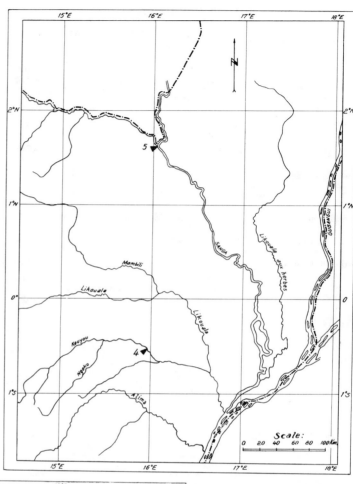

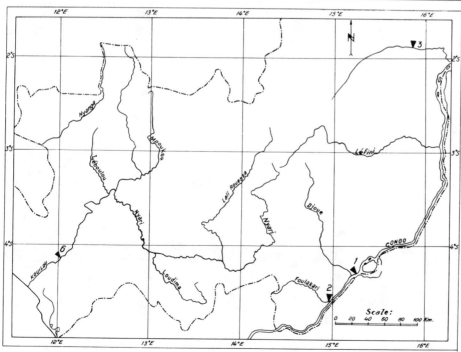

TABLE I — CHARACTERISTICS OF BASIN

No.	River / River system	Name	Period of records	Co-ordinates Lat.	Long.	Distance (km) from gauging site to remotest point of river system L_{rs}	to projection of centre of basin on main course L_{ca}	Mean slope of river I_r (%)	Area A (km²)	Altitude (m) Mean H_m	Max. H_{max}	Min. H_{min}
1	2	3	4	5	6	7	8	9	10	11	12	13
					E							
1	Congo	Brazzaville	1902–73	4:16S	15:19	4640			3480000			270
2	Foulakary	Kimpanzou	1947–73	4:36S	14:56	135			2810	500		380
3	Nkeni	Gamboma	1951–73	1:54S	15:51	125			6200			300
4	Kouyou	Linnegue	1952–73	0:30S	15:56	225			10800			300
5	Sangha	Ouesso	1947–73	1:37N	16:03	750			158000	600		350
6	Kouilou	Sounda	1955–73	4:06S	12:08	710		0.13	55000	400	950	8

No.	Width (km) Mean B_m	Max. B_{max}	Mean slope I_b (%)	Soils	Cover	Weighted lake area P_L (%)	Swamps R_s (%)	Mean annual precipitation P (mm)	Annual runoff Q (mm)	Mean annual temperature T (°C)	Regulating capacity of reservoirs α
1	14	15	16	17	18	19	20	21	22	23	24
1	750	2550							360		
2	21	45						1460	652		
3	50	85						1850	1050		
4	48	70						1620	710		
5	210	570						1600	358		
6	77	270						1500	540		

TABLE II — ANNUAL MAXIMUM DISCHARGES AND VOLUMES

Country:	Congo (1)
River:	Congo
Gauging Station:	Brazzaville Beach

Date	Maximum discharge (m³/s) resulting from:		Maximum volume (10⁶m³) corresponding to max. discharge resulting from:	
	Rainfall	Snowmelt	Rainfall	Snowmelt
1	2	3	4	5
17—11—61	76000			
26—12—62	74500			
10—12—64	68500			
05—12—67	66000			
16—12—68	65500			
15—12—69	64900			
02—12—70	64700			
12—25	63600			
12—24	63500			
18—12—34	62800			
05—12—48	62300			

Country:	Congo (2)
River:	Foulakary
Gauging Station:	Kimpanzou

Date	Maximum discharge (m³/s) resulting from:		Maximum volume (10⁶m³) corresponding to max. discharge resulting from:	
	Rainfall	Snowmelt	Rainfall	Snowmelt
1	2	3	4	5
02—05—66	470			
27—04—55	442			
07—05—65	393			
26—11—51	386			
15—04—53	374			
19—04—73	371			

Country:	Congo (3)
River:	Nkeni
Gauging Station:	Gamboma

Date	Maximum discharge (m³/s) resulting from:		Maximum volume (10⁶m³) corresponding to max. discharge resulting from:	
	Rainfall	Snowmelt	Rainfall	Snowmelt
1	2	3	4	5
29—03—67	282			
01—05—63	268			
19—03—65	264			
02—05—69	264			
06—11—70	264			
04—12—71	264			

Country:	Congo (4)
River:	Kougou
Gauging Station:	Linnegue

Date	Maximum discharge (m³/s) resulting from:		Maximum volume (10⁶m³) corresponding to max. discharge resulting from:	
	Rainfall	Snowmelt	Rainfall	Snowmelt
1	2	3	4	5
18—03—61	597			
27—05—69	594			
31—05—64	567			
12—06—62	525			
11—03—57	487			
23—04—66	486			

TABLE II — ANNUAL MAXIMUM DISCHARGES AND VOLUMES

Country:	**Congo (5)**
River:	**Sangha**
Gauging Station:	**Ouesso**

Date	Maximum discharge (m³/s) resulting from:		Maximum volume (10⁶m³) corresponding to max. discharge resulting from:	
	Rainfall	Snowmelt	Rainfall	Snowmelt
1	2	3	4	5
06—11—60	4680			
02—11—62	4670			
25—10—57	4500			
10—11—59	4450			
09—11—70	4350			

Country:	**Congo (6)**
River:	**Kouilou**
Gauging Station:	**Sounda**

Date	Maximum discharge (m³/s) resulting from:		Maximum volume (10⁶m³) corresponding to max. discharge resulting from:	
	Rainfall	Snowmelt	Rainfall	Snowmelt
1	2	3	4	5
28—04—64	3150			
13—03—61	3090			
27—03—67	3020			
07—05—70	2780			

TABLE IV — CHARACTERISTICS OF RAINFALL FLOODS

No.	River	Gauging station	Q_{max} (m^3/s)	Date	h (mm)	T_T (hours)	t_i (hours)	P_W (%)	$P_{Q_{max}}$ (%)	Type of probability curve for P_W	for $P_{Q_{max}}$
1	2	3	4	5	6	7	8	9	10	11	12
1	Congo	Brazzaville	76000	17—11—61					1.5	Empirical curve	
			74500	26—12—62					2.3	"	
			68500	10—12—64					4.1	"	
			66000	05—12—67					6.2	"	
			65500	16—12—08					7.3	"	
			64900	15—12—69					8.5	"	
			64700	02—12—70					9.0	"	
			63600	12—25					11.3	"	
2	Foulakary	Kimpanzou	470	02—05—66					3.5	Empirical curve	
			442	27—04—55					7.5	"	
			393	07—05—65					11.5	"	
			386	26—11—51					14.0	"	
3	Nkeni	Gamboma	282	29—03—67					2.0	Empirical curve	
			268	01—05—63					11.0	"	
			264	19—03—65					16.5	"	
4	Kouyou	Linnegue	597	18—03—61					6.5	Empirical curve	
			594	27—05—69					7.0	"	
5	Sangha	Ouesso	4680	06—11—60					2.6	Gauss' Law	
			4670	02—11—62					8.0	"	
			4500	25—10—57					13.0	"	
			4450	10—11—59					18.0	"	
			4350	09—11—70					24.0	"	
6	Kouilou	Sounda	3150	28—04—64					9.5	Empirical curve	
			3090	13—03—61					11.0	"	

Czechoslovakia / Tchécoslovaquie / Checoslovaquia / Чехословакия

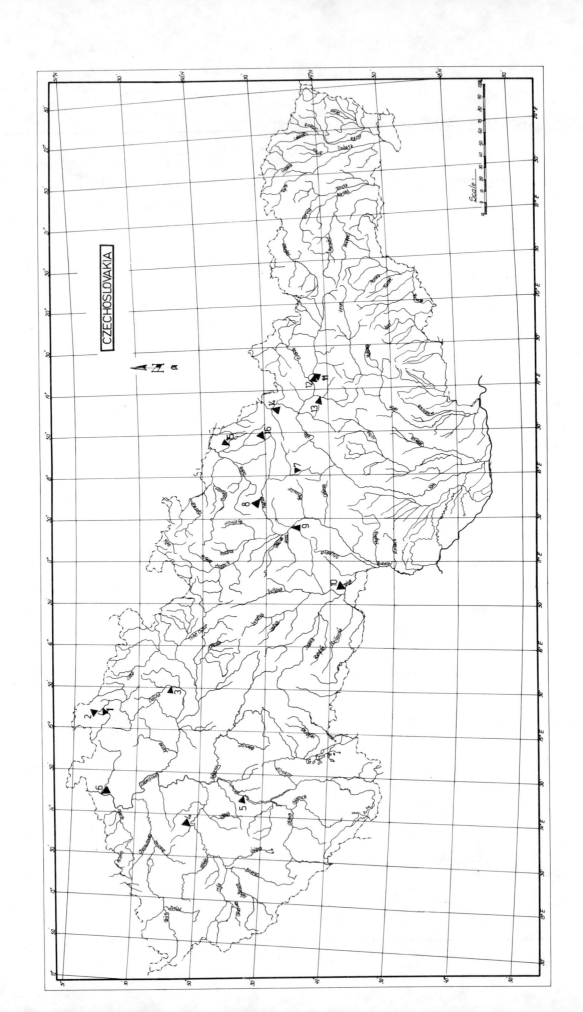

TABLE I.— CHARACTERISTICS OF BASIN

	GAUGING STATION								BASIN				
						Distance (km) from gauging site					Altitude (m)		
	River River system	Name	Period of records	Co-ordinates Lat.	Long.	to remotest point of river system L_{rs}	to projection of centre of basin on main course L_{ca}	Mean slope of river I_r (%)	Area A (km^2)	Mean H_m	Max. H_{max}	Min. H_{min}
No.	2	3	4	5	6	7	8	9	10	11	12	13
1				N	E							
1	Kamenice Labe	Josefův důl	1911–72	50:46	15:14	8	3.5	6.09	26.0	852	1080	591
2	Smědava Odra	Bílý potok	1956–72	50:51	15:14	9	3.8	8.07	26.1	768	1120	398
3	Cidlina Labe	Nový Bydžov	1932–69	50:14	15:30	38	15	1.10	452	361	642	224
4	Berounka Vltava	Křivoklát	1886–70	50:01	13:53	179	57	2.87	7422	460	1340	233
5	Vltava Labe	Kamýk nad Vltavou	1877–54	49:38	14:15	301	61	1.80	12200	563	1380	266
6	Labe	Děčín	1851–70	50:47	14:13	343	106	0.43	51100	465	1600	121
7	Zděchovka Bečva	Zděchov	1928–72	49:15:53	18:04:47	2.9	0.9	10.5	4.08	611	783	479
8	Bečva Morava	Teplice	1920–72	49:32	17:44	79.5	25.1	0.89	1280	539	952	242
9	Morava Danube	Kroměříž	1916–72	49:18	17:24	144	36.4	0.86	7010	492	1420	184

	BASIN										
	Width (km)		Mean slope I_b(%)			Weighted lake area P_L (%)	Swamps R_s (%)	Mean annual precipitation P (mm)	Annual runoff Q (mm)	Mean annual temperature T (°C)	Regulating capacity of reservoirs α
	Mean B_m	Max. B_{max}		Soils	Cover						
No.	14	15	16	17	18	19	20	21	22	23	24
1	3.26	5.0	17.8	4(100)	F(90), C(10)	0	0	1420	1130	5	0
2	2.9	6.5	14.1	2(100)	F(90), C(10)	0	0	1470	1020	5.5	0
3	11.9	28	6.3	2(26), 4(59), 5(15)	F(20), C(80)	0	0	642	138	7.5	0
4	41.4	100	8.2	2, 4(100)	F(30), C(65), U(5)	0	0	593	135	8.2	0.03
5	40.6	149		2(92), 4(2), 5(6)	F(34), C(66)	0	0	687	201	6.6	0.03
6	148	330		2(63), 4(20), 5(2)	F(30), C(62), U(8)	1	0.5	676	189	7.4	0.05
7	1.4	1.9	22.6	4(100)	F(6), C(90), U(4)	0	0	971	474	6.5	0
8	16.0	42.6	9.4	2(47), 4(50), 5, 7(3)	F(47), C(53)	0	0	888	377	6.0	0
9	49.1	124	7.2	2(34), 4(42), 5(24)	F(36), C(64)	0	0	718	222	6.4	0

TABLE I — CHARACTERISTICS OF BASIN (cont'd)

| | | | | | | GAUGING STATION | | | BASIN | | | |
| | | | | | | Distance (km) from gauging site | | | | Altitude (m) | | |
No.	River River system	Name	Period of records	Co-ordinates Lat.	Co-ordinates Long.	to remotest point of river system L_{rs}	to projection of centre of basin on main course L_{ca}	Mean slope of river I_r (%)	Area A (km^2)	Mean H_m	Max. H_{max}	Min. H_{min}
1	2	3	4	5	6	7	8	9	10	11	12	13
10	Dyje Morava	Dolní Věstonice	1921–72	N 48:53	E 17:39	228	53.3	0.22	11700		676	165
11	Váh Danube	Lubochna	1921–72	49:20	19:10	97.2	38.0	1.23	2130	1090	2550	445
12	Lubochnianka Váh	Lubochňa	1931–72	49:20	19:10	24.0	12.5	4.39	118	936	1450	445
13	Turiec Váh	Martin	1931–72	49:04	18:56	59.6	19.0	1.11	827	1530	1530	390
14	Kysuca Váh	Cadca	1920–72	49:26	18:47	35.4	10.0	1.70	484	641	1050	410
15	Celadénka Ostravice	Čeladná	1952–72	49:50	18:20	9.5	3.7	0.79	31.1	809	1260	507
16	Ostravice Odra	Šance	1926–68	49:30	18:24	18.5	6.0	0.48	146	707	1320	440

| | | BASIN | | | | | | | | | | |
No.	Width (km) Mean B_m	Width (km) Max. B_{max}	Mean slope I_b(%)	Soils	Cover	Weighted lake area P_L (%)	Swamps R_s (%)	Mean annual precipitation P (mm)	Annual runoff Q (mm)	Mean annual temperature T (°C)	Regulating capacity of reservoirs α	
1	14	15	16	17	18	19	20	21	22	23	24	
10	51.3	130	4.5	2(46), 4(29), 5(25)	F(27), C(73)	0	0	590	112	7.5	0.04	
11	21.9	34	31.0	2,4(100)	F(60),C(13),U(27)	0	0	1020	562	5.4	0	
12	4.9	8	48.0	2(100)	F(90), U(10)	0	0	1180	635	3.9	0	
13	13.9	30	12.0	2,4(90), 5(10)	F(60), C(30), U(10)	0	0	945	410	5.6	0	
14	13.6	18	23.0	2,4(100)	F(50), C(15), U(35)	0	0	910	547	5.7	0	
15	3.3	5	21.6	2(100)	F(100)	0	0	1320	842	6.5	0	
16	7.9	14	24.2	4(100)	F(100)	0	0	1200	671	6.2	till 1968 0 from 1968 0.64	

Czechoslovakia / Tchécoslovaquie / Checoslovaquia / Чехословакия

TABLE II – ANNUAL MAXIMUM DISCHARGES AND VOLUMES

Country: Czechoslovakia (1)
River: Kamenice
Gauging Station: Josefův Důl

Date	Maximum discharge (m³/s) resulting from:		Maximum volume (10⁶m³) corresponding to max. discharge resulting from:	
	Rainfall	Snowmelt	Rainfall	Snowmelt
1	2	3	4	5
06–04–12	17.5		1.58	
16–08–13	46.0		4.83	
10–07–14	20.7		0.54	
05–09–15	49.8		2.48	
21–07–16	17.9		0.68	
11–08–17	20.3		0.99	
05–07–18	36.5		1.38	
27–06–19	22.6		1.97	
28–08–20	68.5		7.11	
30–10–21	9.1		0.62	
11–01–22		15.4		0.72
12–10–23	16.2		1.18	
14–06–24	66.4		1.60	
04–08–25	33.7		1.60	
17–06–26	42.4		4.48	
12–01–27		11.9		1.72
27–05–28	49.8		2.66	
01–10–30	21.6		1.37	
01–11–31	18.8		2.53	
08–08–32	21.6		0.96	
03–08–33	17.9		1.53	
27–06–34	38.9		2.22	
28–10–35	31.6		1.48	
22–10–36	11.9		0.81	
14–07–37	24.0		1.67	
24–08–38	39.5		5.72	
01–12–39		19.3		2.01
16–07–40	25.0		0.90	
29–05–41	58.6		5.46	
16–05–42	31.6		3.56	

Country: Czechoslovakia (1) cont'd
River: Kamenice
Gauging Station: Josefův Důl

Date	Maximum discharge (m³/s) resulting from:		Maximum volume (10⁶m³) corresponding to max. discharge resulting from:	
	Rainfall	Snowmelt	Rainfall	Snowmelt
1	2	3	4	5
25–11–44	16.6		1.35	
01–10–45	34.8		1.65	
14–08–48	106		10.4	
01–07–49	68.8		8.99	
20–04–50	34.3		18.0	
06–05–51	37.1		4.32	
13–09–52	35.4		4.62	
20–07–54	11.3		1.10	
29–12–55		13.7		2.19
29–10–56	33.0		1.45	
23–07–57	63.7		2.41	
04–07–58	126		7.04	
21–07–59	18.2		1.34	
13–08–60	21.0		0.91	
14–03–61		19.6		2.05
08–05–62	10.6		0.35	
16–06–63	7.34		0.09	
22–04–64	21.0		0.77	
11–05–65	31.0		3.35	
29–06–66	62.0		1.53	
18–05–67	26.4		1.64	
11–06–68	16.2		1.37	
12–04–69	13.4		1.12	
28–05–70	13.6		0.81	

TABLE II – ANNUAL MAXIMUM DISCHARGES AND VOLUMES   (cont'd)

Country:	Czechoslovakia (2)
River:	Smedava
Gauging Station:	Bílý potok

Date	Maximum discharge (m³/s) resulting from:		Maximum volume (10⁶m³) corresponding to max. discharge resulting from:	
	Rainfall	Snowmelt	Rainfall	Snowmelt
1	2	3	4	5
07−06−56	62		3.26	
23−07−57	69		4.68	
04−07−58	118		9.18	
20−07−59	29		3.69	
13−08−60	43		1.35	
31−07−61	42		1.08	
08−05−62	23		1.71	
16−06−63	12		0.47	
11−08−64	69		4.14	
29−05−65	40		1.80	
27−05−66	33		1.98	
17−05−67	38		2.07	
11−06−68	24		1.45	
12−04−69		10		0.86
20−04−70		16		0.88
01−07−71	52		4.86	
21−08−72	44		1.89	

Country:	Czechoslovakia (3)
River:	Cidlina
Gauging Station:	Nový Bydzov

Date	Maximum discharge (m³/s) resulting from:		Maximum volume (10⁶m³) corresponding to max. discharge resulting from:	
	Rainfall	Snowmelt	Rainfall	Snowmelt
1	2	3	4	5
05−01−32		27.5		9.4
07−02−33		8.28		1.5
25−02−34		5.26		1.4
18−02−35		33.4		7.3
02−02−36		18.0		4.8
01−03−37		33.0		11.7
12−09−38	23.7		6.0	
19−01−39		17.4		9.5
24−03−40		48.4		26.5
09−03−41		47.5		40.6
26−03−42		40.5		19.6
16−02−43		26.0		6.8
22−03−44		10.4		4.1
27−02−45		41.9		17.4
09−02−46		57.1		16.5
18−03−47		51.7		41.2
10−02−48		33.4		17.3
16−03−49		17.4		3.6
22−02−50		14.7		2.9
10−05−51	12.3		6.1	
26−02−52		8.28		3.9
31−01−53		37.4		13.8
07−01−54		2.70		0.9
29−12−54		32.1		9.4
03−03−56		50.8		17.4
06−12−56		34.3		12.8
17−02−58		41.0		20.2
27−02−59		3.54		1.5
23−10−60	5.62		1.4	
11−02−61		47.5		23.1

TABLE II – ANNUAL MAXIMUM DISCHARGES AND VOLUMES (cont'd)

Country:	Czechoslovakia (3) cont'd
River:	Cidlina
Gauging Station:	Nový Bydžov

Date	Maximum discharge (m³/s) resulting from:		Maximum volume (10⁶m³) corresponding to max. discharge resulting from:	
	Rainfall	Snowmelt	Rainfall	Snowmelt
1	2	3	4	5
01–04–62		29.3		11.6
13–03–63		19.6		5.6
29–03–64		12.6		3.3
19–03–65		36.9		33.6
13–02–66		36.0		26.0
04–02–67		47.9		19.8
25–12–67		54.6		14.1
15–03–69		28.6		9.9

Country:	Czechoslovakia (4)
River:	Berounka
Gauging Station:	Křivoklát

Date	Maximum discharge (m³/s) resulting from:		Maximum volume (10⁶m³) corresponding to max. discharge resulting from:	
	Rainfall	Snowmelt	Rainfall	Snowmelt
1	2	3	4	5
03–09–90	1300		308	
03–08–01	525		64.0	
19–12–02		670		31.4
07–01–03		323		63.0
04–03–06	344		76.5	
20–03–07		236		87.5
05–02–09		897		120
05–02–13		254		49.3
18–07–14	400		40.3	
07–03–15		520		106
18–02–16		333		89.0
01–01–17		245		134
15–01–20		732		244
02–02–23		521		158
28–03–24		494		235
30–12–25		270		129
17–06–26	410		167	
08–04–27		295		117
02–03–31		432		120
31–05–32	475		132	
05–02–33	223		91.1	
11–04–34	188		46.0	
19–04–35	192		65.7	
08–06–36		419		86.2
24–02–37	241		177	
15–01–38	227		60.1	
19–06–39		251		82.2
15–03–40		816		244
03–03–41	569		260	
22–03–42	461		290	

51

TABLE II — ANNUAL MAXIMUM DISCHARGES AND VOLUMES   (cont'd)

Country:	Czechoslovakia (4) cont'd
River:	Berounka
Gauging Station:	Křivoklát

Date	Maximum discharge (m³/s) resulting from:		Maximum volume (10⁶m³) corresponding to max. discharge resulting from:	
	Rainfall	Snowmelt	Rainfall	Snowmelt
1	2	3	4	5
12–06–43		113		36.6
07–04–44	374		217	
14–02–45	282		199	
10–02–46	234		105	
15–03–47		854		139
02–06–49		305		78.0
12–02–50	246		39.9	
20–01–51	151		46.2	
27–03–52	206		214	
31–01–53	208		96.0	
09–07–54	824		260	
26–03–55	427		170	
04–03–56	515		197	
03–04–57	139		72.5	
05–07–58		368		145
05–05–59		151		48.9
01–03–60	120		77.7	
11–02–61	204		172	
01–04–62	153		52.9	
17–06–63		94.7		25.6
23–03–64	68.0		33.3	
11–06–65		347		195
23–07–66		297		114
22–12–66	219		278	
17–01–68	252		112	
16–03–69	233		141	
24–02–70	340		102	

Country:	Czechoslovakia (5)
River:	Vltava — Labe
Gauging Station:	Kamýk nad Vltavou

Date	Maximum discharge (m³/s) resulting from:		Maximum volume (10⁶m³) corresponding to max. discharge resulting from:	
	Rainfall	Snowmelt	Rainfall	Snowmelt
1	2	3	4	5
04–09–90	2310		972	
05–05–96	1690		848	
08–04–00	1180			742
08–10–15	1650		763	
04–07–26	853		1470	
07–04–27		339		526
27–05–28	464		150	
22–03–29		702		429
01–05–30	235		70	
22–11–31	341		128	
31–05–32	953		298	
05–02–33		418		202
12–04–34		202		112
19–04–35		374		412
08–06–36	643		305	
23–02–37		501		188
26–08–38	588		347	
19–06–39	422		347	
14–03–40		1370		34.8
08–04–41		1030		1110
19–03–42		673		787
02–04–43		277		88
07–04–44		798		939
15–02–45		413		399
10–02–46		676		786
15–03–47		1080		1100
30–12–47 48	735		408	
02–06–49	455		525	
13–02–50		255		203
12–05–51	450		257	
27–03–52		553		689
31–01–53		264		94.8
09–07–54	1970		699	

TABLE II — ANNUAL MAXIMUM DISCHARGES AND VOLUMES   (cont'd)

Country: Czechoslovakia (6)
River: Labe
Gauging Station: Děčín

Date	Maximum discharge (m³/s) resulting from:		Maximum volume (10⁶m³) corresponding to max. discharge resulting from:	
	Rainfall	Snowmelt	Rainfall	Snowmelt
1	2	3	4	5
30—03—45		5600		
22—03—51		1700		
08—02—52		1930		
30—04—53		2110		
09—02—54		1930		
03—03—55		3170		
11—02—56		2370		
03—08—58	1850			
08—03—59		1850		
02—04—60		2280		
29—01—61		1200		
03—02—62		1820		
18—02—64		2300		
10—04—65		3340		
29—01—67		4060		
08—03—68		1920		
14—02—69		1250		
04—03—70		1530		
22—02—71		2360		
27—05—72	2040			
25—12—75	1270			
20—02—76		4140		
16—02—77		2040		
05—03—78		1470		
08—03—80		1720		
13—03—81		2850		
30—12—82	2940			
04—01—83		2810		
09—03—85		1040		
25—03—86		2880		

Country: Czechoslovakia (6) cont'd
River: Labe
Gauging Station: Děčín

Date	Maximum discharge (m³/s) resulting from:		Maximum volume (10⁶m³) corresponding to max. discharge resulting from:	
	Rainfall	Snowmelt	Rainfall	Snowmelt
1	2	3	4	5
19—05—87	1180			
13—03—88		2720		1570
22—03—89		1630		1990
06—09—90	4450		2640	
08—03—91		2540		2060
02—02—92		1560		919
05—03—93		1140		891
06—10—94	1550		694	
28—03—95		2940		4150
07—05—96	3100		2070	
19—05—97	1650		1620	
21—03—98		988		419
15—09—99	2160		721	
10—04—00		3780		3580
08—03—01		1300		687
20—12—02	1550		149	
08—01—03		1400		456
25—02—04		1060		497
07—02—05		2380		338
19—03—06		1640		1270
22—03—07		1510		1160
30—01—08		1500		531
07—02—09		2640		672
13—09—10	1120		795	
21—02—11		1280		498
19—12—12	1050		572	
07—02—13		1180		348
10—03—14		1600		1180
09—03—15		2570		972
19—02—16		1320		571

TABLE II – ANNUAL MAXIMUM DISCHARGES AND VOLUMES   (cont'd)

Country:	Czechoslovakia (6) cont'd
River:	Labe
Gauging Station:	Děčín

Date	Maximum discharge (m³/s) resulting from:		Maximum volume (10⁶m³) corresponding to max. discharge resulting from:	
	Rainfall	Snowmelt	Rainfall	Snowmelt
1	2	3	4	5
19–04–17		2400		1680
07–07–18	914		218	
27–11–19	1310		1080	
16–01–20		3770		3130
29–01–21		854		956
26–02–22		1370		1310
05–02–23		2940		2110
30–03–24		2250		2070
28–08–25	1460		670	
21–06–26	2690		2610	
17–04–27		1580		1340
18–02–28		1490		974
26–03–29		1270		1660
02–11–30	1350		1060	
03–03–31		1450		594
02–06–32	1840		703	
07–02–33		1180		580
02–03–34		610		491
19–02–35		1270		583
09–06–36	1110		356	
25–02–37		1610		801
03–09–38	1610		1690	
04–12–39	2150		2490	
17–03–40		3600		3680
09–04–41		2980		4230
21–03–42		1870		1540
18–02–43		553		393
09–04–44		2120		2750
16–02–45		1560		574
11–02–46		2410		1690

Country:	Czechoslovakia (6) cont'd
River:	Labe
Gauging Station:	Děčín

Date	Maximum discharge (m³/s) resulting from:		Maximum volume (10⁶m³) corresponding to max. discharge resulting from:	
	Rainfall	Snowmelt	Rainfall	Snowmelt
1	2	3	4	5
17–03–47		2550		4160
12–02–48		2390		2500
24–05–49	1370		465	
15–02–50		1220		235
13–05–51	1180		335	
28–03–52		1170		1160
02–02–53		1430		656
12–07–54	2520		1570	
27–03–55		1770		1030
05–03–56		2040		787
21–03–57		1200		677
07–07–58	2080		1110	
31–12–58	755		704	
15–08–60	1170		372	
12–02–61		1160		778
03–04–62		1300		938
13–03–63		543		362
27–10–64	595		622	
13–06–65	2020		3340	
11–02–66		1360		1100
06–02–67		1560		1280
18–01–68		1220		734
17–03–69		1090		536
28–03–70		1420		1080

Czechoslovakia / Tchécoslovaquie / Checoslovaquia / Чехословакия

TABLE II – ANNUAL MAXIMUM DISCHARGES AND VOLUMES (cont'd)

Country:	Czechoslovakia (7)
River:	Zděchovka
Gauging Station:	Zděchov

Date	Maximum discharge (m³/s) resulting from:		Maximum volume (10⁶m³) corresponding to max. discharge resulting from:	
	Rainfall	Snowmelt	Rainfall	Snowmelt
1	2	3	4	5
24–06–28	8.18		0.10	
29–05–29	1.94		0.05	
30–10–30	3.72		0.51	
11–06–31	4.93		0.05	
01–04–32		1.38		0.39
05–03–33		1.07		0.17
17–05–34	2.54		0.09	
23–02–35		2.18		0.53
01–06–36	2.14		0.15	
13–09–37	2.91		0.26	
15–09–38	14.7		0.17	
16–06–39	6.68		0.35	
17–06–40	2.30		0.09	
09–08–41	2.63		0.30	
15–05–42	1.49		0.18	
09–07–43	2.27		0.21	
30–06–44	13.0		0.21	
27–06–45	1.20		0.03	
08–02–46		0.92		0.13
19–03–47		1.14		0.44
29–12–47		1.66		0.28
19–07–49	4.70		0.35	
10–12–50		0.93		0.28
26–06–51	1.14		0.28	
01–04–52		3.00		0.95
03–07–53	1.50		0.04	
05–03–54		0.73		0.10
21–07–55	3.82		0.18	
23–03–56		1.60		0.43
05–12–56		1.17		0.13

Country:	Czechoslovakia (7) cont'd
River:	Zděchovka
Gauging Station:	Zděchov

Date	Maximum discharge (m³/s) resulting from:		Maximum volume (10⁶m³) corresponding to max. discharge resulting from:	
	Rainfall	Snowmelt	Rainfall	Snowmelt
1	2	3	4	5
06–07–58	3.09		0.35	
08–03–59		1.42		0.22
26–07–60	0.60		0.21	
28–06–61	1.39		0.09	
02–06–62	0.97		0.11	
05–10–63	0.60		0.18	
11–07–64	0.74		0.09	
16–03–65		0.83		0.56
09–02–66		1.78		0.48
28–02–67		1.09		0.82
23–12–67		1.37		0.17
13–03–69		0.94		0.35
18–07–70	2.00		0.40	
16–11–70	0.75		0.16	
29–07–72	2.70		0.26	

TABLE II – ANNUAL MAXIMUM DISCHARGES AND VOLUMES (cont'd)

Country: Czechoslovakia (8)
River: Bečva
Gauging Station: Teplice

Date	Maximum discharge (m³/s) resulting from:		Maximum volume (10⁶m³) corresponding to max. discharge resulting from:	
	Rainfall	Snowmelt	Rainfall	Snowmelt
1	2	3	4	5
18–01–20		480		182
23–04–21	120		65	
01–03–22		170		120
03–02–23		200		82
27–03–24		190		110
04–08–25	640		66	
05–06–26	340		72	
16–04–27		190		56
23–09–28	140		10	
15–04–29		160		48
31–10–30	485		168	
25–09–31	485		113	
07–01–32		170		37
06–02–33		140		43
27–02–34		153		44
24–02–35		260		116
02–08–36	150		29	
13–09–37	650		88	
02–09–38	540		74	
27–07–39	660		88	
20–05–40	625		82	
01–04–41		238		94
16–05–42	129		38	
09–07–43	533		72	
23–06–44	265		35	
09–12–44		168		57
09–02–46		289		105
20–03–47		169		138
05–06–48	230		48	
20–07–49	550		79	

Country: Czechoslovakia (8) cont'd
River: Bečva
Gauging Station: Teplice

Date	Maximum discharge (m³/s) resulting from:		Maximum volume (10⁶m³) corresponding to max. discharge resulting from:	
	Rainfall	Snowmelt	Rainfall	Snowmelt
1	2	3	4	5
17–09–50	104		8	
11–05–51	199		67	
02–04–52		267		179
20–09–52	213	76		
03–07–54	250		40	
29–12–54		258		63
23–03–55		140		82
18–03–57		208		46
30–06–58	360		90	
01–07–59	225		48	
26–07–60	630		126	
28–06–61	161		28	
06–03–62		203		60
12–03–63		115		44
29–03–64		71.5		47
12–06–65	286		83	
26–08–66	385		81	
03–02–67		200		55
28–07–68	280		46	
01–04–69		141		24
19–07–70	480		79	
22–01–71		195		35
22–07–72	456		93	

Czechoslovakia / Tchécoslovaquie / Checoslovaquia / Чехословакия

TABLE II – ANNUAL MAXIMUM DISCHARGES AND VOLUMES (cont'd)

Country: Czechoslovakia (9)
River: Morava
Gauging Station: Kroměříž

| Date | Maximum discharge (m³/s) resulting from: | | Maximum volume (10⁶m³) corresponding to max. discharge resulting from: | |
| | Rainfall | Snowmelt | Rainfall | Snowmelt |
1	2	3	4	5
11−10−16	360		359	
08−04−17		578		900
30−07−18	285		52	
11−07−19	480		328	
14−01−20		580		465
23−04−21	220		135	
02−03−22		370		318
05−02−23		458		279
27−03−24		370		327
05−08−25	446		154	
20−06−26	489		593	
16−04−27		358		356
18−02−28		243		195
01−04−29	239		284	
21−03−30	295		152	
01−09−30	670		588	
09−01−32		335		189
10−02−33		222		105
01−03−34		205		91
24−02−35		372		308
02−08−36	253		106	
14−09−37	681		267	
03−09−38	725		559	
27−02−39	515		154	
01−06−40	492		124	
12−03−41		626		572
16−05−42	309		193	
10−07−43	440		105	
13−04−44	327		512	
01−03−45		387		202

Country: Czechoslovakia (9) cont'd
River: Morava
Gauging Station: Kroměříž

| Date | Maximum discharge (m³/s) resulting from: | | Maximum volume (10⁶m³) corresponding to max. discharge resulting from: | |
| | Rainfall | Snowmelt | Rainfall | Snowmelt |
1	2	3	4	5
10−02−46		576		359
23−03−47		530		716
30−12−48		372		217
21−07−49	471		214	
27−02−50		183		190
12−05−51	332		210	
02−04−52		355		602
01−02−53		305		150
03−07−54	500		213	
30−12−54		500		201
05−03−56		287		113
19−03−57		242		139
06−07−58	428		289	
09−03−59		241		119
27−07−60	565		191	
28−06−61	196		36	
15−06−62	550		654	
13−03−63		285		118
29−03−64		190		142
13−06−65	444		498	
26−07−66	480		426	
05−02−67		465		251
11−06−68	315 ·		89	
02−04−69		345		262
20−07−70	509		138	
23−11−70	275		145	
23−08−72	490		142	

TABLE II – ANNUAL MAXIMUM DISCHARGES AND VOLUMES   (cont'd)

Country: Czechoslovakia (10)
River: Dyje
Gauging Station: Dolní Věstonice

Country: Czechoslovakia (10) cont'd
River: Dyje
Gauging Station: Dolní Věstonice

Date	Maximum discharge (m³/s) resulting from:		Maximum volume (10⁶m³) corresponding to max. discharge resulting from:		Date	Maximum discharge (m³/s) resulting from:		Maximum volume (10⁶m³) corresponding to max. discharge resulting from:	
	Rainfall	Snowmelt	Rainfall	Snowmelt		Rainfall	Snowmelt	Rainfall	Snowmelt
1	2	3	4	5	1	2	3	4	5
06–02–21		170		387	14–05–51	133		187	
13–01–22		300		67	03–04–52		124		257
04–02–23		200		193	02–02–53		222		132
28–03–24		200		613	10–07–54	230		157	
06–08–25	240		89		28–03–55		240		267
18–06–26	550		595		30–12–56		240		70
14–01–27		223		264	05–04–57		158		159
18–02–28		189		130	01–04–58		153		144
26–03–29		228		259	23–07–59	107		57	
01–11–30	420		352		21–08–60	230		157	
25–03–31		390		377	10–07–61	168		190	
07–01–32		300		179	16–05–62	358		377	
09–02–33		156		90	01–03.04–63		129		299
01–03–34		155		83	27–10–64	101		53	
19–02–35		200		200	08–06–65	297		672	
03–06–36	170		135		14–02–66		174		247
03–03–37		340		667	07–02–67		174		177
04–09–38	510		539		19–01–68		177		150
31–10–39	221		241		16–03–69		275		400
17–03–40		290		450	11–04–70		246		569
12–03–41		820		865	24–11–71	146		61	
04–04–42		195		515	23–05–72	200		189	
03–04–43	160		29						
13–04–44		320		393					
27–02–45		390		575					
10–02–46		239		151					
22–03–47		815		862					
14–02–48		450		713					
24–05–49	88		32						
18–02–50		90		109					

TABLE II — ANNUAL MAXIMUM DISCHARGES AND VOLUMES (cont'd)

Country:	Czechoslovakia (11)
River:	Váh
Gauging Station:	Lubochňa

Date	Maximum discharge (m³/s) resulting from:		Maximum volume (10⁶m³) corresponding to max. discharge resulting from:	
	Rainfall	Snowmelt	Rainfall	Snowmelt
1	2	3	4	5
19—04—21	152		15.6	
24—03—22	153		16.0	
16—04—23	226		29.8	
10—05—24	307		39.1	
04—08—25	564		54.3	
01—08—26	365		27.0	
10—05—27	227		33.8	
09—05—28	336		38.4	
13—08—29	164		13.7	
04—11—30	295		26.6	
22—04—31	371		118	
06—04—32	377		52.7	
17—07—33	147		32.5	
17—07—34	351		65.1	
13—04—35		185		67.8
21—05—36	243		63.9	
25—08—37	342		71.4	
23—08—38	430		112	
15—05—39	267		65.4	
28—03—40		207		33.3
01—04—41	192		35.8	
09—04—42	164		34.6	
09—07—43	255		62.8	
18—04—44		200		102
03—05—45	179		38.3	
24—06—46	380		76.6	
20—03—47	180		22.6	
08—06—48	544		134	
13—04—49	179		50	
27—02—50		115		26.6

Country:	Czechoslovakia (11) cont'd
River:	Váh
Gauging Station:	Lubochňa

Date	Maximum discharge (m³/s) resulting from:		Maximum volume (10⁶m³) corresponding to max. discharge resulting from:	
	Rainfall	Snowmelt	Rainfall	Snowmelt
1	2	3	4	5
11—05—51	290		79.0	
13—04—52		285		36.7
30—05—53	182		68.4	
09—07—54	180		60.8	
06—08—55	229		57.9	
19—04—56	138		83.5	
19—03—57	184		75.5	
30—06—58	840		71.8	
01—07—59	255		87.1	
26—07—60	618		130	
19—10—61	81.5		5.21	
06—03—62		299		23.1
05—10—63	220.0		19.8	
13—10—64	227.0		25.9	
11—06—65	408.0		69.5	
10—02—66		225		19.9
05—05—67	266		21.1	
08—04—68		216		28.6
30—04—69	123		20.0	
19—07—70	561		53.6	
06—04—71	115		18.9	
22—08—72	257		25.6	

TABLE II — ANNUAL MAXIMUM DISCHARGES AND VOLUMES   (cont'd)

Country: **Czechoslovakia (12)**
River: **Lubochnianka**
Gauging Station: **Lubochňa**

Date	Maximum discharge (m³/s) resulting from:		Maximum volume (10⁶m³) corresponding to max. discharge resulting from:	
	Rainfall	Snowmelt	Rainfall	Snowmelt
1	2	3	4	5
21—04—31	19.4		4.12	
06—04—32	15.4		2.13	
30—10—33	6.3		1.37	
15—10—34	12.2		2.42	
14—04—35	13.9		3.10	
22—07—36	9.5		1.14	
15—03—37	17.8		4.43	
23—08—38	19.5		4.12	
15—05—39	14.2		3.22	
02—12—39		9.70		2.81
19—10—41	17.8		2.42	
09—04—42	12.3		2.39	
14—07—43	14.4		2.71	
18—04—44		24.2		8.10
09—12—44	11.2		1.73	
15—02—46		15.6		4.98
07—04—47	17.4		1.77	
14—01—48		20.4		5.40
13—04—49	23.1		3.93	
24—11—50	8.3		1.15	
20—03—51	17.8		2.82	
12—04—52	20.0		3.41	
30—04—53	20.0		1.77	
02—07—54	17.4		3.18	
27—03—55		14.9		3.07
17—04—56	15.7		5.02	
18—03—57	24.9		2.79	
29—06—58	51.3		4.68	
01—07—59	13.1		1.61	
26—07—60	60.5		10.6	

Country: **Czechoslovakia (12) cont'd**
River: **Lubochnianka**
Gauging Station: **Lubochňa**

Date	Maximum discharge (m³/s) resulting from:		Maximum volume (10⁶m³) corresponding to max. discharge resulting from:	
	Rainfall	Snowmelt	Rainfall	Snowmelt
1	2	3	4	5
11—11—61	14.9		2.03	
19—04—62	21.8		1.90	
05—10—63	13.3		1.23	
02—04—64	13.1		0.60	
12—06—65	15.5		1.30	
09—02—66		15.4		1.93
10—04—67	14.2		1.93	
25—11—68	11.1		0.69	
13—04—69	9.91		1.87	
20—04—70	16.6		2.24	
13—11—71	9.04		0.72	
22—08—72	9.62		1.29	

Czechoslovakia / Tchécoslovaquie / Checoslovaquia / Чехословакия

TABLE II – ANNUAL MAXIMUM DISCHARGES AND VOLUMES (cont'd)

Country: Czechoslovakia (13)
River: Turiec
Gauging Station: Martin

Date	Maximum discharge (m³/s) resulting from:		Maximum volume (10⁶m³) corresponding to max. discharge resulting from:	
	Rainfall	Snowmelt	Rainfall	Snowmelt
1	2	3	4	5
22–04–31	136		27.3	
06–04–32	119		20.2	
07–02–33		45.0		8.4
15–10–34	47.2		8.5	
05–03–35		132.0		7.0
02–06–36	145		22.7	
15–03–37		144		38.4
11–03–38		54.1		16.7
28–03–39	127		21.1	
26–03–40	117		11.2	
01–04–41	158		16.6	
09–04–42	88.8		13.7	
10–07–43	83.3		25.2	
04–02–44	81.5		16.0	
27–03–45	127		36.6	
08–02–46		184		34.9
20–03–47	95.2		11.2	
14–01–48		101		21.0
14–04–49	78.2		13.3	
24–11–50	48.7		8.3	
20–03–51	114		26.1	
01–04–52	169		27.6	
12–05–54	60.8		9.0	
03–07–54	67.7		9.8	
02–04–55	59.8		38.4	
23–04–56	33.1		25.0	
25–03–57	64.7		6.8	
11–07–58	79.3		16.2	
19–08–59	60.8		10.0	
31–07–60	327		64.5	

Country: Czechoslovakia (13) cont'd
River: Turiec
Gauging Station: Martin

Date	Maximum discharge (m³/s) resulting from:		Maximum volume (10⁶m³) corresponding to max. discharge resulting from:	
	Rainfall	Snowmelt	Rainfall	Snowmelt
1	2	3	4	5
02–11–61	39.3		3.24	
06–03–62	135		26.9	
07–10–63	124		16.4	
01–12–64	36.5		10.0	
12–06–65	154		44.8	
20–08–66	134		23.8	
12–03–67		65.7		36.75
25–02–68	43.1		18.3	
13–04–69	32.4		10.4	
27–03–70	80.7		25.4	
23–03–71		45.0		15.41
18–04–72	54.3		15.8	

TABLE II – ANNUAL MAXIMUM DISCHARGES AND VOLUMES   (cont'd)

Country:	Czechoslovakia (14)
River:	Kysuca
Gauging Station:	Cadca

Date	Maximum discharge (m³/s) resulting from:		Maximum volume (10⁶m³) corresponding to max. discharge resulting from:	
	Rainfall	Snowmelt	Rainfall	Snowmelt
1	2	3	4	5
18–01–20	258		13.4	
17–04–21		76.5		9.38
30–12–22	100		14.5	
02–02–23	136		30.6	
10–05–24	197		12.2	
03–08–25	506		39.4	
06–06–26	198		19.1	
25–09–31	243		20.0	
04–04–32	198		12.8	
16–09–33	114		10.4	
28–02–34		102		14.7
23–07–35	168		17.5	
29–02–36	92.0		7.7	
14–03–37	186		9.81	
31–03–38	117		16.0	
27–07–39	268		23.9	
22–08–40	255		24.8	
01–04–41	169		15.7	
12–04–42	107		16.2	
09–07–43	275		27.6	
01–03–44		252		60.2
26–03–45	87.0		7.6	
09–02–46		133		19.1
29–12–47		128		30.1
14–01–48	164		21.4	
01–07–49	242		34.5	
17–09–50	163		21.1	
01–04–51	95.0		21.0	
12–04–52	166		22.9	
30–04–53	110		11.9	

Country:	Czechoslovakia (14) cont'd
River:	Kysuca
Gauging Station:	Cadca

Date	Maximum discharge (m³/s) resulting from:		Maximum volume (10⁶m³) corresponding to max. discharge resulting from:	
	Rainfall	Snowmelt	Rainfall	Snowmelt
1	2	3	4	5
29–12–54	188		32.8	
06–08–55	110		8.8	
05–12–56	110		22.0	
16–07–57	95.0		11.2	
29–06–58	331		24.5	
01–07–59	334		27.6	
09–07–60	287		28.8	
28–06–61	113		14.2	
02–06–62	151		18.4	
30–08–63	106		15.2	
11–07–64	101		14.5	
13–06–65	235		13.5	
25–07–66	243		36.3	
03–12–67		147		21.8
24–12–68		157		21.8
09–07–69	136		16.9	
19–07–70	433		44.1	
20–03–71		121		31.7
19–11–72	147		11.4	

TABLE II − ANNUAL MAXIMUM DISCHARGES AND VOLUMES   (cont'd)

Country:	Czechoslovakia (15)
River:	Čeladénka
Gauging Station:	Čeladná

Date	Maximum discharge (m³/s) resulting from:		Maximum volume (10⁶m³) corresponding to max. discharge resulting from:	
	Rainfall	Snowmelt	Rainfall	Snowmelt
1	2	3	4	5
01−11−52	13.0		2.54	
03−07−54	6.66		1.88	
11−08−55	28.0		3.69	
17−01−56		7.62		4.42
24−07−57	6.78		1.40	
19−08−58	45.0		2.15	
01−07−59	26.0		3.62	
26−07−60	83.0		7.13	
15−03−61		3.30		1.58
19−04−62		6.40		3.35
06−10−63	7.68		1.64·	
11−07−64	4.43		0.77	
12−06−65	16.9		4.12	
25−07−66	63.0		4.22	
11−04−67		11.0		3.90
28−07−68	46.0		5.32	
13−04−69		5.35		2.08
19−07−70	29.8		4.98	
03−07−71	17.8		3.56	
21−08−72	50.4		9.74	

Country:	Czechoslovakia (16)
River:	Ostravice
Gauging Station:	Šance

Date	Maximum discharge (m³/s) resulting from:		Maximum volume (10⁶m³) corresponding to max. discharge resulting from:	
	Rainfall	Snowmelt	Rainfall	Snowmelt
1	2	3	4	5
31−07−26	150		20.5	
24−07−27	53		6.14	
23−09−28	48		3.89	
17−06−29	136		4.32	
13−08−30	· 62		7.03	
25−09−31	132		17.8	
08−08−32	52		6.7	
04−09−33	66		10.8	
15−10−34	30		4.31	
23−07−35	88		3.45	
13−07−36	62		6.40	
13−09−37	154		11.0	
31−03−38		72		9.28
26−07−39	200		20.8	
31−05−40	220		21.0	
06−04−41		46		11.1
12−04−42		53.3		11.0
09−07−43	142		14.4	
18−04−44	71		22.0	
28−03−45		41.0		8.61·
08−02−46		68.9		9.90
20−03−47		48.8		20.7
15−08−48	73		4.98	
02−07−49	100		15.0	
17−09−50	73		6.97	
11−05−51	53.9		8.76	
12−04−52		48.0		42.2
10−07−53	34.0		1.70	
29−12−53		68.2		11.3
31−07−55	70		2.92	

TABLE II – ANNUAL MAXIMUM DISCHARGES AND VOLUMES (cont'd)

Country: **Czechoslovakia (16) cont'd**
River: **Ostravice**
Gauging Station: **Šance**

Date	Maximum discharge (m³/s) resulting from:		Maximum volume (10⁶m³) corresponding to max. discharge resulting from:	
	Rainfall	Snowmelt	Rainfall	Snowmelt
1	2	3	4	5
17–04–56		30.8		11.9
05–12–56		44.3		4.68
29–06–58	270		18.3	
01–07–59	90		11.3	
26–07–60	173		22.6	
28–06–61	32.8		3.79	
07–04–62		35.8		32.7
25–06–63	71.5		5.20	
01–04–64		41.8		12.1
12–06–65	136		18.6	
25–07–66	159		11.5	
03–02–67		53.0		6.40
28–07–68	105		20.4	
13–04–69	29.8			
13–08–69		29.8		
19–07–70	110			
20–11–70	81.2			
22–08–72	70.3			

Country:
River:
Gauging Station:

Date	Maximum discharge (m³/s) resulting from:		Maximum volume (10⁶m³) corresponding to max. discharge resulting from:	
	Rainfall	Snowmelt	Rainfall	Snowmelt
1	2	3	4	5

Czechoslovakia / Tchécoslovaquie / Checoslovaquia / Чехословакия

TABLE III — CHARACTERISTICS OF SNOWMELT FLOODS

No.	River	Gauging station	Q_{max} (m³/s)	Date	h (mm)	T_T (hours)	t_i (hours)	P_W (%)	$P_{Q_{max}}$ (%)	Type of probability curve for P_W	for $P_{Q_{max}}$
1	2	3	4	5	6	7	8	9	10	11	12
1	Kamenice	Josefův důl	19.6	14—03—61	78	93	12	43	59	Empirical	
2	Smědava	Bílý potok	16	20—04—70	34	83	00	82	85	''	
3	Cidlina	Nový Bydžov	51.7	18—03—47	91	442	17	3	10	Pearson type III	
			50.8	03—02—56	38	190	17	27.2	10.5	''	
			36.9	19—03—65	74	506	08	6.3	29	''	
			47.9	04—02—67	31	143	09	22	14	''	
4	Berounka	Křivoklát	732	15—01—20	33	185	00	11.4	7.6	Empirical	Pearson III
			816	15—03—40	33	146	03	11.4	5.6		
			854	15—03—47	19	89	04	40	4.8		
5	Vltava	Kamýk	1 180	08—04—00 ∨	61	480	23	19.8	13.8	Pearson type III	
6	Labe (Elbe)	Děčín	3780	10—06—00	70	670	16	6	5.1	''	
			3770	16—01—20	61	500	19	8.3	6.0	''	
			3600	17—03—40	72	550		4.8	6.8	''	
7	Zděchovka	Zděchov	1.38	01—04—32	96.6	240	17	24	80	''	
8	Bečva	Teplice	480	18—01—20	119	290	12	14	20	Empirical	Pearson III
9	Morava	Kroměříž	626	12—03—41	81	580	06	9.4	9.5	Pearson type III	
			580	14—01—20	66	530	07	16.5	17	''	

No.	Method of curve fitting for W	for Q_{max}	Snow cover Water equivalent (mm)	Layer thickness (cm)	Rainfall during snowmelt (mm)	Monthly precipitation before soil freezing (mm)	Mean monthly temperature before snowmelt (°C)
1	13	14	15	16	17	18	19
1				20	52.5	72.5	0.7
2				120	22.5	100	-0.8
3	ʄ	Alexeev	16	10	15.5	32.8	
		''	32.8	23	48.9	30.8	-11.4
		''		17	23.1	32.0	
		''	6.5	25	37.6	24.9	-2.1
4		Alexeev		5	60	55	-1.1
				4	8	62	-6.1
			39.0	18	22	20	-6.5
5		Alexeev		53	27	51.4	-1.6
6		''		35	29	81	-0.8
		''		11	56	69	-1.3
		''		27	8	77	-9.8
7		''	57.6	20	13.8	71	-4.8
8		Alexeev		13	84	87.8	-0.5
9		Alexeev		21	40	82	-1.1
		''		11	73	83	-0.9

TABLE III — CHARACTERISTICS OF SNOWMELT FLOODS (cont'd)

No.	River	Gauging station	Q_{max} (m^3/s)	Date	h (mm)	T_T (hours)	t_i (hours)	P_W (%)	$P_{Q_{max}}$ (%)	Type of probability curve for P_W	for $P_{Q_{max}}$
1	2	3	4	5	6	7	8	9	10	11	12
10	Dyje	Dolni Věstonice	820	12—03—41	74	1250	16	3.0	1.9	Pearson type III	
			815	23—03—47	73	1100	12—07	3.2	2.0	"	
			450	11—02—48	61	1200	12	6.5		"	
11	Lubochňa	Váh	229	06—03—62	11	158	18	82	51	"	
12	Lubochnianka	Lubochňa	20.4	14—01—48	47	200	20	58	37	"	
13	Turiec	Martin	101	14—01—48	26	96	7	40	38	"	
14	Kysuca	Čadca	157	24—12—68	45	190	12	68	13	"	
15	Čeladenka	Čeladná	11	11—04—67	126	192	16—01	32	58	Empirical	
16	Ostravice	Šance	72	31—03—38	63	125	10	56	46	Empirical	Pearson III

No.	Method of curve fitting for W	for Q_{max}	Snow cover Water equivalent (mm)	Layer thickness (cm)	Rainfall during snowmelt (mm)	Monthly precipitation before soil freezing (mm)	Mean monthly temperature before snowmelt (°C)
1	13	14	15	16	17	18	19
10	Ale	Alexeev		21	43	59	−1.6
		"		41	11	65	−3.4
		"		3	60	64	−0.8
11	Ale	"	9	14	5	66	−3.5
12	Ale	"	28	19	55	116	−0.3
13	Alε	"		5	54	21	−0.3
14	Alε	"		10	9	43	−6.2
15		"	204	55	0	36.5	
16		Alexeev	169	77	79.8	36.7	

TABLE IV — CHARACTERISTICS OF RAINFALL FLOODS

			Characteristic element							Type of probability curve	
No.	River	Gauging station	Q_{max} (m³/s)	Date	h (mm)	T_T (hours)	t_i (hours)	P_W (%)	$P_{Q_{max}}$ (%)	for P_W	for $P_{Q_{max}}$
1	2	3	4	5	6	7	8	9	10	11	12
1	Kamenice	Josefův důl	126	04—07—58	270	96	5	15	1.6	Empirical	
			62	29—06—66	59	59	21	54	12	"	
2	Smědava	Bílý potok	118	04—07—58	351	65	10.2	6.3	7.5	"	
3	Cidlina	Nový Bydžov	23.7	12—09—38	13	140	11	67	58	Pearson type III	
4	Berounka	Křivoklát	1310	03—09—90	42	131	19	2.4	5.4	Empirical	Alexeev
			824	09—07—54	35	174	14	8.5			
5	Vltava	Kamýk nad Vltavou	2310	04—09—90	80	312	23	11	1.4	Pearson type III	
			1690	05—05—96	70	312	10	15	4.6	"	
			1650	08—10—15	63	336	14	19	5.1	"	
			1970	09—07—54	57	432	9	22	2.6	"	
6	Labe	Děčín	4450	06—09—90	51.7	432	12	4	2.5	"	
			3100	07—05—96	40.6	432	3	17	9.4	"	
7	Zděchovka	Zděchov	14.7	15—09—38	35	40	18	67	2.3	"	
			13.0	30—06—44	41	38	15	56	2.8	"	
			8.18	24—06—28	21	30	16	87	7.6	"	
			6.68	16—06—39	29	25	14	30	10	"	
8	Bečva	Teplice	650	13—09—37	69	380	15	33	7.0	Empirical	Pearson III
			660	27—07—39	69	240	2	33	6.0		
			640	04—08—25	52	240	2	51	7.9		
			625	20—05—40	64	290	5	38	9.0		

	Method of curve fitting		Rainfall forming flood (mm)	Snowmelt during floods (mm)	Maximum daily rainfall (mm)	Date	Hourly maximum rainfall (mm)	Date	Antecedent precipitation for	
No.	for W	for Q_{max}							10 days (mm)	30 days (mm)
1	13	14	15	16	17	18	19	20	21	22
1			473		153	03—07—58	8.0	03—07—58	284	328
			169		54	29—06—66	3.8	29—06—66	130	221
2			330		68.7	03—07—58	8.0	03—07—58	105	157
3	Alexeev		39.6		35.5	10—09—38			30.9	162
4		Alexeev	84		64	03—09—90			66	174
		"	130		55	08—07—54	8.2	08—07—54	50	70
5	Alexeev		134		97.6	02—09—90			150	248
	"		119		66.5	04—05—96			126	163
	"		146		62.3	03—10—15			14.6	68
	"		108		114	08—07—54	20.0	08—07—54	65.6	112
6	"		75		98	02—09—90			102	186
	"		66		66	04—05—96			71	99
7	"		52.4		41.3	15—09—38	27.4	15—09—38	85.7	209
	"		74.3		55.2	30—06—44	55.2	30—06—44	93.5	118
	"		63.9		47.3	24—06—28	28.4	24—06—28	62.2	124
	"		31.1		31.1	16—06—39	29.7	16—06—39	93.5	134
8	"		122				23.5	09—09—37	163	185
	"		113		55	12—09—37			109	241
	"		77		50	03—08—25	16.0	03—08—25	100	188
	"		81		46	19—05—40	15.8	19—05—40	91	128

TABLE IV — CHARACTERISTICS OF RAINFALL FLOODS (cont'd)

No.	River	Gauging station	Q_{max} (m³/s)	Date	h (mm)	T_T (hours)	t_i (hours)	P_W (%)	$P_{Q_{max}}$ (%)	Type of probability curve for P_W	for $P_{Q_{max}}$
1	2	3	4	5	6	7	8	9	10	11	12
9	Morava	Kroměříž	725	03–09–38	79	620	14	10	1.6	Pearson type III	
			681	14–09–37	38	480	18	51	4.5	''	
			670	01–09–30	22	670	7	74	5.2	''	
10	Dyje	Dolní Věstonice	550	18–06–26	51	860	4	11	8.0	''	
			510	04–09–38	46	840	12	14	9.5	''	
11	Váh	Lubochňa	255	01–07–59	41	264	14	13	44	''	
			840	30–06–58	34	94	00.30	21	1.2	''	
			290	11–05–51	33	133	19	17	36	''	
12	Lubochnianka	Lubochňa	60.5	26–07–60	89	214	21	1.8	2.5	''	
			51.3	29–06–58	39.5	90	21	17	4.0	''	
13	Turiec	Martin	327	26–07–60	78	320	13	2.0	0.3	''	
			145	02–06–36	27.5	228	8	36	14	''	
14	Kysuca	Čadca	433	18–07–70	91	108	24	4.0	2.5	''	
			334	29–06–59	57	63	8	23	6.0	''	
			331	29–06–58	50.5	86	21	31	6.0	''	
			268	27–07–39	49	104	7	33	13	''	
			506	03–08–25	81	103	19	6.5	1.3	''	
15	Čeladenka	Čeladná	83	26–07–60	229	102	1	9.0	5.0	Empirical	
			63	25–07–66	136	104	20	28	9.5	''	
			50.4	21–08–72	313	105	14	4.5	14	''	

No.	Method of curve fitting for W	for Q_{max}	Rainfall forming flood (mm)	Snowmelt during floods (mm)	Maximum daily rainfall (mm)	Date	Hourly maximum rainfall (mm)	Date	Antecedent precipitation for 10 days (mm)	30 days (mm)
1	13	14	15	16	17	18	19	20	21	22
9	Alexeev		167		37	01–09–38			158	213
	''		92		40.2	12–09–37	23.5	09–09–37	100	216
	''		136		37				119	172
10	''		69		32	14–06–26	32.4	13–06–26	91	156
	''		155		40	25–08–38	7.4	25–08–38	57	193
11	''		88		51	30–06–59			24	116
	''		117		80	29–06–58	7.0	28–06–58	37	79
	''		54		28	11–05–51			36	57
12	''		120		64	26–07–60	14.0	25–07–60	86	182
	''		82		66	29–06–58	10.0	29–06–58	46	103
13	''		113		59	25–07–60	10.0	23–07–60	81	167
	''		36		23	01–06–36	6.0	31–05–36	53	119
14	''		119		82	18–07–70			79	139
	''		103		49	30–06–59	11.0	29–06–59	121	182
	''		77		46	29–06–58	10.0	28–06–58	61	93
	''				22	26–07–39			39	88
	''				28	01–08–25			59	92
15			268		208	25–07–60			267	543
			150		57.4	25–07–66			143	387
			364		170	20–08–72			317	460

TABLE IV — CHARACTERISTICS OF RAINFALL FLOODS (cont'd)

No.	River	Gauging station	Q_{max} (m^3/s)	Date	h (mm)	T_T (hours)	t_i (hours)	P_W (%)	$P_{Q_{max}}$ (%)	Type of probability curve for P_W	for $P_{Q_{max}}$
1	2	3	4	5	6	7	8	9	10	11	12
16	Ostravice	Šance	270	29—06—58	125	90	22	20	2.2	Empirical	Pearson type III
			173	26—07—60	155	150	2	12	9.5	"	"
			154	13—09—37	75	145	5	47	13	"	"
			150	31—07—26	140	105	18	16	14	"	"
			142	09—07—43	98	140	16	32	15		

No.	Method of curve fitting for W	for Q_{max}	Rainfall forming flood (mm)	Snowmelt during floods (mm)	Maximum daily rainfall (mm)	Date	Hourly maximum rainfall (mm)	Date	Antecedent precipitation for 10 days (mm)	30 days (mm)
1	13	14	15	16	17	18	19	20	21	22
16		Alexeev	175		117	29—06—58	25.7		240	287
		"	215		180	25—07—60			361	578
		"	120		62.9	11—09—37			126	352
		"	134		48	09—07—43			129	291

Dahomey / Дагомея

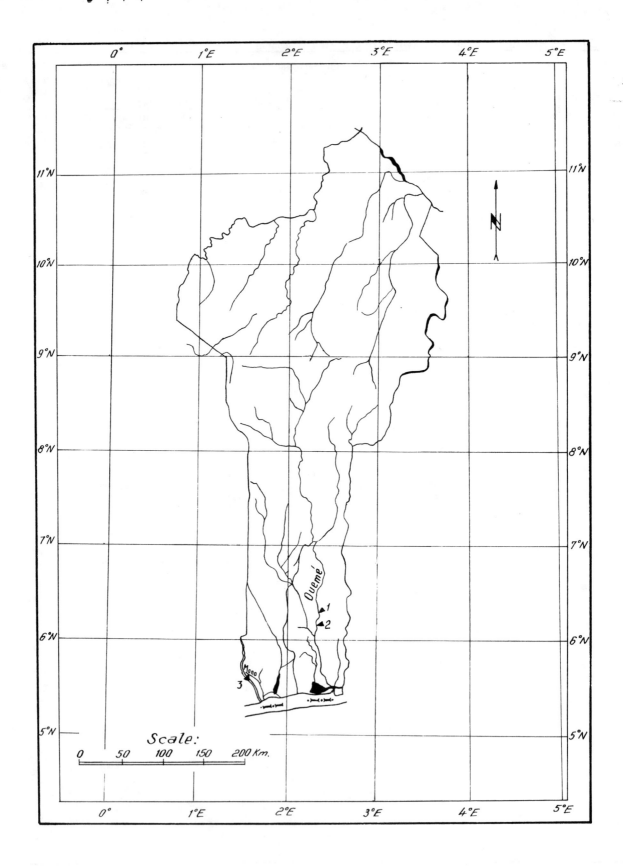

TABLE I – CHARACTERISTICS OF BASIN

			GAUGING STATION						**BASIN**			
						Distance (km) from gauging site						
						to remotest point of river system L_{rs}	to projection of centre of basin on main course L_{ca}	Mean slope of river I_r (%)		Altitude (m)		
No.	River / River system	Name	Period of records	Co-ordinates					Area A (km^2)	Mean H_m	Max. H_{max}	Min. H_{min}
				Lat.	Long.							
1	2	3	4	5	6	7	8	9	10	11	12	13
1	Ouemé	Sagon	1951–72	N 07:10	E 02:26				38000			

TABLE II – ANNUAL MAXIMUM DISCHARGES AND VOLUMES

Country: **Dahomey (1)**
River: **Oueme**
Gauging Station: **Sagon**

Date	Maximum discharge (m^3/s) resulting from:		Maximum volume (10^{6}m^3) corresponding to max. discharge resulting from:	
	Rainfall	Snowmelt	Rainfall	Snowmelt
1	2	3	4	5
06–09–63	1050			
14–09–68	1020			

Country: **Dahomey (3)**
River: **Mono**
Gauging Station: **Athieme**

Date	Maximum discharge (m^3/s) resulting from:		Maximum volume (10^{6}m^3) corresponding to max. discharge resulting from:	
	Rainfall	Snowmelt	Rainfall	Snowmelt
1	2	3	4	5
08–09–63	800			
10–09–68	800			

Country: **Dahomey (2)**
River: **Oueme**
Gauging Station: **Bonou**

Date	Maximum discharge (m^3/s) resulting from:		Maximum volume (10^{6}m^3) corresponding to max. discharge resulting from:	
	Rainfall	Snowmelt	Rainfall	Snowmelt
1	2	3	4	5
16–09–63	1380			
17–09–68	1230			

Finland / Finlande / Finlandia / Финляндия

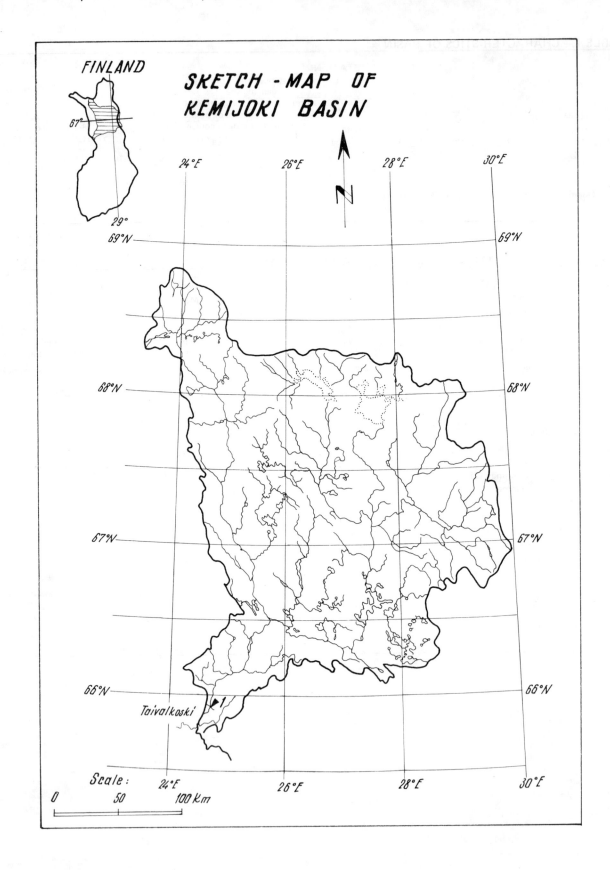

FINLAND

SKETCH - MAP OF
KEMIJOKI BASIN

Scale:

0   50   100 Km

TABLE I — CHARACTERISTICS OF BASIN

		GAUGING STATION								BASIN			
							Distance (km) from gauging site		Mean slope of river I_r (%)	Area A (km^2)	Altitude (m)		
	River River system	Name	Period of records	Co-ordinates		to remotest point of river system L_{rs}	to projection of centre of basin on main course L_{ca}				Mean H_m	Max. H_{max}	Min. H_{min}
No.				Lat.	Long.								
1	2	3	4	5	6	7	8	9	10	11	12	13	
1	Kemijoki	Taivalkoski	1912—73	N 65:57	E 24:42	323	276	0.05	50800		300	0	

							BASIN					
	Width (km)		Mean slope I_b(%)	Soils	Cover	Weighted lake area P_L (%)	Swamps R_s (%)	Mean annual precipitation P (mm)	Annual runoff Q (mm)	Mean annual temperature T (°C)	Regulating capacity of reservoirs α	
No.	Mean B_m	Max. B_{max}										
1	14	15	16	17	18	19	20	21	22	23	24	
1	157	217	2	2		11.6	55	503	341	+0.1		

TABLE II – ANNUAL MAXIMUM DISCHARGES AND VOLUMES

Country:	Finland			
River:	Kemijoki			
Gauging Station:	Taivalkoski			

	Maximum discharge (m³/s) resulting from:		Maximum volume (10⁶m³) corresponding to max. discharge resulting from:	
Date	Rainfall	Snowmelt	Rainfall	Snowmelt
1	2	3	4	5
08–05–12		2770		5860
18–04–13		2220		6190
06–05–14		2950		5810
06–05–15		1930		4630
19–04–16		2200		7060
14–05–17		4130		7170
26–04–18		2460		4600
18–04–19		2450		5920
04–04–20		3660		9060
13–04–21		2820		6910
01–05–22		3650		5160
14–05–23		3630		6250
03–05–24		3310		8040
18–04–25		2840		5070
03–05–26		2450		3750
08–05–27		3550		6330
30–04–28		1620		2150
05–05–29		2840		4240
01–05–30		3590		6280
26–04–31		2900		7030
24–04–32		2950		5520
21–04–33		2680		4860
01–05–34		4060		5520
11–05–35		3360		7930
18–04–36		3110		4740
13–04–37		2170		4170
29–04–38		2310		4350
12–05–39		2590		4760
02–05–40		3090		4370
11–05–41		2040		2570

Country:	Finland cont'd			
River:	Kemijoki			
Gauging Station:	Taivalkoski			

	Maximum discharge (m³/s) resulting from:		Maximum volume (10⁶m³) corresponding to max. discharge resulting from:	
Date	Rainfall	Snowmelt	Rainfall	Snowmelt
1	2	3	4	5
22–04–42		2000		3390
29–04–43		3770		6060
04–05–44		3110		5890
30–04–45		2750		6690
27–04–46		1540		2800
19–04–47		1900		2710
08–04–48		3650		5870
17–04–49		2620		7070
13–04–50		2700		6160
21–04–51		1930		3650
24–04–52		3470		8460
23–04–53		4030		8580
30–04–54		2390		3090
05–05–55		3660		8240
02–05–56		3440		5930
27–04–57		3220		5980
02–05–58		3380		4050
26–04–59		4090		5430
18–04–60		2470		3540
08–05–61		3100		4460
24–04–62		3270		6360
23–04–63		2580		3700
01–05–64		3480		5070
19–04–65		2500		5120
01–05–66		3860		6080
01–05–67		4160		7030
05–05–68		2890		4400
02–05–69		3740		6490
03–05–70		2590		4550
05–05–71		2180		3830

TABLE II — ANNUAL MAXIMUM DISCHARGES AND VOLUMES (cont'd)

Country:	**Finland** cont'd
River:	**Kemijoki**
Gauging Station:	**Taivalkoski**

	Maximum discharge (m³/s) resulting from:		Maximum volume (10⁶m³) corresponding to max. discharge resulting from:	
Date	Rainfall	Snowmelt	Rainfall	Snowmelt
1	2	3	4	5
02—05—72		2560		4130
01—05—73		4820		8000

Country:	
River:	
Gauging Station:	

	Maximum discharge (m³/s) resulting from:		Maximum volume (10⁶m³) corresponding to max. discharge resulting from:	
Date	Rainfall	Snowmelt	Rainfall	Snowmelt
1	2	3	4	5

TABLE III — CHARACTERISTICS OF SNOWMELT FLOODS

			Characteristic elements							Type of probability curve	
No.	River	Gauging station	Q_{max} (m³/s)	Date	h (mm)	T_T (hours)	t_i (hours)	P_W (%)	$P_{Q_{max}}$ (%)	for P_W	for $P_{Q_{max}}$
1	2	3	4	5	6	7	8	9	10	11	12
1	Kemijoki	Taivalkoski	4820	26—05—73	157	1340	624	9.5	1.6		Empirical
			4160	25—05—67	138	1200	600	19.0	3.2		"
			4130	06—10—17	139	2230	840	12.7	4.8		"
			4090	05—10—59	107	1220	360	52.4	6.3		"
			4060	14—05—34	109	1270	336	50.8	7.9		"
			3660	21—05—20	178	2210	1150	1.6	17.5		"

	Method of curve fitting		Snow cover		Rainfall during snowmelt (mm)	Monthly precipitation before soil freezing (mm)	Mean monthly temperature before snowmelt (°C)
No.	for W	for Q_{max}	Water equivalent (mm)	Layer thickness (cm)			
1	13	14	15	16	17	18	19
1		Empirical	223		72	49	−1.5
		"	194		20	78	−0.7
		"	152				−4.9
		"	147		39	42	−2.7
		"	152				−3.2
		"	210				+0.2

France / Francia / Франция

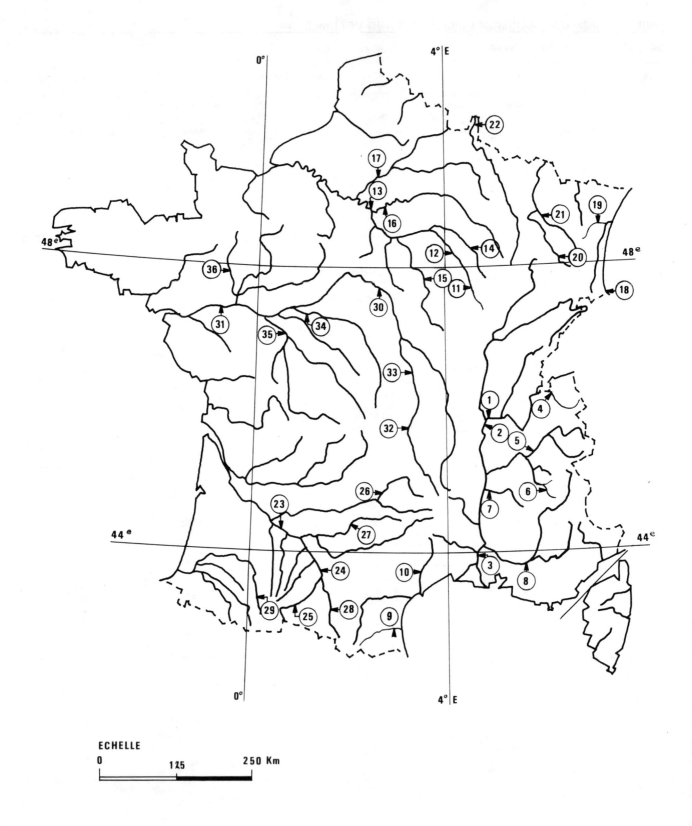

ECHELLE

0   1 25   250 Km

TABLE I — CHARACTERISTICS OF BASIN

| | GAUGING STATION | | | | | | | | BASIN | | | |
| | | | | | | Distance (km) from gauging site | | | | | Altitude (m) | | |
No.	River / River system	Name	Period of records	Co-ordinates Lat.	Long.	to remotest point of river system L_{rs}	to projection of centre of basin on main course L_{ca}	Mean slope of river I_r (%)	Area A (km²)	Mean H_m	Max. H_{max}	Min. H_{min}
1	2	3	4	5	6	7	8	9	10	11	12	13
1	Rhône	Lyon-Pt Morand	1877–72	N 45:46	E 04:50				20300			
2	Rhône	Lyon-Mulatière	1895–72	45:42	04:49				50200			
3	Rhône	Beaucaire	1877–72						95600			
4	Arve	Pt de Carouge (GENEVE)	1896–72	46:13	06:09				1990	1400		367
5	Isère	Grenoble	1877–72						5720	1350	3480	220
6	Drac	Le Sautet	1904–72	44:49	05:56			before 04-48	990	1760	3650	650
								after 04-48	1020			
7	Drome	Livron							1640			
8	Durance	Pont Mirabeau	1904–72						11900			
9	Tet	Perpignan (Pt Joffre)	1876–72	42:42	02:06	100		2.89	1300	1080	2920	25
10	Hérault	Gignac	1875–72	42:39	03:33	90		1.39	1320	550	1570	34
11	Seine	Polisy	1949–72						1460	310	537	
12	Seine	Troyes	1957–72						3410	280	537	

| | BASIN | | | | | | | | | | |
| | Width (km) | | Mean slope I_b(%) | | | Weighted lake area P_L (%) | Swamps R_s (%) | Mean annual precipitation P (mm) | Annual runoff Q (mm) | Mean annual temperature T (°C) | Regulating capacity of reservoirs α |
No.	Mean B_m	Max. B_{max}		Soils	Cover						
1	14	15	16	17	18	19	20	21	22	23	24
1											
2											
3										660	
4										1300	
5									1800	984	
6									1490	1030	
7										510	
8											
9	13	29									
10	18	45	1.30						1250		
11					C(45), F(40)					316	
12					C(50), F(30)					260	0.24

TABLE I — CHARACTERISTICS OF BASIN (cont'd)

No.	River River system	Name	Period of records	Co-ordinates Lat.	Co-ordinates Long.	Distance (km) from gauging site to remotest point of river system L_{rs}	Distance (km) from gauging site to projection of centre of basin on main course L_{ca}	Mean slope of river I_r (%)	Area A (km²)	Altitude (m) Mean H_m	Altitude (m) Max. H_{max}	Altitude (m) Min. H_{min}
1	2	3	4	5	6	7	8	9	10	11	12	13
13	Seine	Paris-Austerlitz		N	E				44300	170	902	
14	Aube	Blaincourt	1953–72						1640	290	504	69
15	Yonne	Gurgy	1953–72						3740	260	902	47
16	Marne	Noisiel	1956–72						12600	180	516	26.4
17	Oise	Venette (Compiegne)							13000		346	
18	Rhin	Bale	1808–72	47:33	07:36				35900	1050	4270	
19	Bruche	Volxheim	1891–72			48		6	615	400	835	
20	Moselle	Epinal	1952–72						1220	674		
21	Meurthe	Malzeville	1960–72						2930	398		
22	Meuse	Chooz	1954–72						10100			
23	Garonne	Agen		44:13	00:36	351		0.52	34900		3400	36.1
24	Garonne	Portet	1910–72	43:22	01:25	201		0.86	9980		3400	139

No.	Width (km) Mean B_m	Width (km) Max. B_{max}	Mean slope I_b (%)	Soils	Cover	Weighted lake area P_L (%)	Swamps R_s (%)	Mean annual precipitation P (mm)	Annual runoff Q (mm)	Mean annual temperature T (°C)	Regulating capacity of reservoirs α
1	14	15	16	17	18	19	20	21	22	23	24
13					C(60), F(20)				192	10.5	
14					C(45), F(35)				344		
15					C(45), F(20)				318		
16					C(70), F(15)				241		
17											
18		124									
19											
20											
21											
22											
23	115							915			
24	45							1100	551		

TABLE I – CHARACTERISTICS OF BASIN (cont'd)

No.	River River system	Name	Period of records	Co-ordinates Lat.	Co-ordinates Long.	Distance (km) from gauging site to remotest point of river system L_{rs}	Distance (km) from gauging site to projection of centre of basin on main course L_{ca}	Mean slope of river I_r (%)	Area A (km²)	Altitude (m) Mean H_m	Altitude (m) Max. H_{max}	Altitude (m) Min. H_{min}
1	2	3	4	5	6	7	8	9	10	11	12	13
				N	E							
25	Garonne	Valentine	1912–72	43:06	00:42	100		1.5	2230		3400	357
26	Truyère	Sarrans	1917–62	44:50	02:45	110		0.8	2460			554
27	Aveyron	Laguepie	1914–69	44:10	01:57	178		0.3	1540		1160	148
28	Ariège	Foix	1906–72	42:58	01:36	68		˙2.6	1340	1500	3120	370
29	Adour	Pointe	1912–72	43:03	00:10	23		7	272	1500	2800	600
30	Loire	Gien	1825–72			445			35900	565	1880	120
31	Loire	Montjean	1866–72			772			1100		1880	9.10
32	Allier	Vieille-Brioude	1872–72			142			2260	1037	1550	428
33	Allier	Moulins	1790–72			335			13000		1890	206
34	Cher	Savonnieres				365			13700			
35	Vienne	Nouatre				300			19700			32
36	Mayenne	Chambellay	1881–72	47:41	00:41	173		0.158	4250	120	417	21.3

No.	Width (km) Mean B_m	Width (km) Max. B_{max}	Mean slope I_b (%)	Soils	Cover	Weighted lake area P_L (%)	Swamps R_s (%)	Mean annual precipitation P (mm)	Annual runoff Q (mm)	Mean annual temperature T (°C)	Regulating capacity of reservoirs α
1	14	15	16	17	18	19	20	21	22	23	24
25	22								854		
26	22								489		
27	9								395		
28	20	32							893		
29	10								1070		
30								845	294		
31											
32								872	402	7.4	
33											
34											
35											
36	24.6	62						780	285	9.9	

TABLE IV — CHARACTERISTICS OF RAINFALL FLOODS

No.	River	Gauging station	Q_{max} (m³/s)	Date	h (mm)	T_T (hours)	t_i (hours)	P_W (%)	$P_{Q_{max}}$ (%)	Type of probability curve for P_W	for $P_{Q_{max}}$
1	2	3	4	5	6	7	8	9	10	11	12
1	Rhône	Lyon (Pont Morand)	4500	31—05—56*							
			4400	16—02—28		144	72				
			4250	25—11—44							
			4190	25—12—18		120	54				
			3890	21—01—10		156	60				
			3700	26—02—57		162	68				
			3400	12—02—45		288	184				
			3910	28—12—52*							
			3350	15—06—89							
			3480	10—03—96							
			3200	27—09—96							
			3110	04—02—97							
			3800	15—01—99							
2	Rhône	Lyon (Mûlatière)	6000	31—01—56*							
			5500	17—02—28							
			5350	26—02—57		148	72				
			5350	25—12—18		148	60				
			4800	27—11—44		288	130				
			4700	21—01—10							
			4700	12—02—45		360	212				
			5100	20—01—55		480	288				
			5170	28—12—82							

No.	Method of curve fitting for W	for Q_{max}	Rainfall forming flood (mm)	Snowmelt during floods (mm)	Maximum daily rainfall (mm)	Date	Hourly maximum rainfall (mm)	Date	Antecedent precipitation for 10 days (mm)	30 days (mm)
1	13	14	15	16	17	18	19	20	21	22
1			—							
			124	68	99	14—02—28				
			—							
			105	13	166	24—12—18				
			129	21	120	19—01—10				
			—							
			—							
			100							
			96							
			139	27						
			101							
			73	57						
			111	31						
2										

TABLE IV — CHARACTERISTICS OF RAINFALL FLOODS (cont'd)

				Characteristic element						Type of probability curve	
No.	River	Gauging station	Q_{max} (m^3/s)	Date	h (mm)	T_T (hours)	t_i (hours)	P_W (%)	$P_{Q_{max}}$ (%)	for P_W	for $P_{Q_{max}}$
1	2	3	4	5	6	7	8	9	10	11	12
3	Rhône	Beaucaire	12000	31—05—56*							
			11000	05—11—40*							
			9600	14—11—35		384	132				
			9170	22—11—51		264	96				
			7970	08—10—60							
			7820	02—01—36							
			7600	06—10—24							
			7240	22—01—55		480	216				
			9470	09—11—86							
			8880	—07—00							
			8800	—12—10							
4	Arve	Pont de Carouge	876	06—08—14							
			870	26—06—10							
			861	24—12—18		144	44				
			840	22—09—68		105	22				
5	Isère	Grenoble	2500	11—11—51***							
			2000	20—12—40**							
			1800	02—11—59*							
			1000	22—09—68		29	11.5				
			920	26—11—44		115	69				
			880	24—12—18							
			884	09—02—55		48	24				
			872	15—01—55		126	72				
			868	08—06—55		100	22.5				

No.	Method of curve fitting		Rainfall forming flood (mm)	Snowmelt during floods (mm)	Maximum daily rainfall (mm)	Date	Hourly maximum rainfall (mm)	Date	Antecedent precipitation for	
	for W	for Q_{max}							10 days (mm)	30 days (mm)
1	13	14	15	16	17	18	19	20	21	22
3										
4			—							
			—							
			110							
			100							
5			—							
			—							
			—							
			80		149	21—09—68				
			—							
			74							
			—							
			200							
			—							

TABLE IV — CHARACTERISTICS OF RAINFALL FLOODS (cont'd)

			Characteristic element							Type of probability curve	
No.	River	Gauging station	Q_{max} (m^3/s)	Date	h (mm)	T_T (hours)	t_i (hours)	P_W (%)	$P_{Q_{max}}$ (%)	for P_W	for $P_{Q_{max}}$
1	2	3	4	5	6	7	8	9	10	11	12
6	Drac	Le Sautet	850	28—09—28		26	8				
			800	22—10—28		68	20				
			540	07—06—55		26.5	6.5				
			495	06—10—60		28.5	5.5				
			440	19—06—48		34	15				
			425	09—10—33		33	9				
			615	16—11—63		31	15				
7	Drôme	Livron	1300	—09—42*							
			1000	13—11—55							
			790	09—12—54		30	11				
			770			71	37				
			760	10—11—51		37	18				
8	Durance	Pont Mirabeau	5100	25—10—82							
			4040	24—10—86							
			3700	04—11—06							
			2980	29—05—17							
			2950	07—11—07							
			2800	11—11—51							
			2500	10—12—54							
9	Têt	Perpignan	3600	18—10—40	193	92	14				
			2080	09—11—92					0.4		Galton
			1860	20—02—20							
			1600	20—10—76							
			1480	20—11—98							

	Method of curve fitting		Rainfall forming flood (mm)	Snowmelt during floods (mm)	Maximum daily rainfall (mm)	Date	Hourly maximum rainfall (mm)	Date	Antecedent precipitation for	
No.	for W	for Q_{max}							10 days (mm)	30 days (mm)
1	13	14	15	16	17	18	19	20	21	22
6			94		161	28—09—28				
			165		275	21—10—28				
			77		102	07—06—55				
7			—							
			180							
			120							
			170							
8			87							
			142							
			127							
			115							
			137							
			110							
9		—	—							
		Moments	—							
			136							

TABLE IV – CHARACTERISTICS OF RAINFALL FLOODS (cont'd)

No.	River	Gauging station	Q_{max} (m³/s)	Date	h (mm)	T_T (hours)	t_i (hours)	P_W (%)	$P_{Q_{max}}$ (%)	Type of probability curve for P_W	for $P_{Q_{max}}$
1	2	3	4	5	6	7	8	9	10	11	12
10	Hérault	Gignac	3750	13–09–75*					0.99		Gumbel
			3150	21–09–90							
			3050	26–09–07	505						
			2900	31–10–63							
			2700	01–10–58							
11	Seine	Polisy	61.6	24–02–58							
			64.0	–08–60							
			98.0	–01–59							
12	Seine	Troyes	458	–01–10							
13	Seine	Paris-Austerlitz	2500	27–02–58***			200				
			2180	28–01–10		>240					
14	Aube	Blaincourt	214	–01–55							
15	Yonne	Gurgy	408	16–01–55							
16	Marne	Noisiel	853	–01–10							
17	Oise	Venette (Compiegne)	580	–02–50*							
			531	18–03–76*							
			515	–12–82							
			473	31–01–10							
18	Rhin	Bâle	6000	16–06–76*							

No.	Method of curve fitting for W	for Q_{max}	Rainfall forming flood (mm)	Snowmelt during floods (mm)	Maximum daily rainfall (mm)	Date	Hourly maximum rainfall (mm)	Date	Antecedent precipitation for 10 days (mm)	30 days (mm)
1	13	14	15	16	17	18	19	20	21	22
10		Moments								
11			>1000				150	18–10–40		
					323	17–10–40	60	17–10–40		
12			136							
13										
14										
15										
16										
17			—							
			—							
			83							
18	244									

TABLE IV — CHARACTERISTICS OF RAINFALL FLOODS (cont'd)

No.	River	Gauging station	Q_{max} (m³/s)	Date	h (mm)	T_T (hours)	t_i (hours)	P_W (%)	$P_{Q_{max}}$ (%)	Type of probability curve for P_W	for $P_{Q_{max}}$
1	2	3	4	5	6	7	8	9	10	11	12
19	Bruche	Volxheim	157	24—12—19					2		
20	Moselle	Epinal	1100	29—12—47							
21	Meurthe	Malzeville	1350	30—12—47							
22	Meuse	Chooz	1500	31—12—25							
23	Garonne	Agen	8500	—06—75*	59						
			7700	—03—30	54						
			7000	—02—52	57						
			5000	—03—27	62						
24	Garonne	Portet	4300	03—02—52							
			3280	18—05—11							
			3050	13—03—30							
			2500	29—11—31							
			2350	02—01—20							
			2570	20—02—71							
25	Garonne	Valentine	815	20—10—37							
			675	13—07—32							
			605	02—02—52							
			571	29—11—31							
			810	20—01—07							

No.	Method of curve fitting for W	for Q_{max}	Rainfall forming flood (mm)	Snowmelt during floods (mm)	Maximum daily rainfall (mm)	Date	Hourly maximum rainfall (mm)	Date	Antecedent precipitation for 10 days (mm)	30 days (mm)
1	13	14	15	16	17	18	19	20	21	22
19	139	14	20							
20										
21										
22										
23										
24										
25										

TABLE IV — CHARACTERISTICS OF RAINFALL FLOODS (cont'd)

No.	River	Gauging station	Q_{max} (m³/s)	Date	h (mm)	T_T (hours)	t_i (hours)	P_W (%)	$P_{Q_{max}}$ (%)	Type of probability curve for P_W	for $P_{Q_{max}}$
1	2	3	4	5	6	7	8	9	10	11	12
26	Truyère	Sarrans	775	06—12—43							
			760	09—10—20							
			645	08—12—44							
27	Aveyron	Laguepie	745	02—12—32							
			655	03—03—30							
			640	07—12—37							
			505	11—12—40							
28	Ariège	Foix	480	23—05—10							
			386	24—11—28							
			310	13—05—08							
			299	07—10—19							
			269	24—10—30							
29	Adour	Pointe d'Aste	156	06—02—19							
			121	03—02—52							
			80	11—05—15							
			75	21—01—36							
			75	27—11—31							
30	Loire	Gien	8500	02—06—56							
			2810	29—12—68							
31	Loire	Montjean	6540	—12—10							
			6160	—01—36							
			5960	—03—23							
			5550	—04—19							

No.	Method of curve fitting for W	for Q_{max}	Rainfall forming flood (mm)	Snowmelt during floods (mm)	Maximum daily rainfall (mm)	Date	Hourly maximum rainfall (mm)	Date	Antecedent precipitation for 10 days (mm)	30 days (mm)
1	13	14	15	16	17	18	19	20	21	22

TABLE IV — CHARACTERISTICS OF RAINFALL FLOODS (cont'd)

No.	River	Gauging station	Q_{max} (m³/s)	Date	h (mm)	T_T (hours)	t_i (hours)	P_W (%)	$P_{Q_{max}}$ (%)	Type of probability curve for P_W	for $P_{Q_{max}}$
1	2	3	4	5	6	7	8	9	10	11	12
32	Allier	Vieille Brioude	2500 1340	24—09—66* 25—11—43							
33	Allier	Moulins	4700	—05—56*							
34	Cher	Savonnieres	1690	—05—56*							
35	Vienne	Nouatre	4000 2100	16—07—92** 14—05—10							
36	Mayenne	Chambellay	715	26—10—66	42	240	62		1.1		Gumbel

No.	Method of curve fitting for W	for Q_{max}	Rainfall forming flood (mm)	Snowmelt during floods (mm)	Maximum daily rainfall (mm)	Date	Hourly maximum rainfall (mm)	Date	Antecedent precipitation for 10 days (mm)	30 days (mm)
1	13	14	15	16	17	18	19	20	21	22
32										
33										
34										
35										
36			82		45	25—10—66			120	250

Gabon / Gabón / Габон

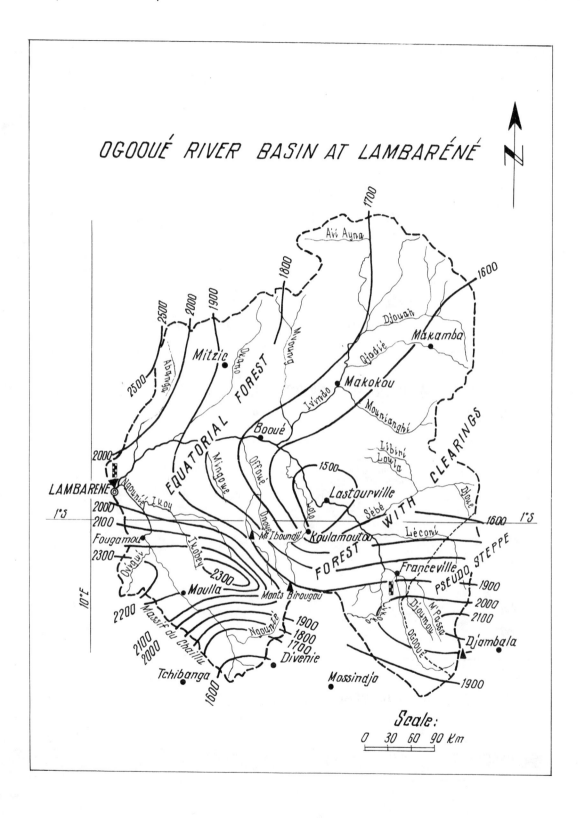

OGOOUÉ RIVER BASIN AT LAMBARÉNÉ

TABLE I — CHARACTERISTICS OF BASIN

		GAUGING STATION								BASIN			
No.	River / River system	Name	Period of records	Co-ordinates Lat.	Long.	Distance (km) from gauging site to remotest point of river system L_{rs}	to projection of centre of basin on main course L_{ca}	Mean slope of river I_r (%)	Area A (km²)	Mean H_m	Max. H_{max}	Min. H_{min}	
1	2	3	4	5	6	7	8	9	10	11	12	13	
1	Ogooué	Lambaréné	1929–72	S 0:42:22	E 10:13:27	820	330	0.7	204000	450	980	10	

	BASIN											
No.	Width (km) Mean B_m	Max. B_{max}	Mean slope I_b(%)	Soils	Cover	Weighted lake area P_L (%)	Swamps R_s (%)	Mean annual precipitation P (mm)	Annual runoff Q (mm)	Mean annual temperature T (°C)	Regulating capacity of reservoirs α
1	14	15	16	17	18	19	20	21	22	23	24
1	250	570	16		F(75), U(25)	0	0.2	1850	850	25	0.0

TABLE II — ANNUAL MAXIMUM DISCHARGES AND VOLUMES

Country: **Gabon (1)**
River: **Ogooué**
Gauging Station: **Lambaréné**

	Maximum discharge (m³/s) resulting from:		Maximum volume (10⁶m³) corresponding to max. discharge resulting from:	
Date	Rainfall	Snowmelt	Rainfall	Snowmelt
1	2	3	4	5
1934	13400			
1939	13000			
1949	11300			
1960	11500			
18–11–61	13600			

Country:
River:
Gauging Station:

	Maximum discharge (m³/s) resulting from:		Maximum volume (10⁶m³) corresponding to max. discharge resulting from:	
Date	Rainfall	Snowmelt	Rainfall	Snowmelt
1	2	3	4	5

TABLE IV — CHARACTERISTICS OF RAINFALL FLOODS

			Characteristic element							Type of probability curve	
No.	River	Gauging station	Q_{max} (m³/s)	Date	h (mm)	T_T (hours)	t_i (hours)	P_W (%)	$P_{Q_{max}}$ (%)	for P_W	for $P_{Q_{max}}$
1	2	3	4	5	6	7	8	9	10	11	12
1	Ogooué	Lambaréné	13600	17–11–61					2.27		Pearson III
			13400	–34					2.73		
			13000	–39					3.90		
			11500	–60					13.0		
			11300	–49					14.9		

Federal Republic of Germany / République fédérale d'Allemagne / República Federal de Alemania / Федеративная Республика Германии

TABLE I — CHARACTERISTICS OF BASIN

| | | GAUGING STATION | | | | | | | BASIN | | | |
No.	River / River system	Name	Period of records	Co-ordinates Lat.	Long.	Distance (km) from gauging site to remotest point of river system L_{rs}	to projection of centre of basin on main course L_{ca}	Mean slope of river I_r (%)	Area A (km²)	Altitude (m) Mean H_m	Max. H_{max}	Min. H_{min}
1	2	3	4	5	6	7	8	9	10	11	12	13
1	Rhein	Maxau	1815—72	N 49:03	E 8:20	310	160	0.08	50300		1490	85
2	Rhein	Kaub	1883—72	50:05	7:46	410	190	0.05	104000		1490	67
3	Rhein	Köln	1816—72	50:55	6:58	515	220	0.05	145000		1490	36
4	Wesser Wesser-Ems	Intschede	1901—72	52:58	9:08	290	150	0.15	37800		982	40
5	Ems Wesser-Ems	Rheine	1946—72	52:17	7:27	105	50	0.08	3740	50	450	24
6	Lippe Rhein	Lippstadt	1950—72	51:41	8:21	45	22	0.09	1390	70	488	30
7	Donau	Hofkirchen	1901—72	48:40	13:07	380	170	0.1	47500		1240	600

| | BASIN | | | | | | | | | | |
No.	Width (km) Mean B_m	Max. B_{max}	Mean slope I_b(%)	Soils	Cover	Weighted lake area P_L (%)	Swamps R_s (%)	Mean annual precipitation P (mm)	Annual runoff Q (mm)	Mean annual temperature T (°C)	Regulating capacity of reservoirs α
1	14	15	16	17	18	19	20	21	22	23	24
1	162	270		4	F(40), C(30), U(30)	1	0				
2	253	450		4	F(50), C(25), U(25)	0.6	0				
3	281	450		4	F(40), C(30), U(30)	0.3	0				
4	13	210		Sand	F(40), C(30), U(30)	<0.1	5	713	288		
5	36	95	0.08	Sand	F(30), C(30), U(40)	0	<0.1	805	350		
6	31	42	0.1	Sand	F(30), C(30), U(40)	0	0	0	1040	434	
7	125	280		4	F(40), C(30), U(30)	<0.1	0	986	373	8	

Federal Republic of Germany / République fédérale d'Allemagne / República Federal de Alemania /
Федеративная Республика Германии

TABLE II — ANNUAL MAXIMUM DISCHARGES AND VOLUMES

Country: **Federal Republic of Germany (1)**
River: **Rhein**
Gauging Station: **Maxau**

| Date | Maximum discharge (m³/s) resulting from: | | Maximum volume (10⁶m³) corresponding to max. discharge resulting from: | |
| | Rainfall | Snowmelt | Rainfall | Snowmelt |
1	2	3	4	5
31—12—82		4550		
30—12—25		3450		

Country: **Federal Republic of Germany (2)**
River: **Rhein**
Gauging Station: **Kaub**

| Date | Maximum discharge (m³/s) resulting from: | | Maximum volume (10⁶m³) corresponding to max. discharge resulting from: | |
| | Rainfall | Snowmelt | Rainfall | Snowmelt |
1	2	3	4	5
05—01—83		7400		
02—01—26		5880		

Country: **Federal Republic of Germany (3)**
River: **Rhein**
Gauging Station: **Köln**

| Date | Maximum discharge (m³/s) resulting from: | | Maximum volume (10⁶m³) corresponding to max. discharge resulting from: | |
| | Rainfall | Snowmelt | Rainfall | Snowmelt |
1	2	3	4	5
02—01—26		11100		

Country: **Federal Republic of Germany (4)**
River: **Weser**
Gauging Station: **Intschede**

| Date | Maximum discharge (m³/s) resulting from: | | Maximum volume (10⁶m³) corresponding to max. discharge resulting from: | |
| | Rainfall | Snowmelt | Rainfall | Snowmelt |
1	2	3	4	5
12—02—46		3040		

Country: **Federal Republic of Germany (5)**
River: **Ems**
Gauging Station: **Rheine**

| Date | Maximum discharge (m³/s) resulting from: | | Maximum volume (10⁶m³) corresponding to max. discharge resulting from: | |
| | Rainfall | Snowmelt | Rainfall | Snowmelt |
1	2	3	4	5
10—02—46		1030		

Country: **Federal Republic of Germany (6)**
River: **Lippe**
Gauging Station: **Lippstadt**

| Date | Maximum discharge (m³/s) resulting from: | | Maximum volume (10⁶m³) corresponding to max. discharge resulting from: | |
| | Rainfall | Snowmelt | Rainfall | Snowmelt |
1	2	3	4	5
17—07—65		113		

Country: **Federal Republic of Germany (7)**
River: **Donau**
Gauging Station: **Hofkirchen**

| Date | Maximum discharge (m³/s) resulting from: | | Maximum volume (10⁶m³) corresponding to max. discharge resulting from: | |
| | Rainfall | Snowmelt | Rainfall | Snowmelt |
1	2	3	4	5
13—07—54		3880		

Ghana / Гана

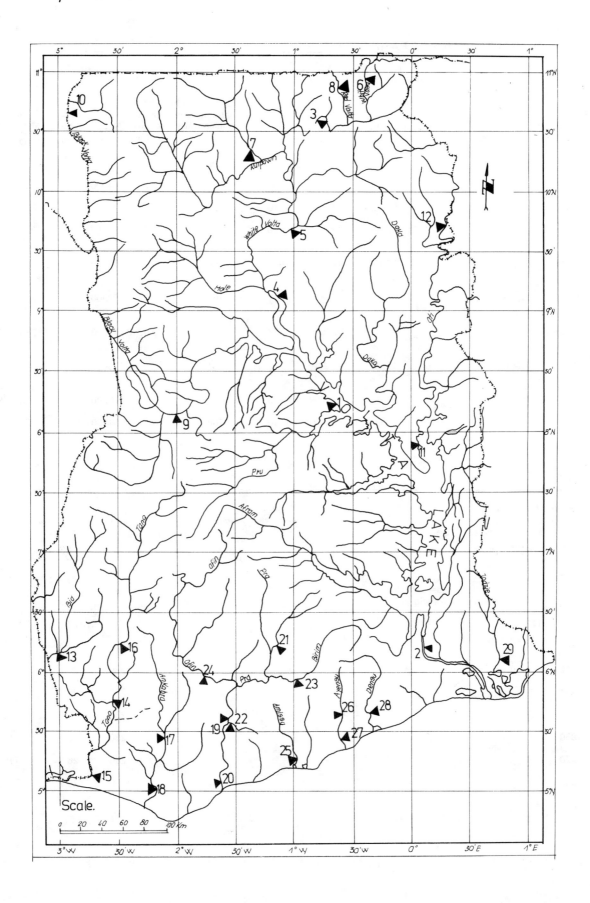

Scale.

o 20 40 60 80 100 Km

TABLE I — CHARACTERISTICS OF BASIN

No.	River / River system	Name	Period of records	Co-ordinates Lat.	Co-ordinates Long.	L_{rs} (to remotest point of river system)	L_{ca} (to projection of centre of basin on main course)	Mean slope of river I_r (%)	Area A (km²)	Altitude (m) Mean H_m	Altitude (m) Max. H_{max}	Altitude (m) Min. H_{min}
1	2	3	4	5	6	7	8	9	10	11	12	13
1	Volta	Yeji	22	N 08:14	00:39W	1090	71.1	0.03	284000		335	SL.
2	Volta	Senchi Halcrow	19	06:12	00:06E	1410	358	0.03	394000		335	SL.
3	White Volta	Pwalugu	22	10:35	00:51W	620	310	0.03	63300		335	SL.
4	White Volta	Yapei	22	09:09	01:10W	952	55.8	0.03	102000		335	SL.
5	White Volta	Nawuni (Dalon)	20	09:42	01:05W	812	165	0.03	92900		335	SL.
6	White Volta	Yarugu	11	10:59	00:24W	477		0.03	41500		335	SL.
7	Kulpawn White Volta	Wiasi	15	10:20	01:26W	215	284		9490		335	SL.
8	Red Volta	Nangodi	3	10:52	00:37W	270			16800		335	SL.
9	Black Volta	Bamboi	23	08:09	02:02W	1110	208		134000		335	SL.

No.	Width (km) Mean B_m	Width (km) Max. B_{max}	Mean slope I_b (%)	Soils	Cover	Weighted lake area P_L (%)	Swamps R_s (%)	Mean annual precipitation P (mm)	Annual runoff Q (mm)	Mean annual temperature T (°C)	Regulating capacity of reservoirs α
1	14	15	16	17	18	19	20	21	22	23	24
1	366			Laterite-ochrosol intergrades savannah ochrosols acid gleisols	U(50), C(50)				1230	26.7	7190
2	282	773		"	"				1230	26.7	7190
3	642			"	"				1230	26.7	7190
4	419			"	"				1230	26.7	7190
5	491			"	"			766	1230	26.7	7190
6	835			"	"				1230	26.7	7190
7	1850			"	"				1230	26.7	7190
8	1470			"	"				1230	26.7	7190
9	360			"	"				1230	26.7	7190

TABLE I – CHARACTERISTICS OF BASIN (cont'd)

No.	River / River system	Name	Period of records	Co-ordinates Lat.	Long.	Distance (km) from gauging site to remotest point of river system L_{rs}	to projection of centre of basin on main course L_{ca}	Mean slope of river I_r (%)	Area A (km²)	Altitude (m) Mean H_m	Max. H_{max}	Min. H_{min}
1	2	3	4	5	6	7	8	9	10	11	12	13
10	Black Volta	Lawra	22	N 10:38	02:55W	746	533		94000		335	SL.
11	Oti	Kpetchu	21	07:56	00:04E	816			70600			
12	Oti	Saboba	20	09:36	00:19E	425			50300			
13	Bia	Dadieso	10	06:08	03:04W	192	69.5	0.10	6200	127	305	122
14	Tano	Jomuro	17	05:46	02:34W	428	178	0.07	10800		488	0
15	Tano	Alenda	17	05:07	02:45W	583	361	0.07	15800		488	0
16	Tano	Wiawso	16	06:14	02:29W	188	30.4	0.07	8440		488	
17	Ankobra	Prestea	19	05:27	02:07W	175	28.6	0.15	4260	56.4	335	SL.
18	Ankobra	Dominasi	11	05:00	02:11W	256	86.3	0.15	6220	56.4		SL.

No.	Width (km) Mean B_m	Max. B_{max}	Mean slope I_b(%)	Soils	Cover	Weighted lake area P_L (%)	Swamps R_s (%)	Mean annual precipitation P (mm)	Annual runoff Q (mm)	Mean annual temperature T (°C)	Regulating capacity of reservoirs α
1	14	15	16	17	18	19	20	21	22	23	24
10	534			Laterite-ochrosol intergrades savannah ochrosols acid gleisols	U(50), C(50)				1230	26.7	7190
11	20										
12	38										
13	34	69						1440	30	25.8	
14	84			Forest-ochrosols forest oxysols forest ochrosol oxysols intergrades	F(50), C(50)						
15	41	95		"	"			1540	145	25.8	
16	489			"	"						
17	48	89	38.5	"	F(70), C(25), U(5)						
18	33	89	38.5		"			1770	41.2	25.6	

TABLE I — CHARACTERISTICS OF BASIN (cont'd)

No.	River River system	Name	Period of records	Co-ordinates Lat.	Co-ordinates Long.	Distance (km) from gauging site to remotest point of river system L_{rs}	Distance (km) from gauging site to projection of centre of basin on main course L_{ca}	Mean slope of river I_r (%)	Area A (km^2)	Altitude (m) Mean H_m	Altitude (m) Max. H_{max}	Altitude (m) Min. H_{min}
1	2	3	4	5	6	7	8	9	10	11	12	13
19	Pra	Twifu Praso	30	05:36 N	01:33W	275	102	0.24	20800		488	SL.
20	Pra	Daboasi	19	05:10	01:38W	346	163	0.24	22700		488	SL.
21	Pra	Brenasi	18	06:12	01:10W	105	12.7	0.24	2110		488	SL.
22	Obuo Pra	Mampong	30	05:33	01:33W	46.7	108	0.24	378		488	SL.
23	Birim Pra	Oda	19	05:57	00:59W	182	66	0.24	3290		488	SL.
24	Ofin Pra	Dunkwa	16	05:59	01:47W	306	104	0.24	8530		488	SL.
25	Ochi Amissa	Mankesim	18	05:16	01:00W	82.1		0.24	1250	52.4	488	SL.

No.	Width (km) Mean B_m	Width (km) Max. B_{max}	Mean slope I_b(%)	Soils	Cover	Weighted lake area P_L (%)	Swamps R_s (%)	Mean annual precipitation P (mm)	Annual runoff Q (mm)	Mean annual temperature T (°C)	Regulating capacity of reservoirs α
1	14	15	16	17	18	19	20	21	22	23	24
19	84	196		Forest ochrosol oxysol ochrosol intergrades	F(40), C(40), U(20)						
20	67	196		"	"			1520	299	25.6	
21	222	196		"	"						
22	497	196		"	"						
23	128	196		"	"						
24	76	196		"	"						
25	28	196		"	"						

TABLE I — CHARACTERISTICS OF BASIN (cont'd)

				GAUGING STATION					BASIN			
						Distance (km) from gauging site		Mean slope of river I_r (%)	Area A (km²)	Altitude (m)		
No.	River River system	Name	Period of records	Co-ordinates		to remotest point of river system L_{rs}	to projection of centre of basin on main course L_{ca}			Mean H_m	Max. H_{max}	Min. H_{min}
				Lat.	Long.							
1	2	3	4	5	6	7	8	9	10	11	12	13
26	Ayensu	Oketsew	13	N 05:38	00:37W	72.4	4.5	0.59	728	78.9	610	SL.
27	Ayensu	Winneba Rd.	11	05:23	00:36W	109	41.2		1660	78.9	610	SL.
28	Densu	Manhia	6	05:46	00:22W	109	33.0	0.39	2120	95.7	488	SL.
29	Todzie	Todzienu Tove		06:05	00:45E	114	54.7	0.58	2180	5.6	853	SL.

	BASIN										
	Width (km)		Mean slope I_b (%)	Soils	Cover	Weighted lake area P_L (%)	Swamps R_s (%)	Mean annual precipitation P (mm)	Annual runoff Q (mm)	Mean annual temperature T (°C)	Regulating capacity of reservoirs α
No.	Mean B_m	Max. B_{max}									
1	14	15	16	17	18	19	20	21	22	23	24
26	24	31	2.89	Forest ochrosol forest rubrisol ochrosol forest ochrosol regosolic ground water laterites savannah ochrosols	C(50), F(20), U(30)				14.5		
27	16	31	2.89	"	"						
28	23	43	1.29	"	F(30), U(30), C(40)			1490	23.0	26.9	
29	15	30	29×10^{-6}	"	C(60), U(40)		20	1160	12.0	27.4	

TABLE II – ANNUAL MAXIMUM DISCHARGES AND VOLUMES

Country:	Ghana (2)
River:	Volta
Gauging Station:	Senchi

	Maximum discharge (m³/s) resulting from:		Maximum volume (10⁶m³) corresponding to max. discharge resulting from:	
Date	Rainfall	Snowmelt	Rainfall	Snowmelt
1	2	3	4	5
09—10—36	7530		28000	
08—10—37	6880		31800	
06—10—38	4550			
26—10—39	7460		38900	
05—10—40	4810		28600	
28—10—41	8450		37400	
19—10—42	3420		12700	
07—10—43	4890		23200	
20—09—44	5730		28500	
08—10—45	9020		46900	
10—10—46	4760		23000	
23—09—47	12400		51100	
25—09—48	6630		26500	
14—09—49	9730		50100	
10—50	3340		16900	
07—11—51	9950		55900	
14—10—52	10100		48200	
06—10—53	7590		45600	
18—10—54	5270		26300	
10—10—55	9610		62000	
09—10—56	5470		18800	
12—10—57	9920		65300	
27—09—58	2550		9360	
05—10—59	6680		29100	
10—10—60	9090		40400	
05—10—61	4810		22300	
02—10—62	9220		53600	
23—09—63	14300		94400	
1964			Start of construction of Coffer dam	

Country:	Ghana (2) cont'd
River:	Volta
Gauging Station:	Senchi

	Maximum discharge (m³/s) resulting from:		Maximum volume (10⁶m³) corresponding to max. discharge resulting from:	
Date	Rainfall	Snowmelt	Rainfall	Snowmelt
1	2	3	4	5
19—09—68	10300			
19—09—69	5100		Regulated releases from dam	
19—09—70	5150			
19—09—71	3290			

TABLE II – ANNUAL MAXIMUM DISCHARGES AND VOLUMES (cont'd)

Country:	Ghana (3)
River:	White Volta
Gauging Station:	Pwalugu

Date	Maximum discharge (m³/s) resulting from:		Maximum volume (10⁶m³) corresponding to max. discharge resulting from:	
	Rainfall	Snowmelt	Rainfall	Snowmelt
1	2	3	4	5
22–08–51	1130		2970	
12–09–52	1190		3890	
12–09–53	9080		1760	
04–09–54	8340		1920	
16–09–55	1230			
21–09–56	1070		3990	
02–10–57	1060			
31–08–58	1370			
59			3690	
23–09–60	1080		2620	
16–09–62	1610		4750	
30–08–63	1000		2730	
08–09–64	1410		5010	
18–08–65	692		1680	
27–08–66	676		1250	
16–09–67	1240		4140	
20–07–68	979		2180	
13–09–69	1520		4270	
10–09–70	1240		3920	
29–08–71	962		3200	
17–08–72	432			

Country:	Ghana (5)
River:	White Volta
Gauging Station:	Nawuni

Date	Maximum discharge (m³/s) resulting from:		Maximum volume (10⁶m³) corresponding to max. discharge resulting from:	
	Rainfall	Snowmelt	Rainfall	Snowmelt
1	2	3	4	5
20–09–53	1720			
16–09–54	1510			
27–09–55	1890		9650	
22–09–56	1630		7000	
19–09–57	1810		9760	
18–09–58	1160			
03–10–59	1580		6180	
27–09–60	1920		7360	
25–09–61	1820		6790	
18–09–62	1920		8400	
05–09–63	2060		10800	
29–09–64	1710		7160	
25–09–65	1270		6150	
06–09–66	1370			
22–09–67	1780		7460	
06–08–68	1440		7240	
19–09–69	2000		7440	
14–09–70	1900		7450	
18–09–71	1780		6680	
07–09–72	394			

TABLE II – ANNUAL MAXIMUM DISCHARGES AND VOLUMES (cont'd)

Country:	Ghana (9)
River:	Black Volta
Gauging Station:	Bamboi

Date	Maximum discharge (m³/s) resulting from:		Maximum volume (10⁶m³) corresponding to max. discharge resulting from:	
	Rainfall	Snowmelt	Rainfall	Snowmelt
1	2	3	4	5
05–10–50	734		3180	
21–09–53	1080		4240	
29–09–54	1300		6060	
15–10–55	1970		10500	
09–10–56	1290		3750	
01–10–59	1700		3980	
06–10–60	1320		5750	
19–09–61	613		2010	
12–10–62	1470		7380	
17–09–63	3190		15700	
19–09–64	1390		5210	
06–10–65	1330		6850	
20–09–67	680		2850	
14–09–68	2560		133000	
04–10–69	1290		7750	
19–09–70	1220		5540	
30–09–71	1230		5100	

Country:	Ghana (12)
River:	Oti
Gauging Station:	Saboba

Date	Maximum discharge (m³/s) resulting from:		Maximum volume (10⁶m³) corresponding to max. discharge resulting from:	
	Rainfall	Snowmelt	Rainfall	Snowmelt
1	2	3	4	5
17–09–53	2580		11200	
01–10–54	1520		4080	
03–09–55	2460		1490	
21–09–56	1350		5790	
01–10–57	2870		13200	
01–10–58	238		617	
29–09–59	2350		8020	
08–10–60	2600		8580	
23–09–61	1530		3890	
18–09–62	2840		6290	
15–09–63	2700		14900	
05–10–64	2170		9450	
18–09–65	1140		3580	
27–08–66	1340		6510	
02–10–67	1740		8720	
12–09–68	1780		8550	
23–09–69	2660		10600	
30–09–70	2830			
14–09–71	2200		8960	
13–09–72	1430			

TABLE II – ANNUAL MAXIMUM DISCHARGES AND VOLUMES (cont'd)

Country:	Ghana (19)				Country:	Ghana (22)			
River:	Pra				River:	Pra			
Gauging Station:	Twitu praso				Gauging Station:	Mampong			

Date	Maximum discharge (m³/s) resulting from:		Maximum volume (10⁶m³) corresponding to max. discharge resulting from:		Date	Maximum discharge (m³/s) resulting from:		Maximum volume (10⁶m³) corresponding to max. discharge resulting from:	
	Rainfall	Snowmelt	Rainfall	Snowmelt		Rainfall	Snowmelt	Rainfall	Snowmelt
1	2	3	4	5	1	2	3	4	5
19–11–43	580		653		06–07–44	56		50	
04–07–44	703		795		20–10–45	48		18	
21–10–45	580		695		12–06–46	40		30	
23–10–46	425		792		22–05–47	35		34	
27–09–47	812		1620		21–11–48	12		14	
14–06–48	511		915		10–07–49	34		11	
26–07–49	703		1200		12–11–50	40		30	
19–10–50	295		444		03–11–51	40		22	
08–11–51	756		1200		22–09–52	56		76	
24–09–52	729		1360		15–10–53	34		25	
14–07–53	1020		947		20–05–54	28		22	
02–07–54	580		1410		25–06–55	52		53	
01–11–55	789		1750		31–05–56	84		36	
13–06–56	756		790		13–06–57	32		26	
17–07–57	1020		1690		13–05–58	34		16	
19–06–58	789		1060		31–05–59	27		38	
06–10–59	584		1130		09–05–60	88		29	
30–06–60	1290		1630		13–06–61	44		21	
23–07–61	880		2150		05–06–62	35		23	
04–07–62	1330		3210		07–10–63	52		31	
12–10–63	1390		3330		17–06–64	40		34	
02–07–64	545		521		15–06–65	61		46	
19–07–65	901		2120		17–05–66	37		22	
10–07–66	877				28–09–68	78		37	
68	2000				13–07–69	27		10	
12–06–69	936		874		27–06–70	55		18	
28–05–70	583		631		16–07–71	27		41	
25–07–71	384		354						
12–06–72	712								

TABLE IV — CHARACTERISTICS OF RAINFALL FLOODS

No.	River	Gauging station	Q_{max} (m³/s)	Date	h (mm)	T_T (hours)	t_i (hours)	P_W (%)	$P_{Q_{max}}$ (%)	Type of probability curve for P_W	for $P_{Q_{max}}$
1	2	3	4	5	6	7	8	9	10	11	12
1	Volta	Yeji	6180	18–09–63	14.0	3670	1920	Not available	5.5	Not available	Empirical curve
			4370	06–10–65	8.5	3050	1970	"	25	"	"
2	Volta	Senchi	143000	23–09–63	23.6	3430	1800	"	3.4	"	"
			12400	23–09–47	12.6	2160	1080	"	6.7	"	"
			10100	14–10–52	12.0	3070	2060	"	14	"	"
			9950	07–11–51	13.3	2640	2200	"	15	"	"
3	White Volta	Pwalugu	1610	16–09–62	7.5	1940	1130	"	9	"	"
			1520	12–09–69	4.7	888	504	"	12.5	"	"
4	White Volta	Yapei	3000	09–09–63	13.2	2950	1220	"	6	"	"
			2510	21–09–62	7.6	2210	1250	"	14	"	"
5	White Volta	Nawuni (Dalon)	2060	07–09–63	11.8	3070	1410	"	14	"	"
			2000	14–09–69	7.9	2350	1220	"	20	"	"
6	White Volta	Yarugu	1940	09–09–62	8.3	1130	672	"	6	"	"
			1910	28–07–64	9.5	1440	120	"	8	"	"
7	White Volta	Wiasi	391	23–08–66	10.4	2450	528	"	14	"	"
			387	23–07–68	11.9	1850	192	"	20	"	"
8	Red Volta	Nangodi	503	19–09–64	3.1	600	408	"	3.7	"	"
			430	11–09–69	3.9	672	312	"	9	"	"

No.	Method of curve fitting for W	for Q_{max}	Rainfall forming flood (mm)	Snowmelt during floods (mm)	Maximum daily rainfall (mm)	Date	Hourly maximum rainfall (mm)	Date	Antecedent precipitation for 10 days (mm)	30 days (mm)
1	13	14	15	16	17	18	19	20	21	22
1				68.9	7.98	28–08–63	5.49	28–08–63	9.7	34.7
				61.5	9.1	10–08–55	4.39		2.6	16.9
2										
3				53.6	9.53	12–08–62			10.2	30.7
				54.2	7.59	20–08–64			8.4	24.5
4				42.7	6.73	21–07–63			8.9	25.8
				33.4	5.89	24–08–62			3.4	20.6
5				45.8	7.06	21–07–63			7.6	23.0
				37.6	4.17	16–08–69			6.6	24.9
6				56.1	9.55	05–08–62			9.0	35.7
				20.9	5.66	23–07–64			11.5	24.5
7										
8				—						
				61.5	10.4	30–07–64			22.1	39.4

TABLE IV — CHARACTERISTICS OF RAINFALL FLOODS (cont'd)

No.	River	Gauging station	Q_{max} (m³/s)	Date	h (mm)	T_T (hours)	t_i (hours)	P_W (%)	$P_{Q_{max}}$ (%)	Type of probability curve for P_W	for $P_{Q_{max}}$
1	2	3	4	5	6	7	8	9	10	11	12
9	Black Volta	Bamboi	3190	17–09–63	9.8	3670	1900	Not available	2.5	Not available	Empirical curve
			2560	14–09–68	8.07	3310	1460	"	5.5	"	"
			1970	15–10–55	7.7	3580	2350	"	14	"	"
10	Black Volta	Lawra	934	09–08–63	5.1	2470	480	"	7	"	"
			898	20–10–51	6.1	3670	2690	"	9	"	"
			881	10–10–52	5.5	2880	2060	"	10	"	"
			712	01–10–64	3.3	3070	1630	"	20	"	"
			680	01–10–55	3.9	2380	1650	"	25	"	"
11	Oti	Kpetchu	4470	13–09–63	11.8	3670	1800	"	8	"	"
			4290	01–10–62	5.7	2570	1490	"	12.5	"	"
12	Oti	Saboba	2870	01–10–57	26.4	2590	1390	"	16	"	"
			2840	18–09–62	12.9	2930	1180	"	20	"	"
14	Tano	Jomuro	779	12–08–68	4.5	336	120	"	2	"	"
			523	04–07–59	8.5	1460	456	"	12.5	"	"
16	Tano	Wiawso	321	11–09–68	4.9	408	144	"	4.3	"	"
			310	31–10–63	6.2	936	192	"	5.3	"	"
17	Ankobra	Prestea	609	22–07–61	14.6	1700	1250	"	7	"	"
			519	07–10–63	29.0	1460	192	"	14	"	"

No.	Method of curve fitting for W	for Q_{max}	Rainfall forming flood (mm)	Snowmelt during floods (mm)	Maximum daily rainfall (mm)	Date	Hourly maximum rainfall (mm)	Date	Antecedent precipitation for 10 days (mm)	30 days (mm)
1	13	14	15	16	17	18	19	20	21	22
9				45.7	6.25	25–08–63	3.56	14–09–63	12.8	25.0
				52.4	7.24	23–08–68	2.16	07–09–68	12.9	29.2
				53.0	7.29	14–07–55			6.2	21.8
10				48.3	13.69	04–08–63			41.0	48.3
				47.0	6.07	03–09–64			6.1	23.1
				45.7	6.07	02–09–55			6.4	24.9
				—						
				—						
11				65.6	9.09	27–07–63			7.5	31.3
				48.8	6.25	11–09–62			10.5	30.4
12				57.7	8.18	11–08–57			8.3	28.7
				—						
14				—						
				25.2	6.43	30–06–59			16.3	25.2
16				4.6	2.26	24–10–63				
				8.4	5.00	06–09–68				
17				50.9	9.45	20–07–61			16.0	28.5
				48.7	6.63	05–09–63			15.1	36.0

Ghana / Гана

TABLE IV – CHARACTERISTICS OF RAINFALL FLOODS (cont'd)

No.	River	Gauging station	Q_{max} (m³/s)	Date	h (mm)	T_T (hours)	t_i (hours)	P_W (%)	$P_{Q_{max}}$ (%)	Type of probability curve for P_W	for $P_{Q_{max}}$
1	2	3	4	5	6	7	8	9	10	11	12
19	Pra	Twifu Praso	2000					Not available	0.7	Not available	Empirical curve
			1390	12–10–63	22.9	1700	1010	"	6.2	"	"
			1330	04–07–62	16.8	1460	816	"	7.7	"	"
			1290	30–06–60	8.4	1080	600	"	9	"	"
			1020	17–07–57	16.1	2330	1510	"	20	"	"
21	Pra	Brenasi	234	10–07–57	10.0	744	240	"	1.3	"	"
			171	12–09–68	24.9	1460	1030	"	6	"	"
22	Obuo	Mampong	835	31–05–56	16.2	1180	312	"	5.3	"	"
			779	09–05–60	7.2	840	456	"	7.1	"	"
			779	28–09–68	9.8	264	96	"	7.1	"	"
23	Birim	Oda	473	19–07–68	23.0	840	624	"	2.9	"	"
			404	16–08–66	12.9	672	168	"	6	"	"
24	Ofin	Dunkwa	979	17–09–68	44.2	1580	864	"	1.0	"	"
			672	10–10–63	23.0	1390	816	"	5.9	"	"
25	Ochi Amissa	Mankesim	268	25–06–62	13.4	600	408	"	2.9	"	"
			231	23–07–61	8.2	768	240	"	5.9	"	"
26	Ayensu	Oketsew	191	25–06–60	20.0	552	264	"	4	"	"
			162	22–07–61	6.7	336	96	"	7.7	"	"

No.	Method of curve fitting for W	for Q_{max}	Rainfall forming flood (mm)	Snowmelt during floods (mm)	Maximum daily rainfall (mm)	Date	Hourly maximum rainfall (mm)	Date	Antecedent precipitation for 10 days (mm)	30 days (mm)
1	13	14	15	16	17	18	19	20	21	22
19				57.0	7.39	10–06–57			10.3	27.1
				25.6	6.50	27–06–60			13.3	28.0
				23.6	4.62	05–06–62			8.8	17.3
				43.4	7.09	21–09–63			8.5	30.9
21				10.2	5.44	07–07–57			9.8	
				43.4	8.31	16–09–68	6.71	06–09–68	16.6	35.8
22				19.9	5.84	25–05–56			19.9	28.8
				16.6	5.08	04–05–60			16.6	21.1
23				50.9	9.07	08–07–68	1.02	08–07–68	4.6	29.2
				37.5	8.38	06–06–62			18.3	34.2
24				65.4	6.07	05–06–68			9.0	27.9
				43.5	6.43	05–09–63			11.5	33.4
25				23.9	5.87	06–07–68				
				20.9	4.52	08–10–62			5.5	21.5
26				17.6	6.65	00–07–68			15.8	31.8
				12.6	11.4	10–07–61			12.9	31.7

Guyana / Guyane / Guayana / Гвиана

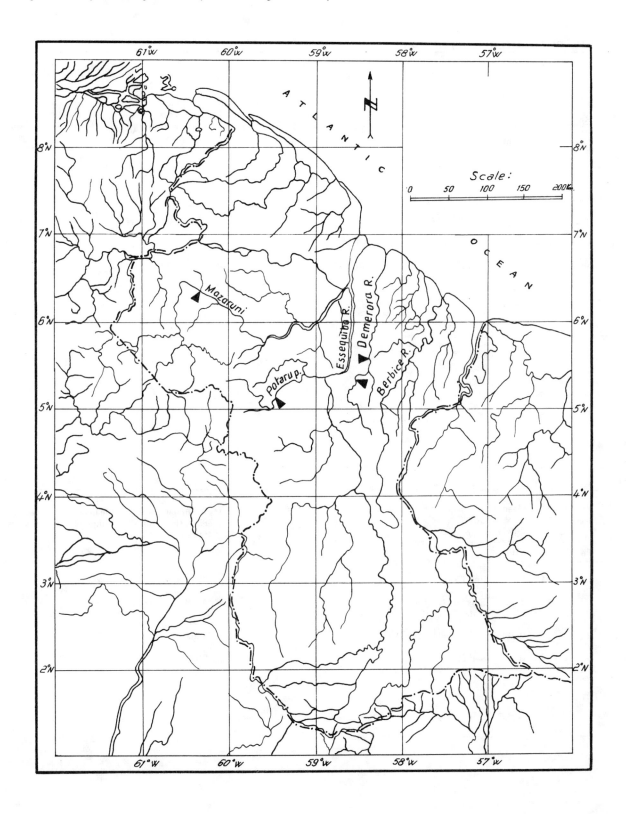

TABLE I – CHARACTERISTICS OF BASIN

No.	River River system	Name	Period of records	Co-ordinates Lat.	Co-ordinates Long.	to remotest point of river system L_{rs}	to projection of centre of basin on main course L_{ca}	Mean slope of river I_r (%)	Area A (km^2)	Mean H_m	Max. H_{max}	Min. H_{min}
				GAUGING STATION		Distance (km) from gauging site			BASIN		Altitude (m)	
1	2	3	4	5	6	7	8	9	10	11	12	13
1	Mazaruni	Apaikwa	1950–72	N 06:22	W 60:23	249	121	0.18	14000		1040	91
2	Potaro	Kaieteur	1950–72	05:09	59:29	97	32	0.25	2640		1370	405
3	Demerara	Great Falls	1950–72	05:18:30	58:32	129	80	0.37	2460		381	45.7
4	Demerara	Saka	1950–72	05:34:10	58:21:55	201	129	1.00	4040		381	15.2

No.	Mean B_m	Max. B_{max}	Mean slope I_b(%)	Soils	Cover	Weighted lake area P_L (%)	Swamps R_s (%)	Mean annual precipitation P (mm)	Annual runoff Q (mm)	Mean annual temperature T (°C)	Regulating capacity of reservoirs α
	Width (km)							BASIN			
1	14	15	16	17	18	19	20	21	22	23	24
1	56	171	0.80	Red Latosols	F			2914	1680	26.5	
2	27	55	1.88	Ragosols & Ground Water Rodzols	F			4138	2340	26.5	
3	19	36	0.68	Red & Yellow Latosols	F			2361	968	27	
4	20	46	0.58	Red & Yellow Latosols	F			2371	891	27	

Guyana / Guyane / Guayana / Гвиана

TABLE II – ANNUAL MAXIMUM DISCHARGES AND VOLUMES

Country:	Guyana (1)
River:	Mazaruni
Gauging Station:	Apaikwa

Date	Maximum discharge (m³/s) resulting from:		Maximum volume (10⁶m³) corresponding to max. discharge resulting from:	
	Rainfall	Snowmelt	Rainfall	Snowmelt
1	2	3	4	5
29—01—50	2390			
02—07—51	1830			
27—06—52	1790			
05—02—53	2350			
22—06—54	2610			
29—05—55	2090			
18—06—56	2590			
27—07—57	1840			
06—05—58	1880			
24—06—59	2000			
04—06—60	2090			
19—06—61	2200			
16—06—62	1840			
12—05—63	1970			
07—06—64	1330			
09—06—65	1850			
04—07—66	2060			
08—06—67	2310			
26—06—68	2380			
27—06—69	1710			
17—05—70	1880			
04—07—71	2640			
02—05—72	2380			

Country:	Guyana (2)
River:	Potaro
Gauging Station:	Kaieteur

Date	Maximum discharge (m³/s) resulting from:		Maximum volume (10⁶m³) corresponding to max. discharge resulting from:	
	Rainfall	Snowmelt	Rainfall	Snowmelt
1	2	3	4	5
18—06—50	985			
27—06—51	869			
27—05—52	801			
05—02—53	911			
27—04—54	920			
26—07—55	710			
05—06—56	962			
23—06—57	713			
04—05—58	727			
24—06—59	801			
04—06—60	852			
17—06—61	804			
14—06—62	773			
31—05—63	773			
28—05—64	812			
24—05—65	662			
04—06—66	730			
31—05—67	668			
18—06—68	1120			
20—06—69	617			
15—05—70	654			
07—07—71	911			
01—06—72	872			

TABLE II – ANNUAL MAXIMUM DISCHARGES AND VOLUMES (cont'd)

Country:	Guyana (3)
River:	Demerara
Gauging Station:	Great Falls

Date	Maximum discharge (m³/s) resulting from:		Maximum volume (10⁶m³) corresponding to max. discharge resulting from:	
	Rainfall	Snowmelt	Rainfall	Snowmelt
1	2	3	4	5
18—06—50	323			
26—06—51	314			
06—08—52	240			
21—06—53	213			
27—08—54	236			
27—07—55	365			
26—06—56	320			
11—07—57	202			
30—06—58	212			
23—07—59	128			
04—06—60	274			
17—07—61	289			
29—06—62	153			
08—06—63	311			
17—07—64	139			
17—06—65	110			
29—07—66	188			
09—07—67	275			
29—06—68	320			
26—06—69	194			
17—08—70	306			
16—07—71	317			
16—06—72	365			

Country:	Guyana (4)
River:	Demerara
Gauging Station:	Saka

Date	Maximum discharge (m³/s) resulting from:		Maximum volume (10⁶m³) corresponding to max. discharge resulting from:	
	Rainfall	Snowmelt	Rainfall	Snowmelt
1	2	3	4	5
21—06—50	388			
02—07—51	447			
06—08—52	337			
27—06—53	291			
31—08—54	374			
04—08—55	425			
28—06—56	396			
24—07—57	317			
05—07—58	253			
18—07—59	171			
07—06—60	320			
19—07—61	323			
05—07—62	226			
24—06—63	385			
20—07—64	180			
16—06—65	183			
31—07—66	231			
12—07—67	351			
11—06—68	405			
28—08—69	261			
21—08—70	357			
20—07—71	391			
20—06—72	399			

Hungary / Hongrie / Hungría / Венгрия

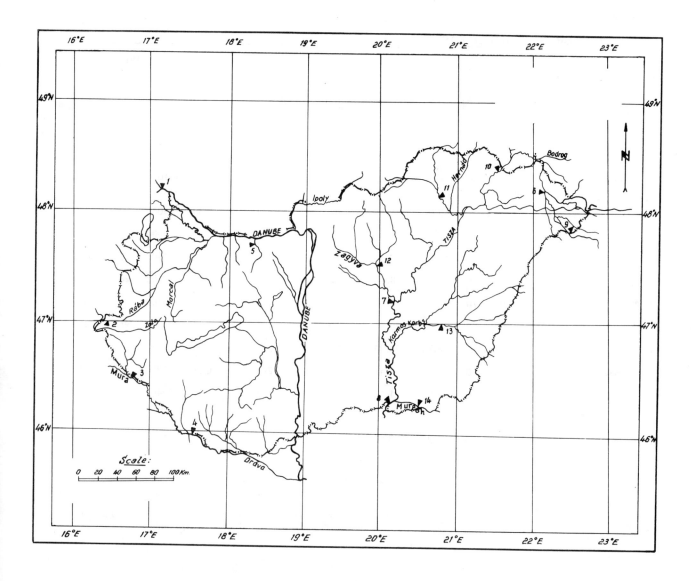

TABLE I — CHARACTERISTICS OF BASIN

				GAUGING STATION					BASIN			
	River River system	Name	Period of records	Co-ordinates		Distance (km) from gauging site		Mean slope of river I_r (%)	Area A (km²)	Altitude (m)		
No.				Lat.	Long.	to remotest point of river system L_{rs}	to projection of centre of basin on main course L_{ca}			Mean H_m	Max. H_{max}	Min. H_{min}
1	2	3	4	5	6	7	8	9	10	11	12	13
1	Danube	Bratislava (Czechoslovakia)	1823—70	N 48:09	E 17:06	990	453	0.43	131000	800	4060	135
2	Rába	Szentgotthárd	1882—70	46:57	16:17	101	73	0.89	3080	523	1780	112
3	Mura	Letenye	1891—70	46:27	16:42	430	187	0.36	13000	845	3060	130
4	Dráva	Barcs	1872—70	45:57	17:26	541	273	0.20	34000	780	3800	83
5	Átalér	Tatabánya	1950—70	47:40	18:19	41	12	0.24	462	280	555	109
6	Tisza	Vásárosnamény	1851—70	47:07	22:19	268	155	0.56	25100	819	2310	103
7	Tisza	Szolnok	1854—70	47:11	20:11	628	358	0.24	73100	455	2310	77
8	Tisza	Szeged	1823—70	46:16	20:09	790	322	0.19	138000	431	2510	74
9	Szamos	Csenger	1875—70	47:49	22:41	369	263	0.38	15300	553	2310	90
10	Bodrog	Felsöberecki	1931—70	48:22	21:42	220	32	0.28	12400	409	1680	90
11	Sajó	Felsözsolca	1879—70	48:07	20:21	179	104	0.49	6440	423	1940	89
12	Zagyva	Jásztelek	1898—70	47:28	20:00	119	60	0.34	4210	198	1020	80

				BASIN								
	Width (km)		Mean slope I_b(%)	Soils	Cover	Weighted lake area P_L (%)	Swamps R_s (%)	Mean annual precipitation P (mm)	Annual runoff Q (mm)	Mean annual temperature T (°C)	Regulating capacity of reservoirs α
No.	Mean B_m	Max. B_{max}									
1	14	15	16	17	18	19	20	21	22	23	24
1	130	380				<1 %		1500	475	9.0	
2	30	36		4	F(65), C(35)	''		859	210	9.0	<1 %
3	30	60		4	F(60), C(40)	''		951	360	8.9	''
4	62	160		4	F(45), C(55)	''		975	530	9.1	''
5	11	20		5	F(10), C(90)	''		678	110	10.2	''
6	108	270		4	F(80), C(20)	''		1070	613	8.1	''
7	116	250		4	F(60), C(40)	''		746	230	9.8	''
8	175	350				''		709	185	10.0	''
9	41	150		4	F(50), C(50)	''		756	240	8.4	''
10	56	100		4	F(45), C(55)	''		761	290	8.5	''
11	36	71		4	F(40), C(60)	''		693	155	8.7	''
12	35	77		4	F(20), C(80)	''		565	53	9.8	''

TABLE I — CHARACTERISTICS OF BASIN (cont'd)

						GAUGING STATION					BASIN			
No.	River / River system	Name	Period of records	Co-ordinates		Distance (km) from gauging site		Mean slope of river I_r (%)	Area A (km^2)	Altitude (m)			
				Lat.	Long.	to remotest point of river system L_{rs}	to projection of centre of basin on main course L_{ca}			Mean H_m	Max. H_{max}	Min. H_{min}	
1	2	3	4	5	6	7	8	9	10	11	12	13	
13	Hármas-Körös	Gyoma	1873–70	46:57	20:50	283	136	0.31	19700	229	1850	77	
14	Maros	Makó	1864–70	46:13	20:09	730	456	0.12	30100	642	2510	74	

					BASIN							
No.	Width (km)		Mean slope I_b (%)	Soils	Cover	Weighted lake area P_L (%)	Swamps R_s (%)	Mean annual precipitation P (mm)	Annual runoff Q (mm)	Mean annual temperature T (°C)	Regulating capacity of reservoirs α
	Mean B_m	Max. B_{max}									
1	14	15	16	17	18	19	20	21	22	23	24
13	70	160		4	F(30), C(70)	<1 %		653	120	9.2	<1%
14	41	125		4	F(55), C(45)	,,		707	160	9.0	,,

TABLE II — ANNUAL MAXIMUM DISCHARGES AND VOLUMES

Country:	Hungary (1)
River:	Danube
Gauging Station:	Pozsony

Date	Maximum discharge (m³/s) resulting from:		Maximum volume (10⁶m³) corresponding to max. discharge resulting from:	
	Rainfall	Snowmelt	Rainfall	Snowmelt
1	2	3	4	5
13—05—51		5130		
28—03—52		5170		
13—07—53	4420			
15—07—54	10900			
13—07—55	6330			
25—06—56	4370			
27—07—57	6280			
20—02—58		6200		
17—08—59	7320			
15—08—60	4430			
15—12—61		5690		
22—05—62		4970		
26—06—63	3990			
20—11—64	5300			
16—06—65	9220			
27—07—66	7320			
02—06—67	5050			
05—10—68	5240			
09—06—69	4150			

Country:	Hungary (2)
River:	Rába
Gauging Station:	Szentgotthárd

Date	Maximum discharge (m³/s) resulting from:		Maximum volume (10⁶m³) corresponding to max. discharge resulting from:	
	Rainfall	Snowmelt	Rainfall	Snowmelt
1	2	3	4	5
15—11—61	155			
20—11—62	157			
14—03—63		202		
25—10—64	280			
02—08—65	531			
21—08—66	168			
01—06—67	297			
01—09—68	92			
16—03—69		190		

TABLE II — ANNUAL MAXIMUM DISCHARGES AND VOLUMES (cont'd)

Country: Hungary (6)
River: Tisza
Gauging Station: Vásárosnamény

Date	Maximum discharge (m³/s) resulting from:		Maximum volume (10⁶m³) corresponding to max. discharge resulting from:	
	Rainfall	Snowmelt	Rainfall	Snowmelt
1	2	3	4	5
04—04—52	2600			
02—01—53		2050		
04—05—54	974			
21—02—55		2010		
21—01—56		1780		
21—03—57		1890		
19—02—58		2610		
31—12—59		1170		
10—11—60	1470			
03—04—61	784			
03—04—62	2900			
15—05—63	960			
01—04—64	3170			
14—06—65	2360			
29—08—66	1820			
14—03—67		2550		
27—02—68		2750		
29—11—69	1540			
15—05—70	3930			

Country: Hungary (7)
River: Tisza
Gauging Station: Szolnok

Date	Maximum discharge (m³/s) resulting from:		Maximum volume (10⁶m³) corresponding to max. discharge resulting from:	
	Rainfall	Snowmelt	Rainfall	Snowmelt
1	2	3	4	5
21—05—51	1440			
15—04—52	1950			
14—01—53		2600		
17—06—54	994			
09—04—55	1640			
04—05—56	1800			
28—02—57		1630		
07—03—58		1650		
13—03—59		1050		
02—08—60	1270			
01—01—61		878		
18—04—62	2560			
19—04—63	1270			
14—04—64	2730			
26—06—65	2190			
04—03—66		2750		
22—03—67		3030		
16—04—68	1500			
02—12—69	1190			
30—05—70	2730			

TABLE II — ANNUAL MAXIMUM DISCHARGES AND VOLUMES (cont'd)

Country:	Hungary (8)
River:	Tisza
Gauging Station:	Szeged

Date	Maximum discharge (m³/s) resulting from:		Maximum volume (10⁶m³) corresponding to max. discharge resulting from:	
	Rainfall	Snowmelt	Rainfall	Snowmelt
1	2	3	4	5
23–05–51	1830			
23–04–52	2210			
17–01–53		2510		
09–05–54	1490			
03–03–55		2220		
07–05–56	2410			
04–06–57	2000			
07–03–58		2600		
15–03–59		1320		
01–03–60		1870		
01–01–61		1280		
22–04–62	3100			
28–03–63	1930			
16–04–64	2770			
22–06–65	2690			
05–03–66		2940		
25–03–67	2900			
14–04–68	1980			
07–07–69	1780			
01–06–70	3880			

Country:	Hungary (9)
River:	Szamos
Gauging Station:	Csenger

Date	Maximum discharge (m³/s) resulting from:		Maximum volume (10⁶m³) corresponding to max. discharge resulting from:	
	Rainfall	Snowmelt	Rainfall	Snowmelt
1	2	3	4	5
23–03–51		371		
04–04–52	878			
04–01–53		612		
04–05–54	322			
16–01–55		898		
21–01–56		512		
01–06–57	681			
20–02–58		1040		
31–12–59		503		
10–11–60	528			
15–03–61		273		
03–04–62		1230		
14–03–63		672		
31–03–64		1440		
14–06–65	791			
15–02–66		985		
03–04–67	575			
27–02–68		956		
03–07–69	562			
14–05–70	4700			

Hungary / Hongrie / Hungría / Венгрия

TABLE II — ANNUAL MAXIMUM DISCHARGES AND VOLUMES (cont'd)

Country: **Hungary (11)**
River: **Sajó**
Gauging Station: **Felsözsolca**

| Date | Maximum discharge (m³/s) resulting from: | | Maximum volume (10⁶m³) corresponding to max. discharge resulting from: | |
| | Rainfall | Snowmelt | Rainfall | Snowmelt |
1	2	3	4	5
14—05—51	267			
04—04—52	254			
04—01—53		422		
07—07—54	148			
10—08—55	195			
05—04—56	107			
18—02—57		74		
03—07—58	227			
11—01—59		216		
29—07—60	319			
08—01—61		116		
09—04—62	224			
17—03—63		191		
25—03—64		141		
13—06—65		379		
26—02—66		303		
10—04—67	318			
27—02—68		108		
19—03—69		133		

Country: **Hungary (12)**
River: **Zagyva**
Gauging Station: **Jásztelek**

| Date | Maximum discharge (m³/s) resulting from: | | Maximum volume (10⁶m³) corresponding to max. discharge resulting from: | |
| | Rainfall | Snowmelt | Rainfall | Snowmelt |
1	2	3	4	5
01—04—51	45			
15—12—52	123			
10—01—53		282		
13—06—54	141			
19—02—55		56		
01—01—56		32		
17—02—57		54		
14—06—58	80			
10—01—59		62		
14—12—60	29			
12—06—61	24			
08—04—62	23			
15—03—63		154		
25—03—64		28		
12—06—65	181			
10—02—66		165		
02—03—67		44		
21—12—68	18			
21—02—69		145		

113

TABLE II – ANNUAL MAXIMUM DISCHARGES AND VOLUMES (cont'd)

Country:	Hungary (14)			
River:	Maros			
Gauging Station:	Makó			

	Maximum discharge (m³/s) resulting from:		Maximum volume (10⁶m³) corresponding to max. discharge resulting from:	
Date	Rainfall	Snowmelt	Rainfall	Snowmelt
1	2	3	4	5
13–05–51	416			
08–04–52	634			
16–04–53	515			
10–06–54	523			
01–03–55		720		
03–05–56	771			
03–06–57	745			
03–05–58	828			
26–05–59	495			
01–08–60	559			
10–06–61	468			
13–04–62	778			
18–04–63	487			
08–04–64	710			
21–06–65	725			
01–06–66	602			
07–04–67	745			
01–03–68		552		
17–07–69	682			
20–05–70	2130			

Country:				
River:				
Gauging Station:				

	Maximum discharge (m³/s) resulting from:		Maximum volume (10⁶m³) corresponding to max. discharge resulting from:	
Date	Rainfall	Snowmelt	Rainfall	Snowmelt
1	2	3	4	5

TABLE IV — CHARACTERISTICS OF RAINFALL FLOODS

			Characteristic element							Type of probability curve	
No.	River	Gauging station	Q_{max} (m^3/s)	Date	h (mm)	T_T (hours)	t_i (hours)	P_W (%)	$P_{Q_{max}}$ (%)	for P_W	for $P_{Q_{max}}$
1	2	3	4	5	6	7	8	9	10	11	12
1	Danube	Bratislava	9220	16—06—65	137	1080	384		2.3		Gamma
2	Rába	Szentgotthárd	329	12—07—72	58	120	48		20.0		"
3	Mura	Letenye	1580	19—07—72	110	480	240		0.1		"
4	Dráva	Barcs	3040	19—07—72	110	720	240		0.1		"
5	Általér	Tatabánya	164	09—06—53	25	26	8		0.1		"
6	Tisza	Vásárosnamény	3930	15—05—70	108	268	72		0.95		"
7	Tisza	Szolnok	2450	28—05—70	35	600	192		7.75		"
8	Tisza	Szeged	3830	30—05—70	50	600	360		2.5		"
9	Szamos	Csenger	4700	14—05—70	120	192	48		0.07		"
10	Bodrog	Felsöberecki	652	06—04—70	93	792	240		17.3		"
11	Sajó	Felsözsolca	379	13—06—65	39	120	72		16.8		"
12	Zagyva	Jásztelek	181	12—06—65	25	312	132		0.70		"
13	H. Körös	Gyoma	1550	14—06—70	104	1220	480		0.27		"
14	Maros	Makó	2440	20—05—70	54	1320	240		0.07		"

	Method of curve fitting		Rainfall forming flood (mm)	Snowmelt during floods (mm)	Maximum daily rainfall (mm)	Date	Hourly maximum rainfall (mm)	Date	Antecedent precipitation for	
No.	for W	for Q_{max}							10 days (mm)	30 days (mm)
1	13	14	15	16	17	18	19	20	21	22
1		Moments	220						50	230
2		"	80						30	80
3		"	130						120	180
4		"	160						100	150
5		"	60							
6		"	95							
7		"	35							
8		"	72						40	
9		"	93							
10		"	41							
11		"	76							
12		"	130						40	60
13		"	54						18	66
14		"	110						40	

India / Inde / Индия

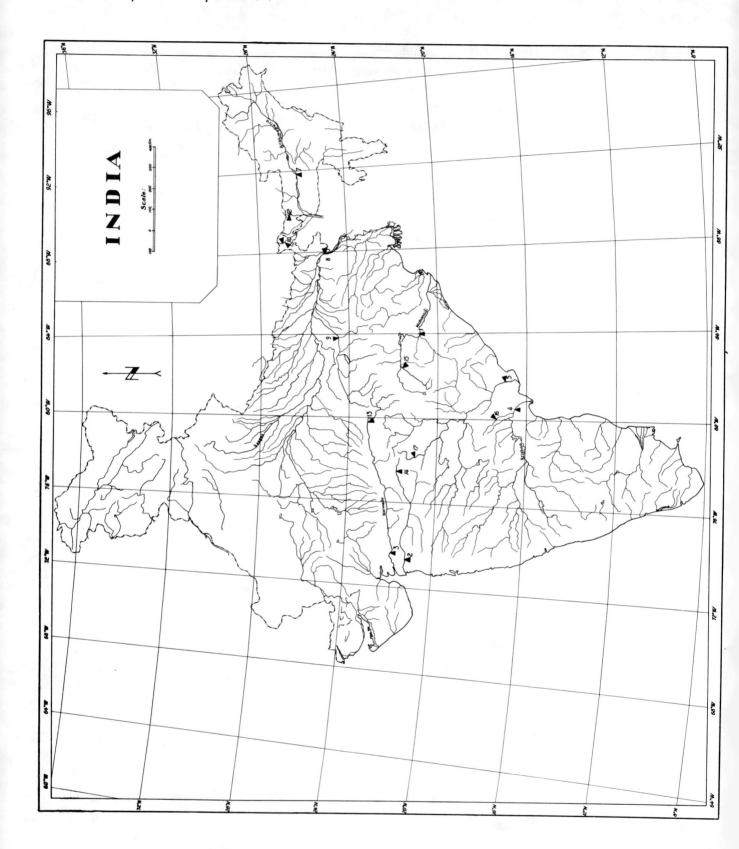

116

TABLE I — CHARACTERISTICS OF BASIN

				GAUGING STATION					BASIN				
	River River system	Name	Period of records	Co-ordinates		Distance (km) from gauging site		Mean slope of river I_r (%)	Area A (km²)	Altitude (m)			
				Lat.	Long.	to remotest point of river system L_{rs}	to projection of centre of basin on main course L_{ca}			Mean H_m	Max. H_{max}	Min. H_{min}	
No.													
1	2	3	4	5	6	7	8	9	10	11	12	13	
1	Mahanadi	Baramul	1946–68	N 20:30	E 84:50	628	343	0.062	127000		442	49.6	
2	Tapi	Kathore	1940–67	21:17	72:57	653	341	0.092	64400		600	0	
3	Narmada	Garudeshwar	1948–68	21:45	73:55	1006	436	0.054	87800		900	361	
4	Krishna	Vijayawada	1894–1958	16:31	80:37	1014	547	0.063	257000		900	250	
5	Godavari	Dowlaishwaram	1941–58	16:55	81:47	1175	467	0.046	309000		600	60	
6	Kosi	Sunakhambhi Khola	1947–67	26:55	87:06	483	161	1.03	66900		5100	106	
7	Brahmaputra	Pandu	1955–70	26:12	91:30	2221	1159	0.25	404000		5700	150	
8	Ganga	Farrakka	1948–67	25:00	87:55	2012	982	0.266	935000		5500		
9	Bankinadi Ganga	Br. No.171	1958–67	24:19	83:51	52.3	22.1	0.36	373	250	344	158	
10	Chell Brahmaputra	Br. No.95	1964, 66, 67	26:57	88:38	28.7	17.5	7.38	119	981	2260	148	

					BASIN							
	Width (km)		Mean slope I_b (%)	Soils	Cover	Weighted lake area P_L (%)	Swamps R_s (%)	Mean annual precipitation P (mm)	Annual runoff Q (mm)	Mean annual temperature T (°C)	Regulating capacity of reservoirs α	
	Mean B_m	Max. B_{max}										
No.												
1	14	15	16	17	18	19	20	21	22	23	24	
1	202	463						1410	436	26.9		
2	91	201						759	265	26.7		
3	87	175						1320	419	24.7		
4	254	563						1390	217	25.9		
5	263	595						1120	332	26.2		
6	138	386						1670	777			
7	182	676						2410	1222	24		
8	465	917						1100	398	25.1		
9	7.2	12.9	3.6	Red Soil	F(75), C(22), U(03)			1200				
10	4.2	9.2	24	Loam & Clay	F(78), C(08), U(14)			3400				

TABLE I – CHARACTERISTICS OF BASIN (cont'd)

				GAUGING STATION					BASIN			
						Distance (km) from gauging site						
						to remotest point of river system L_{rs}	to projection of centre of basin on main course L_{ca}	Mean slope of river I_r (%)	Area A (km²)	Altitude (m)		
	River _River system_	Name	Period of records	Co-ordinates						Mean H_m	Max. H_{max}	Min. H_{min}
No.				Lat.	Long.							
1	2	3	4	5	6	7	8	9	10	11	12	13
				N	E							
11	Gish _Brahmaputra_	Br. No.91	1966–68	26:53	88:37	33.2	14.4	6.40	133	1010	2280	153
12	Kalajani _Brahmaputra_	Br. No.242	1961–62, 68, 69	26:41	89:25	32.0	19.2	7.02	230	670	2350	100
13	Tairhia _Narmada_	Br. No.253	1966–69	22:52	79:50	30.6	13.8	0.63	114	526	610	417
14	Uma _Tapti_	Br. No.394	1958–59 61–65	20:46	77:29	43.2	17.9	0.37	350	343	442	284
15	Lilagar _Mahanadi_	Br. No.12	1962–65	22:02	82:20	64.0	27.3	0.20	647	291	366	240
16	Bhooga Vagu _Krishna_	Br. No.642	1958–59 61–64	17:23	80:11	40.1	18.5	0.38	326	189	274	125
17	Kulbera _Godavari_	Br. No.228	1966–69	21:58	78:57	44.6	25.4	0.50	503	717	854	631

					BASIN						
	Width (km)		Mean slope I_b (%)			Weighted lake area P_L (%)	Swamps R_s (%)	Mean annual precipitation P (mm)	Annual runoff Q (mm)	Mean annual temperature T (°C)	Regulating capacity of reservoirs α
No.	Mean B_m	Max. B_{max}		Soils	Cover						
1	14	15	16	17	18	19	20	21	22	23	24
11	4.0	8.0	42	Loam & Clay	F(95), C(02), U(03)				3350		
12	7.2	16.5	23	Hilly Latrite	F(60), C(20), U(20)				3900		
13	3.7	7.2	8.1	Black Cotton	F(84), C(10), U(06)				1470		
14	8.1	12.8	2.1						900		
15	10.1	19.2	2.0						1270		
16	8.1	13.1	1.8	Black Cotton	F(50), C(30), U(20)				915		
17	11.3	19.2	4.7	Clay Loam & Red soil	F(25), C(40), U(35)				1100		

TABLE II — ANNUAL MAXIMUM DISCHARGES AND VOLUMES

Country:	India (1)
River:	Mahanadi
Gauging Station:	Baramul

Date	Maximum discharge (m³/s) resulting from:		Maximum volume (10⁶m³) corresponding to max. discharge resulting from:	
	Rainfall	Snowmelt	Rainfall	Snowmelt
1	2	3	4	5
25–08–46	39400		17100	
02–09–47	39200		17400	
18–08–48	28800		18000	
09–09–49	20600		5140	
06–08–50	30500		17900	
06–08–51	17600		13800	
12–08–52	28600		17700	
11–08–53	28700		24100	
17–09–54	16500		4310	
05–09–55	30900		16500	
22–08–56	16800		9290	
26–08–57	16600		13400	
17–08–58	28100		11700	
13–09–59	34200		15600	
17–08–60	36300		10900	
11–07–61	30100		27100	
05–08–62	21300		7010	
14–09–63	26400		10300	
28–08–64	24600		31400	
27–08–65	14400		2060	
30–07–66	19600		8650	
02–08–67	21900		13900	
15–08–68	20500		14200	

Country:	India (2)
River:	Tapi
Gauging Station:	Kathore

Date	Maximum discharge (m³/s) resulting from:		Maximum volume (10⁶m³) corresponding to max. discharge resulting from:	
	Rainfall	Snowmelt	Rainfall	Snowmelt
1	2	3	4	5
01–08–40	6880		2550	
14–07–41	13600		3390	
06–08–42	21500		5140	
20–08–43	5070			
24–08–44	25500		14500	
05–09–45	6230		989	
04–08–46	7800		4300	
30–09–47	8270		1630	
02–09–48	7210		1560	
27–09–49	13600		9320	
18–09–50	11300		1210	
10–08–51	4580		897	
06–08–52	3270		488	
07–08–53	6680		734	
02–09–58	8680		2350	
01–09–59	15000		5040	
06–08–60	3850		956	
18–08–61	18500		3230	
11–07–63	4900		642	
24–09–64	3480		1170	
28–07–65	7140		1690	
08–09–66	10500		3040	
03–07–67	9580		1980	

TABLE II – ANNUAL MAXIMUM DISCHARGES AND VOLUMES (cont'd)

Country: India (3)   **River:** Narmada   **Gauging Station:** Garudeshwar

Date	Maximum discharge (m³/s) resulting from: Rainfall	Snowmelt	Maximum volume (10⁶m³) corresponding to max. discharge resulting from: Rainfall	Snowmelt
1	2	3	4	5
06–08–48	20100		7420	
17–09–49	35100		8070	
17–09–50	36800		7100	
09–08–51	11900		2020	
05–08–52	11900		5640	
07–08–53	19100		3900	
24–09–54	29900		11400	
01–09–55	27000		15100	
08–08–56	13400		13400	
23–08–57	25300		4600	
01–09–58	20300		4000	
15–09–59	43200		21000	
19–08–60	19700		11200	
17–09–61	47700		21800	
17–09–63	14800		3280	
13–08–64	22900		12500	
30–07–65	16200		2890	
03–08–66	12700		3100	
01–09–07	22600		10300	
06–08–68	58000		10700	

Country: India (4)   **River:** Krishna   **Gauging Station:** Vijayawada

Date	Maximum discharge (m³/s) resulting from: Rainfall	Snowmelt	Maximum volume (10⁶m³) corresponding to max. discharge resulting from: Rainfall	Snowmelt
1	2	3	4	5
28–07–94	16400		15800	
14–08–95	14000		13400	
07–08–96	21500		30200	
16–08–97	15800		9310	
27–07–98	17600		13200	
17–09–99	11500		6470	
20–07–00	20300		11600	
17–08–01	18900		8870	
23–07–02	15500		6960	
07–10–03	30000		9780	
11–07–04	13600		5730	
30–07–05	13700		5030	
30–07–06	13100		7730	
01–08–07	14000		16400	
29–09–08	16200		7730	
30–07–09	18500		12300	
30–09–10	10500		1680	
23–07–11	9050		2790	
30–07–12	15400		15600	
24–07–13	11800		11300	
11–08–14	26900		5650	
06–08–15	16400		10100	
09–08–16	16200		8330	
04–09–17	14100		8490	
23–09–18	7190		2540	
01–10–19	12900		3390	
14–07–20	11100		16200	
05–08–21	15800		9810	
28–07–22	14100		6960	
26–07–23	17700		9060	

TABLE II – ANNUAL MAXIMUM DISCHARGES AND VOLUMES (cont'd)

Country: India (4) cont'd
River: Krishna
Gauging Station: Vijayawada

Date	Maximum discharge (m³/s) resulting from:		Maximum volume (10⁶m³) corresponding to max. discharge resulting from:	
	Rainfall	Snowmelt	Rainfall	Snowmelt
1	2	3	4	5
05–09–24	18000		5990	
24–09–25	24500		11700	
15–08–26	16600		6190	
02–08–27	15900		8680	
02–10–28	13100		2520	
07–10–29	13000		2850	
27–07–30	10500		3370	
18–08–31	13300		9910	
08–08–32	14500		6140	
11–08–33	17900		8910	
20–08–34	10900		4130	
02–09–35	10200		3200	
04–07–36	9910		2520	
30–07–37	11100		5910	
27–09–38	10500		8380	
20–07–39	11400		7520	
26–08–40	10000		1410	
11–07–41	10800		5680	
12–07–42	10800		8530	
18–07–43	12100		4360	
19–07–44	10900		11000	
14–07–45	10600		9390	
13–08–46	13500		18000	
28–09–47	12600		8760	
22–08–48	10500		5990	
24–09–49	25900		14800	
27–07–50	16000		19300	
31–07–51	10200		8610	
01–08–52	11500		11300	
21–08–53	13500		8450	

Country: India (4) cont'd
River: Krishna
Gauging Station: Vijayawada

Date	Maximum discharge (m³/s) resulting from:		Maximum volume (10⁶m³) corresponding to max. discharge resulting from:	
	Rainfall	Snowmelt	Rainfall	Snowmelt
1	2	3	4	5
22–07–54	14500		14200	
12–08–55	14200		7680	
11–08–56	23500		10000	
20–07–57	16800		10500	
28–07–58	21000		10100	

TABLE II — ANNUAL MAXIMUM DISCHARGES AND VOLUMES (cont'd)

Country: India (5)
River: Godavari
Gauging Station: Dowlaishwaram

| Date | Maximum discharge (m³/s) resulting from: | | Maximum volume (10⁶m³) corresponding to max. discharge resulting from: | |
	Rainfall	Snowmelt	Rainfall	Snowmelt
1	2	3	4	5
16—07—41	17000		11500	
06—08—42	57300		16000	
14—09—43	16700		10100	
26—09—44	16500		4400	
24—09—45	33000		7800	
21—08—46	58500		21100	
27—09—47	32700		14600	
31—08—48	29000		3700	
16—08—49	28400		5830	
28—07—50	17600		12200	
06—08—51	24200		5740	
11—08—52	14100		2950	
16—08—53	78000		23300	
10—08—54	30700		14800	
01—07—55	11500		11100	
06—08—56	42800		15300	
25—08—57	48100		25700	
04—09—58	64000		27300	

Country: India (6)
River: Kosi
Gauging Station: Sunakhambhi Khola

| Date | Maximum discharge (m³/s) resulting from: | | Maximum volume (10⁶m³) corresponding to max. discharge resulting from: | |
	Rainfall	Snowmelt	Rainfall	Snowmelt
1	2	3	4	5
31—07—47	8850		3330	
13—07—48	11400		3700	
19—07—49	10600		1550	
20—08—50	9850		3660	
24—08—51	6810		3020	
24—09—52	8680		2610	
27—08—53	5420		1470	
27—07—54	17400		4950	
07—07—55	5630		1760	
26—08—56	4580		1110	
12—08—57	7170		4980	
25—08—58	7480		1630	
16—08—59	5110		1770	
28—09—60	6790		556	
19—08—61	6540		6200	
02—08—62	8560		2190	
21—08—63	6470		1010	
04—08—64	8720		1510	
11—08—65	6440		1910	
24—08—66	9870		3010	
10—08—67	9360		950	

TABLE II – ANNUAL MAXIMUM DISCHARGES AND VOLUMES   (cont'd)

Country:	India (7)					Country:	India (8)			
River:	Brahmaputra					River:	Ganga			
Gauging Station:	Pandu					Gauging Station:	Farrakka			

Date	Maximum discharge (m³/s) resulting from:		Maximum volume (10⁶m³) corresponding to max. discharge resulting from:		Date	Maximum discharge (m³/s) resulting from:		Maximum volume (10⁶m³) corresponding to max. discharge resulting from:	
	Rainfall	Snowmelt	Rainfall	Snowmelt		Rainfall	Snowmelt	Rainfall	Snowmelt
1	2	3	4	5	1	2	3	4	5
29–07–55	52700		60000		23–08–49	56600		86600	
28–06–56	52500		55200		21–08–50	58100		96900	
10–08–57	58400		45200		29–08–51	45900		17100	
29–08–58	62000		66200		05–09–52	55200		63400	
24–06–59	53500		40300		28–08–53	61700		34100	
18–09–60	58700		49600		22–08–54	72900		70200	
17–07–61	51800		23000		27–08–55	67900		61300	
24–08–62	72700				19–09–56	62900		25900	
25–08–63	43400				09–09–57	55700		17700	
09–08–65	31800				19–08–58	59100		109000	
29–08–66	52200		113000		19–08–59	54200		49400	
11–07–67	45600		36500		02–09–60	59700		89500	
25–06–68	36200		49600		31–08–61	53000		124000	
21–07–69	40500		21500		01–10–62	58800		15100	
27–07–70	49400				08–09–63	50700		24300	
					11–09–64	48800		34700	
					15–09–65	39400		8350	
					30–08–66	44500		40400	
					18–09–67	54500		30700	

TABLE II — ANNUAL MAXIMUM DISCHARGES AND VOLUMES (cont'd)

Country: India (9)
River: Bankinadi
Gauging Station: Bridge No. 171

| Date | Maximum discharge (m³/s) resulting from: | | Maximum volume (10⁶m³) corresponding to max. discharge resulting from: | |
| | Rainfall | . Snowmelt | Rainfall | Snowmelt |
1	2	3	4	5
01–08–60	246		8.3	
05–08–61	134		6.2	
23–09–62	427		29	
12–07–64	319		8.4	
06–09–65	157		6.5	
15–08–67	179		9.6	

Country: India (10)
River: Chell
Gauging Station: Bridge No. 95

| Date | Maximum discharge (m³/s) resulting from: | | Maximum volume (10⁶m³) corresponding to max. discharge resulting from: | |
| | Rainfall | Snowmelt | Rainfall | Snowmelt |
1	2	3	4	5
01–07–66	495		40	
18–07–67	787		70	

Country: India (11)
River: Gish
Gauging Station: Bridge No. 91

| Date | Maximum discharge (m³/s) resulting from: | | Maximum volume (10⁶m³) corresponding to max. discharge resulting from: | |
| | Rainfall | . Snowmelt | Rainfall | Snowmelt |
1	2	3	4	5
26–07–66	385		6.8	
18–07–67	479		13	
13–07–68	1170		36	

Country: India (12)
River: Kalajani
Gauging Station: Bridge No. 242

| Date | Maximum discharge (m³/s) resulting from: | | Maximum volume (10⁶m³) corresponding to max. discharge resulting from: | |
| | Rainfall | Snowmelt | Rainfall | Snowmelt |
1	2	3	4	5
20–06–68	250		5.4	
15–07–69	143		12	

Country: India (13)
River: Tairhla
Gauging Station: Bridge No. 253

| Date | Maximum discharge (m³/s) resulting from: | | Maximum volume (10⁶m³) corresponding to max. discharge resulting from: | |
| | Rainfall | . Snowmelt | Rainfall | Snowmelt |
1	2	3	4	5
31–07–67	191		8.2	
31–07–69	165		8.0	

Country: India (14)
River: Uma
Gauging Station: Bridge No. 394

| Date | Maximum discharge (m³/s) resulting from: | | Maximum volume (10⁶m³) corresponding to max. discharge resulting from: | |
| | Rainfall | Snowmelt | Rainfall | Snowmelt |
1	2	3	4	5
01–09–58	365		7.9	
30–08–59	790		12	
25–07–61	423		9.3	
19–09–62	822		31	
16–08–63	380		20	
20–07–64	326		12	

India / Inde / Индия

TABLE II — ANNUAL MAXIMUM DISCHARGES AND VOLUMES (cont'd)

Country: India (15)
River: Lilagar
Gauging Station: Bridge No. 12

| Date | Maximum discharge (m³/s) resulting from: | | Maximum volume (10⁶m³) corresponding to max. discharge resulting from: | |
| | Rainfall | Snowmelt | Rainfall | Snowmelt |
1	2	3	4	5
11—09—62	595		67	
11—08—63	940		72	
05—07—64	581		51	
23—09—65	496		39	

Country: India (16)
River: Bhooga Vagu
Gauging Station: Bridge No. 642

| Date | Maximum discharge (m³/s) resulting from: | | Maximum volume (10⁶m³) corresponding to max. discharge resulting from: | |
| | Rainfall | Snowmelt | Rainfall | Snowmelt |
1	2	3	4	5
30—09—58	318		9.1	
23—07—59	295		17	
25—07—61	397		16	
23—09—64	242		11	

Country: India (17)
River: Kulbera
Gauging Station: Bridge No. 228

| Date | Maximum discharge (m³/s) resulting from: | | Maximum volume (10⁶m³) corresponding to max. discharge resulting from: | |
| | Rainfall | Snowmelt | Rainfall | Snowmelt |
1	2	3	4	5
22—07—66	340		7.7	
14—09—68	1910		67	
25—08—69	640		9.7	

TABLE IV — CHARACTERISTICS OF RAINFALL FLOODS

No.	River	Gauging station	Q_{max} (m³/s)	Date	h (mm)	T_T (hours)	t_i (hours)	P_W (%)	$P_{Q_{max}}$ (%)	Type of probability curve for P_W	for $P_{Q_{max}}$
1	2	3	4	5	6	7	8	9	10	11	12
1	Mahanadi	Baramul	28800	18—08—48	143	480	72	29	32	Extreme value distribution	
			28700	11—08—53	191	600	216	13	32		"
			34200	13—09—59	124	288	120	40	16		"
			36300	17—08—60	86	408	48	66	13		"
			24600	28—08—64	250	792	528	4.2	49		"
2	Tapi	Kathore	13600	14—07—41	53	288	48	30	46		"
			21500	06—08—42	83	216	48	10	33		"
			25500	24—08—44	226	360	168	3.5	5.3		"
			7800	04—08—46	67	432	48	59	39		"
			6680	07—08—53	12	168	72	65	71		"
3	Narmada	Garudeshwar	30000	24—09—54	128	336	192	31	31		"
			43200	15—09—59	241	696	504	8.0	11		"
			47700	17—09—61	249	576	384	6.8	7.7		"
			22900	13—08—64	142	696	96	27	48		"
			58000	06—08—68	122	312	144	36	3.2		"
4	Krishna	Vijayawada	16700	27—07—98	51	720	168	13	21		"
			20300	19—07—00	45	576	384	21	13		"
			30000	07—10—03	38	336	216	36	1.3		"
			25900	24—09—49	58	480	120	7.9	3.5		"
			16000	27—07—50	75	576	264	1.4	36		"

No.	Method of curve fitting for W	for Q_{max}	Rainfall forming flood (mm)	Snowmelt during floods (mm)	Maximum daily rainfall (mm)	Date	Hourly maximum rainfall (mm)	Date	Antecedent precipitation for 10 days (mm)	30 days (mm)
1	13	14	15	16	17	18	19	20	21	22
1	Eye fitting		250		90.0	15—08—48			218	420
	"		254		50.8	04—08—63			234	465
	"		253		50.3	13—09—59			208	437
	"		240		46.2	01—08—60			134	363
	"		434		54.9	16—08—64			144	477
2	Least squares		108		97.5	12—07—41			151	315
	"		129		68.5	04—08—42			181	338
	"		268		172	17—08—44			277	419
	"		183		42.2	27—07—46			162	276
	"		71		34.0	05—08—53	11.9	05—08—53	140	281
3	"		206		60.0	23—09—54	52.8	16—09—54	199	472
	"		314		38.1	04—09—59	37.5	14—09—59	186	415
	"		501		117	09—09—61	63.0	15—09—61	378	695
	"		311		53.5	12—08—64	17.8	16—08—64	170	310
	"		212		99.0	05—08—68	70.5	13—08—68	302	497
4	Eye fitting		179		32.3	27—07—98			187	378
	"		220		55.4	14—07—00			196	409
	"		118		24.4	03—10—03			141	278
	"		198		39.6	23—09—49	19.3	23—09—49	199	347
	"		257		43.7	27—07—50	33.5	20—07—50	205	392

TABLE IV — CHARACTERISTICS OF RAINFALL FLOODS (cont'd)

No.	River	Gauging station	Q_{max} (m³/s)	Date	h (mm)	T_T (hours)	t_i (hours)	P_W (%)	$P_{Q_{max}}$ (%)	Type of probability curve for P_W	for $P_{Q_{max}}$
1	2	3	4	5	6	7	8	9	10	11	12
5	Godavari	Dowlaishwaram	57300	06—08—42	52	288	144	9.1	15	Extreme value distribution	
			16700	14—09—43	33	528	144	59	81	"	
			58500	21—08—46	68	480	240	18	14	"	
			77900	16—08—53	75	216	120	13	4.8	"	
			64000	04—09—58	88	384	192	7.3	10	"	
6	Kosi	Sunakhambhi Khola	11400	13—07—48	50.0	462	264	25	10	"	
			10600	19—07—49	23.1	286	120	71	14	"	
			17400	27—07—54	74.0	328	192	9.5	0.6	"	
			9650	20—08—50	54.8	462	144	24	27	"	
			8720	04—08—64	22.6	336	192	73	50	"	
7	Brahmaputra	Pandu	52700	29—07—55	148	1320	648	25	38	"	
			52500	28—06—56	137	744	360	34	40	"	
			58400	10—08—57	112	1080	840	63	19	"	
			62000	29—08—58	164	768	240	14	12	"	
			72700	24—08—62					2.5	"	
8	Ganga	Farrakka	58100	21—08—50	104	1540	696	12	36	"	
			62900	19—09—56	28	504	240	80	20	"	
			59100	19—08—58	117	1560	552	8.3	30	"	
			59700	02—09—60	96	1320	672	16	29	"	
			53000	31—08—61	133	1440	720	5.0	60	"	

No.	Method of curve fitting for W	for Q_{max}	Rainfall forming flood (mm)	Snowmelt during floods (mm)	Maximum daily rainfall (mm)	Date	Hourly maximum rainfall (mm)	Date	Antecedent precipitation for 10 days (mm)	30 days (mm)
1	13	14	15	16	17	18	19	20	21	22
5	Eye fitting		68		38.9	05—08—42			135	375
	"		126		31.3	18—09—43			104	266
	"		109		22.6	19—08—46			94	394
	"		86		28.7	13—08—53	29.2	12—08—53	151	408
	"		116		43.0	31—08—58	49.4	27—08—58	198	394
6	Least squares		265		38.6	13—07—48	37.8	20—07—48	133	355
	"		375		28.5	01—07—49	35.6	17—07—49	138	416
	"		499		80.3	26—07—54	31.0	26—07—54	276	528
	"		382		43.7	18—08—50	25.4	14—08—50	185	423
	"		185		50.2	04—08—64	17.1	25—07—64	160	517
7	"		471		32.5	26—07—55	29.5	23—07—55	188	479
	"		341		43.9	15—06—56			169	480
	"		534		41.7	08—07—57	46.7	07—07—57	171	402
	"		361		30.5	25—08—58	50.0	09—08—58	160	490
	"		323		56.6	18—08—62	40.0	24—08—62	113	491
8	"		482		24.6	02—08—50	50.8	13—08—50	126	363
	"		129		20.3	12—08—56	64.5	10—09—56	101	269
	"		536		28.7	10—08—58	59.3	14—09—58	115	409
	"		456		22.5	18—08—60	70.0	17—08—60	120	389
	"		569		23.2	02—08—61	74.8	16—08—61	105	362

India / Inde / Индия

TABLE IV — CHARACTERISTICS OF RAINFALL FLOODS (cont'd)

No.	River	Gauging station	Q_{max} (m^3/s)	Date	h (mm)	T_T (hours)	t_i (hours)	P_W (%)	$P_{Q_{max}}$ (%)	Type of probability curve for P_W	for $P_{Q_{max}}$
1	2	3	4	5	6	7	8	9	10	11	12
9	Bankinadi	Br. No.171	329	08–09–64	19	28	9				
10	Chell	Br. No.95	275	10–07–66	32	25	7				
11	Gish	Br. No.91	479	18–07–67	65	21	9				
12	Kalajani	Br. No.242	250	20–06–68	18	15	6				
13	Tairhia	Br. No.253	191	31–07–67	58	34	9				
14	Uma	Br. No.394	822	18–09–62	83	28	8				
15	Lilagar	Br. No.12	496	22–09–65	43	45	14				
16	Bhooga Vagu	Br. No.642	397	25–07–61	39	40	11				
17	Kulbera	Br. No.228	340	22–07–66	15	28	6				

No.	Method of curve fitting for W	for Q_{max}	Rainfall forming flood (mm)	Snowmelt during floods (mm)	Maximum daily rainfall (mm)	Date	Hourly maximum rainfall (mm)	Date	Antecedent precipitation for 10 days (mm)	30 days (mm)
1	13	14	15	16	17	18	19	20	21	22
9			32		110	01–08–60	57	01–08–60	59	
10			77		222	18–07–67	55	18–07–67	237	
11			216		262	18–07–67	48	21–06–68	412	
12			39		187	26–08–67	33	26–08–67	113	
13			116		128	31–07–67	24	31–07–67	132	
14			111		117	18–09–62	53	26–09–59	70	
15			105		162	10–08–63	69	10–08–63	53	
16			65		183	24–07–61	35	24–07–61	156	
17			38		142	15–09–68	21	15–09–68	100	

128

Italy / Italie / Italia / Италия

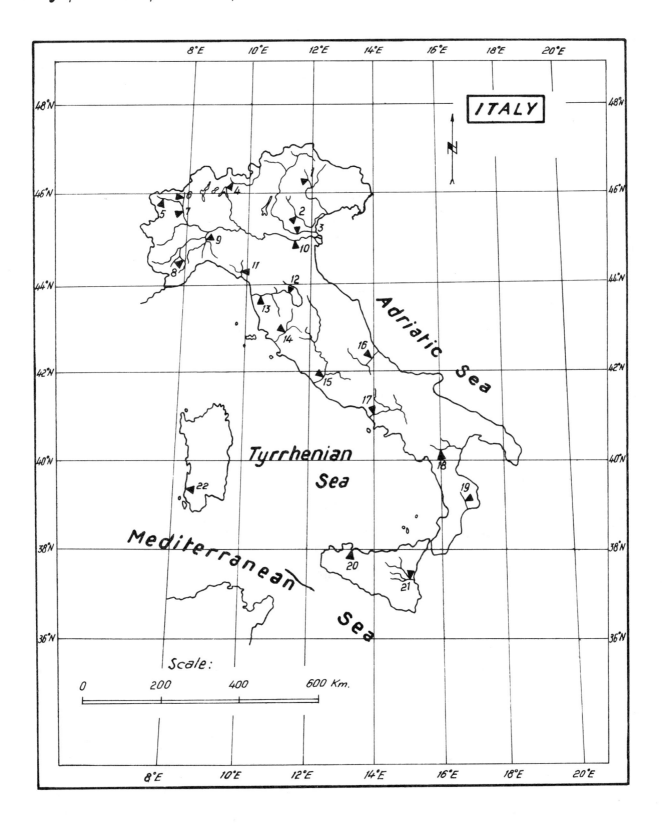

TABLE I — CHARACTERISTICS OF BASIN

		GAUGING STATION							BASIN			
						Distance (km) from gauging site				Altitude (m)		
	River / River system	Name	Period of records	Co-ordinates Lat.	Long.	to remotest point of river system L_{rs}	to projection of centre of basin on main course L_{ca}	Mean slope of river I_r (%)	Area A (km²)	Mean H_m	Max. H_{max}	Min. H_{min}
No.	2	3	4	5	6	7	8	9	10	11	12	13
1				N	E							
1	Boite	Vodo	1930–56	46:25	12:15	42	18		323	1830	3260	818
2	Bacchiglione	Montegaldelia	1930–60	45:26	11:41	80	53		1380	649	2340	15
3	Adige	Boara Pisani	1922–60	45:06	11.48	360	227		12000	1540	900	9
4	Adda	Fuentes	1921–60	46:09	09:25	115	50		2500	1840	4050	198
5	Rutor	Promise	1931–60	45:42	06:55	7	5		49.8	2620	3490	1480
6	Lys	Gressoney S. Jean	1926–53	45:46	07:51	10	7		90.6	2620	4530	1400
7	Dora Baltea	Tavagnasco	1925–60	45:32	07:52	110	50		3310	2080	4810	263
8	Corsaglia	Presa Centrale Molline	1931–59	44:18	07:52	14	8		88.5	1530	2630	620
9	Tanaro	Montecastello	1923–60	44:57	08:43	189	76		7990	663	3300	79
10	Po	Ponte Lagoscuro	1918–60	44:53	11:36	556	285		70100		4810	8
11	Magra	Calamazza	1930–70	44:11	09:57	35	10		939	612	1900	45

	BASIN										
	Width (km)		Mean slope I_b(%)	Soils	Cover	Weighted lake area P_L (%)	Swamps R_s (%)	Mean annual precipitation P (mm)	Annual runoff Q (mm)	Mean annual temperature T (°C)	Regulating capacity of reservoirs α
	Mean B_m	Max. B_{max}									
No.	14	15	16	17	18	19	20*	21	22	23	24
1	7.7	17		Rendzinas and lithosoils	F	0	0	1120	1030.		0
2	17.3	39		Rendzinas, Brown, alluvial s.	F, C	0	0	1480	672		0
3	33.2	107		Brown, podzolic alluvial s.	F, C, U	0.01	1.3	967	639		0.050
4	21.7	40		Brown podzolic s.	F	0.02	3.7	1110	1060		0.122
5	7.1	9		Rankers, lithosoils	F, U	0	23.0	1340	1680		0
6	9.1	8		Brown, podzolic s.	F, U	0.20	16.7	1190	1360		0.038
7	30.1	45		Brown, podzolic, lithosoils	F, C, U	0.01	5.5	965	951		0.034
8	6.3	11		Brown s.	F, C	0	0	1370	1070.		0
9	42.2	95		Brown s.	F, C	0.01	0.01	1030	528		0.004
10	126	240		Brown, podzolic, alluvial s.	F, C, U	0.01	0.01	1110	668		0.033
11	26.8	30		Brown, podzolic s.	F, C	0.01	0	1760	1360		0.004

TABLE I — CHARACTERISTICS OF BASIN (cont'd)

				GAUGING STATION					BASIN			
						Distance (km) from gauging site					Altitude (m)	
						to remotest point of river system L_{rs}	to projection of centre of basin on main course L_{ca}	Mean slope of river I_r (%)	Area A (km^2)	Mean H_m	Max. H_{max}	Min. H_{min}
No.	River / River system	Name	Period of records	Co-ordinates Lat.	Long.							
1	2	3	4	5	6	7	8	9	10	11	12	13
				N	E							
12	Sieve	Fornacina	1931–70	43:48	11:30	54	26		831	490	1660	92
13	Arno	S. Giovanni Alla Vena	1924–70	43:40	10:36	204	85		8190	330	1660	7
14	Ombrone	Sasso D'ombrone	1926–70	42:56	11:21	81	29		2660	346	1730	55
15	Tevere	Roma	1921–60	41:54	12:30	362	137		16600	524	2490	1
16	Pescara	S. Teresa	1922–70	42:26	14:11	136	70		3130	940	2800	5
17	Volturno	Cancello Arnone	1931–60	41:05	14:02	175	78		5560	532	2240	3
18	Agri	Tarangelo	1926–60	40:17	16:00	34	14		507	870	2010	470
19	Alli	Orso	1925–60	39:02	16:34	19	10		46	1080	1520	450
20	Oreto	Parco	1924–70	38:04	13:18	14	5		75.6	608	1330	113
21	Simeto	Giarretta	1923–67	37:27	14:55	122	61		1830	793	3270	17
22	Flumini-maggiore	Flumini-maggiore	1925–70	39:26	8:29	16	8		83	421	1080	40

		BASIN									
	Width (km)		Mean slope I_b(%)			Weighted lake area P_L (%)	Swamps R_s (%)	Mean annual precipitation P (mm)	Annual runoff Q (mm)	Mean annual temperature T (°C)	Regulating capacity of reservoirs α
No.	Mean B_m	Max. B_{max}		Soils	Cover						
1	14	15	16	17	18	19	20*	21	22	23	24
12	15.4	19		Brown, gray podzolics	F, C	0	0	1220	596		0
13	40.1	91		Brown, gray podzolic, regosoils	F, C	0.01	0	1040	381		0.004
14	32.8	76		Brown, regosoils	C	0	0	924	323		0
15	45.7	108		Brown, andosoils	C	0.02	0	1030	444		0.053
16	23.0	67		Brown, rendzinas s.	C	0.01	0	896	534		0.001
17	31.8	54		Brown, rendzinas, alluvial s.	C	0.01	0	1160	557		0.005
18	14.9	24		Brown, rendzinas regosoils	C	0	0	1100	623		0
19	2.4	5		Brown podzolics	F, C	0	0	1560	845		0
20	5.4	10		Brown, rendzinas s.	C	0	0	1080	505		0
21	15.0	42		Brown, andosoils	C, U	0.01	0	747	309		0.26
22	5.2	8		Brown, regosoils	C	0	0	835	389		0

* Column 20 is replaced by glaciers instead of swamps.

TABLE II – ANNUAL MAXIMUM DISCHARGES AND VOLUMES

Country:	Italy (1)
River:	Boite
Gauging Station:	Vodo

Date	Maximum discharge (m³/s) resulting from:		Maximum volume (10⁶m³) corresponding to max. discharge resulting from:	
	Rainfall	Snowmelt	Rainfall	Snowmelt
1	2	3	4	5
30	76.0			
31	60.0			
32	43.5			
33	80.0			
34	82.0			
35	62.0			
37	113			
38	123			
39	97.0			
40	86.0			
41	77.0			
42	149			
43	67.0			
44	53.0			
45	111			
46	92.0			
47	64.0			
48	32.5			
49	25.0			
50	49.5			

Country:	Italy (2)
River:	Bacchiglione
Gauging Station:	Montegaldelia

Date	Maximum discharge (m³/s) resulting from:		Maximum volume (10⁶m³) corresponding to max. discharge resulting from:	
	Rainfall	Snowmelt	Rainfall	Snowmelt
1	2	3	4	5
30	230			
31	285			
32	100			
33	160			
34	325			
35	450			
36	289			
37	250			
38	143			
39	234			
40	315			
41	355			
42	183			
43	69			
44	205			
45	164			
46	158			
47	225			
48	306			
49	250			
50	189			
51	563			
52	288			
53	492			
54	227			
55	177			
56	353			
57	393			
58	324			
59	383			
60	403			

TABLE II — ANNUAL MAXIMUM DISCHARGES AND VOLUMES (cont'd)

Country: Italy (3)
River: Adige
Gauging Station: Boara Pisani

Date	Maximum discharge (m³/s) resulting from:		Maximum volume (10⁶m³) corresponding to max. discharge resulting from:	
	Rainfall	Snowmelt	Rainfall	Snowmelt
1	2	3	4	5
22	525			
23	680			
24	990			
25	750			
26	1650			
27	1070			
28	1700			
29	570			
30	850			
31	990			
32	725			
33	1200			
34	1110			
35	1280			
36	985			
37	1380			
38	1340			
39	1090			
40	1150			
41	1050			
42	1560			
43	500			
44	425			
45	1000			
46	1260			
47	676			
48	996			
49	598			
51	1440			
52	950			

Country: Italy (3) cont'd
River: Adige
Gauging Station: Boara Pisani

Date	Maximum discharge (m³/s) resulting from:		Maximum volume (10⁶m³) corresponding to max. discharge resulting from:	
	Rainfall	Snowmelt	Rainfall	Snowmelt
1	2	3	4	5
53	1650			
54	920			
55	625			
56	514			
57	804			
58	822			
59	667			
60	1500			

TABLE II — ANNUAL MAXIMUM DISCHARGES AND VOLUMES (cont'd)

Country:	Italy (4)
River:	Adda
Gauging Station:	Fuentes

Date	Maximum discharge (m³/s) resulting from:		Maximum volume (10⁶m³) corresponding to max. discharge resulting from:	
	Rainfall	Snowmelt	Rainfall	Snowmelt
1	2	3	4	5
27	1160			
28	860			
29	502			
30	517			
31	517			
32	581			
33	688			
34	429			
35	1000			
36	525			
37	930			
38	418			
39	759			
40	502			
41	443			
42	863			
43	329			
44	510			
45	541			
46	682			
47	457			
48	1060			
49	225			
50	334			
51	878			
52	715			
53	475			
54	820			
55	556			
56	779			

Country:	Italy (4) cont'd
River:	Adda
Gauging Station:	Fuentes

Date	Maximum discharge (m³/s) resulting from:		Maximum volume (10⁶m³) corresponding to max. discharge resulting from:	
	Rainfall	Snowmelt	Rainfall	Snowmelt
1	2	3	4	5
57	744			
58	643			
59	248			
60	1070			

TABLE II – ANNUAL MAXIMUM DISCHARGES AND VOLUMES (cont'd)

Country:	Italy (5)
River:	Rutor
Gauging Station:	Promise

Date	Maximum discharge (m³/s) resulting from:		Maximum volume (10⁶m³) corresponding to max. discharge resulting from:	
	Rainfall	Snowmelt	Rainfall	Snowmelt
1	2	3	4	5
33		18.0		
34		16.8		
35		22.5		
36		27.0		
37		14.1		
38		16.6		
39		12.5		
40		24.3		
41		11.8		
42		11.7		
43		13.3		
52		17.1		
53		12.8		
54		14.8		
55		12.6		
56		16.7		
57		16.0		
58		12.2		
59		11.9		
60		11.9		

Country:	Italy (6)
River:	Lys
Gauging Station:	Gressoney St. Jean

Date	Maximum discharge (m³/s) resulting from:		Maximum volume (10⁶m³) corresponding to max. discharge resulting from:	
	Rainfall	Snowmelt	Rainfall	Snowmelt
1	2	3	4	5
33		18.2		
34		25.6		
35		39.4		
36		23.3		
37		33.2		
38		23.2		
39		26.3		
40		19.5		
41		20.7		
42		23.0		
48		65.4		
49		19.0		
50		20.0		
51		29.6		
52		17.8		
53		33.5		

TABLE II — ANNUAL MAXIMUM DISCHARGES AND VOLUMES (cont'd)

Country:	Italy (7)
River:	Dora Baltea
Gauging Station:	Tavagnasco

| Date | Maximum discharge (m³/s) resulting from: | | Maximum volume (10⁶m³) corresponding to max. discharge resulting from: | |
| | Rainfall | Snowmelt | Rainfall | Snowmelt |
1	2	3	4	5
29	570			
30	492			
31	478			
32	797			
33	464			
34	785			
35	744			
36	746			
37	915			
38	1080			
39	679			
40	598			
41	699			
42	715			
43	449			
44	1130			
45	1050			
46	710			
47	1070			
48	1950			
49	665			
50	323			
51	860			
52	350			
53	560			
54	1210			
55	595			
56	980			
57	1310			
58	690			

Country:	Italy (7) cont'd
River:	Dora Baltea
Gauging Station:	Tavagnasco

| Date | Maximum discharge (m³/s) resulting from: | | Maximum volume (10⁶m³) corresponding to max. discharge resulting from: | |
| | Rainfall | Snowmelt | Rainfall | Snowmelt |
1	2	3	4	5
59	498			
60	865			

TABLE II – ANNUAL MAXIMUM DISCHARGES AND VOLUMES (cont'd)

Country:	Italy (8)
River:	Corsaglia
Gauging Station:	Presa Centrale Molline

Date	Maximum discharge (m³/s) resulting from:		Maximum volume (10⁶m³) corresponding to max. discharge resulting from:	
	Rainfall	Snowmelt	Rainfall	Snowmelt
1	2	3	4	5
32	18.5			
33	16.6			
34	37.3			
35	21.6			
36	30.6			
37	35.5			
38	29.6			
39	33.9			
40	29.8			
41	29.9			
42	34.0			
43	20.2			
44	24.8			
45	50.8			
46	28.0			
47	133			
48	64.6			
49	42.4			
50	22.7			
52	20.0			
53	51.5			
54	34.8			
55	36.0			
56	33.0			
59	43.2			

Country:	Italy (9)
River:	Tanaro
Gauging Station:	Montecastello

Date	Maximum discharge (m³/s) resulting from:		Maximum volume (10⁶m³) corresponding to max. discharge resulting from:	
	Rainfall	Snowmelt	Rainfall	Snowmelt
1	2	3	4	5
33	1700			
35	3000			
36	1780			
37	2670			
38	1150			
39	922			
40	1220			
41	1750			
42	2030			
43	1460			
44	1440			
45	2400			
46	1420			
47	1760			
48	2200			
49	1850			
50	1660			
51	3170			
53	1600			
54	2130			
55	1400			
56	2030			
57	2300			
58	1820			
59	2480			
60	2330			

Italy / Italie / Italia / Италия

TABLE II – ANNUAL MAXIMUM DISCHARGES AND VOLUMES (cont'd)

Country: Italy (10)
River: Po
Gauging Station: Ponte Lagoscuro

Country: Italy (10) cont'd
River: Po
Gauging Station: Ponte Lagoscuro

Date	Maximum discharge (m³/s) resulting from:		Maximum volume (10⁶m³) corresponding to max. discharge resulting from:		Date	Maximum discharge (m³/s) resulting from:		Maximum volume (10⁶m³) corresponding to max. discharge resulting from:	
	Rainfall	Snowmelt	Rainfall	Snowmelt		Rainfall	Snowmelt	Rainfall	Snowmelt
1	2	3	4	5	1	2	3	4	5
18	5490				48	6760			
19	4240				49	7330			
20	7240				50	3260			
21	3000				51	10300			
22	2590				53	7440			
23	2980				54	4490			
24	3920				55	2410			
25	3510				56	5130			
26	8850				57	7070			
27	4240				58	5740			
28	8770				59	7770			
29	2230				60	6570			
30	5500								
31	3720								
32	4150								
33	4740								
34	6810								
35	6620								
36	6830								
37	7740								
38	4500								
39	3960								
40	5440								
41	6980								
42	4600								
43	3270								
44	3660								
45	6960								
46	5200								
47	5460								

TABLE II — ANNUAL MAXIMUM DISCHARGES AND VOLUMES (cont'd)

Country:	Italy (11)
River:	Magra
Gauging Station:	Calamazza

Date	Maximum discharge (m³/s) resulting from:		Maximum volume (10⁶m³) corresponding to max. discharge resulting from:	
	Rainfall	Snowmelt	Rainfall	Snowmelt
1	2	3	4	5
30	410			
31	1150			
32	899			
33	420			
34	3100			
35	2530			
36	758			
37	1220			
38	1330			
39	1410			
40	3100			
41	2470			
42	929			
43	586			
44	450			
46	1040			
47	1470			
48	1070			
49	2050			
50	1430			
51	3070			
52	2360			
53	1050			
54	1900			
55	1130			
56	674			
57	683			
58	1500			
59	2600			
60	3480			

Country:	Italy (11) cont'd
River:	Magra
Gauging Station:	Calamazza

Date	Maximum discharge (m³/s) resulting from:		Maximum volume (10⁶m³) corresponding to max. discharge resulting from:	
	Rainfall	Snowmelt	Rainfall	Snowmelt
1	2	3	4	5
61	1430			
62	809			
63	1010			
64	1510			
65	1650			
66	1880			
67	1470			
68	1920			
69	2530			
70	1490			

TABLE II – ANNUAL MAXIMUM DISCHARGES AND VOLUMES   (cont'd)

Country:	Italy (12)			
River:	Sieve			
Gauging Station:	Fornacina			

	Maximum discharge (m³/s) resulting from:		Maximum volume (10⁶m³) corresponding to max. discharge resulting from:	
Date	Rainfall	Snowmelt	Rainfall	Snowmelt
1	2	3	4	5
31	337			
32	212			
33	261			
34	462			
35	279			
36	346			
37	481			
38	170			
39	347			
40	454			
41	389			
42	386			
46	293			
47	312			
48	360			
49	551			
50	301			
51	679			
52	598			
53	1080			
54	402			
55	457			
56	173			
57	322			
58	445			
59	398			
60	763			
61	458			
62	334			

Country:	Italy (12) cont'd			
River:	Sieve			
Gauging Station:	Fornacina			

	Maximum discharge (m³/s) resulting from:		Maximum volume (10⁶m³) corresponding to max. discharge resulting from:	
Date	Rainfall	Snowmelt	Rainfall	Snowmelt
1	2	3	4	5
63	504			
64	427			
65	414			
66	1340			
67	527			
68	509			
69	478			
70	506			

Italy / Italie / Italia / Италия

TABLE II – ANNUAL MAXIMUM DISCHARGES AND VOLUMES (cont'd)

Country:	Italy (13)			
River:	Arno			
Gauging Station:	S. Giovanni Alla Vena			

Date	Maximum discharge (m³/s) resulting from:		Maximum volume (10⁶m³) corresponding to max. discharge resulting from:	
	Rainfall	Snowmelt	Rainfall	Snowmelt
1	2	3	4	5
24	1240			
25	1670		419	
26	1970		1030	
27	1460			
28	2030		1020	
29	2230			
30	1130			
31	2070		725	
32	1630		771	
33	1960		454	
34	2080		676	
35	1930			
36	1340			
37	1650			
38	764			
39	1460			
40	1520		598	
41		1570		1220
42	1550			
43	998			
46	1110			
47	1880			
48	1810			
49	2270			
50	820			
51	2010			
52	1100			
53	1500			
54	1360			
55	960			

Country:	Italy (13) cont'd			
River:	Arno			
Gauging Station:	S. Giovanni Alla Vena			

Date	Maximum discharge (m³/s) resulting from:		Maximum volume (10⁶m³) corresponding to max. discharge resulting from:	
	Rainfall	Snowmelt	Rainfall	Snowmelt
1	2	3	4	5
56	761			
57	756			
58	1610			
59	1280			
60	1690			
61	1370			
62	813			
63	1300			
64	1080			
65	934			
66	2290			
67	505			
68	1320			
69	966			
70	635			

141

TABLE II – ANNUAL MAXIMUM DISCHARGES AND VOLUMES (cont'd)

Country:	Italy (14)
River:	Ombrone
Gauging Station:	Sasso D'ombrone

| Date | Maximum discharge (m³/s) resulting from: | | Maximum volume (10⁶m³) corresponding to max. discharge resulting from: | |
	Rainfall	Snowmelt	Rainfall	Snowmelt
1	2	3	4	5
26	951			
27	680			
28	1610		531	
29	1460			
30	1190			
31	1150			
32	1570		281	
33	1370		98	
34	1480			
35	1760			
36	994			
37	1680			
38	1250		114	
39	2000			
40	2380			
41	1060			
42	1020			
49	972			
50	1110			
51	573			
52	346			
53	788			
54	607			
55	424			
56	668			
57	665			
58	1010			
59	747			
60	1570			
61	795			

Country:	Italy (14) cont'd
River:	Ombrone
Gauging Station:	Sasso D'ombrone

| Date | Maximum discharge (m³/s) resulting from: | | Maximum volume (10⁶m³) corresponding to max. discharge resulting from: | |
	Rainfall	Snowmelt	Rainfall	Snowmelt
1	2	3	4	5
62	535			
63	944			
64	843			
65	1700			
66	3110			
67	514			
68	857			
69	741			
70	477			

TABLE II — ANNUAL MAXIMUM DISCHARGES AND VOLUMES   (cont'd)

Country:	Italy (15)
River:	Tevere
Gauging Station:	Roma

Date	Maximum discharge (m³/s) resulting from:		Maximum volume (10⁶m³) corresponding to max. discharge resulting from:	
	Rainfall	Snowmelt	Rainfall	Snowmelt
1	2	3	4	5
22	1290			
23	2350			
24	1180			
25	1620			
26	1130			
27	945			
28	1680			
29	2090			
30	850			
31	1200			
32	1010			
33	1540			
34	1960			
35	1750			
36	1720			
37	2800			
38	1490			
39	1100			
40	1420			
41	1590			
42	1610			
43	787			
44	1400			
45	944			
46	1660			
47	2250			
48	1620			
49	772			
50	1020			
51	1490			

Country:	Italy (15) cont'd
River:	Tevere
Gauging Station:	Roma

Date	Maximum discharge (m³/s) resulting from:		Maximum volume (10⁶m³) corresponding to max. discharge resulting from:	
	Rainfall	Snowmelt	Rainfall	Snowmelt
1	2	3	4	5
52	1060			
53	1330			
54	1320			
55	917			
56	1400			
57	744			
58	977			
59	1330			
60	1390			

TABLE II — ANNUAL MAXIMUM DISCHARGES AND VOLUMES   (cont'd)

Country:	Italy (16)
River:	Pescara
Gauging Station:	S. Teresa

Date	Maximum discharge (m³/s) resulting from:		Maximum volume (10⁶m³) corresponding to max. discharge resulting from:	
	Rainfall	Snowmelt	Rainfall	Snowmelt
1	2	3	4	5
22	104			
23	134			
24	126			
25	128			
26	166			
27	120			
28	181			
29	366			
30	270			
36	218			
37	390			
38	314		58	
39	269			
40	654		145	
41	300			
42	376			
45	158			
46	247			
47	169			
48	314			
49	363			
50	144			
51	247			
52	183			
53	660			
54	291			
55	590			
56	414			
57	346			
58	225			

Country:	Italy (16) cont'd
River:	Pescara
Gauging Station:	S. Teresa

Date	Maximum discharge (m³/s) resulting from:		Maximum volume (10⁶m³) corresponding to max. discharge resulting from:	
	Rainfall	Snowmelt	Rainfall	Snowmelt
1	2	3	4	5
59	796			
60	354			
61	398			
65	152			
66	222			
67	224			
68	162			
69	252			
70	217			

TABLE II — ANNUAL MAXIMUM DISCHARGES AND VOLUMES   (cont'd)

Country:	Italy (17)
River:	Volturno
Gauging Station:	Cancello Arnone

Date	Maximum discharge (m³/s) resulting from:		Maximum volume (10⁶m³) corresponding to max. discharge resulting from:	
	Rainfall	Snowmelt	Rainfall	Snowmelt
1	2	3	4	5
31	1130			
32	672		152	
33	1240			
34	782			
35	1650			
37	1010			
39	982			
40	1250			
41	1130			
42	1190			
50	1290			
51	900			
52	1380		438	
53	1040		277	
54	680			
55	770			
56	808			
57	1040			
58	1120			
59	1050			
60	1620			

Country:	Italy (18)
River:	Agri
Gauging Station:	Tarangelo

Date	Maximum discharge (m³/s) resulting from:		Maximum volume (10⁶m³) corresponding to max. discharge resulting from:	
	Rainfall	Snowmelt	Rainfall	Snowmelt
1	2	3	4	5
26	116			
27	149			
28	156			
29	126			
30	165			
31	320			
32	134			
33	161			
34	124			
35	430		68	
36	155			
37	296		24	
38	265		25	
39	201			
40	327		42	
41	164		41	
42	113			
46	106			
47	135			
48	116			
49	98			
50	125			
51	194			
52	419			
53	240			
54	134			
55	82			
56	108			
58	111			
59	254			
60	262			

TABLE II – ANNUAL MAXIMUM DISCHARGES AND VOLUMES (cont'd)

Country:	Italy (19)
River:	Alli
Gauging Station:	Orso

Date	Maximum discharge (m³/s) resulting from: Rainfall	Snowmelt	Maximum volume (10⁶m³) corresponding to max. discharge resulting from: Rainfall	Snowmelt
1	2	3	4	5
28	20.6			
29	5.1			
30	18.1		4.9	
32	15.9			
33	37.6			
34	8.5			
35	7.4			
36	20.3			
37	8.5			
38	4.0			
39	11.4			
40	24.7			
41	7.8			
42	19.7			
44	20.0			
47	11.4			
48	4.7			
49	20.6			
50	8.8			
51	7.3			
52	6.0			
53	7.6			
55	11.8			
56	12.8			
57	10.6			
58	16.3			
59	27.0			
60	10.6			

Country:	Italy (20)
River:	Oreto
Gauging Station:	Parco

Date	Maximum discharge (m³/s) resulting from: Rainfall	Snowmelt	Maximum volume (10⁶m³) corresponding to max. discharge resulting from: Rainfall	Snowmelt
1	2	3	4	5
25	166			
27	232			
28	56			
29	48			
30	140			
31	248		23	
32	81			
33	134			
34	53			
35	36			
36	43			
37	40			
38	64			
39	303		12	
40	139		3	
41	87			
42	48			
43	87			
44	138			
46	58			
47	74			
48	129			
49	47			
50	76			
51	352		3	
52	176			
53	272			
54	146			
55	183		8	
56	122			

TABLE II – ANNUAL MAXIMUM DISCHARGES AND VOLUMES (cont'd)

Country:	Italy (20) cont'd
River:	Oreto
Gauging Station:	Parco

Date	Maximum discharge (m³/s) resulting from:		Maximum volume (10⁶m³) corresponding to max. discharge resulting from:	
	Rainfall	Snowmelt	Rainfall	Snowmelt
1	2	3	4	5
57	178			
58	140			
59	54			
60	109			
61	68			
62	89			
63	58			
64	60			
65	69			
66	113			
67	87			
68	81			
69	86			
70	50			

Country:	Italy (21)
River:	Simeto
Gauging Station:	Giarretta

Date	Maximum discharge (m³/s) resulting from:		Maximum volume (10⁶m³) corresponding to max. discharge resulting from:	
	Rainfall	Snowmelt	Rainfall	Snowmelt
1	2	3	4	5
25	1060			
26	150			
27	2130		298	
28	1360		144	
29	309			
30	474			
31	1740			
32	1200		98	
33	2260		168	
34	1510		145	
35	2020		176	
36	2330		115	
37	416			
38	842			
39	993		81	
40	1260			
41	774			
42	781			
49	2060			
50	1650		203	
51	2390			
52	132			
53	1440			
54	1470		110	
55	2230			
56	1340			
57	1390			
58	1920			
59	797			
60	579			

TABLE II — ANNUAL MAXIMUM DISCHARGES AND VOLUMES (cont'd)

Country:	Italy (21) cont'd
River:	Simeto
Gauging Station:	Giarretta

Date	Maximum discharge (m³/s) resulting from:		Maximum volume (10⁶m³) corresponding to max. discharge resulting from:	
	Rainfall	Snowmelt	Rainfall	Snowmelt
1	2	3	4	5
61	1010			
62	155			
63	448			
64	1130			
65	921			
66	572			
67	309			

Country:	Italy (22)
River:	Fluminimaggiore
Gauging Station:	Fluminimaggiore

Date	Maximum discharge (m³/s) resulting from:		Maximum volume (10⁶m³) corresponding to max. discharge resulting from:	
	Rainfall	Snowmelt	Rainfall	Snowmelt
1	2	3	4	5
27	60.0			
35	7.5			
36	41.0			
37	21.0			
40	36.0			
43	4.1			
46	31.6			
47	29.0			
48	26.9			
50	26.4			
51	85.0			
53	25.4			
55	60.5			
57	83.0			
62	16.5			
65	19.5			
66	17.2			

TABLE IV – CHARACTERISTICS OF RAINFALL FLOODS

No.	River	Gauging station	Q_{max} (m³/s)	Date	h (mm)	T_T (hours)	t_i (hours)	P_W (%)	$P_{Q_{max}}$ (%)	Type of probability curve for P_W	for $P_{Q_{max}}$
1	2	3	4	5	6	7	8	9	10	11	12
10	Po	Pontelagoscuro	8850	20–05–26		1270	103		7.7		Gumbel
			8770	05–11–28		839	349		8.3		"
11	Magra	Calamazza	3480	15–10–60	89	143	19		3.2		"
13	Arno	S. Giovanni Alla Vena	1670	28–02–25	51	240	63		14.3		Galton-Gibrat
			1970	22–11–26	125	720	92		5.7		"
			2030	08–11–28	150	480	268		4.7		"
			2070	21–02–31	89	.384	245		4.3		"
			1630	01–12–32	94	624	132		15.9		"
			1960	14–12–33	56	264	75		6.1		"
			2080	14–12–34	83	264	116		4.2		"
			2010	06–02–51		240	72		5.1		"
			2290	04–11–66		240	44		2.2		"
14	Ombrone	Sasso D'ombrone	2380	25–10–40	90	312	126		16.4		Gumbel
			3110	04–11–66		240	38		3.9		"
15	Tevere	Roma	2800	17–12–37		78	34		6.3		"
16	Pescara	S. Teresa	654	29–06–40	46	384	32		14.9		"
			796	02–04–59		144	38		6.4		"
17	Volturno	Cancello Arnone	1380	16–12–52	79	216	54		47.6		"
18	Agri	Tarangelo	430	01–03–35	134	192	136		10.2		"
			327	24–01–40	83	120	61		28.6		"

No.	Method of curve fitting for W	for Q_{max}	Rainfall forming flood (mm)	Snowmelt during floods (mm)	Maximum daily rainfall (mm)	Date	Hourly maximum rainfall (mm)	Date	Antecedent precipitation for 10 days (mm)	30 days (mm)
1	13	14	15	16	17	18	19	20	21	22
10		Least squares	388		47.5	22–10–28				
11		"			205	14–10–60	49.8	15–10–60		
13		"	70		27.9	28–02–25				
		"	166		41.1	21–11–26				
		"	275							
		"	130							
		"	150							
		"	140							
		"	115		55.9	13–12–34				
		"			211	05–02–51				
		"			338	04–11–66	36.0	04–11–66		
14		"	163		97.8	24–10–40	40.0	24–10–40		
		"			237	03–11–66	40.0	03–11–66		
15		"								
16		"	114		174	28–06–40	35.0	28–06–40		
		"			196	01–04–59	21.0	02–04–59		
17		"	167		122	14–12–52				
18		"	170							
		"	79							

TABLE IV — CHARACTERISTICS OF RAINFALL FLOODS (cont'd)

No.	River	Gauging station	Q$_{max}$ (m^3/s)	Date	h (mm)	T$_T$ (hours)	t$_i$ (hours)	P$_W$ (%)	P$_{Q_{max}}$ (%)	Type of probability curve for P$_W$	for P$_{Q_{max}}$
1	2	3	4	5	6	7	8	9	10	11	12
						Characteristic element					
19	Alli	Orso	18.1	19—12—30	107	192	36				Gumbel
20	Oreto	Parco	248	21—02—31	299	144	14		18.9		"
			303	01—06—39	157	84	12		7.0		"
			352	26—10—51	33	36	6		3.2		"
21	Simeto	Giarretta	2130	30—11—27	163	312	60		11.2		"
			2260	01—12—33	92	144	20		5.7		"
			2330	10—12—36	63	216	16		4.0		"
			2390	17—10—51	110	120			2.9		"

No.	Method of curve fitting for W	for Q$_{max}$	Rainfall forming flood (mm)	Snowmelt during floods (mm)	Maximum daily rainfall (mm)	Date	Hourly maximum rainfall (mm)	Date	Antecedent precipitation for 10 days (mm)	30 days (mm)
1	13	14	15	16	17	18	19	20	21	22
19		Least squares	317		144	19—12—30				
20		"	485		412	21—02—31				
		"	156		78.0	01—06—39	11.0	31—05—39		
		"	47							
		"								
21		"	155		200					
		"	202		151	01—12—33				
		"	116		146	10—12—36	33.0	10—12—36		
		"	348		402	17—10—51	54.8	16—10—51		
		"								

Ivory Coast / Côte-d'Ivoire / Costa de Marfil / Берег Слоновой Кости

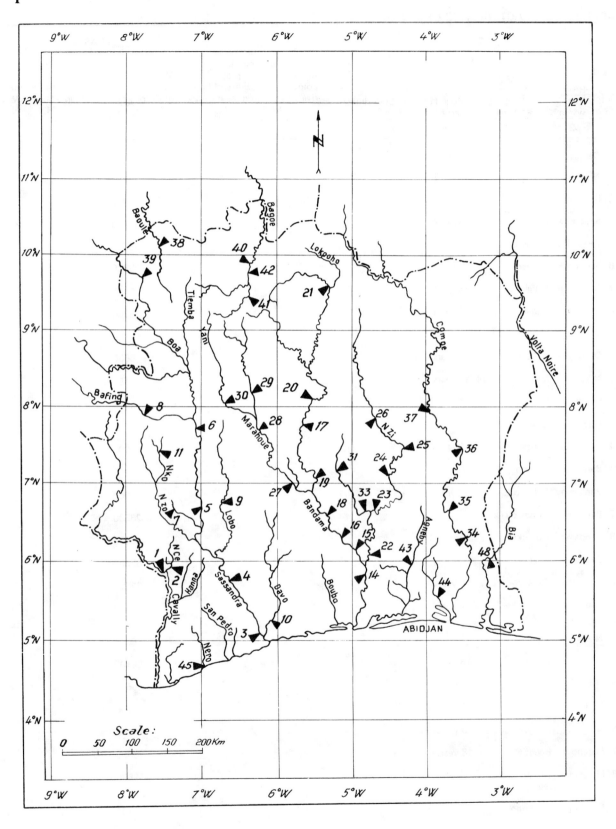

TABLE I — CHARACTERISTICS OF BASIN

			GAUGING STATION							BASIN			
							Distance (km) from gauging site					Altitude (m)	
No.	River River system	Name	Period of records	Co-ordinates Lat.	Long.		to remotest point of river system L_{rs}	to projection of centre of basin on main course L_{ca}	Mean slope of river I_r (%)	Area A (km²)	Mean H_m	Max. H_{max}	Min. H_{min}
1	2	3	4	5	6		7	8	9	10	11	12	13
1	Cavally	Tai	1955–73							13800			
2	N'ce	Tai	1955–73							1240			
3	Sassandra	Gaoulou								66000			
4	Sassandra	Soubre	1954–73							62000			
5	Sassandra	Guessabo	1953–73							35000			
6	Sassandra	Semien	1954–73							28800			
7	N'zo	Guiglo	16 years							6410			
8	Bafing	Badala	11 years							6200			
9	Lobo	Nibehibe	11 years							7280			
10	Davo	Dakpadou	4 years							6630			
11	N'ko	Man	11 years							153			
12	Guemon	Duekoue	4 years							182			
13	Gueri	Gagnoa								700			
14	Bandama	Tiassale	1954–70							94300			
15	Bandama	Brimbo	10 years							60200			
16	Bandama	Bafecao	9 years							59500			
17	Bandama	Kotiessou								26800			
18	Bandama	Kumukro	1955–73							55000			
19	Bandama	Bozi								32600			
20	Bandama	Bada	10 years							22600			
21	Bandama	Rte Ferke-kerhogo	12 years							7000			
22	N'zi	Zienoa	19 years							35000			
23	N'zi	Dimbokro	16 years							24100			
24	N'zi	Bocanda	16 years							20500			
25	N'zi	M'bahiakro	15 years							15700			
26	N'zi	Fetekro	13 years							10000			
27	Marahoue	Bouafle	18 years							19800			
28	Marahoue	Rte Beoumi-seguela								12500			
29	Marahoue	Mankono								6700			

TABLE I – CHARACTERISTICS OF BASIN (cont'd)

				GAUGING STATION						BASIN			
						Distance (km) from gauging site					Altitude (m)		
No.	River River system	Name	Period of records	Co-ordinates Lat.	Long.	to remotest point of river system L_{rs}	to projection of centre of basin on main course L_{ca}	Mean slope of river I_r (%)	Area A (km²)		Mean H_m	Max. H_{max}	Min. H_{min}
1	2	3	4	5	6	7	8	9	10		11	12	13
30	Yani	Seguela							3000				
31	Kan	Tiebissou	14 years						1200				
32	Kohoua	Farandougou	10 years						630				
33	Kan	Zanoafla	4 years						182				
34	Comoe	M'basso	13 years						70500				
35	Comoe	Aniassue	1953–73						66500				
36	Comoe	Akakomoekro	1955–70						57000				
37	Comoe	Serebou	1954–73						49000				
38	Baoule	Djirila	10 years						3970				
39	Kouroukelle	Iradougou	11 years						1990				
40	Bagoe	Kouto	13 years						4740				
41	Niangboue	Ponondougou	13 years						706				
42	Loa	Dembasso	10 years						54.4				
43	Agneby	M'podi							6930				
44	Kavi	M'basse	13 years						975				
45	Tabou	Yaka	8 years						800				
46	San Pedro	Prise d'eau	8 years						3310				
47	Nero	Rte Grand-Bereby							985				
48	Bia	Bianouan	9 years						6770				

Ivory Coast / Côte-d'Ivoire / Costa de Marfil / Берег Слоновой Кости

TABLE II — ANNUAL MAXIMUM DISCHARGES AND VOLUMES

Country: **Ivory Coast (1)**
River: **Cavally**
Gauging Station: **Tai**

| Date | Maximum discharge (m³/s) resulting from: | | Maximum volume (10⁶m³) corresponding to max. discharge resulting from: | |
| | Rainfall | Snowmelt | Rainfall | Snowmelt |
1	2	3	4	5
1955	1210			
1956	504			
1957	1040			
1958	328			
1959	787			
1960	740			
1961	108			
1962	610			
1963	890			
1964	509			
1965	1040			
1966	1320			
1967	698			
1968	862			
1969	853			
1970	859			
1971	868			
1972	504			
1973	960			

Country: **Ivory Coast (2)**
River: **N'ce**
Gauging Station: **Tai**

| Date | Maximum discharge (m³/s) resulting from: | | Maximum volume (10⁶m³) corresponding to max. discharge resulting from: | |
| | Rainfall | Snowmelt | Rainfall | Snowmelt |
1	2	3	4	5
1955	174			
1956	67.6			
1957	172			
1958	46.8			
1959	129			
1960	113			
1961	62.0			
1962	85.1			
1963	143			
1964	79.9			
1965	182			
1966	285			
1967	101			
1968	170			
1969	111			
1970	260			
1971	96.8			
1972	88.3			
1973	131			

TABLE II — ANNUAL MAXIMUM DISCHARGES AND VOLUMES (cont'd)

Country:	Ivory Coast (4)
River:	Sassandra
Gauging Station:	Soubre

Date	Maximum discharge (m³/s) resulting from:		Maximum volume (10⁶m³) corresponding to max. discharge resulting from:	
	Rainfall	Snowmelt	Rainfall	Snowmelt
1	2	3	4	5
1954	1690			
1955	2440			
1956	1360			
1957	2280			
1958	1520			
1959	2280			
1960	1580			
1961	1460			
1962	1550			
1963	2200			
1964	1860			
1965	1980			
1966	2300			
1967	1710			
1968	2230			
1969	1560			
1970	1530			
1971	1690			
1972	846			
1973	1310			

Country:	Ivory Coast (5)
River:	Sassandra
Gauging Station:	Guessabo

Date	Maximum discharge (m³/s) resulting from:		Maximum volume (10⁶m³) corresponding to max. discharge resulting from:	
	Rainfall	Snowmelt	Rainfall	Snowmelt
1	2	3	4	5
1953	1590			
1954	1370			
1955	1790			
1956	389			
1957	1900			
1958	1140			
1959	1680			
1960	1210			
1961	1310			
1962	1440			
1963	1560			
1964	1500			
1965	1640			
1966	1870			
1967	1570			
1968	1680			
1969	1050			
1970	1220			
1971	1800			
1972	976			
1973	820			

TABLE II — ANNUAL MAXIMUM DISCHARGES AND VOLUMES (cont'd)

Country:	Ivory Coast (6)
River:	Sassandra
Gauging Station:	Semien

| Date | Maximum discharge (m³/s) resulting from: | | Maximum volume (10⁶m³) corresponding to max. discharge resulting from: | |
	Rainfall	Snowmelt	Rainfall	Snowmelt
1	2	3	4	5
1954	1560			
1955	1880			
1956	1170			
1957	1730			
1958	829			
1959	605			
1960	1160			
1961	1030			
1962	1340			
1963	1230			
1964	1580			
1965	1610			
1966	1640			
1967	1640			
1968	1690			
1969	930			
1970	1650			
1971	1580			
1972	896			
1973	578			

Country:	Ivory Coast (14)
River:	Bandama
Gauging Station:	Tiassale

| Date | Maximum discharge (m³/s) resulting from: | | Maximum volume (10⁶m³) corresponding to max. discharge resulting from: | |
	Rainfall	Snowmelt	Rainfall	Snowmelt
1	2	3	4	5
1954	1520			
1955	2020			
1956	1160			
1957	2930			
1958	737			
1959	2560			
1960	2350			
1961	1190			
1962	1370			
1963	2380			
1964	2520			
1965	1860			
1966	1550			
1967	1290			
1968	2290			
1969	1240			
1970	2310			

TABLE II – ANNUAL MAXIMUM DISCHARGES AND VOLUMES (cont'd)

Country:	Ivory Coast (18)
River:	Bandama
Gauging Station:	Kumukro

Date	Maximum discharge (m³/s) resulting from:		Maximum volume (10⁶m³) corresponding to max. discharge resulting from:	
	Rainfall	Snowmelt	Rainfall	Snowmelt
1	2	3	4	5
1955	1690			
1956	1040			
1957	2370			
1958	362			
1959	1880			
1960	2390			
1961	1090			
1962	1120			
1963	1630			
1964	2170			
1965	1570			
1966	1220			
1967	1170			
1968	1370			
1969	1040			
1970	1900			
1971	921			
1972	196			
1973	478			

Country:	Ivory Coast (35)
River:	Comoe
Gauging Station:	Aniassue

Date	Maximum discharge (m³/s) resulting from:		Maximum volume (10⁶m³) corresponding to max. discharge resulting from:	
	Rainfall	Snowmelt	Rainfall	Snowmelt
1	2	3	4	5
1953	1140			
1954	2370			
1955	1470			
1956	563			
1957	1710			
1958	550			
1959	1980			
1960	1140			
1961	419			
1962	1250			
1963	2220			
1964	1810			
1965	1560			
1966	1350			
1967	1100			
1968	2250			
1969	1250			
1970	1540			
1971	1320			
1972	321			
1973	650			

TABLE II — ANNUAL MAXIMUM DISCHARGES AND VOLUMES (cont'd)

Country:	Ivory Coast (36)
River:	Comoe
Gauging Station:	Akakomoekro

| Date | Maximum discharge (m³/s) resulting from: | | Maximum volume (10⁶m³) corresponding to max. discharge resulting from: | |
	Rainfall	Snowmelt	Rainfall	Snowmelt
1	2	3	4	5
1955	1640			
1956	650			
1957	1880			
1958	334			
1959	1850			
1960	1250			
1961	378			
1962	1310			
1963	2440			
1964	2070			
1965	1770			
1966	1470			
1967	1180			
1968	2470			
1969				
1970	1750			
1971	1450			
1972	269			
1973				

Country:	Ivory Coast (37)
River:	Comoe
Gauging Station:	Serebou

| Date | Maximum discharge (m³/s) resulting from: | | Maximum volume (10⁶m³) corresponding to max. discharge resulting from: | |
	Rainfall	Snowmelt	Rainfall	Snowmelt
1	2	3	4	5
1954	2000			
1955	1440			
1956	734			
1957	1540			
1958	204			
1959	1500			
1960	1100			
1961	480			
1962	1210			
1963	1780			
1964	1650			
1965	1380			
1966	1250			
1967	1110			
1968	1740			
1969	1270			
1970	1480			
1971	1280			
1972	143			
1973	524			

Ivory Coast / Côte-d'Ivoire / Costa de Marfil / Берег Слоновой Кости

TABLE IV — CHARACTERISTICS OF RAINFALL FLOODS

No.	River	Gauging station	Q_{max} (m³/s)	Date	h (mm)	T_T (hours)	t_i (hours)	P_W (%)	$P_{Q_{max}}$ (%)	Type of probability curve for P_W	for $P_{Q_{max}}$
1	2	3	4	5	6	7	8	9	10	11	12
1	Cavally	Tai	1320	12—10—66							
2	N'ce	Tai	285	05—10—66							
3	Sassandra	Gaoulou	2910	14—10—63							
4	Sassandra	Soubre	2440	19—09—55							
5	Sasandra	Guessabo	1900	25—09—57							
6	Sasandra	Semien	1880	13—09—55							
7	N'zo	Guiglo	618	06—09—68							
8	Bafing	Badala	385	29—09—63							
9	Lobo	Nibehibe	196	07—10—71							
10	Davo	Dakpadou	255	20—06—72							
11	N'ko	Man	40.8	08—10—63							
12	Guemon	Duekoue	19.4	01—11—72							
13	Gueri	Gagnoa	180	10—09—63							
14	Bandama	Tiassale	2930	07—10—57							
15	Bandama	Brimbo	2210	05—10—57							
16	Bandama	Bafecao	2120	22—08—68							
17	Bandama	Kotiessou	940	19—09—71							
18	Bandama	Kumukro	2390	04—10—60							
19	Bandama	Bozi	1260	21—09—64							
20	Bandama	Bada	1390	15—09—64							
21	Bandama	Rte Ferkekorhogo	886	19—09—64							
22	N'zi	Zienca	845	30—09—68							
23	N'zi	Dimbokro	598	01—10—68							
24	N'zi	Bocanda	614	15—09—68							
25	N'zi	M'bahiakro	608	21—09—57							
26	N'zi	Fetekro	544	10—09—68							
27	Marahoue	Bouafle	922	16—09—64							
28	Marahoue	Rte Beoumiseguela	748	08—09—64							

TABLE IV — CHARACTERISTICS OF RAINFALL FLOODS (cont'd)

No.	River	Gauging station	Q_{max} (m^3/s)	Date	h (mm)	T_T (hours)	t_i (hours)	P_W (%)	$P_{Q_{max}}$ (%)	Type of probability curve for P_W	for $P_{Q_{max}}$
1	2	3	4	5	6	7	8	9	10	11	12
29	Marahoue	Mankono	488	05—08—64							
30	Yani	Seguela	137	23—09—60							
31	Kan	Tiebissou	55.1	14—10—63							
32	Kohoua	Farandougou	86.6	16—09—65							
33	Kan	Zancafla	8.5	09—11—69							
34	Comoe	M'basso	2280	01—10—68							
35	Comoe	Aniassue	2370	29—09—54							
36	Comoe	Akakomoekro	2470	26—09—68							
37	Comoe	Serebou	2000	05—10—54							
38	Baoule	Djirila	366	11—09—71							
39	Kouroukelle	Iradougou	120	14—09—70							
40	Bagoe	Kouto	510	02—09—70							
41	Niangboue	Ponondougou	52.4	19—09—55							
42	Loa	Dembasso	12.6	26—08—70							
43	Agneby	M'podi	320	30—09—63							
44	Kavi	M'besse	186	08—09—68							
45	Tabou	Yaka	305	19—05—63							
46	San Pedro	Prise d'eau	510	08—69							
47	Nero	Rte Grand-Bereby	207	10—06—72							
48	Bia	Bianouan	293	26—08—68							

Japan / Japon / Japón / Япония

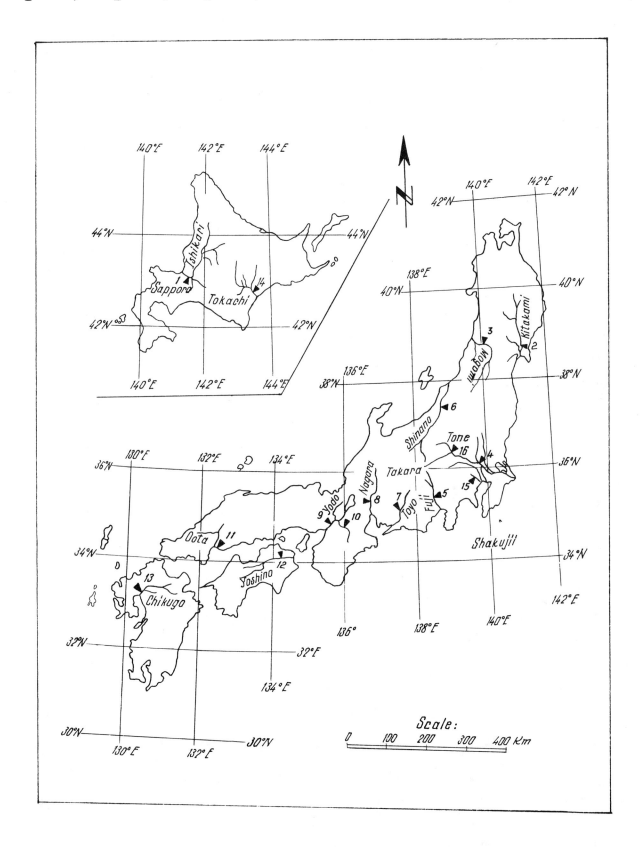

Scale:

0   100   200   300   400 Km

TABLE I — CHARACTERISTICS OF BASIN

	GAUGING STATION									BASIN			
	River River system	Name	Period of records	Co-ordinates		Distance (km) from gauging site		Mean slope of river I_r (%)	Area A (km²)	Altitude (m)			
				Lat.	Long.	to remotest point of river system L_{rs}	to projection of centre of basin on main course L_{ca}			Mean H_m	Max. H_{max}	Min. H_{min}	
No.	2	3	4	5	6	7	8	9	10	11	12	13	
1	2	3	4	5	6	7	8	9	10	11	12	13	
1	Ishikari	Ishikari-oohashi	1954–72	N 43:07	E 143:33	236	118	0.84	12800	390	1980	1	
2	Kitakami	Kozenji	1897–72	38:55	141:10	161	76	0.22	6990	433	2040	12	
3	Mogami	Shimono	1927–72	38:25	140:20	135	54	1.7	3530	516	2040	80	
4	Tone	Yattajima	1936–72	36:15	139:15	110	30	1.61	5110	853	1810	45	
5	Fuji	Shimizubata	1922–72	35:32	138:27	71	20	3.9	2120	1000	3000	234	
6	Shinano	Ojiya	1951–72	37:18	138:48	232	109	1.4	9720	911	3190	43	
7	Toyo	Ishida	1919–72	34:53	137:30	65	15	2.3	724	335	1100	19	
8	Nagara	Chusetsu	1924–72	35:25	136:45	108	47	1.57	1610	512	1710	11	
9	Yodo	Hirakata	1898–72	34:48	135:39	142	72	0.15	7280	192	1240	5	
10	Kizu Yodo	Kamo	1899–72	34:45	135:52	62	32	0.66	1460	263	1030	33	
11	Oota	Kumura	1952–72	34:29	132:31	94	30	1.4	1690	550	1340	11	
12	Yoshino	Iwatsu	1961–72	34:04	134:12	153	60	0.72	2810	710	1130	25	

	BASIN											
	Width (km)		Mean slope I_b (%)	Soils	Cover	Weighted lake area P_L (%)	Swamps R_s (%)	Mean annual precipitation P (mm)	Annual runoff Q (mm)	Mean annual temperature T (°C)	Regulating capacity of reservoirs α	
No.	Mean B_m	Max. B_{max}										
1	14	15	16	17	18	19	20	21	22	23	24	
1	54	126	22.6	4 + peat	F(66), C(18), U(16)	0	1.0	1330	1210	7.6	0.033	
2	41	94	18	4	C(20), F(60), U(20)	0	0	1610	1300	9.5	0.027	
3	31	57	18	4	C(15), F(83), U(2)	0	0	2240	1540	10.8	0.027	
4	47	124	3.0	Loam	F(72), C(13), U(15)	0		1500	1180	13.6	0.057	
5	30	60	5.8	4	F(89), C+U(11)			1130	900	13.6		
6	46	90	1.7	4	F(76), C, U(24)	0	0	1500	1490	11.8		
7	11	22	33	4 + Yellow soils	F(86), C(14)	0		2360	729	14.4	0.030	
8	15	39	10	4 + Yellow soils	F(63), C, U(37)	0	0	2530	2320	13.9	0	
9	59	104	15	4	F(79), C(19), U(2)	52		1450	1310	15.5	0.191	
10	28	52	23	4	F(85), C(13), U(2)	0	0	1360	1050	13.4	0.059	
11	18	45	3.0	4	F(80), C(10), U(10)	0		2000	1570	16.0	0.025	
12	18	55	4.9	Alluvial soil	F(88), C(10), U(2)	0	0	2020	1630	14.8	0.021	

TABLE I — CHARACTERISTICS OF BASIN (cont'd)

						GAUGING STATION				BASIN			
						Distance (km) from gauging site					Altitude (m)		
	River River system	Name	Period of records	Co-ordinates Lat.	Long.	to remotest point of river system L_{rs}	to projection of centre of basin on main course L_{ca}	Mean slope of river I_r (%)	Area A (km²)	Mean H_m	Max. H_{max}	Min. H_{min}
No.													
1	2	3	4	5	6	7	8	9	10	11	12	13
13	Chikugo	Senoshita	1874–72	33:19	130:30	102	41	1.7	2300	436	1790	3
14	Tokachi	Moiwa	1954–72	42:47	143:31	158	48	0.35	8400	413	2080	4
15	Shakujii Ara	Nemura-bashi	1958–72	35:45	139:30	23	10	0.2	48.0	52	81	23
16	Takara Tone	Takara-gawa	1937–64	36:51	139:01	7.56	4.49	9.6	19.1	1390	1950	800

						BASIN						
	Width (km) Mean B_m	Max. B_{max}	Mean slope I_b (%)	Soils	Cover	Weighted lake area P_L (%)	Swamps R_s (%)	Mean annual precipitation P (mm)	Annual runoff Q (mm)	Mean annual temperature T (°C)	Regulating capacity of reservoirs α
No.											
1	14	15	16	17	18	19	20	21	22	23	24
13	23	43	17	4	F(54), C(15), U(31)			2040	1450	15.1	0.029
14	53	140	8.9	Peat Clay	F(61), C(21), U(15)	0		1020	850	6.3	0.024
15	23	3.6	0.2	Loam	U(100)	0	0	1500	920	15.0	
16	2.6	4.8	46.4	2(30), 4(50) 5(20)	F(70), U(30)	0	0	3670	3110	8.3	0

TABLE II – ANNUAL MAXIMUM DISCHARGES AND VOLUMES

Country: **Japan (1)**
River: **Ishikari**
Gauging Station: **Ishikari-oohashi**

Date	Maximum discharge (m³/s) resulting from:		Maximum volume (10^6 m³) corresponding to max. discharge resulting from:	
	Rainfall	Snowmelt	Rainfall	Snowmelt
1	2	3	4	5
21–08–54	3500		840	
10–04–55		3500		1470
18–04–56		3500		1260
19–09–57	2700		780	
24–07–58	3100		450	
06–04–59		2300		830
27–07–60	2200		830	
27–07–61	6810		1000	
04–08–62	8150		1150	
18–04–63		1850		520
18–08–64	2400		380	
19–09–65	3840		1230	
21–08–66	4530		1260	
02–05–67		2760		980
02–04–68		1880		500
02–09–69	2440		370	
12–05–70		3660		1420
06–09–71	2,100		270	
18–04–72		3800		1200

Country: **Japan (2)**
River: **Kitakami**
Gauging Station: **Kozenji**

Date	Maximum discharge (m³/s) resulting from:		Maximum volume (10^6 m³) corresponding to max. discharge resulting from:	
	Rainfall	Snowmelt	Rainfall	Snowmelt
1	2	3	4	5
16–09–47	7900		1100	
17–09–48	6700		770	
05–08–50	4600		500	
26–08–52	2100			
24–07–53	2600		200	
08–06–54	2100			
26–06–55	3900		610	
22–06–56	2500		155	
09–07–57	2900		250	
19–09–58	4100		660	
28–09–59	3100		340	
21–04–60		1300		
28–06–61	2000		123	
18–07–62	1400			
18–07–63	1500			
06–09–64	1800			
16–07–65	2700		300	
29–06–66	2800		260	
21–04–67		2400		160
12–08–68	2600		179	
31–07–69	2500		330	
01–02–70		1300		73
04–07–71	1600		95	
09–07–72	2200		210	

TABLE II – ANNUAL MAXIMUM DISCHARGES AND VOLUMES   (cont'd)

Country: **Japan (3)**
River: **Mogami**
Gauging Station: **Shimono**

| Date | Maximum discharge (m³/s) resulting from: | | Maximum volume (10⁶m³) corresponding to max. discharge resulting from: | |
	Rainfall	Snowmelt	Rainfall	Snowmelt
1	2	3	4	5
28–08–13	3400		390	
06–04–27		2300		320
04–04–28		940		
24–05–29		2400		350
06–07–30	1800		200	
30–04–31		1440		107
21–07–32	2300		310	
10–04–33		1030		
12–07–34	2200		270	
10–03–35		1320		56
26–04–36		1730		220
04–03–37		880		
01–09–38	1700		190	
24–04–39		750		
12–07–40	1530			
23–07–41	1530		220	
15–03–42		870		
03–10–43	1050			
20–07–44	2600		440	
10–10–45	1500			
25–06–46	1290			
15–09–47	1690		195	
17–09–48	1290		132	
02–09–49	870			
04–08–50	1400		40	
27–12–51	810			
17–07–52	1610		127	
14–08–53	1410		68	
09–07–54	770			
26–06–55	1110			

Country: **Japan (3) cont'd**
River: **Mogami**
Gauging Station: **Shimono**

| Date | Maximum discharge (m³/s) resulting from: | | Maximum volume (10⁶m³) corresponding to max. discharge resulting from: | |
	Rainfall	Snowmelt	Rainfall	Snowmelt
1	2	3	4	5
17–07–56	2500		340	
08–07–57	2600		290	
27–09–58	2200		310	
22–07–59	1940		70	
31–03–60		1420		
05–04–61		1680		
04–04–62		1490		
18–04–63		1290		
13–07–64	2400		230	
18–07–65	2600		260	
18–07–66	2600		300	
29–08–67	3900		420	
31–03–68		1010		59
08–08–69	3100		240	
18–04–70		970		65
16–07–71	1450		70	
21–03–72		1150		59

TABLE II – ANNUAL MAXIMUM DISCHARGES AND VOLUMES (cont'd)

Country:	Japan (4)
River:	Tone
Gauging Station:	Yattajima

Date	Maximum discharge (m³/s) resulting from: Rainfall	Snowmelt	Maximum volume (10⁶m³) corresponding to max. discharge resulting from: Rainfall	Snowmelt
1	2	3	4	5
03−10−36	2180			
16−07−37	4950			
29−06−38	6720		410	
06−08−39	2140		250	
27−08−40	5820		400	
23−07−41	8990		600	
03−10−43	4252			
08−10−44	3560			
05−10−45	3980			
15−09−47	16900		1350	
01−09−49	9680		820	
05−08−50	8770		590	
07−04−51	422			
24−06−52	555			
26−09−53	3600		420	
19−09−54	2930		280	
11−10−55	2300		230	
27−09−56	2030		290	
09−08−57	840			
18−09−58	9730		660	
14−08−59	7070		860	
14−07−60	782			
28−10−61	3470			
14−06−62	1480			
11−07−63	745			
09−07−64	1040			
18−09−65	4510			
25−09−66	6040			
10−07−67	1330			
28−08−68	1160			

Country:	Japan (4) cont'd
River:	Tone
Gauging Station:	Yattajima

Date	Maximum discharge (m³/s) resulting from: Rainfall	Snowmelt	Maximum volume (10⁶m³) corresponding to max. discharge resulting from: Rainfall	Snowmelt
1	2	3	4	5
12−08−69	1780			
12−05−70	1040			
31−08−71	2560			
17−09−72	5370			

TABLE II — ANNUAL MAXIMUM DISCHARGES AND VOLUMES (cont'd)

Country:	Japan (5)
River:	Fuji
Gauging Station:	Shimizubata

	Maximum discharge (m³/s) resulting from:		Maximum volume (10⁶m³) corresponding to max. discharge resulting from:	
Date	Rainfall	Snowmelt	Rainfall	Snowmelt
1	2	3	4	5
08−22	3000			
06−23	1300			
07−24	400			
08−25	5000			
09−26	1020			
09−27	770			
10−28	2400			
09−29	1350			
07−30	4200			
10−31	420			
09−32	1240			
10−33	480			
08−34	680			
09−35	3300			
09−36	3000			
07−37	3700			
06−38	1870			
09−39	530			
06−40	1250			
07−41	1350			
09−42	1100			
10−43	1290			
10−44	1350			
10−45	4700			
04−46	210			
09−47	7300			
09−48	3800			
08−49	1050			
08−50	2800			
06−51	550			

Country:	Japan (5) cont'd
River:	Fuji
Gauging Station:	Shimizubata

	Maximum discharge (m³/s) resulting from:		Maximum volume (10⁶m³) corresponding to max. discharge resulting from:	
Date	Rainfall	Snowmelt	Rainfall	Snowmelt
1	2	3	4	5
24−06−52	820			
25−09−53	1610			
09−09−54	2300			
11−10−55	590			
27−09−56	1980			
03−07−57	1180			
18−09−58	2000		51	
14−08−59	5600		330	
14−08−60	1010			
28−06−61	2700		240	
14−06−62	620			
04−06−63	470			
25−09−64	590		36	
18−09−65	2800		174	
25−09−66	2900		128	
10−07−67	500		18	
30−08−68	660		36	
05−08−69	1650		69	
16−06−70	1670		174	
27−09−71	400		7	
17−09−72	2500		117	

TABLE II — ANNUAL MAXIMUM DISCHARGES AND VOLUMES (cont'd)

Country:	Japan (6)
River:	Shinano
Gauging Station:	Ojiya

Date	Maximum discharge (m³/s) resulting from:		Maximum volume (10⁶m³) corresponding to max. discharge resulting from:	
	Rainfall	Snowmelt	Rainfall	Snowmelt
1	2	3	4	5
01−03−51		3520		
01−07−52	3260			
26−09−53	3890			
28−02−54		1580		
11−10−55	2830			
27−09−56	2690			
24−04−57		2560		
18−09−58	5550			
15−08−59	6000			
14−07−60	3750			
30−06−61	3990			
14−06−62	3240			
05−06−63	2660			
09−07−64	3530			
18−09−65	4570			
05−03−66		3140		
04−04−67		2790		
29−08−68	2250			
09−08−69	3470			
16−07−70	2590			
07−09−71	3200			
17−09−72	2500			

Country:	Japan (7)
River:	Toyo
Gauging Station:	Ishida

Date	Maximum discharge (m³/s) resulting from:		Maximum volume (10⁶m³) corresponding to max. discharge resulting from:	
	Rainfall	Snowmelt	Rainfall	Snowmelt
1	2	3	4	5
16−09−19	2720			
04−08−20	1500			
08−09−21	2050			
04−07−22	1480			
09−06−23	3140			
12−09−24	1440			
11−09−25	2880			
04−09−26	1860			
14−09−27	1470			
25−06−28	950			
16−08−29	3080			
01−08−30	2880			
15−03−31	1090			
04−06−32	1700			
20−10−33	980			
20−06−34	1410			
29−08−35	2420			
27−09−36	1660			
15−07−37	3140			
23−03−38	1700			
11−03−39	740			
03−04−40	670			
12−07−41	2500			
06−03−42	1060			
18−06−43	1600			
07−08−44	3550			
29−07−45	3310			
18−09−46	810			
15−09−47	670			
20−06−48	1120			

TABLE II — ANNUAL MAXIMUM DISCHARGES AND VOLUMES (cont'd)

Country:	Japan (7) cont'd
River:	Toyo
Gauging Station:	Ishida

Date	Maximum discharge (m³/s) resulting from:		Maximum volume (10⁶m³) corresponding to max. discharge resulting from:	
	Rainfall	Snowmelt	Rainfall	Snowmelt
1	2	3	4	5
23—09—49	1540			
13—06—50	1200			
31—03—51	310			
24—07—52	1780		46	
25—09—53	1860		50	
28—09—54	1770		65	
31—08—55	1300			
27—09—56	1640		47	
28—07—57	1540		82	
26—08—58	2980		87	
27—09—59	3310		78	
13—08—60	1690		181	
27—06—61	2260		298	
28—07—62	3280		94	
17—05—63	1760		110	
27—06—64	800		23	
18—09—65	3360		88	
12—10—66	1120		32	
28—06—67	840		28	
29—08—68	3660		80	
05—08—69	4770		100	
16—06—70	870		77	
31—08—71	2660		118	
17—09—72	1480			

Country:	Japan (8)
River:	Nagara
Gauging Station:	Chusetsu

Date	Maximum discharge (m³/s) resulting from:		Maximum volume (10⁶m³) corresponding to max. discharge resulting from:	
	Rainfall	Snowmelt	Rainfall	Snowmelt
1	2	3	4	5
17—08—25	6980			
30—01—26	2910			
09—08—27	4340			
25—06—28	3380			
10—09—29	3360			
02—06—32	6060			
27—06—33	4010			
21—09—34	4130			
29—06—35	4890			
03—10—36	4140			
15—07—37	3150			
05—07—38	4190			
17—09—39	3620			
12—09—40	2500			
25—05—41	2400			
22—09—42	4400			
04—04—43	2590			
10—08—44	2330			
17—09—45	3720			
29—03—46	1740			
02—04—47	2670		68	
04—05—48	2980		125	
22—06—49	4220		223	
21—07—50	2290		68	
15—07—51	3610		411	
23—06—52	3990		121	
08—06—53	4290		178	
02—09—54	3890		187	
31—08—55	3280		126	
13—03—56	2310		131	

169

TABLE II – ANNUAL MAXIMUM DISCHARGES AND VOLUMES (cont'd)

Country:	Japan (8) cont'd
River:	Nagara
Gauging Station:	Chusetsu

	Maximum discharge (m³/s) resulting from:		Maximum volume (10⁶m³) corresponding to max. discharge resulting from:	
Date	Rainfall	Snowmelt	Rainfall	Snowmelt
1	2	3	4	5
08–08–57	3110		174	
26–08–58	4170		190	
27–09–59	7340		273	
13–08–60	7970		195	
27–06–61	6830		320	
10–06–62	3300		80	
04–06–63	2150		111	
25–09–64	3710		128	
18–09–65	1790		132	
08–07–66	1640		73	
29–06–67	2860		102	
29–08–68	3070		103	
30–06–69	2790		165	
16–06–70	2600		177	
17–09–71	2760		197	
12–07–72	3930			

Country:	Japan (9)
River:	Yodo
Gauging Station:	Hirakata

	Maximum discharge (m³/s) resulting from:		Maximum volume (10⁶m³) corresponding to max. discharge resulting from:	
Date	Rainfall	Snowmelt	Rainfall	Snowmelt
1	2	3	4	5
25–09–53	7800		460	
06–07–54	3900			
27–09–56	4600			
26–08–58	4200			
27–09–59	7200			
30–08–60	3800			
28–10–61	7800			
18–09–65	7000			
17–09–72	4800			

TABLE II — ANNUAL MAXIMUM DISCHARGES AND VOLUMES   (cont'd)

Country:	Japan (10)
River:	Kizu
Gauging Station:	Kamo

Date	Maximum discharge (m³/s) resulting from:		Maximum volume (10⁶m³) corresponding to max. discharge resulting from:	
	Rainfall	Snowmelt	Rainfall	Snowmelt
1	2	3	4	5
25–09–53	5800			
18–09–54	2190			
27–09–56	3850			
26–09–58	3700			
26–09–59	6200		184	
22–06–60	1260			
28–10–61	5220			
18–09–65	5300			
17–09–72	3400			

Country:	Japan (11)
River:	Oota
Gauging Station:	Kumura

Date	Maximum discharge (m³/s) resulting from:		Maximum volume (10⁶m³) corresponding to max. discharge resulting from:	
	Rainfall	Snowmelt	Rainfall	Snowmelt
1	2	3	4	5
20–09–43	6700		310	
02–07–52	1800			
28–06–53	2400			
25–09–54	3100			
30–09–55	2100		78	
17–08–56	1400		79	
03–07–57	2700		187	
22–08–58	890		148	
14–07–59	2000		114	
08–07–60	3500		260	
26–10–61	830		63	
05–07–62	3100		310	
11–07–63	3000		173	
27–06–64	3000		161	
23–07–65	4300		270	
20–06–66	1810		94	
09–07–67	2100		140	
29–07–68	1380		65	
08–07–69	2600		179	
15–08–70	2300		57	
06–08–71	2000		141	
12–07–72	6800		410	

TABLE II — ANNUAL MAXIMUM DISCHARGES AND VOLUMES (cont'd)

Country:	Japan (12)
River:	Yoshino
Gauging Station:	Iwatsu

	Maximum discharge (m³/s) resulting from:		Maximum volume (10⁶m³) corresponding to max. discharge resulting from:	
Date	Rainfall	Snowmelt	Rainfall	Snowmelt
1	2	3	4	5
16—09—61	12300		388	
10—06—62	1310		49	
10—08—63	9450		755	
25—09—64	8070		285	
10—09—65	3510		160	
18—09—66	5220		327	
10—07—67	7920		382	
29—08—68	9330		574	
26—06—69	3390		163	
21—08—70	11600		681	
31—08—71	4900		344	
16—09—72	8500			

Country:	Japan (13)
River:	Chikugo
Gauging Station:	Senoshita

	Maximum discharge (m³/s) resulting from:		Maximum volume (10⁶m³) corresponding to max. discharge resulting from:	
Date	Rainfall	Snowmelt	Rainfall	Snowmelt
1	2	3	4	5
14—09—50	2530			
14—07—51	2680			
14—09—52	1615			
26—06—53	6070			
30—06—54	2280		238	
16—04—55	1780		294	
28—08—56	1670		245	
03—07—57	2600		410	
14—08—58	1870		227	
07—07—59	2700		416	
22—06—60	2390		367	
05—07—61	2180		247	
06—07—62	3190		518	
11—05—63	3700		330	
20—06—65	3700		320	
20—06—66	1000		62	
09—07—67	1580		164	
02—07—68	2900		240	
01—07—69	2600		510	
15—08—70	1400		109	
22—07—71	2600		340	
23—06—72	2900		240	

TABLE II — ANNUAL MAXIMUM DISCHARGES AND VOLUMES (cont'd)

Country:	Japan (14)
River:	Tokachi
Gauging Station:	Moiwa

Date	Maximum discharge (m³/s) resulting from:		Maximum volume (10⁶m³) corresponding to max. discharge resulting from:	
	Rainfall	Snowmelt	Rainfall	Snowmelt
1	2	3	4	5
04—07—54	800		40	
04—09—55	1500		140	
14—07—56	1000			
19—09—57	1500			
28—09—58	1700		140	
24—04—59		1600		100
14—05—60		800		
05—08—62	5400		500	
18—04—63		1600		140
27—08—64	2700		330	
19—09—65	1800		80	
29—10—66	1700		110	
21—04—67		1400		110
15—05—68		1000		70
24—08—69	800		30	
12—05—70		1700		80
13—09—71	1300		110	
18—09—72	4600		280	

Country:	Japan (15)
River:	Shakujii
Gauging Station:	Nemura-bashi

Date	Maximum discharge (m³/s) resulting from:		Maximum volume (10⁶m³) corresponding to max. discharge resulting from:	
	Rainfall	Snowmelt	Rainfall	Snowmelt
1	2	3	4	5
28—06—66	112		6.2	

TABLE II – ANNUAL MAXIMUM DISCHARGES AND VOLUMES (cont'd)

Country:	Japan (16)					**Country:**				
River:	Takara					**River:**				
Gauging Station:	Takara-gawa					**Gauging Station:**				

Date	Maximum discharge (m³/s) resulting from:		Maximum volume (10⁶m³) corresponding to max. discharge resulting from:		Date	Maximum discharge (m³/s) resulting from:		Maximum volume (10⁶m³) corresponding to max. discharge resulting from:	
	Rainfall	Snowmelt	Rainfall	Snowmelt		Rainfall	Snowmelt	Rainfall	Snowmelt
1	2	3	4	5	1	2	3	4	5
21–09–39	38		0.65						
24–10–40	34		0.55						
23–07–41	21		0.62						
16–07–42	46		0.60						
03–10–43	30		1.26						
20–07–44	40		0.16						
07–06–45		30		0.97					
01–08–46	26		0.04						
15–09–47	98		3.4						
16–09–48	79		3.2						
01–09–49	59		2.6						
08–07–50	112		0.74						
03–11–51	46		1.13						
04–08–52	68		0.34						
25–09–53	31		1.83						
18–04–54		24		1.14					
06–08–55	25		0.15						
11–11–57	17		0.33						
18–09–58	53		2.78						
26–09–59	108		1.61						
13–07–60	58		2.6						
27–06–61		77		1.77					
13–07–62	23		0.67						
31–08–63	31		0.60						
25–09–64	54		0.78						

TABLE III – CHARACTERISTICS OF SNOWMELT FLOODS

No.	River	Gauging station	Q_{max} (m³/s)	Date	h (mm)	T_T (hours)	t_i (hours)	P_W (%)	$P_{Q_{max}}$ (%)	Type of probability curve for P_W	for $P_{Q_{max}}$
1	2	3	4	5	6	7	8	9	10	11	12
1	Ishikari	Ishikari-oohashi	3800	18–04–72	94	114	68		1.6		Empirical
			3700	12–05–70	115	144	104		1.7		"
2	Kitakami	Kozenzi	2400	21–04–67	23	50	22		53		Gumbel
			1300	01–02–70	10	55	16		99.7		"
3	Mogami	Shimono	2400	24–05–29	99	49	22		2.1		Empirical
			2300	06–04–27	91	54	24		2.4		"
6	Shinano	Ojiya	3100	21–04–52	66	96	17		7		"
			2800	24–04–57	220	336	320		12		"
14	Tokachi	Moiwa	1700	12–05–70	10	73	42		57		"
			1600	18–04–63	17	97	44		60		"
16	Takara	Takara-gawa	77	27–06–61	93	49	16				
			30	07–06–45	51	45	16				
			24	06–05–56	50	42	24				
			24	18–04–54	60	76	32				

No.	Method of curve fitting for W	for Q_{max}	Snow cover Water equivalent (mm)	Layer thickness (cm)	Rainfall during snowmelt (mm)	Monthly precipitation before soil freezing (mm)	Mean monthly temperature before snowmelt (°C)
1	13	14	15	16	17	18	19
1		Least squares		30	31	98	7
		"		520	38	174	14
2		Kadoya's method		0	86	180	2
		"		23		86	–3
3		Least squares		54	180	240	8
		"		34	170	150	1
6		"		108			9.2
		"		169			9.2
14		by eye		0	33	68	4
		"		0	15	15	–3
16			740	180	134		9
			2200	490	60		6
			550	180	21		1
				220			

TABLE IV — CHARACTERISTICS OF RAINFALL FLOODS

No.	River	Gauging station	Q_{max} (m³/s)	Date	h (mm)	T_T (hours)	t_i (hours)	P_W (%)	$P_{Q_{max}}$ (%)	Type of probability curve for P_W	for $P_{Q_{max}}$
1	2	3	4	5	6	7	8	9	10	11	12
1	Ishikari	Ishikari-oohashi	8100	04–08–62	91	72	42		1.1		Empirical
			6800	27–07–61	79	96	35		1.2		"
2	Kitakami	Kozenji	7900	16–09–47	157	88	41		1.5		Gumbel
			6700	17–09–48	110	64	29		5.6		"
3	Mogami	Shimono	3900	29–08–67	119	35	17		0.95		Empirical
			3400	28–08–13	110	46	9		1.9		"
			3100	08–08–69	68	26	12		4.0		"
			2600	20–07–44	124	54	21		9.5		"
4	Tone	Yattajima	16900	15–09–47	270	66	18		3.1		Gumbel
			9700	18–09–58	130	57	10		13.6		"
			9700	01–09–49	161	69	21		13.7		"
			7100	14–08–69	168	72	36		15.5		"
5	Fuji	Shimizubata	5600	14–08–59	155	87	36		4.0		Exponential function
			2800	18–09–65	81	121	66		19		"
6	Shinano	Ojiya	6200	18–09–58	105	48	8		6.7		Empirical
			6100	12–08–69	98	52	30		7.7		"
7	Toyo	Ishida	4800	05–08–69	183	24	7		3		"
			3300	27–09–59	143	26	9		12		"
			2300	27–06–61	295	39	12		31		"

No.	Method of curve fitting for W	for Q_{max}	Rainfall forming flood (mm)	Snowmelt during floods (mm)	Maximum daily rainfall (mm)	Date	Hourly maximum rainfall (mm)	Date	Antecedent precipitation for 10 days (mm)	30 days (mm)
1	13	14	15	16	17	18	19	20	21	22
1	Least squares	"	210		120	03–08–62	18	03–08–62	70	157
					100	25–07–61	37	25–07–61	33	95
2	Kadoya's method	"	300		100	15–09–47	25	15–09–47	48	64
			200		140	16–09–48	35	16–09–48	30	190
3	Least squares	"	170		160	28–08–67	14	29–08–67	47	140
		"	180		90	27–08–13	26	27–08–13	20	110
		"	120		80	07–08–69	10	07–08–69	160	180
		"	110		80	19–07–44	17	19–07–44	110	230
4		"	320		170	14–09–47	30	15–09–47	72	240
		"	170		130	17–09–58	20	18–09–58	73	160
		"	200		140	31–08–49	33	31–08–49	130	180
		"	210		120	13–08–59	15	14–08–59	150	230
5		"	250		200	13–08–59	24	14–08–59	80	180
		"	160		110	17–09–65	19	17–09–65	87	130
6		"	140		100	17–09–58	15	18–09–58	185	198
		"	120		40	11–08–69	5.2	11–08–69	132	144
7		"	320		280	04–08–69	68	04–08–69	360	450
		"	220		190	26–09–59	48	26–09–59	270	330
		"	410		200	27–06–61	24	27–06–61	460	640

TABLE IV — CHARACTERISTICS OF RAINFALL FLOODS (cont'd)

No.	River	Gauging station	Q_{max} (m³/s)	Date	h (mm)	T_T (hours)	t_i (hours)	P_W (%)	$P_{Q_{max}}$ (%)	Type of probability curve for P_W	for $P_{Q_{max}}$
1	2	3	4	5	6	7	8	9	10	11	12
8	Nagara	Chusetsu	8000	13–08–60	121	32	12		2.7	Gumbel	
			7300	27–09–59	170	63	38		4.0		"
			6800	27–06–61	199	58	36		5.5		"
9	Yodo	Hirakata	7800	25–09–53	165	76	28		2.0	Empirical	
			7800	28–10–61	156	78	30		2.0	"	
			7200	27–09–59	156	72	26		3.0	"	
			7000	18–09–65	127	58	24		4.0	"	
10	Kizu	Kamo	6200	26–09–59	183	55	24		1.7	"	
			5800	25–09–53	170	60	26		2.0	"	
			5300	18–09–65	139	40	12		3.0	"	
			5200	28–10–61	200	70	28		4.0	"	
11	Oota	Kumura	6800	12–07–72	270	86	54		2.7	Gumbel	
			4300	23–07–65	179	79	20		12	"	
12	Yoshino	Iwazu	12300	16–09–61	141	36	76		14	"	
			11600	21–08–70	250	60	14		18	"	
13	Chikugo	Senosita	3800	20–06–65	141	64	20		9.0	Empirical	
			3700	11–05–63	144	107	46		9.1	"	
14	Tokachi	Moiwa	5400	04–08–62	61	65	24		3.7	"	
			4600	18–09–72	34	50	19		6.0	"	

No.	Method of curve fitting for W	for Q_{max}	Rainfall forming flood (mm)	Snowmelt during floods (mm)	Maximum daily rainfall (mm)	Date	Hourly maximum rainfall (mm)	Date	Antecedent precipitation for 10 days (mm)	30 days (mm)
1	13	14	15	16	17	18	19	20	21	22
8		Least square	390		190	13–08–60	28	13–08–60	440	510
		"	260		150	26–09–59	45	26–09–59	300	470
		"	390		200	26–06–61	21	27–06–61	390	600
9			250		170	25–09–53	27	25–09–53		
			240		180	28–10–61	15	28–10–61		
			240		170	26–09–59	22	26–09–59		
			200		150	17–09–65	20	17–09–65		
10			280		230	26–09–59	28	26–09–54		
			260		180	25–09–53	28	25–09–53		
			210		180	17–09–65	25	17–09–65		
			310		210	28–10–61	24	28–10–61		
11		Least squares	400		170	11–07–72	24	11–07–72	140	280
		"	240		190	22–07–65	20	22–07–65	200	330
12			320		130	15–09–61	33	16–09–61	7	310
			420		380	21–08–70	62	21–08–70	390	490
13		by eyes	370		230	19–06–65	15	20–06–65	67	230
		"	210		110	10–05–63	13	09–05–63	130	240
14		"	136		113	03–08–62	13	03–08–62	56	155
		"	166		106	17–09–72	22	17–09–72	17	36

Japan / Japon / Japón / Япония

TABLE IV — CHARACTERISTICS OF RAINFALL FLOODS (cont'd)

No.	River	Gauging station	Q_{max} (m^3/s)	Date	h (mm)	T_T (hours)	t_i (hours)	P_W (%)	$P_{Q_{max}}$ (%)	Type of probability curve for P_W	for $P_{Q_{max}}$
1	2	3	4	5	6	7	8	9	10	11	12
15	Shakujii	Nemurabashi	112	28–06–66	130	35	18				
			108	27–09–58	197	45	18				
16	Takara	Takara-gawa	112	08–07–50	39	72	6				
			108	26–09–59	85	94	13				
			98	15–09–47	176	86	22				
			79	16–09–48	166	91	10				
			46	16–07–42	31	17	3				

No.	Method of curve fitting for W	for Q_{max}	Rainfall forming flood (mm)	Snowmelt during floods (mm)	Maximum daily rainfall (mm)	Date	Hourly maximum rainfall (mm)	Date	Antecedent precipitation for 10 days (mm)	30 days (mm)
1	13	14	15	16	17	18	19	20	21	22
15			200							
			380		350	26–09–58	68	26–09–58	200	
16			80		80	08–07–50	52	08–07–50	20	260
			122		71	26–09–59	29	26–09–59		
			240		230	15–09–47	35	15–09–47		
			200		152	16–09–48	30	16–09–48	110	370
			166		55	16–07–42	14	16–07–42		

178

Jordan / Jordanie / Jordania / Иордания

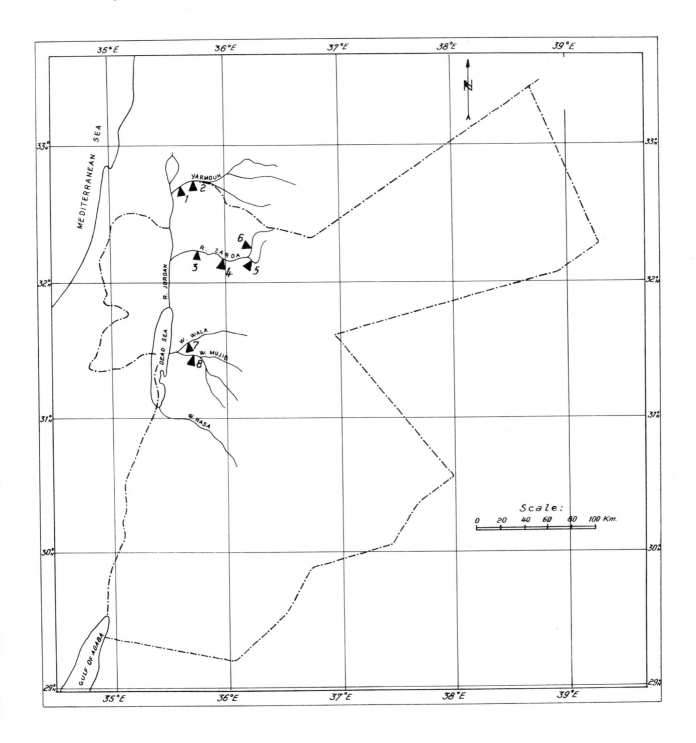

TABLE I – CHARACTERISTICS OF BASIN

	GAUGING STATION								BASIN			
						Distance (km) from gauging site						
	River					to remotest point of river system	to projection of centre of basin on main course	Mean slope of river		Altitude (m)		
No.	River system	Name	Period of records	Co-ordinates Lat.	Long.	L_{rs}	L_{ca}	I_r (%)	Area A (km^2)	Mean H_m	Max. H_{max}	Min. H_{min}
1	2	3	4	5	6	7	8	9	10	11	12	13
				N	E							
1	Yarmouk	Adasiya	1954–72	32:41	35:38:10	105	50	1.04	6790	710	1500	400
2	Yarmouk	Maqarin	1961–72	32:43:54	35:51:30	83	30		5950			
3	Wadi Zerqa	Deir Alla	1959–72	32:12	35:39:36	110	45	0.45	3400	683	1000	500
4	Zerqa	Jerash Bridge	1963–72	32:11:35	35:49:40	92	30		3100			
5	Zerqa	Sukhneh	1971–72	32:08:25	36:03:30	80	8		870			
6	Zerqa	Dhuleil	1972	32:08:50	36:03:45	79	8		1640			
7	Wala	Bridge	1965–72	31:33:15	35:46:15	60	25	0.25	1810	763	850	700
8	Mojib	Kerak Road Bridge	1965–72	31:26:50	35:48:45	100	43	0.2	4380	855	1000	800

	BASIN										
	Width (km)		Mean slope								
No.	Mean B_m	Max. B_{max}	I_b(%)	Soils	Cover	Weighted lake area P_L (%)	Swamps R_s (%)	Mean annual precipitation P (mm)	Annual runoff Q (mm)	Mean annual temperature T (°C)	Regulating capacity of reservoirs α
1	14	15	16	17	18	19	20	21	22	23	24
1	61	100	1.8	(Red Mediterranean, Lithosols, Basalt, Yellow Mediterranean, Regosols)	U			405	32.6		
2					U			427	15.2		
3	31	54	2.74	(Yellow Mediterranean, Red Mediterranean, Lithosols (Sandstone), Regosols)	U			271	9.8		
4					U			342	7.2		
5					U			163	12.6		
6					U			100	1.9		
7	30	50	1.06	(Yellow Mediterranean, Regosols + Alluvial, Yellow)	U			240	9.2		
8	44	68	0.86	(Yellow Mediterranean, Regosols, Lithosols, Basalt)	U			157	3.7		

TABLE II — ANNUAL MAXIMUM DISCHARGES AND VOLUMES

Country: Jordan (1)
River: Yarmouk
Gauging Station: Adasiya

| Date | Maximum discharge (m³/s) resulting from: | | Maximum volume (10⁶m³) corresponding to max. discharge resulting from: | |
| | Rainfall | Snowmelt | Rainfall | Snowmelt |
1	2	3	4	5
08–02–54	1310		141	
15–03–55	43		14	
27–01–56	310		58	
30–01–57	233		32	
24–02–59	106		27	
07–01–60	10		4.6	
22–12–61	300		44	
25–01–63	222		32	
04–02–64	333		58	
19–01–65	473		56	
30–01–66	230		9.1	
06–03–67	650		60	

Country: Jordan (2)
River: Yarmouk
Gauging Station: Maqarin

| Date | Maximum discharge (m³/s) resulting from: | | Maximum volume (10⁶m³) corresponding to max. discharge resulting from: | |
| | Rainfall | Snowmelt | Rainfall | Snowmelt |
1	2	3	4	5
21–12–61	78		13	
11–02–63	72		8.2	
04–02–64	216		17	
19–01–65	242		28	
20–03–66	49.5		7.4	
06–03–67	251		27	
20–03–69	330		57	
22–03–70	134		13	
13–04–71	283		89	
06–02–72	66.9		5.3	

Country: Jordan (3)
River: Zerqa
Gauging Station: Deir Alla

| Date | Maximum discharge (m³/s) resulting from: | | Maximum volume (10⁶m³) corresponding to max. discharge resulting from: | |
| | Rainfall | Snowmelt | Rainfall | Snowmelt |
1	2	3	4	5
20–01–59	72		9.3	
11–02–63	300		17	
09–12–63	122		8.3	
19–01–65	525		26	
22–03–66	138		10	
13–11–66	240		12	
25–01–68	77		4.2	
07–12–71	93.7		5.6	
25–11–72	36.8		0.6	

Country: Jordan (4)
River: Zerqa
Gauging Station: Jerash Bridge

| Date | Maximum discharge (m³/s) resulting from: | | Maximum volume (10⁶m³) corresponding to max. discharge resulting from: | |
| | Rainfall | Snowmelt | Rainfall | Snowmelt |
1	2	3	4	5
12–02–63	43.4		2.1	
18–01–64	106		3.6	
19–01–65	209		11	
22–03–66	100		17	
22–03–69	180		26	
10–01–70	73.4		1.8	
13–04–71	352		22	
09–04–72	88.7		2.5	
25–11–72	27.7		0.9	

TABLE II — ANNUAL MAXIMUM DISCHARGES AND VOLUMES (cont'd)

Country: **Jordan (7)**
River: **W. Wala**
Gauging Station: **Bridge**

| Date | Maximum discharge (m³/s) resulting from: | | Maximum volume (10⁶m³) corresponding to max. discharge resulting from: | |
| | Rainfall | Snowmelt | Rainfall | Snowmelt |
1	2	3	4	5
19—01—65	117		6.8	
22—03—66	113		3.7	
20—12—66	111		5.6	
12—05—68	32.5		0.5	
25—11—68	35.9		1.5	
10—10—69	37.3		0.8	
13—04—71	445		44	
07—12—71	704		21	

Country: **Jordan (8)**
River: **W. Mojib**
Gauging Station: **Kerak Road Bridge**

| Date | Maximum discharge (m³/s) resulting from: | | Maximum volume (10⁶m³) corresponding to max. discharge resulting from: | |
| | Rainfall | Snowmelt | Rainfall | Snowmelt |
1	2	3	4	5
19—01—65	1590		80	
22—03—66	34.3		1.8	
12—10—66	695		4.4	
12—05—68	68.5		1.4	
23—03—69	197		12	
23—03—70	89.8		2.3	
13—11—71	1890		125	
27—12—71	271		27	
13—01—73	30.1		3	

Jordan / Jordanie / Jordania / Иордания

TABLE IV — CHARACTERISTICS OF RAINFALL FLOODS

No.	River	Gauging station	Q_{max} (m^3/s)	Date	h (mm)	T_T (hours)	t_i (hours)	P_W (%)	$P_{Q_{max}}$ (%)	Type of probability curve for P_W	for $P_{Q_{max}}$
1	2	3	4	5	6	7	8	9	10	11	12
1	Yarmouk	Adasiya	1310	08—02—54	20.8	144	68				
			650	06—03—67	8.9	72	28				
2	Yarmouk	Maqarin	330	20—03—69	9.6	132	80				
			283	13—04—71	14.9	192	114				
3	Zerqa	Dier Alla	525	19—01—65	7.5	168	40				
			300	11—02—63	5.0	120	32				
4	Zerqa	Jerash Bridge	352	13—04—71	7.1	168	35				
			209	19—01—65	3.6	72	37				
5	Zerqa	Sukhnek	60.0	06—12—71	3.9	96	24				
			16.9	07—03—73	0.74	72	20				
6	Zerqa	Dhuleil	87.0	09—04—72	1.5	72	5				
			17.4	25—11—72	0.24	48	3				
7	Wala	Bridge	704	07—12—71	11.7	96	28				
			445	13—04—71	24.4	120	38				
8	Mojib	Kerak Road Bridge	1890	13—11—71	28.5	120	36				
			1590	19—01—65	18.3	72	40				

183

Madagascar / Мадагаскар

TABLE I — CHARACTERISTICS OF BASIN

No.	River / River system	Name	Period of records	Co-ordinates Lat.	Co-ordinates Long.	Distance (km) from gauging site to remotest point of river system L_{rs}	Distance (km) from gauging site to projection of centre of basin on main course L_{ca}	Mean slope of river I_r (%)	Area A (km²)	Altitude (m) Mean H_m	Altitude (m) Max. H_{max}	Altitude (m) Min. H_{min}
1	2	3	4	5	6	7	8	9	10	11	12	13
				S	E							
1	Ikopa	Bevomanga		18:48	47:19				4150			
2	Ikopa	Bac de Fiadonana		18:10	46:57				9450			
3	Ikopa	Antsatrana		17:10	47:01				18600			
4	Betsiboka	Ambodiroka		16:56	46:57				11800			
5	Mania	Fasimena		20:17	46:48				6680			
6	Ihosy	Ihosy		21:23	46:07				1500			
7	Zomanbo	Ankaramena		21:57	46:39				610			
8	Sahanivotry	PK 197		20:06	47:05				427			
9	Manandona	Sahanivotry		20:08	47:05				973			
10	Onive	Tsinjoarivo		19:37	47:42				2990			
11	Namorona	Vohiparara		21:14	47:23				445			
12	Mangoro	Mangoro		18:53	48:06				3600			
13	Faraony	Vohilava		21:04	48:00				2000			
14	Mananara	Maroagaty		22:57	46:55				14200			
15	Ivoanana	Fatihita		21:03	47:45				835			
16	Vohitra	Rogez		18:48	48:36				1830			
17	Ivondro	Ringaringa		18:11	49:15				2550			
18	Rianila	Fetraomby		18:40	48:56				1820			
19	Mangoky	Banian		25:49	44:12				50000			
20	Menarandra	Bekily		24:13	45:19				1830			

Madagascar / Мадагаскар

TABLE IV – CHARACTERISTICS OF RAINFALL FLOODS

No.	River	Gauging station	Q_{max} (m^3/s)	Date	h (mm)	T_T (hours)	t_i (hours)	P_W (%)	$P_{Q_{max}}$ (%)	Type of probability curve for P_W	for $P_{Q_{max}}$
1	2	3	4	5	6	7	8	9	10	11	12
1	Ikopa	Bevomanga	600	1932							
2	Ikopa	Bac de Fiadonana	1840	1964							
3	Ikopa	Antsatrana	3850	1961							
4	Betsiboka	Ambodiroka	16500	1959							
5	Mania	Fasimena	1400	1970							
6	Ihosy	Ihosy	414	1970							
7	Zomanbao	Ankaramena	2500	1970							
8	Sahanivotry	PK 197	93	1969							
9	Manandona	Sahanivotry	353	1970							
10	Onive	Tsinjoarivo	1500	1959							
11	Namorona	Vohiparara	1200	1970							
12	Mangoro	Mangoro	2800	1959							
13	Ivoanana	Fatihita	5000	1945							
14	Vohitra	Rogez	3400	1970							
15	Ivondro	Ringaringa	1000	1970							
16	Rianila	Fetraomby	5250	1959							
17	Mangoky	Banian	32000	1970							
18	Menarandra	Bekily	3500	1971							

Malaysia / Malaisie / Malasia / Малайзия

TABLE I — CHARACTERISTICS OF BASIN

No.	River River system	Name	Period of records	Co-ordinates Lat.	Co-ordinates Long.	Distance (km) from gauging site — to remotest point of river system L_{rs}	Distance (km) from gauging site — to projection of centre of basin on main course L_{ca}	Mean slope of river I_r (%)	Area A (km²)	Altitude (m) Mean H_m	Altitude (m) Max. H_{max}	Altitude (m) Min. H_{min}
1	2	3	4	5	6	7	8	9	10	11	12	13
1	Kelantan	Guillemard Bridge	1949–74	N 05:46	E 102:09	251	73.4	0.26	11900	747	1870	25.4
2	Trengganu	Kampong Tanggol	1947–74	05:08	103:03	122	35.4	0.26	3380	513	1430	11.4
3	Perak	Iskandar Bridge	1915–74	04:49	100:58	232	66	0.29	7770	837	1870	44.2
4	Klang	Kuala Lumpur	1910–74	03:09	101:42	29	12	0.93	457	496	1420	30.5

No.	Width (km) Mean B_m	Width (km) Max. B_{max}	Mean slope I_b (%)	Soils	Cover	Weighted lake area P_L (%)	Swamps R_s (%)	Mean annual precipitation P (mm)	Annual runoff Q (mm)	Mean annual temperature T (°C)	Regulating capacity of reservoirs α
1	14	15	16	17	18	19	20	21	22	23	24
1	99	140	1.52					2500	1360	27.9	
2	41	88	4.17					3300	1440	26.4	
3	65	90	2.13					2150	646	26.4	
4	19	24	2.31					2300	965	28	

TABLE II — ANNUAL MAXIMUM DISCHARGES AND VOLUMES

Country:	Malaysia (1)
River:	Kelantan
Gauging Station:	Guillemard Bridge

Date	Maximum discharge (m³/s) resulting from:		Maximum volume (10⁶m³) corresponding to max. discharge resulting from:	
	Rainfall	Snowmelt	Rainfall	Snowmelt
1	2	3	4	5
01—12—49	5900			
24—01—51	7200			
06—01—52	2500			
07—12—53	1900			
13—12—54	4300			
28—11—56	3400			
20—12—57	5000			
05—11—58	1500			
18—12—59	3300			
10—12—60	3600		582	
30—12—61	2900		417	
04—01—63	3300			
23—12—64	1600			
03—12—65	5900			
07—01—67	14800			
28—12—68	1700			
30—11—69	6500			

Country:	Malaysia (2)
River:	Trengganu
Gauging Station:	Kampong Tanggol

Date	Maximum discharge (m³/s) resulting from:		Maximum volume (10⁶m³) corresponding to max. discharge resulting from:	
	Rainfall	Snowmelt	Rainfall	Snowmelt
1	2	3	4	5
16—12—47	4200			
16—11—48	2400			
30—11—49	3000			
05—03—50	2700			
23—01—51	3600			
27—12—53	2800			
12—12—54	3400			
14—12—55	2100			
22—12—56	3000			
19—12—57	4100			
28—11—59	2100			
09—12—60	3100		782	
27—12—61	3700		328	
03—01—63	2500			
03—12—65	4900			
30—12—66	10500		1770	
06—01—67	12500		1620	

TABLE II — ANNUAL MAXIMUM DISCHARGES AND VOLUMES (cont'd)

Country: Malaysia (3)
River: Perak
Gauging Station: Iskandar Bridge

Date	Maximum discharge (m³/s) resulting from:		Maximum volume (10⁶m³) corresponding to max. discharge resulting from:	
	Rainfall	Snowmelt	Rainfall	Snowmelt
1	2	3	4	5
08–11–48	870			
01–12–49	1400			
24–01–51	2200			
17–10–53	1200			
16–12–54	1300			
07–11–55	880			
12–11–56	1300			
20–12–57	1000			
25–11–58	700			
18–12–59	1000			
11–12–60	1200			
26–11–61	700			
19–12–62	1200		165	
20–10–63	880			
07–09–64	600		84	
04–11–65	1300			
06–01–67	6300		1420	
01–12–69	2500			

Country: Malaysia (4)
River: Klang
Gauging Station: Kuala Lumpur

Date	Maximum discharge (m³/s) resulting from:		Maximum volume (10⁶m³) corresponding to max. discharge resulting from:	
	Rainfall	Snowmelt	Rainfall	Snowmelt
1	2	3	4	5
21–10–48	139			
21–11–51	194			
28–04–52	211			
26–10–57	173			
17–05–59	186			
07–11–60	125			
30–04–61	130			
03–12–63	159		12	
14–09–64	130			
10–05–65	164			
12–07–66	140			
30–11–67	122			

TABLE IV — CHARACTERISTICS OF RAINFALL FLOODS

No.	River	Gauging station	Q_{max} (m^3/s)	Date	h (mm)	T_T (hours)	t_i (hours)	P_W (%)	$P_{Q_{max}}$ (%)	Type of probability curve for P_W	for $P_{Q_{max}}$
1	2	3	4	5	6	7	8	9	10	11	12
1	Kelantan	Guillemard Bridge	14800 8100	07—01—1967 27—11—1967	131	116	62		1 9.1		Gumbel ''
2	Trengganu	Kampong Tanggol	12500	06—01—1967	682	126	48		4.2		''
3	Perak	Iskandar Bridge	6300 2800	06—01—1967 27—11—1967	83	192	36		1< 17		'' ''
4	Klang	Kuala Lumpur	566 211	05—01—1971 28—04—1952	99	70	20		<1 3.6		'' ''

No.	Method of curve fitting for W	for Q_{max}	Rainfall forming flood (mm)	Snowmelt during floods (mm)	Maximum daily rainfall (mm)	Date	Hourly maximum rainfall (mm)	Date	Antecedent precipitation for 10 days (mm)	30 days (mm)
1	13	14	15	16	17	18	19	20	21	22
1		least squares ''								
2		''	607		257	04—01—1967			889	1016
3		'' ''	183		94 66	03—01—1967 25—11—1967			59 33	216 381
4		'' ''	201		171	04—01—1971	13.2	04—01—1971	>117	>117

Note: Rainfall estimates are based on catchment mean figures.

Morocco / Maroc / Marruecos / Марокко

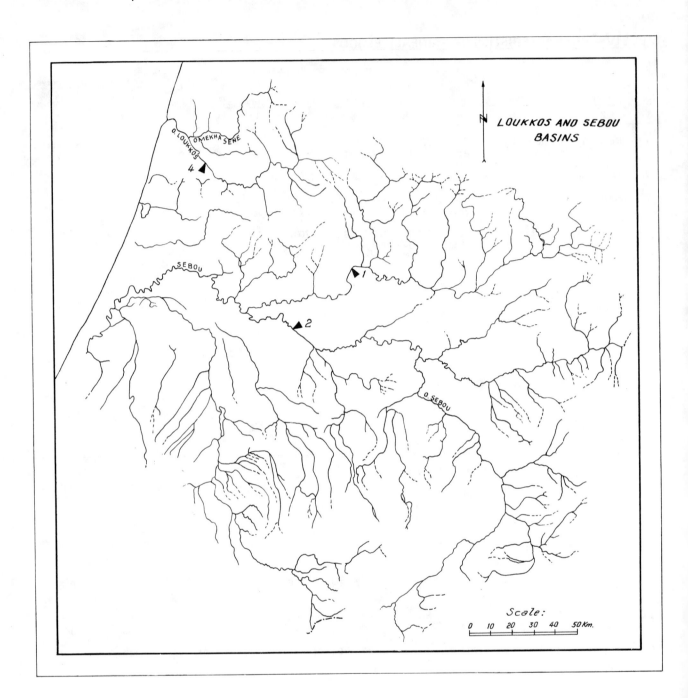

LOUKKOS AND SEBOU
BASINS

TABLE I — CHARACTERISTICS OF BASIN

	River River system	Name	Period of records	Lat.	Long.	L_{rs}	L_{ca}	I_r (%)	Area A (km²)	Mean H_m	Max. H_{max}	Min. H_{min}
						to remotest point of river system	to projection of centre of basin on main course	Mean slope of river			Altitude (m)		
No.	2	3	4	5	6	7	8	9	10	11	12	13
				N	E							
1	Ouergha	Mjara	40 years			194	110	0.8	6190	750	2460	85
2	Sebou	Azib Soltane	21 years			333	148	0.5	16400	985	2700	45
3	Ziz	Ait Athmane	1960–70	32:00:35	04:27:10	165	65.2	0.86	4310	1900	3500	1060
4	Loukkos	M'Rissa	12 years			130	80	0.01	2120	290	1690	20

BASIN

No.	Mean B_m	Max. B_{max}	Mean slope I_b(%)	Soils	Cover	Weighted lake area P_L (%)	Swamps R_s (%)	Mean annual precipitation P (mm)	Annual runoff Q (mm)	Mean annual temperature T (°C)	Regulating capacity of reservoirs α
1	14	15	16	17	18	19	20	21	22	23	24
1	32	65						1260	560		
2	49	165						720	144		
3	26.2	67.5	13		F(16), C(1), U(83)			308	45.2	10.7	
4	11	53			F, C			1130	510	18.0	

Morocco / Maroc / Marruecos / Марокко

TABLE II — ANNUAL MAXIMUM DISCHARGES AND VOLUMES

Country: **Marocco (1)**
River: **Ouergha**
Gauging Station: **Mjara**

| Date | Maximum discharge (m³/s) resulting from: | | Maximum volume (10⁶m³) corresponding to max. discharge resulting from: | |
| | Rainfall | Snowmelt | Rainfall | Snowmelt |
1	2	3	4	5
29—01—33	1380			
07—04—34	2720			
15—11—34	2320			
26—01—36	2540			
28—01—37	2340			
15—12—37	4400			
21—12—38	1130			
05—02—40	3840			
18—02—41	6120			
24—02—42	2870			
18—12—42	1230			
29—02—44	1590			
01—45	800			
21—12—45	4000			
28—02—47	2940			
	4000			
01—49	800			
31—12—49	1640			
29—12—50	7950			
19—11—51	4300			
30—12—52	1050			
14—03—54	900			
26—02—55	2440			
17—02—56	3210			
08—05—57	665			
12—12—57	2470			
20—12—58	3040			
15—01—60	3390			
08—12—60	940			
27—12—61	2160			

Country: **Marocco (1) cont'd**
River: **Ouergha**
Gauging Station: **Mjara**

| Date | Maximum discharge (m³/s) resulting from: | | Maximum volume (10⁶m³) corresponding to max. discharge resulting from: | |
| | Rainfall | Snowmelt | Rainfall | Snowmelt |
1	2	3	4	5
06—01—63	6380			
18—12—63	7030			
01—03—65	2320			
22—02—66	2910			
16—02—67	1300			
18—02—68	1190			
14—01—69	3440			
12—01—70	6820			
03—04—71	4240			
17—01—72	1360			
13—10—72	1160			

192

TABLE II – ANNUAL MAXIMUM DISCHARGES AND VOLUMES (cont'd)

Country:	Marocco (2)
River:	Sebou
Gauging Station:	Azib Soltane

Date	Maximum discharge (m³/s) resulting from:		Maximum volume (10⁶m³) corresponding to max. discharge resulting from:	
	Rainfall	Snowmelt	Rainfall	Snowmelt
1	2	3	4	5
26–03–33	445			
11–12–33	1410			
17–11–34	475			
13–03–36	978			
18–12–36	461			
15–12–37	362			
08–04–39	530			
04–02–40	350			
21–02–41	1100			
25–02–42	980			
20–12–42	575			
29–02–44	694			
21–12–44	612			
24–12–45	540			
15–05–47	381			
11–05–48	334			
11–05–49	670			
01–01–50	769			
30–12–50	1570			
26–01–52	512			
20–01–53	613			
13–03–54	750			
27–02–55	603			
08–04–56	880			
03–01–57	485			
15–12–58	812			
23–12–59	1420			
16–01–60	4090			
26–01–61	376			
24–03–62	904			

Country:	Marocco (2) cont'd
River:	Sebou
Gauging Station:	Azib Soltane

Date	Maximum discharge (m³/s) resulting from:		Maximum volume (10⁶m³) corresponding to max. discharge resulting from:	
	Rainfall	Snowmelt	Rainfall	Snowmelt
1	2	3	4	5
07–01–63	4120			
21–12–63	1740			
02–03–65	973			
23–02–66	378			
11–10–66	827			
01–04–68	626			
28–02–69	3170			
13–01–70	2790			
04–04–71	1130			
18–01–72	437			
16–02–73	312			

Country:	Marocco (4)
River:	Loukkos
Gauging Station:	M'Rissa

Date	Maximum discharge (m³/s) resulting from:		Maximum volume (10⁶m³) corresponding to max. discharge resulting from:	
	Rainfall	Snowmelt	Rainfall	Snowmelt
1	2	3	4	5
12–01–61	1620		370	
07–01–63	1380		930	
17–12–63	1650		680	
24–12–64	1090			
21–01–66	1130			
16–02–67	805		225	
18–02–68	595			
27–02–69	1190		220	
06–01–70	1260		1320	
03–04–71	1260			
01–01–72	796			
18–01–73	310			

TABLE IV — CHARACTERISTICS OF RAINFALL FLOODS

			Characteristic element							Type of probability curve	
No.	River	Gauging station	Q_{max} (m^3/s)	Date	h (mm)	T_T (hours)	t_i (hours)	P_W (%)	$P_{Q_{max}}$ (%)	for P_W	for $P_{Q_{max}}$
1	2	3	4	5	6	7	8	9	10	11	12
1	Ouergha	Mjara	6380	06—01—73	348	160	60			Pearson III	
			7030	18—12—63	309	190	70				
			6820	12—01—70	312	240	90				
2	Sebou	Azib Soltane	4120	07—01—63	55	150	60			Pearson III	
			1740	21—12—63	36	245	95				
			2790	13—01—70	54	240	95				
3	Ziz	Ait Athmane Aval	4600	06—11—65	31.4	40.5	16.5				
4	Loukkos	M'Rissa	1650	17—12—63	321	280	60			Gumbel	
			1620	25—12—61	175	240	12				

	Method of curve fitting		Rainfall forming flood (mm)	Snowmelt during floods (mm)	Maximum daily rainfall (mm)	Date	Hourly maximum rainfall (mm)	Date	Antecedent precipitation for	
No.	for W	for Q_{max}							10 days (mm)	30 days (mm)
1	13	14	15	16	17	18	19	20	21	22
1		Max. Likelihood	292		85				286	330
			310		132				98	248
			342		95				550	595
2		Max. Likelihood	126		35.5				95	132
			243		83.4				32	110
			112		45				270	368
3			72.7		65	05—11—65	13	05—11—65	21.7	84.9
4		Moments	420		267	12—63			74.5	268
					93	12—61			24	137

Norway / Norvège / Noruega / Норвегия

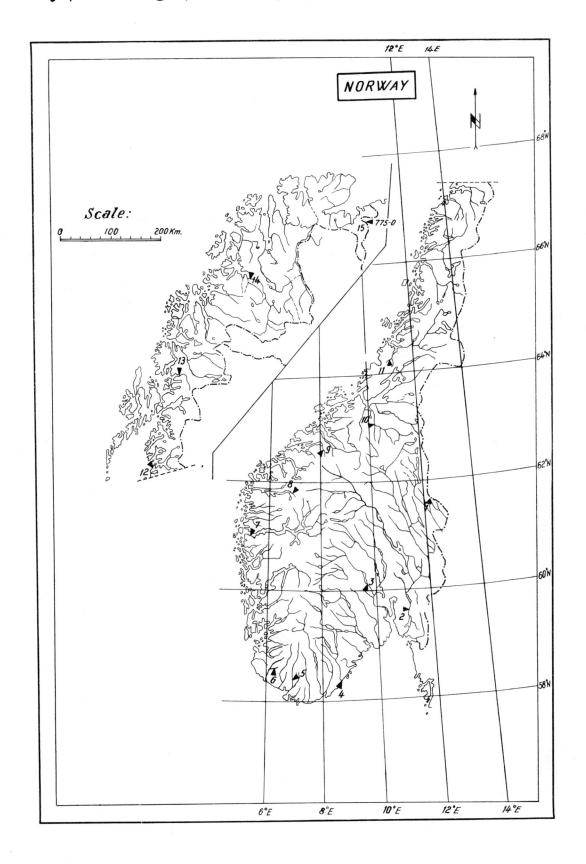

TABLE I – CHARACTERISTICS OF BASIN

		GAUGING STATION							BASIN			
						Distance (km) from gauging site				Altitude (m)		
	River / River system	Name	Period of records	Co-ordinates Lat.	Long.	to remotest point of river system L_{rs}	to projection of centre of basin on main course L_{ca}	Mean slope of river I_r (%)	Area A (km²)	Mean H_m	Max. H_{max}	Min. H_{min}
No.												
1	2	3	4	5	6	7	8	9	10	11	12	13
1	Engera Klara	Engeren 374–0	1911–72	N 61:03	E 12:36	43	17	1.6	394	830	1210	472
2	Glomma	Langnes 395–0	1901–64	59:36	11:07	371	203	0.45	40000	700	2470	76
3	Snarumselv Dramselv	Krødern 458–0	1889–65	60:08	09:47	149	104	1.2	5090	1130	1930	129
4	Nioelv	Lunde Mølle 518-12	1899–72	58:24	08:38	129	87	0.73	3840	550	1520	10
5	Fedeelv	Refsti 560–11	1896–72	58:17	06:49	27	9.6	2.2	211	280	599	0
6	Hellelandselv	Gya 919–0	1933–72	58:36	06:21	14	7.6	5.3	60	590	906	165
7	Klóvtveitelv	Klóvtveitvatn 603–0	1922–72	60:58	05:18	2.3	1.0	7.7	4	460	637	407
8	Loelv	Lovatn 622–11	1900–72	61:51	06:53	23	9.4	8.5	261	1470	2080	49
9	Aura	Eikesdalsvatn 640–0	1902–72	62:38	08:07	60	39	2.3	1090	1220	1950	23

	BASIN										
	Width (km)		Mean slope I_b(%)	Soils	Cover	Weighted lake area P_L (%)	Swamps R_s (%)	Mean annual precipitation P (mm)	Annual runoff Q (mm)	Mean annual temperature T (°C)	Regulating capacity of reservoirs α
No.	Mean B_m	Max. B_{max}									
1	14	15	16	17	18	19	20	21	22	23	24
1	9.2					3.0			594		
2	108					0.7			520		
3	34					0.8			710		
4	30					1.6			968		
5	7.8					2.4			1460		
6	4.3					0.4			2780		
7	1.8					18.3			4500		
8	11					3.9			2000		
9	18					2.2			1180		

TABLE I — CHARACTERISTICS OF BASIN (cont'd)

				GAUGING STATION					BASIN			
						Distance (km) from gauging site		Mean slope of river I_r (%)	Area A (km²)	Altitude (m)		
	River / River system	Name	Period of records	Co-ordinates		to remotest point of river system L_{rs}	to projection of centre of basin on main course L_{ca}			Mean H_m	Max. H_{max}	Min. H_{min}
No.				Lat.	Long.							
1	2	3	4	5	6	7	8	9	10	11	12	13
				N	E							
10	Gaula	Haga Bru 661—0	1907—72	63:04	10:17	82	39	1.2	3060	740	1380	54
11	Argaroselv	Øyungen 685—0	1916—72	64:15	11:05	21	7.4	2.4	235	310	686	107
12	Strandvassa	Stranda 726—0	1916—72	67:32	14:53	7.8	4.0	8.7	24	150	953	0
13	Salangselv	Vassas 756—0	1913—72	68:53	17:53	40	29	2.4	580	520	1480	0
14	Altaelv	Stengelsen 764—0	1915—69	69:52	23:18	136	107	0.5	6260	450	1040	20
15	Pasvikelv	Bjørnvatn 775—0	1911—72	69:31	30:06				18200			19

					BASIN							
	Width (km)		Mean slope I_b (%)	Soils	Cover	Weighted lake area P_L (%)	Swamps R_s (%)	Mean annual precipitation P (mm)	Annual runoff Q (mm)	Mean annual temperature T (°C)	Regulating capacity of reservoirs α
No.	Mean B_m	Max. B_{max}									
1	14	15	16	17	18	19	20	21	22	23	24
10	37					0.9			1650		
11	11					0.11			783		
12	3.1					1.8			1550		
13	15					1.0			1180		
14	46					0.4			390		
15						5.5			295		

TABLE III — CHARACTERISTICS OF SNOWMELT FLOODS

No.	River	Gauging station	Q_{max} (m^3/s)	Date	h (mm)	T_T (hours)	t_i (hours)	P_W (%)	$P_{Q_{max}}$ (%)	Type of probability curve for P_W	for $P_{Q_{max}}$
1	2	3	4	5	6	7	8	9	10	11	12
1	Engera	Engeren 374—0	117	07—05—34	292	60	23		1.1		Log-normal
			102	20—05—66	321	62	21		2.8		"
			112	27—05—67	434	60	27		1.5		"
2	Glomma	Langnes 395—0	3190	07—07—27	518	127	64		2.0		"
			3220	14—05—34	277	100	30		1.8		"
			3540	06—06—67	346	109	41		0.7		"
3	Snarumselv	Krødern 458—0	1020	12—05—16	633	141	41		2.3		"
			998	13—06—26	543	103	72		2.5		"
			1090	30—06—27	605	106	78		1.3		"
4	Nidelv	Lunde Mølle 518—12	706	30—05—25	312	52	30		5.3		"
			869	23—04—37	740	78	24		1.8		"
			701	07—05—54	373	81	49		5.6		"
5	Fedeelv	Refsti 560—11	84.3	24—03—03	441	48	10		5.6		"
			77.7	04—03—26	425	34	9		9.1		"
6	Hellelandselv	Gya 919—0	45.5	10—01—36	159	23	3		9.1		"
			50.5	06—05—42	186	15	3		5.0		"
7	Kløvtveitelv	Kløvtveitvatn 603—0	2.38	12—02—39	920	30	11		5.0		2PGAMA

No.	Method of curve fitting for W	for Q_{max}	Snow cover Water equivalent (mm)	Layer thickness (cm)	Rainfall during snowmelt (mm)	Monthly precipitation before soil freezing (mm)	Mean monthly temperature before snowmelt (°C)
1	13	14	15	16	17	18	19
1		Maximum Likelihood					
		"					
		"					
2		"					
		"					
		"					
3		"					
		"					
		"					
4		"					
		"					
		"					
5		"					
		"					
6		"					
		"					
7		"					

TABLE III — CHARACTERISTICS OF SNOWMELT FLOODS (cont'd)

No.	River	Gauging station	Q_{max} (m³/s)	Date	h (mm)	T_T (hours)	t_i (hours)	P_W (%)	$P_{Q_{max}}$ (%)	Type of probability curve for P_W	for $P_{Q_{max}}$
1	2	3	4	5	6	7	8	9	10	11	12
8	Loelv	Lovatn 622—11	133	25—07—01	708	24	9		1.7		2PGAMA
			127	07—07—14	1147	56	31		2.3		"
			145	14—07—41	834	41	31		1.1		"
9	Aura	Eikesdalsvatn 640—0	409	22—06—05	848	75	50		2.9		"
			364	11—06—26	868	94	27		7.7		"
			393	25—06—35	758	67	33		4.0		"
11	Argaroselv	Øyungen 685—0	521	28—01—32	514	18	12		0.1		"
			248	04—04—46	476	19	10		5.4		"
			335	25—03—53	433	14	6		0.9		"
10	Gaula	Haga Bru 661—0	1300	13—05—17	324	35	27		2.2		"
			1490	06—05—34	395	46	23		0.6		"
			1600	10—06—44	467	31	16		0.3		"
12	Strandvassa	Stranda 726—0	18.6	02—03—30	191	9	5		1.7		"
			14.2	05—03—48	375	23	16		10.5		"
			19.8	06—03—53	713	40	12		1.0		"
13	Salangselv	Vassas 756—0	217	16—06—17	670	50	26		1.1		"
			227	21—06—39	583	69	43		0.7		"
			208	17—06—53	608	40	18		2.2		"
14	Altaelv	Stengelsen 764—0	1230	18—06—17	254	53	31		4.8		"
			1310	23—05—20	286	85	60		3.3		"
			1040	23—05—53	153	36	24		10.0		"

No.	Method of curve fitting for W	for Q_{max}	Snow cover Water equivalent (mm)	Layer thickness (cm)	Rainfall during snowmelt (mm)	Monthly precipitation before soil freezing (mm)	Mean monthly temperature before snowmelt (°C)
1	13	14	15	16	17	18	19
8		Maximum Likelihood					
		"					
		"					
9		"					
		"					
		"					
11		"					
		"					
		"					
10		"					
		"					
		"					
12		"					
		"					
		"					
13		"					
		"					
		"					
14		"					
		"					
		"					

TABLE III — CHARACTERISTICS OF SNOWMELT FLOODS (cont'd)

No.	River	Gauging station	Q_{max} (m³/s)	Date	h (mm)	T_T (hours)	t_i (hours)	P_W (%)	$P_{Q_{max}}$ (%)	Type of probability curve for P_W	for $P_{Q_{max}}$
1	2	3	4	5	6	7	8	9	10	11	12
15	Pasvikelv	Bjørnvatn 775—0	670	16—05—43	90	64	23		2.3		2PGAMA
			741	20—05—49	176	83	29		1.0		"
			823	04—06—52	121	52	25		0.3		"

No.	Method of curve fitting for W	for Q_{max}	Snow cover Water equivalent (mm)	Layer thickness (cm)	Rainfall during snowmelt (mm)	Monthly precipitation before soil freezing (mm)	Mean monthly temperature before snowmelt (°C)
1	13	14	15	16	17	18	19
15		Maximum liklihood					
		"					
		"					

TABLE IV — CHARACTERISTICS OF RAINFALL FLOODS

No.	River	Gauging station	Q_{max} (m³/s)	Date	h (mm)	T_T (hours)	t_i (hours)	P_W (%)	$P_{Q_{max}}$ (%)	Type of probability curve for P_W	for $P_{Q_{max}}$
1	2	3	4	5	6	7	8	9	10	11	12
1	Engera	Engeren 374-0	48.9	24—08—12	139	26	16		0.4		2PGAMA
			39.4	29—07—50	97	23	6		2.0		"
2	Glomma	Langnes 395-0	2390	27—08—12	187	64	25		2.5		"
			2420	19—09—57	106	34	16		2.2		"
3	Snarumselv	Krødern 458-0	1010	04—09—34	162	22	6		0.5		"
			798	26—07—39	187	22	10		2.2		"
4	Nidelv	Lunde Mølle 518-12	1450	04—11—53	252	34	13		2.1		"
			916	17—11—59	114	17	9		7.7		"
5	Fedeelv	Refsti 560-11	125	03—11—98	269	42	13		2.2		"
			132	25—10—29	184	11	3		1.4		"
			116	07—10—43	205	20	7		3.0		"
6	Hellelandselv	Gya 919-0	71.0	29—09—44	215	8	5		20.0		"
7	Kløvtveitelv	Kløvtveitvatn 603-0	2.49	11—09—23	746	23	9		2.4		"
			2.82	11—10—53	1020	37	15		0.4		"
8	Loelv	Lovatn 622-11	118	30—09—01	399	31	15		2.7		"
			125	04—10—08	418	44	9		1.5		"
9	Aura	Eikesdalsvatn 640-0	225	01—08—05	666	91	14		0.4		"
			246	03—09—38	155	15	5		0.2		"

No.	Method of curve fitting for W	for Q_{max}	Rainfall forming flood (mm)	Snowmelt during floods (mm)	Maximum daily rainfall (mm)	Date	Hourly maximum rainfall (mm)	Date	Antecedent precipitation for 10 days (mm)	30 days (mm)
1	13	14	15	16	17	18	19	20	21	22
1		Maximum Likelihood								
		"								
2		"								
		"								
3		"								
		"								
4		"								
		"								
5		"								
		"								
		"								
6		"								
7		"								
		"								
8		"								
		"								
9		"								
		"								

TABLE IV — CHARACTERISTICS OF RAINFALL FLOODS (cont'd)

No.	River	Gauging station	Characteristic element							Type of probability curve	
			Q_{max} (m^3/s)	Date	h (mm)	T_T (hours)	t_i (hours)	P_W (%)	$P_{Q_{max}}$ (%)	for P_W	for $P_{Q_{max}}$
1	2	3	4	5	6	7	8	9	10	11	12
11	Argaroselv	Øyungen 685—0	236 275	29—09—32 20—10—47	224 293	19 17	3 6		2.3 0.6		2PGAMA "
10	Gaula	Haga Bru 661—0	1200 903	14—08—09 08—09—41	81 94	11 13	8 10		2.8 11.1		" "
12	Strandvassa	Stranda 726—0	14.4 17.2	28—08—42 04—10—45	134 306	8 22	3 4		9.1 3.2		" "
13	Salangselv	Vassas 756—0	199 407	21—09—39 07—10—59	106 186	16 11	4 4		5.9 0.1		" "
14	Altaelv	Stengelsen 764—0	353 596	05—08—32 12—08—36	109 81	43 37	14 24		1.3 0.1		" "
15	Pasvikelv	Bjornvatn 775—0	405 450	12—08—31 11—09—51	92 107	56 64	5 32		9.1 5.6		" "

No.	Method of curve fitting		Rainfall forming flood (mm)	Snowmelt during floods (mm)	Maximum daily rainfall (mm)	Date	Hourly maximum rainfall (mm)	Date	Antecedent precipitation for	
	for W	for Q_{max}							10 days (mm)	30 days (mm)
1	13	14	15	16	17	18	19	20	21	22
11		Maximum Likelihood "								
10		" "								
12		" "								
13		" "								
14		" "								
15		" "								

Panama / Panamá / Панама

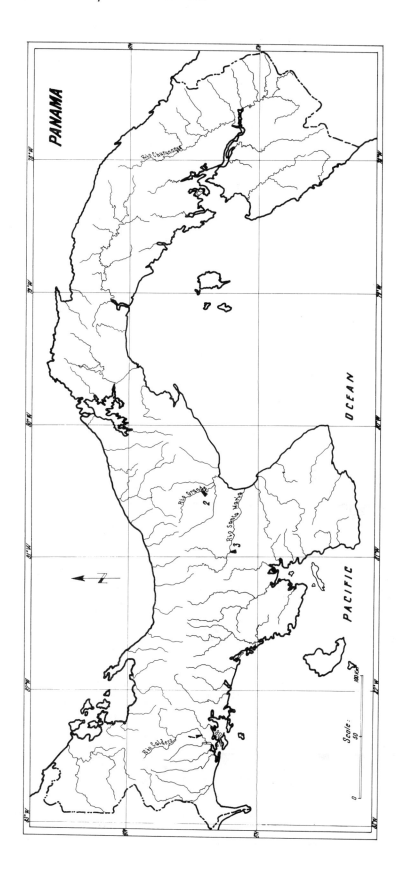

TABLE I — CHARACTERISTICS OF BASIN

		GAUGING STATION							BASIN				
						Distance (km) from gauging site		Mean			Altitude (m)		
	River / River system	Name	Period of records	Co-ordinates		to remotest point of river system L_{rs}	to projection of centre of basin on main course L_{ca}	slope of river I_r (%)	Area A (km²)	Mean H_m	Max. H_{max}	Min. H_{min}
No.				Lat.	Long.							
1	2	3	4	5	6	7	8	9	10	11	12	13
1	Chiriquí	David	1955–73	N 08:25	W 82:21	108	68	1.86	1200	894	2020	12
2	Grande	Grande	1955–73	08:26	80:30	46	22	3.09	471	581	1450	15
3	Santa María	San Francisco	1955–73	08:13	80:58	65	46	2.25	1200	626	1520	55

				BASIN								
	Width (km)		Mean slope I_b(%)	Soils	Cover	Weighted lake area P_L (%)	Swamps R_s (%)	Mean annual precipitation P (mm)	Annual runoff Q (mm)	Mean annual temperature T (°C)	Regulating capacity of reservoirs α
No.	Mean B_m	Max. B_{max}									
1	14	15	16	17	18	19	20	21	22	23	24
1	12.4	50	1.50	14(34), 15(11) 16(55)	F(30) F(70)			4030	3400	21	
2	10.7	34	1.62	15(54), 16(19) Sandy marine deposits (27)	C(100)			2220	1400	23	
3	20.5	46	1.28	15(24), 16(76)	C(100)			3290	2300	23	

TABLE IV — CHARACTERISTICS OF RAINFALL FLOODS

										Type of probability curve	
			Characteristic element							for P_W	for $P_{Q_{max}}$
No.	River	Gauging station	Q_{max} (m³/s)	Date	h (mm)	T_T (hours)	t_i (hours)	P_W (%)	$P_{Q_{max}}$ (%)		
1	2	3	4	5	6	7	8	9	10	11	12
1	Chiriquí	David	2310	09–04–70	238	297	29		4.7		Gumbel
2	Grande	Grande	1900	21–11–60	64.8	217	72		3.9		"
3	Santa María	San Francisco	3550	14–08–69	71.1	70	4		4.2		"

	Method of curve fitting		Rainfall forming flood (mm)	Snowmelt during floods (mm)	Maximum daily rainfall (mm)	Date	Hourly maximum rainfall (mm)	Date	Antecedent precipitation for	
									10 days (mm)	30 days (mm)
No.	for W	for Q_{max}								
1	13	14	15	16	17	18	19	20	21	22
1		Least squares			246	08–04–70			370	481
2		"			46	20–11–60			104	275
3		"			51	14–08–69			237	482

Poland / Pologne / Polonia / Польша

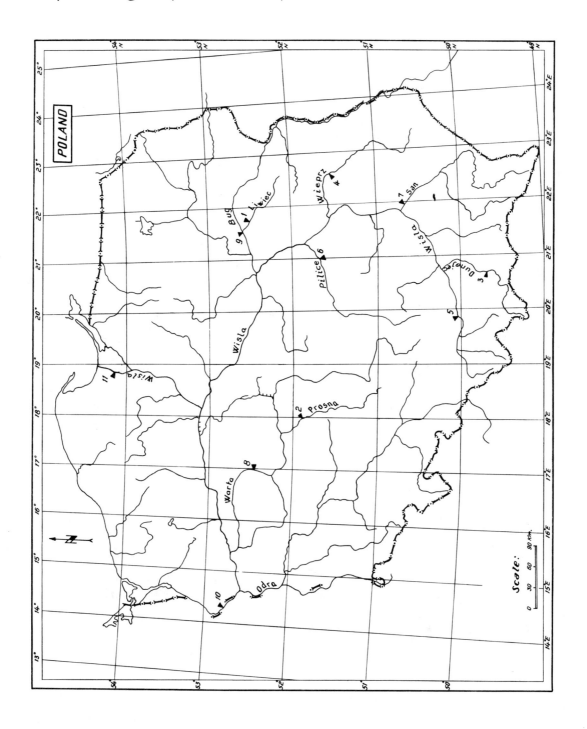

TABLE I – CHARACTERISTICS OF BASIN

		GAUGING STATION							BASIN			
						Distance (km) from gauging site						
	River River system	Name	Period of records	Co-ordinates Lat.	Long.	to remotest point of river system L_{rs}	to projection of centre of basin on main course L_{ca}	Mean slope of river I_r (%)	Area A (km^2)	Altitude (m) Mean H_m	Max. H_{max}	Min. H_{min}
No.	2	3	4	5	6	7	8	9	10	11	12	13
1				N	E							
1	Liwieo Vistula	Łoahów	1931–70	52:30:50	21:40:50	77	45	0.06	2460	152	223	90
2	Prosna Oder	Bogusław	1951–70	51:54:05	17:57:40	105	48	0.10	4300	162	284	90
3	Dunajec Vistula	Nowy Sacz	1921–70	49:37:50	20:42:30	78	34	0.87	4340	799	2500	281
4	Wieprz Vistula	Lubartów	1951–70	51:30:00	22:38:45	122	60	0.06	6360	222	385	150
5	Vistula	Tyniec	1951–70	50:01:15	19:48:15	86	35	0.54	7530	405	1730	205
6	Pilica Vistula	Białobrezegi	1951–70	51:39:30	20:57:10	162	77	0.09	8670	225	504	113
7	San Vistula	Radomyśl	1921–70	50:40:30	21:56:10	199	95	0.16	16800		1350	150
8	Warta Oder	Poznán	1951–70	52:24:40	16:56:30	271	115	0.06	39100		401	50
9	Bug Vistula	Wyszków	1921–70	52:35:00	21:27:00	385	183	0.03	39100		470	81

	BASIN										
	Width (km) Mean B_m	Max. B_{max}	Mean slope I_b(%)	Soils	Cover	Weighted lake area P_L (%)	Swamps R_s (%)	Mean annual precipitation P (mm)	Annual runoff Q (mm)	Mean annual temperature T (°C)	Regulating capacity of reservoirs α
No.	14	15	16	17	18	19	20	21	22	23	24
1	32	48	0.12	2(84), 17(16)	F(34), C(40), U(26)			553	131	7.2	
2	41	60	0.20	2(78), 4(14), 5(2)	F(25), C(55), U(20)			543	107	8.2	
3	56	60	2.56	2(6), 4(47), 17(10), 18(37)	F(40), C(37), U(23)	0.07		874	446	6.1	
4	52	85	0.21	2(73), 4(7), 17(14), 19(6)	F(14), C(69), U(17)			585	108	7.5	
5	88	115	1.24	2(48), 4(26), 17(9), 18(18)	F(32), C(44), U(24)			884	371	7.2	0.035
6	54	95	0.30	2(86), 4(9) 17(5)	F(24), C(58), U(18)			625	167	7.5	
7	84	150	0.65	2(52),4(28),5(4) 17(10), 18(6)	F(31), C(42), U(27)			721	251	7.2	0.019
8	95	120	0.20	2(79), 4(9), 5(4), 17(8)	F(22), C(58), U(20)	0.23		561	109	8.1	
9	102	140	0.14	2(74),4(4),5(4), 17(15), 19(3)	F(23), C(52), U(25)	0.04		556	110	7.4	

Poland / Pologne / Polonia / Польша

TABLE I — CHARACTERISTICS OF BASIN (cont'd)

		GAUGING STATION							BASIN			
	River River system	Name	Period of records	Co-ordinates		Distance (km) from gauging site		Mean slope of river I_r (%)	Area A (km²)	Altitude (m)		
No.				Lat.	Long.	to remotest point of river system L_{rs}	to projection of centre of basin on main course L_{ca}			Mean H_m	Max. H_{max}	Min. H_{min}
1	2	3	4	5	6	7	8	9	10	11	12	13
10	Oder	Gozdowice	1921–70	N 52:45:50	E 14:19:30	467	90	0.09	110000		1600	4
11	Vistula	Tczew	1921–70	54:05:40	18:48:20	625	125	0.11	194000		2500	5

	BASIN										
	Width (km)		Mean slope I_b(%)	Soils	Cover	Weighted lake area P_L (%)	Swamps R_s (%)	Mean annual precipitation P (mm)	Annual runoff Q (mm)	Mean annual temperature T (°C)	Regulating capacity of reservoirs α
No.	Mean B_m	Max. B_{max}									
1	14	15	16	17	18	19	20	21	22	23	24
10	237	350	0.34			0.94		597	146	7.8	0.006
11	311	390	0.43			0.71		611	162	7.3	0.008

TABLE II – ANNUAL MAXIMUM DISCHARGES AND VOLUMES

Country: Poland (1)
River: Liwiec
Gauging Station: Łoahów

Date	Maximum discharge (m³/s) resulting from:		Maximum volume (10⁶m³) corresponding to max. discharge resulting from:	
	Rainfall	Snowmelt	Rainfall	Snowmelt
1	2	3	4	5
03–04–51		162		180
29–10–52	21.4		19.3	
24–02–53		262		124
08–03–54		108		32.7
26–03–55		73.6		44.4
02–04–56		120		95.6
09–01–57		104		43.0
11–04–58		259		206
03–03–59		19.4		18.8
28–07–60	94.4		41.3	
16–07–61		30.8		25.6
04–04–62		153		102
31–03–63		79.0		39.0
30–04–64		146		126
21–03–65		150		101
26–02–66		91.8		83.3
03–03–67		138		158
25–03–68		62.7		63.9
03–04–69		46.1		62.2
03–04–70		230		175

Country: Poland (2)
River: Prosna
Gauging Station: Bogusław

Date	Maximum discharge (m³/s) resulting from:		Maximum volume (10⁶m³) corresponding to max. discharge resulting from:	
	Rainfall	Snowmelt	Rainfall	Snowmelt
1	2	3	4	5
25–03–51		25.9		20.3
03–03–52		32.6		58.0
31–01–53		237		130
05–03–54		52.2		35.7
16–04–55		38.0		44.7
04–03–56		89.3		75.2
08–01–57		71.8		64.7
10–03–58		86.5		73.4
28–02–59		39.6		61.1
17–08–60	55.6		45.3	
14–02–61		76.0		100
03–04–62		74.8		95.2
14–03–63		136		151
30–03–64		68.8		118
21–03–65		128		101
25–02–66		103		148
07–02–67		150		135
20–01–68		102		162
03–04–69		49.0		55.9
26–03–70		121		167

TABLE II — ANNUAL MAXIMUM DISCHARGES AND VOLUMES (cont'd)

Country:	Poland (3)
River:	Dunajec
Gauging Station:	Nowy Sacz

Date	Maximum discharge (m³/s) resulting from: Rainfall	Snowmelt	Maximum volume (10⁶m³) corresponding to max. discharge resulting from: Rainfall	Snowmelt
1	2	3	4	5
28–03–21		120		84
14–10–22	230		95	
02–02–23		285		145
01–08–24	1650		188	
30–06–25	1240		365	
01–08–26	956		177	
01–09–27	1010		193	
09–05–28	865		119	
13–07–29	700		119	
10–08–30	669		93	
25–09–31	1340		336	
06–04–32		1150		334
15–10–33	581		112	
17–07–34	3300		613	
14–04–35		220		80
02–03–36		343		178
25–08–37	959		225	
11–07–38	1170			
24–05–39	679			
20–05–40	1820			
21–10–41	1040			
05–01–42		353		
09–07–43	1040			
12–04–44		546		
28–03–45		560		
09–02–46		700		147
20–03–47		532		189
08–06–48	2190		458	
23–07–49	672		209	
08–08–50	138		37	

Country:	Poland (3) cont'd
River:	Dunajec
Gauging Station:	Nowy Sacz

Date	Maximum discharge (m³/s) resulting from: Rainfall	Snowmelt	Maximum volume (10⁶m³) corresponding to max. discharge resulting from: Rainfall	Snowmelt
1	2	3	4	5
11–05–51	1460		106	
02–04–52		542		94
02–11–53	300		61	
23–04–54		213		70
06–08–55	1970		347	
04–04–56		364		195
17–07–57	420		92	
30–06–58	3300		403	
01–07–59	850		195	
27–07–60	1900		578	
31–07–61	186		42	
06–06–62	1400		395	
13–04–63		434		153
03–04–64		544		315
11–06–65	1120		376	
24–02–66		999		236
23–05–67	566		169	
30–07–68	1010		205	
19–08–69	362		92	
19–07–70	2680		435	

Poland / Pologne / Polonia / Польша

TABLE II — ANNUAL MAXIMUM DISCHARGES AND VOLUMES (cont'd)

Country:	Poland (4)
River:	Wieprz
Gauging Station:	Lubartów

| | Maximum discharge (m^3/s) resulting from: | | Maximum volume ($10^6 m^3$) corresponding to max. discharge resulting from: | |
| Date | Rainfall | Snowmelt | Rainfall | Snowmelt |
1	2	3	4	5
22—02—51		38.7		43.9
07—04—52		75.0		109
28—02—53		146		156
06—03—54		136		99.9
31—03—55		58.2		86.1
03—04—56		250		230
11—01—57		57.3		81.3
11—04—58		154		177
22—01—59		28.0		53.4
10—01—60		30.6		39.2
24—01—61		26.6		48.6
08—06—62	67.9		85.4	
14—03—63		65.9		158
06—04—64		465		398
27—03—65		54.6		79.4
01—03—66		89.6		192
02—03—67		130		306
24—03—68		51.7		84.0
05—04—69		231		253
30—03—70		66.1		130

Country:	Poland (5)
River:	Vistula
Gauging Station:	Tyniec

| | Maximum discharge (m^3/s) resulting from: | | Maximum volume ($10^6 m^3$) corresponding to max. discharge resulting from: | |
| Date | Rainfall | Snowmelt | Rainfall | Snowmelt |
1	2	3	4	5
12—05—51	1310		354	
14—04—52		502		220
30—01—53		604		274
21—04—54		262		176
07—08—55	720		243	
24—06—56	240		180	
18—07—57	470		221	
30—06—58	1200		466	
02—07—59	679		245	
27—07—60	1640		687	
01—04—61		295		164
06—06—62	804		550	
06—05—63	605		314	
30—03—64		421		421
13—06—65	795		463	
31—05—66	888		369	
04—02—67		454		245
30—07—68	948		410	
12—07—69	362		190	
19—07—70	2260		598	

TABLE II – ANNUAL MAXIMUM DISCHARGES AND VOLUMES (cont'd)

Country:	Poland (7)
River:	San
Gauging Station:	Radomyśl

| Date | Maximum discharge (m³/s) resulting from: | | Maximum volume (10⁶m³) corresponding to max. discharge resulting from: | |
	Rainfall	Snowmelt	Rainfall	Snowmelt
1	2	3	4	5
05–04–51		143		85
28–02–52		116		134
01–02–53		464		220
07–03–54		380		161
28–03–55		166		142
06–03–56		183		129
10–01–57		289		56.9
08–04–58		344		291
28–02–59		150		94.8
01–08–60	436		233	
15–02–61		177		168
09–06–62	387		268	
15–03–63		186		152
29–03–64		436		328
19–03–65		310		241
31–07–66	362		331	
08–02–67		471		196
16–06–68	236		151	
05–04–69		101		97.6
28–03–70		268		416

Country:	Poland (7) cont'd
River:	San
Gauging Station:	Radomyśl

| Date | Maximum discharge (m³/s) resulting from: | | Maximum volume (10⁶m³) corresponding to max. discharge resulting from: | |
	Rainfall	Snowmelt	Rainfall	Snowmelt
1	2	3	4	5
27–06–21	1070		382	
27–02–22		1900		1320
05–02–23		1310		790
29–03–24		3340		2170
03–07–25	1940		1110	
26–07–26		2150		885
03–09–27	1940		811	
10–02–28		2150		640
16–07–29	1440		450	
20–03–30		1050		1020
26–09–31	980		630	
08–04–32		1420		1670
11–07–33	1310		751	
19–07–34	2040		2100	
22–02–35		1370		818
02–03–36		2600		997
02–03–37		1040		1520
20–01–38		1270		1340
27–05–39	1730		744	
27–03–40		2720		2640
20–02–41		1070		1380
21–03–42		1180		1750
17–02–43		304		167
14–04–44		980		1220
17–03–46		770		984
18–03–47		2790		2100
10–06–48	2120		2190	
25–07–49	986		427	
17–02–50		1610		959
22–03–51		512		360

TABLE II – ANNUAL MAXIMUM DISCHARGES AND VOLUMES   (cont'd)

Country:	Poland (7) cont'd
River:	San
Gauging Station:	Radomyśl

Date	Maximum discharge (m³/s) resulting from:		Maximum volume (10⁶m³) corresponding to max. discharge resulting from:	
	Rainfall	Snowmelt	Rainfall	Snowmelt
1	2	3	4	5
04–04–52		1180		1170
31–01–53		1110		391
04–03–54		2480		542
10–07–55	1400		692	
02–04–56		926		1310
12–05–57	1150		637	
06–04–58		1140		1620
11–03–59		896		721
30–07–60	1440		649	
17–11–61	830		482	
08–06–62	1820		1160	
15–04–63		1180		496
02–04–64		1930		2140
29–08–65	1250		445	
26–02–66		1600		1580
14–03–67		1240		1480
24–03–68		842		518
11–07–69	872		169	
22–07–70	1710		680	

Country:	Poland (8)
River:	Warta
Gauging Station:	Poznań

Date	Maximum discharge (m³/s) resulting from:		Maximum volume (10⁶m³) corresponding to max. discharge resulting from:	
	Rainfall	Snowmelt	Rainfall	Snowmelt
1	2	3	4	5
28–03–51		150		307
08–03–52		148		192
06–02–53		706		513
17–03–54		207		162
07–04–55		182		537
18–03–56		214		629
15–02–57		299		808
15–04–58		437		1970
09–03–59		185		320
11–08–60	201		547	
22–02–61		293		691
12–04–62		350		302
25–03–63		350		755
08–04–64		305		644
27–03–65		469		717
02–03–66		544		1520
12–02–67		634		928
28–01–68		434		1140
08–04–69		193		678
02–04–70		508		1530

TABLE II – ANNUAL MAXIMUM DISCHARGES AND VOLUMES (cont'd)

Country:	Poland (9)	Country:	Poland (9) cond'd
River:	Bug	River:	Bug
Gauging Station:	Wyszków	Gauging Station:	Wyszków

Date	Maximum discharge (m³/s) resulting from:		Maximum volume (10⁶m³) corresponding to max. discharge resulting from:		Date	Maximum discharge (m³/s) resulting from:		Maximum volume (10⁶m³) corresponding to max. discharge resulting from:	
	Rainfall	Snowmelt	Rainfall	Snowmelt		Rainfall	Snowmelt	Rainfall	Snowmelt
1	2	3	4	5	1	2	3	4	5
06–03–21		418		635	03–04–51		797		1420
17–03–22		633		951	30–04–52		269		650
05–02–23		782		378	26–02–53		828		2260
06–04–24		1500		3190	09–03–54		269		269
11–03–25		228		274	05–04–55		547		1410
10–03–26		539		864	17–04–56		891		2130
13–03–27		756		2280	18–01–57		564		1070
12–02–28		690		684	17–04–58		1430		2760
15–04–29		455		795	02–03–59		287		528
30–03–30		340		635	21–03–60		311		526
11–04–31		813		1890	16–07–61		321		724
16–04–32		1080		1890	14–04–62		769		1720
19–03–33		455		851	01–04–63		524		1430
24–03–34		596		1770	16–04–64		1050		2000
21–02–35		596		461	24–03–65		722		1680
15–03–36		619		1090	08–03–66		1260		2730
16–03–37		802		1660	14–03–67		1170		3140
05–02–38		430		234	26–03–68		584		1420
01–03–39		237		650	05–04–69		590		1930
09–04–40		1230		2340	06–04–70		1300		2320
13–03–41		979		1420					
12–04–42		1140		1760					
02–03–43		184		376					
25–03–44		344		1180					
20–03–45		573		1070					
01–04–46		676		1270					
24–03–47		1090		1730					
09–02–48		374		522					
19–02–49		533		600					
26–02–50		515		614					

TABLE II – ANNUAL MAXIMUM DISCHARGES AND VOLUMES (cont'd)

Country:	Poland (10)
River:	Oder
Gauging Station:	Gozdowice

Date	Maximum discharge (m³/s) resulting from:		Maximum volume (10⁶m³) corresponding to max. discharge resulting from:	
	Rainfall	Snowmelt	Rainfall	Snowmelt
1	2	3	4	5
30–07–21		1460		257
03–03–22		1170		1740
13–02–23		1620		2690
07–04–24		2380		4220
17–08–25	991		1190	
26–06–26	2450		5690	
22–01–27		1710		5190
18–01–28		1660		2790
25–03–29		1860		2390
30–06–30		646		836
08–11–31	2660		8120	
17–01–32		1140		3650
08–02–33		1170		1040
19–01–34		850		372
10–03–35		866		5380
11–03–36		707		2150
25–03–37		1350		7250
11–09–38	2140		4140	
04–06–39	1930		3070	
22–03–40		3720		7420
26–02–46		1370		7800
26–03–47		1710		4800
28–02–48		1810		4920
27–03–49		860		3210
15–02–50		1320		414
17–02–51		1080		1850
23–04–52		915		1960
12–02–53		1690		5350
20–07–54	830		1560	
21–02–55		920		3730

Country:	Poland (10) cont'd
River:	Oder
Gauging Station:	Gozdowice

Date	Maximum discharge (m³/s) resulting from:		Maximum volume (10⁶m³) corresponding to max. discharge resulting from:	
	Rainfall	Snowmelt	Rainfall	Snowmelt
1	2	3	4	5
14–03–56		1400		2080
06–01–57		998		1470
12–07–58	1830		2330	
17–03–59		726		1720
08–08–60	799		739	
08–02–61		890		2290
31–05–62	1210		3120	
23–03–63		1160		2530
15–04–64		885		2680
09–06–65	1800		3780	
01–03–66		1200		2020
17–02–67		1400		5510
27–01–68		1300		3390
10–04–69		1050		2380
20–04–70		1480		5330

Poland / Pologne / Polonia / Польша

TABLE II — ANNUAL MAXIMUM DISCHARGES AND VOLUMES (cont'd)

Country:	Poland (11)
River:	Vistula
Gauging Station:	Tczew

Date	Maximum discharge (m³/s) resulting from:		Maximum volume (10⁶m³) corresponding to max. discharge resulting from:	
	Rainfall	Snowmelt	Rainfall	Snowmelt
1	2	3	4	5
16–03–21		2500		4850
07–03–22		4520		6440
12–02–23		4570		3710
01–04–24		9550		12400
10–07–25	3980		4190	
12–08–26	3280		3560	
18–04–27		3580		6510
19–02–28		3410		4300
01–04–29		4130		4310
28–03–30		2530		4300
04–10–31	4790		5970	
13–04–32		4470		8370
14–02–33		2040		1580
27–07–34	5710		6800	
04–03–35		3650		5470
09–03–36		3530		5780
18–03–37		4030		10200
10–04–38		2490		
03–06–39	3670		3630	
02–04–40		8920		14000
12–03–41		3030		
03–04–42		4800		11100
19–07–43	1770		1120	
21–04–44		2480		3910
24–03–45		4730		
23–03–46		3830		9130
27–03–47		6790		11030
17–06–48	4260		2740	
25–03–49		2620		2640
25–02–50		4010		6590

Country:	Poland (11) cont'd
River:	Vistula
Gauging Station:	Tczew

Date	Maximum discharge (m³/s) resulting from:		Maximum volume (10⁶m³) corresponding to max. discharge resulting from:	
	Rainfall	Snowmelt	Rainfall	Snowmelt
1	2	3	4	5
11–04–51		3990		9210
11–04–52		3270		6260
03–03–53		5090		11100
13–03–54		3290		2400
03–04–55		3780		4740
09–04–56		3160		6690
25–02–57		2540		6900
15–04–58		5000		14800
08–03–59		2450		4760
04–08–60	6640		8300	
21–07–61		2110		3000
13–06–62	7840		11600	
22–03–63		2730		3870
05–04–64		5660		10100
26–03–65		5180		8290
04–03–66		5310		12300
10–03–67		5190		17600
31–03–68		2850		8830
10–04–69		2430		6780
28–03–70	5050		16500	

TABLE III — CHARACTERISTICS OF SNOWMELT FLOODS

No.	River	Gauging station	Q_{max} (m^3/s)	Date	h (mm)	T_T (hours)	t_i (hours)	P_W (%)	$P_{Q_{max}}$ (%)	Type of probability curve for P_W	for $P_{Q_{max}}$
1	2	3	4	5	6	7	8	9	10	11	12
1	Liwieo	Łoahów	262	24–02–53	50	480	68	27.0	6.9	Pearson type III	Pearson type III
2	Prosna	Bogusław	237	31–01–53	30	408	107	24.0	2.1	"	"
4	Wieprz	Lubartów	465	06–04–64	63	816	240	3.4	1.3	"	"
6	Pilica	Białobrezegi	471	08–02–67	23	240	130	43.0	9.8	"	"
7	San	Radomyśl	3340	29–03–24	129	624	144	7.0	1.4	"	"
8	Warta	Poznań	706	06–02–53	20	480	168	60.0	5.7	"	"
9	Bug	Wyszków	1500	06–04–24	82	1340	299	3.8	3.3	"	"
			1430	17–04–58	71	1180	288	6.5	3.8	"	"
			1300	06–04–70	59	1010	384	12.5	6.5	"	"
10	Oder	Gozdowice	3720	22–03–40	68	1080	144	5.1	0.5	"	"
11	Vistula	Tczew	9550	01–04–24	63	792	96	12.5	0.7	"	"

No.	Method of curve fitting for W	for Q_{max}	Snow cover Water equivalent (mm)	Layer thickness (cm)	Rainfall during snowmelt (mm)	Monthly precipitation before soil freezing (mm)	Mean monthly temperature before snowmelt (°C)
1	13	14	15	16	17	18	19
1	Method of quantiles	Method of quantiles	62	22	11	88	–3.4
2	"	"	43	18	6	13	–2.4
4	"	"	63	18	35	35	–3.3
6	"	"	18	6	16	73	–3.8
7	"	"					
8	"	"	43	18	6	13	–2.4
9	"	"					
	"	"	45	30	44	24	–3.2
	"	"	64	22	43	22	+0.2
10	"	"					
11	"	"					

TABLE IV — CHARACTERISTICS OF RAINFALL FLOODS

No.	River	Gauging station	Q_{max} (m³/s)	Date	h (mm)	T_T (hours)	t_i (hours)	P_W (%)	$P_{Q_{max}}$ (%)	Type of probability curve for P_W	for $P_{Q_{max}}$
1	2	3	4	5	6	7	8	9	10	11	12
3	Dunajec	Nowy Sacz	3300	17—07—34	141	192	46	2.3	1.7	Pearson III	Pearson III
			3300	30—06—58	93	144	44	10.2	1.7	"	"
			2680	19—07—70	100	192	82	7.5	3.8	"	"
5	Vistula	Tyniec	2260	19—07—70	79	192	30	8.0	3.1	"	"

No.	Method of curve fitting for W	for Q_{max}	Rainfall forming flood (mm)	Snowmelt during floods (mm)	Maximum daily rainfall (mm)	Date	Hourly maximum rainfall (mm)	Date	Antecedent precipitation for 10 days (mm)	30 days (mm)
1	13	14	15	16	17	18	19	20	21	22
3	Method of quantiles	Method of quantiles	180		120	16—07—34	19.7	16—07—34	34	193
	"	"	141		109	28—06—58			18	130
	"	"	158		101	18—07—70	13.2	18—07—70	9	114
5	"	"	172		108	18—07—70	10.8	18—07—70	27	65

Romania / Roumanie / Rumania / Румыния

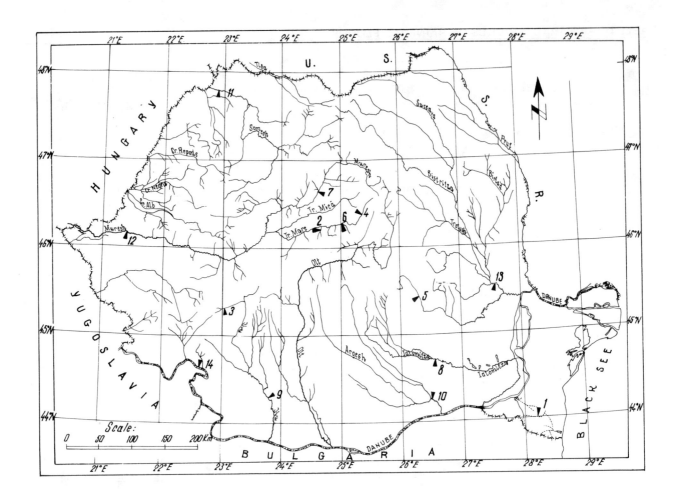

Romania / Roumanie / Rumania / Румыния

TABLE I — CHARACTERISTICS OF BASIN

			GAUGING STATION						BASIN			
						Distance (km) from gauging site		Mean slope of river I_r (%)	Area A (km²)	Altitude (m)		
	River River system	Name	Period of records	Co-ordinates		to remotest point of river system L_{rs}	to projection of centre of basin on main course L_{ca}			Mean H_m	Max. H_{max}	Min. H_{min}
No.				Lat.	Long.							
1	2	3	4	5	6	7	8	9	10	11	12	13
1	Iris	Cocargea	1960–72	44:08	28:01	4.5	2.1	1.04	10.5	106	130	86
2	Laslea	Laslea	1964–72	46:10	24:30	21	9.3	1.4	83	510	580	330
3.	Jiu	Cîmpul lui Neag	1957–72	45:20	23:04	21	8	5.55	140	1350	2510	806
4	Tîrnava Mare	Odorhei	1956–72	46:17	25:17	55	27	2.06	657	893	1800	450
5	Buzău	Nehoiu	1949–72	45:23	26:17	80	30	2.01	1570	1040	1960	352
6	Tîrnava Mare	Topa	1955–72	46:15	25	110	45	1.1	1670	692	1800	345
7	Mureş	Tg. Mureş	1950–72	46:32	24:35	170	90	0.29	4050	833	1790	307
8	Ialomiţa	Coşereni	1950–72	44:42	26:35	210	118	1.12	6470	488	2510	50.7
9	Jiu	Podari	1950–72	44:30	23:32	270	131	0.63	9240	484	2520	61.2
10	Argeş	Budeşti	1950–72	44:10	26:27	310	140	0.66	9370	391	2540	26.6
11	Someş	Satu Mare	1925–72	47:48	22:53	340	140	0.44	15200	540	2310	118
12	Mureş	Arad	1925–72	45:14	20:11	697	180	0.11	27600	618	2510	105

	BASIN											
	Width (km)		Mean slope I_b (%)	Soils	Cover	Weighted lake area P_L (%)	Swamps R_s (%)	Mean annual precipitation P (mm)	Annual runoff Q (mm)	Mean annual temperature T (°C)	Regulating capacity of reservoirs α
No.	Mean B_m	Max. B_{max}									
1	14	15	16	17	18	19	20	21	22	23	24
1	2.34	3.5	0.9	5	C(70), U(30)			400	20	12.0	
2	5.3	9.4	14.0	4	F(35), C(15), U(50)			650	150	8.2	
3	9.2	12.5	31.7	4	F(70), U(30)			1080	770	4	
4	13.5	22.5	19.0	4	F(60), U(40)			816	262	4.8	
5	21.5	52.4	24.4	4	F(80), U(20)			840	386	5	
6	16.6	31	16.4	4	F(60), U(40)			730	162	5.2	
7	21.5	52	20.0	4	F(60), U(40)			810	261	5.8	
8	30.4	85	7.6	4(70) Meadow(30)	F(40), C(40), U(20)			710	176	7.5	
9	35.7	98	10.5	2(75), 4(25)	F(40), C(40), U(20)			790	296	10.2	
10	30.8	67	9.5	Meadow(25) 4(75)	F(35), C(35), U(30)			671	168	9	0.26
11	46	250	17.1	2(65), 4(35)	F(45), C(40), U(15)			770	237	9	
12	40	95	I7.9	2(80), 4(20)	F(37), C(53), U(10)			730	175	9.2	

TABLE I — CHARACTERISTICS OF BASIN (cont'd)

			GAUGING STATION						BASIN			
	River / River system	Name	Period of records	Co-ordinates		Distance (km) from gauging site		Mean slope of river I_r (%)	Area A (km²)	Altitude (m)		
				Lat.	Long.	to remotest point of river system L_{rs}	to projection of centre of basin on main course L_{ca}			Mean H_m	Max. H_{max}	Min. H_{min}
No.	2	3	4	5	6	7	8	9	10	11	12	13
1												
13	Siret	Lungoci	1951–72	45:33	27:30	652	246	0.19	36500	540	2280	19
14	Danube	Orşova	1834–72	44:43	22:24				575000	495	4060	46.4

				BASIN							
	Width (km)		Mean slope I_b (%)	Soils	Cover	Weighted lake area P_L (%)	Swamps R_s (%)	Mean annual precipitation P (mm)	Annual runoff Q (mm)	Mean annual temperature T (°C)	Regulating capacity of reservoirs α
No.	Mean B_m	Max. B_{max}									
1	14	15	16	17	18	19	20	21	22	23	24
13	55.4	171	11.6	Meadow(10) 5(20), 3(20) 4(20)	F(45), C(40), U(15)			660	135	8.2	0.28
14	300	750						881	350	8.5	

TABLE II — ANNUAL MAXIMUM DISCHARGES AND VOLUMES

Country:	Romania (1)
River:	Iris
Gauging Station:	Cocargea

Date	Maximum discharge (m³/s) resulting from:		Maximum volume (10⁶m³) corresponding to max. discharge resulting from:	
	Rainfall	Snowmelt	Rainfall	Snowmelt
1	2	3	4	5
23—06—60	2.7		0.019	
13—06—61	14.9		0.110	
20—06—62	2.3		0.018	
03—02—63		1.6		0.014
25—06—64	29.8		0.216	
10—07—65	6.9		0.042	
16—07—66	8.1		0.044	
21—06—67	26.6		0.105	
01—09—68	63.5		0.341	
31—05—71	3.0		0.140	
20—07—72	97.5		0.431	

Country:	Romania (2)
River:	Laslea
Gauging Station:	Laslea

Date	Maximum discharge (m³/s) resulting from:		Maximum volume (10⁶m³) corresponding to max. discharge resulting from:	
	Rainfall	Snowmelt	Rainfall	Snowmelt
1	2	3	4	5
21—10—64	2.5		0.128	
04—03—65		8.6		0.282
10—02—66		3.7		0.698
01—04—67	22.7		1.100	
29—08—68	6.3		0.270	
12—07—69	5.3		0.786	
06—07—70	20.5		0.830	
16—09—71	1.3		0.184	
22—09—72	2.7		0.213	

TABLE II — ANNUAL MAXIMUM DISCHARGES AND VOLUMES (cont'd)

Country: Romania (3)
River: Jiul de Vest
Gauging Station: Cimpul Lui Neag

| Date | Maximum discharge (m³/s) resulting from: | | Maximum volume (10⁶m³) corresponding to max. discharge resulting from: | |
| | Rainfall | Snowmelt | Rainfall | Snowmelt |
1	2	3	4	5
22—08—57	22.5		4.6	
14—01—58		30.9		5.8
15—08—59	75.6		15.5	
11—12—60	107		19.5	
07—11—61	210		17.3	
26—04—62		26.0		19.2
05—05—63		26.5		10.4
21—10—64	95.0		14.0	
05—06—65	160		16.2	
27—07—66	237		18.7	
23—05—67	37.5		8.5	
06—09—68	22.3		6.1	
30—07—69	43.6		6.7	
11—06—70	122		11.3	
30—07—71	31.4		3.0	
09—10—72	55.5		18.7	

Country: Romania (4)
River: Tîrnava Mare
Gauging Station: Odorhei

| Date | Maximum discharge (m³/s) resulting from: | | Maximum volume (10⁶m³) corresponding to max. discharge resulting from: | |
| | Rainfall | Snowmelt | Rainfall | Snowmelt |
1	2	3	4	5
26—04—56	140		24.3	
13—07—57	83.0		12.0	
17—02—58		103		20.3
20—07—59	79		13.7	
20—02—60		44.2		17.4
26—05—61	29		6.7	
07—03—62		46.7		11.8
13—04—63		33.2		11.2
26—11—64	85.9		9.8	
07—06—65	68.8		15.5	
13—02—66		47.5		11.3
01—04—67		58.8		14.6
26—03—68		54.2		11.1
01—06—69	41		11.6	
13—05—70	305		33.9	
05—07—71	48.9		16.5	
20—09—72	59.4		17.3	

TABLE II – ANNUAL MAXIMUM DISCHARGES AND VOLUMES   (cont'd)

Country:	Romania (5)
River:	Buzau
Gauging Station:	Nehoiu

Date	Maximum discharge (m³/s) resulting from:		Maximum volume (10⁶m³) corresponding to max. discharge resulting from:	
	Rainfall	Snowmelt	Rainfall	Snowmelt
1	2	3	4	5
20–08–49	271		53.8	
06–04–60	92		41.6	
12–06–51	108		38.1	
20–01–52		153		18.6
01–06–53	158		49.8	
25–08–54	195		19.3	
18–09–55	253		54.1	
17–04–56		229		148
13–07–57	448		36.7	
01–04–58	243		25.8	
23–05–59	302		47.4	
29–05–60	313		58.1	
01–05–61	189		28.8	
30–04–62		166		37.5
06–02–63		143		19.3
24–09–64	434		92.5	
20–01–65		508		58.0
14–11–66	400		34.4	
15–06–67	254		51.8	
21–08–68	237		30.5	
13–07–69	1120		190	
14–05–70	506		82.9	
02–07–71	1320		86.4	
11–10–72	267		59.4	

Country:	Romania (6)
River:	Tîrnava Mare
Gauging Station:	Topa

Date	Maximum discharge (m³/s) resulting from:		Maximum volume (10⁶m³) corresponding to max. discharge resulting from:	
	Rainfall	Snowmelt	Rainfall	Snowmelt
1	2	3	4	5
08–08–55	191		39.3	
25–04–56	451		52.4	
13–07–57	74		11.5	
25–04–58	225		50.2	
20–07–59	108		25.9	
28–07–60	189		30.5	
24–05–61	81		23.2	
07–04–62	210		34.7	
13–03–63		54		14.1
06–04–64	94		16.3	
15–06–65	205		33.1	
14–02–66		149		39.1
02–04–67	153		25.4	
26–02–68		74		15.2
13–07–69	98		16.6	
14–05–70	700		135	
05–07–71	126		39.5	
11–10–72	111		26.5	

TABLE II — ANNUAL MAXIMUM DISCHARGES AND VOLUMES (cont'd)

Country: Romania (7)
River: Mures
Gauging Station: Tg. Mures

Date	Maximum discharge (m³/s) resulting from:		Maximum volume (10⁶m³) corresponding to max. discharge resulting from:	
	Rainfall	Snowmelt	Rainfall	Snowmelt
1	2	3	4	5
08–12–50	133		31	
21–03–61	179		36	
01–04–52		425		202
03–04–53		311		170
22–05–54	111		170	
29–03–55		246		128
26–04–56		426		176
10–05–57	335		106	
17–02–58		565		150
08–03–59	444		60	
21–02–60		276		69
14–03–61		99		17
07–04–62		403		132
14–04–63	205		80	
02–04–64		336		209
15–06–65	340		96	
04–04–66	195		36	
01–04–67	540		103	
17–02–68	280		43	
10–06–69	272		102	
03–05–70	1210		337	
05–06–71	340		130	
14–10–72	257		67	

Country: Romania (8)
River: Ialomița
Gauging Station: Coșereni

Date	Maximum discharge (m³/s) resulting from:		Maximum volume (10⁶m³) corresponding to max. discharge resulting from:	
	Rainfall	Snowmelt	Rainfall	Snowmelt
1	2	3	4	5
20–12–50	380		50	
28–07–51	188		54	
24–11–52	166		31	
02–06–53	467		127	
20–05–54	344		71	
11–03–55		488		174
03–03–56		337		183
05–08–57	278		52	
02–04–58	346		55	
24–05–59	195		46	
30–05–60	633		134	
30–05–61	401		78	
08–03–62	299		56	
02–04–63		209		80
14–11–64	191		40	
21–01–65	518		100	
15–11–66	578		102	
16–06–67	605		124	
21–11–68	116		35	
28–06–69	568		81	
19–01–70	572		96	
08–05–71	939		259	
06–10–72	1170		590	

TABLE II — ANNUAL MAXIMUM DISCHARGES AND VOLUMES (cont'd)

Country:	Romania (9)	Country:	Romania (10)
River:	Jiu	River:	Argeş
Gauging Station:	Podari	Gauging Station:	Budeşti

Date	Maximum discharge (m³/s) resulting from:		Maximum volume (10⁶m³) corresponding to max. discharge resulting from:		Date	Maximum discharge (m³/s) resulting from:		Maximum volume (10⁶m³) corresponding to max. discharge resulting from:	
	Rainfall	Snowmelt	Rainfall	Snowmelt		Rainfall	Snowmelt	Rainfall	Snowmelt
1	2	3	4	5	1	2	3	4	5
21–12–50	700		284		08–11–50	346		51	
23–02–51		640		285	19–05–51	259		53	
17–12–52	695		169		19–05–52	523		95	
09–01–53	1500		428		18–02–53		788		119
29–03–54		1190		652	30–03–54		638		247
12–03–55	970		223		13–03–55	585		195	
03–04–56		737		387	05–04–56		900		425
30–05–57	963		406		31–05–57	532		114	
16–01–58	630		190		13–04–58	260		81	
16–08–59	508		123		25–05–59	246		63	
15–12–60	910		368		31–05–60	640		221	
09–06–61	1320		434		31–05–61	589		75	
27–03–62		892		337	09–03–62	350		84	
12–03–63		625		269	03–04–63	408		125	
22–10–64	739		202		23–10–64	553		92	
24–01–65		868		289	04–06–65	269		66	
14–02–66		775		265	06–11–66	189		44	
02–04–67	517		143		16–06–67	377		88	
23–11–68	613		194		23–12–68	150		28	
17–03–69	946		426		17–03–69		361		238
14–04–70		782		460	07–07–70	635		285	
01–04–71	575		170		08–05–71	526		201	
11–10–72	2000		1200		12–10–72	1540		1290	

TABLE II – ANNUAL MAXIMUM DISCHARGES AND VOLUMES (cont'd)

Country:	Romania (11)
River:	Somes
Gauging Station:	Satu-Mare

| Date | Maximum discharge (m³/s) resulting from: | | Maximum volume (10⁶m³) corresponding to max. discharge resulting from: | |
	Rainfall	Snowmelt	Rainfall	Snowmelt
1	2	3	4	5
12–12–25	1890		691	
02–08–26	573		180	
19–01–27		306		121
30–03–28		843		487
16–07–29	673		232	
24–11–30	794		419	
30–10–31	734		422	
07–03–32		2350		1400
11–07–33	1300		407	
05–03–34		587		282
30–04–35	1110		426	
07–04–36		622		284
04–03–37		756		241
11–05–38	740		339	
31–10–39	831		236	
19–03–40		2600		1420
30–04–41	1560		613	
01–03–50		739		248
23–03–51		436		159
04–04–52	1290		738	
04–01–53		806		387
06–03–54		442		134
16–01–55		766		515
05–03–56	572		123	
01–06–57	784		359	
20–02–58	1420		838	
31–12–59	549		203	
23–02–60	1180		483	
15–03–61		282		113
02–04–62	1590		974	

Country:	Romania (11) cont'd
River:	Somes
Gauging Station:	Satu-Mare

| Date | Maximum discharge (m³/s) resulting from: | | Maximum volume (10⁶m³) corresponding to max. discharge resulting from: | |
	Rainfall	Snowmelt	Rainfall	Snowmelt
1	2	3	4	5
14–03–63		930		317
31–03–64	2090		871	
14–06–65	980		467	
15–02–66	1290		772	
05–03–67	1390		716	
27–02–68	1020		395	
04–07–69	562		192	
15–05–70	3340		1350	
03–01–71		659		342
17–11–72	678		228	

TABLE II – ANNUAL MAXIMUM DISCHARGES AND VOLUMES (cont'd)

Country:	Romania (12)
River:	Mureş
Gauging Station:	Arad

	Maximum discharge (m³/s) resulting from:		Maximum volume (10⁶m³) corresponding to max. discharge resulting from:	
Date	Rainfall	Snowmelt	Rainfall	Snowmelt
1	2	3	4	5
28–12–25	1550		1090	
04–07–26	934		536	
26–05–27	372		318	
01–04–28	533		449	
18–07–29	460		268	
22–05–30	779		670	
16–03–31		612		552
07–04–32		2150		2170
16–07–33	957		629	
21–03–34		431		358
04–05–35	844		528	
03–11–36	393		151	
01–05–37	612		401	
14–05–38	881		1040	
01–04–39		889		460
09–06–40	1000		683	
06–05–41	1040		1040	
19–04–50		284		240
12–05–51	475		296	
08–04–52		783		730
15–04–53		605		667
09–06–54	660		446	
27–02–55		806		643
02–05–56	832		904	
01–06–57	794		689	
01–05–58	870		753	
25–05–59	521		204	
26–02–60		645		594
10–06–61	464		344	
12–04–62		731		696

Country:	Romania (12) cont'd
River:	Mureş
Gauging Station:	Arad

	Maximum discharge (m³/s) resulting from:		Maximum volume (10⁶m³) corresponding to max. discharge resulting from:	
Date	Rainfall	Snowmelt	Rainfall	Snowmelt
1	2	3	4	5
17–04–63	464		247	
07–04–64	718		680	
16–06–65	755		840	
31–05–66	769		416	
06–04–67	741		476	
20–02–68		600		367
17–07–69	797		473	
18–05–70	2320		2250	
09–07–71	549		309	
29–11–72	969		615	

Romania / Roumanie / Rumania / Румыния

TABLE II – ANNUAL MAXIMUM DISCHARGES AND VOLUMES (cont'd)

Country:	Romania (13)
River:	Siret
Gauging Station:	Lungoci

| Date | Maximum discharge (m³/s) resulting from: | | Maximum volume (10⁶m³) corresponding to max. discharge resulting from: | |
	Rainfall	Snowmelt	Rainfall	Snowmelt
1	2	3	4	5
15–06–51	821		508	
05–04–52		602		511
04–04–53		800		1240
11–05–54	625		618	
16–08–55	1500		2320	
05–05–56	956		963	
13–05–57	808		441	
05–09–58	883		381	
09–06–59	1120		1040	
01–06–60	1830		998	
22–05–61	678		450	
09–04–62		771		1280
15–04–63		756		779
27–09–64	943		318	
15–05–65	1290		857	
06–06–66	639		368	
02–03–67		664		278
04–09–68	556		210	
18–07–69	2670		1600	
19–05–70	3190		3270	
31–05–71	2550		952	
12–10–72	2100		1580	

Country:	Romania (14)
River:	Danube
Gauging Station:	Orşova

| Date | Maximum discharge (m³/s) resulting from: | | Maximum volume (10⁶m³) corresponding to max. discharge resulting from: | |
	Rainfall	Snowmelt	Rainfall	Snowmelt
1	2	3	4	5
04–06–39		15000		94.2
15–02–40		6840		21.1
14–04–41		9880		49.4
23–04–42		9020		70.8
01–03–43		7480		45.8
29–03–44		9660		102
02–05–45		14000		132
27–04–46		9720		56.2
12–05–47		9630		61.3
23–03–48		10200		62.7
04–05–48		7590		73.0
19–05–50		10400		95.9
04–12–51	9390		51.3	
28–04–52		7900		60.5
07–05–53		13700		189
27–05–54		6490		25.6
20–04–55		11600		129
01–03–56		7660		43.8
06–04–57		7480		72.0
17–04–58		7660		53.4
05–06–59		8460		75.2
29–04–60		11800		79.7
07–04–61		7710		53.3
10–03–62		9300		80.3
17–03–63		5200		49.2
29–06–64		9150		116
05–05–65		10900		64.4
01–04–66		5850		46.9
14–05–67		11100		144
27–05–68		10200		84.0

228

Romania / Roumanie / Rumania / Румыния

TABLE II — ANNUAL MAXIMUM DISCHARGES AND VOLUMES (cont'd)

Country: Romania (14) cont'd
River: Danube
Gauging Station: Orşova

Date	Maximum discharge (m³/s) resulting from: Rainfall	Snowmelt	Maximum volume (10⁶m³) corresponding to max. discharge resulting from: Rainfall	Snowmelt
1	2	3	4	5
31—12—69	8100		62.7	
29—11—70	9630		112	
07—07—71		9940		65.8
16—04—72		7060		111
03—06—73		8910		83.0
04—06—74		9540		71.0
20—04—75		9150		70.7
01—04—76		14100		151
26—05—77		12000		141
14—12—78	10700		68.5	
23—05—79		13000		71.9
20—03—80		7040		63.2
21—04—81		11200		113
26—12—82	10400		87.4	
28—05—83		9000		84.0
09—04—84		7730		41.6
01—11—85	6800		45.4	
23—04—86		9180		45.0
27—05—87		7830		75.9
17—05—88		15500		82.1
30—04—89		11800		81.1
03—12—90	7040		26.7	
02—04—91		9390		64.1
24—05—92		8770		126
13—03—93		11200		46.0
27—03—94		6490		53.5
17—04—95		15900		124
20—11—96	8180		24.7	
07—06—97		15400		71.4
19—04—98		8460		60.0

Country: Romania (14) cont'd
River: Danube
Gauging Station: Orşova

Date	Maximum discharge (m³/s) resulting from: Rainfall	Snowmelt	Maximum volume (10⁶m³) corresponding to max. discharge resulting from: Rainfall	Snowmelt
1	2	3	4	5
11—06—99		8490		79.5
11—05—00		10400		76.6
03—04—01		10600		55.4
07—06—02		8710		118
18—12—03	8910		27.5	
06—03—04		7530		81.7
21—04—05		9660		90.6
26—06—06		10500		58.4
26—04—07		13600		94.3
18—04—08		8680		75.1
16—05—09		8260		64.8
20—05—11		8380		83.7
17—04—11		8380		87.5
26—11—12	10200		31.4	
04—08—13	11400		66.1	
03—04—14		13600	66.1	58.1
31—03—15		12400		79.8
05—01—16	10700		87.7	
19—01—17	11200		53.3	
20—01—19	8630		24.6	
08—03—19		14000		71.9
29—01—20	11500		43.8	
18—05—21		7440		27.0
29—04—22		10300		92.6
19—03—23		10500		80.9
19—04—24		14200		101
17—01—26	11800		33.4	
10—07—26		13100		71.9
26—04—27		8290		69.0
20—05—28		8940		62.7

229

Romania / Roumanie / Rumania / Румыния

TABLE II — ANNUAL MAXIMUM DISCHARGES AND VOLUMES (cont'd)

Country: **Romania (14) cont'd**
River: **Danube**
Gauging Station: **Orşova**

Date	Maximum discharge (m³/s) resulting from:		Maximum volume (10⁶m³) corresponding to max. discharge resulting from:	
	Rainfall	Snowmelt	Rainfall	Snowmelt
1	2	3	4	5
22—05—29		8600		78.0
18—11—30	8380		42.7	
24—03—31		10300		80.2
22—04—32		13800		82.8
26—05—33		9420		66.9
28—03—34		7950		42.4
08—03—35		10900		85.5
09—03—36		9390		72.4
02—03—37		13300		126
02—06—38		9420		86.0
09—06—39		10300		46.7
13—04—40		15100		132
17—05—41		12500		94.6
05—04—42		14700		113
25—06—43		7160		35.5
04—05—44		13500		57.7
12—04—45		8890		90.4
13—02—46		8260		50.8
03—04—47		12800		63.1
18—01—48	9780		48.3	
21—12—49	7020		26.5	
26—12—50	8100		40.3	
12—04—51		9630		94.0
15—04—52		10000		43.6
08—01—53	10700		62.0	
21—05—54		10100		53.9
22—04—55		12000		42.2
21—05—56		11000		113
06—06—57		9600		38.7
06—05—58		11400		80.0

Country: **Romaia (14) cont'd**
River: **Danube**
Gauging Station: **Orşova**

Date	Maximum discharge (m³/s) resulting from:		Maximum volume (10⁶m³) corresponding to max. discharge resulting from:	
	Rainfall	Snowmelt	Rainfall	Snowmelt
1	2	3	4	5
25—06—59		7590		40.1
27—02—60		8080		37.6
28—05—61		9270		42.4
19—04—62		13700		87.3
03—04—63		10700		53.0
15—04—64		8600		58.1
27—06—65		12900		146
24—02—66		11500		42.5
30—04—67		11800		113
22—02—68		8000		63.0
05—03—69		9720		94.5
19—05—70		13800		150
01—04—71		9000		42.6
30—11—72	9500		24.0	
16—05—73		9680		45.3

TABLE III – CHARACTERISTICS OF SNOWMELT FLOODS

No.	River	Gauging station	Characteristic elements							Type of probability curve	
			Q_{max} (m³/s)	Date	h (mm)	T_T (hours)	t_i (hours)	P_W (%)	$P_{Q_{max}}$ (%)	for P_W	for $P_{Q_{max}}$
1	2	3	4	5	6	7	8	9	10	11	12
11	Someş	Satu Mare	2350	07–04–32	92.5	340	170	4.9	7	Kritzki Menkel	Kritzki Menkel
			2600	19–03–40	93.6	480	120	2.4	5	''	''
12	Mureş	Arad	2150	07–04–32	78.5	500	170	4.9	1.6	''	''
14	Danube	Orşova	14000	02–05–45	230	3840	1440		5.0	''	''
			13700	07–05–53	328	6000	2520		6.0	''	''
			14100	01–04–76	261	4800	960		4.7	''	''
			15500	17–05–88	142	2280	840		2.0	''	''
			15900	17–04–95	216	3840	1080		1.5	''	''
			15400	07–06–97	124	1920	840		2.1	''	''
			14000	08–05–19	125	1920	720		5.0	''	''
			14200	19–04–24	175	2880	720		4.5	''	''
			13800	22–04–32	145	2640	960		5.7	''	''
			15100	13–04–40	230	4080	960		2.5	''	''
			14700	05–04–42	196	3120	840		3.4	''	''
			13800	19–05–70	260	3600	1440		5.7	''	''

No.	Method of curve fitting		Snow cover		Rainfall during snowmelt (mm)	Monthly precipitation before soil freezing (mm)	Mean monthly temperature before snowmelt (°C)
	for W	for Q_{max}	Water equivalent (mm)	Layer thickness (cm)			
1	13	14	15	16	17	18	19
11				45.3	35.9	65.2	–4.4
				31.0	40.3	54.4	–6.1
12				40.0	22.0	52.0	–3.3

TABLE IV — CHARACTERISTICS OF RAINFALL FLOODS

No.	River	Gauging station	Characteristic element									
			Q_{max} (m^3/s)	Date	h (mm)	T_T (hours)	t_i (hours)	P_W (%)	$P_{Q_{max}}$ (%)	Type of probability curve	
										for P_W	for $P_{Q_{max}}$
1	2	3	4	5	6	7	8	9	10	11	12
1	Iris	Cocargea	63.5	01—09—68	32	9	2	14	9	Kritzki-Menkel	Kritzki-Menkel
			97.5	20—07—72	41	8	2	7	4.4	"	"
2	Laslea	Laslea	22.7	01—04—67	12.7	75	38	10	22	"	"
			20.5	06—07—70	10.2	75	20	20	24	"	"
3	Jiu	Cîmpul lui Neag	210	07—11—61	124	90	15	30	12	"	"
			237	29—07—66	133	90	10	24	9	"	"
4	Tîrnava Mare	Odorhei	140	25—04—56	37	120	20	11	19	"	"
			305	13—05—70	51.5	190	15	5.5	3.5	"	"
5.	Buzäu	Nehoiu	1120	13—07—69	120	140	25	16	3	"	"
			1320	02—07—71	55	100	17	4	1.7	"	"
6.	Tîrnava Mare	Topa	451	25—04—56	31.3	140	38	11	6	"	"
			700	14—05—70	80.6	190	25	5	1.5	"	"
7	Mureş	Tg. Mureş	540	01—04—67	25.3	170	60	50	13	"	"
			1210	13—05—70	83	240	40	4	0.5	"	"
8	Ialomiţa	Coşereni	939	08—05—71	40	216	60	8.3	5	"	"
			1170	06—10—72	91	384	50	4	1.7	"	"
9	Jiu	Podari	1320	09—06—61	47	220	65	16.5	15	"	"
			2000	11—10—72	130	360	120	4.2	2.2	"	"

No.	Method of curve fitting		Rainfall forming flood (mm)	Snowmelt during floods (mm)	Maximum daily rainfall (mm)	Date	Hourly maximum rainfall (mm)	Date	Antecedent precipitation for	
	for W	for Q_{max}							10 days (mm)	30 days (mm)
1	13	14	15	16	17	18	19	20	21	22
1									0	34
									2.0	19.5
2			34.2		23.4	01—04—67			1.1	16.4
			60.2		60.2	06—07—72			34.9	59.2
3			194		40.0	07—11—61			0	19
									62.4	70.3
4			60.5		45.0	25—04—56			0	17.3
			89.4		50.1	13—05—70			55	58.5
5			140		70	13—07—69			20	90
			97.6		79.9	02—07—70			18.7	44.7
6			56		40.0	25—04—56			0	20
			161		56.8	13—05—70			64.6	72.8
7			36.6		17.3	01—04—67			7.2	16.3
			120		53	13—05—70			36.6	45.1
8			101		68.5	06—05—71			11.4	14
			144		47.4	04—10—72			31	109
9			80		49	07—06—61			62	120
			228		35.6	09—10—72			25.2	85.2

Romania / Roumanie / Rumania / Румыния

TABLE IV — CHARACTERISTICS OF RAINFALL FLOODS (cont'd)

No.	River	Gauging station	Q_{max} (m³/s)	Date	h (mm)	T_T (hours)	t_i (hours)	P_W (%)	$P_{Q_{max}}$ (%)	Type of probability curve for P_W	for $P_{Q_{max}}$
1	2	3	4	5	6	7	8	9	10	11	12
10	Argeş	Budeşti	635	07—07—70	30.4	260	40	12.5	25	Kritzki-Menkel	Kritzki-Menkel
			1540	12—10—72	138	650	190	4	3	''	''
11	Someş	Satu Mare	2090	31—03—64	57	340	100	12.2	10	''	''
			3340	15—05—70	89	290	90	7.3	1.5	''	''
12	Mureş	Arad	1040	06—05—41	37.8	400	200	7.5	20	''	''
			2320	18—05—70	81.3	500	150	2.4	1.2	''	''
13	Siret	Lungoci	2670	18—07—69	43.6	360	150	13	6	''	''
			3186	19—05—70	89.5	700	230	4.3	3.5	''	''

No.	Method of curve fitting for W	for Q_{max}	Rainfall forming flood (mm)	Snowmelt during floods (mm)	Maximum daily rainfall (mm)	Date	Hourly maximum rainfall (mm)	Date	Antecedent precipitation for 10 days (mm)	30 days (mm)
1	13	14	15	16	17	18	19	20	21	22
10			96		56	06—07—70			0	21.7
			209		70	04—10—72			33	110
11			38	40	22	29—03—64			23.3	40.3
			140		67.5	13—05—70			29.4	47.6
12			78.5		19	07—04—41			35.1	63
			92.7		35	13—05—70			36.7	43
13			81		52	12—07—69			25	68
			152		31	18—07—70			17	42

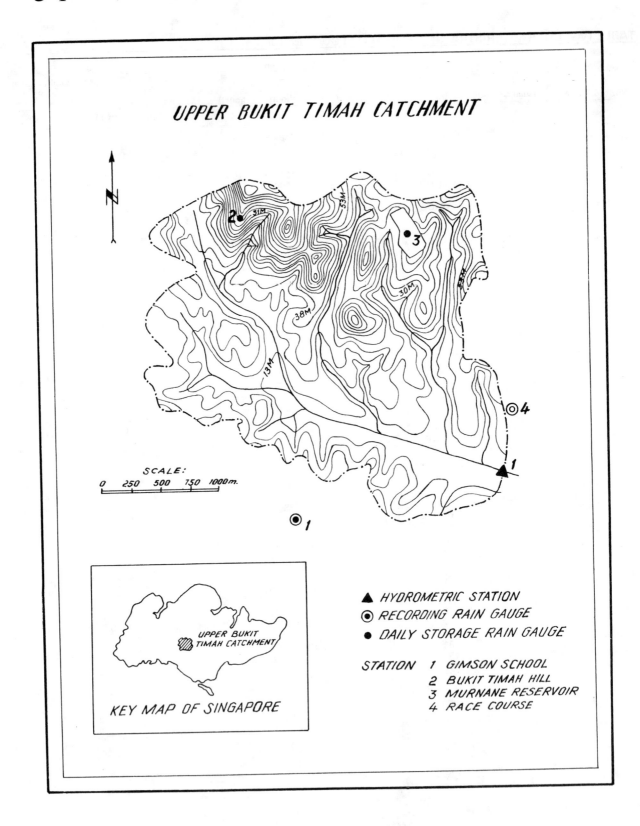

UPPER BUKIT TIMAH CATCHMENT

SCALE:
0   250   500   750   1000 m.

▲ HYDROMETRIC STATION
◉ RECORDING RAIN GAUGE
● DAILY STORAGE RAIN GAUGE

STATION   1 GIMSON SCHOOL
          2 BUKIT TIMAH HILL
          3 MURNANE RESERVOIR
          4 RACE COURSE

UPPER BUKIT
TIMAH CATCHMENT

KEY MAP OF SINGAPORE

TABLE I — CHARACTERISTICS OF BASIN

No.	River / River system	Name	Period of records	Co-ordinates Lat.	Long.	Distance (km) from gauging site to remotest point of river system L_{rs}	to projection of centre of basin on main course L_{ca}	Mean slope of river I_r (%)	Area A (km²)	Mean H_m	Max. H_{max}	Min. H_{min}
1	2	3	4	5	6	7	8	9	10	11	12	13
1	Bukit Timah							1.0	6.35	30.8		

No.	Mean B_m	Max. B_{max}	Mean slope I_b(%)	Soils	Cover	Weighted lake area P_L (%)	Swamps R_s (%)	Mean annual precipitation P (mm)	Annual runoff Q (mm)	Mean annual temperature T (°C)	Regulating capacity of reservoirs α
1	14	15	16	17	18	19	20	21	22	23	24
1	1.88		4	14	U(97), F(3)	0	0				

TABLE IV — CHARACTERISTICS OF RAINFALL FLOODS

No.	River	Gauging station	Q_{max} (m³/s)	Date	h (mm)	T_T (hours)	t_i (hours)	P_W (%)	$P_{Q_{max}}$ (%)	Type of probability curve for P_W	for $P_{Q_{max}}$
1	2	3	4	5	6	7	8	9	10	11	12
1	Bukit Timah			10—12—69	65	20	6				
				23—09—71	60	4.0	1				

No.	Method of curve fitting for W	for Q_{max}	Rainfall forming flood (mm)	Snowmelt during floods (mm)	Maximum daily rainfall (mm)	Date	Hourly maximum rainfall (mm)	Date	Antecedent precipitation for 10 days (mm)	30 days (mm)
1	13	14	15	16	17	18	19	20	21	22
1			121				57	10—12—69		
			108				44	23—09—71		

Sri Lanka / Шри Ланка

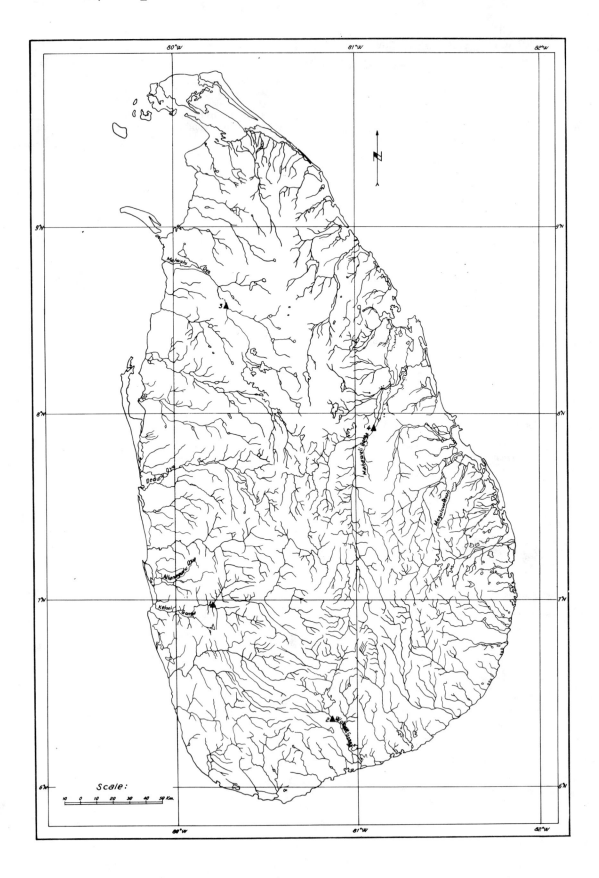

TABLE I — CHARACTERISTICS OF BASIN

	GAUGING STATION									BASIN			
	River River system	Name	Period of records	Co-ordinates Lat.	Long.	Distance (km) from gauging site to remotest point of river system L_{rs}	to projection of centre of basin on main course L_{ca}	Mean slope of river I_r (%)	Area A (km^2)	Altitude (m) Mean H_m	Max. H_{max}	Min. H_{min}	
No.	2	3	4	5	6	7	8	9	10	11	12	13	
1				N	E								
1	Kelani	Glencourse	1944—71	07:01:30	80:16:25	26	20.9	1.85	2310	129	2240	0	
2	Walawe	Embilipitiya	1942—64	06:20:45	80:53:50	78.8	22.5	1.32	2490	210	1830	0	
3	Malwathu	Kapachchi	1944—73	08:36:03	80:16:25	93.4	34	1.4	3300	35	199	0	
4	Mahaweli	Manampitiya	1941—71	07:54:46	80:05:12	208	45	0.7	10600	92	2250	0	

	BASIN										
No.	Width (km) Mean B_m	Max. B_{max}	Mean slope I_b(%)	Soils	Cover	Weighted lake area P_L (%)	Swamps R_s (%)	Mean annual precipitation P (mm)	Annual runoff Q (mm)	Mean annual temperature T (°C)	Regulating capacity of reservoirs α
1	14	15	16	17	18	19	20	21	22	23	24
1	44.4	55.1	5.5	2, 14	C(78), U(13), F(09)	0.27		4050	3360	23.6	
2	50.9	31.5	5.9	2, loam	C(49), U(11), F(40)	6.7		2140	863	23.7	
3	38.0	35.1	4.2	loam		1.2		1490	252	25.8	
4	77.9	50.7	3.4	loam	C(46), U(10), F(44)	0.04		2510	1020	22.3	

TABLE II — ANNUAL MAXIMUM DISCHARGES AND VOLUMES

Country:	Sri Lanka (1)
River:	Kelani
Gauging Station:	Glencourse

Date	Maximum discharge (m³/s) resulting from:		Maximum volume (10⁶m³) corresponding to max. discharge resulting from:	
	Rainfall	Snowmelt	Rainfall	Snowmelt
1	2	3	4	5
49	1700			
50	1020			
51	891			
52	1660			
53	1330			
02—05—54	722		224	
16—05—55	1300		650	
19—06—56	1100		616	
31—05—57	1250		408	
25—12—58	1230		1133	
22—06—59	1700		586	
17—06—60	894		128	
23—05—61	736		185	
20—05—62	843		343	
25—10—63	957		384	
22—10—64	1950		438	
07—05—65	1730		423	
20—05—67	3790		578	
68	3080			
69	1900			
20—10—70	982		167	
71	2040			
72	1400			
73	824			

Country:	Sri Lanka (2)
River:	Walawe Ganga
Gauging Station:	Embilipitiya

Date	Maximum discharge (m³/s) resulting from:		Maximum volume (10⁶m³) corresponding to max. discharge resulting from:	
	Rainfall	Snowmelt	Rainfall	Snowmelt
1	2	3	4	5
14—05—43	787		130	
22—04—44	665		73.4	
28—11—45	934		114	
15—08—46	1130			
15—08—47	2250		251	
04—12—48	254		68.5	
07—04—49	637		258	
08—03—50	538		81.7	
24—01—51	1130		89.5	
29—05—52	1060		225	
24—11—53	538		76	
26—12—54	521		74.5	
22—11—55	622		129	
23—06—56	322		29.5	
18—11—57	1130		103	
12—11—58	1560		124	
05—11—59	600		55.6	
09—04—60	509		45.6	
30—04—61	679		49.7	
18—11—62	1160		57.0	
11—01—63	1870		176	
22—10—64	707		70.2	

TABLE II – ANNUAL MAXIMUM DISCHARGES AND VOLUMES (cont'd)

Country:	Sri Lanka (3)			
River:	Malwathu			
Gauging Station:	Kapachchi			

| Date | Maximum discharge (m³/s) resulting from: | | Maximum volume (10⁶m³) corresponding to max. discharge resulting from: | |
| | Rainfall | Snowmelt | Rainfall | Snowmelt |
1	2	3	4	5
09–12–45	305		82.0	
01–03–46	1420		191	
08–12–47	504		112	
01–01–48	2730		556	
07–12–49	96		18.8	
08–02–50	107		18.0	
21–11–51	492		56.6	
04–10–52	87		12.5	
02–04–53	283		23.8	
09–12–54	580		42.7	
03–12–55	110		16.7	
15–11–56	22		4.71	
26–12–57	6510		1180	
17–01–58	104		18.2	
30–11–59	124		8.32	
18–01–60	1120		244	
24–01–61	113		35.6	
08–01–62	1270		324	
10–12–63	1450		571	
23–12–64	158		13.2	
25–12–65	1370		275	
11–11–66	1530		35.7	
08–12–67	1810		434	
21–12–68	39		5.24	
02–01–69	257		54.0	
30–11–70	215		23.1	
11–12–71	192		54.1	

Country:	Sri Lanka (4)			
River:	Mahaweli			
Gauging Station:	Manampitiya			

| Date | Maximum discharge (m³/s) resulting from: | | Maximum volume (10⁶m³) corresponding to max. discharge resulting from: | |
| | Rainfall | Snowmelt | Rainfall | Snowmelt |
1	2	3	4	5
15–05–43	2830		91.0	
01–03–44	1980		68	
09–12–45	1250		44.5	
26–03–46	1870		55.1	
05–12–47	2270		98.5	
14–12–48	3000		102	
12–01–49	2490		213	
09–01–50	1130		25.4	
18–01–51	2440		69.9	
06–01–52	2830		121	
22–01–53	1870		57.2	
08–12–54	2460		66.7	
24–06–56	1270		54.0	
26–12–57	1890		645	
22–06–59	1740		65.1	
22–02–60	5920		419	
15–01–61	3740		181	
06–03–63	2100		69.9	
03–01–64	3620		156	
15–12–65	2970		133	
05–02–67	2100		93.2	
28–12–69	1690		152	
13–12–70	2120		66.7	
13–12–71	1700		124	

TABLE IV — CHARACTERISTICS OF RAINFALL FLOODS

No.	River	Gauging station	Q_{max} (m^3/s)	Date	h (mm)	T_T (hours)	t_i (hours)	P_W (%)	$P_{Q_{max}}$ (%)	Type of probability curve for P_W	for $P_{Q_{max}}$
1	2	3	4	5	6	7	8	9	10	11	12
1	Kelani	Glencourse	1950	22—10—64	189	144	63	7	8	Gumbel	
2	Walawe	Embilipitiya	2250	15—08—47	101	168	51	6	3	″	
3	Malwathu	Kappachchi	1450	10—12—63	173	168	109	8	21	″	
4	Mahaweli	Manampitiya	5920	22—02—60	39.7	84	12	9	8	″	
			3620	03—01—64	14.7	96	40	18	12	″	

No.	Method of curve fitting for W	for Q_{max}	Rainfall forming flood (mm)	Snowmelt during floods (mm)	Maximum daily rainfall (mm)	Date	Hourly maximum rainfall (mm)	Date	Antecedent precipitation for 10 days (mm)	30 days (mm)
1	13	14	15	16	17	18	19	20	21	22
1			236.7		123.9	21—10—64			241	715
2			256.7		137.4	14—08—47			23	23
3			405.3		76.4	09—12—63			157	434
4			359.1		96.7	21—02—60			201	532
						02—01—60			153	285

Sweden / Suède / Suecia / Швеция

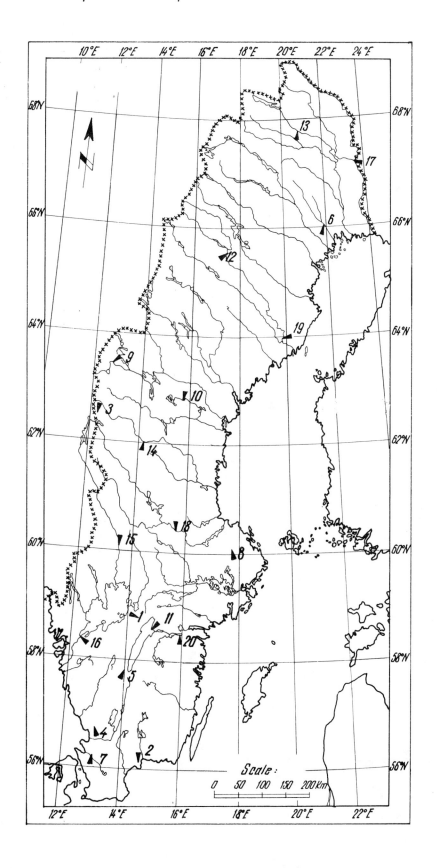

TABLE I — CHARACTERISTICS OF BASIN

	GAUGING STATION								BASIN				
							Distance (km) from gauging site					Altitude (m)	
No.	River River system	Name	Period of records	Co-ordinates Lat.	Long.		to remotest point of river system L_{rs}	to projection of centre of basin on main course L_{ca}	Mean slope of river I_r (%)	Area A (km²)	Mean H_m	Max. H_{max}	Min. H_{min}
1	2	3	4	5	6		7	8	9	10	11	12	13
				N	E								
1	Velenån 67 Motala ström	1662 Velen 2	1937–72	58:42:50	14:18:00		17.5	8	0.023	45	136	180	120
2	Vesanån K 86/87	736 Hålabäck	1927–72	56:07:20	14:37:20		3.2	1.5	0.041	4.7	78	153	10
3	Tännån 48 Ljusnan	1083 Lillglän	1932–72	62:38:25	12:08:20		5.0	5	0.111	63	945	1180	825
4	Esmaån 100 Fylleån	1207 Gårdsilt	1927–72	56:42:00	13:09:15		14.5	6	0.021	55	160	197	140
5	Dummeån 67 Motala ström	818 Risbro	1915–42	57:51:20	14:01:90		11.5	6	0.025	50	235	310	215
6	Råneälv 7 Råneälv	20 Niemisel	1900–72	66:00:50	21:59:40		130	70	0.026	3770	285	686	17
7	Bäljaneå 96 Rönneån	1635 Klippan 2	1890–72	56:08:40	13:06:40		26	15	0.037	239	90	151	9
8	Vattholmaån 61 Norrström	563 Vattholma	1916–72	60:01:10	17:44:00		30	16	0.014	284	35	72	21

	BASIN										
	Width (km)		Mean slope I_b (%)			Weighted lake area P_L (%)	Swamps R_s (%)	Mean annual precipitation P (mm)	Annual runoff Q (mm)	Mean annual temperature T (°C)	Regulating capacity of reservoirs α
No.	Mean B_m	Max. B_{max}		Soils	Cover						
1	14	15	16	17	18	19	20	21	22	23	24
1	2.6	4.5	0.042	2	F	69	12	650	255	+6.0	
2	1.5	2.0	0.080	2	F	0.33		600	215	+7.5	
3	12.6	4.0	0.081	2	U	38	9	800	630	-1.0	
4	3.7	5.0	0.035	2	F	11	30	1000	735	+6.5	
5	4.3	7.0	0.024	2	U	0	38	650	385	+6.0	
6	30	35	0.019	2	F	3.2	27	540	330	+0.2	
7	9.2	14.0	0.009	2	F	2.0	15	790	435	+7.0	
8	9.5	14.0	0.011	2	F	18	8	570	240	+5.5	

TABLE I — CHARACTERISTICS OF BASIN (cont'd)

				GAUGING STATION						BASIN		
						Distance (km) from gauging site		Mean slope of river I_r (%)	Area A (km²)	Altitude (m)		
	River / River system	Name	Period of records	Co-ordinates		to remotest point of river system L_{rs}	to projection of centre of basin on main course L_{ca}			Mean H_m	Max. H_{max}	Min. H_{min}
No.				Lat.	Long.							
1	2	3	4	5	6	7	8	9	10	11	12	13
				N	E							
9	Åreälven 40 Indalsälven	1328 Ö. Norn	1900–72	63:28:05	12:48:00	60	25	0.056	2390	745	1800	398
10	97 Gimån 42 Ljungan	97 Gimdalsby	1910–72	62:50:15	15:40:25	50	25	0.017	2180	365	555	261
11	Motala ström 67 Motala ström	154 Motala	1858–1939	58:32:05	15:02:35	120	40	0.017	6360	145	367	88
12	Vindelälven 28 Umeälv	56 Sorsele	1909–72	65:32:30	17:31:15	125	75	0.035	6110	720	1610	340
13	Torneälv 1 Torneälv	3 Jukkasjärvi	1915–67	67:50:40	20:37:10	135	80	0.055	6000	705	1980	322
14	Ljusnan 48 Ljusnan	106 Sveg	1914–61	62:02:10	14:22:45	140	45	0.040	8490	680	1590	348
15	Klarälven 108 Götaälv	1703 Edsforsens krv	1910–52	60:03:50	13:33:45	290	150	0.025	8580	640	1750	130
16	Götaälv 108 Götaälv	243 Sjötorp	1807–1937	58:50:20	13:59:00	450	170	0.017	46800	250	1750	44

						BASIN					
	Width (km)		Mean slope I_b (%)	Soils	Cover	Weighted lake area P_L (%)	Swamps R_s (%)	Mean annual precipitation P (mm)	Annual runoff Q (mm)	Mean annual temperature T (°C)	Regulating capacity of reservoirs α
No.	Mean B_m	Max. B_{max}									
1	14	15	16	17	18	19	20	21	22	23	24
9	40	50	0.058	2	F	7.0		935	835	+0.8	
10	44	52	0.025	2	F	12.8		575	255	+2.5	
11	53	45	0.013	2	F	35.7		600	210	+6.1	
12	49	35	0.062	2	F	4.1		755	630	-1.5	
13	44	65	0.071	2	F	10.6		535	535	-1.9	
14	61	75	0.044	2	F	1.9	10	655	450	+0.5	
15	30	70		2	F	5.9	10	700	470	+1.6	
16	104	175		2	F	18.6		690	363	+4.6	

TABLE I — CHARACTERISTICS OF BASIN (cont'd)

				GAUGING STATION					BASIN			
						Distance (km) from gauging site				Altitude (m)		
No.	River / River system	Name	Period of records	Co-ordinates Lat.	Long.	to remotest point of river system L_{rs}	to projection of centre of basin on main course L_{ca}	Mean slope of river I_r (%)	Area A (km²)	Mean H_m	Max. H_{max}	Min. H_{min}
1	2	3	4	5	6	7	8	9	10	11	12	13
17	Muonioälv 1 Torneälv	589 Kallio	1911–72	N 67:13:05	E 23:34:56	230	120	0.024	14300	480	1520	135
18	Dalälven 53 Dalälven	121 Norslund	1851–1918	60:24:00	15:41:15	275	120	0.022	25300	445	1460	106
19	Vindelälven 28 Umeälv	1545 Renfors	1911–72	64:13:25	19:42:25	320	170	0.019	11900	525	1610	159
20	Motala ström 67 Motala ström	172 Norsholm	1873–1927	58:30:30	15:58:35	150	90	0.015	13200	145	367	33

	BASIN										
	Width (km)		Mean slope I_b(%)			Weighted lake area P_L (%)	Swamps R_s (%)	Mean annual precipitation P (mm)	Annual runoff Q (mm)	Mean annual temperature T (°C)	Regulating capacity of reservoirs α
No.	Mean B_m	Max. B_{max}		Soils	Cover						
1	14	15	16	17	18	19	20	21	22	23	24
17	62	90		2	F	3.2	24	500	350	-1.3	
18	92	130		2	F	5.6	20	675	435	+2.4	
19	37	70		2	F	5.2	10	750	550	-0.1	
20	88	170		2	F	22.3		580	205	+6.1	

TABLE II – ANNUAL MAXIMUM DISCHARGES AND VOLUMES

Country: Sweden (1)
River: Velenån
Gauging Station: 67–1662 Velen 2

Date	Maximum discharge (m³/s) resulting from:		Maximum volume (10⁶m³) corresponding to max. discharge resulting from:	
	Rainfall	Snowmelt	Rainfall	Snowmelt
1	2	3	4	5
10–02–38		0.80		
10–12–38	0.50			
14–02–39		1.30		
12–12–39	0.52			
30–04–40		0.75		
07–12–40	0.86			
01–01–41		0.42		
01–05–41	0.28			
26–04–42		0.59		
27–02–42	0.52			
15–02–43		1.20		
30–11–43	0.70			
02–02–44		1.10		
03–12–44	1.80			
01–01–45		1.10		
07–05–45	0.93			
09–04–46		0.72		
21–09–46	2.20			
01–01–47		0.49		
01–05–47	0.61			
04–04–48		0.63		
24–12–48	0.28			
22–04–49		0.65		
31–12–49	1.40			
23–04–50		1.50		
11–12–50	0.96			
20–04–51		2.70		
17–12–51	0.75			
01–01–52		0.66		
12–05–52	0.86			
15–04–53		0.86		
25–10–53	0.62			
16–04–54		1.30		
06–12–54	1.30			
10–02–55		0.66		
20–05–55	0.96			
18–01–56		0.56		
12–05–56	0.58			
06–04–57		0.86		
29–09–57	0.68			
21–05–58		1.22		
14–11–58	0.57			
09–03–59		2.16		
30–12–59	0.25			
01–02–60		0.51		
04–12–60	1.54			
01–01–61		1.09		
19–11–61	0.91			
24–04–62		1.12		
15–09–62	1.89			
25–04–63		0.83		
30–11–63	1.03			
01–01–64		0.45		
20–12–64	0.78			
28–04–65		0.66		
12–11–65	0.38			
28–03–66		1.05		
05–05–66	2.97			
15–03–67		2.09		
31–10–67	1.54			

Country: Sweden (1) cont'd
River: Velenån
Gauging Station: 67–1662 Velen 2

TABLE II – ANNUAL MAXIMUM DISCHARGES AND VOLUMES (cont'd)

Country: Sweden (1) cont'd				
River: Velenån				
Gauging Station: 67–1662 Velen 2				

	Maximum discharge (m³/s) resulting from:		Maximum volume (10⁶m³) corresponding to max. discharge resulting from:	
Date	Rainfall	Snowmelt	Rainfall	Snowmelt
1	2	3	4	5
04–04–68		2.31		
10–11–68	0.73			
27–04–69		1.49		
30–11–69	0.24			
30–04–70		2.31		
30–11–70	1.70			
01–01–71		0.66		
09–12–71	0.78			
14–04–72		1.35		
16–12–72	0.86			

Country: Sweden (2)				
River: Vesanån				
Gauging Station: K 86/87–736 Hålabäck				

	Maximum discharge (m³/s) resulting from:		Maximum volume (10⁶m³) corresponding to max. discharge resulting from:	
Date	Rainfall	Snowmelt	Rainfall	Snowmelt
1	2	3	4	5
17–02–28		0.211		
22–11–28	0.343			
23–03–29		0.235		
31–12–29	0.125			
15–04–30		0.235		
22–11–30	0.300			
17–01–31		0.682		
26–04–31	0.267			
07–01–32		0.117		
24–10–32	0.190			
20–03–33		0.169		
28–06–33	0.133			
18–01–34		0.117		
31–12–34	0.211			
16–02–35		0.391		
11–04–35	0.169			
13–04–36		1.046		
16–11–36	0.069			
15–03–37		0.248		
16–04–37	0.169			
17–01–38		0.248		
25–07–38	0.088			
16–01–39		0.391		
30–11–39	0.116			
31–03–40		0.477		
30–05–40	0.258			
15–03–41		0.133		
15–12–41	0.179			
10–04–42		0.706		
08–11–42	0.141			

TABLE II – ANNUAL MAXIMUM DISCHARGES AND VOLUMES (cont'd)

Country:	Sweden (2) cont'd
River:	Vesanån
Gauging Station:	K 86/87–736 Hålabäck

	Maximum discharge (m³/s) resulting from:		Maximum volume (10⁶m³) corresponding to max. discharge resulting from:	
Date	Rainfall	Snowmelt	Rainfall	Snowmelt
1	2	3	4	5
01–02–43		0.358		
31–12–43	0.048			
14–01–44		0.211		
12–05–44	0.160			
01–03–45		0.343		
23–11–45	0.069			
23–03–46		0.960		
03–10–46	0.063			
02–04–47		0.211		
23–11–47	0.032			
01–02–48		0.343		
29–05–48	0.058			
08–04–49		0.141		
17–12–49	0.252			
16–02–50		0.248		
21–11–50	0.260			
12–01–51		0.407		
04–04–51	0.358			
22–02–52		0.133		
20–11–52	0.235			
21–02–53		0.151		
06–04–53	0.069			
01–04–54		0.300		
12–12–54	0.235			
07–04–55		0.286		
07–05–55	0.486			
01–04–56		0.125		
01–05–56	0.101			
13–02–57		0.179		
10–11–57	0.086			

Country:	Sweden (2) cont'd
River:	Vesanån
Gauging Station:	K 86/87–736 Hålabäck

	Maximum discharge (m³/s) resulting from:		Maximum volume (10⁶m³) corresponding to max. discharge resulting from:	
Date	Rainfall	Snowmelt	Rainfall	Snowmelt
1	2	3	4	5
16–02–58		0.496		
24–08–58	0.248			
22–01–59		0.424		
31–06–59	0.643			
04–03–60		0.141		
19–11–60	0.343			
04–01–61		0.202		
06–04–61	0.160			
22–01–62		0.274		
10–05–62	0.101			
23–04–63		0.300		
25–11–63	0.224			
01–02–64		0.141		
13–12–64	0.048			
18–04–65		0.202		
10–12–65	0.429			
26–02–66		0.538		
25–04–66	0.446			
06–02–67		0.349		
08–04–67	0.349			
01–02–68		0.349		
11–10–68	0.114			
31–01–69		0.279		
05–05–69	0.166			
19–06–70		0.412		
03–12–70	0.334			
25–03–71		0.176		
28–05–71	0.043			
05–04–72		0.130		
11–12–72	0.016			

TABLE II – ANNUAL MAXIMUM DISCHARGES AND VOLUMES (cont'd)

Country:	Sweden (3)
River:	Tännån
Gauging Station:	48–1083 Lillglän

Date	Maximum discharge (m³/s) resulting from:		Maximum volume (10⁶m³) corresponding to max. discharge resulting from:	
	Rainfall	Snowmelt	Rainfall	Snowmelt
1	2	3	4	5
23–05–33		12.7		
26–07–33	7.7			
08–05–34		39		
07–09–34	6.4			
09–06–35		19.3		
20–07–35	7.1			
17–05–36		13.5		
28–07–36	5.5			
06–05–37		10.5		
18–06–37	4.6			
01–06–38		21		
03–09–38	14.8			
26–05–39		14.4		
03–07–39	5.0			
23–05–40		20		
24–08–40	10.1			
27–05–41		20		
08–09–41	5.0			
29–05–42		19.8		
25–09–42	3.0			
24–05–43		12.3		
15–07–43	4.0			
10–06–44		33		
27–09–44	6.1			
31–05–45		22		
26–08–45	4.2			
26–05–46		13.9		
27–06–46	10.1			
16–05–47		19.3		
17–06–47	7.1			

Country:	Sweden (3) cont'd
River:	Tännån
Gauging Station:	48–1083 Lillglän

Date	Maximum discharge (m³/s) resulting from:		Maximum volume (10⁶m³) corresponding to max. discharge resulting from:	
	Rainfall	Snowmelt	Rainfall	Snowmelt
1	2	3	4	5
16–05–48		9.1		
25–10–48	1.7			
22–05–49		21		
31–07–49	4.0			
17–06–50		22		
28–07–50	14.4			
27–06–51		11.5		
13–08–51	2.0			
21–06–52		24		
30–09–52	2.4			
21–05–53		17.2		
30–08–53	1.9			
23–05–54		17.2		
16–07–54	12.7			
23–06–55		18.2		
09–10–55	1.7			
28–05–56		17.2		
13–09–56	11.5			
18–05–57		12.3		
15–09–57	6.9			
01–06–58		19.3		
29–10–58	8.2			
04–05–59		12.7		
25–09–69	2.0			
29–05–60		14.4		
18–08–60	11.2			
02–06–61		17.2		
05–08–61	9.5			
09–06–62		10.8		
04–07–62	6.9			

TABLE II – ANNUAL MAXIMUM DISCHARGES AND VOLUMES (cont'd)

Country: Sweden (3) cont'd
River: Tannån
Gauging Station: 48-1083 Lillglän

Date	Maximum discharge (m³/s) resulting from:		Maximum volume (10⁶m³) corresponding to max. discharge resulting from:	
	Rainfall	Snowmelt	Rainfall	Snowmelt
1	2	3	4	5
13–05–63		14.8		
16–07–63	3.5			
14–05–64		12.3		
31–08–64	7.7			
08–06–65		21		
20–09–65	4.4			
24–05–66		9.8		
08–08–66	8.8			
27–05–67		23		
14–08–68	7.7			
04–06–68		18.7		
28–10–68	1.1			
25–09–69		9.5		
14–09–69	3.0			
27–05–70		13.1		
06–10–70	5.5			
19–05–71		14.8		
09–10–71	3.2			
26–05–72		16.7		
09–07–72	4.8			

Country: Sweden (4)
River: Esmaån
Gauging Station: 100-1207 Gårdsilt

Date	Maximum discharge (m³/s) resulting from:		Maximum volume (10⁶m³) corresponding to max. discharge resulting from:	
	Rainfall	Snowmelt	Rainfall	Snowmelt
1	2	3	4	5
10–02–28		9.7		
25–11–28	7.9			
23–03–29		2.9		
27–10–29	5.0			
05–01–30		4.4		
14–08–30	6.3			
13–01–31		7.7		
29–12–31	4.1			
07–01–32		11.0		
27–10–32	4.5			
19–03–33		4.6		
16–07–33	8.6			
20–01–34		3.3		
14–10–34	5.5			
22–02–35		11.3		
21–10–35	7.3			
02–01–36		2.9		
28–07–36	4.3			
05–01–37		6.9		
05–12–37	3.7			
18–01–38		8.6		
14–10–38	7.0			
18–01–39		7.5		
04–12–39	5.0			
07–03–40		5.6		
14–08–40	6.6			
15–04–41		2.5		
15–12–41	3.3			
10–04–42		8.2		
10–12–42	6.7			

TABLE II – ANNUAL MAXIMUM DISCHARGES AND VOLUMES (cont'd)

Country:	Sweden (4) cont'd
River:	Esmaån
Gauging Station:	100-1207 Gårdsilt

| Date | Maximum discharge (m³/s) resulting from: | | Maximum volume (10⁶m³) corresponding to max. discharge resulting from: | |
| | Rainfall | Snowmelt | Rainfall | Snowmelt |
1	2	3	4	5
07–02–43		8.0		
06–10–43	6.4			
24–01–44		8.0		
29–09–44	6.1			
01–03–45		10.4		
18–08–45	10.5			
05–02–46		6.5		
21–09–46	8.2			
27–03–47		4.8		
25–10–47	6.8			
03–02–48		7.4		
15–12–48	4.3			
24–01–49		6.0		
04–08–49	6.2			
19–02–50		9.7		
02–12–50	6.1			
14–04–51		14.3		
10–12–51	7.2			
24–02–52		4.0		
26–09–52	7.2			
24–02–53		8.6		
13–11–53	7.3			
17–01–54		6.6		
23–09–54	9.3			
15–04–55		5.5		
29–12–55	14.9			
19–01–56		8.3		
17–12–56	7.9			
24–01–57		7.1		
15–09–57	7.8			

Country:	Sweden (4) cont'd
River:	Esmaån
Gauging Station:	100-1207 Gårdsilt

| Date | Maximum discharge (m³/s) resulting from: | | Maximum volume (10⁶m³) corresponding to max. discharge resulting from: | |
| | Rainfall | Snowmelt | Rainfall | Snowmelt |
1	2	3	4	5
17–02–58		10.1		
31–12–58	4.7			
24–01–59		14.4		
29–12–59	3.3			
15–04–60		4.2		
27–12–60	5.6			
08–04–61		3.9		
04–11–61	6.3			
23–01–62		9.7		
28–08–62	7.4			
13–04–63		4.4		
14–08–63	8.2			
02–02–64		5.1		
11–12–64	6.6			
19–01–65		5.2		
03–11–65	5.9			
11–03–66		9.0		
19–12–66	8.5			
04–03–67		8.5		
25–12–67	4.9			
02–02–68		9.6		
29–11–68	2.9			
03–02–69		2.3		
14–11–69	4.0			
24–04–70		17.4		
02–11–70	8.9			
27–03–71		3.9		
10–11–71	8.1			
10–04–72		4.2		
11–11–72	6.6			

TABLE II – ANNUAL MAXIMUM DISCHARGES AND VOLUMES   (cont'd)

Country:	Sweden (5)
River:	Dummeån
Gauging Station:	67-818 Risbro

Date	Maximum discharge (m³/s) resulting from:		Maximum volume (10⁶m³) corresponding to max. discharge resulting from:	
	Rainfall	Snowmelt	Rainfall	Snowmelt
1	2	3	4	5
02–04–16		8.4		
21–08–16	2.8			
25–04–17		5.7		
07–12–17	2.9			
28–01–18		4.7		
01–10–18	4.9			
10–04–19		6.6		
05–12–19	3.8			
12–02–20		3.8		
26–07–20	4.9			
01–02–21		3.6		
23–12–21	3.6			
07–03–22		3.0		
16–09–22	3.6			
04–02–23		2.5		
21–08–23	3.8			
04–05–24		5.2		
24–09–24	3.2			
12–02–25		4.5		
25–10–25	3.8			
03–03–26		4.5		
12–06–26	6.8			
29–02–27		0.94		
29–06–27	15.0			
02–04–28		3.9		
12–11–28	5.3			
24–03–29		5.0		
09–07–29	2.8			
14–03–30		2.9		
08–10–30	3.8			

Country:	Sweden (5) cont'd
River:	Dummeån
Gauging Station:	67-818 Risbro

Date	Maximum discharge (m³/s) resulting from:		Maximum volume (10⁶m³) corresponding to max. discharge resulting from:	
	Rainfall	Snowmelt	Rainfall	Snowmelt
1	2	3	4	5
27–04–31		3.8		
30–05–31	4.0			
07–04–32		1.4		
05–11–32	3.2			
19–03–33		2.4		
31–11–33	1.5			
18–03–34		2.9		
08–11–34	3.2			
20–02–35		2.8		
27–09–35	3.1			
24–03–36		3.4		
27–07–36	6.9			
06–04–37		10.9		
22–09–37	2.2			
04–02–38		4.5		
20–05–38	2.4			
18–01–39		6.2		
30–11–39	1.7			
06–04–40		4.5		
29–09–40	2.8			
14–04–41		8.9		
09–11–41	1.3			

TABLE II — ANNUAL MAXIMUM DISCHARGES AND VOLUMES   (cont'd)

Country:	Sweden (6)
River:	Råneälv
Gauging Station:	7-20 Niemisel

Date	Maximum discharge (m³/s) resulting from:		Maximum volume (10⁶m³) corresponding to max. discharge resulting from:	
	Rainfall	Snowmelt	Rainfall	Snowmelt
1	2	3	4	5
29—05—00		577		
16—08—00	88			
16—05—01		414		
31—10—01	48			
30—05—02		248		
20—09—02	198			
26—05—03		674		
26—08—03	183			
31—05—04		362		
04—07—04	74			
15—05—05		454		
11—08—05	111			
10—05—06		685		
25—07—06	48			
28—05—07		272		
25—10—07	68			
26—05—08		528		
10—08—08	31			
03—06—09		307		
28—10—09	123			
16—05—10		700		
09—07—10	86			
12—05—11		472		
03—10—11	96			
20—05—12		331		
01—07—12	131			
12—05—13		381		
17—08—13	36			
20—05—14		290		
13—07—14	33			

Country:	Sweden (6) cont'd
River:	Råneälv
Gauging Station:	7-20 Niemisel

Date	Maximum discharge (m³/s) resulting from:		Maximum volume (10⁶m³) corresponding to max. discharge resulting from:	
	Rainfall	Snowmelt	Rainfall	Snowmelt
1	2	3	4	5
29—05—15		235		
29—07—15	103			
21—05—16		293		
07—09—16	23			
02—06—17		547		
30—10—17	153			
18—05—24		416		
16—09—24	171			
16—05—25		471		
10—09—25	51			
23—05—26		329		
14—10—26	118			
29—08—27		480		
08—10—27	105			
16—06—28		276		
01—08—28	101			
23—05—29		342		
24—09—29	223			
14—05—30		353		
31—10—30	72			
07—05—31		388		
19—08—31	167			
21—05—32		413		
19—10—32	106			
21—05—33		278		
18—10—33	65			
11—05—34		763		
30—10—34	115			
11—06—35		583		
16—10—35	157			

TABLE II – ANNUAL MAXIMUM DISCHARGES AND VOLUMES (cont'd)

Country:	Sweden (6) cont'd
River:	Råneälv
Gauging Station:	7-20 Niemisel

Date	Maximum discharge (m³/s) resulting from:		Maximum volume (10⁶m³) corresponding to max. discharge resulting from:	
	Rainfall	Snowmelt	Rainfall	Snowmelt
1	2	3	4	5
15—05—36		548		
25—07—36	136			
29—04—37		413		
29—09—37	18			
17—05—38		232		
12—07—38	95			
24—05—39		332		
03—06—39	51			
14—05—40		230		
27—09—40	205			
27—05—41		345		
20—09—41	80			
04—06—42		142		
25—10—42	169			
16—05—43		439		
16—09—43	84			
20—05—44		413		
24—10—44	169			
25—05—45		322		
03—09—45	17			
09—05—46		180		
10—10—46	433			
13—05—47		293		
16—06—47	81			
16—05—48		471		
25—10—48	41			
31—05—49		324		
19—11—49	43			
15—05—50		393		
25—10—50	57			

Country:	Sweden (6) cont'd
River:	Rånealv
Gauging Station:	7-20 Niemisel

Date	Maximum discharge (m³/s) resulting from:		Maximum volume (10⁶m³) corresponding to max. discharge resulting from:	
	Rainfall	Snowmelt	Rainfall	Snowmelt
1	2	3	4	5
22—05—51		245		
11—07—51	149			
15—05—52		319		
04—10—52	122			
06—05—53		462		
09—09—53	106			
13—05—54		203		
06—08—54	171			
06—06—55		570		
04—10—55	86			
18—05—56		445		
04—06—56	46			
18—05—57		413		
10—09—57	90			
31—05—58		439		
10—08—58	95			
07—05—59		445		
06—06—59	62			
12—05—60		419		
27—08—60	78			
20—05—61		355		
29—07—61	203			
21—05—62		283		
19—09—62	88			
10—05—63		283		
01—09—63	53			
15—05—64		396		
05—09—64	61			
13—05—65		293		
07—06—65	293			

253

TABLE II — ANNUAL MAXIMUM DISCHARGES AND VOLUMES (cont'd)

Country:	Sweden (6) cont'd
River:	Råneälv
Gauging Station:	7-20 Niemisel

Date	Maximum discharge (m³/s) resulting from:		Maximum volume (10⁶m³) corresponding to max. discharge resulting from:	
	Rainfall	Snowmelt	Rainfall	Snowmelt
1	2	3	4	5
20—05—66		495		
20—09—66	61			
24—05—67		570		
11—11—67	213			
02—06—68		281		
03—07—68	62			
21—05—21		305		
06—10—69	18			
22—05—70		340		
27—10—70	76			
16—05—71		532		
04—06—71	144			

Country:	Sweden (7)
River:	Bäljaneå
Gauging Station:	96-1635 Klippan 2

Date	Maximum discharge (m³/s) resulting from:		Maximum volume (10⁶m³) corresponding to max. discharge resulting from:	
	Rainfall	Snowmelt	Rainfall	Snowmelt
1	2	3	4	5
28—01—90		14		
25—11—90	11			
05—02—91		15		
05—09—91	24			
31—01—92		26		
04—10—92	29			
08—03—93		41		
31—10—93	12			
11—03—94		19		
21—04—94	15			
21—03—95		31		
10—08—95	33			
19—03—96		23		
06—09—96	14			
27—02—97		23		
07—09—97	18			
01—02—98		12		
30—06—98	16			
20—01—99		19		
12—11—99	4			
20—03—00		15		
15—12—00	15			
07—03—01		14		
26—12—01	10			
05—01—02		12		
17—10—02	9.7			
08—01—03		15		
11—10—03	17			
15—01—04		16		
03—05—04	7.1			

TABLE II — ANNUAL MAXIMUM DISCHARGES AND VOLUMES   (cont'd)

Country:	Sweden (7) cont'd			
River:	Bäljaneå			
Gauging Station:	96-1635 Klippan 2			

Date	Maximum discharge (m³/s) resulting from:		Maximum volume (10⁶m³) corresponding to max. discharge resulting from:	
	Rainfall	Snowmelt	Rainfall	Snowmelt
1	2	3	4	5
07—02—05		14		
31—08—05	21			
18—03—06		15		
05—12—06	9.3			
19—03—07		18		
05—07—07	12			
27—03—09		15		
30—12—09	18			
19—02—10		24		
16—11—10	15			
25—02—11		21		
21—11—11	17			
29—02—12		15		
15—12—12	20			
09—02—13		15		
29—12—13	12			
09—01—14		27		
14—11—14	11			
17—01—15		12		
01—08—15	20			
03—01—16		22		
28—08—16	17			
05—01—17		13		
30—11—17	31			
27—01—18		14		
02—10—18	15			
06—01—19		14		
05—02—19	23			
19—01—20		26		
23—03—20	20			

Country:	Sweden (7) cont'd			
River:	Bäljaneå			
Gauging Station:	96-1635 Klippan 2			

Date	Maximum discharge (m³/s) resulting from:		Maximum volume (10⁶m³) corresponding to max. discharge resulting from:	
	Rainfall	Snowmelt	Rainfall	Snowmelt
1	2	3	4	5
12—01—21		18		
06—11—21	11			
19—04—24		21		
08—05—24	12			
31—12—25		21		
31—12—25	23			
18—01—56		12.4		
15—12—56	9.1			
23—01—57		14.2		
30—10—57	15.7			
16—02—58		33		
28—04—58	14.2			
22—01—59		27		
11—04—59	20			
02—02—60		16.8		
05—12—60	14.2			
06—04—61		11.9		
26—10—61	12			
23—01—62		24		
19—08—62	14.2			
24—04—63		15.2		
23—11—63	43			
02—02—64		16.8		
14—12—64	22			
19—01—65		12.4		
09—09—65	21			
27—02—66		25		
19—12—66	24			
05—02—67		19.6		
24—12—67	23			

TABLE II — ANNUAL MAXIMUM DISCHARGES AND VOLUMES   (cont'd)

Country:	Sweden (7) cont'd
River:	Bäljaneå
Gauging Station:	96-1635 Klippan 2

Date	Maximum discharge (m³/s) resulting from:		Maximum volume (10⁶m³) corresponding to max. discharge resulting from:	
	Rainfall	Snowmelt	Rainfall	Snowmelt
1	2	3	4	5
01—02—68		24		
11—11—68	8.4			
01—02—69		10.3		
22—06—69	12.8			
20—04—70		37		
03—12—70	17.3			
26—03—71		19		
17—11—71	23			
06—04—72		11		
02—12—72	7.9			

Country:	Sweden (8)
River:	Vattholmaån
Gauging Station:	61-563 Vattholma

Date	Maximum discharge (m³/s) resulting from:		Maximum volume (10⁶m³) corresponding to max. discharge resulting from:	
	Rainfall	Snowmelt	Rainfall	Snowmelt
1	2	3	4	5
27—04—17		8.2		
30-12—17	3.1			
25—04—18		10.0		
09—11—18	4.9			
18—04—19		13.0		
12—12—19	4.2			
15—03—20		9.2		
13—09—20	1.0			
23—03—21		3.5		
31—12—21	0.9			
02—05—22		25.0		
18—10—22	2.5			
01—02—23		2.7		
01—11—23	5.2			
11—05—24		24.0		
10—12—24	3.2			
20—04—25		6.9		
14—12—25	1.3			
26—04—26		8.0		
27—11—26	1.5			
17—04—27		5.1		
10—10—27	7.3			
10—04—28		5.5		
30—11—28	4.6			
08—05—29		5.1		
31—12—29	3.5			
24—04—30		6.7		
15—12—30	4.9			
06—05—31		9.6		
25—11—31	2.8			

TABLE II — ANNUAL MAXIMUM DISCHARGES AND VOLUMES (cont'd)

Country:	Sweden (8) cont'd
River:	Vattholmaån
Gauging Station:	61-563 Vattholma

Date	Maximum discharge (m³/s) resulting from:		Maximum volume (10⁶m³) corresponding to max. discharge resulting from:	
	Rainfall	Snowmelt	Rainfall	Snowmelt
1	2	3	4	5
21—01—32		9.8		
23—12—32	1.7			
05—04—33		3.6		
20—11—33	1.8			
25—04—34		4.6		
18—11—34	11.0			
15—04—35		5.9		
28—12—35	4.6			
03—04—36		7.5		
18—11—36	4.9			
19—03—37		18.0		
28—11—37	2.3			
07—01—38		5.2		
02—12—38	3.9			
03—04—39		5.5		
14—12—39	2.8			
22—04—40		6.1		
04—12—40	3.6			
02—05—41		7.5		
03—12—41	3.9			
20—04—42		6.3		
28—12—42	2.8			
18—02—43		5.4		
13—12—43	4.7			
03—05—44		13.0		
19—12—44	9.8			
04—07—45		12.0		
19—11—45	3.4			
06—04—46		5.5		
10—12—46	3.6			

Country:	Sweden (8) cont'd
River:	Vattholmaån
Gauging Station:	61-563 Vattholma

Date	Maximum discharge (m³/s) resulting from:		Maximum volume (10⁶m³) corresponding to max. discharge resulting from:	
	Rainfall	Snowmelt	Rainfall	Snowmelt
1	2	3	4	5
03—05—47		7.5		
08—12—47	1.0			
14—04—48		7.5		
23—11—48	2.0			
17—04—49		3.5		
18—11—49	5.0			
29—03—50		9.4		
19—12—50	3.0			
20—04—51		15.3		
31—12—51	0.7			
15—04—52		4.4		
01—12—52	5.0			
07—04—53		12.5		
27—10—53	1.3			
17—04—54		9.2		
16—12—54	6.9			
13—05—55		6.7		
31—12—55	2.1			
09—05—56		14.1		
18—12—56	2.5			
14—04—57		5.7		
11—10—57	10.9			
08—05—58		11.1		
24—12—58	2.2			
18—04—59		13.2		
28—12—59	1.4			
29—04—60		8.5		
30—12—60	9.9			
01—01—61		9.5		
24—08—61	4.3			

TABLE II – ANNUAL MAXIMUM DISCHARGES AND VOLUMES   (cont'd)

Country:	Sweden (8) cont'd
River:	Vattholmaån
Gauging Station:	61-563 Vattholma

Date	Maximum discharge (m³/s) resulting from:		Maximum volume (10⁶m³) corresponding to max. discharge resulting from:	
	Rainfall	Snowmelt	Rainfall	Snowmelt
1	2	3	4	5
23–04–62		15.0		
13–09–62	1.8			
06–05–63		4.9		
17–10–63	2.5			
23–04–64		2.8		
14–12–64	3.7			
19–04–65		7.2		
04–10–65	5.5			
04–05–66		22.0		
21–12–66	5.3			
19–03–67		12.6		
15–11–67	5.5			
07–04–68		10.5		
30–11–68	5.0			
22–04–69		13.4		
26–11–69	3.6			
02–05–70		16.3		
27–11–70	3.5			
22–04–71		8.2		
26–10–71	1.1			
18–04–72		4.4		
20–11–72	1.0			

Country:	Sweden (9)
River:	Äreälven
Gauging Station:	40-1328 Ö. Norn

Date	Maximum discharge (m³/s) resulting from:		Maximum volume (10⁶m³) corresponding to max. discharge resulting from:	
	Rainfall	Snowmelt	Rainfall	Snowmelt
1	2	3	4	5
17–05–01		234		
28–08–01	76			
07–06–02		267		
01–07–02	203			
03–09–03		454		
04–07–03	146			
30–06–04		203		
01–09–04	58			
21–06–05		337		
15–08–05	188			
13–05–06		337		
27–11–06	173			
16–06–07		383		
10–08–07	188			
02–06–08		383		
01–07–08	188			
05–06–09		275		
05–09–09	188			
24–05–10		241		
10–10–10	179			
18–05–11		279		
18–07–11	167			
31–05–12		220		
23–09–12	121			
06–05–13		248		
21–10–13	200			
16–06–14		287		
11–10–14	220			
13–06–15		337		
31–07–15	248			

TABLE II – ANNUAL MAXIMUM DISCHARGES AND VOLUMES (cont'd)

Country:	Sweden (9) cont'd
River:	Åreälven
Gauging Station:	40-1328 Ö. Norn

Date	Maximum discharge (m³/s) resulting from:		Maximum volume (10⁶m³) corresponding to max. discharge resulting from:	
	Rainfall	Snowmelt	Rainfall	Snowmelt
1	2	3	4	5
13–05–16		291		
20–07–16	149			
05–06–17		418		
30–09–17	125			
24–05–18		259		
11–09–18	129			
12–05–19		210		
21–09–19	132			
20–05–20		316		
31–07–20	138			
18–05–21		341		
18–08–21	154			
29–05–22		413		
26–07–22	141			
13–07–23		291		
01–10–23	101			
25–06–24		259		
24–08–24	207			
02–06–25		267		
20–08–25	223			
09–06–26		341		
13–09–26	136			
01–07–27		341		
10–10–27	146			
05–05–28		241		
31–07–28	191			
29–05–29		379		
20–06–29	223			
30–05–30		283		
07–10–30	99			
20–05–31		311		
11–10–31	245			
02–06–32		291		
02–10–32	245			
25–05–33		252		
23–08–33	156			
11–05–34		715		
06–12–34	76			
19–06–35		351		
01–08–35	129			
18–05–36		237		
09–08–36	129			
01–05–37		138		
23–10–37	97			
04–06–38		560		
06–09–38	134			
04–06–39		173		
11–10–39	74			
29–05–40		351		
27–08–40	179			
01–06–41		420		
20–09–41	185			
31–05–42		366		
27–11–42	151			
29–05–43		378		
02–09–43	70			
11–06–44		536		
10–10–44	121			
06–06–45		369		
19–10–45	209			

Sweden / Suède / Suecia / Швеция

TABLE II — ANNUAL MAXIMUM DISCHARGES AND VOLUMES (cont'd)

Country: **Sweden (9) cont'd**
River: **Åreälven**
Gauging Station: **40-1328 Ö. Norn**

Date	Maximum discharge (m³/s) resulting from:		Maximum volume (10⁶m³) corresponding to max. discharge resulting from:	
	Rainfall	Snowmelt	Rainfall	Snowmelt
1	2	3	4	5
02—06—46		406		
21—10—46	120			
18—05—47		268		
23—10—47	255			
19—05—48		317		
06—12—48	203			
22—05—49		490		
07—10—49	131			
11—06—50		364		
01—08—50	276			
29—06—51		228		
31—07—51	91			
14—05—52		293		
24—06—52	257			
24—05—53		420		
11—09—53	163			
26—05—54		323		
15—08—54	134			
28—06—55		378		
24—11—55	111			
15—06—56		399		
24—10—56	142			
22—05—57		323		
13—10—57	166			
05—06—58		404		
29—10—58	235			
04—05—59		301		
25—09—59	163			
31—05—60		278		
03—07—60	211			

Country: **Sweden (9) cont'd**
River: **Åreälven**
Gauging Station: **40-1328 Ö. Norn**

Date	Maximum discharge (m³/s) resulting from:		Maximum volume (10⁶m³) corresponding to max. discharge resulting from:	
	Rainfall	Snowmelt	Rainfall	Snowmelt
1	2	3	4	5
07—06—61		389		
23—11—61	153			
29—06—62		259		
24—10—62	166			
15—05—63		415		
03—10—63	108			
15—05—64		334		
03—09—64	155			
13—05—65		359		
21—10—65	164			
22—05—66		451		
26—09—66	194			
02—06—67		543		
06—07—67	218			
08—06—68		427		
25—10—68	120			
02—06—69		205		
13—10—69	99			
02—06—70		299		
10—09—70	112			
20—05—71		352		
04—11—71	170			
28—05—72		346		
06—07—72	114			

TABLE II – ANNUAL MAXIMUM DISCHARGES AND VOLUMES (cont'd)

Country:	Sweden (10)
River:	Gimån
Gauging Station:	42-97 Gimdalsby

Date	Maximum discharge (m³/s) resulting from:		Maximum volume (10⁶m³) corresponding to max. discharge resulting from:	
	Rainfall	Snowmelt	Rainfall	Snowmelt
1	2	3	4	5
16–05–10		62		
10–12–10	4.5			
20–05–11		32		
31–10–11	7.1			
15–06–12		46		
31–09–12	17.3			
09–05–13		109		
07–09–13	30			
11–05–14		38		
11–09–14	6.6			
07–06–15		14		
10–08–15	39			
21–05–16		124		
24–07–16	49			
30–05–17		21		
21–11–17	17.3			
16–05–18		30		
17–07–18	42			
12–05–19		27		
12–07–19	38			
13–05–20		70		
03–08–20	29			
21–05–21		23		
07–09–21	118			
23–05–22		75		
01–07–22	50			
26–06–23		38		
31–10–23	49			
08–06–24		68		
08–07–24	57			

Country:	Sweden (10) cont'd
River:	Gimån
Gauging Station:	42-97 Gimdalsby

Date	Maximum discharge (m³/s) resulting from:		Maximum volume (10⁶m³) corresponding to max. discharge resulting from:	
	Rainfall	Snowmelt	Rainfall	Snowmelt
1	2	3	4	5
22–06–25		31		
20–12–25	10.6			
24–05–26		109		
18–12–26	18.0			
27–05–32		27		
04–08–32	19.3			
22–05–33		18		
25–08–33	16.7			
09–05–34		29		
19–17–34	18.6			
16–05–35		59		
08–07–35	45			
14–05–36		102		
09–11–36	6.8			
07–05–37		39		
09–10–37	23			
17–05–38		61		
26–07–38	52			
22–05–39		29		
01–10–39	8.4			
29–05–40		29		
13–10–40	11.9			
21–06–41		40		
01–09–41	54			
14–06–42		43		
19–12–42	13			
08–05–43		32		
25–09–43	10.6			
19–06–44		56		
23–11–44	23			

TABLE II – ANNUAL MAXIMUM DISCHARGES AND VOLUMES (cont'd)

Country: **Sweden (10) cont'd**
River: **Gimån**
Gauging Station: **42-97 Gimdalsby**

Date	Maximum discharge (m³/s) resulting from:		Maximum volume (10⁶m³) corresponding to max. discharge resulting from:	
	Rainfall	Snowmelt	Rainfall	Snowmelt
1	2	3	4	5
06–05–45		127		
20–10–45	14.6			
07–05–46		69		
24–09–46	17.3			
22–05–47		30		
01–07–47	21			
03–05–48		56		
09–09–48	13.0			
09–05–49		34		
12–12–49	8.4			
05–05–50		71		
06–08–50	35			
23–05–51		60		
08–08–51	19.3			
24–06–52		60		
19–11–52	21			
06–05–53		74		
23–10–53	14.6			
05–06–54		25		
05–07–54	29			
02–06–55		74		
10–08–55	18.0			
20–05–56		67		
12–09–56	23			
15–06–57		34		
18–09–57	45			
27–06–58		34		
30–11–58	15.6			
09–05–59		94		
30–11–59	5.3			
11–06–60		32		
28–08–60	97			
16–05–61		73		
13–08–61	50			
24–05–62		62		
19–09–62	31			
27–05–63		37		
13–07–63	18.0			
24–05–64		20		
22–09–64	39			
09–05–65		65		
02–10–65	15.6			
25–05–66		125		
22–08–66	36			
26–05–67		108		
07–12–67	14			
16–05–68		75		
04–07–68	15.6			
24–05–69		53		
13–11–69	15.6			
25–05–70		71		
23–11–70	29			
22–05–71		65		
01–12–71	9.9			
21–06–72		45		
13–09–72	11.0			

TABLE II — ANNUAL MAXIMUM DISCHARGES AND VOLUMES (cont'd)

Country:	Sweden (11)
River:	Motala Ström
Gauging Station:	67-154 Motala

Date	Maximum discharge (m³/s) resulting from:		Maximum volume (10⁶m³) corresponding to max. discharge resulting from:	
	Rainfall	Snowmelt	Rainfall	Snowmelt
1	2	3	4	5
13–01–58		29		
31–09–58	31			
30–04–59		29		
18–07–59	35			
05–02–60		29		
19–07–60	64			
10–04–61		61		
25–08–61	61			
03–04–62		31		
20–07–62	77			
27–01–63		77		
22–04–63	59			
30–01–64		37		
21–10–64	48			
20–04–65		36		
08–07–65	44			
21–02–66		37		
07–10–66	72			
20–02–67		63		
05–06–67	100			
31–03–68		79		
05–05–68	85			
20–03–69		53		
07–07–69	53			
20–04–70		37		
11–06–70	44			
31–03–71		33		
25–08–71	51			
13–04–72		31		
07–11–72	79			

Country:	Sweden (11) cont'd
River:	Motala Ström
Gauging Station:	67-154 Motala

Date	Maximum discharge (m³/s) resulting from:		Maximum volume (10⁶m³) corresponding to max. discharge resulting from:	
	Rainfall	Snowmelt	Rainfall	Snowmelt
1	2	3	4	5
12–02–73		66		
25–06–73	63			
26–01–74		63		
20–04–74	61			
16–04–75		44		
14–08–75	63			
22–03–76		27		
29–10–76	51			
21–03–77		44		
24–08–77	79			
15–04–78		58		
26–06–78	66			
01–01–79		33		
29–08–79	61			
24–03–80		42		
03–05–80	51			
05–04–81		29		
21–08–81	63			
11–01–82		56		
25–08–82	61			
26–02–83		44		
26–10–83	72			
20–01–84		63		
30–05–84	66			
31–03–85		53		
18–11–85	66			
30–04–86		53		
23–06–86	63			
04–02–87		35		
08–08–87	33			

TABLE II – ANNUAL MAXIMUM DISCHARGES AND VOLUMES (cont'd)

Country: Sweden (11) cont'd
River: Motala Ström
Gauging Station: 67-154 Motala

Date	Maximum discharge (m³/s) resulting from:		Maximum volume (10⁶m³) corresponding to max. discharge resulting from:	
	Rainfall	Snowmelt	Rainfall	Snowmelt
1	2	3	4	5
01–01–88		189		
09–08–88	48			
04–01–89		39		
23–08–89	44			
15–01–90		44		
29–06–90	51			
01–01–91		39		
22–12–91	53			
06–01–92		53		
07–07–92	58			
31–03–93		31		
31–05–93	33			
11–02–94		37		
31–07–94	48			
01–01–95		35		
27–08–95	63			
01–01–96		41		
06–10–96	51			
01–01–97		35		
20–06–97	51			
18–01–98		37		
31–08–98	61			
15–03–99		63		
01–06–99	63			
23–01–00		35		
25–08–00	46			
16–01–01		46		
01–07–01	51			
10–01–02		33		
01–11–02	50			

Country: Sweden (11) cont'd
River: Motala Ström
Gauging Station: 67-154 Motala

Date	Maximum discharge (m³/s) resulting from:		Maximum volume (10⁶m³) corresponding to max. discharge resulting from:	
	Rainfall	Snowmelt	Rainfall	Snowmelt
1	2	3	4	5
29–03–03		43		
10–09–03	67			
01–01–04		48		
22–05–04	70			
10–01–05		48		
14–08–05	52			
28–01–06		39		
28–06–06	44			
24–01–07		29		
11–09–07	61			
01–03–08		41		
30–07–08	61			
18–01–09		33		
31–07–09	51			
31–01–10		44		
31–05–10	58			
03–01–11		42		
31–05–11	51			
03–01–12		42		
31–12–12	68			
31–01–13		71		
17–10–13	56			
05–01–14		51		
30–04–14	66			
20–01–15		30		
28–08–15	46			
19–02–16		37		
13–10–16	71			
02–01–17		53		
24–06–17	58			

TABLE II — ANNUAL MAXIMUM DISCHARGES AND VOLUMES (cont'd)

Country:	Sweden (11) cont'd
River:	Motala Ström
Gauging Station:	67-154 Motala

	Maximum discharge (m³/s) resulting from:		Maximum volume (10⁶m³) corresponding to max. discharge resulting from:	
Date	Rainfall	Snowmelt	Rainfall	Snowmelt
1	2	3	4	5
10—02—18		50		
23—08—18	60			
25—01—19		41		
29—06—19	48			
18—03—20		46		
25—07—20	66			
22—01—21		33		
24—07—21	35			
10—03—22		19.9		
31—05—22	33			
26—01—23		21		
17—11—23	42			
27—01—24		34		
07—08—24	91			
03—01—25		74		
31—05—25	56			
09—03—26		31		
23—06—26	53			
28—04—27		61		
25—07—27	91			
09—02—28		62		
08—12—28	69			

Country:	Sweden (12)
River:	Vindelälven
Gauging Station:	28-56 Sorsele

	Maximum discharge (m³/s) resulting from:		Maximum volume (10⁶m³) corresponding to max. discharge resulting from:	
Date	Rainfall	Snowmelt	Rainfall	Snowmelt
1	2	3	4	5
24—05—10		905		
04—07—10	446			
31—05—11		755		
04—07—11	381			
30—05—12		577		
15—09—12	165			
10—06—13		841		
09—08—13	223			
27—06—14		688		
28—07—14	236			
13—06—15		655		
31—07—15	432			
14—06—16		959		
16—09—16	119			
06—06—17		947		
23—07—17	188			
09—07—18		688		
29—09—18	280			
28—05—19		531		
17—09—19	153			
04—06—20		923		
07—08—20	639			
03—06—21		566		
20—08—21	502			
23—06—22		1230		
05—08—22	336			
24—06—23		541		
08—09—23	173			
26—06—24		959		
13—10—24	389			

TABLE II – ANNUAL MAXIMUM DISCHARGES AND VOLUMES (cont'd)

Country:	Sweden (12) cont'd
River:	Vindelälven
Gauging Station:	28-56 Sorsele

Date	Maximum discharge (m³/s) resulting from:		Maximum volume (10⁶m³) corresponding to max. discharge resulting from:	
	Rainfall	Snowmelt	Rainfall	Snowmelt
1	2	3	4	5
03–06–25		841		
05–08–25	344			
10–06–26		983		
25–08–26	107			
23–06–27		947		
24–09–27	294			
15–06–28		502		
21–08–28	242			
30–05–29		882		
07–09–29	269			
28–06–30		1170		
30–09–30	116			
22–05–31		634		
28–08–31	432			
29–06–32		507		
21–09–32	259			
12–06–33		639		
13–08–33	381			
13–05–34		650		
11–10–34	324			
20–06–35		1010		
16–10–35	217			
22–05–36		900		
09–08–36	320			
22–05–37		623		
26–09–37	170			
07–06–38		1370		
15–10–38	236			
22–06–39		977		
06–08–39	273			

Country:	Sweden (12) cont'd
River:	Vindelälven
Gauging Station:	28-56 Sorsele

Date	Maximum discharge (m³/s) resulting from:		Maximum volume (10⁶m³) corresponding to max. discharge resulting from:	
	Rainfall	Snowmelt	Rainfall	Snowmelt
1	2	3	4	5
29–05–40		613		
24–09–40	450			
02–06–41		536		
24–08–41	432			
04–06–42		602		
15–10–42	252			
16–06–43		900		
06–11–43	147			
18–06–44		1090		
19–10–44	191			
17–06–45		1050		
23–08–45	191			
22–06–46		716		
25–09–46	239			
17–06–47		492		
18–10–47	90			
07–06–48		784		
28–08–48	197			
01–06–49		1050		
11–08–49	197			
10–06–50		1010		
01–08–50	239			
28–06–51		789		
07–09–51	183			
10–06–52		882		
05–10–52	160			
07–06–53		905		
28–08–53	450			
30–05–54		613		
16–08–54	517			

Sweden / Suède / Suecia / Швеция

TABLE II – ANNUAL MAXIMUM DISCHARGES AND VOLUMES (cont'd)

Country:	Sweden (12) cont'd
River:	Vindelälven
Gauging Station:	28-56 Sorsele

Date	Maximum discharge (m³/s) resulting from:		Maximum volume (10⁶m³) corresponding to max. discharge resulting from:	
	Rainfall	Snowmelt	Rainfall	Snowmelt
1	2	3	4	5
06–07–55		613		
18–10–55	77			
16–06–56		841		
01–09–56	103			
15–06–57		629		
18–09–57	242			
23–06–58		801		
11–08–58	302			
17–05–59		672		
19–09–59	69			
01–06–60		894		
27–08–60	410			
07–06–61		929		
09–08–61	469			
27–05–62		473		
14–09–62	156			
17–05–63		699		
27–07–63	214			
19–06–64		502		
06–09–64	287			
12–06–65		755		
06–08–65	211			
15–06–66		694		
01–08–66	502			
05–06–67		1130		
07–08–67	194			
09–06–68		1040		
30–09–68	40			
13–06–69		699		
23–10–69	100			

Country:	Sweden (12) cont'd
River:	Vindelälven
Gauging Station:	28-56 Sorsele

Date	Maximum discharge (m³/s) resulting from:		Maximum volume (10⁶m³) corresponding to max. discharge resulting from:	
	Rainfall	Snowmelt	Rainfall	Snowmelt
1	2	3	4	5
03–06–70		882		
23–10–70	170			
05–06–71		1280		
01–08–71	144			
11–06–72		876		
16–09–72	211			

267

TABLE II − ANNUAL MAXIMUM DISCHARGES AND VOLUMES (cont'd)

Country:	Sweden (13)
River:	Torneälv
Gauging Station:	1-3 Jukkasjärvi

Date	Maximum discharge (m³/s) resulting from:		Maximum volume (10⁶m³) corresponding to max. discharge resulting from:	
	Rainfall	Snowmelt	Rainfall	Snowmelt
1	2	3	4	5
25−07−15		605		
13−09−15	100			
13−07−16		293		
02−08−16	184			
26−06−17		439		
03−08−17	236			
08−07−18		653		
05−11−18	51			
28−06−19		396		
26−08−19	180			
04−06−20		516		
23−09−20	166			
11−08−21		503		
01−09−21	296			
23−06−22		590		
13−08−22	227			
28−07−23		534		
29−08−23	191			
08−07−24		448		
15−09−24	147			
13−07−25		407		
08−09−25	182			
05−06−26		334		
15−10−26	114			
02−07−27		507		
23−09−27	120			
31−07−28		380		
14−09−28	138			
25−06−29		396		
24−09−29	191			

Country:	Sweden (13) cont'd
River:	Torneälv
Gauging Station:	1-3 Jukkasjärvi

Date	Maximum discharge (m³/s) resulting from:		Maximum volume (10⁶m³) corresponding to max. discharge resulting from:	
	Rainfall	Snowmelt	Rainfall	Snowmelt
1	2	3	4	5
30−05−30		327		
31−08−30	160			
11−07−31		407		
26−08−31	254			
09−07−32		490		
14−09−32	229			
24−06−33		396		
28−09−33	116			
17−07−34		464		
10−09−34	154			
15−06−35		567		
18−10−35	123			
20−05−36		403		
29−09−36	114			
24−06−37		281		
23−09−37	142			
13−06−38		486		
12−10−38	136			
23−06−39		366		
27−09−39	128			
29−06−40		236		
22−09−40,	270			
08−05−41		348		
11−09−41	142			
03−06−42		373		
01−09−42	182			
24−06−43		633		
05−09−43	246			
19−06−44		281		
30−09−44	122			

TABLE II − ANNUAL MAXIMUM DISCHARGES AND VOLUMES   (cont'd)

Country:	Sweden (13) cont'd
River:	Torneälv
Gauging Station:	1-3 Jukkasjärvi

Date	Maximum discharge (m³/s) resulting from:		Maximum volume (10⁶m³) corresponding to max. discharge resulting from:	
	Rainfall	Snowmelt	Rainfall	Snowmelt
1	2	3	4	5
17−06−45		431		
22−08−45	156			
03−06−46		473		
23−09−46	172			
26−06−47		308		
18−09−47	116			
10−06−48		344		
26−08−48	217			
05−07−49		419		
02−09−49	160			
03−07−50		411		
12−10−50	87			
20−07−51		503		
19−10−51	99			
26−06−52		648		
10−09−52	123			
24−06−53		576		
01−09−53	166			
02−08−54		490		
01−10−54	136			
19−07−55		388		
19−09−55	168			
16−06−56		376		
01−09−56	147			
04−08−57		439		
24−08−57	380			
24−06−58		494		
05−08−58	373			
12−06−59		324		
11−10−59	195			

Country:	Sweden (13) cont'd
River:	Torneälv
Gauging Station:	1-3 Jukkasjärvi

Date	Maximum discharge (m³/s) resulting from:		Maximum volume (10⁶m³) corresponding to max. discharge resulting from:	
	Rainfall	Snowmelt	Rainfall	Snowmelt
1	2	3	4	5
03−06−60		229		
24−08−60	202			
29−06−61		396		
28−09−61	122			
25−06−62		311		
14−09−62	142			
23−07−63		314		
01−10−63	197			
15−07−64		331		
02−09−64	231			
30−06−65		456		
08−11−65	116			
14−06−66		281		
01−08−66	182			
05−06−67		331		
10−08−67	351			

TABLE II -- ANNUAL MAXIMUM DISCHARGES AND VOLUMES   (cont'd)

Country:	Sweden (14)
River:	Ljusnan
Gauging Station:	48-106 Sveg

	Maximum discharge (m³/s) resulting from:		Maximum volume (10⁶m³) corresponding to max. discharge resulting from:	
Date	Rainfall	Snowmelt	Rainfall	Snowmelt
1	2	3	4	5
11—05—14		491		
19—10—14	50			
28—05—15		478		
02—08—15	529			
12—05—16		1150		
17—07—16	734			
30—05—17		719		
01—09—17	260			
13—05—18		649		
10—07—18	512			
07—05—19		750		
03—07—19	167			
21—05—20		931		
23—08—20	294			
14—05—21		468		
06—09—21	668			
25—05—22		893		
27—08—22	383			
26—05—23		604		
22—09—23	319			
27—05—24		1100		
21—08—24	649			
15—05—25		529		
12—07—25	368			
25—05—26		944		
29—07—26	325			
06—06—27		1040		
27—09—27	389			
07—05—28		680		
20—08—28	333			

Country:	Sweden (14) cont'd
River:	Ljusnan
Gauging Station:	48-106 Sveg

	Maximum discharge (m³/s) resulting from:		Maximum volume (10⁶m³) corresponding to max. discharge resulting from:	
Date	Rainfall	Snowmelt	Rainfall	Snowmelt
1	2	3	4	5
17—05—29		699		
29—10—29	414			
31—05—30		539		
28—10—30	149			
17—05—31		1070		
26—08—31	302			
21—05—32		730		
18—10—32	211			
24—05—33		297		
30—07—33	302			
08—05—34		1040		
04—09—34	389			
11—05—35		653		
12—10—35	278			
15—05—36		1070		
23—07—36	356			
28—04—37		672		
20—09—37	465			
19—05—38		811		
05—09—38	746			
18—05—39		488		
27—07—39	362			
21—05—40		676		
26—08—40	327			
28—05—41		707		
19—08—41	362			
22—05—42		377		
01—07—42	236			
10—05—43		539		
30—10—43	217			

TABLE II — ANNUAL MAXIMUM DISCHARGES AND VOLUMES   (cont'd)

Country:	Sweden (14) cont'd
River:	Ljusnan
Gauging Station:	48-106 Sveg

Date	Maximum discharge (m³/s) resulting from:		Maximum volume (10⁶m³) corresponding to max. discharge resulting from:	
	Rainfall	Snowmelt	Rainfall	Snowmelt
1	2	3	4	5
12–05–44		1010		
03–10–44	300			
17–05–45		1030		
27–08–45	220			
06–05–46		426		
23–09–46	426			
15–05–47		575		
15–07–47	195			
15–05–48		495		
09–09–48	325			
08–05–49		515		
06–08–49	423			
14–05–50		974		
30–07–50	754			
22–05–51		864		
29–06–51	623			
23–06–52		543		
14–08–52	198			
04–05–53		536		
12–07–53	439			
14–05–54		445		
19–07–54	442			
06–06–55		626		
15–11–55	156			
14–05–56		593		
16–09–56	311			
18–05–57		703		
17–09–57	695			

Country:	Sweden (14) cont'd
River:	Ljusnan
Gauging Station:	48-106 Sveg

Date	Maximum discharge (m³/s) resulting from:		Maximum volume (10⁶m³) corresponding to max. discharge resulting from:	
	Rainfall	Snowmelt	Rainfall	Snowmelt
1	2	3	4	5
30–05–58		719		
05–10–58	200			
02–05–59		1080		
25–11–59	93			
17–05–60		742		
19–08–60	852			
09–05–61		660		
06–08–61	478			

271

TABLE II – ANNUAL MAXIMUM DISCHARGES AND VOLUMES (cont'd)

Country:	Sweden (15)					Country:	Sweden (15) cont'd		
River:	Klarälven					River:	Klarälven		
Gauging Station:	108-1703 Edsforsens krv					Gauging Station:	108-1703 Edsforsens krv		

Date	Maximum discharge (m³/s) resulting from:		Maximum volume (10⁶m³) corresponding to max. discharge resulting from:		Date	Maximum discharge (m³/s) resulting from:		Maximum volume (10⁶m³) corresponding to max. discharge resulting from:	
	Rainfall	Snowmelt	Rainfall	Snowmelt		Rainfall	Snowmelt	Rainfall	Snowmelt
1	2	3	4	5	1	2	3	4	5
18–05–10		759			01–06–25		695		
04–07–10	211				31–10–25	239			
07–05–11		815			03–06–26		603		
04–07–11	119				29–07–26	474			
24–08–12		649			07–06–27		771		
21–10–12	235				05–10–27	549			
04–05–13		753			09–05–28		669		
15–08–13	141				19–08–28	495			
12–05–14		405			16–05–29		505		
04–06–14	220				14–11–29	505			
28–05–15		384			28–05–30		532		
01–08–15	495				07–11–30	220			
13–05–16		1320			21–05–31		1020		
11–11–16	352				19–07–31	323			
02–06–17		410			24–05–32		479		
01–09–17	362				17–10–32	415			
29–04–18		451			27–05–33		239		
27–09–18	364				14–10–33	292			
08–05–19		492			08–05–34		870		
30–09–19	129				09–09–34	418			
22–05–20		863			27–04–35		573		
24–08–20	778				13–10–35	445			
30–04–21		297			15–05–36		617		
06–09–21	286				28–07–36	524			
10–05–22		581			26–04–37		606		
27–08–22	376				27–06–37	318			
25–05–23		559			20–05–38		369		
31–10–23	490				11–10–38	595			
05–05–24		876			14–05–39		430		
27–07–24	784				26–07–39	369			

TABLE II — ANNUAL MAXIMUM DISCHARGES AND VOLUMES   (cont'd)

Country:	Sweden (15) cont'd
River:	Klarälven
Gauging Station:	108-1703 Edsforsens krv

Date	Maximum discharge (m³/s) resulting from: Rainfall	Snowmelt	Maximum volume (10⁶m³) corresponding to max. discharge resulting from: Rainfall	Snowmelt
1	2	3	4	5
12—05—40		546		
10—07—40	303			
14—06—41		247		
01—09—41	241			
22—04—42		393		
03—11—42	237			
10—05—43		508		
30—08—43	336			
17—06—44		595		
03—10—44	557			
17—05—45		482		
11—06—45	355			
05—05—46		451		
22—09—46	381			
18—05—47		398		
14—07—47	201			
21—04—48		328		
09—09—48	404			
29—04—49		444		
05—08—49	269			
14—05—50		522		
30—07—50	648			
21—05—51		634		
03—09—51	313			
08—05—52		557		
24—06—52	326			

Country:	Sweden (16)
River:	Götaälv
Gauging Station:	108-243 Sjötorp

Date	Maximum discharge (m³/s) resulting from: Rainfall	Snowmelt	Maximum volume (10⁶m³) corresponding to max. discharge resulting from: Rainfall	Snowmelt
1	2	3	4	5
29—06—07		492		
13—11—07	407			
22—06—08		481		
13—01—08	419			
25—06—09		500		
14—09—09	415			
16—06—10		405		
16—01—10	393			
06—07—11		564		
28—11—11	514			
30—07—12		621		
10—11—12	597			
18—06—13		557		
10—01—13	578			
09—06—14		438		
24—12—14	487			
05—06—15		648		
18—11—15	535			
30—06—16		660		
22—10—16	735			
20—06—17		735		
06—09—17	761			
26—06—18		759		
03—12—18	564			
18—06—19		529		
15—09—19	436			
30—06—20		584		
11—11—20	553			
12—06—21		541		
31—12—21	483			

TABLE II – ANNUAL MAXIMUM DISCHARGES AND VOLUMES (cont'd)

Country:	Sweden (16) cont'd
River:	Götaälv
Gauging Station:	108-243 Sjötorp

	Maximum discharge (m³/s) resulting from:		Maximum volume (10⁶m³) corresponding to max. discharge resulting from:	
Date	Rainfall	Snowmelt	Rainfall	Snowmelt
1	2	3	4	5
17–05–22		560		
30–12–22	574			
19–06–23		586		
15–11–23	654			
22–05–24		673		
31–12–24	615			
15–06–25		768		
31–12–25	613			
10–06–26		677		
26–12–26	450			
14–06–27		607		
27–08–27	586			
28–06–28		568		
10–10–28	547			
20–06–29		636		
13–10–29	648			
30–07–30		677		
18–10–30	737			
19–06–31		780		
31–12–31	681			
01–06–32		601		
31–10–32	566			
31–05–33		564		
25–12–33	623			
22–05–34		745		
15–09–34	650			
05–06–35		543		
11–12–35	444			
10–06–36		658		
15–10–36	611			

Country:	Sweden (16) cont'd
River:	Götaälv
Gauging Station:	108-243 Sjötorp

	Maximum discharge (m³/s) resulting from:		Maximum volume (10⁶m³) corresponding to max. discharge resulting from:	
Date	Rainfall	Snowmelt	Rainfall	Snowmelt
1	2	3	4	5
24–06–37		644		
05–09–37	597			
28–06–38		665		
27–11–38	712			
23–06–39		677		
27–10–39	687			
31–05–40		588		
07–01–40	636			
29–08–41		718		
31–12–41	772			
08–06–42		737		
04–01–42	772			
12–06–43		475		
08–08–43	461			
27–05–44		413		
30–11–44	535			
01–06–45		506		
19–12–45	588			
13–06–46		751		
09–11–46	630			
22–06–47		595		
29–12–47	487			
13–06–48		588		
22–12–48	675			
06–06–49		582		
18–08–49	584			
25–06–50		609		
28–08–50	570			
05–08–51		774		
28–10–51	720			

Sweden / Suède / Suecia / Швеция

TABLE II – ANNUAL MAXIMUM DISCHARGES AND VOLUMES (cont'd)

Country:	Sweden (16) cont'd
River:	Götaälv
Gauging Station:	108-243 Sjötorp

Date	Maximum discharge (m³/s) resulting from:		Maximum volume (10⁶m³) corresponding to max. discharge resulting from:	
	Rainfall	Snowmelt	Rainfall	Snowmelt
1	2	3	4	5
01−07−52		726		
31−12−52	689			
06−06−53		720		
31−01−53	768			
12−05−54		481		
06−11−54	366			
01−08−55		419		
20−11−55	413			
11−06−56		426		
17−12−56	450			
27−06−57		481		
30−10−57	430			
27−07−58		389		
01−01−58	399			
18−06−59		407		
03−12−59	341			
16−07−60		708		
22−11−60	817			
31−05−61		751		
01−01−61	774			
24−07−62		677		
29−11−62	597			
26−06−63		671		
30−11−63	615			
20−07−64		590		
20−12−64	481			
15−06−65		494		
15−11−65	413			
16−07−66		628		
09−10−66	708			

Country:	Sweden (16) cont'd
River:	Götaälv
Gauging Station:	108-243 Sjötorp

Date	Maximum discharge (m³/s) resulting from:		Maximum volume (10⁶m³) corresponding to max. discharge resulting from:	
	Rainfall	Snowmelt	Rainfall	Snowmelt
1	2	3	4	5
27−07−67		794		
25−09−67	766			
09−06−68		782		
20−10−68	605			
04−07−69		648		
27−11−69	557			
29−06−70		570		
30−11−70	496			
31−07−71		504		
05−09−71	483			
05−07−72		586		
31−12−72	722			
20−06−73		735		
06−12−73	817			
08−04−74		722		
09−11−74	611			
23−06−75		592		
06−09−75	520			
30−06−76		473		
28−10−76	477			
21−09−77		599		
24−12−77	628			
26−06−78		636		
30−11−78	502			
22−08−79		570		
08−11−79	597			
22−05−80		508		
02−01−80	557			
05−07−81		473		
31−12−81	539			

TABLE II – ANNUAL MAXIMUM DISCHARGES AND VOLUMES (cont'd)

Country: Sweden (16) cont'd
River: Götaälv
Gauging Station: 108-243 Sjötorp

| Date | Maximum discharge (m³/s) resulting from: | | Maximum volume (10⁶m³) corresponding to max. discharge resulting from: | |
| | Rainfall | Snowmelt | Rainfall | Snowmelt |
1	2	3	4	5
08–09–82		731		
19–11–82	693			
07–06–83		628		
04–12–83	669			
25–06–84		658		
03–09–84	603			
25–06–85		605		
04–11–85	634			
23–06–86		630		
09–12–86	471			
09–06–87		473		
21–09–87	424			
27–06–88		522		
22–09–88	535			
15–06–89		510		
07–11–89	448			
17–07–90		588		
01–09–90	582			
30–06–91		576		
31–12–91	580			
29–06–92		574		
20–11–92	504			
16–06–93		485		
06–11–93	504			
21–06–94		642		
28–11–94	572			
05–06–95		625		
08–09–95	693			
22–06–96		636		
11–11–96	572			

Country: Sweden (16) cont'd
River: Götaälv
Gauging Station: 108-243 Sjötorp

| Date | Maximum discharge (m³/s) resulting from: | | Maximum volume (10⁶m³) corresponding to max. discharge resulting from: | |
| | Rainfall | Snowmelt | Rainfall | Snowmelt |
1	2	3	4	5
16–06–97		625		
30–10–97	580			
27–08–98		739		
23–12–98	689			
12–06–99		731		
03–09–99	632			
11–07–00		599		
28–12–00	529			
04–06–01		522		
01–01–01	529			
05–04–02		308		
31–10–02	487			
21–06–03		592		
22–11–03	382			
19–06–04		716		
16–08–04	650			
31–05–05		469		
03–01–05	500			
30–06–06		512		
26–11–06	438			
19–07–07		551		
06–09–07	601			
23–06–08		634		
30–09–08	568			
21–07–09		609		
19–12–09	702			
02–06–10		829		
17–08–10	757			
31–05–11		671		
01–09–11	568			

Sweden / Suède / Suecia / Швеция

TABLE II – ANNUAL MAXIMUM DISCHARGES AND VOLUMES (cont'd)

Country: Sweden (16) cont'd
River: Götaälv
Gauging Station: 108-243 Sjötorp

Date	Maximum discharge (m³/s) resulting from:		Maximum volume (10⁶m³) corresponding to max. discharge resulting from:	
	Rainfall	Snowmelt	Rainfall	Snowmelt
1	2	3	4	5
08–07–12		531		
31–12–12	646			
27–05–13		677		
30–11–13	518			
25–05–14		568		
04–09–14	457			
26–08–15		467		
02–10–15	436			
17–07–16		615		
31–12–16	584			
08–06–17		543		
15–12–17	525			
01–06–18		537		
25–11–18	506			
28–05–19		518		
04–10–19	442			
05–06–20		726		
24–09–20	689			
20–04–21		531		
22–01–21	564			
01–06–22		419		
21–09–22	415			
07–07–23		413		
12–12–23	551			
30–06–24		710		
22–11–24	784			
06–06–25		698		
17–01–25	774			
24–05–26		551		
16–08–26	545			

Country: Sweden (16) cont'd
River: Götaälv
Gauging Station: 108-243 Sjötorp

Date	Maximum discharge (m³/s) resulting from:		Maximum volume (10⁶m³) corresponding to max. discharge resulting from:	
	Rainfall	Snowmelt	Rainfall	Snowmelt
1	2	3	4	5
26–07–27		813		
05–11–27	836			
22–05–28		665		
08–12–28	710			
20–06–29		640		
31–12–29	691			
04–06–30		671		
24–01–30	718			
23–06–31		728		
20–08–31	687			
08–06–32		518		
28–12–32	494			
30–05–33		463		
03–10–33	370			
31–05–34		397		
31–12–34	516			
17–06–35		615		
31–12–35	632			
01–06–36		706		
20–11–36	595			
28–05–37		652		
03–09–37	568			

277

TABLE II — ANNUAL MAXIMUM DISCHARGES AND VOLUMES (cont'd)

Country:	Sweden (17)
River:	Muonioälv
Gauging Station:	1-589 Kallio

	Maximum discharge (m³/s) resulting from:		Maximum volume (10⁶m³) corresponding to max. discharge resulting from:	
Date	Rainfall	Snowmelt	Rainfall	Snowmelt
1	2	3	4	5
30—05—11		1120		
03—10—11	312			
28—05—12		1360		
16—09—12	281			
28—05—13		1020		
12—08—13	118			
03—06—14		696		
03—10—14	144			
14—06—15		969		
19—09—15	89			
10—06—16		912		
27—08—16	98			
07—06—17		1650		
28—10—17	360			
02—06—18		835		
01—10—18	380			
25—05—19		974		
12—09—19	732			
22—05—20		1600		
24—09—20	252			
24—05—21		1040		
03—09—21	664			
05—05—22		965		
24—09—22	321			
30—05—23		1190		
03—10—23	466			
01—06—24		1010		
19—09—24	278			
22—05—25		1030		
21—08—25	387			

Country:	Sweden (17) cont'd
River:	Muonioälv
Gauging Station:	1-589 Kallio

	Maximum discharge (m³/s) resulting from:		Maximum volume (10⁶m³) corresponding to max. discharge resulting from:	
Date	Rainfall	Snowmelt	Rainfall	Snowmelt
1	2	3	4	5
24—05—26		961		
14—10—26	337			
25—06—27		1450		
09—10—27	264			
17—06—28		887		
05—09—28	244			
28—05—29		1100		
26—09—29	357			
27—05—30		1270		
01—11—30	208			
22—05—31		1000		
30—08—31	228			
16—06—32		1220		
16—09—32	704			
13—06—33		904		
20—10—33	121			
12—05—34		1410		
11—10—34	290			
16—06—35		1490		
16—10—35	290			
22—05—36		1590		
08—08—36	557			
09—05—37		716		
30—09—37	146			
09—06—38		1100		
14—10—38	194			
29—05—39		939		
01—10—39	81			
16—05—40		961		
16—05—40	614			

TABLE II – ANNUAL MAXIMUM DISCHARGES AND VOLUMES (cont'd)

Country:	Sweden (17) cont'd
River:	Muonioälv
Gauging Station:	1-589 Kallio

Date	Maximum discharge (m³/s) resulting from:		Maximum volume (10⁶m³) corresponding to max. discharge resulting from:	
	Rainfall	Snowmelt	Rainfall	Snowmelt
1	2	3	4	5
27−05−41		1030		
15−08−41	169			
04−06−42		878		
21−08−42	261			
09−06−43		1010		
01−09−43	303			
19−05−44		912		
22−10−44	176			
21−05−45		1120		
07−09−45	167			
13−06−46		728		
29−09−46	272			
14−05−47		756		
19−09−47	258			
16−05−48		1370		
31−08−48	350			
18−05−49		874		
26−10−49	182			
16−05−50		736		
14−10−50	180			
29−06−51		625		
07−09−51	380			
04−06−52		1270		
03−10−52	306			
25−05−53		1380		
07−10−53	341			
30−05−54		509		
19−08−54	407			
05−06−55		1440		
02−10−55	163			

Country:	Sweden (17) cont'd
River:	Muonioälv
Gauging Station:	1-589 Kallio

Date	Maximum discharge (m³/s) resulting from:		Maximum volume (10⁶m³) corresponding to max. discharge resulting from:	
	Rainfall	Snowmelt	Rainfall	Snowmelt
1	2	3	4	5
21−05−56		1090		
04−10−56	126			
22−05−57		748		
19−09−57	367			
06−06−58		1130		
07−08−58	404			
09−05−59		1390		
31−08−59	146			
14−05−60		752		
07−09−60	131			
28−05−61		736		
10−08−61	568			
25−05−62		943		
15−09−62	417			
16−05−63		1120		
04−10−63	299			
18−05−64		797		
08−08−64	502			
10−06−65		1120		
11−08−65	584			
23−05−66		1320		
21−09−66	172			
02−06−67		1320		
11−08−67	645			
10−06−68		1720		
23−08−68	148			
14−06−69		706		
04−10−69	157			
03−06−70		908		
20−09−70	205			

TABLE II — ANNUAL MAXIMUM DISCHARGES AND VOLUMES (cont'd)

Country:	Sweden (17) cont'd
River:	Muonioälv
Gauging Station:	1-589 Kallio

Date	Maximum discharge (m³/s) resulting from:		Maximum volume (10⁶m³) corresponding to max. discharge resulting from:	
	Rainfall	Snowmelt	Rainfall	Snowmelt
1	2	3	4	5
05—06—71		760		
18—08—71	161			

Country:	Sweden (18)
River:	Dalälven
Gauging Station:	53-121 Norslund

Date	Maximum discharge (m³/s) resulting from:		Maximum volume (10⁶m³) corresponding to max. discharge resulting from:	
	Rainfall	Snowmelt	Rainfall	Snowmelt
1	2	3	4	5
22—05—52		1500		
18—12—52	518			
04—06—53		1250		
29—10—53	421			
27—05—54		394		
11—11—54	394			
26—05—55		968		
17—11—55	643			
31—05—56		790		
11—10—56	413			
29—05—57		711		
31—07—57	638			
21—05—58		643		
04—06—58	518			
03—06—59		840		
07—10—59	401			
01—06—60		2640		
01—11—60	927			
31—05—61		901		
10—08—61	559			
20—05—62		1160		
11—07—62	730			
22—05—63		1100		
10—07—63	830			
20—05—64		628		
08—07—64	740			
19—05—65		686		
14—07—65	303			
31—05—66		911		
21—09—66	1050			

TABLE II – ANNUAL MAXIMUM DISCHARGES AND VOLUMES (cont'd)

Country:	Sweden (18) cont'd
River:	Dalälven
Gauging Station:	53-121 Norslund

Date	Maximum discharge (m³/s) resulting from:		Maximum volume (10⁶m³) corresponding to max. discharge resulting from:	
	Rainfall	Snowmelt	Rainfall	Snowmelt
1	2	3	4	5
14–06–67		1600		
20–09–67	382			
22–05–68		1280		
09–10–68	441			
04–06–69		1030		
24–09–69	532			
20–05–70		937		
19–07–70	462			
02–06–71		765		
04–08–71	454			
10–05–72		1260		
18–10–72	1015			
05–06–73		876		
12–09–73	835			
05–06–74		559		
30–10–74	653			
14–05–75		765		
28–08–75	324			
19–05–76		619		
22–09–76	906			
08–06–77		1250		
31–08–77	755			
26–05–78		1060		
08–11–78	371			
27–06–79		1210		
01–08–79	711			
30–04–80		466		
20–08–80	307			
27–05–81		1070		
16–09–81	725			
12–05–82		1190		
11–08–82	770			
18–05–83		906		
13–09–83	937			
13–06–84		1030		
01–08–84	532			
05–06–85		1120		
16–10–85	984			
28–05–86		624		
06–08–86	349			
27–05–87		881		
01–10–87	409			
25–05–88		1380		
22–09–88	433			
17–05–89		850		
09–11–89	559			
09–05–90		1630		
11–07–90	825			
28–05–91		1050		
31–10–91	578			
10–06–92		715		
07–11–92	382			
10–06–93		462		
11–10–93	891			
06–05–94		1160		
30–07–94	496			
07–05–95		1540		
23–08–95	994			
13–05–96		916		
22–10–96	619			

TABLE II – ANNUAL MAXIMUM DISCHARGES AND VOLUMES (cont'd)

Country:	Sweden (18) cont'd
River:	Dalälven
Gauging Station:	53-121 Norslund

Date	Maximum discharge (m³/s) resulting from:		Maximum volume (10⁶m³) corresponding to max. discharge resulting from:	
	Rainfall	Snowmelt	Rainfall	Snowmelt
1	2	3	4	5
08–05–97		1280		
09–10–97	550			
21–05–98		1280		
14–08–98	916			
25–05–99		2030		
18–10–99	382			
30–05–00		942		
23–11–00	327			
17–05–01		715		
04–11–01	238			
31–05–02		840		
06–09–02	1050			
30–05–03		865		
04–11–03	587			
25–05–04		1190		
30–11–04	168			
13–05–05		765		
02–09–05	483			
16–05–06		1160		
06–06–06	1160			
25–05–07		1130		
12–08–07	550			
03–06–08		942		
20–09–08	293			
09–06–09		1430		
03–11–09	891			
20–05–10		1540		
07–07–10	559			
13–05–11		1280		
22–11–11	164			

Country:	Sweden (18) cont'd
River:	Dalälven
Gauging Station:	53-121 Norslund

Date	Maximum discharge (m³/s) resulting from:		Maximum volume (10⁶m³) corresponding to max. discharge resulting from:	
	Rainfall	Snowmelt	Rainfall	Snowmelt
1	2	3	4	5
26–06–12		629		
19–08–12	958			
09–05–13		1100		
23–08–13	479			
15–05–14		619		
29–12–14	93			
30–05–15		653		
05–08–15	815			
18–05–16		2410		
16–11–16	657			
31–05–17		624		
05–09–17	587			
23–05–18		760		
30–09–18	615			

TABLE II — ANNUAL MAXIMUM DISCHARGES AND VOLUMES (cont'd)

Country:	Sweden (19)
River:	Vindelälven
Gauging Station:	28-1545 Renfors

Date	Maximum discharge (m³/s) resulting from:		Maximum volume (10⁶m³) corresponding to max. discharge resulting from:	
	Rainfall	Snowmelt	Rainfall	Snowmelt
1	2	3	4	5
03—06—11		856		
07—10—11	171			
31—05—12		712		
18—09—12	219			
12—06—13		886		
13—08—13	302			
01—07—14		732		
28—09—14	137			
16—06—15		652		
10—09—15	167			
16—06—16		1070		
21—09—16	137			
09—06—17		1010		
18—10—17	186			
11—07—18		678		
30—09—18	321			
31—05—19		537		
08—07—19	360			
06—06—20		1090		
10—08—20	736			
06—06—21		598		
21—08—21	515			
25—06—22		1370		
01—08—22	398			
27—06—23		521		
25—07—23	432			
28—06—24		1040		
17—10—24	508			
06—06—25		973		
16—07—25	427			

Country:	Sweden (19) cont'd
River:	Vindelälven
Gauging Station:	28-1545 Renfors

Date	Maximum discharge (m³/s) resulting from:		Maximum volume (10⁶m³) corresponding to max. discharge resulting from:	
	Rainfall	Snowmelt	Rainfall	Snowmelt
1	2	3	4	5
13—06—26		1130		
30—08—26	164			
26—06—27		1110		
09—10—27	342			
19—06—28		634		
22—08—28	309			
02—06—29		968		
12—09—29	319			
01—07—30		1190		
05—09—30	155			
23—05—31		797		
30—08—31	486			
07—06—32		560		
25—09—32	302			
16—06—33		627		
16—08—33	438			
15—05—34		648		
13—10—34	429			
22—06—35		1230		
20—10—35	309			
24—05—36		1100		
11—08—36	331			
25—05—37		671		
02—10—37	213			
09—06—38		1650		
19—10—38	281			
25—06—39		1040		
09—07—39	552			
30—05—40		643		
18—10—40	444			

TABLE II – ANNUAL MAXIMUM DISCHARGES AND VOLUMES   (cont'd)

Country:	Sweden (19) cont'd
River:	Vindelälven
Gauging Station:	28-1545 Renfors

Date	Maximum discharge (m³/s) resulting from:		Maximum volume (10⁶m³) corresponding to max. discharge resulting from:	
	Rainfall	Snowmelt	Rainfall	Snowmelt
1	2	3	4	5
22–06–41		608		
24–08–11	593			
13–07–42		659		
21–10–42	396			
18–06–43		1050		
16–11–43	212			
21–06–44		1400		
01–11–44	343			
21–06–45		1500		
18–09–45	201			
14–06–46		738		
07–10–46	287			
22–06–47		664		
01–10–47	123			
10–06–48		976		
26–10–48	232			
11–06–49		1240		
27–10–49	258			
12–06–50		1020		
08–08–50	270			
01–07–51		972		
16–09–51	206			
14–06–52		1030		
11–10–52	184			
13–06–53		1080		
05–09–53	465			
04–06–54		582		
14–08–54	728			
21–06–55		721		
30–10–55	96			

Country:	Sweden (19) cont'd
River:	Vindelälven
Gauging Station:	28-1545 Renfors

Date	Maximum discharge (m³/s) resulting from:		Maximum volume (10⁶m³) corresponding to max. discharge resulting from:	
	Rainfall	Snowmelt	Rainfall	Snowmelt
1	2	3	4	5
19–06–56		877		
07–08–56	160			
18–06–57		725		
03–08–57	775			
26–06–58		909		
14–08–58	323			
20–05–59		721		
03–07–59	251			
04–06–60		976		
29–08–60	563			
10–06–61		1030		
13–08–61	542			
30–05–62		633		
14–09–62	249			
20–05–63		693		
31–07–63	243			
22–06–64		545		
05–09–64	342			
15–06–65		824		
05–08–65	217			
18–06–66		816		
04–08–66	563			
08–06–67		1300		
14–11–67	243			
12–06–68		1110		
14–10–68	75			
15–06–69		761		
29–10–69	112			
06–06–70		960		
26–10–70	214			

TABLE II – ANNUAL MAXIMUM DISCHARGES AND VOLUMES   (cont'd)

Country:	Sweden (19) cont'd
River:	Vindelälven
Gauging Station:	28-1545 Renfors

Date	Maximum discharge (m³/s) resulting from:		Maximum volume (10⁶m³) corresponding to max. discharge resulting from:	
	Rainfall	Snowmelt	Rainfall	Snowmelt
1	2	3	4	5
08–06–71		1480		
02–08–71	184			
13–06–72		993		
21–09–72	209			

Country:	Sweden (20)
River:	Motala ström
Gauging Station:	67-172 Norsholm

Date	Maximum discharge (m³/s) resulting from:		Maximum volume (10⁶m³) corresponding to max. discharge resulting from:	
	Rainfall	Snowmelt	Rainfall	Snowmelt
1	2	3	4	5
25–01–73		177		
06–12–73	122			
17–04–74		154		
29–08–74	86			
24–04–75		203		
05–06–75	164			
22–04–76		108		
14–10–76	105			
05–05–77		210		
17–11–77	148			
15–04–78		134		
07–06–78	102			
31–05–79		136		
16–08–79	190			
24–04–80		86		
11–08–80	70			
21–05–81		164		
21–09–81	134			
07–01–82		134		
29–07–82	122			
28–04–83		134		
08–12–83	151			
22–03–84		167		
10–05–84	128			
07–03–85		125		
07–11–85	134			
08–04–86		136		
12–05–86	134			
01–03–87		53		
09–06–87	57			

TABLE II – ANNUAL MAXIMUM DISCHARGES AND VOLUMES (cont'd)

Country:	Sweden (20) cont'd
River:	Motala ström
Gauging Station:	67-172 Norsholm

Date	Maximum discharge (m³/s) resulting from:		Maximum volume (10⁶m³) corresponding to max. discharge resulting from:	
	Rainfall	Snowmelt	Rainfall	Snowmelt
1	2	3	4	5
09–05–88		134		
12–06–88	119			
30–04–89		112		
28–11–89	69			
31–05–90		119		
27–11–90	98			
31–04–91		98		
29–12–91	164			
01–01–92		164		
01–05–92	134			
19–03–93		85		
22–10–93	65			
17–05–94		88		
22–11–94	86			
18–04–95		164		
17–08–95	134			
01–05–96		95		
24–08–96	108			
25–04–97		164		
10–07–97	108			
12–05–98		134		
05–08–98	126			
26–02–99		157		
25–07–99	86			
24–04–00		173		
29–12–00	120			
23–04–01		120		
02–07–01	97			
27–05–02		98		
01–01–02	119			

Country:	Sweden (20) cont'd
River:	Motala ström
Gauging Station:	67-172 Norsholm

Date	Maximum discharge (m³/s) resulting from:		Maximum volume (10⁶m³) corresponding to max. discharge resulting from:	
	Rainfall	Snowmelt	Rainfall	Snowmelt
1	2	3	4	5
16–05–03		141		
01–11–03	106			
21–04–04		210		
24–12–04	126			
01–01–05		125		
28–11–05	113			
13–05–06		97		
06–08–06	73			
20–06–07		106		
03–09–07	112			
18–05–08		139		
24–12–08	59			
16–05–09		142		
07–11–09	67			
27–03–10		129		
25–12–10	131			
07–05–11		134		
29–12–11	92			
24–04–12		109		
31–12–12	215			
01–01–13		224		
30–11–13	113			
25–03–14		151		
11–08–14	60			
16–05–15		119		
28–08–15	80			
09–04–16		163		
12–07–16	153			
07–05–17		188		
15–12–17	81			

TABLE II – ANNUAL MAXIMUM DISCHARGES AND VOLUMES (cont'd)

Country:	Sweden (20) cont'd
River:	Motala ström
Gauging Station:	67-172 Norsholm

Date	Maximum discharge (m³/s) resulting from:		Maximum volume (10⁶m³) corresponding to max. discharge resulting from:	
	Rainfall	Snowmelt	Rainfall	Snowmelt
1	2	3	4	5
14–02–18		134		
25–04–18	114			
21–04–19		136		
10–08–19	73			
18–03–20		126		
01–05–20	102			
25–03–21		86		
23–07–21	65			
17–03–22		95		
09–05–22	111			

Country:	
River:	
Gauging Station:	

Date	Maximum discharge (m³/s) resulting from:		Maximum volume (10⁶m³) corresponding to max. discharge resulting from:	
	Rainfall	Snowmelt	Rainfall	Snowmelt
1	2	3	4	5

TABLE III — CHARACTERISTICS OF SNOWMELT FLOODS

No.	River	Gauging station	Q_{max} (m³/s)	Date	h (mm)	T_T (hours)	t_i (hours)	P_W (%)	$P_{Q_{max}}$ (%)	Type of probability curve for P_W	for $P_{Q_{max}}$
1	2	3	4	5	6	7	8	9	10	11	12
1	Velenån	Velen	2.7	20–04–51		1900	410		2.8		Empirical
			2.3	04–04–68		1130	280		5.6		"
			2.3	30–04–70		2450	910		8.4		"
			2.2	09–03–59		840	340		11.1		"
			2.1	15–03–67		1750	480		13.9		"
2	Vesanån	Hålabäck	1.04	13–04–36		340	100		2.2		Empirical
			0.96	23–03–46		310	120		4.3		"
			0.70	10–04–42		410	100		6.4		"
			0.68	17–01–31		290	190		8.5		"
			0.53	26–02–66		310	140		10.6		"
3	Tännån	Lillglän	39	08–05–34		650	170		2.5		Empirical
			33	10–06–44		980	580		4.9		"
			24	21–06–52		1780	1270		7.3		"
			23	27–05–67		770	380		9.8		"
			22	31–05–45		1010	580		12.2		"
4	Esmaån	Gårdsilt	17.4	24–04–70		820	380		1.9		Lognormal
			14.4	24–01–59		380	100		4.6		"
			14.3	14–04–51		700	310		4.8		"
			11.3	22–02–35		600	220		13.6		"
			11.0	07–01–32		260	120		14.1		"
5	Dummeån	Risbro	10.9	06–04–37		1370	550		1.7		Lognormal
			8.9	14–04–41		790	190		4.6		"
			8.4	02–04–16		340	120		6.8		"

No.	Method of curve fitting for W	for Q_{max}	Water equivalent (mm)	Layer thickness (cm)	Rainfall during snowmelt (mm)	Monthly precipitation before soil freezing (mm)	Mean monthly temperature before snowmelt (°C)
1	13	14	15	16	17	18	19
1				120	110	50	–4
				70	50	130	–4
				80	150	80	–2
				70	50	40	–2
				50	100	60	–1
2				20	50	70	+2
				25	20	70	0
				30	20	25	–5
				10	50	80	+1
				25	20	110	–3
3				100	30	30	–1
				100	100	70	–3
				150	240	70	+2
				140	70	100	–2
				110	90	40	0
4				70	110	170	–1
				20	60	30	0
				60	100	140	–1
				10	100	50	–1
				20	70	80	+1
5				25	50	60	–1
				30	10	30	–2
				40	20	10	–3

TABLE III — CHARACTERISTICS OF SNOWMELT FLOODS (cont'd)

No.	River	Gauging station	Q_{max} (m³/s)	Date	h (mm)	T_T (hours)	t_i (hours)	P_W (%)	$P_{Q_{max}}$ (%)	Type of probability curve for P_W	for $P_{Q_{max}}$
1	2	3	4	5	6	7	8	9	10	11	12
6	Råneälv	Niemisel	763	11−05−34		960	170		1.8		Lognormal
			700	16−05−10		1200	550		3.8		,,
			685	10−05−06		430	220		4.3		,,
			674	16−05−03		1180	620		4.5		,,
			583	11−06−35		1580	980		9.5		,,
7	Bäljaneå	Klippan 2	41	08−03−93*		1180	240		2.0		Empirical
			37	20−04−70		1460	910		3.9		,,
			33	16−02−58		600	410		5.9		,,
			31	21−04−95*		890	260		7.8		,,
			27	09−01−14		890	480		9.8		,,
8	Vattholmaån	Vattholma	25	02−05−22		840	410		1.6		Lognormal
			24	11−05−24		1300	580		1.8		,,
			22	04−05−66		1730	790		3.0		,,
			18	10−03−37		1920	310		6.5		,,
			16.3	02−05−70		2180	740		9.0		,,
9	Åreälven	Ö. Norn	715	11−05−54		960	480		0.6		Gumbel
			560	04−06−38		770	340		4.0		,,
			543	02−06−67		910	500		4.5		,,
			536	11−06−44		2020	720		4.9		,,
			490	22−05−49		1510	770		8.5		,,

No.	Method of curve fitting for W	for Q_{max}	Water equivalent (mm)	Layer thickness (cm)	Rainfall during snowmelt (mm)	Monthly precipitation before soil freezing (mm)	Mean monthly temperature before snowmelt (°C)
1	13	14	15	16	17	18	19
6				90	30	25	−2
				100	60	60	−1
					20	40	+1
					30	90	−1
				110	70	75	−1
7					40	10	−4
				50	150	140	−3
				30	100	30	−2
					60	40	−6
				10	60	70	−1
8				50	60	40	−2
				60	110	70	−1
				75	50	60	−1
				20	110	35	−3
				50	90	20	−1
9				110	50	40	−1
				100	120	150	+1
				90	70	180	−2
				110	100	70	−3
				120	180	120	0

TABLE III — CHARACTERISTICS OF SNOWMELT FLOODS (cont'd)

No.	River	Gauging station	Q_{max} (m³/s)	Date	h (mm)	T_T (hours)	t_i (hours)	P_W (%)	$P_{Q_{max}}$ (%)	Type of probability curve for P_W	for $P_{Q_{max}}$
1	2	3	4	5	6	7	8	9	10	11	12
10	Gimån	Gimdalsby	127	06—05—45		1560	860		1.7		Empirical
			125	25—05—66		1460	550		3.4		"
			124	21—05—16		1560	580		5.1		"
			109	09—05—13		1940	670		6.8		"
			109	24—05—26		1610	710		8.5		"
11	Motala ström	Motala	79	31—03—68*		840	530		1.9		Lognormal
			77	27—01—63*		190	100		2.6		"
			74	03—01—25		2280	170		3.8		"
			71	31—01—13		3360	1320		4.6		"
			66	12—02—73*		1610	960		7.6		"
12	Vindelälven	Sorsele	1370	07—06—38		2540	860		1.6		Lognormal
			1280	05—06—71		1800	580		3.5		"
			1230	23—06—22		1900	1180		4.7		"
			1170	28—06—30		2330	1420		6.5		"
			1140	05—06—67		1940	580		8.0		"
13	Torneälv	Jukkasjärvi	653	08—07—18		2590	1440		3.5		Lognormal
			648	26—06—52		2640	1340		4.2		"
			633	24—06—43		2640	1100		4.5		"
			605	25—07—15		2640	1610		6.0		"
			590	23—06—22		1970	1270		8.0		"

No.	Method of curve fitting for W	for Q_{max}	Snow cover Water equivalent (mm)	Layer thickness (cm)	Rainfall during snowmelt (mm)	Monthly precipitation before soil freezing (mm)	Mean monthly temperature before snowmelt (°C)
1	13	14	15	16	17	18	19
10				70	140	25	−1
				110	60	25	−1
				100	120	10	+2
				80	80	50	−2
				80	120	50	+1
11					50	30	−1
					50	30	+1
				20	80	25	+3
				20	150	100	+2
					70	40	+1
12				110	300	130	−1
				110	140	50	−3
				80	290	50	−3
				90	150	100	0
				120	170	100	−1
13				110	125	50	−3
				100	260	80	−2
				140	220	80	−4
				90	200	50	0
				70	190	60	−3

TABLE III — CHARACTERISTICS OF SNOWMELT FLOODS (cont'd)

No.	River	Gauging station	Q_{max} (m³/s)	Date	h (mm)	T_T (hours)	t_i (hours)	P_W (%)	$P_{Q_{max}}$ (%)	Type of probability curve for P_W	for $P_{Q_{max}}$
1	2	3	4	5	6	7	8	9	10	11	12
14	Ljusnan	Sveg	1150	12—05—16		1180	530		4.3		Pearson III
			1090	27—05—24		980	670		6.0		"
			1080	02—05—59		1100	380		6.5		"
			1070	17—05—31		790	430		7.2		"
			1070	15—05—36		1300	670		7.2		"
15	Klarälven	Edsforsen	1320	13—05—16		2180	1010		0.6		Lognormal and Gumbel
			1020	21—05—31		1940	720		4.2		"
			876	05—06—24		1460	1010		9.0		"
			870	08—05—34		1560	530		9.3		"
			863	22—05—20		2590	1820		9.6		"
16	Götaölv	Sjötorp	829	02—06—10		6960	2520		0.8		Empirical
			813	26—07—27		6240	4970		1.5		"
			794	27—07—67*		3900	2180		2.3		"
			782	09—06—68*		5100	2020		3.0		"
			780	19—06—31*		4680	1870		3.8		"
17	Muonioälv	Kallio	1720	10—06—68		1750	500		3.6		Pearson III
			1650	07—06—17		1560	500		4.7		"
			1600	22—05—20		1220	550		6.0		"
			1590	22—05—36		820	530		6.5		"
			1490	16—06—35		1460	790		9.5		"

No.	Method of curve fitting for W	for Q_{max}	Water equivalent (mm)	Layer thickness (cm)	Rainfall during snowmelt (mm)	Monthly precipitation before soil freezing (mm)	Mean monthly temperature before snowmelt (°C)
1	13	14	15	16	17	18	19
14		Maximum likelihood		100	120	60	+2
		"		90	100	90	−1
		"		90	40	90	0
		"		80	40	50	−1
		"		100	60	90	0
15		"		100	190	50	−4
		"		100	100	70	+1
		"		90	180	110	−1
		"		60	100	100	+1
		"		100	210	20	−3
16		"		60	600	50	−1
		"		60	700	60	−4
		"			300	80	−5
		"			400	20	−2
		"					
17		"		70	70	30	−1
		"		60	80	50	−5
		"		40	50	100	−2
		"		90	10	50	−5
		"		60	110	50	−2

TABLE III — CHARACTERISTICS OF SNOWMELT FLOODS (cont'd)

No.	River	Gauging station	Q_{max} (m^3/s)	Date	h (mm)	T_T (hours)	t_i (hours)	P_W (%)	$P_{Q_{max}}$ (%)	Type of probability curve for P_W	for $P_{Q_{max}}$
1	2	3	4	5	6	7	8	9	10	11	12
18	Dalälven	Norslund	2640	01—06—60*		2930	1200		1.5		Empirical
			2410	18—05—16		2260	1050		2.9		"
			2030	25—05—99*		2060	1370		4.4		"
			1630	09—05—90*		1990	1300		5.8		"
			1600	14—06—67*		1920	1370		7.3		"
19	Vindelälven	Renfors	1650	09—06—38		1730	1390		1.8		Gumbel
			1500	21—06—45		1730	1220		4.2		"
			1480	08—06—71		2110	910		4.4		"
			1400	21—06—44		790	500		5.5		"
			1370	25—06—22		2090	1340		7.0		"
20	Motala ström	Norsholm	224	04—01—13		2570	790		4.2		Lognormal
			210	05—05—77*		2470	820		4.4		"
			210	21—04—04		3050	600		4.4		"
			203	24—04—75*		1460	820		6.0		"
			188	07—05—17		3290	980		9.8		"

No.	Method of curve fitting for W	for Q_{max}	Snow cover Water equivalent (mm)	Layer thickness (cm)	Rainfall during snowmelt (mm)	Monthly precipitation before soil freezing (mm)	Mean monthly temperature before snowmelt (°C)
1	13	14	15	16	17	18	19
18					220		−8
				100	200	70	−5
					110	30	−8
					140	70	−2
					130	30	−6
19				100	170	120	−2
				110	180	70	+2
				100	160	70	−2
				70	90	60	+3
				70	250	40	−1
20				20	130	110	
					130	40	0
					170	20	−2
					50	30	−4
				40	170	90	−5

TABLE IV — CHARACTERISTICS OF RAINFALL FLOODS

						Characteristic element						Type of probability curve	
No.	River	Gauging station	Q_{max} (m^3/s)	Date	h (mm)	T_T (hours)	t_i (hours)	P_W (%)	$P_{Q_{max}}$ (%)			for P_W	for $P_{Q_{max}}$
1	2	3	4	5	6	7	8	9	10			11	12
1	Velenån	Velen	2.97	05–05–66		1780	260		1.8				Lognormal
			2.20	21–09–46		1750	530		4.8				"
			1.88	15–09–62		2690	1010		8.5				"
			1.80	03–12–44		2570	770		9.5				"
			1.70	30–11–70		2710	1440		11.5				"
2	Vesanån	Hålabäck	0.64	31–07–59		510	50		2.5				Pearson III
			0.48	07–05–55		220	20		5.0				"
			0.44	24–04–66		360	140		7.0				"
			0.42	10–12–65		220	50		8.2				"
			0.35	04–04–51		380	120		12.5				"
3	Tännån	Lillglän	14.8	03–09–38		360	170		3.5				"
			14.4	28–07–50		310	100		3.9				"
			12.7	16–07–54		190	70		6.5				"
			11.5	13–09–56		380	50		9.3				"
			11.2	18–08–60		410	100		9.6				"
4	Esmaån	Gårdsilt	14.9	29–12–55		430	120		2.2				Empirical
			10.5	18–08–45		670	170		4.4				"
			9.3	23–09–54		840	380		6.5				"
			8.9	02–11–70		550	120		8.7				"
			8.6	16–07–33		410	100		10.9				"

No.	Method of curve fitting		Rainfall forming flood (mm)	Snowmelt during floods (mm)	Maximum daily rainfall (mm)	Date	Hourly maximum rainfall (mm)	Date	Antecedent precipitation for	
	for W	for Q_{max}							10 days (mm)	30 days (mm)
1	13	14	15	16	17	18	19	20	21	22
1										
2		Maximum likelihood								
		"								
		"								
		"								
3										
4										

TABLE IV — CHARACTERISTICS OF RAINFALL FLOODS (cont'd)

No.	River	Gauging station	Q_{max} (m^3/s)	Date	h (mm)	T_T (hours)	t_i (hours)	P_W (%)	$P_{Q_{max}}$ (%)	Type of probability curve for P_W	for $P_{Q_{max}}$
1	2	3	4	5	6	7	8	9	10	11	12
5	Dummeån	Risbro	15.0	29—06—27		410	50		3.7		Empirical
			6.9	27—07—36		220	50		7.5		"
			6.8	12—06—26		340	50		11.1		"
			5.3	12—11—28		460	260		14.8		"
			4.9	26—07—20		240	50		18.5		"
6	Råneälv	Niemisel	433	10—10—46		940	500		0.9		Lognormal
			293	07—06—65		580	290		4.3		"
			223	24—09—29		430	100		9.7		"
			213	11—11—67		670	220		9.8		"
			205	27—09—40		480	190		10.0		"
7	Bäljaneå	Klippan 2	43	23—11—63		1100	410		2.0		"
			33	10—08—95*		360	50		7.5		"
			31	30—11—17		260	170		9.1		"
			29	04—10—92*		170	50		11.9		"
			24	05—09—91*		340	100		20.0		"
8	Vattholmaån	Vattholma	11.0	18—11—34		720	240		1.8		Empirical
			10.9	11—10—57		2450	1030		3.5		"
			9.9	30—12—60		1270	430		5.3		"
			9.8	19—12—44		1250	430		7.0		"
			7.3	10—10—27		980	770		8.8		"

No.	Method of curve fitting for W	for Q_{max}	Rainfall forming flood (mm)	Snowmelt during floods (mm)	Maximum daily rainfall (mm)	Date	Hourly maximum rainfall (mm)	Date	Antecedent precipitation for 10 days (mm)	30 days (mm)
1	13	14	15	16	17	18	19	20	21	22

TABLE IV — CHARACTERISTICS OF RAINFALL FLOODS (cont'd)

No.	River	Gauging station	Q_{max} (m³/s)	Date	h (mm)	T_T (hours)	t_i (hours)	P_W (%)	$P_{Q_{max}}$ (%)	Type of probability curve for P_W	for $P_{Q_{max}}$
1	2	3	4	5	6	7	8	9	10	11	12
9	Åreälven	Ö. Norn	276	01—08—50		430	170		2.8		Pearson III
			257	24—06—52		1030	290		4.7		"
			255	23—10—47		980	100		4.9		"
			248	31—07—15		670	140		6.0		"
			245	02—10—32		910	100		7.0		"
10	Gimån	Gimdalsby	118	07—09—21		1010	550		0.8		Lognormal
			97	28—08—60		1250	340		2.5		"
			57	08—07—24		600	60		8.5		"
			54	01—09—41		1580	480		9.3		"
			52	26—07—38		1420	600		9.8		"
11	Motala ström	Motala	100	05—06—67*		70	20		0.8		"
			91	07—08—24		960	360		2.8		"
			91	25—07—27		2090	650		2.8		"
			85	05—05—68*		1900	500		4.7		"
			79	24—08—77*		600	290		8.3		"
12	Vindelälven	Sorsele	639	07—08—20		500	340		1.8		Gumbel
			517	16—08—54		790	480		4.7		"
			502	20—08—21		1270	310		5.5		"
			502	01—08—66		700	140		5.5		"
			469	09—08—61		480	140		8.0		"

No.	Method of curve fitting for W	for Q_{max}	Rainfall forming flood (mm)	Snowmelt during floods (mm)	Maximum daily rainfall (mm)	Date	Hourly maximum rainfall (mm)	Date	Antecedent precipitation for 10 days (mm)	30 days (mm)
1	13	14	15	16	17	18	19	20	21	22
9										
10										
11										
12		Maximum likelihood								
		"								
		"								
		"								

TABLE IV — CHARACTERISTICS OF RAINFALL FLOODS (cont'd)

No.	River	Gauging station	Q_{max} (m^3/s)	Date	h (mm)	T_T (hours)	t_i (hours)	P_W (%)	$P_{Q_{max}}$ (%)	Type of probability curve for P_W	for $P_{Q_{max}}$
1	2	3	4	5	6	7	8	9	10	11	12
13	Torneälv	Jukkasjärvi	380	24—08—57		550	120		1.4		Lognormal
			373	05—08—58		840	290		1.6		''
			351	10—08—67		670	140		1.9		''
			296	01—09—21		1010	100		6.0		''
			270	22—09—40		550	190		9.0		''
14	Ljusnan	Sveg	852	19—08—60		600	290		2.5		Pearson III
			754	30—07—50		500	190		4.3		''
			746	05—09—38		550	240		4.7		''
			734	17—07—16		550	260		5.9		''
			695	17—09—57		1660	550		6.8		''
15	Klarälven	Edsforsen	784	27—07—24		500	70		2.3		Gumbel
			778	24—08—20		410	120		2.9		''
			648	30—07—50		430	140		7.0		''
			595	11—10—38		670	170		9.5		''
			557	03—10—44		430	220		14.0		''
16	Götaälv	Sjötorp	836	05—11—27		2280	960		1.8		Pearson III
			817	22—11—60*		5400	2330		3.5		''
			817	06—12—73*		5350	2520		3.5		''
			784	22—11—24		2930	1970		4.6		''
			774	17—01—25		3180	360		5.0		''

No.	Method of curve fitting for W	for Q_{max}	Rainfall forming flood (mm)	Snowmelt during floods (mm)	Maximum daily rainfall (mm)	Date	Hourly maximum rainfall (mm)	Date	Antecedent precipitation for 10 days (mm)	30 days (mm)
1	13	14	15	16	17	18	19	20	21	22
13										
14		Maximum likelihood								
		''								
		''								
		''								
15		''								
		''								
		''								
		''								
		''								
16										

296

Sweden / Suède / Suecia / Швеция

TABLE IV — CHARACTERISTICS OF RAINFALL FLOODS (cont'd)

No.	River	Gauging station	Q_{max} (m^3/s)	Date	h (mm)	T_T (hours)	t_i (hours)	P_W (%)	$P_{Q_{max}}$ (%)	Type of probability curve for P_W	for $P_{Q_{max}}$
1	2	3	4	5	6	7	8	9	10	11	12
17	Muonioälv	Kallio	732	12—09—19		1490	550		3.5	Lognormal	
			704	16—09—32		840	290		4.2	"	
			664	03—09—21		1320	820		4.6	"	
			645	11—08—67		650	120		4.9	"	
			614	24—09—40		460	170		6.5	"	
18	Dalälven	Norslund	1160	06—06—06		1320	190		1.5	Empirical	
			1050	21—09—66*		1660	500		4.4	"	
			1050	06—09—02		1150	290		4.4	"	
			1020	18—10—72*		1010	670		5.8	"	
			994	23—08—95*		1510	980		7.3	"	
19	Vindelälven	Renfors	775	03—08—57		1320	410		3.0	Lognormal	
			736	10—08—20		910	380		3.8	"	
			728	14—08—54		1150	720		4.1	"	
			593	24—08—41		2040	380		8.2	"	
			563	29—08—60		1780	240		8.8	"	
20	Motala ström	Norsholm	215	31—12—12		2570	790		1.2	"	
			190	16—08—79*		2350	670		3.5	"	
			164	05—06—75*		340	170		8.0	"	
			164	29—12—91*		1730	840		8.0	"	
			153	12—07—16		1100	170		11.0	"	

No.	Method of curve fitting for W	for Q_{max}	Rainfall forming flood (mm)	Snowmelt during floods (mm)	Maximum daily rainfall (mm)	Date	Hourly maximum rainfall (mm)	Date	Antecedent precipitation for 10 days (mm)	30 days (mm)
1	13	14	15	16	17	18	19	20	21	22

297

Thailand / Thaïlande / Tailandia / Таиланд

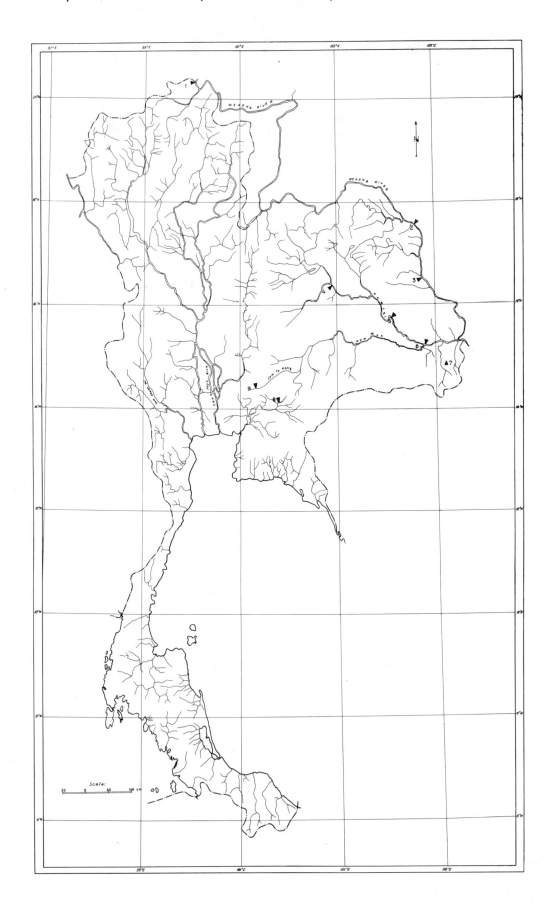

TABLE I — CHARACTERISTICS OF BASIN

No.	River / River system	Name	Period of records	Co-ordinates Lat.	Long.	L_{rs}	L_{ca}	Mean slope of river I_r (%)	Area A (km²)	Mean H_m	Max. H_{max}	Min. H_{min}
						to remotest point of river system	to projection of centre of basin on main course				Altitude (m)	
1	2	3	4	5	6	7	8	9	10	11	12	13
1	Mekong River	Chiang Saen	1960–74	N 20:16.4	E 100:06.0	2080	880		189000			
2	Mekong River	Nakhon Phanom	1960–74	17:23.9	104:48.2	3120	1330		373000			
3	Mekong River	Mukdahan	1959–74	16:32.3	104:42.2	3200	1330		391000			
4	Nam Chi	Ban Kok	1966–74	16:21.0	102:57.8	285	157	0.4	28500		1320	150
5	Nam Chi	Yasothon	1960–74	15:46.9	104:08.5	448	224	0.3	43100		1320	125
6	Nam Mum	Ubon	1950–74	15:13.3	104:51.7	653	352	0.2	104000		1320	125
7	Lam Dom Yai	Det Udom	1961–74	15:53.9	105:04.8	126	71	0.5	3340	216	753	120
8	Sai Yai	Ban Saphan Hin	1963–74	14:08.0	101:44.0	109	46.8	1.2	636	608	1330	20
9	Lam Takong	Khao Yai	1964–74	14:26.4	101:22.2	18.7	7.8	0.2	60.7	872	1140	740

No.	Mean B_m	Max. B_{max}	Mean slope I_b(%)	Soils	Cover	Weighted lake area P_L (%)	Swamps R_s (%)	Mean annual precipitation P (mm)	Annual runoff Q (mm)	Mean annual temperature T (°C)	Regulating capacity of reservoirs α
	Width (km)										
1	14	15	16	17	18	19	20	21	22	23	24
1	91	336			C, F			1960	505	23.2	
2	120	608			C, F				648		
3	122	624			C, F			1510	662		
4	100	256			C, F			1200	102		
5	96	256			C, F				186		
6	159	377			C, F			1590	183		
7	26.5	80.4	4.2		C, F			1610	390		
8	5.8	21.0	16.1		C, F			2060	906		
9	3.2	8.0	22.6		F			2190	718	21.9	

TABLE II — ANNUAL MAXIMUM DISCHARGES AND VOLUMES

Country: Thailand (1)
River: Mekong
Gauging Station: Nong Khai (Vientiame)

Date	Maximum discharge (m³/s) resulting from:		Maximum volume (10⁶m³) corresponding to max. discharge resulting from:	
	Rainfall	Snowmelt	Rainfall	Snowmelt
1	2	3	4	5
04−09−66	26000		2250	

Country: Thailand (6)
River: Nam Mun
Gauging Station: Ubon

Date	Maximum discharge (m³/s) resulting from:		Maximum volume (10⁶m³) corresponding to max. discharge resulting from:	
	Rainfall	Snowmelt	Rainfall	Snowmelt
1	2	3	4	5
18−10−50	4790		414	

Country:
River:
Gauging Station:

Date	Maximum discharge (m³/s) resulting from:		Maximum volume (10⁶m³) corresponding to max. discharge resulting from:	
	Rainfall	Snowmelt	Rainfall	Snowmelt
1	2	3	4	5

TABLE IV — CHARACTERISTICS OF RAINFALL FLOODS

No.	River	Gauging station	Q_{max} (m^3/s)	Date	h (mm)	T_T (hours)	t_i (hours)	P_W (%)	$P_{Q_{max}}$ (%)	Type of probability curve for P_W	for $P_{Q_{max}}$
1	2	3	4	5	6	7	8	9	10	11	12
5	Nam Chi	Yasothorn	1930	10—10—62	95	744	216	5	5	Frequency anal.	Frequency anal
6	Nam Mun	Ubon	4790	18—10—50	107	792	384	3	3	"	"
1	Mekong	Chiang Saen	23600	03—09—66	170	576	312	6	6	"	"
A	Mekong	Nong Khai	26000	04—09—66	154	696	312	3	3	"	"
3	Mekong	Mukdahan	36200	15—09—66	166	696	120	3	3	"	"
B	Lang Suan	Khao Chum Saeng	959	11—07—65	84	120	24	10	10	"	"
9	Lam Ta Kong	Khao Yai	144	12—10—65	60	72	24	10	10	"	"
C	Khlong Langu	Satun	202	06—01—67	250	120	48	10	10	"	"
8	Sai Yai	Ban Saphan Hin	316	17—08—67	43	96	24	10	10	"	"
D	Pa Sak	Kaeng Sida	362	03—09—65	48	120	24	10	10	"	"

No.	Method of curve fitting for W	for Q_{max}	Rainfall forming flood (mm)	Snowmelt during floods (mm)	Maximum daily rainfall (mm)	Date	Hourly maximum rainfall (mm)	Date	Antecedent precipitation for 10 days (mm)	30 days (mm)
1	13	14	15	16	17	18	19	20	21	22
5	Least squares		88.9		63.4	07—10—62			174	361
6	"	"								
1		"	129		43.6	28—08—66			231	674
A		"	46.2		40.7	31—08—66			47.7	152
3		"	73.5		46.0	12—09—66			190	395
B		"	21.3		84.2	11—07—65			21.3	164
9		"	70.3		44.8	12—10—65			106	391
C		"	101		165	05—01—67			219	380
8		"	64.8		70.0	16—08—67			138	507
D		"	70.9		89.0	03—09—65			103	220

Tunisia / Tunisie / Túnez / Тунис

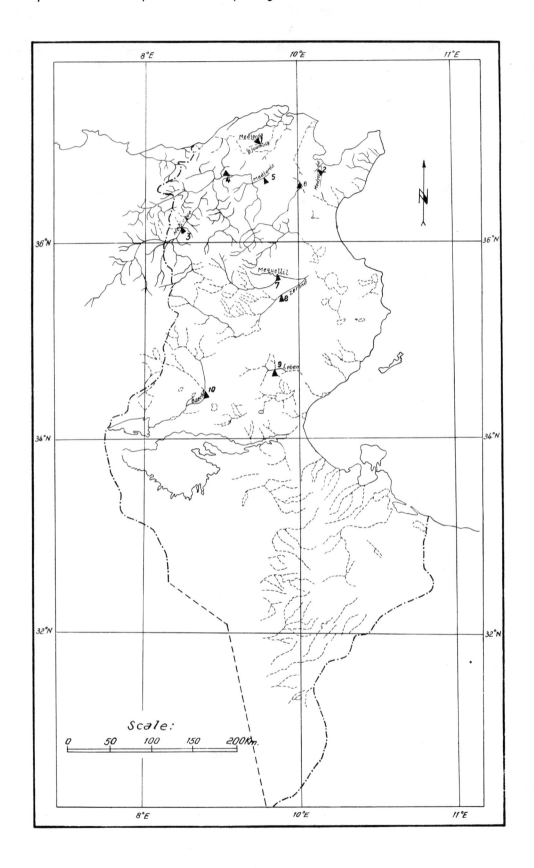

TABLE I – CHARACTERISTICS OF BASIN

No.	River / River system	Name	Period of records	Co-ordinates Lat.	Long.	Distance (km) from gauging site — to remotest point of river system L_{rs}	to projection of centre of basin on main course L_{ca}	Mean slope of river I_r (%)	Area A (km²)	Altitude (m) Mean H_m	Max. H_{max}	Min. H_{min}
1	2	3	4	5	6	7	8	9	10	11	12	13
1	Djoumine	Jebel Antra	1952–73			30		0.73	235	360	716	130
2	Medjerda	Ghardimaou	1948–73			91.8		0.80	1480	805	1320	192
3	Méllégue	PK13 Route le Kef Sakiet	1924–73			212		0.53	9000	810	1710	327
4	Medjerda	Bou Salem	1925–73			327		0.48	16200	710	1710	127
5	Medjerda	Medjez el Bab-Sloughia	1946–73			370		0.33	21000	640	1710	44
6	Miliane	Cheylus	1945–73						1420			
7	Merguellil	Haffouz B3	1966–74					1.1	651	550	1200	270
8	Zéroud	Sidi-Saad	1945–74						8950		1450	230
9	Leben	Maknassy PR				65		1.1	1060	360	898	200
10	Bayech	Gafsa PVF							6360			

No.	Width (km) Mean B_m	Max. B_{max}	Mean slope I_b (%)	Soils	Cover	Weighted lake area P_L (%)	Swamps R_s (%)	Mean annual precipitation P (mm)	Annual runoff Q (mm)	Mean annual temperature T (°C)	Regulating capacity of reservoirs α
1	14	15	16	17	18	19	20	21	22	23	24
1	8			Clay, slate	F, C, U			868	412		
2	15.7		0.97	Clay	F, C			680	112		
3	42.3		0.74	7	C, U			320	15		
4	50		0.61	Clay	F, C, U			440	36		
5	57		0.59	Clay	F, C, U			420	40		
6								450	32		
7					F, C			400	27		
8			7		F, C, U			400	8		
9	17		0.33	7	F, C, U			206	2.3		
10				7	F, C, U			250	4.0		

TABLE IV — CHARACTERISTICS OF RAINFALL FLOODS

No.	River	Gauging station	Q_{max} (m³/s)	Date	h (mm)	T_T (hours)	t_i (hours)	P_W (%)	$P_{Q_{max}}$ (%)	Type of probability curve for P_W	for $P_{Q_{max}}$
1	2	3	4	5	6	7	8	9	10	11	12
1	Djoumine	Jebel Antra	235	20—10—62	70	137	15				
2	Medjerda	Ghardimaou	2370	28—03—73	139	56	18	< 1	< 0.1		Lognormal
3	Méllégue	PK 13 Route le Kef Sakiet	4480	29—09—69	37.2	56	6	< 0.1	< 0.5		,,
4	Medjerda	Bou Salem	3180	29—03—73	43.8	136	52	< 0.1	< 0.1		,,
5	Medjerda	Medjez el Bab-Sloughia	3500	28—03—73	45	·172	38	< 0.3	< 1		,,
6	Miliane	Cheylus	1800	22—10—69	53	96	8				
7	Merguellil	Haffouz B3	2890	24—09—69	120	76	1				
8	Zéroud	Sidi-Saad	17100	27—09—69	134	72	12		1.5		Empirical
9	Leben	Maknassy PR	3500	07—10—69	89						
10	Bayech	Gafsa PVF	2500	13—12—73		60	22				

No.	Method of curve fitting for W	for Q_{max}	Rainfall forming flood (mm)	Snowmelt during floods (mm)	Maximum daily rainfall (mm)	Date	Hourly maximum rainfall (mm)	Date	Antecedent precipitation for 10 days (mm)	30 days (mm)
1	13	14	15	16	17	18	19	20	21	22
1										
2		Graphic	175							
3		,,								
4		,, ,,	123							
5		,, ,,	128							
6										
7			137							
8		Graphic			250					
9					237	06—10—69	70			
10					150					

U.S.S.R. / URSS / CCCP

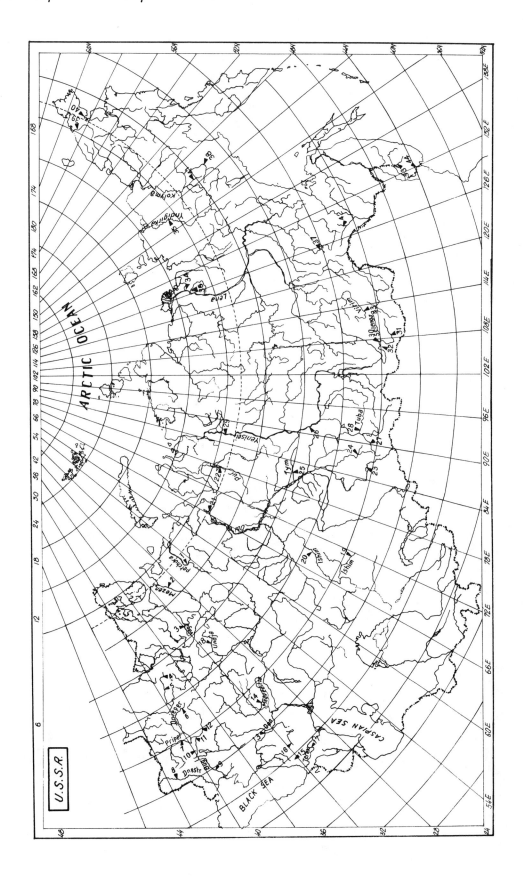

TABLE I — CHARACTERISTICS OF BASIN

				GAUGING STATION					BASIN			
						Distance (km) from gauging site		Mean slope of river I_r (%)	Area A (km²)	Altitude (m)		
No.	River River system	Name	Period of records	Co-ordinates Lat.	Long.	to remotest point of river system L_{rs}	to projection of centre of basin on main course L_{ca}			Mean H_m	Max. H_{max}	Min. H_{min}
1	2	3	4	5	6	7	8	9	10	11	12	13
				N	E							
1	Pechora	Ust-Tsilima	1932–72	65:28	52:15		486		248000		1890	15
2	Mezen	Malonisogorskaya	1920–72	64:57	45:40	780	306	0.48	56400	147	485	25
3	Vaga	Filaevskya	1938–72	61:14	42:15	226	73	0.63	13200	164	245	85
4	Verebushka	Oksotchi	1945–72	58:42	32:49	23	10.6	3.57	96.3	165	195	105
5	Lovat	Kholm	1911–72	57:08	31:17	337	63	0.38	14700	140	215	55
6	Dnieper	Smolensk	1881–72	54:48	32:07	455	180	0.19	14100	225	330	120
7	Pripiat	Mozir	1881–72	51:58	29:14	888	226	0.10	101000	188	375	115
8	Dniester	Zaleschiki	1877–70	48:33	25:45	416		1.5	24600		1840	143
9	Southern Bug	Aleksandrovka	1923–70	47:43	31:11	674		0.5	46200		392	2
10	Dnieper	Kiev	1876–70	50:30	30:27	1320		0.1	328000		220	90
11	Desna	Chernigov	1884–70	51:27	31:21	920		0.14	81400		250	105
12	Golovesnia	Pokoshichi	1928–70	51:53	32:44	7.9		3.5	29.5		200	142

		BASIN										
	Width (km)		Mean slope I_b (%)	Soils	Cover	Weighted lake area P_L (%)	Swamps R_s (%)	Mean annual precipitation P (mm)	Annual runoff Q (mm)	Mean annual temperature T (°C)	Regulating capacity of reservoirs α
No.	Mean B_m	Max. B_{max}									
1	14	15	16	17	18	19	20	21	22	23	24
1		786						734	447		
2	72	355		2	F(89)		6	691	366	−2.4	
3	58	190		2	F(91)		3	724	286	0	
4	4.2	12.1	35.8	2	F(64)	0	3	700	312	3.3	
5	44	142		2	F(85)	0	4	650	228	4.2	
6	31	118	8.22	2	F(36), C(40)	0	5	630	216	4.0	
7	114	365	6.09			0	14	550	117	7.5	
8	59			3				564	289	7.3	
9	68			5	F(93)	1	2	424	58	9.4	
10	250			2,3				610	132	7.2	
11	250			2,3				539	126	6.5	
12	3.7			2	F(15)	0	1	579	178	5.7	

TABLE I – CHARACTERISTICS OF BASIN   (cont'd)

				GAUGING STATION					BASIN			
						Distance (km) from gauging site				Altitude (m)		
No.	River / River system	Name	Period of records	Co-ordinates Lat.	Long.	to remotest point of river system L_{rs}	to projection of centre of basin on main course L_{ca}	Mean slope of river I_r (%)	Area A (km^2)	Mean H_m	Max. H_{max}	Min. H_{min}
1	2	3	4	5	6	7	8	9	10	11	12	13
13	Don	Razdorskaya	1881–51	N 47:30	E 40:40				378000			5.0
14	Medveditsa	Archedinskaya	1928–72	49:49	43:10	679		0.35	33700	180	332	20
15	Teberda	Teberda	1927–72	43:16	41:38	37	2.7	32	504	2580	4050	1360
16	Kalaus	Svetlograd	1930–72	45:14	42:47	181		1.8	4540	340	687	135
17	Terek	Ordzhonikidze	1912–72	43:04	44:36	93	4.8	26	1490	2540	5050	600
18	Unzha	Makariev	1896–70	57:54	43:40	481	238	0.31	18500	150	293	123
19	Ishim	Tselinograd	1933–72	51:07	71:28	209		1.04	7400	460	843	342
20	Ishim	Petropavlovsk	1932–71	54:58	69:07	1570		0.30	106000	314	834	89.0
21	Ob	Salekhard	1930–72	66:34	66:32				2430000		2180	20
22	Pur	Samburg	1936–72	67:05	78:09	938	320		95100		171	20
23	Biya	Biysk	1894–70	52:31	85:16		190		36900	1370	2620	160
24	Usa	Mezhdourechensk	1936–70	53:39	88:06	171	25	7.00	3320	790	1870	240
25	Tym	Napas	1936–70	59:54	81:55	678	125	0.15	24500	120		

			BASIN								
	Width (km)		Mean slope I_b (%)	Soils	Cover	Weighted lake area P_L (%)	Swamps R_s (%)	Mean annual precipitation P (mm)	Annual runoff Q (mm)	Mean annual temperature T (°C)	Regulating capacity of reservoirs α
No.	Mean B_m	Max. B_{max}									
1	14	15	16	17	18	19	20	21	22	23	24
13	210	870						404	71	7.0	
14	49.6	200		5	F(5), C(75), U			400	61	5.9	
15	13.6	32.3	450	3,4	F(10), C, U(1.1)	0.22		1780	1700	5.5	
16	25.1	116		5	F(5), C(60), U(0.20)	0.11		474	20	9.7	
17	16.0	61.2		3,4	F(10), C, U(1.3)	0.01		852	736	7.6	
18	39	180		2,6	F(80), C(4), U(1)	1	2	525	286	2.0	
19	35.4	88.5	22.7	6	F(1.2), U(0.34)	1.11	0.46	297	27	1.4	0.5
20	67.4			6,5	F(27)	0.9	0.4	312	17	0.5	0.01
21								416	157	-2.8	
22	101	362					50	451	292	-6.8	
23		160		5,3				640	417	0.5	
24	19	60	210	3,5	F(75)	1	0		1390	-0.1	
25				2	F(71)	3	24	531	232	-2.8	

TABLE I – CHARACTERISTICS OF BASIN (cont'd)

				GAUGING STATION					BASIN			
						Distance (km) from gauging site						
						to remotest point of river system L_{rs}	to projection of centre of basin on main course L_{ca}	Mean slope of river I_r (%)	Area A (km²)	Altitude (m)		
No.	River River system	Name	Period of records	Co-ordinates Lat.	Long.					Mean H_m	Max. H_{max}	Min. H_{min}
1	2	3	4	5	6	7	8	9	10	11	12	13
26	Yenisei	Yeniseisk	1902–66	N 58:28	E 92:03	3050	1650		1400000		3510	66
27	Abakan	Abaza	1932–72	52:35	90:10	325	145	5.8	14400	1460	2960	446
28	Tuba	Bugurtak	1911–72	53:46	92:46	390	175	4.7	31800	976	2920	285
29	Graviyka	Igarka	1938–72	67:31	86:37	37.0	20.0	1.6	323	94	136	36
30	Selenga	Mostovoy	1934–72	52:01	107:24	1330			440000			491
31	Khilok	Maleta	1936–72	50:46	108:15	614	215		25700	1040	1740	665
32	Bolshaya	Possolskaya	1929–72	51:46	106:27	54	22.5	12.6	565	1020	1560	478
33	Vitim	Romanovka	1944–72	53:07	112:47	482	199	2.2	18200	1310	2280	880
34	Lena	Kusur	1935–72	70:42	127:39	4690			2430000			
35	Indigirka	Vorontsovo	1937–72	69:35	147:21		475		305000		2960	25
36	Zbitiem	Zbetem	1937–72	70:22	127:57	68	4.0	8.3	1000	410	994	10
37	Timpton	Nagorni	1926–72	55:59	124:45	49	23	10.8	613	1130	1600	1180
38	Kolyma	Ust-Srednikan	1933–72	62:27	152:43	1890	436		99400	970	2590	228

			BASIN									
	Width (km)		Mean slope I_b(%)				Weighted lake area P_L (%)	Swamps R_s (%)	Mean annual precipitation P (mm)	Annual runoff Q (mm)	Mean annual temperature T (°C)	Regulating capacity of reservoirs α
No.	Mean B_m	Max. B_{max}		Soils	Cover							
1	14	15	16	17	18		19	20	21	22	23	24
26	460	1400								174		
27	44	117		2,3	F(75)		1	1	1270	658	-0.4	
28	82	192		2,3	F(58)		1	1	1110	750	-2.3	
29	8.7	19.5	25.0	1,2	F(7)		6	2	705	504	-8.7	
30										67		
31	42	107		2	F(76), C(5)				410	90	-3.6	
32	10.5	20.2	224	2	F(99)		0	1	840	697	-2.2	
33	38	252		2	F(75)		1	5	440	85	-6.0	
34										215		
35		75		1			1		420	162	-14.8	
36	13	7.0	211				1	0	380	420	-13.2	
37	13	14	149	2			1	5	600	489	-8.3	
38	53	400		2	F(100)		1		392	232	-12.2	

TABLE I — CHARACTERISTICS OF BASIN (cont'd)

	GAUGING STATION								BASIN			
	River River system	Name	Period of records	Co-ordinates		Distance (km) from gauging site		Mean slope of river I_r (%)	Area A (km²)	Altitude (m)		
				Lat.	Long.	to remotest point of river system L_{rs}	to projection of centre of basin on main course L_{ca}			Mean H_m	Max. H_{max}	Min. H_{min}
No.	2	3	4	5	6	7	8	9	10	11	12	13
1	2	3	4	5	6	7	8	9	10	11	12	13
39	Amguema	Mouth of the brook Shoumny	1944–72	N 67:40	E 178:30	397	169		26700	550	1840	50
40	Iziskatelski	1.6 km up-stream the mouth	1947–72	66:22	179:15	4.4	2.1	100	13.2	430	739	50
41	Khasyn	Kolyma Road, 79th km	1941–72	64:11	151:18	48	27	16.9	682	650	1440	258
42	Dep	Rychkovo	1942–72	53:25	127:55	259	134	2.2	8440	426	955	237
43	Ussuri	Kirovsky	1927–72	45:01	133:39	353	121	3.7	24400	435	1680	83.6
44	Souyfoun	Terekhovka	1935–72	43:47	131:58	343	147	2.5	15500	434	873	7.0

	BASIN										
	Width (km)		Mean slope I_b(%)	Soils	Cover	Weighted lake area P_L (%)	Swamps R_s (%)	Mean annual precipitation P (mm)	Annual runoff Q (mm)	Mean annual temperature T (°C)	Regulating capacity of reservoirs α
No.	Mean B_m	Max. B_{max}									
1	14	15	16	17	18	19	20	21	22	23	24
39	67	182		1		1			331	−10.9	
40	3.0	4.0	439	1		0	0		836	−6.6	
41	14	27.6	260	1		0			404	−6.6	
42	33	96.0	52.1	2	F(75)		23	650	289	−4.8	
43	69.1	150		2	F(95)	0	5	800	273	1.9	
44	45.2	142		2	F(50), C(18)	0	2	800	150	3.4	

TABLE II – ANNUAL MAXIMUM DISCHARGES AND VOLUMES

Country: U.S.S.R. (1)
River: Pechora
Gauging Station: Ust – Tsilima

Date	Maximum discharge (m³/s) resulting from:		Maximum volume ($10^6 m^3$) corresponding to max. discharge resulting from:	
	Rainfall	Snowmelt	Rainfall	Snowmelt
1	2	3	4	5
20–06–32		21300		1840
12–06–33		11700		1010
06–06–34		34600		2990
14–06–35		32700		2830
10–06–36		20100		1740
16–06–37		21000		1810
17–05–38		19400		1680
11–06–39		30200		2610
22–06–40		25200		2180
03–06–41		29800		2580
11–06–42		26000		2250
23–05–43		24800		2140
02–06–44		18500		1600
08–06–45		23900		2070
24–05–46		26400		2280
11–05–47		19400		1680
20–05–48		21200		1830
22–05–49		26400		2280
05–05–50		20000		1730
30–04–51		19300		1670
08–06–52		39500		3410
02–05–53		18700		1620
29–05–54		16400		1420
08–05–55		21700		1880
30–05–56		28500		2460
16–05–57		25700		2220
22–06–58		30600		2640
20–05–59		22100		1910
25–06–60		16200		1400
02–04–61		24900		2150

Country: U.S.S.R. (1) cont'd
River: Pechora
Gauging Station: Ust – Tsilima

Date	Maximum discharge (m³/s) resulting from:		Maximum volume ($10^6 m^3$) corresponding to max. discharge resulting from:	
	Rainfall	Snowmelt	Rainfall	Snowmelt
1	2	3	4	5
16–05–62		29300		2530
01–06–63		21900		1890
02–06–64		29300		2530
22–05–65		18500		1600
02–06–66		33400		2890
11–05–67		23900		2070
23–05–68		21700		1880
03–07–69		18500		1600
12–06–70		22300		1930
21–06–71		23000		1990
28–06–72		29500		2550

TABLE II – ANNUAL MAXIMUM DISCHARGES AND VOLUMES   (cont'd)

Country:	U.S.S.R. (2)
River:	Mezen
Gauging Station:	Malonisogorskaya

Date	Maximum discharge (m³/s) resulting from:		Maximum volume (10⁶m³) corresponding to max. discharge resulting from:	
	Rainfall	Snowmelt	Rainfall	Snowmelt
1	2	3	4	5
26–04–21		5230		452
11–05–22		5740		496
26–05–23		8820		762
06–05–24		6550		566
16–05–25		5180		448
20–05–26		5040		435
31–05–27		5430		469
15–05–28		7000		605
17–05–29		7610		658
23–05–30		5600		484
08–05–31		3790		327
13–05–32		7330		633
11–05–33		4970		429
14–05–34		6680		577
28–05–35		5450		471
05–05–36		4170		360
29–05–37		2850		246
12–05–38		2930		253
01–05–39		6200		536
23–05–40		3590		310
29–05–41		5670		490
27–05–42		5140		444
15–05–43		7160		619
18–05–44		6640		574
08–06–45		3880		335
14–05–46		7400		635
06–05–47		5020		434
15–05–48		4740		410
15–05–49		6930		599
29–04–50		4300		372

Country:	U.S.S.R. (2) cont'd
River:	Mezen
Gauging Station:	Malonisogorskaya

Date	Maximum discharge (m³/s) resulting from:		Maximum volume (10⁶m³) corresponding to max. discharge resulting from:	
	Rainfall	Snowmelt	Rainfall	Snowmelt
1	2	3	4	5
21–04–51		4310		372
02–06–52		9530		823
29–04–53		7150		618
11–05–54		4750		410
04–05–55		4920		425
21–05–56		4530		391
09–05–57		7210		623
24–05–58		5200		449
10–05–59		6010		519
28–04–60		3600		311
29–05–61		7930		685
08–05–62		5030		435
07–05–63		4040		349
21–05–64		8380		724
13–05–65		5420		468
26–05–66		9040		781
29–04–67		5860		506
14–05–68		5780		499
25–05–69		5090		440
12–05–70		5200		449
01–06–71		6190		535
04–06–72		7540		651

TABLE II — ANNUAL MAXIMUM DISCHARGES AND VOLUMES (cont'd)

Country:	U.S.S.R. (3)
River:	Vaga
Gauging Station:	Filaevskaya

Date	Maximum discharge (m³/s) resulting from:		Maximum volume ($10^6 m^3$) corresponding to max. discharge resulting from:	
	Rainfall	Snowmelt	Rainfall	Snowmelt
1	2	3	4	5
12–05–38		761		65.8
22–05–39		869		75.1
12–05–40		783		67.7
28–05–41		1060		91.6
25–04–42		1050		90.7
29–04–43		1030		89.0
08–05–44		990		85.0
23–06–45	523		45.2	
02–05–46		1340		116
27–04–47		1200		104
05–05–48		1550		134
03–05–49		1450		125
27–04–50		437		37.8
19–04–51		1120		96.8
01–04–52		812		70.2
23–04–53		1740		150
07–05–54		699		60.4
09–05–55		1560		135
12–05–56		1230		106
03–05–57		2090		181
08–05–58		1330		115
03–05–59		1280		111
26–04–60		764		66.0
16–05–61		2100		181
02–05–62		1090		94.2
28–04–63		637		55.0
07–05–64		1070		92.4
13–05–65		833		72.0
11–05–66		1550		134
28–04–67		545		47.1

Country:	U.S.S.R. (3) cont'd
River:	Vaga
Gauging Station:	Filaevskaya

Date	Maximum discharge (m³/s) resulting from:		Maximum volume ($10^6 m^3$) corresponding to max. discharge resulting from:	
	Rainfall	Snowmelt	Rainfall	Snowmelt
1	2	3	4	5
11–05–68		1650		143
23–05–69		1390		120
10–05–70		1180		102
15–05–71		1210		105
05–05–72		959		82.9

TABLE II – ANNUAL MAXIMUM DISCHARGES AND VOLUMES (cont'd)

Country:	U.S.S.R. (4)
River:	Verebushka
Gauging Station:	Oksotchi

Date	Maximum discharge (m³/s) resulting from:		Maximum volume (10⁶m³) corresponding to max. discharge resulting from:	
	Rainfall	Snowmelt	Rainfall	Snowmelt
1	2	3	4	5
27–04–46		18.3		18.6
25–04–47		20.3		15.6
08–04–48		14.5		13.9
19–04–49		9.01		13.7
15–04–50		13.2		14.8
04–04–51		15.5		15.3
15–04–52		11.2		10.3
19–04–53		14.1		15.8
03–04–54		9.75		11.3
09–05–55		25.8		24.0
30–05–56		20.2		23.6
26–04–57		12.9		15.8
19–04–58		13.3		19.0
19–04–59		15.9		17.0
15–04–60		18.9		13.6
18–04–61		11.7		13.9
15–04–62		16.9		21.4
22–04–63		13.8		9.8
23–04–64		15.7		10.1
23–04–65		13.7		16.3
27–04–66		20.5		28.5
12–04–67		9.55		12.8
07–04–68		20.8		21.1
21–04–69		13.7		14.0
28–04–70		9.21		13.5
11–04–71		8.26		12.6
15–04–72		13.2		9.6

Country:	U.S.S.R. (5)
River:	Lovat
Gauging Station:	Kholm

Date	Maximum discharge (m³/s) resulting from:		Maximum volume (10⁶m³) corresponding to max. discharge resulting from:	
	Rainfall	Snowmelt	Rainfall	Snowmelt
1	2	3	4	5
30–03–12		796		1980
26–03–13		1230		1920
16–04–14		747		1440
24–04–15		1310		2590
07–04–16		1470		2210
19–04–17		1480		2380
13–04–18		1400		1720
15–04–19		1400		1720
30–03–20		800		2300
27–03–21		637		1470
23–04–24		670		1030
05–04–25		770		1090
24–03–30		594		1090
23–04–31		2130		2270
14–04–32		1080		2370
23–03–33		606		1780
28–03–34		1110		1810
15–04–35		865		1720
19–04–36		666		2090
01–04–37		516		1180
24–03–38		1200		1980
25–04–39		471		956
20–04–40		784		1050
04–04–45		993		1720
08–04–46		1210		2360
05–04–47		893		1700
09–04–48		1560		1730
10–04–49		748		1460
08–04–50		885		1780
04–04–51		1210		1780

TABLE II – ANNUAL MAXIMUM DISCHARGES AND VOLUMES (cont'd)

Country:	U.S.S.R. (5) cont'd
River:	Lovat
Gauging Station:	Kholm

Date	Maximum discharge (m³/s) resulting from:		Maximum volume (10⁶m³) corresponding to max. discharge resulting from:	
	Rainfall	Snowmelt	Rainfall	Snowmelt
1	2	3	4	5
17–04–52		392		604
04–04–53		1040		2060
09–04–54		388		1180
02–05–55		1400		2430
27–05–56		1270		2300
08–04–57		952		1610
20–04–58		1190		2280
13–04–59		1420		2180
17–04–60		965		1180
14–03–61		614		1560
12–04–62		1720		2600
22–04–63		773		1270
20–04–64		741		1010
22–04–65		1180		1790
07–04–66		1120		2680
12–04–67		495		1430
02–04–68		1280		1880
16–04–69		563		1120
13–04–70		877		2090
06–04–71		599		1120
12–04–72		436		853

Country:	U.S.S.R. (6)
River:	Dnieper
Gauging Station:	Smolensk

Date	Maximum discharge (m³/s) resulting from:		Maximum volume (10⁶m³) corresponding to max. discharge resulting from:	
	Rainfall	Snowmelt	Rainfall	Snowmelt
1	2	3	4	5
02–05–81		1050		2220
06–04–82		435		1430
05–05–83		1120		2880
16–05–84		1030		2240
21–04–85		500		1570
19–04–86		737		1760
23–04–87		524		1250
13–04–88		912		1760
22–04–89		1130		2340
24–03–90		357		1030
27–04–91		638		1710
29–04–92		702		1870
13–05–93		507		1580
22–04–94		710		1380
03–05–95		1340		2510
03–05–96		1190		2420
14–04–97		1050		2090
20–04–98		486		1400
22–04–99		750		1510
27–04–00		1110		2120
25–04–01		1320		2480
12–04–02		615		2580
10–04–03		737		1720
21–04–04		554		1370
01–05–05		824		1680
23–04–06		1000		1910
27–04–07		1120		2220
01–05–08		1820		4110
06–05–09		1190		2850
22–04–10		574		1370

TABLE II – ANNUAL MAXIMUM DISCHARGES AND VOLUMES (cont'd)

Country:	U.S.S.R. (6) cont'd
River:	Dnieper
Gauging Station:	Smolensk

Date	Maximum discharge (m³/s) resulting from:		Maximum volume (10⁶m³) corresponding to max. discharge resulting from:	
	Rainfall	Snowmelt	Rainfall	Snowmelt
1	2	3	4	5
29–04–11		683		1160
12–04–12		538		1790
02–04–13		789		1420
24–04–14		386		1280
21–04–15		1230		2230
13–04–16		1170		2170
22–04–17		1440		2770
22–04–18		1120		1730
22–04–19		938		1600
14–04–20		567		1580
07–04–21		475		970
14–04–22		1190		2510
28–04–23		832		1160
18–04–24		1130		2180
13–04–25		412		880
28–04–26		1180		2150
27–04–27		530		1800
18–04–28		532		1710
09–05–29		1500		2710
29–03–30		340		920
01–05–31		1720		2720
22–04–32		872		2320
02–04–33		466		1750
05–04–34		860		2030
16–04–35		1050		2050
29–04–36		725		2380
05–04–37		772		1680
03–04–38		1040		1900
26–04–39		442		1440
13–04–45		589		1370

Country:	U.S.S.R. (6) cont'd
River:	Dnieper
Gauging Station:	Smolensk

Date	Maximum discharge (m³/s) resulting from:		Maximum volume (10⁶m³) corresponding to max. discharge resulting from:	
	Rainfall	Snowmelt	Rainfall	Snowmelt
1	2	3	4	5
20–04–46		636		1860
12–04–47		1100		2640
19–04–48		710		1440
20–04–49		691		1580
17–04–50		512		1190
09–04–51		1060		2050
29–04–52		606		1190
14–04–53		926		2330
25–04–54		503		1520
03–04–55		962		2260
28–04–56		1200		2520
16–04–57		624		1650
28–04–58		1650		3290
21–04–59		579		1510
26–04–60		525		1130
18–04–61		436		1510
19–04–62		1260		2250
29–04–63		682		1500
29–04–64		597		1270
30–04–65		379		763
14–04–66		780		2290
24–04–67		803		1710
16–04–68		738		1720
29–04–69		467		1080
26–04–70		973		2670
17–04–71		493		1380
19–04–72		411		1210

TABLE II – ANNUAL MAXIMUM DISCHARGES AND VOLUMES   (cont'd)

Country:	U.S.S.R. (7)
River:	Pripiat
Gauging Station:	Mozir

Date	Maximum discharge (m³/s) resulting from:		Maximum volume (10⁶m³) corresponding to max. discharge resulting from:	
	Rainfall	Snowmelt	Rainfall	Snowmelt
1	2	3	4	5
22–04–81		1560		
03–04–82		700		4140
01–05–83		2450		11400
16–04–84		1340		8400
18–04–85		632		3840
22–04–86		2990		8800
26–04–87		855		3840
15–04–88		5100		11900
25–04–89		4700		10100
07–04–90		1820		6870
10–04–91		1620		7370
16–04–92		1120		5550
01–04–93		1200		5250
09–04–94		836		5150
22–04–95		5670		12000
09–04–96		1630		7780
29–03–97		1350		8700
21–04–98		1080		4850
11–04–99		573		4040
18–04–00		2330		7780
18–04–01		429		2420
20–04–02		927		6270
17–03–03		1140		6770
27–04–04		484		3130
28–04–05		1180		6470
03–04–06		1470		7680
20–04–07		3030		9200
31–03–08		1920		9300
16–04–09		2560		8600
31–04–10		653		4350

Country:	U.S.S.R. (7) cont'd
River:	Pripiat
Gauging Station:	Mozir

Date	Maximum discharge (m³/s) resulting from:		Maximum volume (10⁶m³) corresponding to max. discharge resulting from:	
	Rainfall	Snowmelt	Rainfall	Snowmelt
1	2	3	4	5
01–04–11		1720		6460
20–04–12		1860		10300
04–05–13		916		7380
17–04–14		1250		11400
21–04–15		1370		5970
11–04–16		1370		6570
18–04–17		2600		7680
13–04–19		1550		11300
25–03–20		1750		
13–04–21		477		2520
25–03–22		2100		8700
31–03–23		2110		8700
13–04–24		3320		9200
30–03–25		423		2730
16–04–26		1930		7270
27–03–27		1760		9700
29–04–28		2060		8500
29–04–29		1800		7270
12–12–30	662		1620	
18–04–30		477		3840
23–04–31		3840		10900
19–04–32		4220		11600
10–04–33		1240		6370
28–03–34		3100		8900
10–04–35		1850		9200
01–04–36		939		5150
06–04–37		1190		5960
25–03–38		1390		7070
14–03–39		690		5250
23–04–40		4520		9900

TABLE II — ANNUAL MAXIMUM DISCHARGES AND VOLUMES (cont'd)

Country:	U.S.S.R. (7) cont'd
River:	Pripiat
Gauging Station:	Mozir

| Date | Maximum discharge (m³/s) resulting from: | | Maximum volume (10⁶m³) corresponding to max. discharge resulting from: | |
| | Rainfall | Snowmelt | Rainfall | Snowmelt |
1	2	3	4	5
16—04—41		2420		
10—04—43		510		2420
24—04—44		1070		6780
09—04—45		1350		6460
19—04—46		1190		4850
11—04—47		1690		5960
14—02—48	1330		3720	
24—03—48		1170		6470
22—04—49		930		5150
22—03—50		586		3940
09—04—51		1530		7570
06—05—52		411		2320
06—04—53		1950		7670
06—05—54		306		2420
17—04—55		1740		6870
27—04—56		3420		9400
03—04—57		1010		6670
26—04—58		4010		11400
28—04—59		1170		6670
30—12—60	947			
21—04—60		519		3240
29—03—61		940		6060
22—04—62		1910		7380
25—04—63		1740		6470
04—05—64		794		3330
13—04—65		1560		5550
11—03—66		3090		10900
31—03—67		1790		8590
14—04—68		1330		7080
24—04—69		1830		6270

Country:	U.S.S.R. (7) cont'd
River:	Pripiat
Gauging Station:	Mozir

| Date | Maximum discharge (m³/s) resulting from: | | Maximum volume (10⁶m³) corresponding to max. discharge resulting from: | |
| | Rainfall | Snowmelt | Rainfall | Snowmelt |
1	2	3	4	5
08—04—70		4140		13100
06—04—71		2340		8080
15—04—72		598		3740

Country:	U.S.S.R. (11)
River:	Desna
Gauging Station:	Chernigov

| Date | Maximum discharge (m³/s) resulting from: | | Maximum volume (10⁶m³) corresponding to max. discharge resulting from: | |
| | Rainfall | Snowmelt | Rainfall | Snowmelt |
1	2	3	4	5
18—04—17		8090		13300

Country:	U.S.S.R. (12)
River:	Golovesnia
Gauging Station:	Pokoshichi

| Date | Maximum discharge (m³/s) resulting from: | | Maximum volume (10⁶m³) corresponding to max. discharge resulting from: | |
| | Rainfall | Snowmelt | Rainfall | Snowmelt |
1	2	3	4	5
06—04—41		45		32

TABLE II – ANNUAL MAXIMUM DISCHARGES AND VOLUMES (cont'd)

Country:	U.S.S.R. (13)
River:	Don
Gauging Station:	Razdorskaya

Date	Maximum discharge (m³/s) resulting from:		Maximum volume (10⁶m³) corresponding to max. discharge resulting from:	
	Rainfall	Snowmelt	Rainfall	Snowmelt
1	2	3	4	5
26–04–81		13000		1120
01–04–82		2390		206
06–04–83		8600		743
18–04–84		10400		899
03–04–85		2650		229
15–04–86		3810		329
02–05–87		5490		474
26–04–88		11900		1030
05–05–89		8600		743
27–04–90		2730		236
18–03–91		2980		257
18–05–92		3810		329
06–05–93		8420		727
18–05–94		3020		261
10–05–95		6700		579
16–05–96		12300		1060
28–04–97		8420		727
08–05–98		4300		372
10–05–99		6700		579
13–05–00		4820		416
13–05–01		3920		339
30–04–02		5490		474
05–03–03		6870		594
23–05–04		4820		416
12–05–05		3660		316
28–04–06		3550		307
01–05–07		6360		550
18–05–08		9870		853
07–04–09		4070		352
15–05–10		2670		231

Country:	U.S.S.R. (13) cont'd
River:	Don
Gauging Station:	Razdorskaya

Date	Maximum discharge (m³/s) resulting from:		Maximum volume (10⁶m³) corresponding to max. discharge resulting from:	
	Rainfall	Snowmelt	Rainfall	Snowmelt
1	2	3	4	5
16–05–11		2140		185
09–05–12		3810		329
14–04–13		6530		564
19–04–14		1740		150
03–05–15		7530		651
26–04–16		5900		510
26–04–17		13500		1170
16–05–18		2740		237
13–05–19		4390		379
26–04–20		8320		719
30–03–21		2900		251
03–05–22		5450		471
27–05–23		2770		239
05–05–24		7130		616
02–04–25		1800		156
18–05–26		8070		697
07–05–27		7980		689
20–05–28		7520		650
16–05–29		11000		950
30–05–30		2110		182
19–05–31		5980		517
04–05–32		11300		976
23–04–33		3000		259
21–03–34		2140		185
29–04–35		1600		138
20–05–36		3420		295
30–04–37		3350		289
07–05–38		2380		206
01–05–39		2420		209
09–05–40		5070		438

TABLE II – ANNUAL MAXIMUM DISCHARGES AND VOLUMES   (cont'd)

Country:	U.S.S.R. (13) cont'd
River:	Don
Gauging Station:	Razdorskaya

Date	Maximum discharge (m³/s) resulting from:		Maximum volume (10⁶m³) corresponding to max. discharge resulting from:	
	Rainfall	Snowmelt	Rainfall	Snowmelt
1	2	3	4	5
17–05–41		8320		719
13–05–42		13100		1130
15–05–43		2170		187
25–04–44		1790		155
30–04–45		2650		229
06–05–46		8080		698
29–04–47		6380		551
09–05–48		8080		698
13–05–49		1840		159
29–04–50		1650		143
26–04–51		7680		664

Country:	U.S.S.R. (14)
River:	Medveditsa
Gauging Station:	Archedinskaya

Date	Maximum discharge (m³/s) resulting from:		Maximum volume (10⁶m³) corresponding to max. discharge resulting from:	
	Rainfall	Snowmelt	Rainfall	Snowmelt
1	2	3	4	5
02–05–28		1840		159
05–05–29		2070		179
13–04–30		566		48.9
26–04–31		1200		104
22–04–32		1900		164
13–04–33		259		22.4
28–04–34		806		69.6
15–04–35		147		12.7
27–04–36		519		44.8
04–05–37		330		28.5
15–04–38		405		35.0
18–04–39		418		36.1
09–04–40		653		56.4
21–04–41		1480		128
01–05–42		1450		125
15–04–45		320		27.6
21–04–46		1690		146
11–04–47		837		72.3
23–04–48		1960		169
25–04–49		497		42.9
17–04–50		358		30.9
10–04–51		1010		87.3
25–04–52		315		27.2
27–04–53		895		77.3
26–04–54		48.2		4.16
06–04–55		1420		123
29–04–56		927		80.1
22–04–57		1440		124
26–04–58		571		49.3
24–04–59		498		43.0

TABLE II — ANNUAL MAXIMUM DISCHARGES AND VOLUMES   (cont'd)

Country:	U.S.S.R. (14) cont'd
River:	Medveditsa
Gauging Station:	Archedinskaya

Date	Maximum discharge (m³/s) resulting from:		Maximum volume (10⁶m³) corresponding to max. discharge resulting from:	
	Rainfall	Snowmelt	Rainfall	Snowmelt
1	2	3	4	5
16—04—60		661		57.1
11—04—61		697		60.2
29—03—62		358		30.9
27—04—63		1120		96.8
29—04—64		1010		87.3
16—04—65		574		49.6
07—04—66		265		22.9
19—04—67		202		17.5
15—04—68		723		62.5
22—04—69		96.9		8.37
23—04—70		794		68.6
12—04—71		457		39.5
09—04—72		149		12.9
17—11—72	697		60.2	

Country:	U.S.S.R. (15)
River:	Teberda
Gauging Station:	Teberda

Date	Maximum discharge (m³/s) resulting from:		Maximum volume (10⁶m³) corresponding to max. discharge resulting from:	
	Rainfall	Snowmelt	Rainfall	Snowmelt
1	2	3	4	5
28—07—27		272		23.5
24—06—28		84.0		7.26
09—11—29	200		17.3	
12—08—30		117		10.1
26—09—31	210		18.1	
09—08—32		147		12.7
14—08—33		132		11.4
19—08—34		160		13.8
02—08—35		110		9.50
08—07—36		·319		27.6
17—07—37		189		16.3
11—07—38		140		12.1
25—09—39	128		11.1	
03—08—40		243		21.0
07—11—41	187		16.2	
27—06—48		131		11.3
01—08—49		151		13.0
11—07—50		145		12.5
23—07—51		154		13.3
25—09—52	228		19.7	
15—09—53	182		15.7	
20—08—54		177		15.3
08—08—55		134		11.6
25—06—56		171		14.8
25—07—57		127		11.0
26—07—58		141		12.2
07—07—59		124		10.7
06—07—60		155		13.4
20—07—61		246		21.3
04—07—62		233		20.1

TABLE II – ANNUAL MAXIMUM DISCHARGES AND VOLUMES   (cont'd)

Country:	U.S.S.R. (15) cont'd
River:	Teberda
Gauging Station:	Teberda

Date	Maximum discharge (m³/s) resulting from:		Maximum volume (10⁶m³) corresponding to max. discharge resulting from:	
	Rainfall	Snowmelt	Rainfall	Snowmelt
1	2	3	4	5
19–07–63		182		15.7
13–08–64		185		16.0
17–07–65		123		10.6
02–08–66		229		19.8
05–08–67		203		17.5
22–07–68		185		16.0
13–05–69		151		13.0
20–07–70		292		25.2
30–09–72	256		22.1	

Country:	U.S.S.R. (16)
River:	Kalaus
Gauging Station:	Svetlograd

Date	Maximum discharge (m³/s) resulting from:		Maximum volume (10⁶m³) corresponding to max. discharge resulting from:	
	Rainfall	Snowmelt	Rainfall	Snowmelt
1	2	3	4	5
17–07–30	17.5		1.51	
10–03–31		181		15.6
13–04–32	435		37.6	
10–03–33		152		13.1
14–03–34		146		12.6
20–02–35		3.80		0.33
04–06–36	20.3		1.75	
11–03–37		58.8		5.08
13–03–38		69.3		5.99
07–06–39	17.8		1.54	
10–03–40		159		13.7
20–02–41		65.9		5.69
21–06–44	138		11.9	
18–06–45	53.2		4.60	
12–03–46		86.4		7.46
05–03–47		22.7		1.96
26–03–48		37.8		3.27
22–03–49		83.5		7.21
21–02–50		35.9		3.10
12–03–51		22.8		1.97
28–06–52	15.0		1.30	
30–03–53		11.8		1.01
01–04–54		257		22.2
24–12–55	58.5		5.05	
04–06–56	181		15.6	
07–03–57		116		10.0
01–04–58		48.0		4.15
28–03–59		24.7		2.13
20–06–60	192		16.6	
27–06–61	35.7		3.08	

TABLE II – ANNUAL MAXIMUM DISCHARGES AND VOLUMES   (cont'd)

Country:	U.S.S.R. (16) cont'd
River:	Kalaus
Gauging Station:	Svetlograd

Date	Maximum discharge (m³/s) resulting from:		Maximum volume (10⁶m³) corresponding to max. discharge resulting from:	
	Rainfall	Snowmelt	Rainfall	Snowmelt
1	2	3	4	5
05–03–62		123		10.6
21–04–63	61.9		5.35	
13–06–64	500		43.2	
17–05–65	181		15.6	
12–06–66	69.9		6.03	
25–06–67	53.1		4.59	
29–02–68		184		15.9
04–04–69		46.5		4.02
06–06–70	23.9		2.06	
14–03–71		23.7		2.05
30–03–72		129		11.1

Country:	U.S.S.R. (17)
River:	Terek
Gauging Station:	Ordzhonikidze

Date	Maximum discharge (m³/s) resulting from:		Maximum volume (10⁶m³) corresponding to max. discharge resulting from:	
	Rainfall	Snowmelt	Rainfall	Snowmelt
1	2	3	4	5
29–07–12		156		13.5
01–07–13		144		12.4
25–06–25		94.0		8.12
27–06–26		97.0		8.38
22–06–27		136		11.8
26–06–28		173		14.9
05–07–29		168		14.5
29–07–30		152		13.1
15–07–31		281		24.3
28–06–32		214		18.5
18–09–33		130		11.2
14–07–34		173		14.9
22–07–35		100		8.64
07–06–36		197		17.0
09–08–37		228		19.7
10–07–38		115		9.94
24–06–39		146		12.6
14–07–40		207		17.9
12–08–41		121		10.5
10–07–42		170		14.7
23–06–43		124		10.7
03–05–44		240		20.7
17–06–45		152		13.1
21–06–46		138		11.9
23–07–47		120		10.4
05–06–48		150		13.0
05–08–49		181		15.6
11–07–50		156		13.5
24–06–51		131		11.3
10–07–52		128		11.1

U.S.S.R. / URSS / CCCP

TABLE II – ANNUAL MAXIMUM DISCHARGES AND VOLUMES   (cont'd)

Country: U.S.S.R. (17) cont'd
River: Terek
Gauging Station: Ordzhonikidze

Date	Maximum discharge (m³/s) resulting from:		Maximum volume (10⁶m³) corresponding to max. discharge resulting from:	
	Rainfall	Snowmelt	Rainfall	Snowmelt
1	2	3	4	5
17–08–53		369		31.9
10–07–54		154		13.3
24–07–55		88.8		7.67
26–06–56		213		18.4
04–08–57		90.7		7.84
12–07–58		206		17.8
07–08–59		242		20.9
26–06–60		167		14.4
03–07–61		365		31.5
11–07–62		146		12.6
27–07–63		157		13.6
11–07–64		145		12.5
03–08–65		124		10.7
11–06–66		165		14.3
06–08–67		424		36.6
18–07–68		101		8.73
14–05–69		80.6		6.96
15–08–70		107		9.24
06–07–71		137		11.8
06–06–72		65.9		5.69

Country: U.S.S.R. (18)
River: Unzha
Gauging Station: Makariev

Date	Maximum discharge (m³/s) resulting from:		Maximum volume (10⁶m³) corresponding to max. discharge resulting from:	
	Rainfall	Snowmelt	Rainfall	Snowmelt
1	2	3	4	5
16–05–96		1240		2870
11–05–97		845		1850
15–05–98		913		1680
10–05–99		1830		5110
26–05–00		1250		3900
28–04–01		1810		3980
17–05–02		1450		3130
28–04–03		1920		3830
02–05–04		1890		2440
07–05–05		1830		3480
30–04–06		1890		2760
30–04–07		1020		2550
03–05–08		1260		2040
09–05–09		1250		2370
01–05–10		1550		1870
10–05–11		1370		2810
25–05–12		1760		3740
29–04–13		1660		3160
17–05–14		2190		3850
28–04–15		1810		3330
02–05–16		1620		4130
23–04–17		1530		2280
05–05–18		1020		1610
03–05–19		1200		1920
20–04–20		1810		2780
23–04–21		1160		1940
10–05–22		1560		3370
24–05–23		1620		3810
27–04–24		1750		4110
30–04–25		1510		2960

TABLE II – ANNUAL MAXIMUM DISCHARGES AND VOLUMES (cont'd)

Country:	U.S.S.R. (18) cont'd
River:	Unzha
Gauging Station:	Makariev

Date	Maximum discharge (m³/s) resulting from:		Maximum volume (10^6m³) corresponding to max. discharge resulting from:	
	Rainfall	Snowmelt	Rainfall	Snowmelt
1	2	3	4	5
08–05–26		2180		3740
06–05–27		1490		3260
07–05–28		1600		2790
16–05–29		1820		2740
02–05–30		1310		2200
01–05–31		1740		3090
02–05–32		1480		2740
27–04–33		1000		2980
04–05–34		1700		2070
22–04–35		1140		1980
03–05–36		2180		3130
27–04–37		506		1330
30–04–38		1620		2900
03–05–39		1170		1410
27–04–40		1260		1780
15–05–41		1260		2940
01–05–42		1360		2650
30–04–43		1020		2630
04–05–44		1680		3500
12–05–45		925		2070
06–05–46		1740		2850
05–05–47		2520		5270
21–04–48		1490		2900
08–05–49		1520		2460
26–04–50		823		1300
12–04–51		1060		2040
08–05–52		1520		3260
28–04–53		1810		2810
26–04–54		900		2260
03–05–55		1700		5290

Country:	U.S.S.R. (18) cont'd
River:	Unzha
Gauging Station:	Makariev

Date	Maximum discharge (m³/s) resulting from:		Maximum volume (10^6m³) corresponding to max. discharge resulting from:	
	Rainfall	Snowmelt	Rainfall	Snowmelt
1	2	3	4	5
16–05–56		1720		3940
08–05–57		2520		3500
13–05–58		2220		5180
27–04–59		1710		3130
29–04–60		1240		2000
18–05–61		2070		3480
24–04–62		1380		3140
28–04–63		1210		1920
11–05–64		938		2280
07–05–65		1030		3480
28–04–66		2090		4680
21–04–67		600		1630
15–05–68		1660		3740
02–05–69		1480		3420
07–05–70		1170		2650
20–05–71		1050		2650
06–05–72		1120		3220

TABLE II – ANNUAL MAXIMUM DISCHARGES AND VOLUMES (cont'd)

Country:	U.S.S.R. (19)
River:	Ishim
Gauging Station:	Tselinograd

Date	Maximum discharge (m³/s) resulting from:		Maximum volume (10⁶m³) corresponding to max. discharge resulting from:	
	Rainfall	Snowmelt	Rainfall	Snowmelt
1	2	3	4	5
14−04−33		215		163
02−05−34		182		148
23−04−35		286		104
23−04−36		14.2		9.84
01−05−37		221		102
24−04−38		36.0		26.4
18−04−39		17.8		16.5
11−04−40		43.5		25.0
15−04−41		668		346
21−04−42		883		443
16−04−43		1060		323
01−04−44		122		54.4
13−04−45		120		41.4
18−04−46		339		332
08−04−47		299		199
16−04−48		1200		667
19−04−49		1080		489
19−04−50		134		82.5
11−04−51		264		138
22−04−52		117		69.5
15−04−53		135		75.8
27−04−54		472		274
04−04−55		168		162
12−04−56		93.6		42.8
17−04−57		319		119
24−04−58		190		190
18−04−59		531		277
22−04−60		478		284
01−04−61		382		229
04−04−62		249		225

Country:	U.S.S.R. (19) cont'd
River:	Ishim
Gauging Station:	Tselinograd

Date	Maximum discharge (m³/s) resulting from:		Maximum volume (10⁶m³) corresponding to max. discharge resulting from:	
	Rainfall	Snowmelt	Rainfall	Snowmelt
1	2	3	4	5
11−04−63		45.3		27.7
23−04−64		619		276
06−04−65		130		70.4
17−04−66		509		328
08−04−67		1.83		12.1
09−04−68		36.0		33.5
11−04−69		27.0		10.5
03−04−70		78.4		27.6
19−04−71		235		
25−04−72		385		

325

TABLE II − ANNUAL MAXIMUM DISCHARGES AND VOLUMES   (cont'd)

Country:	U.S.S.R. (20)
River:	Ishım
Gauging Station:	Petropavlovsk

Date	Maximum discharge (m³/s) resulting from:		Maximum volume (10⁶m³) corresponding to max. discharge resulting from:	
	Rainfall	Snowmelt	Rainfall	Snowmelt
1	2	3	4	5
23−04−32		394		834
30−04−33		226		571
15−05−34		352		910
30−04−35		196		535
01−05−36		27.4		65.1
11−05−37		35.2		133
24−04−38		107		190
21−04−39		109		164
18−04−40		211		551
23−04−41		3760		5430
14−05−42		3340		4610
25−04−43		484		1880
29−04−44		66.2		347
05−05−45		83.4		389
06−05−46		2030		4500
10−04−47		2890		3870
08−05−48		3750		7030
14−05−49		2320		4980
23−04−50		166		613
14−04−51		216		434
05−05−52		184		292
07−05−53		231		640
07−05−53		2480		5480
02−05−55		1840		1960
25−04−56		234		509
04−05−57		334		890
07−05−58		297		1128
29−04−59		655		1850
01−05−60		476		1740
02−05−61		456		1900

Country:	U.S.S.R. (20) cont'd
River:	Ishim
Gauging Station:	Petropavlovsk

Date	Maximum discharge (m³/s) resulting from:		Maximum volume (10⁶m³) corresponding to max. discharge resulting from:	
	Rainfall	Snowmelt	Rainfall	Snowmelt
1	2	3	4	5
20−04−62		417		1098
26−04−63		393		734
10−05−64		2260		3020
15−04−65		398		805
27−04−66		781		1850
26−04−67		74.6		188
27−04−69		33.5		
26−04−70		444		1330
03−05−71		1210		3060

TABLE II – ANNUAL MAXIMUM DISCHARGES AND VOLUMES   (cont'd)

Country:	U.S.S.R. (21)
River:	Ob
Gauging Station:	Salekhard

Date	Maximum discharge (m³/s) resulting from:		Maximum volume (10⁶m³) corresponding to max. discharge resulting from:	
	Rainfall	Snowmelt	Rainfall	Snowmelt
1	2	3	4	5
				X10³
14–06–30		34000		
08–06–31		32700		
16–06–32		31700		
06–06–33		36600		
09–06–34		32900		
07–06–35		33300		
07–06–36		33500		248
08–06–37		33900		270
31–05–38		35400		292
07–06–39		38900		267
31–05–40		38200		245
07–08–41		42800		411
05–06–42		35900		310
23–05–43		38600		270
23–05–44		37100		282
31–05–45		36000		216
01–06–46		41200		352
25–05–47		41500		440
01–08–48		40000		413
28–05–49		38000		352
27–05–50		37200		338
21–05–51		39800		248
04–06–52		35300		241
28–05–53		29400		231
24–05–54		31700		238
28–05–55		30200		211
01–06–56		35300		245
12–06–57		36900		323
19–06–58		38100		311
31–05–59		38300		311

Country:	U.S.S.R. (21) cont'd
River:	Ob
Gauging Station:	Salekhard

Date	Maximum discharge (m³/s) resulting from:		Maximum volume (10⁶m³) corresponding to max. discharge resulting from:	
	Rainfall	Snowmelt	Rainfall	Snowmelt
1	2	3	4	5
				X10³
03–06–60		37000		333
15–06–61		38000		292
24–05–62		33600		258
03–06–63		34100		224
06–06–64		37800		248
02–05–65		36600		260
07–06–66		27200		333
29–05–67		36200		168
29–05–68		32100		185
15–06–69		40500		304
11–06–70		40900		311
04–07–71		43800		401
01–07–72		39600		316

U.S.S.R. / URSS / CCCP

TABLE II – ANNUAL MAXIMUM DISCHARGES AND VOLUMES (cont'd)

Country: U.S.S.R. (22)
River: Pur
Gauging Station: Samburg

Date	Maximum discharge (m³/s) resulting from:		Maximum volume (10⁶m³) corresponding to max. discharge resulting from:	
	Rainfall	Snowmelt	Rainfall	Snowmelt
1	2	3	4	5
				X10³
07–06–39		7410		17.3
25–06–40		6990		20.4
30–05–41		4490		16.8
06–06–42		6230		15.5
27–05–43		7580		18.6
11–06–44		5300		15.3
02–06–45		4650		14.9
09–06–46		5300		20.7
14–06–47		6160		16.1
08–06–48		7940		14.7
18–06–49		5660		15.1
04–06–50		6410		13.5
01–06–51		6960		16.6
04–06–52		5350		12.5
01–06–53		6360		13.6
08–06–54		5970		12.5
03–06–55		6280		13.9
07–06–56		5630		12.8
09–06–57		7060		15.2
14–07–58		6830		13.6
12–06–59		7400		20.8
05–06–60		4900		11.2
19–06–61		7360		17.2
31–05–62		5660		16.6
19–06–63		7210		19.8
05–06–64		5920		17.3
14–06–65		5880		13.9
12–06–66		6430		14.7
07–06–67		5120		17.1
14–06–68		5200		16.8

Country: U.S.S.R. (22) cont'd
River: Pur
Gauging Station: Samburg

Date	Maximum discharge (m³/s) resulting from:		Maximum volume (10⁶m³) corresponding to max. discharge resulting from:	
	Rainfall	Snowmelt	Rainfall	Snowmelt
1	2	3	4	5
				X10³
14–06–69		5700		14.9
19–06–70		6250		17.4
11–06–71		6400		20.0
19–06–72		6710		16.4

328

TABLE II – ANNUAL MAXIMUM DISCHARGES AND VOLUMES   (cont'd)

Country:	U.S.S.R. (23)
River:	Biya
Gauging Station:	Biysk

Date	Maximum discharge (m³/s) resulting from:		Maximum volume (10⁶m³) corresponding to max. discharge resulting from:	
	Rainfall	Snowmelt	Rainfall	Snowmelt
1	2	3	4	5
16–07–21		3550		16000
15–05–22		4610		17800
30–04–23		3010		11800
30–04–24		2360		11900
23–04–29		2580		12600
16–04–33		1970		6050
10–05–34		1670		6200
24–04–35		2750		12200
15–06–36		4790		19400
12–05–37		5040		14100
19–04–38		3340		16600
25–04–39		2900		10700
01–05–40		2170		12200
21–04–41		3620		14100
01–05–42		3080		13700
18–04–43		2380		6790
26–04–44		1650		10900
17–04–45		3100		6200
07–06–46		4020		10800
15–04–47		2760		9980
28–04–48		2300		11500
12–05–49		2790		10800
07–05–50		3960		11500
11–05–51		2000		10000
14–05–52		3340		13200
06–05–53		1840		9520
10–05–54		2220		12300
07–05–55		2650		9120
19–06–56		2860		10700
18–04–57		2680		14200

Country:	U.S.S.R. (23) cont'd
River:	Biya
Gauging Station:	Biysk

Date	Maximum discharge (m³/s) resulting from:		Maximum volume (10⁶m³) corresponding to max. discharge resulting from:	
	Rainfall	Snowmelt	Rainfall	Snowmelt
1	2	3	4	5
29–06–58		2740		18100
30–04–59		2150		11700
30–04–60		2230		13300
13–04–61		2740		14000
23–05–62		2120		9890
05–06–63		2140		8060
30–04–64		2110		9890
04–05–65		2490		7380
12–06–66		4030		14700
26–04–67		2020		2180
18–05–68		2630		5240
30–04–69		5770		15400
29–05–70		2830		10100
20–04–71		2860		10260
16–07–72		1760		7760

TABLE II — ANNUAL MAXIMUM DISCHARGES AND VOLUMES   (cont'd)

Country:	U.S.S.R. (24)
River:	Usa
Gauging Station:	Mezhdourechensk

Date	Maximum discharge (m³/s) resulting from:		Maximum volume (10⁶m³) corresponding to max. discharge resulting from:	
	Rainfall	Snowmelt	Rainfall	Snowmelt
1	2	3	4	5
29—05—37		1360		3210
24—05—38		1620		3460
02—05—39		1860		2900
29—04—40		1060		2610
08—06—41		1950		51100
13—06—42		1860		3400
06—05—43		1210		2640
09—05—44		988		2730
21—07—45	2520		525	
01—06—46		2440		3300
08—07—47	900		406	
27—05—48		1590		3580
02—05—49		1220		3140
31—05—50		1590		2780
21—05—51		1450		2270
01—06—52		1470		2820
06—06—53		1270		2690
20—06—54		1670		3000
21—05—55		1940		2350
05—10—56	1110		229	
26—05—57		1030		2160
02—06—58		2590		3940
13—05—59		1890		4170
11—06—60		1550		3000
23—05—61		1210		3120
20—05—62		2430		3540
28—05—63	1100	1100	230	3420
27—05—64		1520		3570
20—05—65		1520		3340
05—06—66		1880		5040

Country:	U.S.S.R. (24) cont'd
River:	Usa
Gauging Station:	Mezhdourechensk

Date	Maximum discharge (m³/s) resulting from:		Maximum volume (10⁶m³) corresponding to max. discharge resulting from:	
	Rainfall	Snowmelt	Rainfall	Snowmelt
1	2	3	4	5
16—05—67		884		1770
28—04—68		1260		1550
26—05—69		2400		4490
15—05—70		1950		3920
28—05—71		1220		3030
14—07—72		2200		2660

TABLE II — ANNUAL MAXIMUM DISCHARGES AND VOLUMES (cont'd)

Country:	U.S.S.R. (25)
River:	Tym
Gauging Station:	Napas

Date	Maximum discharge (m³/s) resulting from:		Maximum volume (10⁶m³) corresponding to max. discharge resulting from:	
	Rainfall	Snowmelt	Rainfall	Snowmelt
1	2	3	4	5
08–06–37		790		2720
13–05–38		602		3060
27–05–39		834		3870
09–06–40		784		3940
14–06–41		845		3680
05–06–42		731		3620
22–05–43		782		5380
25–05–44		801		4650
18–05–45		574		4200
08–06–46		808		4890
26–05–47		860		4940
13–06–48		882		4550
24–05–49		742		3300
07–06–50		671		3040
20–05–51		745		3670
03–06–52		601		2130
11–05–53		570		2670
30–05–54		608		2160
24–05–55		544		1930
04–06–56		774		2330
07–06–57		732		3380
12–06–58		918		3040
10–06–59		987		3920
07–06–60		1070		4320
08–06–61		908		3660
03–06–62		829		3460
12–06–63		842		3500
03–06–64		772		2700
04–06–65		815		3220
07–06–66		893		4950

Country:	U.S.S.R. (25) cont'd
River:	Tym
Gauging Station:	Napas

Date	Maximum discharge (m³/s) resulting from:		Maximum volume (10⁶m³) corresponding to max. discharge resulting from:	
	Rainfall	Snowmelt	Rainfall	Snowmelt
1	2	3	4	5
23–05–67		839		2550
20–05–68		568		3480
16–06–69		850		3340
12–06–70		1180		5930
02–06–71		998		4190
04–06–72		656		3320

TABLE II – ANNUAL MAXIMUM DISCHARGES AND VOLUMES   (cont'd)

Country:	U.S.S.R. (26)
River:	Yenisei
Gauging Station:	Yeniseisk

Date	Maximum discharge (m³/s) resulting from:		Maximum volume (10⁶m³) corresponding to max. discharge resulting from:	
	Rainfall	Snowmelt	Rainfall	Snowmelt
1	2	3	4	5
22–05–03		22500		109000
15–05–04		36200		144000
29–05–05		35600		98200
16–05–07		34300		134000
20–05–08		42600		140000
31–05–09		35100		129000
28–05–10		34500		98800
26–05–11		24000		96900
16–05–12		25800		80700
23–05–13		36600		124000
12–05–14		39400		123000
14–05–15		42000		128000
06–06–16		39400		110000
14–05–17		25400		88500
17–05–18		31900		94300
26–05–19		41200		127000
15–05–20		26200		123000
03–06–21		30900		123000
13–05–23		46600		111000
25–05–24		38600		
30–05–25		29600		118000
15–06–26		19900		87700
12–05–27		27600		110000
18–05–28		31600		133000
18–05–29		18800		105000
21–05–30		41800		114000
26–05–31		35500		105000
16–06–32		24800		120000
21–05–33		30500		112000
17–05–34		33900		87000

Country:	U.S.S.R. (26) cont'd
River:	Yenisei
Gauging Station:	Yeniseisk

Date	Maximum discharge (m³/s) resulting from:		Maximum volume (10⁶m³) corresponding to max. discharge resulting from:	
	Rainfall	Snowmelt	Rainfall	Snowmelt
1	2	3	4	5
25–05–35		37300		140000
16–05–36		34700		156000
18–05–37		57400		135000
18–05–38		30200		152000
08–05–39		40800		124000
13–05–40		20200		114000
26–05–41		44700		168000
21–05–42		21900		100000
06–05–43		21700		96800
11–05–44		21500		96700
10–05–45		23200		832000
20–05–46		22200		104000
10–05–47		27900		110000
13–05–48		19900		113000
08–05–49		26700		99000
16–05–50		33300		120000
26–05–51		40000		129000
18–05–52		34800		157000
12–05–53		26000		109000
19–05–54		21800		102000
20–05–55		31900		129000
22–05–56		32800		101000
24–05–57		23900		108000
24–05–58		35700		128000
02–06–59		38400		150000
27–05–60		30400		118000
09–05–61		26900		137000
20–05–62		30200		117000
19–05–63		19600		91800
18–05–64		28100		88500

TABLE II — ANNUAL MAXIMUM DISCHARGES AND VOLUMES   (cont'd)

Country:	U.S.S.R. (26) cont'd				Country:	U.S.S.R. (27)			
River:	Yenisei				River:	Abakan			
Gauging Station:	Yeniseisk				Gauging Station:	Abaza			

	Maximum discharge (m³/s) resulting from:		Maximum volume (10⁶m³) corresponding to max. discharge resulting from:			Maximum discharge (m³/s) resulting from:		Maximum volume (10⁶m³) corresponding to max. discharge resulting from:	
Date	Rainfall	Snowmelt	Rainfall	Snowmelt	Date	Rainfall	Snowmelt	Rainfall	Snowmelt
1	2	3	4	5	1	2	3	4	5
25–05–65		34700		108000	22–06–32	5800	2550	2008	
18–05–66		39400		158000	23–05–33	432	1600		3780
					24–05–34	1220	1180		2930
					09–05–35	1000	3280		4890
					10–05–37	1380	2400		
					25–05–38	1720	2900		
					13–05–39	1300	2340		
					28–05–40	878	1570		
					20–07–41	3750	3660	1203	
					10–06–42	1110	3130		
					30–05–43	414	2440		
					06–05–44	972	1570		
					15–05–45	1020	2220		
					05–06–46	1330	2920		4720
					24–08–47	1420	1360	520	
					27–05–48	2000	2450		
					08–05–49	829	2120		6020
					24–05–50	743	2290		5630
					20–05–51	1140	2020		4080
					21–05–52	1750	1980		4610
					27–05–53	1320	2360		5310
					19–05–54	758	4230		6950
					22–05–55	893	2420		4520
					18–06–56	1380	1790		4360
					28–05–57	567	2280		4370
					27–06–58	1400	2780		3980
					30–05–59	2060	2300		4430
					04–06–60	1280	1630		5120
					31–05–61	988	2460		7500
					21–05–62	795	3650		5000

TABLE II − ANNUAL MAXIMUM DISCHARGES AND VOLUMES   (cont'd)

Country:	U.S.S.R. (27) cont'd
River:	Abakan
Gauging Station:	Abaza

	Maximum discharge (m³/s) resulting from:		Maximum volume (10⁶m³) corresponding to max. discharge resulting from:	
Date	Rainfall	Snowmelt	Rainfall	Snowmelt
1	2	3	4	5
03−05−63	570	2040		3690
27−05−64	785	1960		4580
17−05−65	923	1850		3520
07−06−66	1030	3450		8950
04−07−67	2140	2720		2070
17−05−68	711	3530		3520
29−05−69	1760	6700		8970
25−05−70	917	2520		5630
21−06−71	1230	1920		5010
14−07−72	2580	2000	1292	

Country:	U.S.S.R. (28)
River:	Tuba
Gauging Station:	Bugurtak

	Maximum discharge (m³/s) resulting from:		Maximum volume (10⁶m³) corresponding to max. discharge resulting from:	
Date	Rainfall	Snowmelt	Rainfall	Snowmelt
1	2	3	4	5
23−05−11	1030	5540		16100
31−05−12	2230	3980		15300
06−06−13	2030	4900		14300
05−06−14	1690	5300		18800
14−05−15	1330	4900		18200
02−06−16	721	7750		20600
31−05−17	2300	4440		14300
30−05−18	433	4440		14800
27−05−19	1810	5240		19700
04−06−20	1170	5760		15200
13−06−21	2160	6070		18100
08−06−22	1270	6850		20100
13−05−23	1980	4960		21000
09−06−28	1600	3430		
27−05−30	1710	5620		19800
01−06−31	627	5870		16200
08−06−32	1170	4610		14900
15−06−33	1690	4290		12600
15−06−34	3080	3550		10800
19−05−35	1900	6750		20100
29−05−36	1810	5620		22300
08−05−37	3180	6710		17600
27−05−38	1800	5820		20200
04−05−39	2210	3920		16700
11−06−40	1930	3650		13800
10−06−41	745	6850		24800
11−06−42	981	4950		16200
09−05−43	1010	3200		11500
05−06−44	2370	3370		14400
14−05−45	726	2890		11300

TABLE II – ANNUAL MAXIMUM DISCHARGES AND VOLUMES   (cont'd)

Country:	U.S.S.R. (28) cont'd	Country:	U.S.S.R. (29)
River:	Tuba	River:	Graviyka
Gauging Station:	Bugurtak	Gauging Station:	Igarka

Date	Maximum discharge (m³/s) resulting from:		Maximum volume (10⁶m³) corresponding to max. discharge resulting from:		Date	Maximum discharge (m³/s) resulting from:		Maximum volume (10⁶m³) corresponding to max. discharge resulting from:	
	Rainfall	Snowmelt	Rainfall	Snowmelt		Rainfall	Snowmelt	Rainfall	Snowmelt
1	2	3	4	5	1	2	3	4	5
04–06–46	1970	4260		14100	23–05–38		73.2		84
26–05–47	2300	3100		12200	11–06–39		159		143
28–05–48	1470	3550		12300	02–06–40		126		121
17–06–49	1820	3950		16200	25–05–41		79.0		75
01–06–50	1200	5390		14400	30–05–42		87.2		96
23–05–51	1480	5090		15500	27–05–43		69.0		108
07–06–52	1540	5210		19100	04–06–44		112		94
02–06–53	1310	4140		14200	25–05–45		128		97
10–06–54	1910	4350		14000	05–06–46		51.6		83
28–09–55	5270	5230	16300		06–06–47		85.5		100
30–05–56	2820	3510		15600	08–06–48		87.0		139
07–06–57	3000	4140		13500	13–06–49		81.9		104
05–06–58	934	6700		17200	04–06–50		80.6		84
29–05–59	851	7070		20000	03–06–51		93.8		129
02–06–60	3080	3840		14000	10–06–52		135		117
29–05–61	1610	5730		20600	28–05–53		110		92
22–05–62	943	5760		16700	05–06–54		104		64
05–06–63	1060	3890		15200	12–06–55		84.5		113
28–05–64	753	4350		13400	06–06–56		118		89
22–05–65	2960	8240		17200	06–06–57		166		133
09–06–66	1470	10500		26200	15–06–58		212		100
21–05–67	1870	3660		13700	06–06–59		145		140
14–05–68	905	3870		11300	28–05–60		90.2		54
31–05–69	1420	5410		17100	25–06–61		197		20
10–06–70	1920	6020		18700	16–06–62		127		124
30–05–71	884	3550		12500	14–06–63		144		147
04–06–72	2610	5970		18000	11–06–64		63.5		102
					18–06–65		92.5		120
					09–06–66		41.4		47
					10–06–67		119		108

TABLE II – ANNUAL MAXIMUM DISCHARGES AND VOLUMES   (cont'd)

Country:	U.S.S.R. (29) cont'd
River:	Graviyka
Gauging Station:	Igarka

Date	Maximum discharge (m³/s) resulting from:		Maximum volume (10⁶m³) corresponding to max. discharge resulting from:	
	Rainfall	Snowmelt	Rainfall	Snowmelt
1	2	3	4	5
21–06–68		190		119
09–06–71		68.1		68
12–06–72		156		101

Country:	U.S.S.R. (30)
River:	Selenga
Gauging Station:	Mostovoy

Date	Maximum discharge (m³/s) resulting from:		Maximum volume (10⁶m³) corresponding to max. discharge resulting from:	
	Rainfall	Snowmelt	Rainfall	Snowmelt
1	2	3	4	5
07–05–34		3220		8360
19–07–35	2920		4840	
11–06–36	7620		5280	
14–05–37		3560		7480
21–07–38	3700		4840	
23–04–39		3400		5720
06–08–40	6480		4840	
21–08–41	3490		13600	
20–07–42	4070		8800	
28–05–43	3270		4180	
02–05–44		2200		6160
12–09–45	3270		8800	
22–04–46		2120		6600
28–07–47	2740		4840	
21–09–48	2740		10100	
01–09–49	3440		6600	
24–08–50	2830		7480	
02–06–51		4200		14100
09–08–52	3950		8360	
11–07–53	3100		10100	
19–07–54	2250		4360	
18–05–55		3090		7480
07–08–56	3130		4090	
01–06–57	2680		1670	
22–05–58		2120		6600
28–08–59	4180		10100	
26–08–60	3100		3960	
28–08–61	4080		7040	
26–07–62	4580		11400	
26–07–63	4050		7480	

TABLE II – ANNUAL MAXIMUM DISCHARGES AND VOLUMES   (cont'd)

Country:	U.S.S.R. (30) cont'd
River:	Selenga
Gauging Station:	Mostovoy

| Date | Maximum discharge (m³/s) resulting from: | | Maximum volume (10⁶m³) corresponding to max. discharge resulting from: | |
| | Rainfall | Snowmelt | Rainfall | Snowmelt |
1	2	3	4	5
25–05–64	3840		5720	
19–08–65	3470		9240	
09–08–66	3270		6600	
25–07–67	3030		5720	
06–05–68		3620		8360
08–09–69	4180		14100	
23–05–70	3260		6600	
05–08–71	6370		12500	
10–07–72	1700		3210	

Country:	U.S.S.R. (31)
River:	Khilok
Gauging Station:	Maleta

| Date | Maximum discharge (m³/s) resulting from: | | Maximum volume (10⁶m³) corresponding to max. discharge resulting from: | |
| | Rainfall | Snowmelt | Rainfall | Snowmelt |
1	2	3	4	5
16–09–36	473		1160	
14–05–37		517		1130
07–09–38	795			
23–04–39		936		
12–07–40	770		1590	
15–09–41	411		514	
05–05–42	524	524	642	798
27–04–43		543		642
29–04–44		373		488
23–07–45	289		334	
06–05–46		152		308
27–07–47	281		334	
06–06–48	445		540	
27–05–49	576		591	
11–05–50		358		694
08–05–51		576		1230
05–05–52		591		1180
02–05–53		726		848
07–05–54		242		386
15–05–55		399		642
18–05–56		282		463
30–05–57	525		308	
16–05–58		324		874
17–06–59	242		411	
30–04–60		276		642
29–08–61	298		308	
28–07–62	621		1230	
16–05–63		384		720
21–05–64	420		257	
08–05–65		233		514

TABLE II – ANNUAL MAXIMUM DISCHARGES AND VOLUMES   (cont'd)

Country:	U.S.S.R. (31) cont'd
River:	Khilok
Gauging Station:	Maleta

Date	Maximum discharge (m³/s) resulting from:		Maximum volume (10⁶m³) corresponding to max. discharge resulting from:	
	Rainfall	Snowmelt	Rainfall	Snowmelt
1	2	3	4	5
21–05–66		354		694
28–04–67		288		411
08–05–68		830		1390
09–09–69	753		848	
28–04–70		411		977
08–08–71	530		977	
30–04–72		241		283

Country:	U.S.S.R. (32)
River:	Bolshaya
Gauging Station:	Possolskaya

Date	Maximum discharge (m³/s) resulting from:		Maximum volume (10⁶m³) corresponding to max. discharge resulting from:	
	Rainfall	Snowmelt	Rainfall	Snowmelt
1	2	3	4	5
31–08–29	50.2		29.9	
26–07–30	38.5		9.60	
15–06–36		119*		236
04–07–37	166*		100	
12–07–38	149*		67.8	
19–06–39	53.8*		17.5	
04–07–40	185		84.2	
02–06–41		97.0		211
15–07–42	444*		117	
21–05–43		74.5		125
28–07–44	192		61.6	
22–05–45		51.6		145
25–05–46		47.1		133
25–07–47	60.2		19.2	
03–06–48		74.3		146
29–05–49		45.5		91.0
18–08–50	122		47.5	
28–05–51		85.0		201
01–06–52		147		176
17–06–53	84.2		10.7	
15–07–54	95.4		37.3	
02–06–55		82.0		126
01–06–56		63.0		159
05–08–57	165		44.1	
24–05–58		41.3		105
11–06–59	146		33.3	
22–08–60	108		57.1	
18–08–61	114		83.6	
03–07–62	167		57.1	
31–08–63	93.4		29.4	

TABLE II — ANNUAL MAXIMUM DISCHARGES AND VOLUMES (cont'd)

Country: U.S.S.R. (32) cont'd
River: Bolshaya
Gauging Station: Possolskaya

Date	Maximum discharge (m³/s) resulting from:		Maximum volume (10⁶m³) corresponding to max. discharge resulting from:	
	Rainfall	Snowmelt	Rainfall	Snowmelt
1	2	3	4	5
25–05–64		77.1		158
16–08–65	146		81.4	
04–07–66	145		75.1	
23–05–67		100		170
31–05–68		127		232
01–09–69	53.1		6.22	
12–06–70		139		310
20–07–71	333		206	
14–07–72	41.0		10.2	

* Mean daily valves.

Country: U.S.S.R. (33)
River: Vitim
Gauging Station: Romanovka

Date	Maximum discharge (m³/s) resulting from:		Maximum volume (10⁶m³) corresponding to max. discharge resulting from:	
	Rainfall	Snowmelt	Rainfall	Snowmelt
1	2	3	4	5
15–09–44	1040		655	
23–07–45	1770		473	
20–06–46	361		983	
01–09–47	2370		1060	
20–07–48	2930		1510	
26–08–49	3400		1490	
20–08–50	707		182	
04–07–51	1440		528	
28–06–52	1270		528	
04–07–53	290		118	
10–07–54	1650		510	
07–09–55	603		218	
10–08–56	1730		455	
08–08–57	2820		801	
21–05–58		248		237
20–08–59	1390		855	
22–08–60	1840		528	
27–08–61	546		200	
16–07–62	2270		1260	
17–07–63	1460		692	
23–07–64	2150		546	
29–08–65	272		80.0	
20–07–66	1560		419	
16–07–67	1680		819	
27–06–68	896		200	
19–08–69	1310		692	
08–07–70	1790		400	
31–07–71	3210		1600	
15–07–72	927		218	

TABLE II – ANNUAL MAXIMUM DISCHARGES AND VOLUMES   (cont'd)

Country:	U.S.S.R. (34)
River:	Lena
Gauging Station:	Kusur

Date	Maximum discharge (m³/s) resulting from:		Maximum volume (10⁶m³) corresponding to max. discharge resulting from:	
	Rainfall	Snowmelt	Rainfall	Snowmelt
1	2	3	4	5
05–06–35		78000		328000
05–06–36		103000		304000
03–06–37		113000		216000
09–06–38		110000		360000
05–05–39		122000		267000
12–06–40		96700		243000
09–06–41		143000		297000
14–06–42		137000		274000
23–05–43		102000		299000
03–06–45		141000		224000
14–06–46		106000		242000
06–06–47		152000		262000
13–06–48		165000		309000
08–06–49		163000		348000
08–06–50		155000		313000
10–06–51		164000		296000
07–06–52		161000		367000
02–06–53		134000		299000
10–06–54		92700		260000
11–06–56		123000		279000
04–06–57		134000		284000
10–06–58		143000		422000
04–06–59		130000		304000
08–06–60		123000		262000
06–06–62		166000		364000
20–06–63		136000		391000
09–06–64		140000		287000
09–06–65		132000		299000
06–06–66		159000		381000
08–06–67		189000		340000

Country:	U.S.S.R. (34) cont'd
River:	Lena
Gauging Station:	Kusur

Date	Maximum discharge (m³/s) resulting from:		Maximum volume (10⁶m³) corresponding to max. discharge resulting from:	
	Rainfall	Snowmelt	Rainfall	Snowmelt
1	2	3	4	5
27–05–68		144000		347000
09–06–69		138000		345000
07–06–70		114000		360000
08–06–71		124000		309000
08–05–72		122000		268000

TABLE II — ANNUAL MAXIMUM DISCHARGES AND VOLUMES   (cont'd)

Country: U.S.S.R. (35)
River: Indigirka
Gauging Station: Vorontsovo

Date	Maximum discharge (m³/s) resulting from:		Maximum volume (10⁶m³) corresponding to max. discharge resulting from:	
	Rainfall	Snowmelt	Rainfall	Snowmelt
1	2	3	4	5
24—07—37	5170		7010	
16—06—38		8880		30800
26—07—39	8190		10400	
05—06—40		8880		30500
08—06—41		11500		20400
07—07—42		9240		32900
30—06—43		7290		23500
09—07—44		8080		36900
06—07—45		7310		28100
29—07—46	7250		10700	
03—07—47		10300		37400
13—06—48		6320		17100
15—06—49		6720		18000
03—07—50		8560		24100
03—07—51		10600		30400
10—07—52		7010		18000
02—06—53		8190		23200
06—07—54		9980		42100
07—06—55		7450		14000
26—06—56		10000		25900
16—08—57	8140		13100	
19—06—58		8560		20400
05—08—59	10500		27200	
06—06—60		7010		17400
09—06—61		9550		21600
09—07—62	7590		12200	
20—06—63		9350		25000
19—06—64		8600		19500
06—06—65		7880		27200
04—06—66		7850		18900

Country: U.S.S.R. (35) cont'd
River: Indigirka
Gauging Station: Vorontsovo

Date	Maximum discharge (m³/s) resulting from:		Maximum volume (10⁶m³) corresponding to max. discharge resulting from:	
	Rainfall	Snowmelt	Rainfall	Snowmelt
1	2	3	4	5
15—06—67		11700		35400
31—05—68		11200		27200
05—06—69		8900		24700
06—06—70		8860		29000
17—07—71	6550		17100	
09—07—72	5920		15900	

TABLE II – ANNUAL MAXIMUM DISCHARGES AND VOLUMES (cont'd)

Country:	U.S.S.R. (36)
River:	Zbitiem
Gauging Station:	Zbetem

Date	Maximum discharge (m³/s) resulting from:		Maximum volume (10⁶m³) corresponding to max. discharge resulting from:	
	Rainfall	Snowmelt	Rainfall	Snowmelt
1	2	3	4	5
30–05–37		218		116
06–06–38		429		266
25–06–39		282*		310
11–08–40	289		58	
09–08–41	304		33	
06–07–42	342		37	
27–08–43	251		60	
11–08–44	275		36	
02–06–45		311		187
10–06–46		234		164
18–06–47		278		328
12–06–48		296*		338
22–06–49		349		291
09–07–50	500		58	
11–06–51		336		182
04–08–52	748		72	
05–06–53		356		248
03–07–54	640		112	
09–06–55		479		313
12–06–56		277		194
04–06–57		251		168
12–06–58		394*		194
02–06–59		455		177
06–06–60		232		120
10–06–61		267		160
08–09–62	650		48	
21–06–63		304		184
12–06–64		572		376
04–06–65		336		257
16–06–66		661		274

Country:	U.S.S.R. (36) cont'd
River:	Zbitiem
Gauging Station:	Zbetem

Date	Maximum discharge (m³/s) resulting from:		Maximum volume (10⁶m³) corresponding to max. discharge resulting from:	
	Rainfall	Snowmelt	Rainfall	Snowmelt
1	2	3	4	5
13–06–67		415		260
10–06–68		412		267
03–06–69		299		214
10–06–70		399		258
11–06–71		383		
30–06–72		178		

* Mean daily values

TABLE II – ANNUAL MAXIMUM DISCHARGES AND VOLUMES   (cont'd)

Country:	U.S.S.R. (37)					Country:	U.S.S.R. (37) cont'd			
River:	Timpton					River:	Timptom			
Gauging Station:	Nagorni					Gauging Station:	Nagorni			

	Maximum discharge (m³/s) resulting from:		Maximum volume (10⁶m³) corresponding to max. discharge resulting from:				Maximum discharge (m³/s) resulting from:		Maximum volume (10⁶m³) corresponding to max. discharge resulting from:	
Date	Rainfall	Snowmelt	Rainfall	Snowmelt		Date	Rainfall	Snowmelt	Rainfall	Snowmelt
1	2	3	4	5		1	2	3	4	5
13–07–26	352		61			21–06–61	133		27	
11–07–27	344		66			19–07–62	208		25	
11–06–28		193		70		08–06–63		423		146
12–06–29		193		107		05–07–64	183		47	
25–05–34		510		201		27–08–65	167		26	
22–05–35	296*		60			09–06–66		262		
07–07–36	183		31			24–07–67	150		25	
02–09–37	157		25			02–07–68	231		69	
15–07–38	358		88			08–06–69		122		
01–06–39	414		34			08–06–70		357		
19–09–40	150		27			26–05–71		125	11	
24–06–41	291		17			24–08–72	221		9	
31–08–42	369		54							
21–08–43	304		44			*Mean daily values.				
08–07–44	178		12							
26–08–45	125		16							
21–08–47	260		71							
20–08–48	304		45							
02–06–49		283		175						
03–08–50	240		29							
26–07–51	264		52							
06–09–52	227		59							
23–05–53		285								
23–06–54	169		34							
24–05–55		182		113						
11–07–56	309		54							
16–07–57	344		41							
16–07–58	698*		59							
23–07–59	326		39							
16–07–60	164		20							

TABLE II – ANNUAL MAXIMUM DISCHARGES AND VOLUMES (cont'd)

Country: U.S.S.R. (38)
River: Kolyma
Gauging Station: Ust–Srednikan

Date	Maximum discharge (m³/s) resulting from:		Maximum volume (10⁶m³) corresponding to max. discharge resulting from:	
	Rainfall	Snowmelt	Rainfall	Snowmelt
1	2	3	4	5
04–06–33		5400		
02–06–34		6760		8450
06–06–35		3910		7550
28–05–36		8610		9140
16–08–37	3660		1580	
07–06–38		.10800		13500
24–08–39	17800		8290	
27–08–40	9450		6250	
02–06–41		9260		9740
01–06–42		5610		7650
27–05–43		6930		6660
29–07–44	6090		4810	
28–06–45	5720		4650	
02–09–46	5260		3290	
24–06–47		10500		17200
05–06–48		3900		5670
03–06–49		3970		4270
11–06–50		7770		10600
15–06–51		11800		18700
09–06–52		5370		9640
29–05–53		5430		6360
13–06–54		7770		14600
14–07–55	6880		4590	
15–06–56		13000		23800
03–06–57		5920		5960
01–08–58	8340		2760	
31–05–59		8180		9840
08–06–60		6520		10900
02–07–61	8310		3880	
07–06–62		5380		8350

Country: U.S.S.R. (38) cont'd
River: Kolyma
Gauging Station: Ust–Srednikan

Date	Maximum discharge (m³/s) resulting from:		Maximum volume (10⁶m³) corresponding to max. discharge resulting from:	
	Rainfall	Snowmelt	Rainfall	Snowmelt
1	2	3	4	5
09–06–63		8690		16500
16–08–64	3630		2780	
10–06–65		6820		11500
29–08–66	5220		2190	
01–06–67		6310		13400
25–05–68		10500		9640
06–06–69		7180		12000
02–06–70		3850		9640
30–05–71		4220		6960
25–06–72		5870		12100

TABLE II – ANNUAL MAXIMUM DISCHARGES AND VOLUMES (cont'd)

Country:	U.S.S.R. (39)		Country:	U.S.S.R. (40)
River:	Amguema		River:	Iziskatelski
Gauging Station:	Mouth of the brook Shoumny		Gauging Station:	1.6 km upstream the mouth

Date	Maximum discharge (m³/s) resulting from:		Maximum volume (10⁶m³) corresponding to max. discharge resulting from:		Date	Maximum discharge (m³/s) resulting from:		Maximum volume (10⁶m³) corresponding to max. discharge resulting from:	
	Rainfall	Snowmelt	Rainfall	Snowmelt		Rainfall	Snowmelt	Rainfall	Snowmelt
1	2	3	4	5	1	2	3	4	5
17—06—45		3000		4380	21—07—47	9.48		0.51	
25—06—46		2380			13—09—48	17.0		2.59	
18—06—47		5300		6970	27—06—49		8.18		1.91
12—06—48		2230		4030		8.18		1.70	
04—07—49		4290		4750	09—08—50	19.5		2.76	
27—06—50		4150			06—08—51	11.2		0.95	
23—06—51		2890		5130	19—06—52		8.00		5.04
24—06—52		2890		5930	21—09—53	9.82		0.97	
11—06—53		3260		3340	09—06—54		8.35		4.53
12—06—54		3030		4430		8.35		1.44	
17—06—55		4030		2380	22—07—55	11.0		1.48	
19—06—56		5160		5230	16—06—56		7.05		4.79
16—06—57		5780		5870	12—07—57	16.5		1.49	
12—06—58		2950		3120	03—07—58	12.0		0.68	
11—06—59		3310		5130	12—09—59	14.9		1.62	
20—06—60		3240		5100	25—08—60	9.81		0.82	
11—06—61		3240		4570	18—06—61	10.3		1.08	
24—06—62		6790		8810	24—06—62		13.0		5.98
19—06—63		3730		6010	25—07—63	24.0		0.79	
10—06—64		3720		4620	10—06—64		8.50		3.93
01—07—65		4490		6270	06—07—65	9.98		0.77	
30—06—66		4650		7370	29—06—66		12.3		
12—06—67		2120		7330	20—06—67		10.1		7.18
17—06—68	2250		908		07—08—68	5.35		1.41	
18—06—69		3160		5210	14—09—69	54.0		3.14	
04—06—70		4140		3070	24—09—71	5.46		1.20	
22—06—71		5230		4990	17—06—72		9.96		4.13
01—07—72		2850		5910					

TABLE II – ANNUAL MAXIMUM DISCHARGES AND VOLUMES (cont'd)

Country:	U.S.S.R. (41)
River:	Khasyn
Gauging Station:	Kolyma Road, 79th km

Date	Maximum discharge (m³/s) resulting from:		Maximum volume (10⁶m³) corresponding to max. discharge resulting from:	
	Rainfall	Snowmelt	Rainfall	Snowmelt
1	2	3	4	5
14−08−41	196		31.4	
24−06−42	149		12.1	
25−09−43	300		61.6	
20−09−44	420		51.6	
26−06−45	180		45.7	
29−09−46	126		52.2	
01−07−47	144		27.5	
29−05−48		106		104
02−06−49	79.6		28.7	
19−07−50	514		30.8	
12−06−51		213		267
22−08−52	109		23.9	
23−05−53		52.0		75.0
	52.0		11.5	
06−09−54	120		29.4	
24−09−55	318		44.6	
10−06−56		244		342
20−06−57	71.0		15.6	
30−07−58	234		29.8	
28−05−59		175		131
16−09−60	185		29.3	
24−06−61	194		23.9	
17−05−62		83.2		53.9
	83.2		12.3	
03−10−63	513		32.7	
09−08−64	108		16.4	
14−06−65		157		133
02−09−66	152		40.2	
04−06−67		147		208
25−06−68	249		33.4	

Country:	U.S.S.R. (41) cont'd
River:	Khasyn
Gauging Station:	Kolyma Road, 79th km

Date	Maximum discharge (m³/s) resulting from:		Maximum volume (10⁶m³) corresponding to max. discharge resulting from:	
	Rainfall	Snowmelt	Rainfall	Snowmelt
1	2	3	4	5
11−07−69	196		16.4	
07−06−70		56.0		90.7
24−06−71	181		17.0	
01−09−72	184		43 7	

TABLE II — ANNUAL MAXIMUM DISCHARGES AND VOLUMES (cont'd)

Country: U.S.S.R. (42)
River: Dep
Gauging Station: Rychkovo

Date	Maximum discharge (m³/s) resulting from:		Maximum volume (10⁶m³) corresponding to max. discharge resulting from:	
	Rainfall	Snowmelt	Rainfall	Snowmelt
1	2	3	4	5
10−08−42	668		643	
24−09−43	638		442	
02−08−44	208		203	
24−06−45	376		ʼ ౨	
20−09−46	732		969	
23−08−47	584		260	
13−06−48	902		420	
11−08−49	883		544	
07−05−50		1080		566
11−10−51	648		362	
19−07−52	432		209	
12−07−53	2000		1380	
19−06−54	291		260	
17−08−55	1380		634	
08−06−56	1040		833	
02−09−57	445		236	
30−06−58	725		285	
29−08−59	864		1530	
21−07−60	917		820	
16−07−61	1210		663	
24−09−62	387		419	
05−07−63	1590		596	
07−07−64	3970		1070	
07−06−65	382		175	
30−05−67		950		918
01−07−68	708		285	
29−06−69	480		283	
25−09−70	525		324	
13−07−71	624		445	
26−07−72	1620		854	

Country: U.S.S.R. (43)
River: Ussuri
Gauging Station: Kirovsky

Date	Maximum discharge (m³/s) resulting from:		Maximum volume (10⁶m³) corresponding to max. discharge resulting from:	
	Rainfall	Snowmelt	Rainfall	Snowmelt
1	2	3	4	5
13−08−27	9380			
01−08−28	2570		1230	
01−09−29	1760		1930	
26−08−30	597		747	
19−05−31	5560		2080	
17−08−32	6400		3890	
11−06−33	910		975	
14−09−34	3090		1430	
20−05−35	2950		1600	
24−05−36	3090		1960	
12−05−37	618		562	
03−09−38	6610		3110	
14−07−39	1790		612	
12−06−40	546		655	
06−05−41	2540		1980	
14−10−42	1100		1200	
01−09−43	777		707	
10−05−44	2460		1530	
11−05−45	756		1290	
02−09−46	1540		935	
05−10−47	2350		1630	
10−05−48	1480		2000	
17−10−49	376		506	
24−07−50	10300		3840	
22−09−51	3780		2950	
09−07−52	974		917	
20−05−53	1080		1160	
20−08−54	1020		1210	
04−06−55	779		900	
15−05−56	2640		1960	

TABLE II — ANNUAL MAXIMUM DISCHARGES AND VOLUMES   (cont'd)

Country:	U.S.S.R. (43) cont'd
River:	Ussuri
Gauging Station:	Kirovsky

Date	Maximum discharge (m³/s) resulting from:		Maximum volume (10⁶m³) corresponding to max. discharge resulting from:	
	Rainfall	Snowmelt	Rainfall	Snowmelt
1	2	3	4	5
08—06—57	918		980	
29—05—58	944		748	
14—07—59	888		715	
28—06—60	1700		1240	
24—05—61	594		342	
12—09—62	5520		3770	
30—09—63	540		426	
10—06—64	1290		1270	
27—05—65	913		752	
13—07—66	1820		1280	
05—07—67	677		1100	
05—09—68	4430		3100	
30—05—69	849		1210	
17—05—70	1660		1640	
10—08—71	4820		2560	
16—10—72	1070		743	

Country:	U.S.S.R. (44)
River:	Souyfoun
Gauging Station:	Terekhovka

Date	Maximum discharge (m³/s) resulting from:		Maximum volume (10⁶m³) corresponding to max. discharge resulting from:	
	Rainfall	Snowmelt	Rainfall	Snowmelt
1	2	3	4	5
10—08—28	1380		667	
30—06—29	739		376	
20—07—30	144		90.4	
14—06—31	3940		1740	
03—08—32	4140		1270	
09—06—33	196		98.1	
12—09—34	1080		561	
23—05—36	524		783	
03—06—37	193		153	
31—08—38	5580		3100	
28—06—39	1010		510	
16—06—40	437		474	
31—08—41	713		582	
30—07—42	188		164	
30—08—43	5780		1770	
08—05—44	577		439	
05—06—45	1060		771	
29—08—46	2450		1050	
02—10—47	157		98.8	
10—07—48	941		630	
07—06—49	170		100	
24—07—50	4840		1680	
11—06—51	787		647	
19—10—52	227		204	
23—08—53	281		180	
17—09—54	1450		711	
01—06—55	860		1020	
12—09—56	1600		676	
24—08—57	1890		938	
26—05—58	524		440	

TABLE II – ANNUAL MAXIMUM DISCHARGES AND VOLUMES   (cont'd)

Country:	U.S.S.R. (44) cont'd				Country:				
River:	Souyfoun				River:				
Gauging Station:	Terekhovka				Gauging Station:				

Date	Maximum discharge (m³/s) resulting from:		Maximum volume (10⁶m³) corresponding to max. discharge resulting from:		Date	Maximum discharge (m³/s) resulting from:		Maximum volume (10⁶m³) corresponding to max. discharge resulting from:	
	Rainfall	Snowmelt	Rainfall	Snowmelt		Rainfall	Snowmelt	Rainfall	Snowmelt
1	2	3	4	5	1	2	3	4	5
21–09–59	595		347						
08–06–60	704		705						
08–09–61	1260		735						
10–09–62	511		232						
21–08–63	502		402						
24–08–64	682		341						
09–08–65	3580		1110						
20–08–66	686		524						
16–06–67	141		210						
26–08–68	1930		775						
29–08–69	657		519						
14–05–70	672		290						
20–09–71	1050		701						
13–08–72	2200		1030						

TABLE III — CHARACTERISTICS OF SNOWMELT FLOODS

			Characteristic elements							Type of probability curve	
No.	River	Gauging station	Q_{max} (m^3/s)	Date	h (mm)	T_T (hours)	t_i (hours)	P_W (%)	$P_{Q_{max}}$ (%)	for P_W	for $P_{Q_{max}}$
1	2	3	4	5	6	7	8	9	10	11	12
1	Pechora	Ust-Tsilima	39500	08–06–52	299	78	31	1	37	Binomial	
			34600	06–06–34	322	74	37	5	20	"	
			33400	02–06–66	282	58	29	8	52	"	
			32700	14–06–35	334	79	31	9	12	"	
			30600	22–06–58	356	70	47	15	3	"	
2	Mezen	Malonisogorskaya	9530	02–06–52	197	39	10	2	50	"	
			9040	26–06–66	284	52	25	4	3	"	
			8820	26–05–23	244	57	20	4	20	"	
			8380	21–05–64	224	38	14	7	35	"	
			7930	29–05–61	241	48	18	10	21	"	
3	Vaga	Filaevskaya	2100	16–05–61	222	54	22	3	14	"	
			1090	03–05–62	190	57	28	3	26	"	
			1740	23–04–53	152	49	17	10	50	"	
			1650	11–05–68	188	66	38	14	27	"	
			1560	09–05–55	233	52	21	18	10	"	
4	Verebushka	Oksotchi	18.3	27–04–46	194	58	24	23.2	25.5	"	
			25.8	09–05–55	250	47	25	3.3	8.5	"	
			20.2	30–04–56	246	57	24	14.8	9.4	"	
			16.9	15–04–62	223	45	14	31.5	15.0	"	
			20.5	27–04–66	297	53	28	13.7	2.9	"	

	Method of curve fitting		Snow cover		Rainfall during snowmelt (mm)	Monthly precipitation before soil freezing (mm)	Mean monthly temperature before snowmelt (°C)
No.	for W	for Q_{max}	Water equivalent (mm)	Layer thickness (cm)			
1	13	14	15	16	17	18	19
1	Graphical						
	"						
	"						
	"						
2	"		210	90	56	122	-1.8
	"		225	80	115	157	-2.1
	"		190	70	188	158	-4.9
	"		245	100	62	151	-2.6
	"		245	90	146	104	-4.7
3	"		228	75	74	117	-1.8
	"		269	95	84	196	-8.3
	"		177	60	78	236	-5.0
	"		164	65	118	259	-0.8
	"		194	70	177	225	-6.5
4	"			69	33.5		
	"			62		80.8	-4.8
	"		206	71	72.5	92.6	-10.6
	"			67		72.5	-6.3
	"		252	71	74.4	51.1	-2.4

TABLE III – CHARACTERISTICS OF SNOWMELT FLOODS (cont'd)

No.	River	Gauging station	Q_{max} (m³/s)	Date	h (mm)	T_T (hours)	t_i (hours)	P_W (%)	$P_{Q_{max}}$ (%)	Type of probability curve for P_W	for $P_{Q_{max}}$
1	2	3	4	5	6	7	8	9	10	11	12
5	Lovat	Kholm	1210	08–04–46	160	89	18	28.2	14.5	Binomial	
			1400	02–05–55	165	66	17	16.8	12.0	''	
			1270	27–04–56	156	63	10	24.1	17.0	''	
			1720	12–04–62	177	69	7	6.0	7.2	''	
			1120	07–04–66	182	104	34	35.0	5.7	''	
6	Dnieper	Smolensk	1820	01–05–08	291	58	18	2	0.1	''	
			1720	01–05–31	193	42	15	2	9	''	
			1650	28–04–58	233	58	22	3	2	''	
			1500	09–05–29	191	48	20	4	10	''	
			1440	22–04–17	196	51	20	5	8	''	
7	Pripiat	Mozir	5670	22–04–95	119	97	21	2	3	''	
			5100	05–04–88	118	122	27	2	4	''.	
			4700	25–04–89	100	110	34	3	13	''	
			4520	23–04–40	98	121	41	4	15	''	
			4220	19–04–32	115	126	17	5	5	''	
9	Southern Bug	Aleksandrovka	5320	08–04–32	75	66	31	1	1	''	
10	Dnieper	Kiev	23100	02–05–31	133	87	27	1	3	''	
			18500	21–04–70	155	99	30	2	1	''	
			17500	22–04–17	127	109	26	3	6	''	
11	Desna	Chernigov	8000	20–04–70	173	96	27	2	2	''	

No.	Method of curve fitting for W	for Q_{max}	Snow cover Water equivalent (mm)	Layer thickness (cm)	Rainfall during snowmelt (mm)	Monthly precipitation before soil freezing (mm)	Mean monthly temperature before snowmelt (°C)
1	13	14	15	16	17	18	19
5		Graphical					
		''		24		56.9	–7.6
		''	129	37	42.9	37.6	–6.5
		''		38		35.7	–7.7
		''		23		25.7	–12.2
6		''					
		''					
		''			28	25	–6.8
		''					
		''					
7		''					
		''					
		''					
		''					
		''					
9		''					
10		''	140	70	35	59	–3.1
		''		12		37	–2.7
		''	160	80	40	31	–7.0
11		''		13		45	–3.0

TABLE III — CHARACTERISTICS OF SNOWMELT FLOODS (cont'd)

No.	River	Gauging station	Q_{max} (m^3/s)	Date	h (mm)	T_T (hours)	t_i (hours)	P_W (%)	$P_{Q_{max}}$ (%)	Type of probability curve for P_W	for $P_{Q_{max}}$
1	2	3	4	5	6	7	8	9	10	11	12
12	Golovesnia	Pokoshichi	28	26—03—51	125	64	13	8	20	Binomial	
13	Don	Razdorskaya	11300	04—05—32	92	99	52	5	11	"	
			13100	13—05—42	112	90	48	2	5	"	
14	Medveditsa	Archedinskaya	2070	05—05—29	109	64	30	2.5	3	"	
			1690	21—04—46	89	65	29	7	8	"	
			1960	23—04—48	87	45	18	3.5	9	"	
15	Teberda	Teberda	272	28—07—27	1140	128	97	7.2	82.4	"	
			319	08—07—36	886	99	46	1.9	90.2	"	
			243	03—08—40	1730	180	126	12.6	7	"	
			292	20—07—70	1530	162	108	4.6	27.8	"	
16	Kalaus	Svetlograd	249	13—03—32	29	23	4	4.2	4.2	"	
			257	01—04—54	43	47	7	1.7	1.7	"	
			184	22—02—60	17	60	8	6.7	11.6	"	
17	Terek	Ordzhonikidze	369	17—08—53	846	168	100	2.7	10	"	
			365	29—07—61	758	163	93	3	12	"	
			424	06—03—67	764	141	103	1.5	30	"	
18	Unzha	Makariev	2520	05—05—47	285	95	32	1.1	2.1	"	
			1700	03—05—55	286	97	17	33	2	"	
			2520	08—05—57	189	41	21	1.1	26	"	

No.	Method of curve fitting for W	for Q_{max}	Snow cover Water equivalent (mm)	Layer thickness (cm)	Rainfall during snowmelt (mm)	Monthly precipitation before soil freezing (mm)	Mean monthly temperature before snowmelt (°C)
1	13	14	15	16	17	18	19
12	Graphical			29		42	−3.0
13		"			3.3	31.9	−6.8
		"			8.8	57.8	−7.8
14		"					
		"	64	14	30	33.3	−5.4
		"	79	23	14	46.9	−6.2
15		"					
		"					
		"			27.8		−0.6
		"			0	108	−0.9
					112	48.3	−0.6
16		"			10.6	24.7	−5.5
		"	154	57	6.1	36	−3.0
		"	29	12	0	27.9	−3.2
17		"		15		8	−1.8
		"		16		5.5	−5.0
		"		20		2.8	−0.3
18		Moments		84		31	−6.6
		"		60		76.1	−8.1
		"	207	77	57	53.3	−9.5

TABLE III — CHARACTERISTICS OF SNOWMELT FLOODS (cont'd)

No.	River	Gauging station	Q_{max} (m^3/s)	Date	h (mm)	T_T (hours)	t_i (hours)	P_W (%)	$P_{Q_{max}}$ (%)	Type of probability curve for P_W	for $P_{Q_{max}}$
1	2	3	4	5	6	7	8	9	10	11	12
19	Ishim	Tselinograd	1200	16—04—48	90.1	46	5	3.5	2.1	Binomial	
			1080	19—04—49	66	63	5	4.5	5	"	
			883	21—04—42	60	46	5	8	7	"	
			668	15—04—41	46.7	48	5	14	14	"	
20	Ishim	Petropavlovsk	3760	23—04—41	46	106	7	6	5	"	
			3340	14—05—42	39.1	123	26	7	8	"	
			3750	08—05—48	59.5	117	34	6	2.2	"	
			2480	07—05—54	46.4	118	17	13	5	"	
21	Ob	Salekhard	42800	07—08—41	169	154	86	2.5	5	"	
			41500	25—05—47	181	186	34	6	3	"	
			40000	01—08—48	170	172	99	12.3	5	"	
			43800	04—07—71	165	144	62	1.5	6	"	
22	Pur	Samburg	5300	09—06—46	218	109	40	84	2	"	
			7400	12—06—59	219	69	17	10	1.98	"	
			7210	19—06—63	208	86	28	14	4.5	"	
			6400	11—06—71	210	92	28	41	4.3	"	
23	Biya	Biysk	5770	30—04—69	416	95	20	1	14	"	
			5040	12—05—37	382	141	33	2.2	21	"	
			4790	15—06—36	525	182	61	3.1	2.7	"	
			4610	15—05—22	484	176	38	5.6	5	"	
			4030	12—06—66	398	98	57	7	18	"	

No.	Method of curve fitting for W	for Q_{max}	Snow cover Water equivalent (mm)	Layer thickness (cm)	Rainfall during snowmelt (mm)	Monthly precipitation before soil freezing (mm)	Mean monthly temperature before snowmelt (°C)
1	13	14	15	16	17	18	19
19	Graphical		60	22	4	56	−17.5
	"				13	38	−15.2
		"	109	33		42	
		"		33		10	
20		"		29	25	20	−8.3
		"			20	17	−14.5
		"		20	0.2	24	−17.0
		"	90	33		16	−13.4
21		"					
		"					
		"					
		"					
22		"	257	78	104	334	−20.5
		"	214	86	49	294	−18.9
		"	305	111	36	209	−18.3
		"		77		267	−19.8
23		"	256	60	272	324	−12.4
		"			375	129	−3.5
		"		35	462	23.6	−11.7
		"		54	340	152	−12.7
		"	305	117	294	152	−7.8

TABLE III — CHARACTERISTICS OF SNOWMELT FLOODS (cont'd)

No.	River	Gauging station	Q_{max} (m³/s)	Date	h (mm)	T_T (hours)	t_i (hours)	P_W (%)	$P_{Q_{max}}$ (%)	Type of probability curve for P_W	for $P_{Q_{max}}$
1	2	3	4	5	6	7	8	9	10	11	12
24	Usa	Mezhdourechensk	2590	02—06—58	1200	76	48	3.8	15	Binomial	
			2440	01—06—46	993	97	60	5.7	36	"	
			2430	20—05—62	1070	81	42	6	26	"	
			2400	26—05—69	1350	74	30	7	6.3	"	
			1950	08—06—41	1540	109	54	19	2.2	"	
25	Tym	Napas	1180	12—06—70	242	105	27	1	1	"	
			1070	07—06—60	176	83	31	2.3	20	"	
			987	10—05—59	160	80	42	6.9	33	"	
			918	12—06—58	124	73	36	15	70	"	
26	Yenisei	Yeniseisk	57400	18—05—37	96	83	19	1.1	17.9	"	
			46600	13—05—23	79	78	26	2.6	54.6	"	
			44700	26—05—41	120	90	36	4.1	1.1	"	
27	Abakan	Abaza	6700	29—05—69	622	85	45	1.7	6.7	"	
			4230	19—05—54	483	86	30	4.3	41	"	
			3650	21—05—62	382	85	34	9.4	76	"	
28	Tuba	Bugurtak	10500	09—06—66	819	102	54	1.1	1.2	"	
			8240	22—05—65	538	98	49	2.7	31	"	
			7750	02—06—16	643	101	35	4.3	9.4	"	
29	Graviyka	Igarka	212	15—06—58	309	47	10	2	59	"	
			197	25—06—61	483	51	29	5	2	"	
			190	21—06—68	370	42	14	8.1	32	"	

No.	Method of curve fitting for W	for Q_{max}	Snow cover Water equivalent (mm)	Layer thickness (cm)	Rainfall during snowmelt (mm)	Monthly precipitation before soil freezing (mm)	Mean monthly temperature before snowmelt (°C)
1	13	14	15	16	17	18	19
24	Graphical			109		284	−11.5
	"			122		353	−11.5
	"			104		232	−4.7
	"			138		346	0.7
	"						
25	"		203	72	174	108	−2.3
	"		192	87	186	189	−2.5
	"		260	98	84.4	154	−8.4
	"		203	84	98.3	139	−5.5
26	"						−16.9
	"						−4.6
	"						−5.4
27	"			61	223	30.3	−3.5
	"			40	307	44	−3.8
	"			40	158	50.4	−1.4
28	"			97	272	57.4	−3.4
	"			73	126	32.5	−6.6
	"						
29	"			64	55.7	58.5	−2.7
	"			108	24.9	65.5	−3.2
	"			51	57.7	68.5	−3.9

TABLE III — CHARACTERISTICS OF SNOWMELT FLOODS (cont'd)

No.	River	Gauging station	Q_{max} (m³/s)	Date	h (mm)	T_T (hours)	t_i (hours)	P_W (%)	$P_{Q_{max}}$ (%)	Type of probability curve for P_W	for $P_{Q_{max}}$
1	2	3	4	5	6	7	8	9	10	11	12
30	Selenga	Mostovoy	4200	02–06–51	32	110	58	5	1.2	Binomial	
			3620	06–05–68	19	68	33	9	19	"	
31	Khilok	Maleta	830	08–05–68	54	81	38	4	2	"	
			726	02–05–53	33	83	38	7	21	"	
			591	05–05–52	46	85	36	14	6	"	
32	Bolshaya	Possolskaya	147	01–06–52	311	64	32	2	28	"	
			139	12–06–70	549	75	36	4	0.5	"	
			127	31–05–68	411	80	46	6	6	"	
34	Lena	Kusur	161000	07–06–52	151	92	20	15	16	"	
			143000	09–06–41	174	96	22	35	3	"	
			166000	06–06–62	150	69	15	11	17	"	
			136000	20–06–63	161	72	22	46	7	"	
			159000	06–06–66	157	75	21	16	9	"	
35	Indigirka	Vorontsovo	9240	07–07–42	108	60	40	28	10	"	
			8080	09–07–44	121	70	48	49	4	"	
			10300	03–07–47	122	60	33	15	4	"	
			9980	06–07–54	138	63	39	18	1	"	
			11700	15–06–67	116	50	27	5	5	"	
36	Zbitiem	Zbetem	282	25–06–39	310	37	30	63	11	"	
			278	18–06–47	328	52	21	64	8	"	
			296	12–06–48	338	43	17	58	7	"	
			479	09–06–55	313	46	15	13	11	"	
			572	12–06–64	376	36	11	5	4	"	

No.	Method of curve fitting for W	for Q_{max}	Snow cover Water equivalent (mm)	Layer thickness (cm)	Rainfall during snowmelt (mm)	Monthly precipitation before soil freezing (mm)	Mean monthly temperature before snowmelt (°C)
1	13	14	15	16	17	18	19
30		Graphical					
		"					
31		"	77	35	1.2	37.3	−22.6
		"	36	17	0	34.8	−29.9
		'	46	24	0	43.2	−27.0
32		"				7.5	−18.7
		"		34	0	126	−18.8
		"		61	0	52.1	−21.1
34		"					
		"					
		"					
		"					
		"					
35		"					
		"					
		"					
		"					
		"					
36		"	224	78		44.4	−6.3
		"		39		38.6	−3.0
		"		82		31.3	−4.2
		"	96	48		42.6	−4.3
		"	234	88		47.2	−5.2

TABLE III — CHARACTERISTICS OF SNOWMELT FLOODS (cont'd)

										Type of probability curve	
No.	River	Gauging station	Q_{max} (m^3/s)	Date	h (mm)	T_T (hours)	t_i (hours)	P_W (%)	$P_{Q_{max}}$ (%)	for P_W	for $P_{Q_{max}}$
1	2	3	4	5	6	7	8	9	10	11	12
38	Kolyma	Ust-Srednikan	13000	15—06—56	239	53	25	3	2	Binomial	
			11800	14—06—51	188	49	28	5	6	"	
			10800	07—06—38	136	29	17	8	23	"	
			10500	24—06—47	173	42	25	9	8	"	
			10500	25—05—68	97	20	8	9	42	"	
39	Amguema	Mouth of the Brook Shoumny	6790	24—06—62	330	34	15	3	3	"	
			5780	16—06—57	220	30	15	8	22	"	
			5300	18—06—47	261	42	19	14	10	"	
			5230	22—06—71	187	41	14	15	39	"	
			5160	19—06—56	196	40	8	15	34	"	
40	Iziskatelski	1.6 km upstream the mouth	14.4	05—07—50	516	25	23	4	11	"	
			13.0	24—06—62	453	19	11	7	19	"	
			12.3	29—06—66				10		"	
			11.0	19—06—48	441	36	28	14	20	"	
			10.1	20—06—67	544	40	27	19	9	"	
41	Khasyn	Kolyma Road, 79th km	244	10—06—56	501	64	32	2	2	"	
			213	12—06—51	392	44	28	4	4	"	
			175	28—05—59	192	40	21	7	23	"	
			157	14—06—65	195	38	33	10	22	"	
			147	04—06—67	305	50	35	11	8	"	

	Method of curve fitting		Snow cover		Rainfall during snowmelt (mm)	Monthly precipitation before soil freezing (mm)	Mean monthly temperature before snowmelt (°C)
No.	for W	for Q_{max}	Water equivalent (mm)	Layer thickness (cm)			
1	13	14	15	16	17	18	19
38	Graphical			91		38.6	−19.4
	"			79		76.4	−19.5
	"		176	79	3.9	54.8	−19.0
	"			67		92.6	−17.2
	"		118	54	52.7	54.3	−7.4
39	"			74		54.1	−5.4
	"			47		65.8	−9.2
	"		212	68	7.4	79	−9.6
	"			41		50.6	−11.4
40	"			81		11	−10.1
	"			110		7.3	−6.0
	"		243	76	12.8	21.4	−15.4
	"			57		9.2	−9.5
	"			75		7.1	−11.9
41	"			105		83.3	−12.3
	"			82		68.3	−9.6
	"			55		15.8	−7.0
	"			90		1.6	−9.6
	"			75		114	−10.4

TABLE IV — CHARACTERISTICS OF RAINFALL FLOODS

No.	River	Gauging station	Q_{max} (m³/s)	Date	h (mm)	T_T (hours)	t_i (hours)	P_W (%)	$P_{Q_{max}}$ (%)	Type of probability curve for P_W	for $P_{Q_{max}}$
1	2	3	4	5	6	7	8	9	10	11	12
8	Dniester	Zaleschiki	8040	04—04—71	165	552	120	1	0.1	Binomial	
			5970	10—06—69	99	312	48	2	2	"	
16	Kalaus	Svetlograd	435	13—06—32	22	360	72	2.8	1.8		"
			181	04—06—56	5.7	480	72	10.5	16		"
			192	20—06—60	9.6	216	96	10	8		"
			500	13—06—64	3.7	144	24	2	24		"
			181	17—05—65	4	456	192	10.5	22		"
18	Unzha	Makariev	772	30—06—38	35	25	11	13	20		"
			1170	16—07—52	55	22	10	3	4.5		"
			1070	14—10—53	51	16	8	4.5	5.0		"
			994	11—09—65	51	14	11	6	5		"
27	Abakan	Abaza	5800	22—06—32	139	15	6	1.7	1.7		"
			3750	20—07—41	83.5	11	5	4.2	7.2		"
			2580	14—07—72	89.7	16	9	6.7	6.7		"
28	Tuba	Bugurtak	5270	28—09—55	130	30	14	1.2	2.9		"
			3180	30—09—37	61.4	12	6	2.9	16.6		"
			3080	03—08—60	94.5	23	7	4.6	6.3		"
30	Selenga	Mostovoy	7620	11—06—36	12	288	120	1.1	62		"
			6480	06—08—40	11	336	168	3	68		"
			6370	05—08—71	28	1100	480	4	6		"

No.	Method of curve fitting for W	for Q_{max}	Rainfall forming flood (mm)	Snowmelt during floods (mm)	Maximum daily rainfall (mm)	Date	Hourly maximum rainfall (mm)	Date	Antecedent precipitation for 10 days (mm)	30 days (mm)
1	13	14	15	16	17	18	19	20	21	22
8	Graphical									
	"		110		74	08—06			89	92
16		"	81.2		32.6	13—04			18	28.6
		"	54.9		41.2	02—06			9.8	74.6
		"	63.7		36.1	19—06			37.5	84.6
		"	30.2		13.4	13—06			50.0	92.7
		"	36.6		19	16—05			12	56.2
18	Moments		99.4		35.6	22—06			11.9	35.4
		"	140		52.6	06—07			37.2	81.5
		"	62		17.5	05—10			28.3	192
		"	110		35.2	04—06			28.4	70.5
27	Graphical		221							
		"	257							
		"	218	31						
28		"		67						
		"								
		"		108						
30		"								
		"								
		"								

TABLE IV — CHARACTERISTICS OF RAINFALL FLOODS (cont'd)

No.	River	Gauging station	Q_{max} (m³/s)	Date	h (mm)	T_T (hours)	t_i (hours)	P_W (%)	$P_{Q_{max}}$ (%)	Type of probability curve for P_W	for $P_{Q_{max}}$
1	2	3	4	5	6	7	8	9	10	11	12
31	Khilok	Maleta	795	07—09—38	86	1970	600	6	0.1	Binomial	
			770	12—07—40	62	1440	360	7	0.7	"	
			753	09—09—69	33	408	288	7	10	"	
32	Bolshaya	Possolskaya	444	15—07—42	207	384	72	0.4	1.2		"
			333	20—07—71	365	912	92	2	0.02		"
33	Vitim	Romanovka	3400	26—08—49	82	456	120	6	3		"
			3200	31—07—71	88	336	192	7	2		"
			2930	20—07—48	83	408	144	11	3		"
37	Timpton	Nagorni	352	13—07—26	99	336	72	17	15		"
			344	11—07—27	109	264	120	18	10		"
			358	15—07—38	144	288	120	17	3		"
			260	21—08—47	116	144	72	27	8		"
			231	02—07—68	113	192	72	32	9		"
38	Kolyma	Ust-Srednikan	17800	24—08—39	83	384	88	0.9	2		"
			9450	27—08—40	63	580	180	8	8		"
			9300	27—06—68	41	216	87	9	30		"
			9060	25—06—38	47	264	139	10	21		"
			8340	01—08—58	28	192	56	13	54		"
40	Iziskatelski	1.6 km upstream the mouth	54.0	14—09—69	238	122	30	1	2		"
			24.0	25—07—63	60	56	13	6	75		"
			19.5	09—08—50	210	132	72	11	3		"
			17.0	13—09—48	196	140	2	16	4		"

No.	Method of curve fitting for W	for Q_{max}	Rainfall forming flood (mm)	Snowmelt during floods (mm)	Maximum daily rainfall (mm)	Date	Hourly maximum rainfall (mm)	Date	Antecedent precipitation for 10 days (mm)	30 days (mm)
1	13	14	15	16	17	18	19	20	21	22
31		Graphical	215						35.8	68.7
		"	234						3.6	52.8
		"	70.2						63.4	168
32		"								
		"	411		84.1	20—07			17.6	97.5
33		"	95.4						35.1	159
			140						44.4	62.9
			101						46.2	118
37		"			17.7	11—07			5.9	174
		"	152		51.3	07—07			40.4	144
		"	192		67	15—07			36.3	239
		"			41.4	21—08			48.8	89.4
		"			36.6	01—07			47.1	168
38		"							93.1	133.3
		"							66.8	98.5
		"	59.7						63.4	99.1
		"							29.8	84.1
		"							49.7	92.6
40		"			130	14—09			225	275
		"			48.7	25—07			59.6	121
		"			50.3	09—07			70.5	156
		"			25.2	13—09			52.1	68.4

TABLE IV — CHARACTERISTICS OF RAINFALL FLOODS (cont'd)

			Characteristic element							Type of probability curve	
No.	River	Gauging station	Q_{max} (m^3/s)	Date	h (mm)	T_T (hours)	t_i (hours)	P_W (%)	$P_{Q_{max}}$ (%)	for P_W	for $P_{Q_{max}}$
1	2	3	4	5	6	7	8	9	10	11	12
41	Khasyn	Kolyma Road, 79th km	514	19–07–50	45	96	8	0.9	35	Binomial	
			513	03–10–63	48	280	22	0.9	30	"	
			420	20–09–44	76	216	32	2	7	"	
			318	24–09–55	65	168	54	8	15	"	
			300	25–09–43	90	264	98	9	3	"	
42	Dep	Rychkovo	3970	07–07–64	126	456	144	1	9	Lognormal	
			2000	12–07–53	164	600	216	8	4	"	
			1620	26–07–72	101	312	120	12	17	"	
43	Ussuri	Kirovsky	10300	24–07–50	158	648	144	2.6	4.9	Binomial	
			9380	13–08–27				3.6		"	
			6610	03–09–38	127	695	192	8.2	9.6	"	
			6400	17–08–32	159	408	144	8.5	4.8	"	
44	Souyfoun	Terekhovka	5780	30–08–43	114	1300	216	2.8	8.9	"	
			5580	31–08–38	200	984	408	2.9	1.3	"	
			4840	24–07–50	108	792	96	4.5	9.8	"	

	Method of curve fitting		Rainfall forming flood (mm)	Snowmelt during floods (mm)	Maximum daily rainfall (mm)	Date	Hourly maximum rainfall (mm)	Date	Antecedent precipitation for	
No.	for W	for Q_{max}							10 days (mm)	30 days (mm)
1	13	14	15	16	17	18	19	20	21	22
41	Graphical		57.7		40.9	19–07			80.2	98.1
		"	58.6		30.1	03–10			58.6	66.9
		"	87.4		45.2	20–09			89.1	126
		"			36.9	24–09			74.5	79.4
		"			26.6	24–09			68	116
42		"	257		100	05–07			33.6	52.8
		"	260		75.6	15–07			7.8	46.3
		"	150		37.6	22–07			67.2	113
43		"								
		"								
		"								
		"								
44		"								
		"								
		"								

United Kingdom / Royaume-Uni / Reino Unido / Соединенное Королевство

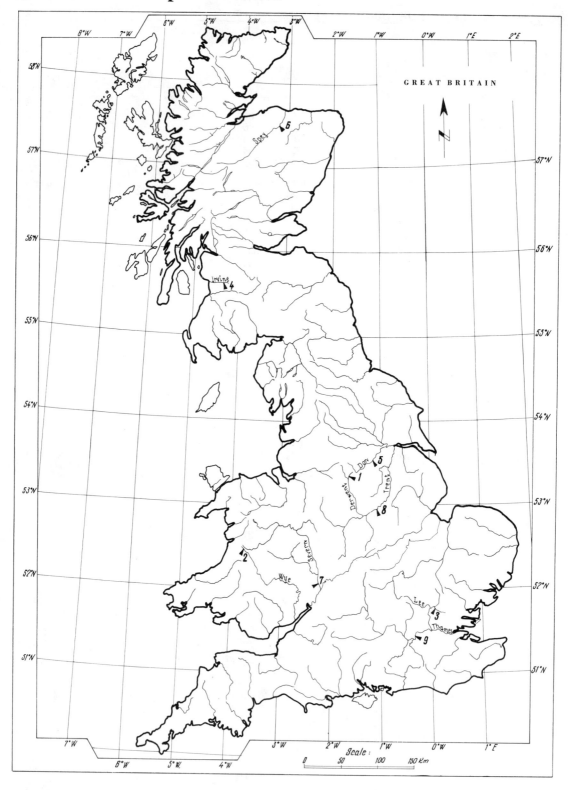

GREAT BRITAIN

TABLE I — CHARACTERISTICS OF BASIN

No.	River / River system	Name	Period of records	Co-ordinates Lat.	Long.	Distance (km) from gauging site to remotest point of river system L_{rs}	to projection of centre of basin on main course L_{ca}	Mean slope of river I_r (%)	Area A (km^2)	Altitude (m) Mean H_m	Max. H_{max}	Min. H_{min}
1	2	3	4	5	6	7	8	9	10	11	12	13
1	Burbage Brook Trent	Burbage	1925–74	N 53:19.1	1:36.7W	4.18	1.93	3.3	9.1	362	442	382
2	Wye	Cefn Brwyn	1950–74	52:26.3	3:43.3W	4.35	2.83	3.7	10.4	496	740	351
3	Canons Brook Lee	Harlow	1950–74	51:46.3	0.4.5E	5.60	2.32	7.5	21.4	75	107	43
4	Irvine	Kilmarnock	1913–74	55:35.9	4:29.6W	24.8	13.3	0.82	218	163	384	23
5	Don	Doncaster	1868–74	53:31.7	1:8.4W	76.2	37.0	0.37	1260	172	547	10.8
6	Spey	Boat O'brig	1952–74	57:33.1	3:8.4W	151	76.2	0.18	2860	453	1310	43
7	Severn	Upton	1955–74	52:3.4	2:11.8W	248	70.4	0.05	6990	165	827	8
8	Trent	Colwick (Trent Bridge)	1883–74	52:57.1	1:4.6W	143	57.1	0.063	7490	139	636	16.8
9	Thames	Teddington	1882–74	51:25.9	0:19.6W	239	131	0.032	9670	111	330	4.7

No.	Width (km) Mean B_m	Max. B_{max}	Mean slope I_b (%)	Soils	Cover	Weighted lake area P_L (%)	Swamps R_s (%)	Mean annual precipitation P (mm)	Annual runoff Q (mm)	Mean annual temperature T (°C)	Regulating capacity of reservoirs α
1	14	15	16	17	18	19	20	21	22	23	24
1	2.2	2.5	10.2	Peaty gley	U	0	0	1000	650	10	0
2	2.4	3.1	19.8	60% Peaty podzols 40% Peaty gleys	U	0	0	2530	2200	10	0
3	3.8	7.5	2.6	Gleyed Silty till	C (20), U (80)	0	0	640	150	10	0
4	8.8	13.7	5.6	4 (90), 2 (10)	C (20), U (80)	0	0	1250	850	10	0
5	16.5	29.0	6.7	4 (90) Peaty gleys (10)	C (50), U (50)	0	0	798	361	10	
6	18.9	38.6	14.2	4 (90) Peaty gley (10)	U	0.1	0	1150	850	9	0
7	28.2	82.1	7.9	2 (50), 4 (35)	C (35), U (65)	0	0	850	420	10	0
8	52.4	113	5.0	4 (40), 2 (20) (40)	C (30), U (70)	0	0	785	300	10	
9	41.3	99.8	3.2	2 (70), Gley (30)	C (40), U (60)	0	0	735	246	10	0

TABLE II — ANNUAL MAXIMUM DISCHARGES AND VOLUMES

Country:	United Kingdom (1)		
River:	Burbage Brook		
Gauging Station:	Burbage		

Date	Maximum discharge (m³/s) resulting from:		Maximum volume (10⁶m³) corresponding to max. discharge resulting from:	
	Rainfall	Snowmelt	Rainfall	Snowmelt
1	2	3	4	5
15—09—27	29.1			
06—01—28	4.99			
25—11—28	3.04			
11—11—29	3.41			
04—09—31	15.2			
21—05—32	11.8			
04—03—33	3.15			
07—10—33	3.41			
04—12—34	2.83			
17—11—35	3.61			
17—03—37	4.32			
02—12—37	5.88			
14—01—39	5.26			
23—02—40	4.04			
08—02—41	6.06			
18—10—41	4.48			
11—01—43	2.99			
02—09—44	4.71			
27—11—44	2.80			
20—09—46	4.65			
21—03—47	4.99			
13—01—48	4.32			
06—04—49	3.70			
09—02—50	1.80			
13—03—51	2.35			
05—11—51	4.13			
13—10—52	4.16			
20—08—54	10.1			
26—03—55	6.18			
02—09—56	4.82			

Country:	United Kingdom (1) cont'd		
River:	Burbage Brook		
Gauging Station:	Burbage		

Date	Maximum discharge (m³/s) resulting from:		Maximum volume (10⁶m³) corresponding to max. discharge resulting from:	
	Rainfall	Snowmelt	Rainfall	Snowmelt
1	2	3	4	5
09—08—57	3.01			
01—07—58	27.8			
16—04—59	4.07			
27—08—60	4.29			
03—12—60	4.55			
10—10—61	3.26			
06—03—63	5.33			
18—07—64	7.20			
12—12—64	6.10			
09—12—65	6.25			
14—05—67	2.91			
16—10—67	5.23			
31—03—69	5.51			
12—04—70	5.14			
17—11—70	1.39			
20—11—71	1.73			
15—07—73	30.0			

TABLE II — ANNUAL MAXIMUM DISCHARGES AND VOLUMES (cont'd)

Country:	United Kingdom (2)
River:	Wye
Gauging Station:	Cefn Brwyn

	Maximum discharge (m³/s) resulting from:		Maximum volume (10⁶m³) corresponding to max. discharge resulting from:	
Date	Rainfall	Snowmelt	Rainfall	Snowmelt
1	2	3	4	5
10–01–52	15.7			
29–08–53	15.7			
13–11–53	19.1			
02–12–54	13.5			
26–01–56	13.8			
05–08–57	48.8			
23–09–58	12.4			
12–10–58	10.2			
26–10–59	18.3			
03–12–60	23.0			
23–08–62	17.6			
25–09–63	10.8			
11–07–64	11.9			
12–12–64	19.6			
27–06–66	18.1			
29–11–66	9.26			
27–02–67	9.26			
13–01–68	10.9			
12–08–69	16.8			
21–02–70	16.0			
11–70	22.9			
11–72	29.7			
05–08–73	57.1			

Country:	United Kingdom (3)
River:	Canons Brook
Gauging Station:	Harlow

	Maximum discharge (m³/s) resulting from:		Maximum volume (10⁶m³) corresponding to max. discharge resulting from:	
Date	Rainfall	Snowmelt	Rainfall	Snowmelt
1	2	3	4	5
08–02–51	4.44			
09–03–52	3.31			
10–02–53	3.40			
03–03–54	4.02			
09–12–54	4.59			
08–07–56	2.12			
01–10–56	4.81			
01–07–58	14.2			
02–11–58	5.46			
19–09–60	8.49			
04–12–60	10.6			
21–01–62	5.46			
31–08–63	3.17			
21–07–64	8.49			
20–07–65	6.09			
22–06–66	7.93			
25–06–67	4.39			
14–07–68	7.50			
03–08–69	10.6			

United Kingdom / Royaume-Uni / Reino Unido / Соединенное Королевство

TABLE II – ANNUAL MAXIMUM DISCHARGES AND VOLUMES (cont'd)

Country:	United Kingdom (4)
River:	Irvine
Gauging Station:	Kilmarnock

Date	Maximum discharge (m³/s) resulting from:		Maximum volume (10⁶m³) corresponding to max. discharge resulting from:	
	Rainfall	Snowmelt	Rainfall	Snowmelt
1	2	3	4	5
03–12–13	65.5			
28–11–14	64.8			
15–02–16	40.0			
14–10–16	55.0			
29–11–17	74.0			
25–09–19	64.1			
10–01–21	66.9			
15–05–22	76.0			
20–08–23	72.6			
02–11–23	65.5			
17–04–25	69.7			
14–09–26	64.1			
28–09–27	62.7			
02–11–27	71.8			
23–11–28	69.7			
19–08–30	62.7			
16–01–31	63.4			
03–01–32	14.1			
16–12–32	74.7			
12–04–34	56.6			
16–02–35	69.7			
25–07–36	52.6			
13–12–36	64.1			
30–07–38	63.4			
03–10–38	70.4			
16–09–40	64.8			
23–05–41	69.0			
03–01–42	53.4			
11–02–43	62.7			
02–07–44	71.1			

Country:	United Kingdom (4) cont'd
River:	Irvine
Gauging Station:	Kilmarnock

Date	Maximum discharge (m³/s) resulting from:		Maximum volume (10⁶m³) corresponding to max. discharge resulting from:	
	Rainfall	Snowmelt	Rainfall	Snowmelt
1	2	3	4	5
03–02–45	84.6			
24–10–45	81.9			
21–11–46	53.4			
15–09–48	96.7			
07–01–49	95.7			
25–10–49	89.4			
16–01–51	84.6			
06–02–52	66.2			
27–01–53	88.4			
15–11–53	109			
15–10–54	98.8			
01–03–56	74.7			
04–12–56	65.5			
07–12–57	81.9			
06–10–58	55.0			
26–10–59	90.4			
08–08–61	227			
08–12–62	54.2			
12–11–63	81.9			
09–01–65	58.2			
15–08–66	102			
19–12–66	129			
02–10–67	85.7			

TABLE II — ANNUAL MAXIMUM DISCHARGES AND VOLUMES (cont'd)

Country: United Kingdom (5)
River: Don
Gauging Station: Doncaster

Date	Maximum discharge (m³/s) resulting from:		Maximum volume (10⁶m³) corresponding to max. discharge resulting from:	
	Rainfall	Snowmelt	Rainfall	Snowmelt
1	2	3	4	5
09—12—68	221			
14—07—72	274			
08—08—75	114			
21—10—75	280			
05—01—77	191			
23—11—77	106			
30—12—78	138			
16—09—80	187			
28—10—80	307			
14—10—81	154			
29—01—83	196			
02—02—84	146			
14—05—86	326			
22—01—87	162			
21—03—89	196			
27—01—90	162			
06—01—91	190			
16—10—92	310			
21—01—95	187			
10—02—97	187			
26—11—98	143			
24—02—00	183			
01—01—01	132			
15—12—01	163			
11—05—03	101			
05—02—04	183			
01—03—06	91.8			
03—06—07	64.8			
17—10—07	154			
03—02—10	153			

Country: United Kingdom (5) cont'd
River: Don
Gauging Station: Doncaster

Date	Maximum discharge (m³/s) resulting from:		Maximum volume (10⁶m³) corresponding to max. discharge resulting from:	
	Rainfall	Snowmelt	Rainfall	Snowmelt
1	2	3	4	5
04—12—10	203			
27—08—12	153			
28—10—12	48.5			
07—10—13	82.5			
29—12—14	111			
18—03—16	224			
30—12—16	91.8			
20—01—18	132			
14—03—19	153			
01—02—20	153			
18—01—21	101			
09—08—22	277			
28—02—23	234			
12—02—25	143			
30—12—25	101			
11—04—27	121			
06—01—28	143			
05—01—29	132			
24—07—30	183			
06—09—31	323			
24—05—32	347			
33	276			
35	204			
36	96.6			
37	168			
38	73.6			
39	193			
40	222			
41	348			
12—09—43	41.0			

TABLE II – ANNUAL MAXIMUM DISCHARGES AND VOLUMES   (cont'd)

Country:	United Kingdom (5) cont'd					Country:	United Kingdom (6)				
River:	Don					River:	Spey				
Gauging Station:	Doncaster					Gauging Station:	Boat O'Brig				

Date	Maximum discharge (m³/s) resulting from:		Maximum volume (10⁶m³) corresponding to max. discharge resulting from:		Date	Maximum discharge (m³/s) resulting from:		Maximum volume (10⁶m³) corresponding to max. discharge resulting from:	
	Rainfall	Snowmelt	Rainfall	Snowmelt		Rainfall	Snowmelt	Rainfall	Snowmelt
1	2	3	4	5	1	2	3	4	5
25–01–44	108				51	341			
29–11–44	101				12–01–53	563			
20–09–46	210				03–12–53	508			
19–03–47	347				19–10–54	517			
13–01–48	143				30–07–56	1150			
07–04–49	98.2				18–08–57	960			
11–02–50	101				28–07–58	924			
17–02–51	98.2				19–01–59	313			
25–11–51	105				25–08–60	980			
18–02–53	85.6				13–10–60	389			
04–08–54	118				11–02–62	585			
27–03–55	153				14–12–62	588			
55	154				18–08–64	341			
56	100				18–09–65	517			
03–07–58	153				24–06–66	588			
17–04–59	81.1				17–12–66	704			
31–01–60	133				05–05–68	572			
05–12–60	217				31–10–68	377			
12–02–62	71.7				17–08–70	1600			
06–03–63	107								
15–03–64	99.5								
08–09–65	118								
10–12–65	267								
15–05–67	189								
23–09–68	205								
02–11–68	192								

TABLE II – ANNUAL MAXIMUM DISCHARGES AND VOLUMES (cont'd)

Country:	United Kingdom (7)
River:	Severn
Gauging Station:	Upton

Date	Maximum discharge (m³/s) resulting from:		Maximum volume (10⁶m³) corresponding to max. discharge resulting from:	
	Rainfall	Snowmelt	Rainfall	Snowmelt
1	2	3	4	5
30–01–56	450			
29–07–57	467			
13–02–58	487			
23–01–59	476			
25–01–60	538			
07–12–60	515			
13–01–62	365			
09–03–63	447			
26–03–64	382			
17–12–64	427			
22–12–65	487			
11–12–66	470			
18–01–68	478			
28–05–69	470			
22–02–70	430			

Country:	United Kingdom (8)
River:	Trent
Gauging Station:	Trent Bridge

Date	Maximum discharge (m³/s) resulting from:		Maximum volume (10⁶m³) corresponding to max. discharge resulting from:	
	Rainfall	Snowmelt	Rainfall	Snowmelt
1	2	3	4	5
18–02–85	271			
15–05–86	951			
21–01–87	867			
22–04–88	186			
10–03–89	823			
28–01–90	527			
25–11–90	484			
14–12–91	538			
23–02–93	371			
18–02–94	221			
22–01–95	787			
15–12–95	196			
07–02–97	802			
06–01–98	276			
22–01–99	325			
21–02–00	618			
01–01–01	967			
02–01–02	595			
19–03–03	338			
29–10–03	527			
15–03–05	119			
09–01–06	368			
03–01–07	410			
15–12–07	493			
25–03–09	221			
24–12–09	720			
03–12–10	908			
28–08–12	681			
25–01–13	360			
11–01–14	200			

United Kingdom / Royaume-Uni / Reino Unido / Соединенное Королевство

TABLE II – ANNUAL MAXIMUM DISCHARGES AND VOLUMES (cont'd)

Country:	United Kingdom (8) cont'd
River:	Trent
Gauging Station:	Trent Bridge

Date	Maximum discharge (m³/s) resulting from:		Maximum volume (10⁶m³) corresponding to max. discharge resulting from:	
	Rainfall	Snowmelt	Rainfall	Snowmelt
1	2	3	4	5
02–01–15	565			
04–03–16	689			
10–01–17	394			
20–01–18	475			
13–03–19	643			
24–12–19	447			
19–01–21	394			
06–08–22	506			
22–12–22	720			
04–06–24	481			
31–10–24	399			
09–02–26	658			
30–01–27	337			
25–01–28	600			
26–11–28	410			
11–12–29	512			
06–09–31	506			
23–05–32	945			
01–03–33	704			
15–01–34	206			
26–02–35	241			
24–12–35	708			
19–03–37	407			
03–12–37	272			
09–01–39	646			
24–02–40	780			
10–02–41	624			
26–01–42	502			
02–02–43	453			

Country:	United Kingdom (8) cont'd
River:	Trent
Gauging Station:	Trent Bridge

Date	Maximum discharge (m³/s) resulting from:		Maximum volume (10⁶m³) corresponding to max. discharge resulting from:	
	Rainfall	Snowmelt	Rainfall	Snowmelt
1	2	3	4	5
24–01–44	319			
02–02–45	561			
09–02–46	1010			
19–03–47	1110			
14–01–48	495			
02–01–49	624			
11–02–50	477			
08–01–51	624			
26–11–51	459			
21–12–52	374			
07–03–54	279			
27–03–55	747			
23–01–59	547			
31–01–60	733			
05–12–60	810			
12–01–62	266			
06–03–63	296			
15–03–64	356			
24–03–65	338			
11–12–65	731			
12–12–66	385			
15–01–68	468			
08–05–69	456			

Additional flood data

Year		ex. prov.
1795	1420 m³/s	0.043%
1875	1270 "	0.233
1852	1130 "	0.886

Ref: POTTER H. R. "Introduction to the history of the floods and droughts of the Trent Basin" Trent River Authority, Nottingham.

TABLE II – ANNUAL MAXIMUM DISCHARGES AND VOLUMES (cont'd)

Country:	United Kingdom (9)
River:	Thames
Gauging Station:	Teddington

Date	Maximum discharge (m³/s) resulting from:		Maximum volume (10⁶m³) corresponding to max. discharge resulting from:	
	Rainfall	Snowmelt	Rainfall	Snowmelt
1	2	3	4	5
03–02–84	231			
18–02–85	228			
07–12–85	244			
14–01–87	284			
28–03–88	208			
10–03–89	237			
30–01–90	205			
01–02–91	171			
25–10–91	339			
28–02–93	300			
19–02–94	173			
18–11–94	1060			
24–03–96	202			
07–02–97	351			
02–01–98	171			
14–02–99	262			
21–02–00	533			
13–04–01	200			
31–12–01	162			
21–06–03	386			
15–02–04	517			
17–03–05	229			
18–01–06	249			
03–01–07	220			
17–12–07	376			
08–03–09	204			
26–02–10	231			
18–12–10	428			
27–01–12	367			
24–01–13	255			

Country:	United Kingdom (9) cont'd
River:	Thames
Gauging Station:	Teddington

Date	Maximum discharge (m³/s) resulting from:		Maximum volume (10⁶m³) corresponding to max. discharge resulting from:	
	Rainfall	Snowmelt	Rainfall	Snowmelt
1	2	3	4	5
11–03–14	256			
05–01–15	585			
29–03–16	374			
26–12–16	327			
23–01–18	351			
08–03–19	334			
01–02–20	251			
05–01–21	240			
10–03–22	198			
14–04–23	231			
26–01–24	298			
04–01–25	522			
08–01–26	370			
02–03–27	375			
07–01–28	526			
30–12–28	235			
13–12–29	552			
01–12–30	228			
25–05–32	274			
28–02–33	479			
16–03–34	94.6			
01–03–35	227			
02–01–36	478			
25–01–37	438			
15–12–37	247			
01–02–39	369			
09–02–40	410			
19–11–40	384			
26–01–42	298			
02–02–43	457			

TABLE II — ANNUAL MAXIMUM DISCHARGES AND VOLUMES (cont'd)

Country:	United Kingdom (9) cont'd
River:	Thames
Gauging Station:	Teddington

	Maximum discharge (m³/s) resulting from:		Maximum volume (10⁶m³) corresponding to max. discharge resulting from:	
Date	Rainfall	Snowmelt	Rainfall	Snowmelt
1	2	3	4	5
24—01—44	115			
19—12—44	261			
30—12—45	257			
20—03—47	714			
31—01—48	227			
03—01—49	299			
04—02—50	324			
06—02—51	385			
20—11—51	377			
22—12—52	263			
14—06—54	231			
01—12—54	453			
01—02—56	316			
09—02—57	314			
26—02—58	317			
23—01—59	375			
25—01—60	308			
04—11—60	456			
23—01—62	344			
11—03—63	286			
16—03—64	369			
26—09—65	132			
26—02—66	324			
10—03—67	313			
17—09—68	600			
18—12—68	369			
24—01—70	233			
27—01—71	362			

Country:	United Kingdom (9) cont'd
River:	Thames
Gauging Station:	Teddington

Additional flood data

Year

1821 — 0.25 m above level of 1894 flood

1774, 1809 — probably greater than 1894

1823 — possibly greater than 1894

(1894 is highest flood in period of record)

Ref: SYMONS, G. J. and CHATTERTON. G. "The November floods of 1894 in the Thames Valley" Quart. Journal. Royal Met. Soc. XXI, 96, Oct. 1895.

TABLE IV — CHARACTERISTICS OF RAINFALL FLOODS

No.	River	Gauging station	Q_{max} (m^3/s)	Date	h (mm)	T_T (hours)	t_i (hours)	P_W (%)	$P_{Q_{max}}$ (%)	Type of probability curve for P_W	for $P_{Q_{max}}$
1	2	3	4	5	6	7	8	9	10	11	12
1	Burbage Brook	Burbage	30.0	16—07—73	64.8	31	3		0.46		G.E.V.
			27.8	01—07—58	21.7	18	1.8		0.57		"
			15.2	04—09—31	50.7	17	2		3.03		"
2	Wye	Cefn Brwyn	57.1	05—08—73	81.6	21	3		2.43		G.E.V.
			48.8	05—08—57	36.4	14			3.54		"
			23.0	03—12—60	85.0	36			11.7		"
3	Canons Brook	Harlow	14.2	01—07—58	20.4	29	5.5		3.12		G.E.V.
			10.6	04—12—60	10.2	27	4.9		9.10		"
4	Irvine	Kilmarnock	227	08—08—61	33.2	40	8		0.12		G.E.V.
			141	03—01—32					2.03		"
			129	19—12—66	24.3	30			3.35		"
5	Don	Doncaster	347	24—05—32					2.35		G.E.V.
			347	19—03—47	32.6	240	50		2.35		"
6	Spey	Boat O'Brig	1600	17—08—70	42.0	70	15		3.03		G.E.V.
			1150	30—07—56	21.7	65	15		8.44		"
			980	25—08—60	11.5	40	10		13.7		"
8	Trent	Trent Bridge (colwick)	1110	19—03—47	85.0	410	110		1.08		G.E.V.
			1010	09—02—46	27.0	180	50		2.47		"
			967	01—01—01	29.5	205	85		3.38		"

No.	Method of curve fitting for W	for Q_{max}	Rainfall forming flood (mm)	Snowmelt during floods (mm)	Maximum daily rainfall (mm)	Date	Hourly maximum rainfall (mm)	Date	Antecedent precipitation for 10 days (mm)	30 days (mm)
1	13	14	15	16	17	18	19	20	21	22
1		M.L.	105	No	105	15—07—73	17.5	15—07—73	28.7	28.7
		"	54.2	"	50	01—07—58	33.0	01—07—58	58	116
		"	82.5	"	43.4	04—09—31	10.8	04—09—31	62.7	210
2		M.L.	104	No	105	05—08—73	20.0	05—08—73	59.6	149
		"	78.2	"	78.2	05—08—57			30.7	265
		"	154	"	95.3	03—12—60			240	421
3		M.L.	36.1	No	35.0	01—07—58	9.6	01—07—58	74.3	365
		"	13.6	"	22.7	03—12—60	3.6	03—12—60	28.8	68.9
		"		"						
4		M.L.	78.7	No	78.7	08—08—61			70.6	199
		"	145	"	65.2	02—01—32			54.2	115
		"	41	"	41	19—12—66			52	181
5		M.L.	43.9	Yes	9.9	17—03—47			20.5	29.0
6		M.L.	66.4	No	47.0	16—08—70			23.4	188
		"	87.6	"	52.8	30—07—66			26.2	78.5
		"	75.9	"	75.9	25—08—60			39.9	151
8		M.L.	92.2	Yes	23.6	12—03—47			44.3	120
		"	31.2	No	16.4	07—02—46			84.0	113
		"	75.4	"	51.3	30—12—00			21.7	71.3

TABLE IV — CHARACTERISTICS OF RAINFALL FLOODS (cont'd)

No.	River	Gauging station	Characteristic element							Type of probability curve	
			Q_{max} (m^3/s)	Date	h (mm)	T_T (hours)	t_i (hours)	P_W (%)	$P_{Q_{max}}$ (%)	for P_W	for $P_{Q_{max}}$
1	2	3	4	5	6	7	8	9	10	11	12
9	Thames	Teddington	1070	18—11—94	36.5	360	110		0.11		G.E.V.
			714	20—03—47	50.0	480	180		1.61		"
			600	17—09—68	15.8	290	80		4.19		"

No.	Method of curve fitting		Rainfall forming flood (mm)	Snowmelt during floods (mm)	Maximum daily rainfall (mm)	Date	Hourly maximum rainfall (mm)	Date	Antecedent precipitation for	
	for W	for Q_{max}							10 days (mm)	30 days (mm)
1	13	14	15	16	17	18	19	20	21	22
9		M.L.	85.3	No	30.5	12—11—94			33.0	154
		"	88.4	Yes	20.6	11—03—47			40.4	47.3
		"	67.6	No	41.4	15—09—68			16.3	46.1

United States of America / États-Unis d'Amérique / Estados Unidos de América /
Соединенные Штаты Америки

ATLANTIC OCEAN

PACIFIC OCEAN

GULF OF MEXICO

Lake Superior

Lake Michigan

Lake Huron

Lake Erie

Lake Ontario

Missouri River

MISSOURI

KANSAS

ARKANSAS

Colorado

RIO GRANDE

Columbia River

Snake River

Ohio

Mississippi

RIVER

Scale:

0   200   400   600   800 km

TABLE I — CHARACTERISTICS OF BASIN

	GAUGING STATION								BASIN			
						Distance (km) from gauging site					Altitude (m)		
No.	River River system	Name	Period of records	Co-ordinates Lat.	Long.	to remotest point of river system L_{rs}	to projection of centre of basin on main course L_{ca}	Mean slope of river I_r (%)	Area A (km²)	Mean H_m	Max. H_{max}	Min. H_{min}
1	2	3	4	5	6	7	8	9	10	11	12	13
1	Cascade Cr.	Petersburg, Alas.	1917—20; 22—28; 46—71	N 57:00:21	E 132:46:45				60			37
2	Colorado	Grand Canyon, Ariz.	1874; 1921—70	36:06:05	112:05:08				357000			737
3	Salt	Chrysotile, Ariz.	1916; 1925—70	33:47:53	110:29:57				7400			1020
4	Arkansas	Little Rock, Ark.	1923; 27, 29—70	34:47:27	92:21:32				409000			68
5	Eel	Scotia, Calif.	1910—71	40:29:30	124:05:55				8100			11
6	Plum Cr.	Louviers, Colo.	1942—72	39:29:04	105:00:07				780			1700
7	Ute Cr.	Fort Garland, Colo.	1916; 23—71	37:26:50	105:25:30				83			2450
8	Altamaha	Doctortown, Ga.	1925—71	31:39:16	81:49:41				35200			9

	BASIN											
	Width (km)		Mean slope I_b(%)			Weighted lake area P_L (%)	Swamps R_s (%)	Mean annual precipitation P (mm)	Annual runoff Q (mm)	Mean annual temperature T (°C)	Regulating capacity of reservoirs α
No.	Mean B_m	Max. B_{max}		Soils	Cover						
1	14	15	16	17	18	19	20	21	22	23	24
1									3760		
2									42		
3									70		
4									86		
5									804		
6									28		
7									220		
8									341		

TABLE I — CHARACTERISTICS OF BASIN (cont'd)

			GAUGING STATION						BASIN			
						Distance (km) from gauging site						
						to remotest point of river system L_{rs}	to projection of centre of basin on main course L_{ca}	Mean slope of river I_r (%)		Altitude (m)		
No.	River / River system	Name	Period of records	Co-ordinates Lat.	Long.				Area A (km²)	Mean H_m	Max. H_{max}	Min. H_{min}
1	2	3	4	5	6	7	8	9	10	11	12	13
9	Kawaikoi Str.	Waimea, Hawaii	1914—16; 20—72	N 22:08:09	E 159:37:22				11			1040
10	Salmon	White Bird, Ida.	1911—17; 20—71	45:45:01	116:19:23				35100			430
11	Ohio	Evansville, Ind.	1974—71	37:58:20	87:34:35				277000			100
12	Red	Alexandria, La.	1872—71	31:18:46	92:26:34				175000			13
13	Connecticut	Montague City, Mass.	1904—71	42:34:48	72:34:30				20400			30
14	Quaboag	West Brimfield, Mass.	1913—71	42:10:56	72:15:51				390			119
15	Mississippi	St. Paul, Minn.	1867—71	44:56:40	93:05:20				95300			208
16	Mississippi	Vicksburg, Miss.	1858; 85; 97—98; 1903—09; 12—13; 16—17; 20—22; 27—70	32:18:45	90:54:25				2960000			14

				BASIN								
	Width (km)		Mean slope I_b (%)			Weighted lake area P_L (%)	Swamps R_s (%)	Mean annual precipitation P (mm)	Annual runoff Q (mm)	Mean annual temperature T (°C)	Regulating capacity of reservoirs α	
No.	Mean B_m	Max. B_{max}		Soils	Cover							
1	14	15	16	17	18	19	20	21	22	23	24	
9									2950			
10									283			
11									415			
12									159			
13									590			
14									539			
15									96			
16									167			

TABLE I — CHARACTERISTICS OF BASIN (cont'd)

						GAUGING STATION				BASIN			
	River / River system	Name	Period of records	Co-ordinates		Distance (km) from gauging site		Mean slope of river I_r (%)	Area A (km²)	Altitude (m)			
No.				Lat.	Long.	to remotest point of river system L_{rs}	to projection of centre of basin on main course L_{ca}			Mean H_m	Max. H_{max}	Min. H_{min}	
1	2	3	4	5	6	7	8	9	10	11	12	13	
17	Salt	Shelbina, Mo.	1909; 28; 31—71	N 39:44:29	E 92:02:26				1250			202	
18	Judith	Utica, Mont.	1920—67	46:53:30	110:13:54				850			1460	
19	Yellowstone	Sidney, Mont.	1911—67	47:40:42	104:09:22				179000			573	
20	Big Blue	Barneston, Nebr.	1903; 25; 29—71	40:03:11	96:35:16				115000			355	
21	Otter Brook	Keene, N.H.	1924—57	42:57:55	72:14:00				110			218	
22	Beetree Cr.	Swannanoa, N.C.	1926; 28—71	35:39:11	82:24:20				14			831	
23	Columbia	The Dalles, Oreg.	1858—1971	45:36:27	121:10:20				614000			24	
24	Cow Creek	Azalea, Oreg.	1928—31; 33—71	42:49:30	123:10:40				202			514	
25	Susquehanna	Harrisburg, Pa.	1786; 1846; 65; 68; 86; 89—1971	40:15:10	76:52:27				62400			88	

			BASIN									
	Width (km)		Mean slope I_b (%)	Soils	Cover	Weighted lake area P_L (%)	Swamps R_s (%)	Mean annual precipitation P (mm)	Annual runoff Q (mm)	Mean annual temperature T (°C)	Regulating capacity of reservoirs α	
No.	Mean B_m	Max. B_{max}										
1	14	15	16	17	18	19	20	21	22	23	24	
17									200			
18									56			
19									65			
20									59			
21									566			
22									657			
23									283			
24									486			
25									482			

TABLE I – CHARACTERISTICS OF BASIN (cont'd)

						GAUGING STATION				BASIN			
						Distance (km) from gauging site					Altitude (m)		
No.	River / River system	Name	Period of records	Co-ordinates Lat.	Long.	to remotest point of river system L_{rs}	to projection of centre of basin on main course L_{ca}	Mean slope of river I_r (%)	Area A (km²)	Mean H_m	Max. H_{max}	Min. H_{min}
1	2	3	4	5	6	7	8	9	10	11	12	13
				N	E							
26	Clinch	Tazewell, Tenn.	1862; 1920–67	36:25:30	83:23:54				3820			323
27	San Saba	San Saba, Tex.	1916–71	31:12:47	98:43:09				7880			354
28	Virgin	Virgin, Utah	1910–71	37:11:54	113:12:25				2420			1050
29	James	Buchanan, Va.	1877; 86; 89; 93–1972	37:31:50	79:40:45				5370			244
30	Skagit	Concrete, Wash.	1897; 1907; 17; 21; 24–28; 30–68	48:31:28	121:46:11				7090			40
31	S Fk. Cedar	Lester, Wash.	1944–71	47:18:30	121:31:00				16			701
32	Middle Crow Cr.	Hecla, Wyo.	1903; 33–67	41:10:30	105:15:05				67			2220

						BASIN						
	Width (km)		Mean slope I_b (%)	Soils	Cover	Weighted lake area P_L (%)	Swamps R_s (%)	Mean annual precipitation P (mm)	Annual runoff Q (mm)	Mean annual temperature T (°C)	Regulating capacity of reservoirs α
No.	Mean B_m	Max. B_{max}									
1	14	15	16	17	18	19	20	21	22	23	24
26									479		
27									27		
28									74		
29									403		
30									1900		
31									2220		
32									62		

TABLE II — ANNUAL MAXIMUM DISCHARGES AND VOLUMES

Country:	U. S. A. (1)
River:	Cascade Creek
Gauging Station:	Petersburg, Alas.

Date	Maximum discharge (m³/s) resulting from:		Maximum volume (10⁶m³) corresponding to max. discharge resulting from:	
	Rainfall	Snowmelt	Rainfall	Snowmelt
1	2	3	4	5
18—11—17	56			
21—09—19	44			
06—08—20	72			
31—08—23	57			
04—09—24	76			
09—12—25	29			
08—09—27	57			
21—07—28	68			
11—09—47	93			
09—09—48	52			
23—09—49	52			
22—09—50	40			
14—06—51	35			
08—07—52	51			
01—10—52	41			
22—09—54	32			
07—08—55	38			
24—08—56	36			
30—09—57	67			
07—08—58	32			
02—10—58	49			
17—10—59	39			
10—10—60	43			
03—10—61	70			
06—09—63	44			
16—08—64	31			
18—10—64	28			
04—09—66	47			
27—09—67	47			
28—09—68	38			

Country:	U. S. A. (1) cont'd
River:	Cascade Creek
Gauging Station:	Petersburg, Alas.

Date	Maximum discharge (m³/s) resulting from:		Maximum volume (10⁶m³) corresponding to max. discharge resulting from:	
	Rainfall	Snowmelt	Rainfall	Snowmelt
1	2	3	4	5
10—07—69	38			
02—11—69	44			
24—08—71	36			

TABLE II — ANNUAL MAXIMUM DISCHARGES AND VOLUMES (cont'd)

Country:	U. S. A. (2)		Country:	U. S. A. (2) cont'd
River:	Colorado		River:	Colorado
Gauging Station:	Grand Canyon, Ariz.		Gauging Station:	Grand Canyon, Ariz.

Date	Maximum discharge (m³/s) resulting from:		Maximum volume (10⁶m³) corresponding to max. discharge resulting from:		Date	Maximum discharge (m³/s) resulting from:		Maximum volume (10⁶m³) corresponding to max. discharge resulting from:	
	Rainfall	Snowmelt	Rainfall	Snowmelt		Rainfall	Snowmelt	Rainfall	Snowmelt
1	2	3	4	5	1	2	3	4	5
08—07—74	8500				06—06—50	1650			
19—06—21	6230				01—06—51	1800			
01—06—22	3250				12—06—52	3450			
19—09—23	3170				17—06—53	1940			
18—06—24	2090				27—05—54	930			
03—06—25	1520				14—06—55	1140			
29—05—26	2420				06—06—56	1900			
02—07—27	3590				13—06—57	3540			
03—06—28	3250				02—06—58	3050			
29—05—29	3140				19—06—59	1080			
04—06—30	2010				10—06—60	1310			
22—05—31	980				06—06—61	1130			
26—05—32	2890				17—05—62	2420			
05—06—33	2310				22—10—62	590			
17—05—34	720				29—04—64	560			
19—06—35	2970				15—06—65	1650			
24—05—36	2160				04—05—66	600			
21—05—37	2410				09—09—67	680			
08—06—38	2830				20—07—68	760			
26—05—39	1390				12—09—69	870			
18—05—40	1320				27—08—70	780			
17—05—41	3400								
31—05—42	2600								
06—06—43	1890								
20—05—44	2640								
17—05—45	1790								
14—06—46	1420								
14—05—47	2270								
26—05—48	2540								
22—06—49	3170								

TABLE II — ANNUAL MAXIMUM DISCHARGES AND VOLUMES (cont'd)

Country:	U. S. A. (3)
River:	Salt
Gauging Station:	Chrysotile, Ariz.

Date	Maximum discharge (m³/s) resulting from:		Maximum volume (10⁶m³) corresponding to max. discharge resulting from:	
	Rainfall	Snowmelt	Rainfall	Snowmelt
1	2	3	4	5
19–01–16	2090			
08–03–25	200			
06–04–26	380			
17–02–27	560			
21–07–28	980			
23–09–29	330			
11–08–30	330			
15–02–31	210			
10–02–32	1130			
28–02–33	80			
20–08–34	110			
09–04–35	440			
17–02–36	370			
07–02–37	1500			
04–03–38	540			
05–04–39	240			
15–08–40	180			
14–03–41	1480			
13–01–42	150			
05–03–43	360			
19–10–43	70			
27–03–45	130			
19–09–46	270			
18–09–47	230			
12–04–48	160			
14–01–49	400			
21–07–50	70			
29–08–51	150			
14–01–52	1460			
30–07–53	100			

Country:	U. S. A. (3) cont'd
River:	Salt
Gauging Station:	Chrysotile, Ariz.

Date	Maximum discharge (m³/s) resulting from:		Maximum volume (10⁶m³) corresponding to max. discharge resulting from:	
	Rainfall	Snowmelt	Rainfall	Snowmelt
1	2	3	4	5
23–03–54	810			
23–08–55	250			
29–01–56	50			
02–08–57	110			
22–03–58	560			
20–08–59	210			
26–12–59	740			
30–08–61	60			
25–01–62	160			
11–02–63	180			
26–07–64	80			
08–01–65	450			
30–12–65	1160			
12–08–67	140			
28–01–68	250			
04–10–68	140			
06–09–70	140			

TABLE II – ANNUAL MAXIMUM DISCHARGES AND VOLUMES (cont'd)

Country:	U. S. A. (4)
River:	Arkansas
Gauging Station:	Little Rock, Ark.

Date	Maximum discharge (m³/s) resulting from:		Maximum volume (10⁶m³) corresponding to max. discharge resulting from:	
	Rainfall	Snowmelt	Rainfall	Snowmelt
1	2	3	4	5
18—06—23	8490			
07—10—27	6230			
19—05—29	7780			
12—05—30	6250			
11—02—31	2750			
26—01—32	6590			
19—05—33	7840			
09—04—34	3590			
22—06—35	11900			
09—12—35	4080			
18—01—37	4810			
21—02—38	13300			
18—04—39	5120			
09—09—40	2610			
24—04—41	8320			
07—11—41	11400			
27—05—43	15200			
04—05—44	7980			
21—04—45	13200			
04—10—45	7580			
13—12—46	8150			
28—06—48	7470			
26—01—49	8520			
15—05—50	10100			
08—07—51	6650			
25—04—52	4730			
19—03—53	4500			
05—05—54	5940			
22—03—55	3680			
10—10—55	2890			

Country:	U. S. A. (4) cont'd
River:	Arkansas
Gauging Station:	Little Rock, Ark.

Date	Maximum discharge (m³/s) resulting from:		Maximum volume (10⁶m³) corresponding to max. discharge resulting from:	
	Rainfall	Snowmelt	Rainfall	Snowmelt
1	2	3	4	5
31—05—57	13000			
11—05—58	5290			
30—07—59	4270			
10—10—59	9910			
13—05—61	8150			
24—11—61	4580			
07—10—62	1850			
07—04—64	3000			
12—04—65	3590			
27—04—66	4190			
07—07—67	2500			
16—05—68	5720			
31—01—69	5150			
27—04—70	6080			

TABLE II — ANNUAL MAXIMUM DISCHARGES AND VOLUMES (cont'd)

Country:	U. S. A. (5)
River:	Eel
Gauging Station:	Scotia, Calif.

Date	Maximum discharge (m³/s) resulting from: Rainfall	Snowmelt	Maximum volume (10⁶m³) corresponding to max. discharge resulting from: Rainfall	Snowmelt
1	2	3	4	5
20−01−11	3850			
26−01−12	4810			
18−01−13	4240			
22−01−14	8740			
02−02−15	9930			
25−02−17	8260			
07−02−18	2220			
17−01−19	4220			
16−04−20	1750			
19−11−20	4190			
19−02−22	3480			
28−12−22	2080			
08−02−24	2080			
06−02−25	3590			
04−02−26	4980			
21−02−27	6250			
27−03−28	6590			
04−02−29	1160			
15−12−29	3400			
23−01−31	2460			
27−12−31	3590			
17−03−33	1640			
29−03−34	1440			
08−04−35	2260			
16−01−36	6110			
05−02−37	3790			
11−12−37	9760			
03−12−38	3760			
28−02−40	8630			
24−12−40	4250			

Country:	U. S. A. (5) cont'd
River:	Eel
Gauging Station:	Scotia, Calif.

Date	Maximum discharge (m³/s) resulting from: Rainfall	Snowmelt	Maximum volume (10⁶m³) corresponding to max. discharge resulting from: Rainfall	Snowmelt
1	2	3	4	5
06−02−42	5910			
21−01−43	8910			
04−03−44	1640			
03−02−45	2800			
27−12−45	6760			
12−02−47	2440			
08−01−48	3230			
18−03−49	3960			
18−01−50	3310			
22−01−51	7050			
27−12−51	7410			
09−01−53	6080			
17−01−54	6930			
31−12−54	1480			
22−12−55	15300			
25−02−57	4330			
25−02−58	5720			
12−01−59	4100			
08−02−60	9710			
11−02−61	3200			
14−02−62	3030			
01−02−63	7130			
21−01−64	5040			
23−12−64	21300			
05−01−66	8800			
05−12−66	4360			
15−01−68	4190			
13−01−69	6310			
24−01−70	8770			
04−12−70	6620			

TABLE II — ANNUAL MAXIMUM DISCHARGES AND VOLUMES (cont'd)

Country:	U. S. A. (6)
River:	Plum Creek
Gauging Station:	Louviers, Colo.

Date	Maximum discharge (m³/s) resulting from:		Maximum volume (10⁶m³) corresponding to max. discharge resulting from:	
	Rainfall	Snowmelt	Rainfall	Snowmelt
1	2	3	4	5
13−05−42	22			
17−10−42	4			
15−05−44	18			
08−08−45	218			
24−08−46	12			
22−07−47	19			
14−03−48	15			
13−06−49	27			
16−04−50	1			
30−07−51	6			
27−05−52	7			
29−07−53	76			
21−07−54	108			
20−05−55	11			
01−08−56	55			
13−07−57	23			
09−05−58	6			
28−04−59	8			
24−03−60	32			
02−08−61	49			
22−04−62	6			
19−09−63	8			
18−03−64	8			
16−06−65	4360			
19−07−66	61			
07−07−67	17			
11−05−68	4			
08−05−69	125			
29−04−70	7			
15−05−71	7			

Country:	U. S. A. (7)
River:	Ute Creek
Gauging Station:	Fort Garland, Colo.

Date	Maximum discharge (m³/s) resulting from:		Maximum volume (10⁶m³) corresponding to max. discharge resulting from:	
	Rainfall	Snowmelt	Rainfall	Snowmelt
1	2	3	4	5
11−05−16		3.0		
08−06−23		2.3		
14−06−24		4.8		
10−08−25		3.3		
06−06−26		4.5		
27−07−27		4.7		
28−05−28		4.3		
23−09−29		6.5		
22−07−30		7.4		
15−09−31		3.6		
12−07−32		6.4		
06−08−33		4.8		
24−09−34		3.3		
13−06−35		7.5		
05−08−36		10.0		
30−06−37		9.1		
06−06−38		4.7		
03−05−39		2.7		
17−05−40		2.2		
15−05−41		17.8		
11−05−42		4.2		
30−06−43		5.0		
16−05−44		5.0		
05−05−45		3.5		
23−08−46		2.2		
11−05−47		4.3		
20−06−48		4.8		
18−06−49		3.9		
11−07−50		3.9		
27−05−51		1.6		

TABLE II – ANNUAL MAXIMUM DISCHARGES AND VOLUMES (cont'd)

Country:	U. S. A. (7) cont'd
River:	Ute Creek
Gauging Station:	Fort Garland, Colo.

Date	Maximum discharge (m³/s) resulting from:		Maximum volume (10⁶m³) corresponding to max. discharge resulting from:	
	Rainfall	Snowmelt	Rainfall	Snowmelt
1	2	3	4	5
08–06–52		6.0		
29–05–53		3.3		
20–05–54		1.9		
19–08–55		2.9		
02–06–56		0.9		
17–07–57		7.6		
24–05–58		4.4		
14–05–59		3.2		
05–06–60		3.8		
30–05–61		3.2		
20–04–62		2.6		
13–08–63		4.4		
15–09–64		5.9		
19–06–65		5.3		
23–07–66		5.7		
01–09–67		3.8		
02–08–68		7.4		
14–08–69		6.8		
13–09–70		4.5		
22–07–71		1.3		

Country:	U. S. A. (8)
River:	Altamaha
Gauging Station:	Doctortown, Ga.

Date	Maximum discharge (m³/s) resulting from:		Maximum volume (10⁶m³) corresponding to max. discharge resulting from:	
	Rainfall	Snowmelt	Rainfall	Snowmelt
1	2	3	4	5
23–01–25	8500			
04–02–26	1530			
02–08–27	650			
25–08–28	3570			
13–03–29	5070			
13–10–29	3760			
18–05–31	910			
21–01–32	1040			
04–03–33	1310			
17–03–34	1310			
15–09–35	610			
18–04–36	5040			
13–05–37	1350			
19–04–38	1920			
11–03–39	2770			
03–03–40	1000			
07–41	780			
03–04–42	2530			
02–04–43	2010			
02–04–44	3170			
10–05–45	1000			
22–01–46	2010			
21–03–47	2010			
04–04–48	2620			
12–12–48	3340			
22–03–50	660			
04–04–51	820			
18–03–52	2020			
16–05–53	1890			
30–12–53	1120			

TABLE II — ANNUAL MAXIMUM DISCHARGES AND VOLUMES (cont'd)

Country:	U. S. A. (8) cont'd
River:	Altamaha
Gauging Station:	Doctortown, Ga.

| Date | Maximum discharge (m³/s) resulting from: | | Maximum volume (10⁶m³) corresponding to max. discharge resulting from: | |
| | Rainfall | Snowmelt | Rainfall | Snowmelt |
1	2	3	4	5
26—04—55	630			
01—04—56	930			
11—04—57	890			
15—03—58	1520			
16—03—59	1250			
12—04—60	2540			
10—03—61	2300			
10—03—62	1520			
04—02—63	1520			
20—04—64	2240			
23—02—65	1870			
12—03—66	3110			
16—01—67	1450			
26—01—68	740			
04—05—69	980			
06—04—70	2240			
16—03—71	2720			

Country:	U. S. A. (9)
River:	Kawaikoi Stream
Gauging Station:	Waima, Hawaii

| Date | Maximum discharge (m³/s) resulting from: | | Maximum volume (10⁶m³) corresponding to max. discharge resulting from: | |
| | Rainfall | Snowmelt | Rainfall | Snowmelt |
1	2	3	4	5
26—09—14	63			
08—01—16	74			
18—12—16	303			
19—03—20	85			
16—01—21	130			
31—01—22	95			
10—01—23	167			
23—12—23	118			
13—12—24	183			
31—01—26	25			
05—03—27	130			
24—12—27	113			
04—11—28	152			
27—02—30	70			
03—08—31	164			
17—02—32	43			
04—03—33	92			
04—06—34	79			
26—02—35	83			
09—12—35	127			
18—03—37	92			
23—12—37	151			
11—05—39	48			
27—11—39	121			
02—10—40	175			
19—02—42	103			
09—03—43	116			
06—12—43	33			
06—04—45	66			
24—04—46	50			

TABLE II — ANNUAL MAXIMUM DISCHARGES AND VOLUMES (cont'd)

Country:	U. S. A. (9) cont'd
River:	Kawaikoi Stream
Gauging Station:	Waima, Hawaii

	Maximum discharge (m³/s) resulting from:		Maximum volume (10⁶m³) corresponding to max. discharge resulting from:	
Date	Rainfall	Snowmelt	Rainfall	Snowmelt
1	2	3	4	5
22–12–46	132			
17–12–47	94			
07–02–49	147			
15–08–50	226			
04–03–51	138			
16–12–51	151			
13–02–53	51			
22–02–54	90			
06–02–55	179			
11–11–55	116			
29–01–57	58			
01–12–57	120			
06–08–59	204			
02–11–59	137			
20–03–61	48			
25–04–62	81			
30–03–63	72			
30–09–64	142			
16–12–64	91			
01–12–65	52			
13–01–67	320			
26–11–67	148			
30–11–68	291			
13–01–70	97			
31–01–71	68			
02–03–72	60			

Country:	U. S. A. (10)
River:	Salmon
Gauging Station:	White Bird, Idaho

	Maximum discharge (m³/s) resulting from:		Maximum volume (10⁶m³) corresponding to max. discharge resulting from:	
Date	Rainfall	Snowmelt	Rainfall	Snowmelt
1	2	3	4	5
15–06–11		2170		
09–06–12		2140		
28–05–13		2300		
24–05–14		1460		
02–06–15		960		
19–06–16		2400		
18–06–17		2180		
17–06–20		1600		
09–06–21		2510		
07–06–22		1900		
12–06–23		1580		
17–05–24		1130		
21–05–25		1660		
05–05–26		870		
09–06–27		2090		
23–05–28		2310		
25–05–29		1360		
30–05–30		1150		
17–05–31		840		
22–05–32		1940		
15–06–33		2330		
25–04–34		990		
02–06–35		1220		
15–05–36		2010		
27–05–37		970		
28–05–38		2160		
05–05–39		1160		
14–05–40		1350		
14–05–41		1120		
27–05–42		1700		

TABLE II — ANNUAL MAXIMUM DISCHARGES AND VOLUMES (cont'd)

Country:	U. S. A. (10) cont'd
River:	Salmon
Gauging Station:	White Bird, Idaho

Date	Maximum discharge (m³/s) resulting from:		Maximum volume (10⁶m³) corresponding to max. discharge resulting from:	
	Rainfall	Snowmelt	Rainfall	Snowmelt
1	2	3	4	5
01−06−43	2090			
01−06−44	1040			
07−06−45	1370			
28−05−46	1320			
09−05−47	2390			
03−06−48	2910			
16−05−49	2160			
22−06−50	1930			
28−05−51	1950			
07−06−52	1790			
14−06−53	2140			
21−05−54	2030			
14−06−55	1910			
24−05−56	3000			
06−06−57	2330			
25−05−58	2370			
15−06−59	1820			
05−06−60	1570			
03−06−61	1690			
19−06−62	1350			
25−05−63	1720			
08−06−64	2240			
12−06−65	2730			
30−05−66	1030			
24−05−67	2150			
04−06−68	1500			
27−05−69	1900			
06−06−70	2400			
29−05−71	2550			

Country:	U. S. A. (11)
River:	Ohio
Gauging Station:	Evansville, Ind.

Date	Maximum discharge (m³/s) resulting from:		Maximum volume (10⁶m³) corresponding to max. discharge resulting from:	
	Rainfall	Snowmelt	Rainfall	Snowmelt
1	2	3	4	5
28−02−74	12500			
10−08−75	14900			
31−01−76	16800			
25−01−77	14700			
17−03−78	7360			
01−04−79	9620			
21−02−80	15100			
19−02−81	12300			
24−02−82	19400			
19−02−83	25900			
19−02−84	26200			
23−01−85	11700			
14−04−86	16900			
09−02−87	16600			
04−04−88	10600			
13−11−88	9030			
31−03−90	18500			
02−03−91	16100			
27−04−92	12000			
24−02−93	14800			
19−02−94	9100			
18−01−95	10800			
08−04−96	11900			
03−03−97	17200			
03−04−98	19200			
12−03−99	16100			
19−02−00	8800			
01−05−01	14800			
11−03−02	13000			
11−03−03	15500			

TABLE II — ANNUAL MAXIMUM DISCHARGES AND VOLUMES (cont'd)

Country: U. S. A. (11) cont'd
River: Ohio
Gauging Station: Evansville, Ind.

Date	Maximum discharge (m³/s) resulting from:		Maximum volume (10⁶m³) corresponding to max. discharge resulting from:	
	Rainfall	Snowmelt	Rainfall	Snowmelt
1	2	3	4	5
04—04—04	12800			
17—03—05	11600			
06—04—06	14000			
25—01—07	21600			
09—04—08	15200			
02—03—09	16600			
10—03—10	12800			
09—02—11	12300			
31—03—12	15800			
05—04—13	25500			
08—04—14	11900			
11—02—15	15800			
18—01—16	17200			
22—03—17	16200			
17—02—18	12800			
09—01—19	13800			
25—03—20	16100			
15—03—21	11200			
30—12—21	16500			
08—02—23	15200			
11—01—24	17100			
22—02—25	9790			
29—01—26	12100			
29—01—27	19200			
24—12—27	12200			
11—03—29	15100			
18—01—30	12900			
11—04—31	10400			
07—02—32	16600			
27—03—33	19900			

Country: U. S. A. (11) cont'd
River: Ohio
Gauging Station: Evansville, Ind.

Date	Maximum discharge (m³/s) resulting from:		Maximum volume (10⁶m³) corresponding to max. discharge resulting from:	
	Rainfall	Snowmelt	Rainfall	Snowmelt
1	2	3	4	5
13—03—34	12100			
20—03—35	16200			
01—04—36	18500			
29—01—37	39900			
21—03—38	11500			
12—02—39	19200			
28—04—40	17400			
12—06—41	7400			
22—03—42	12300			
26—03—43	19800			
19—04—44	13100			
11—03—45	25600			
15—01—46	12600			
26—01—47	11100			
21—04—48	20100			
31—01—49	16100			
09—02—50	19700			
14—12—50	16500			
05—02—52	17500			
09—03—53	10100			
24—04—54	6880			
13—03—55	18500			
21—03—56	15900			
14—04—57	15400			
14—05—58	16200			
28—01—59	16300			
11—04—60	11100			
13—05—61	17900			
07—03—63	20600			
22—03—63	19400			

TABLE II — ANNUAL MAXIMUM DISCHARGES AND VOLUMES (cont'd)

Country:	U. S. A. (11) cont'd
River:	Ohio
Gauging Station:	Evansville, Ind.

Date	Maximum discharge (m³/s) resulting from:		Maximum volume (10⁶m³) corresponding to max. discharge resulting from:	
	Rainfall	Snowmelt	Rainfall	Snowmelt
1	2	3	4	5
16—03—64	25800			
02—04—65	13800			
20—02—66	15200			
15—03—67	19000			
02—06—68	16800			
02—02—69	11700			
08—04—70	15200			
26—02—71	13800			

Country:	U. S. A. (12)
River:	Red
Gauging Station:	Alexandria, La.

Date	Maximum discharge (m³/s) resulting from:		Maximum volume (10⁶m³) corresponding to max. discharge resulting from:	
	Rainfall	Snowmelt	Rainfall	Snowmelt
1	2	3	4	5
29—04—72	3590			
19—06—73	2940			
08—05—74	3960			
27—04—75	1870			
17—04—76	3480			
18—05—77	2070			
13—03—78	2350			
26—05—79	1420			
11—04—80	1610			
20—03—81	2490			
17—03—82	3930			
27—03—83	2070			
30—05—84	4020			
25—01—85	3820			
17—06—86	2520			
24—03—87	960			
27—03—88	2830			
13—02—89	3200			
19—05—90	4440			
17—02—91	2910			
12—06—92	4950			
07—01—93	3340			
12—04—94	4020			
05—08—95	2630			
06—02—96	2240			
14—04—97	2210			
23—01—98	1160			
27—01—99	1250			
25—04—00	1420			
26—04—01	930			

TABLE II – ANNUAL MAXIMUM DISCHARGES AND VOLUMES (cont'd)

Country: U. S. A. (12) cont'd
River: Red
Gauging Station: Alexandria, La.

Date	Maximum discharge (m³/s) resulting from:		Maximum volume (10⁶m³) corresponding to max. discharge resulting from:	
	Rainfall	Snowmelt	Rainfall	Snowmelt
1	2	3	4	5
21–04–02	1420			
28–03–03	4220			
30–06–04	2800			
17–06–05	4100			
05–01–06	2830			
17–06–07	3400			
06–07–08	5800			
04–06–09	1330			
23–04–10	1360			
30–04–11	1670			
22–04–12	3060			
06–04–13	1530			
15–04–14	3310			
17–05–15	3650			
16–02–16	3850			
06–05–17	960			
30–04–18	1980			
01–01–19	1560			
02–06–20	4300			
06–05–21	2910			
10–05–22	3680			
11–02–23	2380			
02–01–24	3940			
05–05–25	1360			
15–05–26	1980			
08–05–27	4900			
02–05–28	2630			
27–05–29	2910			
03–06–30	4270			
13–12–30	2090			

Country: U. S. A. (12) cont'd
River: Red
Gauging Station: Alexandria, La.

Date	Maximum discharge (m³/s) resulting from:		Maximum volume (10⁶m³) corresponding to max. discharge resulting from:	
	Rainfall	Snowmelt	Rainfall	Snowmelt
1	2	3	4	5
03–02–32	5260			
13–03–33	2410			
09–03–34	2330			
04–06–35	4270			
13–12–35	2120			
02–02–37	3030			
05–03–38	4050			
05–03–39	2590			
09–07–40	2520			
15–05–41	3740			
09–05–42	4410			
21–05–43	2390			
14–05–44	4130			
17–04–45	6590			
24–02–46	3880			
28–05–47	3710			
08–03–48	3480			
04–02–49	4100			
21–02–50	4440			
27–02–51	3250			
30–04–52	3910			
19–05–53	5460			
17–05–54	2690			
28–03–55	2540			
23–02–56	2020			
07–05–57	5580			
12–05–58	5660			
13–03–59	1590			
23–12–59	2470			
06–04–61	3790			

United States of America / États-Unis d'Amérique / Estados Unidos de América / Соединенные Штаты Америки

TABLE II – ANNUAL MAXIMUM DISCHARGES AND VOLUMES (cont'd)

Country: U. S. A. (12) cont'd
River: Red
Gauging Station: Alexandria, La.

Date	Maximum discharge (m³/s) resulting from:		Maximum volume (10⁶m³) corresponding to max. discharge resulting from:	
	Rainfall	Snowmelt	Rainfall	Snowmelt
1	2	3	4	5
18–12–61	3200			
03–12–62	1540			
01–05–64	3200			
16–02–65	2530			
08–05–66	4670			
07–06–67	3140			
11–04–68	4500			
01–03–69	3820			
03–05–70	3230			
03–11–70	1230			

Country: U. S. A. (13)
River: Connecticut
Gauging Station: Montague City, Mass.

Date	Maximum discharge (m³/s) resulting from:		Maximum volume (10⁶m³) corresponding to max. discharge resulting from:	
	Rainfall	Snowmelt	Rainfall	Snowmelt
1	2	3	4	5
30–04–04	2090			
01–04–05	3310			
16–04–06	2360			
28–04–07	1830			
07–11–07	2370			
16–04–09	3370			
02–03–10	2780			
16–04–11	1710			
09–04–12	2720			
28–03–13	4080			
21–04–14	3000			
26–02–15	2370			
03–04–16	2270			
30–03–17	1870			
03–04–18	2080			
29–03–19	2410			
28–03–20	3400			
10–03–21	2160			
13–04–22	3760			
07–04–23	2720			
07–04–24	1720			
30–03–25	2830			
26–04–26	2650			
19–03–27	2060			
05–11–27	5070			
25–03–29	2140			
09–04–30	1400			
12–04–31	2050			
13–04–32	2600			
19–04–33	3880			

TABLE II — ANNUAL MAXIMUM DISCHARGES AND VOLUMES (cont'd)

Country: U. S. A. (13) cont'd
River: Connecticut
Gauging Station: Montague City, Mass.

Date	Maximum discharge (m³/s) resulting from:		Maximum volume (10⁶m³) corresponding to max. discharge resulting from:	
	Rainfall	Snowmelt	Rainfall	Snowmelt
1	2	3	4	5
13—04—34	3230			
11—01—35	2620			
19—03—36	6680			
16—05—37	2750			
22—09—38	5520			
23—04—39	2780			
05—05—40	3370			
15—04—41	1310			
09—04—42	2000			
29—04—43	2010			
10—11—43	1970			
22—03—45	2420			
10—03—46	2000			
13—04—47	2710			
23—03—48	3570			
31—12—48	3930			
06—04—50	2250			
01—04—51	2890			
02—06—52	3060			
28—03—53	3480			
18—04—54	2140			
16—04—55	2300			
30—04—56	2810			
24—01—57	1020			
23—04—58	2860			
04—04—59	2650			
06—04—60	4020			
24—04—61	1940			
02—04—62	2600			
03—04—63	2190			

Country: U. S. A. (13) cont'd
River: Connecticut
Gauging Station: Montague City, Mass.

Date	Maximum discharge (m³/s) resulting from:		Maximum volume (10⁶m³) corresponding to max. discharge resulting from:	
	Rainfall	Snowmelt	Rainfall	Snowmelt
1	2	3	4	5
15—04—64	2250			
17—04—65	1150			
26—03—66	1570			
04—04—67	2240			
24—03—68	2860			
23—04—69	2910			
26—04—70	2140			
05—05—71	2160			

392

TABLE II — ANNUAL MAXIMUM DISCHARGES AND VOLUMES (cont'd)

Country:	U. S. A. (14)			
River:	Quaboag			
Gauging Station:	West Brimfield, Mass.			

	Maximum discharge (m³/s) resulting from:		Maximum volume (10⁶m³) corresponding to max. discharge resulting from:	
Date	Rainfall	Snowmelt	Rainfall	Snowmelt
1	2	3	4	5
16—04—13	34.0			
01—03—14	35.9			
07—01—15	47.0			
03—04—16	35.4			
29—03—17	31.1			
07—03—18	28.9			
01—03—19	38.5			
17—03—20	56.0			
03—05—21	27.5			
07—03—22	47.5			
26—03—23	40.5			
07—04—24	49.5			
01—03—25	32.3			
09—04—26	25.2			
22—04—27	25.2			
04—11—27	33.4			
23—04—29	32.3			
26—03—30	15.7			
01—04—31	30.3			
01—04—32	28.2			
18—04—33	42.5			
12—04—34	29.7			
11—01—35	32.5			
18—03—36	102			
20—12—30	29.7			
21—09—38	240			
06—04—39	26.7			
13—04—40	52.4			
08—02—41	22.6			
22—03—42	33.1			

Country:	U. S. A. (14) cont'd			
River:	Quaboag			
Gauging Station:	West Brimfield, Mass.			

	Maximum discharge (m³/s) resulting from:		Maximum volume (10⁶m³) corresponding to max. discharge resulting from:	
Date	Rainfall	Snowmelt	Rainfall	Snowmelt
1	2	3	4	5
20—03—43	27.2			
24—06—44	33.7			
07—03—45	28.2			
09—03—46	29.7			
14—03—47	24.9			
22—03—48	46.7			
06—01—49	19.0			
31—03—50	20.8			
03—04—51	33.4			
28—01—52	27.5			
16—04—53	41.0			
11—09—54	36.2			
19—08—55	362			
18—04—56	42.7			
23—01—57	22.1			
08—04—58	35.1			
06—03—59	30.6			
05—04—60	54.1			
27—02—61	29.4			
03—04—62	38.5			
29—03—63	44.7			
25—01—64	22.6			
14—02—65	15.3			
25—03—66	17.7			
26—05—67	27.9			
21—03—68	52.6			
05—04—69	32.3			
03—02—70	43.6			
07—04—71	19.5			

TABLE II — ANNUAL MAXIMUM DISCHARGES AND VOLUMES (cont'd)

Country:	U. S. A. (15)
River:	Mississippi
Gauging Station:	St. Paul, Minn.

	Maximum discharge (m³/s) resulting from:		Maximum volume (10⁶m³) corresponding to max. discharge resulting from:	
Date	Rainfall	Snowmelt	Rainfall	Snowmelt
1	2	3	4	5
23—07—67	2600			
04—04—68	760			
24—09—69	1960			
11—04—70	2830			
19—05—72	570			
21—04—73	2030			
02—07—74	1100			
16—04—75	2440			
10—04—76	1000			
25—05—77	570			
27—04—78	460			
11—07—79	970			
17—06—80	1760			
29—04—81	3030			
13—04—82	1380			
22—04—83	1240			
06—05—84	890			
18—06—85	530			
29—03—86	630			
17—04—87	800			
14—04—88	1590			
21—05—89	270			
23—06—90	490			
17—04—91	430			
26—05—92	1290			
06—05—93	1660			
21—05—94	1170			
16—06—95	270			
18—04—96	1000			
06—04—97	2440			

Country:	U. S. A. (15) cont'd
River:	Mississippi
Gauging Station:	St.Paul, Minn.

	Maximum discharge (m³/s) resulting from:		Maximum volume (10⁶m³) corresponding to max. discharge resulting from:	
Date	Rainfall	Snowmelt	Rainfall	Snowmelt
1	2	3	4	5
08—06—98	1000			
14—04—99	1040			
24—10—99	730			
12—04—01	560			
26—05—02	560			
03—06—03	1220			
14—10—03	1470			
11—07—05	1690			
12—06—06	1430			
04—04—07	1430			
29—06—08	2070			
04—04—09	1380			
19—03—10	1010			
24—05—11	240			
10—05—12	1100			
27—05—13	450			
03—07—14	1150			
05—04—15	880			
06—04—16	2080			
08—04—17	1940			
24—03—18	640			
22—04—19	1540			
29—03—20	1500			
16—06—21	550			
13—04—22	1300			
07—05—23	370			
27—08—24	370			
20—06—25	480			
28—03—26	410			
19—03—27	990			

TABLE II — ANNUAL MAXIMUM DISCHARGES AND VOLUMES (cont'd)

Country:	U. S. A. (15) cont'd
River:	Mississippi
Gauging Station:	St. Paul, Minn.

Date	Maximum discharge (m³/s) resulting from:		Maximum volume (10⁶m³) corresponding to max. discharge resulting from:	
	Rainfall	Snowmelt	Rainfall	Snowmelt
1	2	3	4	5
29—03—28	930			
23—03—29	1300			
19—05—30	620			
26—06—31	270			
12—04—32	500			
06—04—33	400			
12—04—34	210			
23—03—35	360			
30—03—36	1060			
04—05—37	660			
14—05—38	1100			
31—03—39	1010			
12—04—40	670			
11—04—41	1120			
20—05—42	860			
07—04—43	1650			
21—06—44	1610			
23—03—45	1510			
24—03—46	1160			
06—05—47	1320			
02—04—48	1330			
08—04—49	1220			
13—05—50	1530			
16—04—51	2630			
16—04—52	3540			
27—06—53	1330			
06—05—54	1230			
07—04—55	730			
11—04—56	1000			
29—06—57	2220			

Country:	U. S. A. (15) cont'd
River:	Mississippi
Gauging Station:	St. Paul, Minn.

Date	Maximum discharge (m³/s) resulting from:		Maximum volume (10⁶m³) corresponding to max. discharge resulting from:	
	Rainfall	Snowmelt	Rainfall	Snowmelt
1	2	3	4	5
14—04—58	520			
05—06—59	630			
28—05—60	1230			
22—05—61	640			
11—04—62	1600			
15—06—63	900			
15—05—64	950			
16—04—65	4840			
23—03—66	1400			
06—04—67	1480			
16—06—68	770			
15—04—69	4410			
29—04—70	1010			
12—04—71	1410			

TABLE II – ANNUAL MAXIMUM DISCHARGES AND VOLUMES (cont'd)

Country:	U. S. A. (16)
River:	Mississippi
Gauging Station:	Vicksburg, Miss.

Date	Maximum discharge (m³/s) resulting from: Rainfall	Snowmelt	Maximum volume (10⁶m³) corresponding to max. discharge resulting from: Rainfall	Snowmelt
1	2	3	4	5
24–06–58	35200			
22–01–85	32600			
15–04–97	50300			
23–04–98	41200			
31–03–03	45500			
23–04–04	39100			
25–04–06	43500			
12–02–07	48700			
29–03–09	42900			
12–04–12	50400			
02–05–13	50500			
16–02–16	49100			
20–04–17	43600			
17–04–20	46700			
20–04–22	49600			
01–05–27	64500			
12–07–28	37500			
06–06–29	49000			
03–02–30	32500			
20–04–31	20100			
26–02–32	39900			
10–06–33	38500			
13–04–34	24800			
15–04–35	40200			
29–04–36	36200			
17–02–37	58900			
23–04–38	33700			
09–03–39	39900			
11–05–40	30400			
30–04–41	23000			

Country:	U. S. A. (16) cont'd
River:	Mississippi
Gauging Station:	Vicksburg, Miss.

Date	Maximum discharge (m³/s) resulting from: Rainfall	Snowmelt	Maximum volume (10⁶m³) corresponding to max. discharge resulting from: Rainfall	Snowmelt
1	2	3	4	5
20–04–42	33300			
06–06–43	46600			
13–05–44	45500			
08–04–45	54400			
26–01–46	41900			
04–05–47	36800			
13–04–48	39700			
10–02–49	44500			
23–02–50	53100			
12–03–51	38400			
10–04–52	38700			
27–05–53	27800			
08–05–54	20000			
07–04–55	36300			
03–03–56	31400			
07–06–57	37100			
16–05–58	33700			
01–03–59	27700			
25–04–60	31100			
30–03–61	44700			
02–04–62	40600			
02–04–63	37800			
02–04–64	35900			
22–04–65	36300			
28–02–66	31300			
29–05–67	29300			
12–04–68	32800			
19–02–69	39700			
16–05–70	36900			

TABLE II – ANNUAL MAXIMUM DISCHARGES AND VOLUMES (cont'd)

Country:	U.S.A. (17)
River:	Salt
Gauging Station:	Shelbina, Mo.

Date	Maximum discharge (m³/s) resulting from:		Maximum volume (10⁶m³) corresponding to max. discharge resulting from:	
	Rainfall	Snowmelt	Rainfall	Snowmelt
1	2	3	4	5
07–09	501			
06–28	509			
08–06–31	234			
18–08–32	168			
01–07–33	453			
30–09–34	79			
03–06–35	348			
27–02–36	199			
21–02–37	113			
11–04–38	115			
13–03–39	223			
04–03–40	101			
18–01–41	45			
07–02–42	219			
18–06–43	181			
24–04–44	294			
18–06–45	263			
07–01–46	331			
07–06–47	651			
20–03–48	224			
21–02–49	131			
21–06–50	118			
01–06–51	175			
11–03–52	148			
01–04–53	198			
07–04–54	57			
20–02–55	162			
04–07–56	73			
18–05–57	108			
25–10–57	300			

Country:	U.S.A. (17) cont'd
River:	Salt
Gauging Station:	Shelbina, Mo.

Date	Maximum discharge (m³/s) resulting from:		Maximum volume (10⁶m³) corresponding to max. discharge resulting from:	
	Rainfall	Snowmelt	Rainfall	Snowmelt
1	2	3	4	5
12–02–59	105			
30–03–60	222			
15–09–61	193			
23–03–62	147			
06–03–63	142			
22–04–64	132			
03–01–65	317			
14–06–66	156			
15–06–67	265			
01–11–67	138			
11–07–69	391			
25–09–70	323			
11–10–70	192			

TABLE II — ANNUAL MAXIMUM DISCHARGES AND VOLUMES (cont'd)

Country:	U.S.A. (18)
River:	Judith
Gauging Station:	Utica, Mont.

Date	Maximum discharge (m³/s) resulting from:		Maximum volume (10⁶m³) corresponding to max. discharge resulting from:	
	Rainfall	Snowmelt	Rainfall	Snowmelt
1	2	3	4	5
18—06—20		15.6		
28—05—21		6.2		
09—06—22		19.1		
24—06—23		15.5		
17—05—24		14.5		
22—05—25		12.9		
07—05—26		12.3		
11—06—27		31.7		
09—05—28		17.8		
01—06—29		12.8		
31—05—30		9.3		
04—06—31		1.8		
22—05—32		16.0		
12—05—34		2.8		
13—06—35		3.4		
15—05—36		13.3		
30—05—37		1.9		
29—06—38		26.3		
05—05—39		6.5		
12—07—40		9.1		
08—08—41		30.3		
25—05—42		31.1		
13—06—43		16.4		
19—05—44		13.5		
06—06—45		12.4		
02—07—46		14.8		
11—05—47		18.8		
04—06—48		25.4		
17—05—49		11.9		
19—06—50		17.5		

Country:	U.S.A. (18) cont'd
River:	Judith
Gauging Station:	Utica, Mont.

Date	Maximum discharge (m³/s) resulting from:		Maximum volume (10⁶m³) corresponding to max. discharge resulting from:	
	Rainfall	Snowmelt	Rainfall	Snowmelt
1	2	3	4	5
24—05—51		11.8		
22—05—52		17.4		
04—06—53		25.3		
22—05—54		7.0		
17—06—55		12.0		
28—05—56		10.3		
07—06—57		9.6		
12—05—58		5.1		
07—06—59		20.5		
13—05—60		9.1		
24—05—61		5.5		
26—05—62		16.4		
05—06—63		8.5		
09—06—64		30.3		
17—06—65		27.7		
11—05—66		11.8		
30—05—67		27.7		

TABLE II — ANNUAL MAXIMUM DISCHARGES AND VOLUMES (cont'd)

Country:	U.S.A. (19)
River:	Yellowstone
Gauging Station:	Sidney, Mont.

Date	Maximum discharge (m³/s) resulting from:		Maximum volume (10⁶m³) corresponding to max. discharge resulting from:	
	Rainfall	Snowmelt	Rainfall	Snowmelt
1	2	3	4	5
22—06—11	2220			
29—03—12	3230			
04—06—13	2090			
07—06—14	2260			
13—06—15	2760			
23—06—16	2860			
23—06—17	2680			
20—06—18	3570			
29—05—19	750			
19—06—20	2540			
21—06—21	4500			
17—06—22	2450			
20—06—23	1820			
03—10—24	3790			
02—06—25	2000			
27—05—26	1500			
01—07—27	2860			
01—06—28	2520			
07—06—29	2680			
02—06—30	1150			
11—06—31	1300			
12—05—34	498			
18—06—35	2200			
06—06—36	1780			
14—06—37	1850			
01—07—38	2380			
05—06—39	1600			
09—06—40	1060			
19—06—41	1220			
07—06—42	1930			

Country:	U.S.A. (19) cont'd
River:	Yellowstone
Gauging Station:	Sidney, Mont.

Date	Maximum discharge (m³/s) resulting from:		Maximum volume (10⁶m³) corresponding to max. discharge resulting from:	
	Rainfall	Snowmelt	Rainfall	Snowmelt
1	2	3	4	5
29—03—43	3740			
21—06—44	3400			
30—06—45	1880			
15—06—46	1420			
23—03—47	2770			
09—06—48	2200			
15—06—49	1360			
26—06—50	1910			
21—06—51	1410			
31—03—52	3910			
18—06—53	1850			
01—07—54	1170			
29—06—55	1100			
02—06—56	1830			
10—06—57	1980			
28—05—58	1100			
22—03—59	1620			
23—03—60	1640			
02—06—61	849			
20—06—62	1950			
07—06—63	2430			
19—06—64	2040			
16—06—65	2830			
05—06—66	792			
20—06—67	2340			

TABLE II − ANNUAL MAXIMUM DISCHARGES AND VOLUMES (cont'd)

Country:	U.S.A. (20)
River:	Big Blue
Gauging Station:	Barneston, Nebr.

	Maximum discharge (m³/s) resulting from:		Maximum volume (10⁶m³) corresponding to max. discharge resulting from:	
Date	Rainfall	Snowmelt	Rainfall	Snowmelt
1	2	3	4	5
05−03	1100			
28−09−19	283			
02−10−19	127			
04−07−21	308			
10−07−22	213			
23−04−23	297			
03−10−23	410			
18−06−25	351			
22−06−29	334			
15−05−30	323			
15−09−31	371			
24−11−31	289			
23−08−33	157			
04−09−34	59.4			
02−06−35	368			
25−02−36	351			
25−07−37	91.7			
13−09−38	214			
12−03−39	280			
27−08−40	113			
09−06−41	1630			
12−05−42	444			
12−06−43	668			
14−06−44	461			
22−05−45	761			
16−07−46	248			
23−06−47	974			
22−03−48	487			
28−06−49	761			
10−05−50	603			

Country:	U.S.A. (20) cont'd
River:	Big Blue
Gauging Station:	Barneston, Nebr.

	Maximum discharge (m³/s) resulting from:		Maximum volume (10⁶m³) corresponding to max. discharge resulting from:	
Date	Rainfall	Snowmelt	Rainfall	Snowmelt
1	2	3	4	5
04−06−51	736			
30−06−52	484			
09−06−53	62.5			
08−08−54	801			
19−02−55	175			
03−07−56	501			
22−06−57	473			
11−07−58	628			
04−07−59	419			
28−03−60	832			
13−09−61	345			
25−03−62	481			
26−06−63	526			
22−06−64	252			
01−07−65	583			
12−02−66	233			
19−06−67	756			
20−08−68	286			
24−03−69	577			
16−06−70	185			
22−05−71	308			

TABLE II — ANNUAL MAXIMUM DISCHARGES AND VOLUMES   (cont'd)

Country:	U.S.A. (21)
River:	Otter Brook
Gauging Station:	Keene, N.H.

Date	Maximum discharge (m³/s) resulting from:		Maximum volume (10⁶m³) corresponding to max. discharge resulting from:	
	Rainfall	Snowmelt	Rainfall	Snowmelt
1	2	3	4	5
07—04—24	54.9			
13—02—25	24.7			
25—04—26	12.5			
19—03—27	16.8			
04—11—27	90.0			
03—05—29	37.1			
26—03—30	17.0			
11—04—31	36.8			
01—04—32	28.0			
18—04—33	44.1			
12—04—34	85.5			
10—01—35	27.2			
18—03—36	101			
14—05—37	37.4			
21—09—38	173			
19—04—39	38.5			
12—04—40	48.1			
10—02—41	12.5			
09—03—42	29.4			
28—04—43	13.4			
09—11—43	41.9			
20—06—45	45.8			
09—03—46	34.0			
12—04—47	19.8			
22—03—48	42.2			
06—01—49	23.8			
01—09—50	39.1			
26—11—50	100			
06—04—52	28.6			
16—03—53	26.7			

Country:	U.S.A. (21) cont'd
River:	Otter Brook
Gauging Station:	Keene, N.H.

Date	Maximum discharge (m³/s) resulting from:		Maximum volume (10⁶m³) corresponding to max. discharge resulting from:	
	Rainfall	Snowmelt	Rainfall	Snowmelt
1	2	3	4	5
18—04—54	30.3			
03—11—54	22.1			
30—04—56	37.4			
23—01—57	13.6			

401

TABLE II — ANNUAL MAXIMUM DISCHARGES AND VOLUMES (cont'd)

Country:	U.S.A. (22)
River:	Beetree Creek
Gauging Station:	Swannanoa, N.C.

| Date | Maximum discharge (m³/s) resulting from: | | Maximum volume (10⁶m³) corresponding to max. discharge resulting from: | |
| | Rainfall | Snowmelt | Rainfall | Snowmelt |
1	2	3	4	5
15—11—26	10.2			
15—08—28	23.5			
26—09—29	5.4			
21—10—29	10.7			
22—04—31	5.8			
01—05—32	5.1			
28—12—32	6.8			
03—03—34	5.8			
08—01—35	5.8			
06—04—36	6.2			
16—10—36	6.1			
19—10—37	5.1			
08—07—39	7.4			
13—08—40	38.8			
27—12—40	6.6			
08—03—42	4.3			
29—12—42	5.9			
30—09—44	6.2			
26—03—45	2.9			
10—02—46	4.0			
20—01—47	7.2			
11—07—48	4.5			
16—06—49	16.0			
01—09—50	4.3			
07—12—50	7.5			
23—03—52	7.0			
21—02—53	12.8			
22—01—54	7.7			
22—03—55	2.3			
15—04—56	3.7			

Country:	U.S.A. (22) cont'd
River:	Beetree Creek
Gauging Station:	Swannanoa, N.C.

| Date | Maximum discharge (m³/s) resulting from: | | Maximum volume (10⁶m³) corresponding to max. discharge resulting from: | |
| | Rainfall | Snowmelt | Rainfall | Snowmelt |
1	2	3	4	5
04—04—57	8.0			
20—12—57	4.5			
30—09—59	8.2			
30—03—60	6.7			
24—08—61	7.9			
12—12—61	5.1			
12—03—63	16.0			
29—09—64	13.0			
26—03—65	17.1			
13—02—66	9.6			
04—06—67	7.9			
12—03—68	4.7			
19—10—68	3.7			
30—12—69	5.4			
07—07—71	1.9			

TABLE II -- ANNUAL MAXIMUM DISCHARGES AND VOLUMES (cont'd)

Country:	U.S.A. (23)	Country:	U.S.A. (23) cont'd
River:	Columbia	River:	Columbia
Gauging Station:	The Dalles, Oreg.	Gauging Station:	The Dalles, Oreg.

Date	Maximum discharge (m³/s) resulting from:		Maximum volume (10⁶m³) corresponding to max. discharge resulting from:		Date	Maximum discharge (m³/s) resulting from:		Maximum volume (10⁶m³) corresponding to max. discharge resulting from:	
	Rainfall	Snowmelt	Rainfall	Snowmelt		Rainfall	Snowmelt	Rainfall	Snowmelt
1	2	3	4	5	1	2	3	4	5
58	15900				18–06–88	16000			
59	24700				05–06–89	8550			
60	18900				14–05–90	17900			
61	17500				02–06–91	12700			
62	26800				22–06–92	17200			
63	22000				14–06–93	19200			
64	18500				06–06–94	35100			
65	20200				31–05–95	13400			
66	23700				22–06–96	22200			
67	19000				24–05–97	22100			
68	13700				20–06–98	18400			
69	9280				22–06–99	22300			
70	22000				19–06–00	15500			
71	24200				01–06–01	18700			
72	20900				01–06–02	18200			
73	18100				18–06–03	22300			
74	16500				26–05–04	17800			
75	19400				15–06–05	11700			
76	27100				01–06–06	10600			
77	13800				05–06–07	16600			
12–06–78	13700				18–06–08	18500			
18–06–79	18200				19–06–09	19100			
30–06–80	25900				14–05–10	16000			
17–06–81	16900				17–06–11	16200			
13–06–82	25000				01–06–12	16100			
14–06–83	16200				12–06–13	21500			
13–06–84	19800				27–05–14	14000			
23–06–85	13600				01–06–15	9280			
09–06–86	19100				01–07–16	20600			
19–06–87	25400				20–06–17	20600			

TABLE II – ANNUAL MAXIMUM DISCHARGES AND VOLUMES (cont'd)

Country:	U.S.A. (23) cont'd
River:	Columbia
Gauging Station:	The Dalles, Oreg.

Date	Maximum discharge (m³/s) resulting from:		Maximum volume (10⁶m³) corresponding to max. discharge resulting from:	
	Rainfall	Snowmelt	Rainfall	Snowmelt
1	2	3	4	5
25—06—18	16400			
01—06—19	15700			
26—06—20	12100			
11—06—21	21900			
09—06—22	19200			
14—06—23	16400			
26—05—24	12300			
24—05—25	18200			
08—05—26	7600			
18—06—27	19500			
29—05—28	21700			
19—06—29	13000			
14—06—30	9400			
19—05—31	8700			
24—05—32	16400			
18—06—33	20400			
02—05—34	12800			
10—06—35	13600			
17—05—36	15000			
24—06—37	10700			
31—05—38	17200			
21—05—39	11000			
05—06—40	10500			
10—06—41	7730			
17—06—42	12200			
21—06—43	15500			
19—06—44	9250			
08—06—45	14400			
30—05—46	16500			

Country:	U.S.A. (23) cont'd
River:	Columbia
Gauging Station:	The Dalles, Oreg.

Date	Maximum discharge (m³/s) resulting from:		Maximum volume (10⁶m³) corresponding to max. discharge resulting from:	
	Rainfall	Snowmelt	Rainfall	Snowmelt
1	2	3	4	5
11—05—47	15300			
31—05—48	28500			
18—05—49	17700			
25—06—50	21100			
30—05—51	17000			
28—05—52	15900			
17—06—53	17300			
23—05—54	16100			
26—06—55	15500			
02—06—56	23300			
22—05—57	20000			
31—05—58	16800			
23—06—59	15700			
06—06—60	13300			
08—06—61	19800			
05—06—62	13000			
18—06—63	12400			
18—06—64	18700			
09—06—65	14700			
12—06—66	11200			
10—06—67	17600			
13—06—68	11400			
15—05—69	14600			
28—05—70	12000			
13—05—71	15800			

TABLE II – ANNUAL MAXIMUM DISCHARGES AND VOLUMES   (cont'd)

Country:	U.S.A. (24)			
River:	Cow Creek			
Gauging Station:	Azalea, Oreg.			

Date	Maximum discharge (m³/s) resulting from:		Maximum volume (10⁶m³) corresponding to max. discharge resulting from:	
	Rainfall	Snowmelt	Rainfall	Snowmelt
1	2	3	4	5
27—03—28	21.6			
14—04—29	15.0			
14—12—29	79.2			
01—04—31	11.2			
02—01—33	75.8			
23—01—34	18.1			
07—01—35	18.1			
13—01—36	69.1			
13—04—37	62.3			
06—02—38	109			
12—03—39	52.1			
28—02—40	81.5			
27—01—41	53.5			
18—12—41	81.5			
21—01—43	109			
04—11—43	10.8			
08—02—45	45.0			
28—12—45	125			
10—03—47	35.7			
06—01—48	129			
22—02—49	77.0			
23—01—50	41.6			
29—10—50	168			
01—02—52	80.9			
18—01—53	121			
27—01—54	108			
31—12—54	17.3			
21—12—55	147			
26—02—57	97.9			
29—01—58	116			

Country:	U.S.A. (24) cont'd			
River:	Cow Creek			
Gauging Station:	Azalea, Oreg.			

Date	Maximum discharge (m³/s) resulting from:		Maximum volume (10⁶m³) corresponding to max. discharge resulting from:	
	Rainfall	Snowmelt	Rainfall	Snowmelt
1	2	3	4	5
12—01—59	87.7			
08—02—60	58.9			
10—02—61	86.9			
23—11—61	80.4			
02—12—62	81.2			
20—01—64	109			
22—12—64	239			
05—01—66	94.0			
28—01—67	57.7			
23—02—68	56.6			
12—01—69	96.2			
26—01—70	153			
17—01—71	142			

TABLE II – ANNUAL MAXIMUM DISCHARGES AND VOLUMES (cont'd)

Country:	U.S.A. (25)
River:	Susquehanna
Gauging Station:	Harrisburg, Pa.

	Maximum discharge (m³/s) resulting from:		Maximum volume (10⁶m³) corresponding to max. discharge resulting from:	
Date	Rainfall	Snowmelt	Rainfall	Snowmelt
1	2	3	4	5
05—10—86	13600			
15—03—46	13600			
18—03—65	16200			
19—03—68	11800			
06—01—86	10900			
02—06—89	18500			
19—02—91	11600			
05—04—92	7640			
05—05—93	9170			
22—05—94	17400			
11—04—95	6510			
01—04—96	7500			
26—03—97	5090			
24—03—98	8910			
06—03—99	6450			
02—03—00	6740			
28—11—00	7050			
03—03—02	12700			
02—03—03	7810			
08—03—04	8430			
21—03—05	8660			
04—12—05	5940			
15—03—07	6990			
20—03—08	8410			
02—05—09	8410			
03—03—10	9400			
16—01—11	5040			
04—04—12	7050			
28—03—13	11400			
30—03—14	10100			

Country:	U.S.A. (25) cont'd
River:	Susquehanna
Gauging Station:	Harrisburg, Pa.

	Maximum discharge (m³/s) resulting from:		Maximum volume (10⁶m³) corresponding to max. discharge resulting from:	
Date	Rainfall	Snowmelt	Rainfall	Snowmelt
1	2	3	4	5
26—02—15	8090			
29—03—16	10700			
29—03—17	4390			
16—03—18	8150			
23—05—19	8320			
13—03—20	12000			
11—03—21	5040			
30—11—21	7870			
03—06—23	7390			
08—04—24	9170			
13—02—25	10700			
27—03—26	4700			
27—11—26	9160			
02—05—28	7140			
17—03—29	6650			
28—02—30	5010			
31—03—31	4330			
02—04—32	6930			
25—08—33	7610			
14—04—34	3990			
02—12—34	6850			
19—03—36	20900			
24—01—37	6540			
20—12—37	5040			
23—02—39	5940			
02—04—40	11800			
07—04—41	6910			
24—05—42	8210			
01—01—43	11700			
09—05—44	6000			

TABLE II — ANNUAL MAXIMUM DISCHARGES AND VOLUMES   (cont'd)

Country:	U.S.A. (25) cont'd	Country:	U.S.A. (26)
River:	Susquehanna	River:	Clinch
Gauging Station:	Harrisburg, Pa.	Gauging Station:	Tazewell, Tenn.

Date	Maximum discharge (m³/s) resulting from:		Maximum volume (10⁶m³) corresponding to max. discharge resulting from:		Date	Maximum discharge (m³/s) resulting from:		Maximum volume (10⁶m³) corresponding to max. discharge resulting from:	
	Rainfall	Snowmelt	Rainfall	Snowmelt		Rainfall	Snowmelt	Rainfall	Snowmelt
1	2	3	4	5	1	2	3	4	5
05—03—45	7130				02—62	1870			
29—05—46	14000				24—01—20	801			
07—04—47	6060				15—12—20	365			
16—04—48	8720				11—03—22	589			
01—01—49	6230				04—02—23	1120			
30—03—50	8490				02—01—24	572			
27—11—50	11800				09—12—24	713			
13—03—52	9170				16—02—26	382			
26—03—53	6110				23—12—26	1100			
03—03—54	6850				30—06—28	458			
06—03—55	5010				24—03—29	792			
10—03—56	9570				18—11—29	450			
07—04—57	7080				05—04—31	334			
09—04—58	7950				31—01—32	1070			
24—01—59	6510				29—12—32	665			
02—04—60	10800				24—03—34	637			
27—02—61	11100				02—04—35	637			
02—04—62	7640				07—04—36	637			
28—03—63	7050				19—01—37	750			
12—03—64	13700				23—07—38	450			
11—02—65	3850				04—02—39	826			
15—02—66	7500				15—08—40	688			
17—03—67	5150				13—03—41	258			
15—03—68	5720				10—08—42	526			
20—11—68	3930				31—12—42	722			
04—04—70	9710				19—02—44	1000			
01—03—71	6340				18—02—45	543			
					08—01—46	1070			
					16—01—47	959			
					15—02—48	988			

TABLE II – ANNUAL MAXIMUM DISCHARGES AND VOLUMES   (cont'd)

Country:	U.S.A. (26) cont'd
River:	Clinch
Gauging Station:	Tazewell, Tenn.

Date	Maximum discharge (m³/s) resulting from: Rainfall	Snowmelt	Maximum volume (10⁶m³) corresponding to max. discharge resulting from: Rainfall	Snowmelt
1	2	3	4	5
06–01–49	504			
02–02–50	1060			
08–12–50	430			
24–03–52	569			
21–05–53	722			
17–01–54	390			
18–03–55	841			
16–04–56	937			
31–01–57	1450			
07–05–58	1020			
23–01–59	515			
29–11–59	456			
26–02–61	708			
01–03–62	736			
13–03–63	1600			
16–03–64	475			
27–03–65	877			
03–05–66	484			
03–03–67	1050			

Country:	U.S.A. (27)
River:	San Saba
Gauging Station:	San Saba, Tex.

Date	Maximum discharge (m³/s) resulting from: Rainfall	Snowmelt	Maximum volume (10⁶m³) corresponding to max. discharge resulting from: Rainfall	Snowmelt
1	2	3	4	5
01–05–16	117			
03–06–17	170			
03–06–18	515			
23–09–19	863			
17–10–20	123			
26–11–20	21.1			
26–04–22	201			
17–09–23	580			
02–11–23	184			
11–05–25	132			
16–10–25	245			
09–02–27	245			
02–10–27	239			
30–05–29	211			
14–10–29	245			
07–10–30	1270			
02–07–32	962			
25–05–33	208			
06–04–34	780			
15–06–35	1810			
17–09–36	1900			
26–10–36	145			
23–07–38	5740			
12–01–39	62.0			
09–05–40	158			
28–04–41	770			
06–10–41	713			
05–06–43	577			
02–05–44	132			
05–10–44	135			

TABLE II — ANNUAL MAXIMUM DISCHARGES AND VOLUMES (cont'd)

Country:	U.S.A. (27) cont'd
River:	San Saba
Gauging Station:	San Saba, Tex.

Date	Maximum discharge (m³/s) resulting from: Rainfall	Snowmelt	Maximum volume (10⁶m³) corresponding to max. discharge resulting from: Rainfall	Snowmelt
1	2	3	4	5
27—09—46	416			
19—05—47	70.5			
11—05—48	132			
20—04—49	178			
26—05—50	77.0			
25—05—51	354			
11—09—52	1990			
30—12—52	42.5			
04—10—53	202			
19—05—55	1170			
02—05—56	1010			
13—05—57	778			
14—10—57	906			
03—06—59	89.4			
14—10—59	292			
19—06—61	325			
10—10—61	289			
31—05—63	19.0			
24—09—64	572			
17—05—65	577			
24—04—66	54.3			
21—07—67	132			
21—01—68	492			
07—05—69	120			
05—10—69	1040			
26—07—71	724			

Country:	U.S.A. (28)
River:	Virgin
Gauging Station:	Virgin, Utah

Date	Maximum discharge (m³/s) resulting from: Rainfall	Snowmelt	Maximum volume (10⁶m³) corresponding to max. discharge resulting from: Rainfall	Snowmelt
1	2	3	4	5
01—01—10	78.4			
30—09—11	300			
31—07—12	144			
27—10—12	340			
30—07—14	708			
03—09—15	123			
26—07—16	123			
06—10—16	73.9			
12—03—18	144			
03—09—19	35.1			
19—08—20	311			
22—08—21	75.0			
31—08—22	96.2			
22—07—23	144			
10—09—24	87.7			
25—08—25	47.0			
05—10—25	78.4			
13—09—27	122			
31—10—27	73.6			
31—07—29	119			
04—08—30	84.9			
17—11—30	100			
09—02—32	255			
08—09—33	66.5			
28—07—34	43.9			
08—04—35	49.8			
31—07—36	178			
08—05—37	54.3			
03—03—38	382			
06—09—39	283			

TABLE II – ANNUAL MAXIMUM DISCHARGES AND VOLUMES   (cont'd)

Country: U.S.A. (28) cont'd
River: Virgin
Gauging Station: Virgin, Utah

Date	Maximum discharge (m³/s) resulting from:		Maximum volume (10⁶m³) corresponding to max. discharge resulting from:	
	Rainfall	Snowmelt	Rainfall	Snowmelt
1	2	3	4	5
17–09–40	124			
06–05–41	84.3			
13–10–41	89.1			
09–03–43	26.0			
12–05–44	30.3			
03–05–45	23.9			
12–08–46	48.1			
29–10–46	58.9			
16–09–48	39.6			
08–09–49	28.6			
08–07–50	187			
29–08–51	79.2			
30–12–51	137			
01–08–53	365			
12–09–54	133			
25–08–55	300			
27–01–56	64.0			
10–06–57	40.5			
03–09–58	210			
03–08–59	125			
01–09–60	62.0			
17–09–61	382			
12–02–62	87.7			
18–09–63	129			
12–08–64	131			
05–09–65	195			
23–11–65	111			
06–12–66	645			
07–08–68	194			
25–01–69	387			

Country: U.S.A. (28) cont'd
River: Virgin
Gauging Station: Virgin, Utah

Date	Maximum discharge (m³/s) resulting from:		Maximum volume (10⁶m³) corresponding to max. discharge resulting from:	
	Rainfall	Snowmelt	Rainfall	Snowmelt
1	2	3	4	5
18–08–70	75.3			
21–08–71	81.5			

TABLE II — ANNUAL MAXIMUM DISCHARGES AND VOLUMES   (cont'd)

Country:	U.S.A. (29)				Country:	U.S.A. (29) cont'd			
River:	James				River:	James			
Gauging Station:	Buchanan, Va.				Gauging Station:	Buchanan, Va.			

Date	Maximum discharge (m³/s) resulting from:		Maximum volume (10⁶m³) corresponding to max. discharge resulting from:		Date	Maximum discharge (m³/s) resulting from:		Maximum volume (10⁶m³) corresponding to max. discharge resulting from:	
	Rainfall	Snowmelt	Rainfall	Snowmelt		Rainfall	Snowmelt	Rainfall	Snowmelt
1	2	3	4	5	1	2	3	4	5
11—77	3540				20—03—20	758			
04—86	2410				23—01—21	691			
03—89	2410				11—03—22	685			
04—05—93	1020				07—03—23	532			
14—10—93	623				12—05—24	1700			
09—04—95	1410				12—01—25	331			
30—09—96	1080				19—01—26	812			
23—02—97	1140				26—12—26	1080			
07—05—98	727				16—08—28	1100			
05—03—99	1470				01—03—29	849			
20—03—00	674				19—11—29	1100			
26—11—00	1690				30—03—31	340			
01—03—02	2150				05—02—32	991			
24—03—03	1240				21—03—33	705			
19—05—04	580				28—03—34	906			
13—07—05	1040				23—01—35	1990			
23—01—06	679				18—03—36	2380			
14—06—07	1180				21—01—37	1170			
16—02—08	1410				20—10—37	1110			
14—04—09	1000				31—01—39	1020			
14—06—10	1100				31—05—40	1160			
03—01—11	727				08—07—41	659			
30—03—12	1130				17—05—42	1480			
27—03—13	2970				14—03—43	993			
20—02—14	507				01—03—44	507			
02—02—15	1590				18—09—45	614			
30—12—15	815				08—01—46	954			
05—03—17	1260				15—03—47	730			
14—03—18	1220				15—02—48	1100			
03—01—19	1350				14—04—49	1550			

United States of America / États-Unis d'Amérique / Estados Unidos de América / Соединенные Штаты Америки

TABLE II — ANNUAL MAXIMUM DISCHARGES AND VOLUMES   (cont'd)

Country:	U.S.A. (29) cont'd	Country:	U.S.A. (30)
River:	James	River:	Skagit
Gauging Station:	Buchanan, Va.	Gauging Station:	Concrete, Wash.

	Maximum discharge (m³/s) resulting from:		Maximum volume (10⁶m³) corresponding to max. discharge resulting from:			Maximum discharge (m³/s) resulting from:		Maximum volume (10⁶m³) corresponding to max. discharge resulting from:	
Date	Rainfall	Snowmelt	Rainfall	Snowmelt	Date	Rainfall	Snowmelt	Rainfall	Snowmelt
1	2	3	4	5	1	2	3	4	5
02—02—50	942				19—11—97	7780			
08—12—50	1410				30—11—09	7360			
12—03—52	1190				30—12—17	6230			
22—02—53	1360				13—12—21	6790			
02—03—54	1310				12—12—24	262			
07—03—55	1380				23—12—25	1460			
17—04—56	447				16—10—26	2520			
06—04—57	1310				12—01—28	2700			
31—03—58	835				09—10—28	2100			
13—04—59	569				07—06—30	911			
21—03—60	1270				26—06—31	1710			
26—02—61	640				27—02—32	4160			
21—10—61	1190				13—11—32	3280			
13—03—63	1750				22—12—33	2860			
06—03—64	778				25—01—35	3710			
08—02—65	1010				03—06—36	1700			
14—02—66	1020				19—06—37	1930			
08—03—67	1560				28—10—37	2540			
13—03—68	608				29—05—39	2250			
20—08—69	1860				15—12—39	1360			
01—01—70	1400				19—10—40	1440			
31—05—71	1320				02—12—41	2160			
22—06—72	3140				23—11—42	1530			
					03—12—43	1850			
					08—02—45	2000			
					25—10—45	2890			
					25—10—46	2330			
					19—10—47	2690			
					13—05—49	1580			
					27—11—49	4360			

TABLE II – ANNUAL MAXIMUM DISCHARGES AND VOLUMES (cont'd)

Country:	U.S.A. (30) cont'd
River:	Skagit
Gauging Station:	Concrete,Wash.

Date	Maximum discharge (m³/s) resulting from:		Maximum volume (10⁶m³) corresponding to max. discharge resulting from:	
	Rainfall	. Snowmelt	Rainfall	Snowmelt
1	2	3	4	5
10–02–51	3930			
05–06–52	1230			
01–02–53	1870			
31–10–53	1840			
11–06–55	1590			
03–11–55	2000			
20–10–56	1730			
17–01–58	1170			
30–04–59	2570			
23–11–59	2530			
16–01–61	2240			
03–01–62	1580			
20–11–62	3230			
22–10–63	2090			
01–12–64	1490			
06–05–66	1040			
21–06–67	2050			
28–10–67	2380			

Country:	U.S.A. (31)
River:	South Fork Cedar
Gauging Station:	Lester, Wash.

Date	Maximum discharge (m³/s) resulting from:		Maximum volume (10⁶m³) corresponding to max. discharge resulting from:	
	Rainfall	Snowmelt	Rainfall	Snowmelt
1	2	3	4	5
07–01–45		24.8		
28–12–45		11.3		
11–12–46		17.8		
07–11–47		15.3		
13–05–49		8.6		
27–11–49		14.5		
09–02–51		15.7		
13–05–52		5.6		
31–01–53		14.7		
09–12–53		16.9		
08–02–55		14.1		
11–12–55		14.5		
09–12–56		66.2		
20–04–58		8.0		
12–11–58		15.3		
22–11–59		54.9		
21–02–61		11.5		
06–04–62		11.4		
20–11–62		25.6		
31–05–64		7.5		
29–01–65		14.5		
06–05–66		7.8'		
15–01–67		7.8		
25–12–67		14.7		
05–01–69		9.5		
22–01–70		5.5		
30–01–71		6.8		

TABLE II – ANNUAL MAXIMUM DISCHARGES AND VOLUMES   (cont'd)

Country:	U.S.A. (32)
River:	Middle Crow Creek
Gauging Station:	Hecla, Wyo.

Date	Maximum discharge (m³/s) resulting from:		Maximum volume (10⁶m³) corresponding to max. discharge resulting from:	
	Rainfall	Snowmelt	Rainfall	Snowmelt
1	2	3	4	5
27–04–03			2.72	
08–09–33			14.0	
04–05–34			0.34	
31–05–35			4.16	
24–06–36			4.08	
01–06–37			0.96	
25–08–38			5.18	
04–05–39			0.99	
29–04–40			0.28	
25–07–41			4.78	
11–05–42			3.31	
24–05–43			1.90	
13–05–44			1.75	
05–06–45			1.47	
02–06–46			0.62	
03–05–47			2.26	
04–29–48			0.76	
10–06–49			3.06	
27–05–50			0.91	
31–07–51			1.53	
30–04–52			1.30	
31–07–53			0.65	
07–04–54			0.57	
17–06–55			0.62	
23–05–56			0.76	
04–05–57			2.77	
24–07–58			2.21	
23–05–59			1.08	
07–04–60			0.51	
04–06–61			2.60	

Country:	U.S.A. (32) cont'd
River:	Middle Crow Creek
Gauging Station:	Hecla, Wyo.

Date	Maximum discharge (m³/s) resulting from:		Maximum volume (10⁶m³) corresponding to max. discharge resulting from:	
	Rainfall	Snowmelt	Rainfall	Snowmelt
1	2	3	4	5
16–04–62			1.47	
24–07–63			6.59	
18–05–64			1.13	
17–06–65			4.27	
22–10–65			0.31	
11–07–67			2.80	

414

TABLE III — CHARACTERISTICS OF SNOWMELT FLOODS

			Characteristic elements							Type of probability curve	
No.	River	Gauging station	Q_{max} (m^3/s)	Date	h (mm)	T_T (hours)	t_i (hours)	P_W (%)	$P_{Q_{max}}$ (%)	for P_W	for $P_{Q_{max}}$
1	2	3	4	5	6	7	8	9	10	11	12
7	Ute Creek	Fort Garland, Colo.	17.8	15—05—41					<1		Log Pearson type III
			10.0	05—08—36					4		"
			9.1	30—06—37					6		"
			7.6	17—07—57					13		"
			7.5	13—06—35					15		"
18	Judith	Utica, Mont.	31.7	11—06—27					3		"
			31.1	25—05—42					4		"
			30.3	08—08—41					4		"
			30.3	09—06—64					4		"
			27.7	30—05—67					8		"
31	S. Fk. Cedar	Lester, Wash.	66.2	09—12—56					2		"
			54.9	22—11—59					2		"
			25.6	20—11—62					13		"
32	Middle Crow Cr.	Hecla, Wyo.	14.0	08—09—33					1		"
			6.6	24—07—63					6		"
			5.2	25—08—38					10		"

	Method of curve fitting		Snow cover		Rainfall during snowmelt (mm)	Monthly precipitation before soil freezing (mm)	Mean monthly temperature before snowmelt (°C)
No.	for W	for Q_{max}	Water equivalent (mm)	Layer thickness (cm)			
1	13	14	15	16	17	18	19
7		Method of moments					
		"					
		"					
		"					
		"					
18		"					
		"					
		"					
		"					
		"					
31		"					
		"					
		"					
32		"					
		"					
		"					

TABLE IV — CHARACTERISTICS OF RAINFALL FLOODS

											Type of probability curve	
												Characteristic element
No.	River	Gauging station	Q_{max} (m^3/s)	Date	h (mm)	T_T (hours)	t_i (hours)	P_W (%)	$P_{Q_{max}}$ (%)		for P_W	for $P_{Q_{max}}$
1	2	3	4	5	6	7	8	9	10		11	12
1	Cascade Cr.	Petersburg, Alas.	92.8	11—09—47					2		Log Pearson type III	
			75.8	04—09—24					6		,,	
			71.9	06—08—20					7		,,	
2	Colorado	Grand Canyon, Ariz.	8490	08—07—74					<1		,,	
			6230	19—06—21					2		,,	
			3590	07—02—27					14		,,	
			3540	13—06—57					14		,,	
			3450	06—12—52					15		,,	
3	Salt	Chrysotile, Ariz.	2090	19—01—16					2		,,	
			1500	07—02—37					4		,,	
			1480	14—03—41					4		,,	
			1460	14—01—52					5		,,	
			1160	30—12—65					7		,,	
4	Arkansas	Little Rock, Ark.	15200	27—05—43					3		,,	
			13300	21—02—38					5		,,	
			13200	21—04—45					5		,,	
			13000	31—05—57					5		,,	
5	Eel	Scotia, Calif.	21300	23—12—64					<1		,,	
			15300	22—12—55					2		,,	
			9930	02—02—15					9		,,	
			9760	11—12—37					10		,,	
			9710	08—02—60					10		,,	
			8910	21—01—43					13		,,	

No.	Method of curve fitting for W	for Q_{max}	Rainfall forming flood (mm)	Snowmelt during floods (mm)	Maximum daily rainfall (mm)	Date	Hourly maximum rainfall (mm)	Date	Antecedent precipitation for 10 days (mm)	30 days (mm)
1	13	14	15	16	17	18	19	20	21	22
1		Method of moments								
		,,								
		,,								
2		,,								
		,,								
		,,								
		,,								
		,,								
3		,,								
		,,								
		,,								
		,,								
		,,								
4		,,								
		,,								
		,,								
		,,								
5		,,								
		,,								
		,,								
		,,								
		,,								
		,,								

TABLE IV — CHARACTERISTICS OF RAINFALL FLOODS (cont'd)

No.	River	Gauging station	Q_{max} (m³/s)	Date	h (mm)	T_T (hours)	t_i (hours)	P_W (%)	$P_{Q_{max}}$ (%)	Type of probability curve for P_W	for $P_{Q_{max}}$
1	2	3	4	5	6	7	8	9	10	11	12
6	Plum Cr.	Louviers, Colo.	4360	16–06–65					<1		Log Pearson type III
			218	08–08–45					2		''
			125	08–05–69					12		''
8	Altamaha	Doctortown, Ga.	8490	23–01–25					<1		''
			5070	13–03–29					4		''
			5040	18–04–36					5		''
			3760	13–10–29					10		''
			3570	25–08–28					12		''
9	Kawaikoi Str.	Waimea, Hawaii	320	13–01–67					1		''
			300	18–12–16					2		''
			290	30–11–68					2		''
			230	15–08–50					6		''
			200	06–08–59					9		''
			180	13–12–24					14		''
10	Salmon	White Bird, Ida.	3000	24–05–56					3		''
			2910	03–06–48					4		''
			2730	12–06–65					6		''
			2550	29–05–71					10		''
			2400	19–06–16					15		''
			2400	06–06–70					15		''

No.	Method of curve fitting for W	for Q_{max}	Rainfall forming flood (mm)	Snowmelt during floods (mm)	Maximum daily rainfall (mm)	Date	Hourly maximum rainfall (mm)	Date	Antecedent precipitation for 10 days (mm)	30 days (mm)
1	13	14	15	16	17	18	19	20	21	22
6		Method of moments								
		''								
		''								
8		''								
		''								
		''								
		''								
		''								
9		''								
		''								
		''								
		''								
		''								
		''								
10		''								
		''								
		''								
		''								
		''								
		''								

TABLE IV — CHARACTERISTICS OF RAINFALL FLOODS (cont'd)

No.	River	Gauging station	Q_{max} (m^3/s)	Date	h (mm)	T_T (hours)	t_i (hours)	P_W (%)	$P_{Q_{max}}$ (%)	Type of probability curve for P_W	for $P_{Q_{max}}$
1	2	3	4	5	6	7	8	9	10	11	12
11	Ohio	Evansville, Ind.	39900	29—01—37					<1		Log Pearson type III
			26200	19—02—84					3		"
			25900	19—02—83					3		"
			25800	16—03—64					3		"
			25600	11—03—45					3		"
			25500	05—04—13					3		"
			21600	25—01—07					10		"
			20100	21—04—48					15		"
			19900	27—03—33					15		"
			19670	09—02—50					18		"
12	Red	Alexandria, La.	6590	17—04—45					1		"
			5800	06—07—08					3		"
			5660	12—05—58					4		"
			5580	07—05—57					4		"
			5460	19 05 53					5		"
			5260	03—02—32					6		"
			4950	12—06—92					8		"
			4900	08—05—27					9		"
			4670	08—05—66					10		"
			4500	11—04—68					15		"

No.	Method of curve fitting for W	for Q_{max}	Rainfall forming flood (mm)	Snowmelt during floods (mm)	Maximum daily rainfall (mm)	Date	Hourly maximum rainfall (mm)	Date	Antecedent precipitation for 10 days (mm)	30 days (mm)
1	13	14	15	16	17	18	19	20	21	22
11		Method of moments								
		"								
		"								
		"								
		"								
		"								
		"								
		"								
		"								
12		"								
		"								
		"								
		"								
		"								
		"								
		"								
		"								
		"								

United States of America / États-Unis d'Amérique / Estados Unidos de América / Соединенные Штаты Америки

TABLE IV — CHARACTERISTICS OF RAINFALL FLOODS (cont'd)

No.	River	Gauging station	Q_{max} (m³/s)	Date	h (mm)	T_T (hours)	t_i (hours)	P_W (%)	$P_{Q_{max}}$ (%)	Type for P_W	Type for $P_{Q_{max}}$
1	2	3	4	5	6	7	8	9	10	11	12
13	Connecticut	Montague City, Mass.	6680	19—03—36					<1		Log Pearson type III
			5520	22—09—38					1		"
			5070	05—11—27					2		"
			4080	28—03—13					8		"
			4020	06—04—60					9		"
			3930	31—12—48					9		"
			3880	19—04—33					10		"
14	Quaboag	West Brimfield, Mass.	360	19—08—55					<1		"
			240	21—09—38					1		"
			100	18—03—36					5		"
			56	17—03—20					15		"
			54	05—04—60					15		"
			53	21—03—68					16		"
15	Mississippi	St. Paul, Minn.	4840	16—04—65					<1		"
			4410	15—04—69					<1		"
			3540	16—04—52					2		"
			3030	29—04—81					4		"
			2830	11—04—70					5		"
			2630	16—04—51					6		"
			2600	23—07—67					6		"
			2440	16—04—75					7		"
			2440	06—04—97					7		"
			2220	29—06—57					10		"

No.	Method for W	Method for Q_{max}	Rainfall forming flood (mm)	Snowmelt during floods (mm)	Maximum daily rainfall (mm)	Date	Hourly maximum rainfall (mm)	Date	Antecedent 10 days (mm)	Antecedent 30 days (mm)
1	13	14	15	16	17	18	19	20	21	22
13		Method of moments								
		"								
		"								
		"								
		"								
		"								
		"								
14		"								
		"								
		"								
		"								
		"								
		"								
15		"								
		"								
		"								
		"								
		"								
		"								
		"								
		"								
		"								
		"								

419

TABLE IV — CHARACTERISTICS OF RAINFALL FLOODS (cont'd)

No.	River	Gauging station	Q_{max} (m^3/s)	Date	h (mm)	T_T (hours)	t_i (hours)	P_W (%)	$P_{Q_{max}}$ (%)	Type of probability curve for P_W	for $P_{Q_{max}}$
1	2	3	4	5	6	7	8	9	10	11	12
16	Mississippi	Vicksburg, Miss.	64500	01—05—27					<1	Log Pearson type III	
			58900	17—02—37					2	,,	
			54400	08—04—45					5		,,
			53100	23—02—50					5		,,
			50500	02—05—13					10		,,
			50400	12—04—12					10		,,
17	Salt	Shelbina, Mo.	650	07—06—47					1		,,
			510	06—28					4		,,
			500	07—09					4		,,
			450	01—07—33					6		,,
19	Yellow Stone	Sidney, Mont.	4500	21—06—21					1		,,
			3910	31—03—52					3		,,
			3790	03—10—24					4		,,
			3740	29—03—43					4		,,
			3570	20—06—18					6		,,
20	Big Blue	Barneston, Nebr.	1610	09—06—41					<1		,,
			1100	—05—03					3		,,
			830	28—03—60					10		,,
			800	08—08—54					12		,,
			760	22—05—45					13		,,
21	Otter Brook	Keene, N.H.	173	21—09—38					1		,,
			101	18—03—36					5		,,
			100	26—11—50					5		,,

No.	Method of curve fitting for W	for Q_{max}	Rainfall forming flood (mm)	Snowmelt during floods (mm)	Maximum daily rainfall (mm)	Date	Hourly maximum rainfall (mm)	Date	Antecedent precipitation for 10 days (mm)	30 days (mm)
1	13	14	15	16	17	18	19	20	21	22
16		Method of moments								
		,,								
		,,								
		,,								
		,,								
		,,								
17		,,								
		,,								
		,,								
		,,								
19		,,								
		,,								
		,,								
		,,								
		,,								
20		,,								
		,,								
		,,								
		,,								
		,,								
21		,,								
		,,								
		,,								

TABLE IV — CHARACTERISTICS OF RAINFALL FLOODS (cont'd)

No.	River	Gauging station	Q_{max} (m³/s)	Date	h (mm)	T_T (hours)	t_i (hours)	P_W (%)	$P_{Q_{max}}$ (%)	Type of probability curve for P_W	for $P_{Q_{max}}$
1	2	3	4	5	6	7	8	9	10	11	12
22	Beetree Cr.	Swannanoa, N.C.	39	13—08—40					<1		Log Pearson type III
			24	15—08—28					3		''
			17	26—03—65					7		''
			16	16—06—49					8		''
			16	12—03—63					8		''
23	Columbia	The Dalles, Oreg.	35100	06—06—94					<1		''
			28600	31—05—48					1		''
			25900	30—06—80					4		''
			25400	19—06—87					5		''
			25000	13—06—82					5		''
			23300	02—06—56					9		''
			22300	22—06—99					13		''
			22300	18—06—03					13		''
			22200	22—06—96					13		''
			22100	24—05—97					13		''
24	Cow Creek	Azalea, Oreg.	239	22—12—64					<1		''
			168	29—10—50					6		''
			153	26—01—70					10		''
			147	21—12—55					13		''

No.	Method of curve fitting for W	for Q_{max}	Rainfall forming flood (mm)	Snowmelt during floods (mm)	Maximum daily rainfall (mm)	Date	Hourly maximum rainfall (mm)	Date	Antecedent precipitation for 10 days (mm)	30 days (mm)
1	13	14	15	16	17	18	19	20	21	22
22		Method of moments								
		''								
		''								
		''								
23		''								
		''								
		''								
		''								
		''								
		''								
		''								
		''								
		''								
24		''								
		''								
		''								
		''								

TABLE IV — CHARACTERISTICS OF RAINFALL FLOODS (cont'd)

No.	River	Gauging station	Q_{max} (m³/s)	Date	h (mm)	T_T (hours)	t_i (hours)	P_W (%)	$P_{Q_{max}}$ (%)	Type of probability curve for P_W	for $P_{Q_{max}}$
1	2	3	4	5	6	7	8	9	10	11	12
25	Susquehanna	Harrisburg, Pa.	20900	19—03—36					<1		Log Pearson type III
			18500	02—06—89					2		"
			17400	22—05—94					2		"
			16200	18—03—65					3		"
			14000	29—05—46					6		"
			13700	12—03—64					7		"
			13600	05—10—86					7		"
			13600	15—03—46					7		"
			12700	03—03—02					10		"
26	Clinch	Tazewell, Tenn.	1870	02—62					1		"
			1600	13—03—63					2		"
			1450	31—01—57					4		"
			1120	04—02—23					13		"
			1100	23—12—26					14		"
27	San Saba	San Saba, Tex.	5740	23—07—38					<1		"
			2010	26—04—22					5		"
			1990	11—09—52					5		"
			1900	17—09—36					6		"
			1810	15—06—35					6		"
			1270	07—10—30					12		"

No.	Method of curve fitting for W	for Q_{max}	Rainfall forming flood (mm)	Snowmelt during floods (mm)	Maximum daily rainfall (mm)	Date	Hourly maximum rainfall (mm)	Date	Antecedent precipitation for 10 days (mm)	30 days (mm)
1	13	14	15	16	17	18	19	20	21	22
25		Method of moments								
		"								
		"								
		"								
		"								
		"								
		"								
		"								
26		"								
		"								
		"								
		"								
		"								
27		"								
		"								
		"								
		"								
		"								
		"								

United States of America / États-Unis d'Amérique / Estados Unidos de América / Соединенные Штаты Америки

TABLE IV – CHARACTERISTICS OF RAINFALL FLOODS (cont'd)

No.	River	Gauging station	Q_{max} (m^3/s)	Date	h (mm)	T_T (hours)	t_i (hours)	P_W (%)	$P_{Q_{max}}$ (%)	Type of probability curve for P_W	for $P_{Q_{max}}$
1	2	3	4	5	6	7	8	9	10	11	12
28	Virgin	Virgin, Utah	645	06–12–66					1		Log Pearson type III
			387	25–01–69					5		"
			382	03–03–38					5		"
			382	17–07–61					5		"
			365	01–08–53					5		"
			340	27–10–12					7		"
29	James	Buchanan, Va.	3540	11–77					<1		"
			3140	22–06–72					1		"
			2970	27–03–13					2		"
			2410	04–86					4		"
			2410	03–89					4		"
			2380	18–03–36					4		"
			2150	01–03–02					6		"
			1990	23–01–35					9		"
30	Skagit	Concrete, Wash.	7780	19–11–97					4		"
			7360	30–11–09					5		"
			6790	13–12–21					6		"
			6230	30–12–17					7		"
			4360	27–11–49					15		"

No.	Method of curve fitting for W	for Q_{max}	Rainfall forming flood (mm)	Snowmelt during floods (mm)	Maximum daily rainfall (mm)	Date	Hourly maximum rainfall (mm)	Date	Antecedent precipitation for 10 days (mm)	30 days (mm)
1	13	14	15	16	17	18	19	20	21	22
28		Method of moments								
		"								
		"								
		"								
		"								
29		"								
		"								
		"								
		"								
		"								
		"								
		"								
		"								
30		"								
		"								
		"								
		"								
		"								

Uruguay / Уругвай

TABLE II – ANNUAL MAXIMUM DISCHARGES AND VOLUMES

Country: **Uruguay (1)**
River: **Uruguay**
Gauging Station: **Salto**

Date	Maximum discharge (m³/s) resulting from:		Maximum volume (10⁶m³) corresponding to max. discharge resulting from:	
	Rainfall	Snowmelt	Rainfall	Snowmelt
1	2	3	4	5
09–65	22300			
06–72	27200			

Country: **Uruguay (2)**
River: **Rio Negro**
Gauging Station: **Polmos**

Date	Maximum discharge (m³/s) resulting from:		Maximum volume (10⁶m³) corresponding to max. discharge resulting from:	
	Rainfall	Snowmelt	Rainfall	Snowmelt
1	2	3	4	5
07–67	8320			
09–72	6970			

Country: **Uruguay (3)**
River: **Rio Negro**
Gauging Station: **Poso del Puerto** *

Date	Maximum discharge (m³/s) resulting from:		Maximum volume (10⁶m³) corresponding to max. discharge resulting from:	
	Rainfall	Snowmelt	Rainfall	Snowmelt
1	2	3	4	5
29–04–59	11400			

* Area = 62100 km²